Liaison
1914

Liaison 1914

1914

A NARRATIVE OF THE GREAT RETREAT

EDWARD SPEARS
FOREWORD BY WINSTON CHURCHILL

Pen & Sword
MILITARY

First published in Great Britain in 1930
and reprinted in 1968 by Eyre & Spottiswoode

Reprinted in this format in 2014 and again in 2021 by
PEN & SWORD MILITARY
An imprint of
Pen & Sword Books Ltd
Yorkshire – Philadelphia

ISBN 978 1 52679 690 5

Printed and bound in England by CPI Group (UK) Ltd, Croydon, CR0 4YY

Pen & Sword Books Limited incorporates the imprints of Atlas, Archaeology,
Aviation, Discovery, Family History, Fiction, History, Maritime, Military, Military
Classics, Politics, Select, Transport, True Crime, Air World, Frontline Publishing, Leo
Cooper, Remember When, Seaforth Publishing, The Praetorian Press, Wharncliffe
Local History, Wharncliffe Transport, Wharncliffe True Crime and White Owl.

For a complete list of Pen & Sword titles please contact

PEN & SWORD BOOKS LIMITED
47 Church Street, Barnsley, South Yorkshire, S70 2AS, England
E-mail: enquiries@pen-and-sword.co.uk
Website: www.pen-and-sword.co.uk

Or
PEN AND SWORD BOOKS
1950 Lawrence Rd, Havertown, PA 19083, USA
E-mail: Uspen-and-sword@casematepublishers.com
Website: www.penandswordbooks.com

to my son
MICHAEL

Foreword to the First Edition

BY WINSTON S. CHURCHILL

No part of the Great War compares in interest with its opening. The measured, silent drawing together of gigantic forces, the uncertainty of their movements and positions, the number of unknown and unknowable facts made the first collision a drama never surpassed. Nor was there any other period in the War when the general battle was waged on so great a scale, when the slaughter was so swift or the stakes so high. Moreover, in the beginning our faculties of wonder, horror and excitement had not been cauterized and deadened by the furnace fires of years. In fact the War was decided in the first twenty days of fighting, and all that happened afterwards consisted in battles which, however formidable and devastating, were but desperate and vain appeals against the decision of Fate.

General Spears' account is a definite and new contribution to our knowledge of this opening phase. At the time those who were in responsible positions were absorbed in their own intense preoccupations; and the general public were necessarily left in complete ignorance. Afterwards so much else happened that we all were swept along in the torrent, and the significance of these supreme and awful days has never imprinted itself deeply upon the consciousness of the nation. The Author of this book is well qualified and well suited to light up that part of the immense field in which he moved and acted. It must remain the most arresting theatre in British estimation; it was certainly the scene of the vital dominant events. General Spears, then a Lieutenant of Hussars, was the Liaison Officer between the British Army and the Fifth or most Northerly of the whole line of French Armies. It was his duty to gain and hold the confidence and goodwill of the French Army Command and to preserve so far as possible in frightful circumstances their physical contact and moral relationship. The difficulties were enormous. An intense impression of them can be gained from these pages. That a young Officer should have acquitted himself so effectively in the white heat of this crisis explains his rise from the rank of a Sub-altern to that of a General Officer. There is a passage in Sir John French's Memoirs of 1914 to which no reference is made in General Spears' book, but which I shall take the liberty of reprinting here.

"I have a most vivid and grateful recollection of the invaluable services performed by this intrepid young officer. He is possessed of an extremely acute perception and is able to express himself and deliver his reports in the clearest and most concise terms. He was always exact and accurate, and never failed to bring me back the information I most particularly wanted. I seldom knew him at fault. He was a perfect master of the French language and was popular with the staffs, and made welcome by the various generals to whom he was attached. His unfailing tact, judgement and resource were very marked. His reckless, daring courage often made me anxious for his safety, and, indeed, he was severely wounded on at least five separate occasions.

"I remember well his coming back to report to me late one evening. He spoke with his usual confidence and decision, and the information which he gave me proved to be very important and accurate, but I noticed that his voice was weak and he looked very tired and worn in the face. I sent him away to his quarters as quickly as possible, thinking he wanted rest. All this time he had a bullet in his side, and in that condition he had travelled back several miles to make his report. He fainted after leaving my room, and lay in considerable danger for several days."
"1914," *by Field Marshal Viscount French of Ypres.*

This is a fine tribute, but some of those who read these pages will see that even more resolution and firmness were displayed by Lieutenant Spears when on several occasions he presented on the field of honour the burning case of Britain to France or of France to Britain.

During these convulsions the Author was placed in a position from which he could command a wide view. It was the view of a French and a British Army fighting side by side against overwhelming forces. In all that he writes upon this aspect he makes a contribution to History. There were, however, higher view-points from which the panorama appeared in different proportions. These he could only partially appreci-ate. We have here the military politics of Army Commanders, and wider, though certainly not more exciting, controversies open when we approach the problems of the French High Command and their attempts to solve them. To bring the story into its proper setting and proportion it suffices to repeat that hideous and measureless miscalculation of almost every factor present at the outbreak of the War was made by General Joffre and his officers. In consequence the two armies of the Allied Left were placed in positions of inconceivable peril; and in fact when all the thought and talk was of confident advance, they were hurled back by a tidal wave whose force and volume transcended all imagined dimensions.

It is this that assigns to this account its precise intrinsic value. It is the story of the armies of the Left Wing. It sheds a light upon that story hitherto unseen and almost unrecorded. To those who wish to comprehend the deeper pressures of war and the baffling manner in which they operate upon all subjected to them, these pages will carry a message of profound significance. I have found them so captivating that I could scarcely lay them down, and I commend them to the study of all who seek deeper insight into the most prodigious destructive period of history.

WINSTON S. CHURCHILL

CONTENTS

PART TWO: THE RETREAT
AND THE BATTLE OF THE MARNE

APPENDICES

ILLUSTRATIONS

ACKNOWLEDGEMENTS
FOR ILLUSTRATIONS

Acknowledgements and thanks are due to the following for permission to reproduce copyright material:

Bassano & Vandyk Studios for plate 10; Monsieur René Dazy for plates 2, 28, 32, 35–6, 48; Éstablissement Cinématographique des Armées, Fort d'Ivry, Seine, for plates 21–4, 33, 39–40, 49; The Imperial War Museum for plates 14, 18–19, 26, 37; Paul Popper Limited for plates 20, 25, 27, 30–1; The Radio Times Hulton Picture Library for plates 16, 34, and Ullstein Bilderdienst for plates 8–9.

MAPS

Drawn by W. H. Bromage

These are based on the original maps drawn by Sir Morgan Crofton for the first edition.

Author's Preface to the First Edition

THE object of this book is to contribute something to the true story of the war, and to vindicate the role of the British Expeditionary Force in 1914. It is a narrative based upon what I saw, upon the evidence of eye-witnesses, and upon documents. I have also drawn freely on the information contained in the British and French Official Histories.

The book would never have been written but for the following occurrence. A few years ago I visited the French Senate in company with a Member who had been a Minister during the war. He introduced me to several of his colleagues, who began to talk of 1914. I heard with amazement the opinion expressed that British military participation had been negligible until 1916. Nothing appeared to be known of the part played by the British at Le Cateau and the Battle of the Marne, and some Senators even said that Sir John French had let down his neighbour General Lanrezac at the beginning of the campaign. I knew these statements were fantastically untrue, and said so, but the incident made me resolve to tell the story of the events of those first weeks of the war. Owing to the accident of having been the only British officer attached to General Lanrezac's Army at that time, I happened to have been particularly well placed to observe them.

Inevitably, the book contains criticisms, sometimes of the French, sometimes of our own people, but the British never seemed so fine to me as when I was attached to the French, and I trust that the profound admiration I feel for the French nation and my respect for the French soldier stand out clearly from these pages.

Living with the French, I had a better opportunity of appreciating their qualities than had most Englishmen.

To our men, the French people were represented by the hard-bitten and often grasping peasants of Northern France. Most of them never saw a real French soldier, and thought the posts of old and shabby Territorials guarding bridges and railways were typical of the French

Army. Those who did come in contact with French troops, finding their mentality and methods of fighting entirely different, were apt to conclude they were unreliable. They did not see, as I have seen, French regiments hurrying forward, machine-guns carried on men's backs, anxious not to waste a moment in their eagerness to come to the rescue of the hard-pressed British at Ypres.

The two peoples are different even in their manifestations of courage and heroism.

The British most appreciate action unadorned by words. To the Frenchman, bravery has an enhanced value if accompanied by a gesture.

Typical of this trait is the story of the little French soldier aged twenty, who, acting as a guide, was mortally wounded by a shell splinter. Before dying he turned with a smile to the officer to whom he had been showing the way, and said: "Happily it was not you, *mon Capitaine.*"

My narrative covers the period known as the War of Movement, that is from the outbreak of hostilities to the eve of the Battle of the Aisne. Of the Battle of the Marne I have given only a slight sketch, but even this shows that it was the action of the British in advancing across the river twelve hours before any French infantry that determined the German retreat.

The period of which I have written marks the end of an epoch in military history, for the gigantic struggle known as the Battle of the Marne was more closely related to Waterloo than it could be to any battle of the future, if such a battle there is to be.

In describing what I saw, I have necessarily written mainly of commanders and their problems, and of the results of their orders and calculations, but I hope that something of the spirit of the Armies of those days appears here and there between the lines of my story. The counterpart, though not the compensation, of the horror and stupid waste of the war was the great moral effort it involved. The heroic spirit of the men who fought is the background of this book, as it must be of any account of 1914.

In conclusion, I desire to thank all those who have helped me. I wish particularly to express my gratitude to my cousin Lieut.-General Sir Fenton Aylmer, V.C., K.C.B., and to Lieut.-Commander Fletcher, for many valuable suggestions.

I owe a particular debt of obligation to Colonel Sir Morgan Crofton, Bart., D.S.O., for the very remarkable maps he has drawn. Not only do they elucidate the narrative, but they have saved many tedious explanations in the text. Anyone who reads this book will realize their value.

Author's Preface to the Second Edition

THIS edition of *Liaison 1914*, which was first published in 1930, includes a new chapter, XVI, containing material concerning events on the left of the front on the eve of the Battle of the Marne, which was not available to me when I wrote the book.

It is my hope that this will throw new light on the respective roles of Joffre and Gallieni, which have long been a matter of controversy.

Commandant Maurin, by then Minister of War, gave me his account of what occurred at General Joffre's H.Q. on the evening of September 4th. I also toured the battlefield of the Marne with Marshal Franchet d'Esperey, accompanied by the officers who were writing the French Official History of the War. From them I learnt much. I did my own researches both on the ground and from the increasing documentation that had by then become available. I also had many discussions with Marshal Joffre in his retirement.

In this new chapter I have revised and amplified the account I gave in the original edition, and this is now as complete as I can hope to make it.

LIAISON 1914

PART ONE

THE
OUTBREAK OF WAR
TO
THE BEGINNING OF
THE RETREAT

CHAPTER I

PARIS

July 27th–August 4th, 1914

First impressions – Return of Poincaré from Russia – The President and the Prime Minister – Precautions against frontier incidents – The "télégramme de couverture" – The murder of Jaurés – General mobilization – Doubts concerning the attitude of England – The British declaration of war.

THE room was small, stuffy and gloomy. The low ceiling was dirty, and the pigeonholes lining the walls, full of dust, seemed to scatter their grey impalpable contents over the room. Even the glorious sun that was melting the asphalt in the street outside seemed to neglect or disdain this dismal apartment.

And yet the surroundings, depressing as they were, were not responsible for the tension and nervous strain under which the three men sitting there were labouring.

I was one of them, and my two companions were French officers belonging to the General Staff. We each sat at a table in this stifling corner of the *Ministère de la Guerre* exactly as we had sat the day before, and the day before that. But there was now an enormous difference: today was August 2nd, 1914, France was mobilizing for war, and I, who belonged to the Army of a country that had not declared itself, had ceased to be a comrade and had suddenly become an object of suspicion.

The senior French officer had just informed me in icy tones that, as I was no doubt aware, the ordinary post was being systematically delayed, and would I be so good as to hand him my letters to the War Office open? I had protested with asperity, but I knew he was acting on higher authority and that there was nothing to be done about it. I was cut off from my chiefs. The telephone and telegraph wires were commandeered by the French General Staff. I was virtually a prisoner, and felt strongly the humiliation and helplessness of my position.

A bad moment, followed by equally trying days, but soon to be forgotten in an admiration for the French Army which never ceased to increase during the long period I was to spend with it, an admiration fortified, as time went on and weary months lengthened into seemingly endless years, by personal friendships with many members of that absolutely magnificent body of men, the French officers.

My presence at the *Ministère de la Guerre* was entirely unconnected with the war. I had left England on the 27th July, 1914. That I took my uniform with me was merely a precaution, certainly not a forecast. It had been decided some months before that a British officer should be attached for a few weeks to a certain section of the French War Office, and when war suddenly loomed on the horizon it was felt that there was no disadvantage, and might indeed be a possible advantage, in adhering to the original arrangement.

It is common knowledge now that conversations had taken place between the French and British Staffs upon which certain plans had been based. These plans made it possible for the British forces to take their place beside the French if war broke out and our Government decided upon intervention on land, but it had always been most clearly stated that this did not in the least bind Great Britain to any action whatsoever. Indeed, so strictly was this interpretation enforced, and so anxious were the authorities to prevent any misunderstanding as to the unfettered freedom of action we intended to maintain, that the officers charged with the work of preparing these plans had been much impeded at various times by the anxiety of statesmen who feared and suspected that the soldiers in their zeal might go a step too far, and in some way commit the Government to intervention.

I felt as soon as I landed that France was even more different from England than usual. At home the Irish crisis cast a heavy cloud, but not heavy enough to dim a brilliant London Season or to interfere seriously with the general prosperity of the country. But here it was obvious that the people were fully alive to the great danger that was casting its shadow over their country. There was a tenseness that was almost palpable. Individuals doing their ordinary jobs seemed to be carrying out purely mechanical tasks while inwardly absorbed in the contemplation of some awful possibility as engrossing, as awe-inspiring as a portent in the heavens. Every man and woman seemed simultaneously to have received bad news.

My luggage had "XIth Hussars" written all over it, which resulted in my passing the Customs triumphantly and obtaining an exceptionally good place on the train. I was taken for a French officer returning from leave, porters and others omitting to note the difference between the French and English spelling of the particular branch of light cavalry to which I belonged.

The French friends with whom I was staying lived in a flat at Passy close to the Bois de Boulogne, the only cool place in Paris.

The father, who had been a student at the time of the Siege of Paris, had seen some fighting then. Seated by the green shaded lamp in his study the evening I arrived, he spoke earnestly of those evil days, and described the hopeless struggle, the picquets in the snow, the starvation of the city. France would never fight merely to get back Alsace Lorraine. No, she would only take up arms in self-defence. Let bygones be bygones; the cruel wound was almost healed. They knew how weak they were. Why could not Germany let them alone? All they wanted was peace. But of course if war was inevitable they would fight. This view represented that of the solid middle class of France, and was repeated to me by almost everyone I met at this time. There was no bombast. The streets and homes were subdued. There was a superstitious, apprehensive feeling that any demonstration, even if only meant to keep up one's courage, would bring bad luck. All remembered with a shudder the last time the streets of Paris had rung with the cry *"à Berlin"*, and a picture of Paris cut off from the world, surrounded by Prussians, was conjured up, distressingly, in men's minds.

The only thought that cheered was that of Russia. On all sides people tried to shake off their forebodings by talking of the great Ally on the far side of Germany. There were millions more Germans than French, but there were millions more Russians than Germans; that was the great hope. But when would they be ready? *Voilà la question*, and heads were shaken dubiously. But then there might be no war after all. Things looked very black, it was true, but surely even the German people would see the folly of it and stop before it was too late?

No foreigner can have been in France during those days without his heart going out in admiration to these people who, stoically and without fear, in deep apprehension yet unfaltering, prepared to meet their fate. And they were silent and quiet, very different from what one would have imagined: nothing describes their conduct better than the word quiet.

The *Ministère de la Guerre*, where I worked, was very quiet, ominously so: everyone realized the importance of being calm, of keeping a cool head. *"Sang-froid"* was the motto, and very well it was lived up to in that dismal building, where nothing was up to date save the men who worked in it. It is hard to remember whether sand did not take the place of blotting paper. At any rate that medieval method of dealing with wet ink would have been entirely in keeping with the ancient frowsty atmosphere of the rooms in which so many momentous orders were being penned.

The news I had gathered on the 28th, the day after my arrival, was most disquieting. There seemed to be no doubt that on the 25th, three days before, Germany had taken some preliminary steps closely related to mobilization. Officers on leave had been recalled, and work had been started on the frontier fortresses. This had been answered the same evening by the French Minister of War recalling from leave all general officers and corps commanders.

On the 26th and 27th further news concerning German preparations came in; the railways had been ordered to take the prescribed measures preparatory to the concentration of troops, and the last four classes released from the colours had been ordered to hold themselves in readiness to rejoin. Then, more ominous still, requisitions began, and covering troops were reported to be moving into position. In the Grand Duchy of Baden motor-car owners received a secret order to hold their machines at the disposal of the military authorities. There was also a reliable report that certain Austro-Hungarian Corps were to begin mobilization on the 28th. The French thereupon stopped all furlough and all movement of troops, and steps were taken to keep military information out of the papers.

All this was serious enough, but worse was to come. On returning to the office on the 28th after lunch, we heard that Austria had declared war on Serbia. Then information came trickling in that Germany was surreptitiously calling up her reservists.

France brooded upon her weakness and the known strength of Germany. The news of the Austrian declaration of war cast a deep gloom on the Capital. Some still hoped against hope, but the general tone was one of despondency. The Austrian action appeared utterly unjustified after Serbia's surrender. The only explanation seemed to be that the Central Powers meant to fight whatever happened.

On the 29th it became evident that only a miracle could save the situation. Russia was mobilizing all troops in the districts on the Austrian frontier, while Belgium announced that she would take steps to defend her neutrality, and graver news from Germany came in every hour.

There was an air of mystery that evening in the flat at Passy, a lot of handing up of cases to people on top of ladders, many wrappers marked "*Félix Potin*" strewn about, a general requisitioning of cupboards, the original shabby contents of which lay about untidily with an appearance of protest at being thus rudely thrust into the light of day. Stocks of food were being laid in by my host, who, with the liveliest memories of the Siege of Paris, was determined to put off a diet of rats as long as possible.

The flat was not a cheerful place, but there was nowhere else to go, and no one whom one wished to see. It was impossible to face the questions and the reproaches which one felt were almost ready to burst forth. "Surely you are not going to leave us in the lurch?" Would we? No one knew what England was going to do.

* * *

The President of the Republic, Monsieur Poincaré, and the Prime Minister, Monsieur Viviani, had been on an official visit to Russia when the crisis became acute. They had returned as fast as the battleship transporting them could steam.

They arrived in Paris on July 29th, and were welcomed at the station by an immense crowd which, when the official group appeared, cheered itself hoarse. This was most unusual, for a French crowd is not given to manifesting its feelings in this way: generally there are too many cross-currents, the people are too busy observing and criticizing, to concentrate on any one thing and give that manifestation of enthusiasm, a great roaring cheer. But that day the people of Paris were in earnest; they were concentrated and unanimous as they yelled their welcome. Then, quite spontaneously, with bared heads, they sang the *Marseillaise*. The returned statesmen must have felt deeply moved and heartened by this great and touching welcome, this implicit proof of the confidence their countrymen placed in them.

All the way to the Elysée an immense concourse, for it was the luncheon interval of the workers, carried on the cheers of the crowd at the station.

What all these thousands of men unmistakably conveyed was a feeling of thankfulness at their leaders' safe return, relief at knowing that the hands chosen by the people themselves were again at the helm, and most of all confidence that if it were possible, they, the leaders of France, would know how to translate into action the longing for peace of the whole nation.

The two men, the President and the Prime Minister, on whom the importance of the moment placed a cloak of sacerdotal dignity, were not impressive in appearance.

Réné Viviani stood there big, grey, rather awkward, and a little bent, as if the weight of events were almost crushing him. As one looked at his face one remembered that he was first and foremost a great orator, able to sway thousands by the magic of his eloquence, in a land where great speakers are common, and one wondered what staying power this Radical Prime Minister would show in the crisis. A wave of extreme radicalism had put him at the head of affairs. He represented the anti-clerical, materialist, almost socialistic tendencies of the France of that day. He was neither chauvinist nor militarist, and certainly never contemplated his country's achieving greatness through military feats. He believed in peace and the arts of peace, and knew little or nothing of military matters save as they appeared in the works of the poets, whose verses he learnt by heart for the sake of improving his memory and embellishing his speech.

He showed decision in the crisis, but that day at the station he did not convey the impression of being a great leader.

Very different was Raymond Poincaré, President of the Republic, small, square and precise. This Lorrainer evidently knew his own mind. His view might be limited, but what came within his horizon his small, quick eyes saw with microscopic minuteness. He gave the impression of dogged determination, an impression conveyed more by the automatic quickness of his movements and the squareness of his jaw which was not concealed under his small, thin pointed beard, than by his eyes which, set close together, spoke of obstinacy, of cold relentlessness, rather than of breadth of vision. His turned up nose seemed to convey a challenge.

Later meetings with this remarkable man and great patriot confirmed these impressions. He had the persistence of a leech rather than that of a bulldog. Like a weazel he could follow a trail. His tireless industry was uncanny. Charming though he could be in conversation, cultured and of polished mind and tongue, he was hardly human. His mind, that of a great lawyer trained to deal with abstract questions, appeared to be strangely out of sympathy with human needs, incapable of understanding mere emotions. His objective he could see with the utmost clearness, and towards it he would work, wearing down opposition and even exasperating goodwill by sheer persistency and reiteration. In fact he was, except in appearance, the very opposite of what an Englishman expects a Frenchman to be. Cold, precise, unemotional, implacable, but a typical Frenchman for all that, for he was tenaciously, we would say hopelessly, logical.

The next time I was to see Monsieur Poincaré after his return from Russia was some months later when he came to the front to distribute decorations to the troops. Tireless and automatic, he went from place to place pecking at the cheeks of the bearded warriors whom he was rewarding in the name of France. A certain reserve, shyness perhaps, prevented him from appearing gracious upon these occasions, but he certainly handicapped himself unnecessarily in the eyes of the troops by the kit he had devised for himself. A chauffeur's cap with a dark blue band on which could be discerned the oak leaves that appear in gold on a French General's headdress, a kind of blue Norfolk jacket and black leggings, made up an outfit which would have made Napoleon look ridiculous.

On that afternoon in July, 1914, war was not yet declared, and all hoped that it would not be; but as I watched the President and the Prime Minister I realized afresh the helplessness of great men in the face of overwhelming events. Individuals may appear to tower above their fellows, chance or ability may have placed them at the head of affairs, but confronted by a cataclysm such as war they are helpless, and their actions and reactions are the same as those of any other little people.

When an ocean liner goes down, all on board, great and small alike, struggle with equal futility and for about the same time, against elements so overwhelming that any difference there may be in the strength or ability of the swimmers is insignificant compared to the forces against which they are pitted, and which will engulf them all within a few minutes of each other.

*   *   *

On July 30th, the French Cabinet, sitting for the first time since the crisis with a full attendance of its members, issued an order that no French troops were under any circumstances to move within ten kilometres of the frontier, and that those already beyond this line were to be withdrawn.

The importance attached by the Government to this step was again underlined when on the early afternoon of the 1st August, in spite of a violation of the French frontier by German cavalry at Xure, the French

Minister for War reaffirmed the order, stating that it applied to cavalry
as well as to all other arms, and that anyone transgressing it would be
court-martialled.

No country has ever given a more convincing proof of its will for
peace than this: France abandoned territory within her own frontiers,
left thousands of her citizens unprotected, and in fact chose to invite
attack rather than run the risk of being responsible for the first act of
war.

The troops were told that this measure was taken to ensure British
co-operation; otherwise the morale of the Army might have been affected
by an order that might be construed as having been dictated by fear or
timidity on the part of the Government. That Great Britain should be
considered in this matter was but natural. She was watching events
closely. Her leaders were absolutely opposed to war, and she would undoubtedly have turned from the aggressor.

On August 2nd General Joffre protested, pointing out that the
forbidden zone included important positions which, if the order were
enforced, would have to be abandoned to the enemy and subsequently
retaken with great loss of life. The Government yielded to these arguments, and early that afternoon the interdict was removed and absolute
liberty of movement given to the Commander-in-Chief, who, however,
gave instructions that under no circumstances should the frontier be
crossed except at his express command.*

Meanwhile the peril of France had been increasing hourly. On the
31st the telegraph wires were cut on the German side, the railway line
between Pagny and Novéant was broken, and traffic across the frontier
was everywhere stopped.

In the early afternoon of the 31st came the news that Austria and
Russia had mobilized simultaneously, and that Germany had sent an
ultimatum to the latter.

That same day an unusual spectacle was offered to an incurious and
undemonstrative Paris. Masses of Germans and Austrians besieged the
police stations to obtain the papers necessary to enable them to cross the
frontier. There they were, those enemies of tomorrow, forced to come
out into the open, sullen and scared, forming queues in the streets
outside the Commissariats. They need not have worried. No demonstration, hostile or otherwise, took place, a very interesting symptom in
a city where it takes so little to make a riot, where even a fisherman on

---

* As late as August 3rd General Joffre warned all troops under no circumstances to cross
the frontier. "If there are incidents they must arise and be developed on French territory."

the banks of the Seine collects a crowd. Today people were too preoccupied and too sad even to be made angry by the sight of men who
they knew might in a few days' time be shooting their own kindred
down.

The anxiety felt by the French General Staff at the headway the
Germans were making with their mobilization became so acute that on
July 31st General Joffre, then still only Chief of the General Staff,
although Commander-in-Chief elect, warned the Government that the
Germans were in effect carrying out their plan of mobilization without
actually proclaiming it. He explained that from that evening onwards
every delay of twenty-four hours in calling up the reservists and in putting into force the measures preparatory to a general mobilization,
would mean a loss of territory of from fifteen to twenty kilometres a day,
since the French troops would have to concentrate farther and farther
back. He stated that he could not accept this responsibility. The
Ministers felt they must bow before the reasons set forth by the responsible soldier. A telegram ordering the steps preliminary to mobilization
(*télégramme de couverture*) was sent off at 5 p.m., and the railways were
warned to be in readiness.

Then, on top of everything else, the awful news of the murder of
Jaurès came like a thunderclap, and the heart of France stood still.
What would result from the death of the great Socialist leader? Did it
mean that the forces of disorder would assert themselves, and that the
country would have to defend itself with one hand while with the other
it had to hold down the enemies within its borders? So serious was the
Government view of the news that the orders to the 2nd Regiment of
Cuirassiers stationed in Paris, which was to have moved to the frontier,
were cancelled.

Immense crowds collected for the funeral, but there was perfect order.
All heaved a sigh of relief; France was sound to the core.

On August 1st came the General Mobilization Order. Suddenly at
5.30 p.m. it appeared posted up everywhere.* We had not been told of
it in the obscure corner where we worked, but as we left the *Ministère
de la Guerre* it was quite evident that something had happened.

It was a lovely afternoon. The streets of Paris had the hot, sultry look
they have on summer evenings, relieved only by the shade from rows of
dusty-leaved chestnut-trees. The streets were as they had been the day
before, but one felt that some strange spectre was stalking abroad. The
Boulevard St. Germain was curiously still, there were few people about,

* The Order was only signed by the Minister of War at 3.30 p.m.

and no *fiacres*, a circumstance that caused my companion to explain how *fiacres* came by their name, from a courtyard in which the first cabs that plied for hire in Paris used to stand, over which presided a statue of St. Fiacre, a holy man, who hailed from Scotland, he said.

But what was the matter? That was the second woman hurrying by who seemed to be crying. At the end of the Boulevard St. Germain, near the Chamber of Deputies, by the quays, our attention was at once arrested by something unusual. Paris traffic has never been slow, but now motors fairly whizzed past, driven by men with strained, set faces. No taxi driver would stop: they were all returning to the garages. We turned. There on the walls of the Palais Bourbon, still wet from the bill-poster's brush and shining in the sun, was the Order for General Mobilization. It was to be war after all.

* * *

"You are a military gentleman, can you tell me if we are going to join in this war or not? Because if we don't these Frenchmen will have our heads off, and I don't blame them neither, we'll have deserved it."

Thus quoth the British Embassy porter, evidently prepared to meet his fate like a stoic. Easy enough to be cheerful to him, but would we join in? It was painful beyond words.

I have already hinted that during these days I had to contend with difficulties, both personal and official, but these are best forgotten. My telegrams begging to be recalled were only answered at last by a curt order to remain, so there was nothing to do but to make the best of it.

I watched the citizens of this nation that was at war with poignant curiosity. What were they doing, how did they take it, what were they thinking? Would the people at home react in the same way if we joined in? The first conclusion did not take long to come to; they were wasting no time in vain regrets now that the great machine of war had been set in motion. One realized with surprise how the surrender by the individual of his will contributed to settle jarred nerves. Those who were mobilizable had nothing to do but obey orders. The feeling that they were being embodied in a great machine, and that the machine was running smoothly, was a great help. Every man knew what to do. The man from whom I hired a bicycle – now the only available means of transport – was due to report to his unit on the tenth day of mobilization, the tobacconist, on the other hand, was to go on the fourth. There was no confusion and no fuss. One was to go to Dijon, the other to Belfort. It was in the mobilization order in each man's possession, all he had to do was to go to a station and step into a train. It was noticeable too that everyone was too busy settling up his own private affairs to think much about anything else. It was of course those who remained behind who suffered most. Pathetic groups filled the stations, whole families helped to carry along the porterless platforms the bags of the men who were going.

Mobilization proceeded apace and without the slightest hitch, an enormous relief in view of the vital importance of keeping to schedule.

One of the first steps of the French mobilization had been strikingly carried out in Paris. It had consisted in the police pouncing on all doubtful characters and locking them up. They went about with motor buses which they filled as they went along. This was a very wise step in a cosmopolitan city like Paris at a time when it was essential that no hitch should occur. An anarchist attack on any of the railways, for instance, might have had very serious consequences indeed.

The first four days of August were a time of terrible doubt as to what Great Britain's attitude would be. The French people had been bitterly disappointed at the non-committal answer President Poincaré had received to the urgent appeal he had sent to the King, and the technicians, the responsible soldiers, were in a fever lest the delay should upset all their plans, for their calculations had been based on the assumption that we would come in, if we did so at all, at the same time as the French.

Many hard things were said about the British, and indeed it could hardly have been otherwise. Our situation and peculiar difficulties were not taken into account or even realized except by a very few. To the average Frenchman it looked as if we were turning out to be the worst kind of fair-weather friends, and history, that mirage of the past, was invoked to show how false England was apt to prove. Snatches of conversation overheard in restaurants or in the street indicated how the wind was blowing. "And how do you suppose she came by the name of perfidious Albion?" seemed to bring many discussions to a conclusive end.

It is true that these sentiments were uttered by the same type of person who said, a few days later, when we were in the war and there was no possibility of our withdrawing: "Yes, quite useful of course, but she has no army."

During the whole of this period the only people who gave rein to their excitement, with the exception of some youths who broke a number of windows in shops belonging to Germans, were the foreigners resident in Paris. Bands of Greeks, Roumanians and others paraded the streets waving their national flags and manifesting noisily their enthusiasm for the French cause. They were watched with interest by the indigenous inhabitants, who took no part in these sporadic displays, though the evidence of support did not displease, being taken to mean that abroad the attitude of France was appreciated and understood, and that sympathy was felt for the nation reluctantly compelled to fight. What practical form, if any, this enthusiasm took I do not know, but some Englishmen and a few Americans who had not done so much in the way of processing joined the Foreign Legion.

At last, at the end of what seemed a frightful nightmare of suspense and sickening anxiety, Great Britain sent her ultimatum to Germany. A few hours later we were at war. All France heaved a sigh of relief, but immediately began pessimistic computations of the numerical strength of the armies we could put in the field. Few if any Frenchmen then or later realized the strength inherent in England's sea-power. The people were pleased, however, at hearing the most unfounded rumours that barges loaded with British troops had been seen coming up the Seine to Rouen the day after we declared war. They concluded that although we might not be numerous we were at least prompt!

After the first flush of this new excitement was over hope was again centred on Russia. The French nation said to itself that its own army could hold on until the giant Russian tortoise had begun to advance with devastating sureness, developing an irresistible pressure on the eastern frontier of Prussia. Then the French Armies would have their opportunity, the time to advance would come, and the war would be won.

So thought the people in their simplicity, but they knew nothing of the intentions of the General Staff. They had never heard of Plan XVII, the manœuvre on the success of which their existence as a nation was about to be staked.

Now that Great Britain had declared war, I put on my uniform.

"How funny you look, disguised as a dusty canary," observed the female *concierge* who let me in at one of the more obscure entrances to the *Ministère de la Guerre*, when she saw me for the first time in khaki. This was disappointing, but one became used to the fact that for a long time the French thought that to go to war in a collar and tie represented an attitude of levity quite out of keeping with the seriousness of the situation.

Throughout these days, the country was changing before one's eyes, metamorphosised from a land of commerce and of art into an immense armed camp. Everything that was of peace seemed to be struck by paralysis, whilst new organisms that had existed only in an embryo state in those dusty pigeonholes at the War Office crept out as living things and grew and grew until they swallowed up the nation.

A file was taken out, the red tape tying it was undone, and it was as if some genie had been let loose. The railways were his servants: he scattered himself into a thousand telegrams, trains were stopped, and he laughed to see poor bewildered passengers turned out anywhere but at their right destinations. Engines he collected by the hundred, trains were formed out of cattle-trucks, goods-vans, passenger coaches, anything would do, and all were sent on, oh so slowly, to strange destinations, carrying nothing but men, always men, packed tightly together, not knowing whither they were being sent.

Another genie, barely released, gripped the telegraph wires, the nerves of the nation, only letting loose what he chose: desperate summonses, appeals for help from the sick or dying, these could wait, while he scanned every message, peered into letters, listened with a thousand ears, searching for the spy and the informer, keeping the lines clear for the commands of the new power, grown suddenly omnipotent, of which he was the servant.

Thus the Spirit of War let loose his minions over France, and seizing upon all that lived, man and beast, set his mark upon them.

As one watched the men torn without a moment's warning from their peaceful occupations and from their families, dropping the tool, the pen or the plough, the fisherman his net and the man of fashion his sport, going quietly each to his appointed place, shouldering the heavy pack and rifle and putting on the ill-fitting uniform made shabby by many previous wearers, one realized that each individual as he doffed his civilian clothes had made an immense sacrifice, that the change of clothing was a symbol. For him life as he had known it was over, and at the end of the Calvary that each man knew he was just beginning to ascend, was death in the prime of life.

Yet all came, many too soon, the others at the appointed time, none late, each bringing his life as a gift to his country to do with as she willed.

There is a subtle yet immense difference between a conscripted nation and one free from this incubus. In England, in an emergency, thousands upon thousands of men can be relied upon to come forward at once of their own free will, ready to risk their lives for their country's sake. Nothing can be finer than this. Under our system each man is his own judge, weighs whether he must go or whether he can stay behind. But a nation which adopts conscription denies the right of each man to decide for himself whether he shall fight or not, and, anticipating the act of personal sacrifice, deprives the individual of his opportunity for heroism. Every mother knows that her son's blood must be shed at his country's call without discussion or argument. Every man knows that whether he likes it or not he will automatically become a part of war. The supreme moment when it comes involves him in nothing more spectacular than mute acquiescence. There is no glory in it, no chance for pride. Such a sacrifice of individuality is only possible in a community where civilized man cares enough for the heritage left him by a long line of self-sacrificing forbears, to be willing to lay down his life at any time to preserve it.

It is a mistake to think that conscription makes for militarism. I have never met a conscripted soldier who did not long for his release, who did not find the call of duty an almost intolerable waste of the best years of his life, rendered bearable only by the sense of accomplishing a noble and necessary duty. On the contrary, anti-militarism is born in a barrack-room and gains vigour and strength by strenuous exercise on the square, while pack drill gives added bitterness to its spleen. It is inevitable that anti-militarism should find its disciples amongst all those who suffer real or imaginary wrongs in the Army, among the many men who either never accept the sacrifice conceded by the majority as necessary, or rebel against the discipline the bitter memory of which, superseding all other thoughts, drives them into violent opposition to the Army as such.

Conspicuous in those early days of August, 1914, were the indomitable women of France. I watched them sending their men off to the war: shouldering the responsibility of all that the men were leaving behind, guaranteeing the home, the farm, the business, obstinate, brave, sturdily practical, undertaking to keep the life of France going for the men who were gone. The old men, the fathers, mostly stood by, feebly silent, until the trains had left, unable to find words in which to cloak their misery.

CHAPTER II

GRAND QUARTIER GÉNÉRAL, VITRY-LE-FRANÇOIS

August 5th–8th, 1914

Departure for the G.Q.G. – The G.V.C.s – Le Grand Quartier Général – Joffre – The G.Q.G. offices – The Staff – Some considerations concerning the French pre-war Army – Personalities at the G.Q.G. – Operations and Intelligence.

I WAS ordered to the Grand Quartier Général* on August 5th, and was told I would be taken there in the liaison car leaving the War Office at 1.30 p.m.

Our departure caused some excitement. We piled into the car, a huge racing machine owned by a very nice man who had been mobilized as its chauffeur. His brother was, I think, the extra chauffeur. A gendarme in charge of despatches accompanied us.

As the great doors swung open and the first British officer started for the front, a cheer burst forth from the hundreds of clerks, orderlies, etc., who had just marched back from dinner, *"La Soupe"* at a neighbouring barrack, and were leaning out of the windows or were still in the immense courtyard.

The driver stopped at a bazaar to buy two large Red Ensigns which were secured to the windscreen as a sign that the British really were in the war. On the way I learnt for the first time the secret of our destination: the G.Q.G. had been installed that morning at Vitry-le-François.

The chauffeur, like many wealthy men who owned cars, had been mobilized according to an arrangement whereby motorists were called up with their machines. This system had great advantages in peace time from everybody's point of view: the owners did manœuvres in comparative comfort and the staff had excellent cars; but in war time it became apparent that the arrangement was unfair, and soon nearly all

---

* For convenience in this narrative the Grand Quartier Général will be designated as it was in the war, the G.Q.G.

the amateur chauffeurs joined the ranks. There was a story current in the Army at a later date, of a general, who, recognizing in the chauffeur holding open the door of the car he was about to step into, the heir to one of the great Napoleonic families, said to him: "Allow me to congratulate you, sir. Your grandfather led men; you, I see, drive Generals." A typical example of that smooth and polished irony found only in France, which, uttered in the most polite tones, is quite deadly in its effect, yet so subtle, so insidious, that the writhing victim is entirely deprived of means of retaliation.

The roads were deserted, which was lucky, for our pace was furious. We only pulled up when we met posts of elderly men in plain clothes, armed with shotguns, guarding level crossings and bridges. These were the *"gardes des voies et communications"*, G.V.C.s for short, who did not wear any sort of uniform until later. Those we met upon this occasion were calm and reasonable human beings, in which qualities they differed completely from some other G.V.C.s encountered farther north.

I was soon to learn how dangerous these old gentlemen could be, and how considerable were the delays they imposed on messengers carrying important despatches. They were a nightmare. The less they knew the more suspicious they were sure to be; the greater one's hurry the more slowly would they inspect one's papers, leisurely turning them round and round, painstakingly examining the back.

If you were lucky you spotted the post some way ahead and the car had time to slow down and stop. If not, the risk was great. A sentry, finger on trigger, would bounce out from behind a hedge when the car was almost alongside him, and would fire if it was not stopped immediately. Having no idea how hard it is suddenly to pull up a fast-travelling car, hating all motors, full of tales of Germans tearing about the countryside (we all remember the "blue" car full of spies or the "red" car crammed with Huns that haunted the roads in those days), he was apt to fire first and apologize afterwards.

At night the G.V.C.s were even more dangerous than in the daytime, and the delays they caused were longer. As on some roads these posts were constantly met with, the waste of time they occasioned was often serious, for minutes were often worth more than all the treasure of the Grand Mogul.

Many of these wayside scenes must have been curious to watch: a car in which sat an officer half dead with fatigue, the bearer of urgent orders or news, a sentry covering him with a rifle, whilst three or four

old Territorials, partially illiterate,
handed to them by the light of a lan *1914*

The G.V.C.s went on being more or .
war. They were perfectly useless, and nev
of a pass was required. I remember hearin
nurse who got out of Calais by showin
ticket.*

* * *

We got to Vitry-le-François, a tiny sleepy little to
towards evening, and stopped in the big *Place* in fi
where General Headquarters were lodged.

General Joffre was walking up and down talking
Captain Muller. He said a few words of greeting as I was b
him, then resumed his slow walk. His hands were clasped
broad back, he wore the red and gold cap of a French genei
black tunic that from about the third button down sloped ge
ward. His red breeches were baggy and ill-fitting. The outfit wa
pleted by cylindrical leggings.

He had a big face, rather soft in texture, though not flabby,
hinges and sides of the jaw forming a bold outline. His chin was marke
and determined. The whiteness of his hair, the lightness of his almost
colourless blue eyes, which looked out from under big eyebrows the
colour of salt and pepper, white predominating, and the tonelessness of
his voice coming through the sieve of his big whitish moustache, all gave
the impression of an albino. His cap was worn well forward so that the
peak protected his eyes, which resulted in his having to tilt his head
slightly to look at one.

A bulky, slow-moving, loosely-built man, in clothes that would have
been the despair of Savile Row, yet unmistakably a soldier.

---

* At a later date the G.V.C.s were to a great extent replaced by gendarmes, who were less
dangerous but almost as trying, for as years went by many G.V.C.s realized their uselessness
and were content to gape at passing traffic: not so the gendarmes, whose painstaking con-
scientious stupidity was constantly railed at by the French officers themselves. These tiresome
traits of the gendarmes were not a growth of the war, for the lack of perspicacity of the
species was proverbial and has been sung and rhymed for years.

A typical story of a gendarme was told me during the battle of the Somme. He was from
the interior and had never seen an observation balloon. He gazed at one for some time in
puzzled astonishment, then, espying the cable that held it to earth, an idea struck him. "If a
German shell cut the rope, what an awful fall the poor man up there would have!" He visualized the balloon as precariously balanced on the end of a rope like an apple on the end of a
billiard cue.

GRAND QUARTIER GÉNÉ...m were his dominant charac-
Very often this trait baffled his
He looked placid. Placidity to speak he did not utter a word.
teristics. He was impenetra dquarters, listen in silence to what
subordinates. At times w without opening his mouth, leaving
He has been known to rders buzzing unvoiced in the heads
was said, and step b happened the effect was extremely
queries, questions of generals and staff officers would
of those he left zing in dismay at the fast disappearing
comic to an vanished in a cloud of dust they would
remain riv rnation, turn their hands out in the ex-
motor. means "What will you?" and shrugging
look eadquarters building.
pr en Joffre had something to say he did not
ined silent if he had no positive ideas to put
s to make. He was always prepared to listen,
med to have time upon most occasions to do
gent matters required his attention he would
ie individual speaking to him.

sed was terrific in its concentrated quiet force,
od. There were then a few short gestures of the
ice rose half a tone, whilst the head was thrown
he words that came forth from under the shaggy
ver either disregarded or forgotten. To the very end
he held active command he kept absolute discipline
enerals. A corps commander whom his direct chief, the
nmander, might find difficult to deal with, invariably became
derfully tractable after a talk with General Joffre.

He had another quality, untried as yet, which proved of inestimable value: a great clarity of vision built upon a powerful self-confidence that made him entirely proof against getting "rattled". He was a man of great courage. Events were to show that he possessed a capacity for taking punishment that might have turned Jack Johnson grey with envy. It was perhaps this trait which enabled him to maintain a robust optimism in face of the appalling events now so close upon him. His shoulders appeared strong enough and broad enough to bear any responsibility, as indeed they proved to be. His silence strengthened this impression of strength. He obviously required no confidant, and certainly no commander was ever less under the influence of his Staff.

Such was Papa Joffre, "*Le Grandpère*" as his Army later called him, the man who at the moment carried as crushing a burden as has ever weighed down human shoulders.

This burden had not yet assumed the frightful weight it became a few weeks later, but one could not help a feeling of awe coming over one at the sight of this man, by virtue of his position the greatest of all the great men on the Allied side, in whom the hope of so many nations rested, the centre of interest of a planet, walking up and down, like an elderly bourgeois of the uninteresting little town of Vitry, whose habit it was to stroll of a summer evening before putting on his slippers and lighting his lamp.

A billet was found for me in the house of some rather dazed people who lived in terror of the G.Q.G. Guards. These were the formidable *"Gardes Forestiers"*, who watched over the Government forests in peace time, but who had nothing of the ghilly or the gamekeeper in their composition. They were used to patrolling the great forests of Eastern France on the look-out for smugglers, poachers, and undesirables who might come creeping across the frontier, gentry not slow to use their weapons, and demanding on the part of the representatives of the law who tracked them down qualities of rare determination and sternness.

It was as much as your life was worth not to know the sign and countersign when challenged by the stealthy patrols in constant movement about the town after dark. They nearly did for Colonel Ignatiev, the Russian Military Attaché, one night. That genial soul was the only foreign officer at the G.Q.G. when I arrived; a typical specimen of his race, big, blonde, bulky, fond of a good yarn, good champagne, good cheer and a nap after lunch. He was propelling his large person home to his billet one night, humming some cheerful tune, when he was challenged. *"Qui va là"* rang out sharp as a pistol-shot from an advancing patrol. Now the password was "Austerlitz" and Ignatiev, remembering it, was shocked. He had paid no attention when told it, but now it occurred to him with force that Austerlitz was a word of evil omen, an ill-sounding word in Russian ears, and he said so. Addressing the patrol through the darkness, he inveighed against the tactlessness, the immorality, of insulting Allies upon whom you were lavishing requests to hurry up and fight. To make his point clear to his invisible audience he began to advance, which is a mistake when challenged by *Gardes Forestiers* deeply imbued with a sense of the importance of their functions. Several bolts had clicked before Ignatiev, happily for all concerned, reached his peroration. "Austerlitz, Austerlitz, what a word to inflict on a Russian!" he cried, and the sound of the password, even mixed in this Russian salad, placated the patrol sufficiently to give time for his papers to be examined.

The offices of the G.Q.G. were installed in the large rooms belonging to the school. The 2ème Bureau (Intelligence), where I was given a desk, was in the gymnasium, where the rings and trapezes had been fastened out of reach of athletic officers who might have been tempted to use them.

The officers worked in sections and shifts, each section in its own part of the hall, installed at school desks. The atmosphere was that of a monastery or a factory, if anything so chilly as a factory of ideas can be imagined. The offices were open day and night and each section worked in shifts of eight hours. Each individual was paired with another to whom he handed over at the end of his spell of duty the information that had come in and the work he had done.

At one end of the room was an enormous map on which reports concerning the enemy were marked up. It was revised and brought up to date twice a day, and the only stir there ever was in the great silent room occurred when some important news came in. Then officers would tiptoe up and discuss it in whispers, or stand round square-headed, square-shouldered Colonel Dupont, the remarkable Head of the 2ème Bureau, whilst he briefly expounded his views.

If you had no special job to do it was duller than watching a hunt from a bathchair. Everything at Vitry was subdued and monotonous. No traffic, no sound in the street save the occasional whirr of a great car carrying liaison officers whose mysterious looks gave one clearly to understand that they were the bearers of awe-inspiring secrets. Even the motor-park was abandoned save by the men on the cars next for duty.

The only relief to the endless routine came at meal-times when the whole of the outgoing shift trooped over to the mess, the "*popotte*", where extremely good though simple food was served. After meals we went off to the local Café in the Place and ordered our "*café filtre*" which was served at a little marble table, but not by the usual white-aproned black-coated "*garçon*", the adjunct of every café in France: he was gone with all the other men, and was perhaps thinking at this moment with regret of the sunny shadeless square, where at this time of day he would have been dashing in and out carrying foaming *bocks* on a little metal tray, calling out "*Trois bocks, deux cafés*", as with the incredible agility of his kind he served his civilian customers. These, like the *garçon*, were gone.

Their places were taken by men in uniform, and the *garçon*'s by a very old man who looked like the *doyen* of all the waiters. He waited with shaky hands and would have found it hard to get through his work had he not been helped by a neat young girl, who might well have been the heroine of the song "Madelon".

Gazing out from under the café awning, watching the strolling officers making for the welcome shade, and the few civilians who dared face the sweltering heat, the thought arose of the endless trains with their burden of armed men clanging towards the frontier, and by contrast the silence here at Vitry seemed as tense as a violin string, growing even tauter, until one felt it must break with a nerve-wracking snap.

But it never broke: outwardly at least the G.Q.G. remained till the end of the war as it was at the beginning, infinitely quiet and subdued, turning whatever place it descended upon into a town of whispers.

I found the officers of the G.Q.G. a most interesting body of men. They were all of more than average intelligence. The general tone among them was one of polite reserve, and it was rare that the natural exuberance even of those who hailed from the voluble south was allowed to pierce through the cold professional veneer. When, subsequent to the attacks in Alsace of August 6th, extraordinary reports came in to the effect that the German commissariat had broken down, that the enemy troops were ill-fed and discouraged, that the equipment of their cavalry was so defective as to be already wearing out, and that their artillery fire was utterly ineffective, the curb put by some officers on their optimism showed signs of relaxing. But in the main the general tone of absolute self-control was well maintained by the majority and imposed on the rest. I remember well with what distaste, almost apprehension, this wave of optimism was viewed by some, notably by Lieut.-Colonel Zoppf, Head of the Secret Service.

To anyone not familiar with the French Army the impression created by its professional officers was a strange one. For the first time one realized that there existed in the French body politic a fraternity of several thousand men who seemed to have inherited the qualities of the old orders of warrior knights. They differed from their prototypes in that they had taken no vow of chastity, as was evident from their conversation. Indeed, one of the first things I heard at Vitry was that according to a Papal Ordinance several centuries old, soldiers at war who had crossed three rivers – or was it seven? – were absolved from their marriage vows, and the question arose whether crossing the same river backwards and forwards counted towards the total. But subsequent observation led to the conclusion that however free the talk, this type of Frenchman at any rate was singularly domesticated and had little thought beyond his profession and his wife and family. It was gradually borne in on one that these men, day by day and week by week in each long succeeding year of dull routine in a garrison town, or of intensive work in one of the various colleges or on the Staff, had sacrificed themselves to an immensely high ideal of service to their country.

This was the rule, an invariable one amongst the Staff officers, who formed an aristocracy within the great body of professional officers. Indeed, they seemed to consider themselves the High Priests of the profession, the repositories of the True Faith, the Adepts. But although at the moment I am only concerned with genuine Staff Officers, "patented", as the French say, it is important to explain, lest a wrong impression should be gained, that there were a large number of regimental officers in whom slow promotion and poor prospects had stifled ambition and enterprise. Many of these had become atrophied by the deadly drudgery of life in a small garrison town. On the eastern frontier this was not the case; the stimulus of the neighbouring Germans spurred energy and maintained a high level amongst all the troops stationed in this region, but in other parts of France the endless routine of training recruits was apt to have a soporific effect, and many officers were gradually absorbed into the life of the small town where they lived and where they probably married. These officers, living their lives in one sleepy corner, often became engrossed in the small material interests so characteristic of the French middle class, and from these interests the monotony of their work was hardly a relief. To such men the question of stores and equipment was far more important than tactical training, and the main object of their care became to have no trouble at inspections.

French officers as a class were very ill paid, and unlike the German officers derived no compensation from any special social position granted them by the public. On the contrary they were actually deprived by a large section of the nation of the consideration given in almost every other country to the officers of the Army. Moreover, some of these men had been actually persecuted, for many of them were devout Roman Catholics, and to practise religion had been a black mark against a man's name when the War Office had been administered by General André. During that period Army discipline was shaken to its foundations and the loyalty of officers strained to breaking point.

Incalculable harm was done by the system of *"fiches"* whereby some subordinates were allowed to make reports on their superiors through a secret political organization. The sense of duty of many officers was further tried almost beyond endurance when at the time of the separation of Church and State they were called upon to enforce the law secularizing church property. The Army suffered greatly also from the result of the Dreyfus Trial.

But somehow the tradition survived. The corps of officers remained true to its ideals, and the tradition asserted itself more and more as the war went on. All praise is due to these men who, through years of opposition, had so high a sense of duty that they went doggedly on serving their patriotic ideal, at the cost of great self-abnegation and the sacrifice of all the good things of this world. It is not unlikely that those who suffered most in peace for the sake of what they believed, were able to face the difficulties of war the better for the ordeal. Further, the lack of success early in the war of several officers whose promotion had been attributed by rumour to their political or anti-religious views, did much to clear the way for others who had shunned politics and were not even overwarm in their support of the existing régime. Be this as it may, at the end of the war many of the most important commands were held by men who had never concealed their profound devotion to the Catholic faith, even at a time when to proclaim it had meant to jeopardize their careers. Notable among these were Marshal Foch and General de Castelnau, known throughout the French Army as *"le capucin botté"* (the fighting friar).

Some staffs, and the French were not alone in this, were not entirely free from an unfortunate tendency to form a group round the Commander, to surround him jealously, to filter the very air he breathed. Sometimes such a group was the natural consequence of long service under one Chief, at others it was the result of pure sycophancy, or, it was hinted, was due to a similarity of training, intensely religious and instinctively opposed to radical or even mildly liberal views and to what is implied in France by Freemasonry. Whatever the cause, the effect was always bad, resulting in the Commander being to a certain extent segregated and deprived of direct touch with the great broad feeling of the Army. In the French Army such groups were called *"Petites Chapelles"*.

Naturally enough perhaps, now that the war had come, the professional soldiers had a tendency to look down on the reserve officers, and to believe genuinely that the civilian could never really understand war or fill an important post in the Army even in his speciality, and they barred his way accordingly. This was unfortunate, and in some cases prevented the best use being made of highly qualified men. It must be confessed also that some professionals felt that now at last they were coming into their own, that this was their chance, and that any trespassing within their preserves was an intolerable injustice to be resisted in every possible way.

Natural too was the dislike and mistrust of a capricious and meddlesome Parliament. Deputies were the subject of endless quips and jokes in which there was often more bite and sarcasm than humour. But in spite of this there was a general and absolute respect for the Republican form of government which France of her own free will had chosen.

General Joffre had passed through the storms of previous years unscathed. He was certainly not a religious man and did not practise religion, although he was extremely tolerant of the views of others. On the other hand he owed nothing to politics, save that, his tendencies being known, there had been nothing to stand in the way of his promotion. Moreover he understood how to handle politicians, and his immense and stolid silence, so different from their own garrulity, impressed and even awed them. The Commander-in-Chief was undoubtedly a good republican in the sense given to the words in France. Indeed it is difficult to imagine how he could have been anything else, for he was of humble origin, and it was said that like Ney he was the son of a cooper. He had been born in the distant Catalan country at the foot of the Pyrenees. His extreme simplicity was that of the small *bourgeoisie* which is the embodiment as well as the backbone of the Third Republic.

General Joffre's chief assistant was General Belin, the *Major Général* (Chief of Staff). I had very little to do with this distinguished officer, and I only remember him as vivacious, smart and soldierly. He was oppressed by the immense burden of his task, and I understand that the strain imposed on him by the retreat of the French Armies nearly killed him.

Very different was the *Aide-Major-Général* (Assistant Chief of Staff) General Berthelot, who was the best known and most often quoted of the great men at the G.Q.G. He was a brilliantly clever, amazingly fat man. The tendency was to be so overwhelmed by his bulk that his extremely clever quick eyes escaped notice at first. In his own room he was fond of wearing a blouse, and rumour, perhaps correct for once, proclaimed that this and a pair of slippers was what constituted in his opinion the only sensible uniform for a General Officer who, tactically handicapped by a weight of 17 stone or so, had to wrestle with strategy in a temperature of 90 degrees in the shade. He was always at work and universally popular. His robust temperament and great heart enabled him to face the bad days that were to come, carrying with them the collapse of his calculations and the brushing aside of his dreams, with an optimism that would not be denied.

These were the men around whom the whole of the G.Q.G. revolved. Everyone else existed to provide the material upon which these great ones based their decisions, or to carry out the details of the orders they might give, and no potentates, no captains of industry offering gold or personal gain as an incentive, were ever so well served.

But gradually, as the working of the Staff at Vitry became more familiar, one began to wonder whether there were not serious defects in the system.

Was it well, for instance, that the two most important sections of the Staff, Operations and Intelligence, should work in watertight compartments?

The French and British Armies were alike in this respect, and it did not require much foresight to make one realize that the lack of intimate collaboration between the two sections might prove extremely harmful.

Operations said – "What can be the use of Intelligence knowing our plans? Their sole duty is to watch the enemy and report his movements and numbers." "That's all very well," Intelligence would argue, "but we have to divine the enemy's intentions. These are based largely on what he can guess of ours. He forms his conclusions on what he can see or hear of the movements of our troops, and how can we enter into his mind and read his thoughts if we know nothing of our own Army?" The Intelligence officers were right, but for a long time they had to work in the dark, much to the general hurt. Of course every possible means of preventing leakage of information must be employed, but the absurd handicap of blinkers imposed on your own people should never again be allowed to increase the very great difficulties of the Intelligence in obtaining information as to the enemy's intentions and movements, without which the Commander-in-Chief is like a man groping in the dark.

The pretext for the limitations imposed on the Intelligence during the war was of course secrecy, the fear that information might leak out to the enemy. In those days we lived in a nightmare of secrecy. We may have concealed our plans from the enemy but we certainly befogged our own people. Allies did not communicate their plans to each other; different branches of the staff behaved as if each thought the others only wanted information for the sake of passing it on to Berlin. How ridiculous it all was! Experience has taught that however important it may be to keep information from the enemy, if this can only be achieved by keeping your own people in the dark, thus limiting their scope and fettering their initiative, then the price paid is too high. Better far to run some risk as regards the enemy than forfeit the homogeneous co-operation of all those on your side who must work in the closest harmony to obtain victory, and co-operation is impossible if some officers are kept in ignorance of their Commander's intentions. Moreover, suppose the enemy does gather something of our plans, he will probably be informed too late, and will certainly not know whether or not to believe what he hears, unless the information is confirmed by observed facts such as the movements of troops or trains spotted by his aeroplanes.

The Intelligence officer will generally be found to be an optimist, a cheerful bloke, living with the enemy, whose malevolent shadow he is, deriving an immense amount of *"Schadenfreude"* from all the mishaps that come to his ears. Guessing at the enemy's problems, and to a certain extent aware of his difficulties, his is a more hopeful outlook than that of the Operations officer, who is eternally faced with the difficulties confronting his own side and with problems which he finds it hard to realize confront the enemy as well.

This difference in outlook may easily result in lack of harmony between the two sections of the staff, and harmony is essential if a staff is to give the best results. Who will ever know what harm was done by the often unconscious adoption of a thesis by the 3ème Bureau just because the opposite point of view was advanced by the 2ème? In war, the margin between success and failure is often so slender that nothing can be overlooked with impunity, and even rivalry between officers having the best intentions and the highest motives may have very unfortunate results.

During the battle of the Somme in 1916, General Fayolle, commanding the Sixth French Army, and his Chief of Staff, the brilliant Colonel Duval, seeing the danger of working in watertight compartments, had a daily conference at which all the heads of sections were present as well as representatives from all the corps. They were told exactly what the Army Commander's intentions were, and exchanges of information took place between them there and then, the duties of all being made to dovetail into each other. There was no secrecy, and each officer was able to get on with his job without having to waste time guessing what the other fellow was at.

This was much later in the war, however, and at the time of which I am writing the compartments dividing the staff and the walls dividing Allies had not yet been broken down. The obsession of secrecy was long to endure, and in some quarters outlasted the war, clogging the machinery, obstructing co-ordination and narrowing vision.

CHAPTER III

PLAN XVII

August 9th–14th, 1914

Colonel Huguet – The problem of the detrainment of the B.E.F. – Joffre's decision – French mobilization and concentration – The necessity of a definite plan – Why the French decided on an offensive – The "forward" school – "Plan XVII." – Why it failed – Pre-war talks in Berlin – Errors in French calculations – Departure from Vitry-le-François.

ON the morning of August 9th, I found Colonel Huguet having breakfast in our mess. He was to occupy the extremely important position of Head of the French Mission attached to the British Army. It was through him that General Joffre would communicate with Sir John French, and it was his Mission that would deal with the very complex questions of the relations of the British with the French civil authorities and inhabitants. All French officers attached to the British would be under his orders. His Mission became known as "*La Mission H*", just as the British Army was always alluded to as the "Ws", this name being I believe derived from the code-book in French and English known as Code W which had been compiled for use between the two Armies in case of war, though it is possible, as many thought, that it was derived from the initial of General Wilson's name, for he was well known to and looked upon with particular favour by the French.

I had known Colonel Huguet well in London. An olive-complexioned, dapper, little gunner, whose short hair was brushed forward and apparently glued to his scalp, he was very suave and friendly, professing the greatest admiration for England and all things English. He manipulated the English language fluently, thanks to a plentiful lubrication of the difficult words – and they mostly seemed to be difficult for him – with a shower of "z's".

Huguet was an intimate friend of General Henry Wilson's. On the great question of British co-operation on land with the French he had found a convinced supporter in Wilson. Huguet had been French Military Attaché in London until shortly before the war, and the two men had carried out work together without which the B.E.F. could not have landed when and how it did. They understood each other perfectly, and were at one in their endeavours to prevent the British Government from taking alarm at the extent of their preparations.

Colonel Huguet had just arrived via Paris from London, where he had been trying to persuade Lord Kitchener to alter his decision to postpone the embarkation of the Army until Sunday, August 9th. General Joffre when he heard of this wrote to the President of the Republic begging him to use his influence to prevent any kind of delay, but the British War Office found it impossible to rescind their decision. Now another question had arisen. Where were the British troops to detrain? Lord Kitchener wished them to detrain about Amiens, as he considered concentration in the region between Maubeuge and Le Cateau, as originally planned, somewhat too risky. Sir John French was against this change, so it had been settled in London to refer the matter to General Joffre, hence Huguet's visit. It goes without saying that General Joffre was of Sir John's opinion, so the Le Cateau-Maubeuge area was decided upon.

Colonel Huguet told the Commander-in-Chief the day I saw him at Vitry (August 9th) that he was convinced the dates laid down in the peacetime plan could be anticipated, expressing it as his opinion that the British fighting forces could be in a position to advance on the 21st, whereas the original plan fixed the 23rd as the date on which the last troops of the B.E.F. would detrain in the zone of concentration. He proved to be quite right, and on August 21st the British Army was concentrated and moving forward to its positions. It was actually in contact with the enemy on the 22nd.*

* * *

During the time I was at the G.Q.G. French mobilization and concentration were being steadily proceeded with, with wonderful smoothness and practically without a hitch. The whole of this concentration was

---

* The change in the date of embarkation of the B.E.F. was due to the fact that the August Bank Holiday had necessitated a short delay in the plans for the concentration of the Army.

As is well known, British mobilization was carried out with the utmost smoothness and despatch. On an average thirteen ships a day transported the four divisions and the cavalry division, which was shortly followed by a fifth, the 4th, which arrived in time for the battle of Le Cateau.

based upon the now famous "Plan XVII", and it is necessary to make clear at this stage what the plan was, and how it came to be adopted.

To understand the problem of mobilizing a modern continental army, it is important to realize that the whole process is a race against time. If the mobilization is delayed or slow, the enemy will be enabled to advance with a fully equipped army against an unprepared one, which would be disastrous.

The time factor also makes it essential that the Armies once mobilized should find themselves exactly where they can at once take up the role assigned to them. There is no opportunity for extensive manœuvres: mobilization is in itself a manœuvre at the end of which the armies must be ready to strike according to the pre-arranged plan.

This plan is therefore obviously of vital importance. It has of necessity to be somewhat rigid, for it has to be worked out in every detail beforehand. From the moment mobilization is ordered, every man must know where he has to join, and must get there in a given time. Each unit, once complete and fully equipped, must be ready to proceed on a given day at the appointed hour to a pre-arranged destination in a train awaiting it, which in its turn must move according to a carefully prepared railway scheme. Each unit has also to drop into its place in the higher formations, and these again must find themselves grouped in position according to the fundamental plan. No change, no alteration is possible during mobilization. Improvisation when dealing with nearly three million men and the movements of 4,278 trains, as the French had to do, is out of the question.

It will be understood therefore with what care this plan on which success or failure might depend has to be thought out, weighed and minutely prepared.

The problem was one of especial difficulty and urgency for the French. As regards the time factor, they knew that the Germans would almost certainly be the aggressors, and would probably decide upon war secretly and begin to mobilize surreptitiously before the French became aware of their intentions, thus gaining hours and even days. This was in fact what happened in July, 1914.

Further, the French plan could not and did not envisage the possibility of invading neutral territory, unless Germany, by setting the example, compelled France to follow suit. Germany placed no such limitations upon her own action, and the French knew well that, if it paid Germany to do so, the chances were that she would disregard those Treaty obligations which bound France.

And supposing Germany did violate neutral territory, how could the French know what the extent of the violation would be, or what attitude the governments of the invaded countries would adopt?

A glance at the map will show what a terrible handicap this moral obligation on her own part, this uncertainty concerning the action of a totally unscrupulous enemy, placed upon France and those whose duty it was to prepare a plan for her protection. Unwilling to surrender the initiative to the Germans by awaiting the development of the German plan and holding back until it had been ascertained if this included the violation of neutral territory, the French General Staff concluded that the only possible way out of the difficulty was for France to assume the offensive herself. This decision had the further advantage of coinciding with the theory then prevailing in military circles in France, which laid enormous stress on the importance of the attack.* (Map I, p. 34.)

This theory was so potent a factor in influencing French military policy during the opening stages of the campaign that its importance is worth emphasizing. So enthusiastic were many French officers in its favour, that the perfectly sound axiom that the best way of defending yourself is to attack, was misunderstood, and its basic principle lost sight of. It was interpreted to mean that wherever you met the enemy you should attack him, and that if you attacked with sufficient vigour you were bound to be successful. It was forgotten that an attack if undertaken at all must be made in such numbers as to render success probable, and that this can only be achieved, in the case of opposing armies which are fairly equally matched, by adopting a defensive attitude on the greater portion of the front. In other words, superiority in numbers at any given point can only be achieved by adopting the defensive elsewhere.

In the years preceding the war the doctrine of the "*offensive à outrance*" spread from the staff to the regimental officers, and soon showed itself in its tactical application: the bayonet was hailed as Queen of the battlefield, the lessons of the South African and Russo-Japanese Wars were lost sight of, and this frightful mistake resulted in hecatombs of French soldiers during the first period of the war. Thousands upon thousands of lives were lost before it was realized that infantry however brave cannot

---

* Colonel de Grandmaison was one of the most enthusiastic protagonists, in fact, the leader of the forward school. The following is a typical instance of his theories:

"The offensive spirit of a body of troops charged with an offensive mission will be destroyed if it contains more or less numerous detachments which have been allotted defensive duties. Safety is best obtained by attacking vigorously whenever one can with all one's forces. When one has seized the enemy by the throat one is his master and need not fear him."

Dover

Bruges
•Ghent

Calais
Dunkirk

⊙ BRUSSELS

Boulogne

B E L G I U M

Lille•

Mons   Charleroi   Namur Huy

•Arras

Sambre

Dinant•

Abbeville

Givet•

Somme

ARDENN

Amiens •

St Quentin

Senois

Lanrezac Ⓥ

Serre

Mezières

Meuse

Laon

Compiègne•

Aisne

Langle de Cary

Oise

Soissons

Reims

Ⓘ

F

Seine

Ourcq

Marne

Ste Ménehould• Verdu

R   A   N

Meaux•

Epernay

Châlons

Gd. Morin

PARIS

Bar-le-Duc

Seine

VITRY
le-François
GQG

C

PLAN XVII(a)

Based on the supposition that
the French and German armies
would meet only over the common
frontiers with no violation of
neutral territory

French
armies Ⓘ

WBromage.

charge in close formation over open spaces against concealed infantry and machine-guns, and that to fix bayonets and sound the charge is no magic recipe for victory.

I had attended French manœuvres a couple of years before the war, and had been much struck then by the dislike of the French infantry for digging trenches, in fact their real disdain of this form of protection, and had felt that their mass formations could only have been excused on the ground that a spectacular effect was permissible at the end of manœuvres, and might indeed be useful in conveying a false impression to foreign Military Attachés. As musketry instructor in my own regiment and fully alive to the stopping power of rifles and machine-guns, I had found the display particularly exasperating. I wondered whether they had learnt anything since then, but in the battles that were to come I had the misfortune to see these troops, animated by the highest courage, led to their doom in the same close formations I had watched at manœuvres a few years before.

The sense of the tragic futility of it will never quite fade from the minds of those who saw these brave men, dashing across the open to the sound of drums and bugles, clad in the old red caps and trousers which a parsimonious democracy dictated they should wear, although they turned each man into a target. The gallant officers who led them were entirely ignorant of the stopping power of modern firearms, and many of them thought it chic to die in white gloves.

Interwoven with and perhaps the real cause of this enthusiasm for the attack, was a deep psychological mistake. The Higher Command in the French Army was doubtful if the French infantry, supreme in the enthusiasm of an attack, would be able to stand on the defensive against the more strictly disciplined masses of Germany. The three years service had not been re-introduced until 1913, so that most of the reservists had only been trained for two years with the colours. Several French generals whom I met at this time considered that this placed the French Army at a very real disadvantage compared with the German Army, which they believed to be more highly trained than theirs.

It took the war to reveal the French to themselves, and to prove that French troops could be as stoic and as stubborn in resistance as the most stolid northerners. Years of war, terrible losses, fearful attacks, endless bombardments that seemed as if they would unhinge reason: fatigue, cold, mud, they stood them all. But for four long years France paid dearly in loss of territory for the original mistake of her military leaders, who were justified in believing in an offensive policy, but who were mistaken in the universal application, and particularly in the tactical application they gave to it, and above all were wrong in thinking that French soldiers would prove indifferent in defence.*

* * *

As has been said, the French had had to make their plan before they knew whether or not the Germans would violate neutral territory. Their field of action, therefore, once they had decided upon taking the offensive, was limited to the coterminous frontier between themselves and Germany. Fortresses and natural obstacles further restricted the field of any possible advance to a few very narrow passages in Lorraine. (Map I, p. 35.)

The plan decided upon, Plan XVII, of which General Joffre was the author, had been ratified by the *Conseil Supérieur de la Guerre* and the Government of the day. It envisaged an offensive by two armies, the First and Second, through the passages in Lorraine, with a subsidiary attack in Alsace, whilst another Army, the Fifth, attacked north of Verdun. The Third Army was to act as liaison between the Second and Fifth and undertake the investment of Metz as the campaign proceeded. The Fourth Army was to be in reserve.

The First Army was to advance on Sarrebourg, whilst one Corps, the VII., and a cavalry division invaded Alsace. The Second Army was to advance upon Château Salins and Morhange. Its two left Corps were to watch Metz from the left bank of the Moselle.

Simultaneously the Fifth Army on the left was to close in on Verdun, and passing south of the Belgian frontier was to advance on Thionville, and attack north of that fortress.

The Third Army was to advance on the right of the Fifth, whilst the Fourth Army followed in second line.

In the event of Germany's invading Belgium, certain variations of the main scheme were provided for. In that case the right wing (First and Second Armies) was to keep to the original plan, but the Fourth Army was to reinforce the left, taking up its position between the Third and Fifth Armies, and the three armies were then to advance north-east on a front extending between Thionville and a point north-east of Mézières. (Map II, pp. 38–9.)

As soon as it was clear that Germany had violated Belgium and Luxembourg these modifications were carried out, and orders to that effect were issued on August 2nd.

* See Appendix VII.

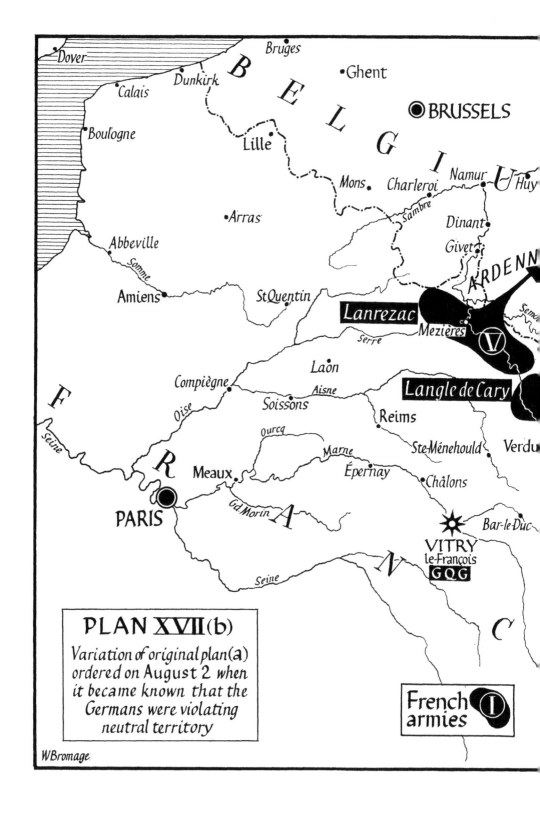

Dover · · Bruges

· Ghent

Dunkirk

Calais

⊚ BRUSSELS

Boulogne

Lille

B E L G I U

Mons · Charleroi Namur U Huy

Sambre

Arras

Dinant ·

Givet ·

Abbeville

Somme

ARDENN

Amiens ·

StQuentin

Lanrezac

Serre

Mezières

V

Sem

Laon

Langle de Cary

Compiègne

Aisne

Oise

Soissons

Reims

F

Seine

Ourcq

Marne

Ste-Ménehould

Verdu

R

Meaux

Épernay

Châlons

A

Gd Morin

Bar-le-Duc

PARIS

Seine

N

☆ VITRY
le-François
GQG

C

PLAN XVII(b)

Variation of original plan (a)
ordered on August 2 when
it became known that the
Germans were violating
neutral territory

French
armies I

WBromage

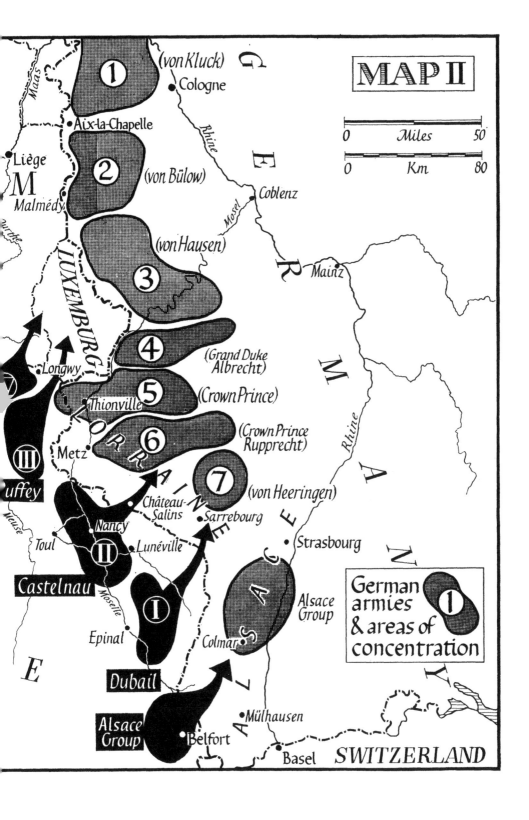

It is now a matter of history that the attacks in Alsace Lorraine carried out under Plan XVII failed disastrously, and indeed it is hard to see how this could have been otherwise, since the Germans were necessarily expecting attacks in these areas, which as has been explained were the only ones open to the French. German knowledge of French military policy must have led them to the conclusion that that policy would be an offensive one. The Germans also knew that the French would never plan to invade neutral territory. It was therefore a foregone conclusion that they should prepare for French attacks exactly where these attacks were actually delivered.

The French had been hypnotized by the belief that the Germans would resort to the famous "*attaque brusquée*", and issuing in great force from the fortress of Metz would attempt to dislocate French mobilization. They considered that Plan XVII was well calculated to meet such a contingency, as indeed it was, but unfortunately the Germans attempted no such manœuvre, and although the French had to a certain extent allowed for a German sweep through Belgium, the main flaw in Plan XVII lay in the fact that it made no allowance whatsoever for an out-flanking movement of the magnitude actually undertaken by the Germans, and was not elastic enough to parry it.

That the French should have been so misled as to German intentions is hard to understand, particularly in view of the fact that British military circles before the war accepted a wide sweep of the enemy through Belgium as possible and even probable. It was not particularly difficult to form an idea of what would be likely to occur, as even I, a mere subaltern and a very junior one at that, accidentally found out.

I happened to spend some time in Berlin during the winter of 1913–14 and there met many German officers studying at their Staff College. Conversation naturally enough often turned on the possibility of war with France. It never occurred to these professional soldiers that there would not be another conflict. It was bound to come. But when? Who could tell? At any rate it was sure to come in their time, which was all that mattered.

The possible attitude of England in such a contingency was often discussed, and these men found it hard to conceal their contempt for Britain's land forces. Yes, she had proved a doughty enemy in the past, but this time she would not have a chance to develop her full strength were she so ill-advised as to side with France and Russia. Her continental Allies would be overwhelmed long before she was ready, long before the slow pressure of her naval supremacy could make itself felt. What account need be taken of a power that had been so long defied by a handful of peasants in South Africa? Several times, in what were perhaps unguarded moments, in the course of animated talks between themselves, operations against France were discussed. From these I gathered that it was an absolute axiom of the Great General Staff that France must be overwhelmed before Russia became really dangerous. It followed that no time could be wasted in reducing the great French fortresses on the German frontier. The strength of these was not under-estimated. I heard it stated several times that although the German guns would make short work of the French forts it would nevertheless take six months to break through the French defensive system. Since they also declared it necessary that the war should be over and won in that time, as France must be beaten to her knees before the Russians became really dangerous, the inference was obvious: Belgium had to be invaded as the only means of turning the French fortresses.

I had occasion to talk these matters over with the French Military Attaché in Berlin, the gallant Colonel Seret, who was killed at Hart-mannsweilerkopf leading his *chasseurs*. He was of the opinion that the Germans were almost certain to violate Belgium. He thought they would attempt as wide a sweep as possible and might even cross the Meuse below Namur.

Nevertheless the French General Staff did not believe that in the event of an invasion of Belgium the Germans had enough troops, in view of the Russian threat, to extend north of the Meuse. Time was soon to show that in this they were mistaken, although events proved that the Germans were in fact planning too wide a movement for the troops they had at their disposal.

How did it happen that the French were so mistaken as to the numbers the Germans could put in the field at the decisive point? It was a fatal mistake, for the false assumption they made completely vitiated their plan.

The following pages will show that despite reports, information and the avalanche of troops overrunning Belgium, the G.Q.G. would not admit the evidence of men who had seen, and air observers who had noted. Why? Because all the reports were in contradiction with their preconceived ideas concerning the German plan and their calculations of the strength of the German Army in the western theatre. In these calculations they placed implicit faith. It did not occur to them that the Germans would gamble on Russia's slowness to the extent of leaving

only 250,000 men on their eastern front. This initial misreading of the
German plan led General Joffre and his advisers to the conclusion that
the Germans did not dispose of enough troops on the Western front for
so ambitious a manœuvre as would be involved in throwing large bodies
of troops across the Meuse east of Namur.

On June 13th, 1914, the French General Staff had carried out a
study of the probable German plan of attack and had estimated the
numbers that would be concentrated against France at twenty active
corps, ten reserve corps, eight cavalry divisions and eight reserve
divisions, a total of sixty-eight divisions, whereas in fact the Germans
brought against them seventy-eight divisions plus fourteen Landwehr
Brigades and ten cavalry divisions.

Further, the French Intelligence had concluded that north of Trèves
there were not sufficient sidings to allow of the simultaneous concentration of more than eleven corps, and it was argued that if the enemy
wanted to make a greater effort than this in Belgium he would have to
withdraw troops intended to defend Alsace and detrain some of these
units as far back as the Rhine. This would have meant delay, and the
French General Staff inferred that the Germans would not adopt a
plan which would necessarily retard their attack, thus robbing it of the
suddenness which the French held to be a tenet of military faith across
the Rhine. For similar reasons, the French believed the Germans would,
from political motives and because of the effect such an attack would
have on French mobilization and on French public opinion, elect to
make a sudden onslaught on the Lorraine plateau.

But when no such attack took place, and ominous reports began to
come in from Belgium, it was strange that the French General Staff,
and in particular the Commander-in-Chief, did not at once infer that
there was probably a mistake in their previsions and take steps to meet
what was likely to prove an unforeseen situation. Nothing was done,
however, and the days went by as if nothing unexpected was happening.
This war was to prove time and again how difficult it is to eradicate a
preconceived idea from the military mind.

*   *   *

My stay at the G.Q.G. was not a long one, and I was unfeignedly glad
when it began to draw to a close.

The only nice thing about Vitry was the Marne. That beautiful river
flowed through a lovely valley, and whilst bathing in it war did not

seem such an unpleasant affair after all. The Germans were so far away, the weather was so wonderfully warm, it was difficult to realize that anything serious was happening. The Marne was just a charming cool stream that none of us in our wildest dreams connected directly with the war. Who but a lunatic or a traitor would have thought that the armies concentrating so far to the north, full of hope and confidence, would soon, with despair and rage gnawing at their hearts, footsore, weary, exhausted, be crossing the river now sparkling like gold in the sun, abandoning the rich and lovely valley to the enemy? Who would have thought that the Germans would occupy luckless Vitry, which certainly felt that at the moment it was doing its bit, in fact as much as any town could be expected to do in wartime, in having ponderous, police-haunted G.Q.G. billeted on it and overflowing into every house in the town?

There was no prophet amongst us to tell us that in years to come the name of the Marne would evoke, not a picture of a broad sleepy stream, but of a gigantic battlefield, to be quoted for ever not only as one of the great turning points in human history, but as one of the sixteen decisive battles of the world.

CHAPTER IV

FIFTH ARMY HEADQUARTERS, RETHEL

August 14th, 1914

Departure for Fifth Army H.Q. – Rethel – The Army Commander – The Staff – The Marquis de Rose – Junior Staff Officers – Colonel d'Alenson – The G.Q.G. liaison officers.

ORDERS arrived from London directing me to proceed to Rethel, the Headquarters of the Fifth French Army, which formed the left of the French line. A British Mission was to arrive shortly at the G.Q.G.

I was at this time working under the direct orders of the Head of the British Intelligence, Colonel Macdonogh, and during my first few days at Rethel my duties were almost exclusively concerned with the organization of our Intelligence in this area, co-ordinating it with the French service and adapting our pre-war organization to war conditions. We were attempting to lay a net along the probable line of a German advance, a net of eyes and ears to watch and listen for the enemy, and to devise a plan whereby the information obtained could be collected and passed on. We also had a number of Intelligence Officers in Belgium with whom it was important to keep in touch. This entailed a great deal of travelling by car over considerable distances, and led to many exciting little adventures in country well beyond our outpost lines.

Individuals had to be found who would be prepared for patriotic or other reasons to run the great risks involved in collecting information. It is a duty to pay tribute to the volunteers, both men and women, who were prepared to risk their lives, fully understanding that risk, and to suffer an ignominious death at the hands of the enemy, for the sake of procuring information of use to their country and its Allies. Information from such sources was of the greatest importance, since besides air reports we had practically nothing else, for the French cavalry, in spite of the exhausting marches it was called upon to carry out, brought in little or no information of value.

I soon found that a great deal of work not connected with duties of the kind just alluded to was expected of me. Our own people kept asking me questions concerning the plans and intentions of the French. Although Colonel Bowes from the Operations Section was more especially charged with the duty of keeping in touch with the Fifth Army, and from August 20th onwards occasionally came over from G.H.Q., I had to devote more and more attention to Operations work, and even before the armies were at grips with the enemy I had little time for real Intelligence work. The fact that I was the only British officer permanently attached to the Fifth Army, and the pressure of entirely unforeseen events, forced me to assume the role of a liaison officer dealing with operations.

The British forces were to concentrate on the left of and in immediate touch with the Fifth Army,* which was called at that time the "*Armée de Paris*". It was thus camouflaged because had the numbers of the armies been known, the fact that there was no army numbered higher than five and that this was on the left of the French line, would have clearly shown the enemy both how many French armies there were in the field and where their left lay.

On the morning of my departure from Vitry-le-François, Captain Muller, General Joffre's A.D.C., told me how lucky I was to be attached to the Fifth Army, for its Commander, General Lanrezac, was a veritable lion. That very morning he had come in to see General Joffre, who had the highest opinion of him. He was the star turn, but high as was his reputation he had enhanced it: all at the G.Q.G. had been impressed by his determination, and by his declarations in favour of early offensive action. The British Army would have to hurry up if they were going to see any of the fun, since General Lanrezac was not going to delay for slowcoaches, declared Muller.

I started off for Rethel in high spirits, delighted to leave behind me the somewhat stifling and restricted atmosphere of the G.Q.G., where the only relaxation had been discussion of the verdict in the Caillaux trial (which in spite of the national emergency still loomed large in men's imaginations) and where the only breath of fresh air had been brought in by liaison officers coming from the Eastern front with accounts of the attacks in Alsace. Their stories of actual encounters with the enemy, of brave deeds carried out under a canopy of German

---

* The Fifth Army numbered about 300,000 men, including lines of communications' troops, and consisted at this date of the I., III., X. and XI. Corps, the 37th and 38th Divisions, the 52nd and 60th Reserve Divisions, the Cavalry Corps and the 4th Cavalry Division. See Appendix II.

shrapnel bursting too high to do any damage, of the welcome given the troops by a population delirious with joy at being delivered from the German yoke, had made sitting in an office appear quite intolerable. I remember, too, the intense satisfaction felt at the appearance of some German prisoners. But my clearest memory of my last days at Vitry is of a map that was brought in one day, dyed deep in blood, its centre pierced by a lancehead. It had been taken from the breast-pocket of a German cavalry officer killed when a French patrol had galloped him down.

I left Vitry in the early afternoon of August 14th.

Towards the end of the long motor journey to Rethel we began to get some relief from the torrid heat of the Champagne plain. The road gradually rose towards the Ardennes, on the first slopes of which nestled the charming little town of Rethel. We arrived towards the end of an evening that appeared to be almost cool in comparison with the furnace of the flat country behind us.

It was a pleasant little place, of some five thousand inhabitants, built on the slope of a hill overlooking the Aisne. There were some attractive seventeenth-century houses here and there in the main street, dating back to the time when the town had been the property of the famous Mazarin family. A few small factories near the river did not detract from the charm of the town, while just beyond rose the great forest of the Ardennes.

Poor Rethel, so soon to be utterly destroyed, how thoroughly we were to learn in due course from the diary of a captured German officer, who with crocodile tears noted in his journal the pity of such destruction. He added that he had had the satisfaction of finding in a half-destroyed house a mackintosh which would make a nice present for Ernst, whoever Ernst might be.

Army Headquarters were lodged in an old house giving on to the pretty little sloping square, by some steps. The Staff, unexpectedly small and homely, were pleasant and welcoming: no question here of being held at arm's length as had been the case with the imposing array at Vitry.

The General commanding the Fifth Army, General Lanrezac, was leaning against the balustrade at the door of his H.Q. looking out on the *Place*. Beside him stood his Chief of Staff, General Hély d'Oissel. The Army Commander was a big flabby man with an emphatic corporation. His moustache had more grey than white in it, as had his hair. His face was weatherbeaten and dark, and his cheeks and lower lip hung rather loosely. He was looking upward, his head tilted forward, and appeared to be in a bad temper, for a reason which will appear later. I was struck by the fact that his eyeglasses were hitched over his right ear, a trick he much favoured. My impression was one of relief when I found Muller's lion did not devour me. His Chief of Staff's manner conveyed that the General was a man whom it might be difficult to approach.

The contrast in the appearance of the two men was striking. Hély d'Oissel was extremely smart and had that trimness, ease of movement, and knowledge of the world, characteristic of the cavalry arm in the Europe of pre-war days. He was tall and slim, with a well-trimmed moustache, and was obviously a gentleman. His manners were good if formal, but it was apparent at once that the coolness of his demeanour did not conceal an exuberant nature, on the contrary it seemed to mask a certain sadness, a somewhat sceptical unhopeful outlook. His attitude towards his Chief was what one would expect in a sensitive well-bred man in constant contact with a person of whose reactions he could not be certain, and whose words might sometimes wound; but later observation proved that if he suffered from the abruptness, even the violence of manner, of General Lanrezac, this never in the least affected his perfect loyalty and devotion to his Chief.

My first impression of the contrast between the two men was strengthened by later observation of differences in manner, which cloaked a similarity of outlook on many points, the discouragement of the one blending into the pessimism of the other in the bad days that were to come.

The "*popotte*" to which I was initiated was installed in a small cinema theatre. A great occasion was made of the arrival of the first Allied officer, and an appropriate speech was delivered by Colonel Ganther, at that time head of the aviation of the Fifth Army. The warmth of the welcome afforded me was very touching. All wished to convey their gratitude to the British nation for standing by them, and the honour they felt at having the British Army for a neighbour. These regular soldiers had the highest opinion of the British Army, and their appreciation was worth having, for they were a fine body of men. They welcomed me as a comrade, and the friendships formed then will last my lifetime.

One officer in particular, Captain de Rose, attracted me instantly. Although not tall he was one of the finest looking men I have ever seen. Very fair, with a long drooping moustache and dancing blue eyes, he looked the Gaul of legend. He was a cavalryman whose extreme outspokenness and independence had got him into serious trouble at the time of the struggle between Church and State. Now he was a flying officer. He had somehow obtained the privilege of wearing a kit personal to himself: a tunic of soft black cloth with deep pockets, into which his hands were generally thrust, a white hunting stock, and the regulation red cap and breeches.

On the night of my arrival I was told of a narrow escape he had had a few days before.

Whilst on a reconnaissance over Belgium he had had to alight for lack of petrol, and had gone into a village to get some when he was told by the inhabitants that German cavalry were approaching. He rushed back to his machine carrying some tins, and was attempting to start the engine when a troop of German cavalry appeared. He had all the difficulty in the world in getting off, but happily for him the Germans, instead of making straight for him, got off their horses behind a wall 150 yards away and proceeded to take pot-shots at him. This had been going on for a good many minutes when at last his propeller began to turn, and clambering in he sailed off triumphantly over their heads.

We were soon great friends, and whenever he was not flying he accompanied me, a self-appointed escort, saying that sooner or later I would be shot by some post of Territorials if there was no French uniform to protect me: this was true enough, and he certainly got me out of some tight places.

Captain the Marquis de Rose became known later throughout the French Army as one of its best and boldest aviators. He was killed flying in 1916, when he was Head of an army. As long as those who knew him live, they will remember him as the very embodiment of the gay and gallant spirit of the French Air Service.

Many junior officers will flit across these pages because, a junior officer myself, I saw a great deal of them, and the picture I wish to draw would be incomplete without them, but there is another reason why I have not omitted some of those I remember.

It is as difficult to exaggerate as it is to describe the influence which even junior staff officers may have on the course of operations. Sometimes their influence is indirect, but it is none the less potent on that account.

This narrative will give instances of how misunderstandings between individuals, and even the moods of commanders, may affect operations on which the fate of nations depends. But it is impossible, except in a few instances, to trace these. To write accurate history it would be necessary to know not only how all those concerned worked together and reacted on each other, but also what was the exact frame of mind of the responsible man, how he understood and mentally digested the information at his disposal, what he saw and what he feared, what he apprehended and what he misunderstood. How can these things be told when the man himself cannot know exactly what his impulses of the day may have been? Even a report drawn up within a few hours of the event it describes may be consciously or unconsciously influenced by after knowledge, by the desire everyone has to place his own actions in the most favourable light.

All the officers I have to mention played a larger or smaller part in the great tragedy of the war. It is impossible to define the role of each man during the Retreat. Quite a junior staff officer reporting events at the front, interpreting the intentions of a commander or the situation of troops, may have largely influenced events. The Intelligence officer who foresaw or discovered a hostile manœuvre, the Operations officer working out the movement of a body of troops, each played a part in the co-ordinated whole, in which it is impossible to attribute individual responsibility, but where the temperament, the training and the morale of each man was an important factor.

For instance, what influence did Colonel Gamelin exercise on General Joffre?

The Commander-in-Chief, so impervious to outside impressions, was said to pay great attention to this smooth, chubby little officer, who looked so young and who exercised such a mastery over himself that it seemed impossible he should ever give himself away. Eloquent and low-voiced, imperturbable and distant, I have seen him in his dark *chasseur* uniform, following Joffre, mute if not asked to speak, precise and logical if called upon to give an opinion, always very much all there. A member of General Joffre's personal staff while I was at Vitry, he became eventually Head of the 3ème Bureau at the G.Q.G.

A very striking example comes to mind when discussing influences, although it is so unique as to be really out of place in the picture I have attempted to draw – I mean Colonel d'Alenson, General Nivelle's *Chef de Cabinet*. I knew him well in 1915, and later on the Somme when as a Major he visited the Armies as liaison officer.

He was immensely tall, as loosely built as a giant I used to hear about in the nursery, who came down the chimney bit by bit and assembled himself as best he could on the floor. At first I disliked this slow-voiced, untidy individual with the sunken face and eyes, who towered above me and gave the impression that he would only notice me if I climbed on to a table to speak at his level. Later, as I knew him better, I grew to like him. His sardonic humour, when it flashed out, was arresting. There was kindness, too, concealed in those eyes that burnt with fever away down in the caverns of the eye-sockets deepset in his high-cheeked, thin, cavernous face. He was dying of phthisis, though we did not know it. When he found himself with General Nivelle, perhaps unconsciously determined to live in history as he knew himself condemned to die, he infused into his Chief his own mad faith in the disastrous offensive of 1917. "Victory must be won before I die, and I have but a short time to live." And the faith of this man working through his Chief overrode all objections, the doubts of soldiers and the qualms of politicians.

Poor, brave, dying d'Alenson! It was not a true light that guided him. False pictures and false values had got into his fever-consumed brain. His responsibility for the terrible massacre of the Chemin des Dames was great, yet his guilt is small, for he believed that he would save France before he died.

Probably the officers who, without having any direct responsibility themselves, most powerfully influenced decisions, were the G.Q.G. liaison officers. They were often relatively junior in rank, but belonged to the 3ème Bureau of the Supreme Staff, and reported personally to the Commander-in-Chief. They were invariably able men, and generally tactful. Sometimes they were humorists, like Major Réquin, who made the most screamingly funny caricatures of all the great men he met. Others, like our own Colonel Alexandre, liaison officer to the Fifth Army, were made of sterner stuff. But whoever they might be, their arrival was an event, and they were treated with the respect due to minor saints, who, having access to the Supreme Presence, could intercede for or damn their respective congregations. I am convinced that in all cases they did their duty according to their lights, and reported as to whether the Commander-in-Chief's orders were being carried out in the letter and in the spirit. Knowing the Commander-in-Chief's intentions, they were able to interpret them; being young and agile they would go and see for themselves up to the very picquet line if necessary, and no one dared say them nay. They were the Commander-in-Chief's eyes and ears, and very useful they proved to be.

The British Army did not take kindly to the idea of liaison, which it may be explained is a general term referring to all liaison, vertical and horizontal. The value of horizontal liaison, i.e., of keeping in touch with neighbouring units, has never been disputed; it was the value of vertical liaison that appeared more doubtful to the British. British commanders resented an officer from a higher formation interviewing their own juniors. Nevertheless I am convinced that the French system was sound. The Commander-in-Chief, the Army Commander, cannot visit all the units in an Army, yet he should know their temper and quality, and no report going through official channels can take the place of someone who has *seen*. A verbal account of a situation, the views of a quite detached individual concerning the mentality of a staff, a report of a conversation with a commander precluded by the situation on his front from reporting personally, often proved invaluable. I have seen the system working under all circumstances, and it is perhaps the only institution that survived the war without modification. Even when there was friction, and it is impossible to conceive of more friction than there was between Alexandre and the Commander of the Fifth Army, the system proved its worth, for fundamental misunderstandings, instead of being concealed, were exposed far sooner than they would otherwise have been. On the other hand, when there was complete unity of view between the higher and lower formations, the liaison officer perfected the accord, and by dealing with minor difficulties, helped the whole machine to run more efficiently.

Throughout the war, the French liaison officer, flitting backwards and forwards with great if undefined powers, was an important figure. The junior officer in whom these powers were vested generally kept them carefully concealed behind the respectful mask of discipline when dealing with the Generals to whom he was sent, but all knew, and all bowed low, for even in the early days of 1914 it was realized that he would have the scalps of many wearers of gold-braided caps, since his comments would be of much weight in quarters where an opinion could make or break a man.

CHAPTER V

THE FIGHTING ABOUT DINANT
AND ITS CONSEQUENCES

August 14th and 15th, 1914

The Germans attack at Dinant – The situation of the French Fifth Army – Joffre's point of view – Lanrezac's doubts – His foresight – The I. Corps ordered to move north – Instruction Particulière No. 6 – Events on the German side – Lanrezac sees Joffre – A misunderstanding – The Fifth Army ordered to move north-west – Changes in the composition of the Fifth Army – Lanrezac's fears vindicated – Plan XVII. abandoned.

ON the evening of my arrival at the Headquarters of the Fifth Army news came in that the Germans had made an attempt to seize the passage of the Meuse at Dinant, but that the attack had been fairly easily repelled.

On the morning of August 15th I started off from Rethel for Dinant with de Rose. It was a wet morning, the first wet day for weeks. When we got there it turned out that the Germans were renewing their attack of the previous day, but Major Cameron, of our Intelligence, who had come down to see me, agreed with us that the attack did not appear to be pressed with any great vigour. How calm we all pretended to be, but how inwardly excited we were! I found I could hardly control my voice when, scanning the scene through glasses, I attempted a casual diagnosis of the situation for the benefit of my companions. So this was war, *real* bullets were flying about, real shells being fired. Somebody might be aiming at *us*, and those were the enemy over there, those cavalrymen who suddenly appeared on the right bank of the river silhouetted against the skyline. (Map IV, pp. 60–1.)

But for all our excitement, the town of Dinant could hardly have been described as "unhealthy" by standards that prevailed later in the war, and viewed from the left bank of the river, looking towards the enemy, our position appeared immensely strong. The greater part of the town was built on the right bank, at the foot of steep cliffs, and was connected with the other side by a bridge under which flowed the broad river, unusually low just now owing to the drought. There were such ample means of concealment on the left bank and such facilities for cross and enfilade fire that it did not look as if anything on two legs could ever get over the bridge.

Things began to look unexpectedly ugly, however, when some territorials and a portion of the 33rd Regiment, which had been holding the houses on the far side of the river, were driven back to the left bank by the enemy. The hostile artillery fire increased, and under its protection a small detachment of German infantry could be seen running across the bridge. We could not make out whether they had brought a machine-gun over or not. At about midday two regiments of the French 2nd Division appeared on the scene and swept down the hill in great style, forcing the Germans back over the Meuse. This counter-attack was carried out with much vigour and zest, and the Germans on our side of the river never had a chance. We learnt in the evening that the attack had been carried out by Saxon Jägers, probably supported by two cavalry divisions.

Very wisely, on the previous day, taking warning from the Germans' first attempt to cross the river, General Franchet d'Esperey, commanding the I. Corps, had made the 2nd Division responsible for guarding the passages between Hastière and Anhée and had moved up the 1st Division in reserve.* But when the attack was renewed on the 15th and he learnt that the enemy had forced his way across, he felt serious alarm and called upon the 37th and 38th Divisions† which had barely detrained a day's march away, to move up in support. It was soon realized that the intervention of these troops would be unnecessary, so the weary men were ordered back whence they came. (Map IV, pp. 60–1.)

Meanwhile the French Cavalry Corps under General Sordet, which had been to the east of the river during the engagement, hearing firing, had come up and attempted to attack the Germans in flank, but confronted with infantry they had withdrawn and crossing over to the left bank of the river at Givet and Hastière had moved north-west of Dinant. (Map IV, pp. 60–1.)

* The I. Corps had been concentrated between Rocroi and the Meuse and had then moved up north, the 1st Division having been drawn up on the Meuse about 20 km. south of Givet, while the 2nd Division was grouped behind the river west of that town. (*See also* p. 57.)

† These divisions, which came from North Africa, were by "*Instruction Particulière No. 6*" placed at the disposal of the Fifth Army. They began detraining about Rocroi and Chimay on the 13th. The II. Corps was upon their arrival transferred to the Fourth Army.

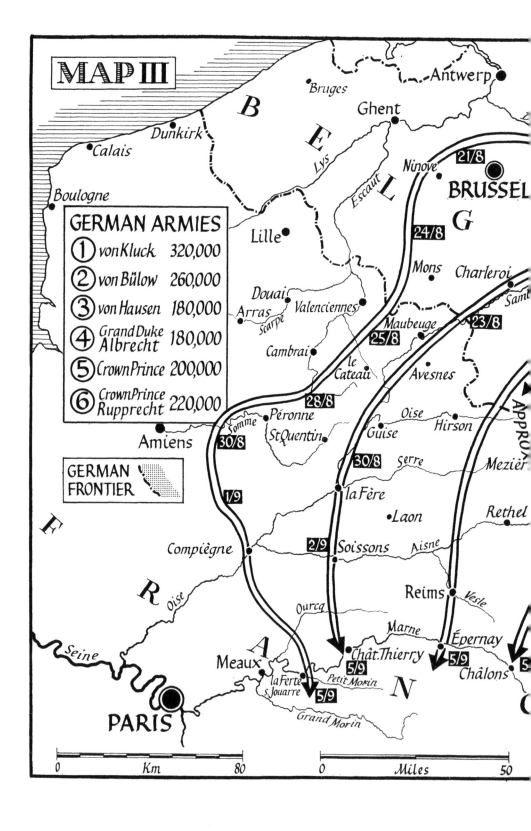

MAP III

Antwerp

Bruges

Ghent

B E L G

Ninove

21/8

BRUSSEL

24/8

Dunkirk

Calais

Boulogne

Lys

Escaut

Mons

Charleroi

Sami

23/8

Lille

GERMAN ARMIES

① von Kluck   320,000

② von Bülow   260,000

③ von Hausen   180,000

④ Grand Duke Albrecht   180,000

⑤ Crown Prince   200,000

⑥ Crown Prince Rupprecht   220,000

Douai

Arras   Scarpe

Valenciennes

Maubeuge

25/8

Avesnes

Cambrai

le Cateau

Oise

Hirson

Mezièr

28/8

Somme

Péronne

StQuentin

Guise

Amiens

30/8

30/8

Serre

la Fère

Laon

Rethel

GERMAN FRONTIER

F

1/9

Compiègne

2/9

Soissons

Aisne

Reims

Vesle

R

Oise

Seine

Meaux

A

Ourcq

Marne

Épernay

5/9

Châlons

5

Chât. Thierry

5/9

Petit Morin

N

la Ferte s.Jouarre

5/9

PARIS

Grand Morin

APPR

0   Km   80

0   Miles   50

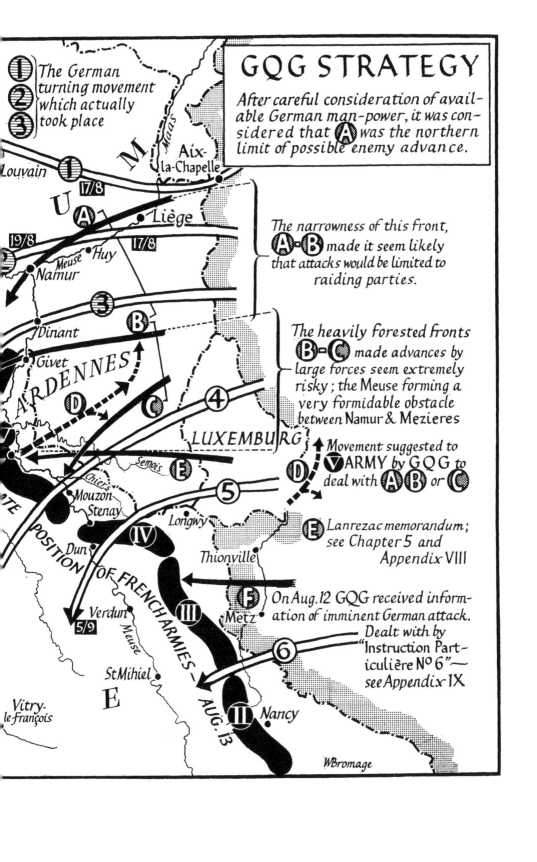

GQG STRATEGY

The German turning movement which actually took place
- ①
- ②
- ③

After careful consideration of available German man-power, it was considered that Ⓐ was the northern limit of possible enemy advance.

The narrowness of this front, Ⓐ-Ⓑ made it seem likely that attacks would be limited to raiding parties.

The heavily forested fronts Ⓑ-Ⓒ made advances by large forces seem extremely risky; the Meuse forming a very formidable obstacle between Namur & Mezieres

Movement suggested to Ⓓ Ⓥ ARMY by GQG to deal with Ⓐ Ⓑ or Ⓒ

Ⓔ Lanrezac memorandum; see Chapter 5 and Appendix VIII

Ⓕ On Aug. 12 GQG received information of imminent German attack. Dealt with by "Instruction Particulière Nᵒ 6"— see Appendix IX

Louvain · Aix-la-Chapelle · Liège · Huy · Namur · Dinant · Givet · ARDENNES · LUXEMBURG · Semois · Mouzon · Stenay · Longwy · Thionville · Dun · Verdun · Metz · StMihiel · Vitry-le-François · Nancy

17/8 · 19/8 · 17/8 · 5/9 · AUG.13

POSITION OF FRENCH ARMIES

WBromage

This action, insignificant as it appeared to anybody witnessing it, turned out to be extremely important in its results. Not only did it have a considerable effect on the Corps and the Army immediately concerned, but, as will be seen, it directly influenced the decisions of the Commander-in-Chief.

To understand the situation as it then appeared it is necessary to summarize events as they affected the Fifth Army up to the 15th.

The Fifth Army was facing north-east between Namur and a point east of Sedan, in readiness to advance across the Ardennes. By the 12th it was practically concentrated according to plan, as was the Fourth Army on its right. (Map III, p. 54.)

General Joffre still expected an attack from the direction of Metz. He was of course fully alive to the possibility of an attack by the German right wing in Belgium, but was still persuaded that it could not possibly attempt to sweep west of the Meuse beyond the north of Namur, believing that the enemy could not have enough troops for so gigantic a manœuvre, which must include the investment of Namur. Nothing could persuade the G.Q.G. that their calculations of the forces Germany would have to leave on her eastern frontier to deal with Russia were mistaken. No French staff officer would have believed that all the troops Germany had left to deal with the Russian hordes were three active and one reserve corps, one reserve division, one cavalry division and some second line formations.*

Having assumed that it was materially impossible for the enemy to extend beyond and north of Namur, the G.Q.G. also thought it unlikely that he would attempt anything more than an attack by raiding forces between Givet and Namur; a large force would have been exposed to attack from the fortress whilst attempting to cross the river, and its flank and rear would have been endangered by a French advance across the Ardennes. It was further thought improbable that the Germans would try to cross the Meuse between Givet and Mézières, for the river presented a formidable obstacle, and the forests and lack of roads on the left bank made the advance of a considerable body of troops a very risky undertaking. The conclusion naturally was that the operations of the German right armies must be confined to an attack across the Ardennes. (Map III, pp. 54-5.)

General Lanrezac was not so ready to accept this view. In a memorandum he had addressed to General Joffre on July 31st, 1914, he mentioned the possibility of the Germans making a wider sweep through Belgium

---

* These were one Erzatz division, one Landwehr division and two Landwehr brigades.

than was anticipated by the General Staff. He qualified his suggestion by saying that it was probable the German right wing would be directed on Sedan, but it must have taken some courage to put forward, however tentatively, a point of view in contravention of the accepted opinion of General Joffre and his advisers, and full credit is due to General Lanrezac for having done so.*†

On August 9th, General Joffre, somewhat taken aback by the unexpected delay in the German advance (for had the Germans been moving as expected there should by then have been some indication of it), but still persuaded that they would act according to his previsions, suggested to General Lanrezac that he should take measures to enable the Fifth Army to cross the Semoy, which flows just north of the Franco-Belgian frontier. General Lanrezac objected unless a simultaneous offensive by the Fourth Army were decided upon. He had always held, very rightly, that before engaging his forces in the defiles of the Ardennes he must be certain of being able not only to get through them without opposition, but to deploy beyond.

On the 11th General Lanrezac began to manifest some anxiety for his left. Numerous patrols had appeared on the Meuse, which seemed to show that there was a powerful force of German cavalry in the neighbourhood which might seize one of the points of passage of the Meuse and cut the communications of the I. Corps. Only one infantry regiment, the 148th, held the Meuse between Namur and Dinant, and the Cavalry Corps which had hitherto covered the left of the Army had moved from the region of Rochefort twelve miles to the south, so that the left of the Fifth Army was now only protected by a single infantry regiment which was very much strung out. (Map IV, p. 60.)

With the object of guarding against this threat to his left General Lanrezac asked leave on the evening of the 11th to move the I. Corps to the neighbourhood of Givet, some nine miles south of Dinant. This suggestion was accepted and orders consequently given, as a result of which we find the I. Corps on the 14th in the region between Givet and Dinant with instructions to hold the passages of the Meuse, the other Corps conforming to this movement.

Once this movement was completed, on the 14th, the Fifth Army was

---

* See Appendix VIII.

† It would seem that Lanrezac did not believe the Germans would sweep north of Namur, for in a conversation he had with General Fournier, Governor of Maubeuge, on June 23rd, 1914, Lanrezac said: "Your fortress is useless, your forts are falling down, but *the Germans will not pass the Sambre;* and in any case I shall come to your help." – Commandant Cassou, "Le Siège de Maubeuge," *Revue de Paris,* July 15th, 1918, p. 257.

ready to carry out the orders issued by General Joffre on the 8th,* that is it was in a position to attack any hostile forces debouching between Mézières and Mouzon or to assume the offensive by crossing the Meuse between these two places and marching to meet the enemy across the Ardennes.†‡

On the assumption that the German right could not possibly attempt an enveloping movement on both banks of the Meuse, the Fifth Army was now ideally placed to meet it, whilst any danger to his left anticipated by General Lanrezac owing to the possibility of the passages of the river being forced between Givet and Namur by large bodies of cavalry, was met by the movement of the I. Corps.

Unfortunately the German strategy had little in common with what the French imagined it to be. It was not until several days later that the G.Q.G. began to have any inkling of the real trend of events.

On the 12th the G.Q.G. had had information which made it appear that a German attack on the front Metz-Thionville was likely, and reports came in that the right of the Fourth Army was also threatened. General Joffre thereupon on the 13th addressed *"Instruction Particulière No. 6"*§ to the Third, Fourth and Fifth Armies, in which he stated that there might not be time to give battle to the enemy under good conditions beyond the Semoy and the Chiers and that steps must be taken to prepare for battle which might be engaged on the 15th or 16th. The Third Army was to be ready to counter-attack hostile forces debouching from Metz and to co-operate with the Fourth Army. The latter was to advance so that the head of its main forces should be on the front Sommauthe (about eleven miles west of Stenay on the Meuse) Dun-sur-Meuse. The Fifth Army was to have the head of its main bodies five to six miles west of the Meuse about Mézières and above it. If the enemy advanced he was to be attacked only after he had engaged a consider-

* Extract from *Instruction Générale No. 1*, dated August 8th, 1914:
"The Fifth Army will close in between Vouziers and Aubenton so as to be able to launch a powerful attack against any forces debouching between Mouzon and Mézieres (inclusive) or possibly to cross the Meuse between these two points."

† It is important to note that the 4th Group of Reserve Divisions which was detraining about Vervins, was ordered by General Joffre on the 8th to prepare a fortified position about that place. The object of this was to establish a strong point in support of the left of the Fifth Army until the British Army was ready to advance.

‡ The XI. Corps was about Sedan, the X. Corps extended from Sedan to Mézières, the III. Corps was immediately to the west of Mézières, the 52nd Reserve Division held the Meuse north of Mézières on a front of some eighteen miles up to Fumay. The 348th Regiment guarded the river passages north of the river from Fumay to the bend above Givet, then came the I. Corps, between it and Namur, with the Cavalry Corps in rear.

§ See Appendix IX.

able part of his forces on the left bank of the river. General Lanrezac was ordered to defend the passages of the Meuse below Mézières as far as Givet, and was given leave to blow up the bridges should he think fit. The I. Corps was to cover the left of the Fifth Army and to support the Cavalry Corps which was only to cross to the left bank of the Meuse if it could no longer maintain itself on the right bank. Finally, this order stated, in case the enemy should still prove to be far distant, all measures should be taken not later than August 15th by the Fourth and Fifth Armies to be in readiness to move forward. (Map III, p. 54.)

That is, if the enemy turned out to be very slow in his advance he was not to be given time to develop his manœuvre, but the French Armies were to advance across the Ardennes to meet him in the open country beyond.

On August 14th the First and Second Armies far to the east were given orders to begin their attacks in Alsace-Lorraine. These were the main attacks under Plan XVII which have already been referred to.

From the foregoing it will be clear that on August 13th the G.Q.G. was still convinced that there was no possibility of the Germans attempting to cross the Meuse in force north of Mézières.

But whilst the French were wondering at the delay in the anticipated German advance, and were inclined to believe that the enemy's plans had gone awry, the Great General Staff of the Imperial Forces was driving on its armies mercilessly, regardless of the sufferings of its own men, ruthlessly overriding opposition, adopting a policy of terrorism towards the civil population, so that the martyred people should not have the spirit to do anything that would delay the immense mass relentlessly advancing on the gigantic arc, the extremity of which pointed to the far left, miles and miles away in the west, beyond where the still absent British Army was to assemble.

The German Armies, delayed only for seventy-two hours by the Belgians' gallant defence of Liège, were in position, the jaws of the immense pincers were wide open, while the French, all unconscious, sat in the middle, their eyes fixed on a still empty area, entirely blind to the fearful danger gathering in the north where the great upper jaw was beginning to close down. (Map III, p. 54.)

Such was the situation when General Lanrezac, on the exposed flank, beginning to conceive suspicions of what was really afoot, decided to go and see the Commander-in-Chief on the 14th to discuss the situation.

General Joffre and General Lanrezac seem to have been at cross-purposes at this interview.

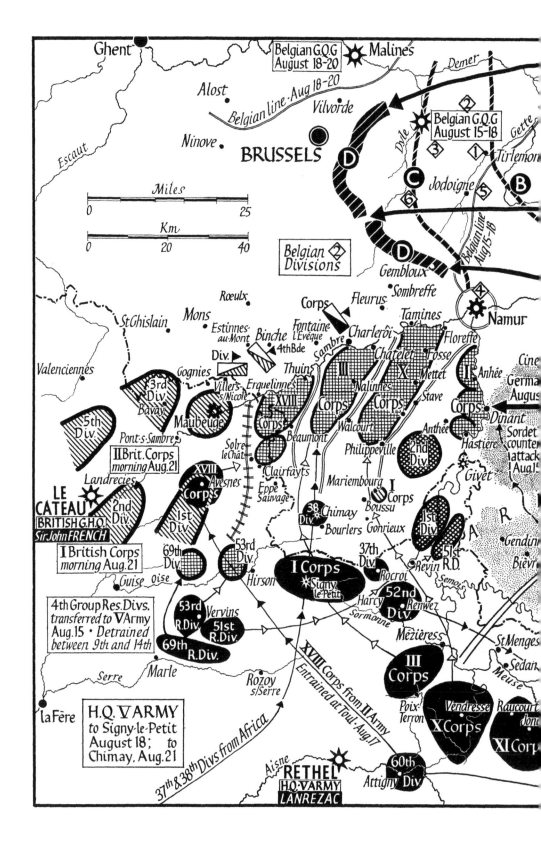

Ghent

Belgian G.Q.G
August 18-20

Malines

Demer

Alost

Belgian line·Aug 18-20

Vilvorde

Dyle

②

Belgian G.Q.G
August 15-18

Gette

Ninove

BRUSSELS

③

①

Tirlemon

D

C

Jodoigne

⑤

B

Escaut

Miles

0   25

Km

0   20   40

Belgian
Divisions

②

⑥

Belgian line Aug 15-18

Gembloux

D

④

Namur

Sombreffe

Roeulx

Corps

Fleurus

Tamines

St Ghislain

Mons

Estinnes-au-Mont

Binche

Fontaine
l'Évêque

Charleroi

Floreffe

Cine

German
Augus

Valenciennes

3rd
Div
Bavay

Gognies

Villers
s/Nicole

Erquelinnes

Thuin

Sambre

III
Corps

Châtelet

Fosse

Mettet

II
Corps

Anhée

Dinant

4thBde

Div ▶

XVIII
Corps

Beaumont

Nalinnes

X
Corps

Stave

Anthée

Sordet
counter
attack
Aug.1

5th
Div

Pont·s·Sambre

Maubeuge

5th
Corps

Walcourt

Givet

II Brit. Corps
morning Aug.21

XVIII
Corps

Solre
le Chât

Clairfayts

Philippeville

2nd
Div

Hastière

Landrecies

Avesnes

Eppe
Sauvage

Mariembourg

I
Corps

1st
Div

Gendin

LE
CATEAU

2nd
Div

1st
Div

38
Div

Chimay

Boussu

Bourlers

Gonrieux

51st
R.D.

Bièvr

BRITISH G.H.Q.
Sir John FRENCH

69th
Div

53rd
Div

Hirson

37th
Div

Rocroi

Revin

I British Corps
morning Aug.21

I Corps

Signy
le Petit

Harcy

52nd
Div

Renwez

St Menges

Guise

Oise

4th Group Res.Divs.
transferred to V Army
Aug.15 · Detrained
between 9th and 14th

53rd
R.Div.

Vervins

51st
R.Div.

Sormonne

Mézières

Sedan

Meuse

69th
R.Div.

III
Corps

Serre

Marle

Rozoy
s/Serre

Poix-
Terron

Vendresse

Raucourt
Jon

la Fère

H.Q. V ARMY
to Signy·le·Petit
August 18;   to
Chimay, Aug.21

X Corps

XI Corp

Aisne

RETHEL

60th
Div

Attigny

37th & 38th Divs from Africa

XVIII Corps from II Army
Entrained at Toul. Aug.17

H.Q. V ARMY
LANREZAC

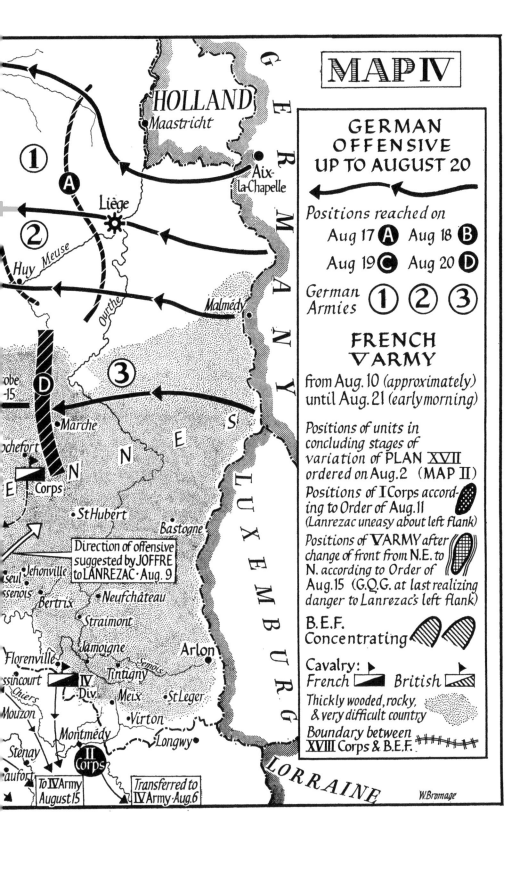

MAP IV

GERMAN OFFENSIVE UP TO AUGUST 20

Positions reached on
Aug 17 (A) Aug 18 (B)
Aug 19 (C) Aug 20 (D)

German Armies (1) (2) (3)

FRENCH ▽ ARMY

from Aug. 10 (approximately) until Aug. 21 (early morning)

Positions of units in concluding stages of variation of PLAN XVII ordered on Aug. 2 (MAP II)

Positions of I Corps according to Order of Aug. 11 (Lanrezac uneasy about left flank)

Positions of V ARMY after change of front from N.E. to N. according to Order of Aug. 15 (G.Q.G. at last realizing danger to Lanrezac's left flank)

B.E.F. Concentrating

Cavalry: French ▶ British

Thickly wooded, rocky, & very difficult country

Boundary between XVIII Corps & B.E.F.

HOLLAND
Maastricht
Aix-la-Chapelle
Liège
Huy Meuse
Ourthe
Malmédy

GERMANY

LUXEMBURG

A R D E N N E S

...obe -15
Marche
...chefort
E
Corps
N
St Hubert
Bastogne

Direction of offensive suggested by JOFFRE to LANREZAC·Aug. 9

...seul Jehonville
...ssenois
Bertrix Neufchâteau
Straimont
Jamoigne
Arlon
Florenville
...ssincourt IV Div. Tintigny Semois
Chiers Meix St Leger
Mouzon Virton
Montmédy Longwy
Stenay II Corps
...aufort

To IV Army August 15

Transferred to IV Army·Aug. 6

LORRAINE

W. Bromage

General Lanrezac put forward the objection that if, whilst he was engaged in a forward movement to the north-east towards Gedinne – Paliseul – Neufchâteau, the Germans assumed the offensive with large forces on the left bank of the Meuse, he would be in a precarious, if not a fatal position, for the enemy, should he succeed in forcing the passages of the river, would be behind his left flank and in a position to march straight down on his communications, whilst his own army, inextricably engaged in the defiles of the Ardennes, would be helpless. (Map IV, p. 60.)

General Joffre, on the other hand, did not believe the left of the Fifth Army to be threatened.

After some discussion the Generalissimo and the Commander of the Fifth Army separated, the latter leaving the impression that he was reassured as to his position and anxious to execute General Joffre's plans, with which he entirely concurred; the former delighted at the way General Lanrezac appeared to have entered into his views.

General Lanrezac convinced those who saw him at Vitry-le-François that he was enthusiastic for the offensive contemplated, and hoped to be in a position to carry it out at an early date. I remember the circumstances well, for this was the day I myself left Vitry for the H.Q. of the Fifth Army at Rethel, an object of envy to those I left behind, who were one and all persuaded that this Army was about to do great things under its most determined and able Commander.

When General Lanrezac returned to Rethel, however, he found awaiting him the Intelligence Summary prepared by the 2ème Bureau of the G.Q.G. for the 14th, which confirmed his worst fears. He immediately wrote to General Joffre:

"I hasten to inform you that I found on my return here Intelligence Summary No. 38 sent out by your Headquarters, which crossed me.

"This summary makes it clear that the German right mass of manœuvre, situated between the northernmost part of Luxembourg and the neighbourhood of Liège, comprises eight army corps and four cavalry divisions (even possibly six cavalry divisions counting the two divisions observed in the region Marche–Rochefort).*

"This information, coming to my knowledge only after my interview with you, seems to me to establish the threat of an enveloping

---

* There were in reality some seventeen Corps. The Corps identified by the 2ème Bureau were the IX., VII., X., XI., VI., III., IV. and Guard.

movement carried out by very considerable forces on both banks of the Meuse."

He concluded:

"I should not be easy in my mind if I did not repeat that in the face of this information emanating from the G.Q.G. the eventual transport of the Fifth Army to the region Givet–Maubeuge (leaving one corps and two reserve divisions on the Meuse in liaison with the Fourth Army) ought it seems to me to be studied immediately."

This information gave definite form in General Lanrezac's mind to what had previously only been vague fears, and dissipated completely the reassuring impression he had taken away that afternoon from Vitry. He was now certain that his Army would run the gravest risk if it advanced north-east across the Ardennes, for in view of the 2ème Bureau's report it looked as if it might walk into the very jaws of an immense trap. From this moment on he tried to persuade the Commander-in-Chief to meet the danger by ordering the Fifth Army to form into line to the north, its right on the Meuse. The effect of this would be to face the danger with an army drawn up to meet it instead of presenting a flank to the coming onrush. To have been caught facing north-east by an enemy descending from the north would have meant being helplessly rolled up, the communications of the left would have been severed, and irremediable defeat would have ensued. As it was, even after General Lanrezac's suggestions had been carried out and the line his Army formed facing north had been prolonged by the British Army, defeat was not averted, for the German outflanking movement was of a magnitude neither Lanrezac nor anyone else had foreseen, and their right spread far beyond the Allied left, making retreat inevitable.

General Lanrezac had just written to General Joffre when I arrived at Rethel. He received me abruptly, but the curtness of his manner was no doubt due to his preoccupation. I was told in awed tones that the General had been very snappy since the day before.

General Lanrezac received that evening an answer to his letter. This message was to the effect that the Commander-in-Chief considered the danger preoccupying General Lanrezac to be still a distant one and in any case by no means certain to materialize. He was, however, granted leave to gain ground to the west so as to be in a position either to advance north on the left bank of the Meuse, or, should the original plan be adhered to, to cross the river and advance north-east.*

It was not long before General Joffre also began to realize the danger. At 9 a.m. on the 15th the Commander-in-Chief authorized General Lanrezac to prepare the movement to the north of two corps in addition to the I. Corps, to be ready to meet the contingency envisaged by General Lanrezac in his letter of the 14th. At the same time General Joffre asked the Minister of War that the three Territorial divisions detailed for coast defence should be employed to form a barrier against German cavalry between Dunkirk and Maubeuge.†

As soon as General Lanrezac received this message he took steps to shift the centre of gravity of his Army towards the north-west. (Map IV, p. 60.)

Later in the day news confirming General Lanrezac's premonitions began to come in fast. Ten thousand German cavalry were reported to have crossed the Meuse north-east of Huy.‡ The Belgians evacuated Huy, blowing up the bridges. A considerable number of German troops were reported in the valley of the Hoyoux.§

Then the Commander-in-Chief became aware of the attacks on Dinant described at the beginning of this chapter.

These attacks, combined with the general trend of the intelligence reports, led General Joffre first to order the Fifth Army to send to the north the two corps (III. and X.) whose movements had been envisaged in the morning, and secondly to issue fresh orders (*Instruction Particulière No. 10*)‖ on August 15th at 8 p.m., which stated that the enemy appeared to be carrying out his main effort by his right wing north of Givet. The Fifth Army, leaving the I. Corps on the Meuse, was to bring up the remainder of its forces to the region Mariembourg–Philippeville, to operate there in concert with the British and Belgian forces against the hostile formations to the north.

The XI. Corps and the 4th Cavalry Division were transferred to the Fourth Army, which also received the IX. Corps from the Second

---

* The text of the G.Q.G.'s reply was as follows: "The Commander-in-Chief sees nothing but advantage in studying a movement such as that suggested, but considers that the danger is far removed and by no means certain to materialize. As preparatory measures all that is necessary is that the Fifth Army should extend towards the left as far as Renwez and Monthermé, from whence it is as easy to advance to Paliseul and Gedinne as to Philippeville."

† This was agreed to, and on the 16th two of these divisions were placed under the command of General d'Amade, whose H.Q. was to be at Arras, with orders to form a barrage as General Joffre had requested.

‡ Sixteen miles below Namur.

§ South of Huy.

‖ See Appendix X.

Army. The XVIII. Corps was to be transferred to the Fifth Army from the Second Army.

These various changes were hardly favourable to the Fifth Army. The II. and XI. Corps had been under General Lanrezac's orders in peacetime, and he had also had time to get to know the 52nd and 60th Reserve Divisions. These were now taken from him, and the latter replaced by the three reserve divisions commanded by General Valabrègue, which he did not know. Nor did he know the two divisions from North Africa (the 37th and 38th) which were allotted to him, although these were a distinct accession of strength to the Army, for they were composed of very fine troops. He knew nothing of the XVIII. Corps either. It cannot be denied that having to work with several entirely new units and with commanders whose mentality was unfamiliar to him increased General Lanrezac's difficulties.

Moreover, the Fifth Army now included five autonomous divisions, that is divisions not organized in corps, each having its own separate transport, which rendered the Army as a whole clumsier and more difficult to manœuvre, although in point of fact this cannot be said to have seriously impeded General Lanrezac, the movement to the north taking place according to schedule. This difficulty only made itself felt to any considerable extent during the retreat.

The orders of the G.Q.G. certainly vindicated General Lanrezac. Much closer to the enemy than was the Commander-in-Chief, he had sensed the danger first.

It did not transpire till afterwards with what apprehension General Lanrezac had faced having to lead his Army through the Ardennes over ground where deployment was very difficult. It matters little whether he instinctively favoured a solution that meant avoiding this. The fact remains that he saw the danger before it was perceived at Vitry-le-François. Happily, thanks to the rapidity with which General Joffre either adopted General Lanrezac's view or came to the same conclusion independently, no time was lost in carrying out a movement which, had it been postponed, would have proved fatal to the French.

*Instruction Particulière No. 10** is very important from another point of view; its issue marks the surrender of the initiative by the French to the Germans.

The attacks on Dinant, General Lanrezac's forebodings, and the Intelligence reports of the enemy's movements, caused General Joffre

* See Appendix X.

to realize that whatever the German plan might be it certainly was not what he had supposed. The carefully laid schemes to overwhelm the German right north and south of the Ardennes had to be abandoned, and the French left extended to the north to face a danger the magnitude of which was not even yet realized, either at the G.Q.G. or anywhere else.

Once the French Commander-in-Chief abandoned his own plans and began to submit to the necessity of moving his troops to parry the German manœuvre, his chance of dealing the enemy the first strategic blow on the ground he had chosen vanished. Although he did not realize it, although he struggled hard to adapt his dispositions to the new situation, he could now do nothing but attempt to ward off the danger until such time as a better knowledge of the German plans might enable him to deliver a counter-thrust. As will be seen, he made a bold attempt, which failed, to turn the tables on the enemy by an attack on his centre; but from the moment General Lanrezac's Army turned north, General Joffre's hands were tied. He was compelled to cast aside his own conceptions. Groping in the dark, he was moving to meet a danger which had not yet assumed a definite form, and was forced to concentrate on parrying the German movements as they gradually revealed themselves.

From this moment Plan XVII went by the board. Tactical and local offensives were still possible, but the great conception whereby the French Armies, in combined strategical and tactical offensive, were to have been hurled at their adversary, compensating by their boldness and dash for inferiority in training and numbers, was perforce abandoned. And out of the ensuing chaos, with the whole of France seeming to crumble in irretrievable disaster, the French soldier was to reveal himself as the stoic and enduring peasant, capable of a stubbornness which was a revelation to his own people and his own leaders; whilst from the utter ruin of his plans the French Commander-in-Chief was to wrest one of the greatest strategic victories in history.

CHAPTER VI

SIR JOHN FRENCH
MEETS GENERAL LANREZAC

August 16th and 17th, 1914

Commandant Schneider – The Staff prepares the move to the north – The difficulties of this operation – Le Système "D" – Visit to British G.H.Q. at Reims – Aviation difficulties – Sir John French – The Rethel interview – Colonel Huguet's account – The misunderstandings – Joffre's memorandum – The billeting areas – The employment of the British Cavalry – Personal relations of French and Lanrezac – Lanrezac's report to Joffre – Joffre's reply – First misgivings about Lanrezac.

SUNDAY August 16th was a day of hard work for the 3ème Bureau.

The Head of this section, a son-in-law of General Maunoury, Major Schneider by name, was a man whom I came to like very much, and whose upright character called for general respect. We got on well, although as representative of the British Army on the Fifth Army Staff I had constantly to put forward a point of view in disagreement with his.

Schneider habitually peered at one through his pince-nez with a worried look. His square face was topped by a heavy crop of grey-white hair "*en brosse*", and was barred by a black moustache. A blunt-headed, rather obstinate, perhaps short-sighted man, he invariably adopted as his own the views of his chiefs, and these were not always clarified by passing through his mind. It was a great misfortune for him that he was in charge of the Operations Section of the Fifth Army during the Retreat, for this was the last kind of work to give him a chance of exhibiting the really admirable qualities he undoubtedly possessed. He was an excellent officer in the wrong place.

The task confronting the 3ème Bureau was that involved in dealing with the very serious difficulties arising out of the change of front of the

Fifth Army from the line Mézières–Mouzon to that of the Lower Sambre.*

The main bodies of the corps had over sixty miles to go, since on account of the lack of roads in the wooded area they had to move to the west of the great forests on the left bank of the Meuse. The road which followed the river could not be used as it was in full view from the right bank, now practically in the possession of the Germans. (Map IV, p. 60.)

This dearth of roads, necessitating a wide detour, meant that the movements of the Army might be slower than under more normal conditions. The seriousness of this is evident, for it was essential that the Army should be placed at the earliest possible moment in a position to meet the enemy's manœuvre should the threat to its left materialize. To have been caught by the German attack whilst engaged in this complicated change of front would have been fatal. There was a real risk of the French being caught "on the hop" and every hour's delay increased this danger.

There were also certain practical difficulties which tended to upset the most careful calculations. The French horse transport at this period of the war was an absolute curse. Manned to a great extent by reservists who had not yet become permeated with army discipline, the convoys were for ever blocking the roads and getting hopelessly jammed. One shuddered to think what would happen if, as seemed extremely likely, the transport of one corps got mixed with that of another.

Luckily no such disaster occurred.

This fortunate result was due less to organization than to the amazing way the French have at times of "getting there" in spite of what would appear to be hopeless confusion. It is the resource and wit displayed by each individual in solving his own problem that does it. "*Le Système D*" – "*Débrouille-toi*" – "muddle through" they called it, and very effective it was. Applied by the men on many occasions during the war, it often retrieved mistakes of higher authorities. It is, however, not a method to be recommended for exportation: its use should be confined to France and its application to Frenchmen.

On this occasion the "*Système D*", combined with good staff work, gave excellent results, and by the 18th the Fifth Army had reached a line

---

* This was the move ordered by *Instruction Particulière No. 10*. See previous chapter, p. 64. During the night of the 15th General Lanrezac, justifiably anxious for his right during the movement to the north, had sent a message to General de Langle commanding the Fourth Army asking that the 52nd Reserve Division should continue to assure the protection of his right flank, and that should the enemy attempt to force the passages of the Meuse he should be allowed to give orders to this division direct.

extending from the neighbourhood of Philippeville to a point immediately south of Maubeuge. The I. Corps on the right was well forward, guarding the passages of the Meuse.

Meanwhile, to return to events on the 16th, reports came in from the I. Corps showing that a good deal of unnecessary alarm had been caused by the attack on Dinant the previous day, as it now transpired that only two or three battalions of Jägers had been engaged. This information could not, however, be assumed to mean that there were only weak enemy forces in the neighbourhood, and it was a serious matter that the morning turned out to be cloudy, making air reconnaissance impossible.

During the afternoon, which was very wet, I had to go north of Rethel. Captain Bénazet, a Reserve Officer, who was also a *Député*, accompanied me. We had to call at Mézières, and whilst we were waiting at the Post Office a small crowd collected to view the first British soldier they had seen. Presently a dear little girl, fair, tiny and very shy, was pushed forward, holding a bouquet of hastily gathered flowers which she presented to me. I can remember to this day how ridiculous I felt. In my embarrassment I entirely neglected to do what was expected of me, namely, to say in a few well chosen words that the war would be over and won by Christmas, and embrace the small person standing on one foot opposite me.

At out next halt, Rocroi, which was packed with troops, we were involved in a very different scene. Bénazet and I became separated, and I suddenly found myself surrounded by a mob of eager, curious and extremely hostile French soldiers. My strange uniform was totally unfamiliar to them, and they jumped to the conclusion that I was a German prisoner. The assurances I gave them that I was not were put down to Teutonic guile and carried no conviction. Things began to look ugly when I had forcibly to prevent an enthusiast from starting to collect my buttons as souvenirs. Happily for me, but much to the disappointment of the crowd, Bénazet appeared and delivered a neat little speech, under the impression of which we quietly slipped away.

I had already suggested that postcards and coloured plates showing British army uniforms should be sent out to the front, and this incident, proving as it did what really serious mistakes might be made, led me to urge their prompt despatch. By some miracle Colonel Macdonogh, Head of our Intelligence, managed to produce great quantities of these, and they were distributed amongst the French troops before the battle of Charleroi.

That the British uniform should have been unfamiliar at this period was perfectly natural, but it is strange that years later one still came upon individuals and units in the French Army who had apparently never seen a British soldier. It was not unusual during '15 or '16 for French battalions to be totally ignorant of the fact that the British Army was fighting within a mile of them. The demarcation between the two armies was rigidly maintained, and even at the actual points of contact the men seldom mixed.

Once in '15 near the Vimy Ridge, within a mile of the British I. Corps, I met a small detachment of French troops in charge of a corporal who mistook me for a German. I confess I was annoyed, and pointed with some asperity to my Legion of Honour, which I used to wear when in the French lines, as much for purposes of identification as for any other reason. This rather took the corporal aback, but only for a moment. "We thought you might have been given that for surrendering," he said.

French and British kept apart, principally of course because they could not understand each other's language, but they had few common interests. Even food, an absorbing topic in wartime, did not bring them together, for they disliked each other's cuisine. When, owing to the sudden German onslaught on Verdun, the Tenth French Army was hurriedly relieved by the British, and during the movement the French Commissariat fed some of our men whilst we supplied some French units, complaints were endless. French and British both declared they were starved. Our people could do nothing with the vegetables for which they were expected to devise sauces. They hated the coffee and threw away in disgust the inordinate quantities of bread served out. On the other hand, the gorge of the French rose at the slabs of beef provided by us. They declared they could not face all this meat and clamoured for more vegetables, bread and coffee. As for tea instead of wine – puah! Had the arrangement continued it might have led to mutiny. Not that our men disliked wine. Soldiers in blue and soldiers in khaki had at any rate that taste in common.

It was reported that the civilians, unlike the poilus, knew how to accommodate themselves to our rations. In some localities at least, a private wishing to enjoy the favours of a young lady, would hold up a tin of jam, and the formula "*Mademoiselle, confiture?*" became well established. This is the only instance I have to record in which the difference of language, far from proving to be an impediment, tended, on the contrary, to closer, more rapid, and generally to more satisfactory relations, in fact to better liaison, between French and English.

*   *   *

On my return to Rethel from my tour with Bénazet, I found a message ordering me to report to Sir John French's Chief of Staff at Reims immediately and to bring with me all available codes and decodes. I at once set out, accompanied by Captain Helbronner, he with French and I with English codes, for we did not know what exactly was wanted.

Helbronner belonged to the Reserve and in civil life was a Member of the *Conseil d'État*. A little later he was often employed to go in liaison to the British, especially to the I. Corps. He was very much liked by our people. His manner, which nothing could ruffle, made him a valuable asset; his invariable courtesy and lucidity of mind and expression enabled him to render much distinguished service both in liaison work and on his own staff.

The weather had cleared and it did not take us much over an hour to tear to Reims, coveys of partridges by the roadside flying off in great numbers as we passed. Helbronner was inclined to think that the war would be over in time for him to come and shoot those very same birds in the late autumn.

These visions of sport could do little to conceal the tragedy written, for all to read, in the fields on either side of the road. There stood the great golden crops of France, ungarnered and abandoned. How were they to be saved, and without them how was France to live? In any other country in the world the autumn rains would have found them drooping and wasted, but in France the love of the soil is so great that somehow the women, the children and the old men found the strength to do the work of their absent menfolk, and to save part at least of the harvest.

At Reims we flashed past the lovely, grey, austere cathedral, which I was to see next under such tragic circumstances. From its towers saints and kings looked down on us. We went straight to the Lion d'Or Hotel, where the British Commander-in-Chief was staying with a small staff. We beheld these great ones with awe. Several of them were wearing the cravat of the Legion of Honour round their necks, which made them look even more imposing than usual.

It transpired that we were wanted because the officer who was responsible for the codes had left them behind somewhere or other, in the luggage rack of a railway carriage, I believe. Several telegrams from the War Office had come in which could not be decoded. Unfortunately none of the decodes we had brought were of any use.

I was taken to the Chief of Staff, Sir Archibald Murray, who greeted me with the kindness he invariably displayed. He was worried, not so much by the situation, which he was trying to unravel on all fours on the floor, where enormous maps were laid out, as by the fact that chambermaids kept coming into the room, and he had only his pants on.

Finding we were not wanted, Helbronner and I returned to Rethel with our codes.

Next day, the weather again made air reconnaissance impossible. It was exasperating to be blind at this critical period in the operations. How could we meet the German manœuvre if we could not see? Should we bump into each other like ships in a fog?

The only good thing about it was that it gave the aviators and their machines a rest. The French had very few aeroplanes at this time, some of these were not particularly reliable, and the aviators were being worked to death. To make matters worse, the French troops were firing more and more at their own airmen: a flying machine was a target they could not resist. Like victims of the drug habit, the more they indulged their craving, the less were they able to resist it. The temptation to let fly at anything that appeared over their heads was overwhelming. The only safe place to alight in was a desert, if one could be found. The Staff were in despair at the reports they received on this subject, and simply did not know what steps to take to educate the troops.

So far, the Germans were proving to be much the least dangerous people in the war. Territorials on roads were apt to shoot you at sight: alighting in your own lines from an aeroplane was far more deadly than flying over the enemy's, and if you happened to be British you ran the risk of being cut into small pieces for souvenirs.

Talking of flying in those early days reminds me of a story told me by a French liaison officer. A German aeroplane appeared flying low over a British Brigade. Thousands of shots were fired at it, and, astonishing to relate, the machine was struck and was seen to lose poise and alight some distance away. Everyone was delighted, even the Brigadier was rubbing his hands, when a rather disreputable old French Territorial appeared from behind a hedge. He approached the General, stood in front of him, and taking a pull-through out of his pocket began slowly and deliberately to clean his rifle. Interrupting his labours for a moment he nonchalantly pointed over his shoulder to where the German machine had fallen, and said: "Rather a good shot of mine, that, wasn't it?"

*   *   *

On the morning of Monday August 17th everyone at the Head-quarters of the Fifth Army was agog with excitement, for all knew that the British Commander-in-Chief was coming to call on General Lanrezac. The orderlies, even the escort, were curious to see the great man, the leader of the strange islanders who were coming from over the sea, from their mysterious foggy land, to fight against the Germans.

The officers were deeply interested, for it was fully realised how vitally important the personal relationship between the two Commanders was bound to be. Each was at the head of a great Army which would do his bidding without question or demur. How would those armies co-operate? Would it be possible for them to work together almost as if they were under one commander? Would the special qualities of each compensate for differences in training and in temperament? It depended on these two men more than on any other factor. No one present doubted the good that would come of this interview, the only matter open to question being that of degree, and of the capacity for co-operation the two generals would show. All guessed the difficulties that might arise between Allies speaking a different tongue and with a totally different tradition and mentality: none realized how great these difficulties would be. As it turned out, there is on record no interview between two individuals similarly situated which by its sheer negative results led to such serious, such disastrous consequences.

Sir John and some of his Staff arrived at about ten o'clock in the morning.

Sir John stepped out of his car looking very spick and span. He was a good deal shorter than General Lanrezac, who came out to greet him. The two men stood for a moment in strong contrast to each other, Lanrezac large, swarthy, revealing his creole origin (he was born in Guadeloupe), Sir John ruddy-faced, his white moustache drooping over the corners of his mouth. His clear penetrating blue eyes, his very up-right bearing and quick movements, made him infinitely the more attractive personality, and gave him the appearance of being by far the more soldierly of the two. You had only to look at him to see that he was a brave, determined man.

At that time I did not know him, but later it fell to my lot to see him often, and at times when he was being as highly tried as any individual could be. I learnt to love and to admire the man who never lost his head, and on whom danger had the effect it has on the wild boar: he would become morose, furious for a time, harsh, but he would face up and never shirk. He knew only one way of dealing with a difficulty, and that was to tackle it. When everything seemed to crumble about him he stood his ground undismayed.

I was told a story of him, I think by General Foch, of how during the bad days at Ypres he once arrived at the latter's headquarters and said: "I have no more reserves. The only men I have left are the sentries at my gates. I will take them with me to where the line is broken, and the last of the English will be killed fighting."

If he had once lost confidence in a man, justly or unjustly, that man could do no right in his eyes. He was as bad an enemy as he was a good friend, and that is saying a great deal. He was deeply attached to the French nation, and after the war, being unable to live in his place in Ireland, which had been sacked, he lived in France from choice. But he judged both French and British by the same standards, and when, at the time of Mons, he came to the conclusion that General Lanrezac was not playing the game with him, it was finished. Once he had lost confidence in the Commander of the Fifth Army he ignored him and acted as if he and his Army did not exist.

Today all was still well.

The two men walked into General Lanrezac's sanctum together, the one short, brisk, taking long strides out of proportion to his size, the other big, bulky, heavy, moving with short steps as if his body were too heavy for his legs.

Owing to the extraordinary importance of this interview I have been at great pains to reconstruct it.

My own personal recollection is that Lanrezac and Sir John disappeared into the former's room, and that General Hély d'Oissel went into the 3ème Bureau with the British staff officers who had accompanied Sir John. There is no doubt whatever that the French Chief of Staff was not present at the interview, and it is my belief that the two generals were closeted alone together. I was outside the building, with a group of French officers who stood about the little square, where as many members of the Fifth Army Staff as could make themselves free were collected. We knew that Lanrezac spoke no English, and Sir John, though he understood a little French, at that time could hardly speak it at all. In fact he never mastered it. Even after the war when he lived in Paris he had the greatest difficulty in such simple things as directing a taxi driver to the hotel where he lived. Our knowledge of the linguistic limitations of the two chiefs led to some mild jokes such as, "I bet they are asking each other what has become of the penknife belonging to the gardener's uncle."

Some of the British officers remember being present at a discussion between Sir John French and Lanrezac, but I am convinced that no English staff officer can have assisted at an interview from which the Chief of Staff of the Fifth Army was excluded. What I think probably happened is that after a time the two generals came out of General Lanrezac's sanctum and joined the waiting British officers in the 3ème Bureau, where some sort of general conversation took place. Presumably the two Chiefs of Staff had a talk while their leaders were in conference, but from the results it would not appear that their conversation was any more satisfactory than the interview between the two Commanders.

A British officer has told me the following incident of which he was a witness. Sir John, stepping up to a map in the 3ème Bureau, took out his glasses, located a place with his finger, and said to Lanrezac: "*Mon Général, est-ce-que —*" His French then gave out, and turning to one of his staff, he asked: "How do you say 'to cross the river' in French?" He was told, and proceeded: "*Est-ce que les Allemands vont traverser la Meuse à - à —*" Then he fumbled over the pronunciation of the name. "Huy" was the place, unfortunately one of the most difficult words imaginable to pronounce, the "u" having practically to be whistled. It was quite beyond Sir John. "Hoy", he said at last, triumphantly. "What does he say? What does he say?" exclaimed Lanrezac. Somebody explained that the Marshal wanted to know whether in his opinion the Germans were going to cross the river at Huy? Lanrezac shrugged his shoulders impatiently. "Tell the Marshal," he said curtly, "that in my opinion the Germans have merely gone to the Meuse to fish." This story gives some idea of Lanrezac's mentality and manners. Evidently his conversation with Sir John had put him out of temper, and he did not hesitate to show it by being deliberately rude.

But perhaps the best illustration of the attitude of General Lanrezac and some of his Staff is given by a Frenchman, Colonel Huguet, who in his book* which is anything but friendly to the British, describes his

* "*L'Intervention Militaire Britannique en 1914.*"

arrival at Rethel and his reception by General Hély d'Oissel. Hély d'Oissel's opening remark to him was: "Well, here you are (meaning the British) – it is just about time. If we are beaten it will be thanks to you." Huguet writes that he was flabbergasted, as well he might be, and he concluded that the Chief of Staff merely reflected the views of his Commander. But what a state of mind! Here was the Commander-in-Chief of the British Army, which was being rushed forward ahead of its time tables, himself ahead of his troops, coming to confer with General Lanrezac, and this was the spirit in which he was met! This remark explains many things. It contains the seeds of the whole series of dismal, sordid misunderstandings. It can only be explained by the fact that the Commander of the Fifth Army was already "rattled".

That none of the many competent officers who were at Rethel that day were called upon to act as interpreters at the main interview is another example of the fetish of secrecy. It was so generally accepted that secrecy was the most important of all factors, that it was applied against all the dictates of common sense. Upon this occasion the veil of secrecy was so tightly drawn that the chief actors were debarred from gaining more than an inkling, and that a distorted one, of each other's intentions, with the result that the plan of operations itself remained blurred and indistinct to those whom it most concerned.

Neither the private conversation between French and Lanrezac, nor the subsequent general conversation between the Staffs, lasted very long: some twenty minutes or half an hour after Sir John's arrival, the two generals appeared on the steps of the Headquarters building, took formal leave of each other, and the Field Marshal drove off to Le Cateau via Vervins.

The staffs of both armies were not slow to realize that the two men had not taken to each other. General Lanrezac did not disguise from his entourage his feelings towards Sir John, and I learnt a few days later at Le Cateau that Sir John had not liked Lanrezac.

The interview had resulted in a complete fiasco.

Amongst the subjects discussed was the date on which the British Army would be in a position to advance. General Joffre had assumed that it would be ready to move forward on the 21st. General Lanrezac on the other hand gathered from the Field Marshal that he could not advance till the 24th, and that even then he would require another week to get his reservists fit. General Lanrezac was all the more inclined to accept the latter assumption since it was generally believed on his staff, in spite of all assurances to the contrary, that the British would not be in a position to move before the 30th or 31st. When General Lanrezac reported his conversation with Sir John to the G.Q.G. and stated that he gathered that the British would only move forward at earliest on the 24th, General Joffre was much concerned. A telephone conversation between the G.Q.G. and G.H.Q.* took place as a result of which General Lanrezac was informed that even supposing the British could not advance before the 24th they could throw out small detachments on the 21st to cover the final concentration.

Facts proved the estimate of G.H.Q. to be too conservative, for the British Army, when the time came, was in position and ready to move forward on the 21st.

One of the strangest things about the Rethel interview is that a memorandum handed to Sir John by General Joffre, which gave the situation of the enemy as it was believed to be on the previous evening, the 16th, and outlined the role to be played by the British and the Fifth Army, was not, according to General Lanrezac, discussed at all. He alleged that Sir John did not even mention this paper, which he (Lanrezac) had neither heard of nor seen.† The explanation may be that the memorandum had not been translated into English, and that Sir John was therefore not in a position to discuss it. This may seem extraordinary, but it was exactly what happened in the case of another equally important order of Joffre's during the Retreat.‡

One of the first proofs that the two generals had not succeeded in understanding each other was afforded by the following incident.

General Lanrezac had asked that some villages in the British zone should be given to the XVIII. Corps for billets, and had thought that Sir John had acquiesced, but the units of the XVIII. Corps found British troops already billeted in these same villages when they arrived there. This was only a minor incident, but it irritated General Lanrezac, not unnaturally, and gave colour to his preconceived idea that the British were difficult if not impossible people to deal with.

The matter is mentioned by General Lanrezac in his book in the following words:

"This incident, unimportant in itself, tended to show that our military relations with the British would be anything but easy, in

---

* General Headquarters. These initials will throughout indicate British General Headquarters.

† See Appendix XI.

‡ See Part Two, Chapter IV, August 26th, p. 230.

spite of undeniable goodwill on both sides. We did not speak the same language, and moreover we had very different ideas on the conduct of war."

But perhaps the most unfortunate misunderstanding of all occurred over the employment of the British Cavalry.

General Lanrezac attached great importance to this question, for he very rightly considered it vital to locate the German columns and determine their line of march. For this purpose Cavalry was essential, especially as air reconnaissance was yielding no results owing to the weather.

General Lanrezac asked Sir John about the employment of his Cavalry, and understood the Field Marshal to answer that he refused to use his cavalry as cavalry, and that not having the number of troops originally contemplated, he intended to employ it as a reserve, and that it would only be engaged as mounted infantry in the line.

This was a complete misunderstanding. It had never entered Sir John French's head to use his Cavalry as mounted infantry. He had himself been a bold and successful cavalry leader, and was the last person to wish to prevent the cavalry fulfilling its proper functions. The British Cavalry Division was pushed forward at the earliest possible moment, and under the orders of General Allenby carried out its work as cavalry in a way which, if it has ever been equalled, has never been surpassed in the annals of the mounted service of any country. It is just possible that Sir John may have mentioned to General Lanrezac that it might be necessary for him to keep the cavalry temporarily as a reserve, in view of the fact that the 4th Division had been kept in England contrary to the original plan, but even this is doubtful, and it is certain that Sir John attached the greatest importance to its operating as cavalry.

It is the fact, however, that General Lanrezac, as is proved by his report to General Joffre* as well as by numerous conversations he had with his staff, believed that Sir John did not intend to use his cavalry for strategic reconnaissances, and was exasperated, all the more so that the French Cavalry Corps, hitherto operating on his front, had now been given a semi-political mission by the G.Q.G. He feared this would deprive him for all practical purposes of its use. Moreover, he was aware that Sordet's horses were in a state of great exhaustion. He (Lanrezac) was persuaded that the French Cavalry could not both give him the

* See Appendix XII.

information he required and carry out the mission assigned to it by the G.Q.G.; hence the great importance he attached to the question, and his brooding exasperation at what he considered to be Sir John French's amateurish and timid conception of the use of cavalry.

That such a misunderstanding should ever have arisen is strange enough, but what is quite extraordinary is that it was not cleared up. It was certainly never mentioned to me either by General Lanrezac or by his Chief of Staff. If General Lanrezac had had a further conversation with Sir John, or had maintained any sort of personal contact with the British, his mistake would have been swiftly corrected.

The explanation of his attitude is that, like so many Frenchmen, he had by training and tradition an instinctive mistrust of foreigners, and, in common with the rest of mankind, disliked what he did not know. That the British should be difficult and unreliable was just what such a man would expect. That an English Commander should not know his job was taken as a matter of course: the contrary would be as noteworthy as it would be surprising. General Lanrezac lived with his *parti pris*. What he had gathered of Sir John's intentions fitted in so well with his preconceived ideas that he made no attempt to dispel the misconceptions upon which his impressions were based. Anyone who has read General Lanrezac's book will see that this is not an unfair comment, and every officer on his staff knew that neither the British, nor the Belgians for that matter, found favour in his eyes. He was apt to lump them in with his own Reserve Divisions as being all equally useless. During the whole period of his command he never saw a British unit.

General Lanrezac never returned Sir John French's call. That he should have been extremely perturbed as a result of their interview is not surprising, but this can hardly be accepted as a reason for never making the least effort to confer again with the British Commander-in-Chief. Quite apart from the question of combined operations, this was a matter of elementary courtesy, and the omission of this formality by an officer of high rank, belonging to an army justly proud of its punctiliousness in such matters, is hard to explain. It was a real slight, and may have been a studied one. The difference between his procedure and that of his successor is worthy of note, and will be told in due course.

The two generals did not see each other again until the 26th August at St. Quentin, after the battles of Charleroi and Mons had been fought and lost. Sir John attempted to see General Lanrezac on the 22nd, but turned back on hearing that the latter was too far away to be reached in the time he could dispose of. When they met at St. Quentin, they did not do so of their own initiative, but were summoned by General Joffre to confer with him.

It was of course the armies that paid the penalty. They were incalculably weakened in the trials they were so soon to face together, by the lack of understanding between their leaders. They endured the same hardships, and they were overwhelmed by the same enemy, to whom a single will and a closely knit plan were not opposed until General Joffre took matters in hand and replaced General Lanrezac. The Allied cause suffered an injury, as the result of the Rethel interview, which was only completely effaced by the victory that was awaited so long, and came only after years of tribulation. Men and the characters of men are what count in war. Their smaller defects turned the scale against the Allies that day.

The lives General Lanrezac and the Earl of Ypres each devoted to the service of his country are over. No one can doubt that all they had to give they gave unsparingly, each in his own way and according to his maximum capacity. But as leaders of Armies at what was perhaps the most crucial period of the war, their actions cannot escape scrutiny and criticism. As far as the Rethel interview is concerned, I feel impelled to state my belief that the English general was far less to blame than General Lanrezac for the evil consequences of their meeting. Far from having a prejudice against the French he liked them. He got on well with General Joffre. No misunderstanding with him ever failed to be cleared up. He was on friendly terms with every French Commander with whom he had dealings, save General Lanrezac, and when the latter had been replaced, in spite of the bitterness he had by that time come to feel, he co-operated with the utmost loyalty with his successor.

*   *   *

I learned later, what I did not know at the time, that General Lanrezac, in reporting his conversation with Sir John to General Joffre, took the opportunity to make a suggestion which illuminates in a significant fashion his subsequent actions.

The message* ran:

"As the area of detrainment of the British Army is very close to the Sambre, the Fifth Army, which in the event of a retirement would not

* See Appendix XII.

have at its disposal enough roads, would be obliged to make incursions into the British area."

To avoid the confusion which would result he suggested that "the possibility of the British Army's concentrating farther back should be studied."

This message seriously disturbed General Joffre, and no wonder. He had been urging the British forward (and General Lanrezac, although ready to discount the value of the B.E.F., had also displayed considerable nervousness lest it should be delayed, as witness Hély d'Oissel's remark to Colonel Huguet). His offensive plan largely depended upon their being in line with the Fifth Army at the earliest possible date, and now it was suggested that they would concentrate farther back, and for what reason? So that they should not block the Fifth Army's possible retirement! General Lanrezac's point of view appeared to be that if the British were not up in time his left would be endangered, while if they hurried to his protection they might obstruct his retreat!*

General Joffre could not understand. He had fallen in with General Lanrezac's suggestions. The Fifth Army was moving into the position indicated by its Commander, who seemed satisfied. This talk of retreat on the part of the General upon whom Joffre had relied more than on any other for his offensive spirit was, to say the least, disconcerting.

Joffre's reply showed the astonishment caused by Lanrezac's communication at the G.Q.G.

"The British Army is protected during detrainment by the Fifth Army and the fortifications of Maubeuge. *There must be no question of doing anything but holding the present positions.* It is only if it should become absolutely impossible to do otherwise that the area in which the British Army is detraining should be modified. At present we know that a German Corps (the IV.) is advancing towards Dinant to force the passage of the Meuse. When we know the movements of the others we will assume the offensive. It is only at the last extremity that we could contemplate giving up the present line."

Lanrezac's message was the first indication General Joffre received that the Commander of the Fifth Army might not be so determined or

* In point of fact the Allies did retire over the ground General Lanrezac was considering, but although in an operation of this nature it is almost always felt that means of evacuation are insufficient, the retreat, in spite of much hardship caused by congestion, was carried out without any disaster being attributable to shortage of roads.

so confident as he had hitherto believed him to be. It revealed for the first time a trait unsuspected by all, probably ignored by General Lanrezac himself. His personality is one of the enigmas of the war. In the early days he was like a hound in leash, straining to get at the enemy, eager to assume the offensive, and up to a much later date everybody believed that this was his firm intention. It was only by degrees that the hesitation in his mind, and the growing pessimism which finally developed into total inactivity, became apparent. Little by little from minute incidents, many of which were too small to make a conscious impression at the time, I came to the conclusion that General Lanrezac did not intend to attack at all. It is probable that at this date he intended to do so, and merely had momentary misgivings.

CHAPTER VII

THE MOVE TO THE NORTH

August 17th, 18th and 19th, 1914

*The captive German airman – The English and Calais – Lord Kitchener's girls'
school – Valuable information concerning the enemy – Commandant Girard –
Fifth Army H.Q. leaves Rethel – Signy-le-Petit – Commandant Duruy – French
infantry – Search for the British Army – Captain Fagalde – Instruction Générale
No. 13 – The G.Q.G.'s miscalculations – General Lanrezac reports his intentions
– A message from the British – Bad news from the Belgians – Duruy brings more
bad news – General Lanrezac's lecture – Impressions of the French infantry –
Northerners and southerners – The French Cavalry Corps – A fiasco in combined
operations – The spirit of the cavalry – General Sordet's difficulties – Useless
manœuvres – More searches for the British – Colonel Huguet's letter – The Fifth
Army on the Sambre – An important report from the Fourth Army – Joffre's
reply – The "Armée de Paris" identified by the enemy.*

ON the evening of the 17th, when I walked into Headquarters at about
seven o'clock, to my utter surprise I found a German officer sitting in the
little hall.

But if I was taken aback, he was much more so, he gasped and nearly
fell off his stool. He was a tall, fair young man, and his astonishment at
seeing a British uniform was comical. He had not known, he said, that
England was in the war!

He was an observer whose machine had been shot down and his
pilot killed, and we were all very sorry for him on account of his grief
when he heard that the pilot was dead.

General Hély d'Oissel walked across the room and said a few kind
words to him, offering him a cigar. Later in the war such a gesture
would have been unthinkable, for when French soil was invaded and
reports of German atrocities began to come in, every German became
the hated representative of a barbaric foe with whom it was absolutely
impossible to have any human relationship.

Several of us walked over to the *"popotte"* together for dinner, which was very gay. There was much chaffing about the insane English who were reported to be taking three-year leases of houses in Rouen. As if the war could possibly last beyond Christmas! Were we seizing a pretext to reconquer France? That night for the first time I heard a joking reference to Calais. "If the English get into Calais —" someone said laughingly, "they will never leave it at the end of the war. They were too upset when they lost it before. It killed *Marie la Sanguinnaire.*" "Yes," I replied, "Allies are apt to be a nuisance when the fighting is over. What about Savoy and Nice?"

Such remarks passed as jokes at the time, but strange as it may seem, a haunting fear developed later in many French minds, as the war dragged on and northern France became a British camp, that we really might refuse to leave Calais when the time came to settle accounts. Few Englishmen realized the immense relief France felt when all these strangers went home, when their own land ceased to be a dumping ground for every nation in the world, and their beloved Paris became French again.

At dinner that night there were of course witticisms concerning the joke of the moment in the French Army – Lord Kitchener's Order to the troops.* "We were shipping over a girls' school instead of an army." "We had evidently much changed since the days of the wars in Spain."

Meanwhile the Intelligence had been busy with the aviator, and had obtained a great deal of valuable information from him. He belonged to the Second German Army, which was commanded by General von Bülow, whose Headquarters had just moved into Liège. He stated that the forts of the town had fallen and that military trains were able to arrive there. He declared that the Second Army included the VII., IX. and X. Corps and the Guard, and that three Reserve Corps were following in second line.

This was very important news. It was the first indication that reserve corps were following on the heels of the active corps. The threat from the north was taking shape. Commander Girard, head of the 2ème Bureau of the Fifth Army, was hot on the trail.

Girard was a very remarkable man. His stern appearance hid a heart of pure gold. Although a Provençal and a typical one, no man ever had his emotions under better control or had a calmer, more icy mind. The only way in which his southern blood asserted itself was in the vividness

* See Appendix XIII.

of word and gesture with which he emphasized his speech. He worked like a galley-slave, as did his officers, and it was wonderful to see growing out of his labours, from information coming in from all sources, air observations, cavalry reconnaissances, secret service reports, or messages from the G.Q.G., an analysis of the situation, astonishingly complete considering the shreds upon which it was based. This was embodied on the map in ever-lengthening red lines called at the time *"chenilles"* (caterpillars), representing the German columns spreading out in a gigantic movement which grew and amplified with each new report, until they seemed to change into long blood-red snakes spreading over the face of Belgium like a plague. And always Girard's eager clutching hand was tearing down the veil of secrecy hiding the movements of the German armies, until his piercing eyes were able to discern the secrets of the overwhelming turning movement. Now he began to sense the weight behind the blow he had foreseen. The information obtained from the airman, following on earlier reports, was certainly alarming. On the previous day Maubeuge had reported that the Belgian staff had information that 200,000 Germans were crossing the Meuse between Maëstricht and Visé. Large forces of German cavalry had been concentrated about Hannut on the 15th, and were apparently intended to cover the German columns on the left bank of the Meuse.

To cap this, Girard was told over the telephone by the G.Q.G. of a report from Brussels that two Cavalry Divisions had appeared at Jodoigne, causing a panic in the Belgian capital which had determined the Government to retire to Antwerp.

The shadow of the coming onrush was beginning to be thrown forward clear and distinct for all who had eyes to see. Great masses of cavalry moving slowly forward could but be covering the advance of numerous columns of infantry. These cavalry divisions were not raiders whose object it was by a sudden dash to throw confusion into the enemy's country and imperil his communications. The German Cavalry had already shown a dislike for excursions and forays far from the protection of their infantry supports. They were obviously merely clearing the way for the Corps following close behind.

Such was the view gradually evolving in the mind of the clear-sighted head of the 2ème Bureau of the Fifth Army, whilst the British Intelligence was drawing a similar conclusion; but their opinion was not shared by the Operations sections, much less by the G.Q.G., which seemed to think that to the west only cavalry raids were threatened.

On the 18th August at 9 a.m., we left Rethel for good. We were to move north to keep in close touch with the Corps now fast advancing towards the Sambre.

I said good-bye gaily to my pleasant hostess and my host the Sous-Préfet, who represented the authority of the Republic in that corner of the Department of the Ardennes, and presently the whole Headquarters Staff departed in the exhilarating atmosphere military moves always engender, provided the enemy is not at one's heels. The entire population of the town turned out to see us go. All was well, we were going northwards, where the enemy was reported to be: a move in the right direction seemed to the townsfolk a good omen, a forecast of victory.

At the last moment, as I was getting into a car, I discovered that neither my bag, which had "*Armée de Paris*" painted on it in great white letters, nor my soldier servant, the "*ordonnance*" who had been told off to look after me, could be found. A hue and cry was started in which the more active natives joined. Not that the man would be hard to find: he could be identified anywhere. He was an amazing little fellow, a mason by trade, and his idea of looking after one's things was to pile them carefully one on top of the other on the floor in a corner of the room, as if he were building a wall. The toothbrush was often the foundation of this edifice, and the boots provided a very satisfactory roof, handily placed so as to be available without stooping, whilst the meaningless little brush was deprived of the opportunity of mislaying itself. His name was Boisvert, but however suggestive it might be of the gay greenwood, he recalled neither Robin Hood by his agility nor Maid Marion by his beauty. He had a terrific squint and was bandy-legged. He was neither useful nor prepossessing, but I soon became very much attached to him, principally because of his extraordinary devotion, which I found to be one of the most touching traits in the French soldier's character.

Upon this occasion he was at last discovered, my bag on his shoulder, having an argument with a washerwoman whom he accused of having lost one of my socks. Neither of them were mincing their words, but the washerwoman got in the last shot, for alluding to his bow legs, she called him a worm in brackets, an insult to which Boisvert could find no answer as he was being bundled away.

We started off with much dignity, the General and his Chief of Staff leading the way in one car, the rest of us following in others at proper intervals, at a slow and stately pace. All went well until we began to meet convoys. Wagons, at times two abreast, blocked the way. Our procession began to advance as if it were a telescope jerkily opening and closing.

There were bumps, we got separated, and finally were stopped altogether. I could see gesticulating people in all the cars. The most animated figure was that of the general himself, whom I could see in the distance waving his arms about. We finally got through, although it had looked as if we should be stuck for hours.

The country was lovely, and the great Ardennes forests were at their very best on this fine sunny day. Rozoy-sur-Serre, Aubenton and Fligny were left behind, and before noon we reached our destination, Signy-le-Petit, a picturesque little place, hardly a town. We were lucky in being able to install our mess, the *"popotte"*, in the establishment of Monsieur Barrachin, who had a fine house and proved to be a very pleasant host.

Commandant Duruy, who had been Military Attaché in Brussels and was therefore obviously the right man for liaison with the Belgians, was sent off to Namur, in pursuance of a suggestion made by the G.Q.G., to get into touch with the 4th Belgian Division commanded by General Michel, who had assumed command of the fortress.

Commandant Duruy, a son of the celebrated Minister of the Third Empire whose name he bore, was a striking personality. He was one of the finest looking men and one of the most distinguished soldiers it has ever been my good fortune to know. He looked magnificent in his tirailleur's uniform, light blue tunic with a yellow collar, and baggy red trousers. I shall have occasion to mention him often, and his name never fails to evoke in my mind the picture of a very tall, strong man, as straight as a die, whose character was as fine as his bearing. We who served with him still feel his loss almost as keenly as we did that day, some months later, when he fell at Ypres.

Bénazet and I shared a billet in the house of an elderly couple, *"rentiers"*, rather timorous and puzzled about the war, not knowing whether to be pleased or scared by this invasion of armed men. They questioned us anxiously and deferentially as to whether it would be wise to move south. Bénazet assured them in eloquent language that Signy-le-Petit was an ideal if not the ideal point of vantage from which to view the war. I do not know whether they took his advice, but some ten days later Signy was in the hands of the enemy.

After getting something to eat, I had to go north, and on my way visited some French units and saw many more on the march. The aspect of French infantry straggling forward anyhow had profoundly shocked me when I first saw the long columns sprawling all over the road, no two men in step, the *"capotes"** unbuttoned, looking much more like a mob than like disciplined men, but it quickly became apparent that although this infantry was not smart to look at, it got there all the same, and that the lack of polish was due more to badly fitting uniforms than to anything else. The French soldier, we were soon to learn, had lost nothing of the wonderful marching powers which had proved so disturbing to us in the days of the Peninsular War. As one became better acquainted with these men, it was impossible not to be impressed by their fire, their determination, their enthusiasm and their endurance.

On my return to Signy, I was requested to accompany Captain Fagalde, who had been ordered to search the country for signs of the British.

We scoured most of Picardy without meeting a single man in khaki, and our reports to this effect seemed to confirm the worst suspicions of those members of the Fifth Army Staff who held that if the British Army was not a myth it must be indulging in one last gorge of roast beef, or be playing out the last game of the summer football season, before starting for the war.

But quite seriously, perhaps no single fact better illustrates the attitude of mind of General Lanrezac and some of his staff at this time than these searches for the British, in which several French officers and I myself frequently took part. There was the French liaison mission attached to the British Army, there was the G.Q.G. itself fully aware of where the British were, arranging in fact for their transport. These authorities could be consulted at any moment, but this did not suffice. The wily sons of Albion might be playing some trick on the trustful French. Advance parties might be pretending to be divisions. It was necessary that a representative of the Fifth Army should see these Britishers for himself, and to make assurance doubly sure, to be quite certain that these troops really were the British and not something else, the British liaison officer must go too and identify his compatriots under the lynx eyes of a French confrère.

Captain Fagalde, my companion upon this occasion, hailed from the Basque country. He was one of the most brilliant members of the Fifth Army Staff. He belonged to the 2ème Bureau, and like everybody else in that section worked eighteen hours a day, deducing the movements of the German Army from information received, or deciphering inter-

---

* The combined tunic and great coat worn by the French soldiers.

cepted code messages, which he was singularly successful in doing. Later he was occasionally sent in liaison to the British Army.

At this time he was suffering from an internal complaint and lived on *tisanes.** It was wonderfully plucky of him to stick to his work in the way he did, considering how ill he often was. It was quite evident that if his health held out he would go far. He ended the war as Head of the French Military Mission in London, and there his health completely recovered, either because the climate suited him, or because of the impossibility of procuring the necessary ingredients for his nauseating *tisanes.*

When we got back to Signy, we found that *Instruction Particulière No. 13* had been received from the G.Q.G.†

This order, which was the last common to the Third, Fourth and Fifth Armies, envisaged two main lines of action by the enemy forces opposed to them, that is the German corps believed to be grouped round Thionville, in Luxembourg and in Belgium.

These forces, it was stated, appeared to comprise from thirteen to fifteen corps formed into two main groups. (Map V, p. 90.)

The first contingency contemplated was that the enemy northern group, which might consist of from seven to eight corps and four cavalry divisions, advancing on both banks of the Meuse, might try to cross between Givet and Brussels and even possibly accentuate still further its movement towards the north.

In this case the Fifth Army and the Cavalry Corps, in liaison with the British and Belgian Armies, were to oppose this movement directly and attempt to outflank the enemy by the north. The Belgian Army and the Cavalry Corps were, it was pointed out, already in position to take part in such an outflanking manœuvre.

Whilst this plan was being carried out in the north, the Third and Fourth French Armies were to attack the enemy's centre, which was estimated at another six or seven corps and two or three cavalry divisions and, having defeated it, the major part of the Fourth Army was to advance immediately against the left flank of the enemy's northern group.

The second contingency provided for was that the enemy might only engage north of the Meuse a fraction of his right wing group, in which case it was thought that whilst the central group was engaging frontally the Third and Fourth French Armies, that part of his northern group which was south of the Meuse might attempt to attack the left flank of

* Infusion of herbs.
† See Appendix XIV.

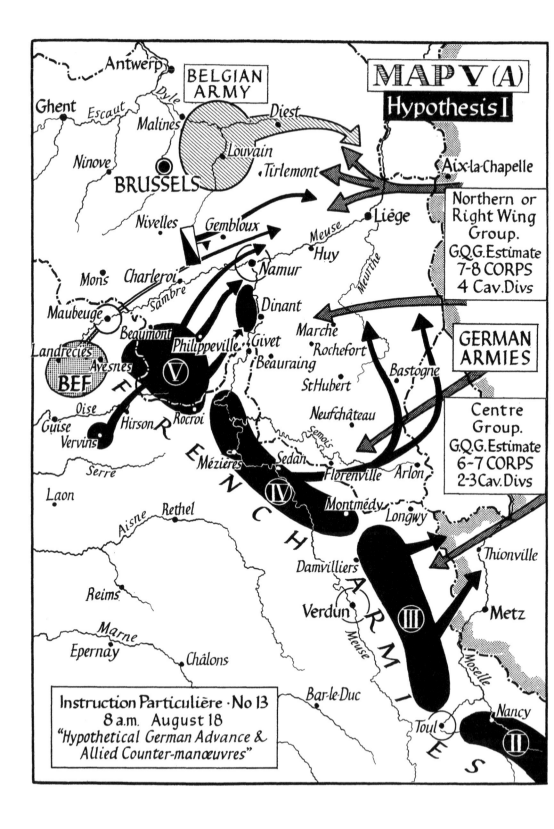

MAP V (A)
Hypothesis I

BELGIAN ARMY

Antwerp
Ghent
Escaut
Malines
Ninove
BRUSSELS
Nivelles
Mons
Charleroi
Maubeuge
Beaumont
Landrecies
Avesnes
BEF
Oise
Guise
Vervins
Hirson
Rocroi
Laon
Reims
Marne
Epernay
Châlons

Dyle
Louvain
Diest
Tirlemont
Gembloux
Namur
Sambre
Philippeville
Givet
Beauraing
Aix-la-Chapelle
Liége
Meuse
Huy
Meurthe
Dinant
Marche
Rochefort
StHubert
Bastogne
Neufchâteau
Semois
Méziéres
Sedan
Florenville
Arlon
Montmédy
Longwy
Damvilliers
Verdun
Meuse
Bar-le-Duc
Toul
Thionville
Metz
Moselle
Nancy

V
IV
III
II

Rethel
Aisne
Serre

FRENCH ARMIES

Northern or
Right Wing
Group.
G.Q.G.Estimate
7-8 CORPS
4 Cav.Divs

GERMAN
ARMIES

Centre
Group.
G.Q.G.Estimate
6-7 CORPS
2-3 Cav.Divs

Instruction Particulière · No 13
8 a.m. August 18
"Hypothetical German Advance &
Allied Counter-manœuvres"

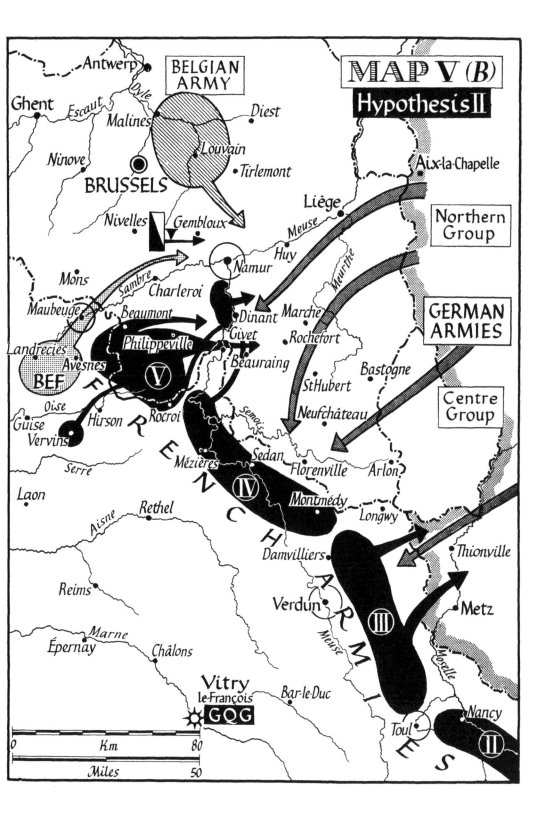

the Fourth Army. If this turned out to be the case, the British and
Belgians were to be left to deal with the German forces north of the
Sambre and Meuse, whilst the Fifth Army, wheeling on Namur and
Givet, was to advance in the general direction of Marche or of St.
Hubert.*

How mistaken the G.Q.G. was at this date both concerning the
German plans and the troops they had available is shown by the fact
that the German forces advancing against the Third, Fourth and Fifth
Armies and the British and Belgians, were, not the fifteen corps esti-
mated in this Order, but a total of twenty-eight corps including the
reserve corps, two cavalry corps, one reserve division and twelve
Landwehr brigades, comprising in all the German First, Second, Third,
Fourth and Fifth Armies. The northern group, estimated by General
Joffre at seven to eight corps, consisted of the First, Second and Third
Armies, a total of sixteen corps, six Landwehr brigades, and five cavalry
divisions organized in two corps.‡ This force proved sufficient not only
to outflank and outnumber the British and the Fifth Army but to drive
in the French centre as well. (Map V, p. 90.)

Before receiving this order General Lanrezac had reported his intentions
to General Joffre that morning (18th) as follows:

* A copy of *Instruction Particulière No. 13* was sent to Sir John French, who acknowledged
it next day in the following terms:
"I have the honour to acknowledge receipt of your Instructions speciales (*sic*) of August
18th, 1914. It appears from it that you envisage two hypotheses:
"(*a*) The first by which a large enemy force (*e.g.* four to six corps) is operating north of the
         Meuse.
"(*b*) The second according to which a relatively weak force (*e.g.* one or two corps at most)
         is located north of the Meuse.
"Under hypothesis (*a*) your intention is to oppose the forward movement of the Germans
by pushing forward the Fifth Army north of the Sambre and Meuse, and you ask me to
co-operate in this movement together with the Belgian Army, and if possible to outflank the
Germans, and you have taken steps to give me the support during these operations of a French
Cavalry Corps.
"Under hypothesis (*b*) you have the intention of transferring the Fifth Army to the other
side of the Meuse between Namur and Givet, so as to take in flank the German Army, and
you ask me as well as the Belgian Army to protect the flank of the Fifth Army and to take as
my objective the German forces north of the river.
"If I have thoroughly understood your intentions, you can rely upon my most cordial
co-operation. I have only to add that under hypothesis (*b*) I would accept with the greatest
pleasure the support of the three reserve divisions to which you allude in the last paragraph
of your letter.†

                                                    (*Signed*) J. FRENCH.
"Dated Le Cateau, August 19th, 1914."
† See Appendix XI.
‡ The IX. Reserve Corps was retained in Schleswig until August 23rd, when it joined the
northern group.

"The I. Corps can hold the Meuse about Dinant so long as it is not outflanked from the north. If need be I shall reinforce it tomorrow with a division from the X. Corps.

"Tomorrow I shall push forward the main bodies of the X. and III. Corps (each reinforced by an African division) to the front Stave–Nalinnes.

"I shall thus be in a position as from the day after tomorrow (the 20th) to counter-attack any enemy forces attempting an outflanking movement west of Namur by crossing the Sambre between Namur and Charleroi, and to throw them back into the Sambre.

"In case the I. Corps should be outflanked before the arrival of the X. and III. Corps, and be compelled to give ground, it would fall back towards the south, resting its right on the Meuse, and once its left was supported by the X. and III. Corps it would resume, together with them, the offensive between the Sambre and the Meuse." (Map IV, p. 60.)

General Lanrezac also drew attention to the weakness of the link between himself and the Fourth Army,* and added that should he be forced to retire he would do so on Vervins and not on Mézières, so as to be in touch with the British. He reiterated that, as Sir John intended to use his cavalry as mounted infantry, it was absolutely essential that he should dispose of Sordet's Cavalry Corps, as this would be the only cavalry both for his Army and for the British.

It would seem from this message that General Joffre's admonition had had its effect, for General Lanrezac was now firm and his intentions clear. He did not allow himself to be unduly perturbed by the temporary weakness of his liaison with the Fourth Army, and seemed to have recovered his confidence. His mind was apparently working on very much the same lines as General Joffre's, with the notable exception that he disregarded any possibility of the enemy's confining his attack to the south of the Meuse. He, no more than his Chief, had as yet the

---

* He stated that his Army was now only weakly protected between Givet and Mézières, and that it was therefore essential that the 52nd Reserve Division, no longer under his orders, should continue to guard the river between Mézières and Revin. One of the Reserve Divisions under General Valabrègue (the 51st) had been despatched to Rocroi, where it was to arrive on the 20th. Its orders were, when it reached the Meuse, to prevent the enemy's passage between Revin and Vireux-Molhein and to establish liaison with the 52nd Reserve Division.

General Lanrezac also pointed out that however important it was to prevent hostile forces slipping in between the Fourth and Fifth Armies by Sedan or Mézières, yet, as he had to manœuvre towards the north to cover the British detrainment, he could assume no responsibility in this respect.

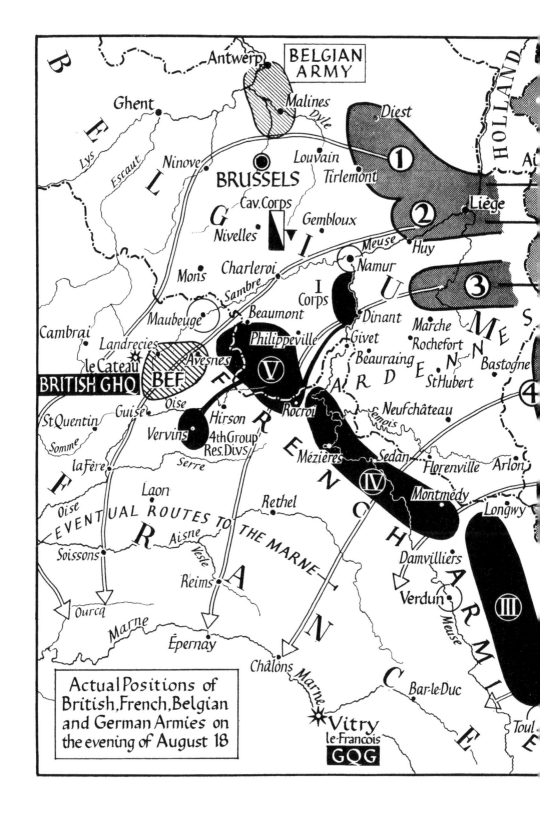

Actual Positions of British, French, Belgian and German Armies on the evening of August 18

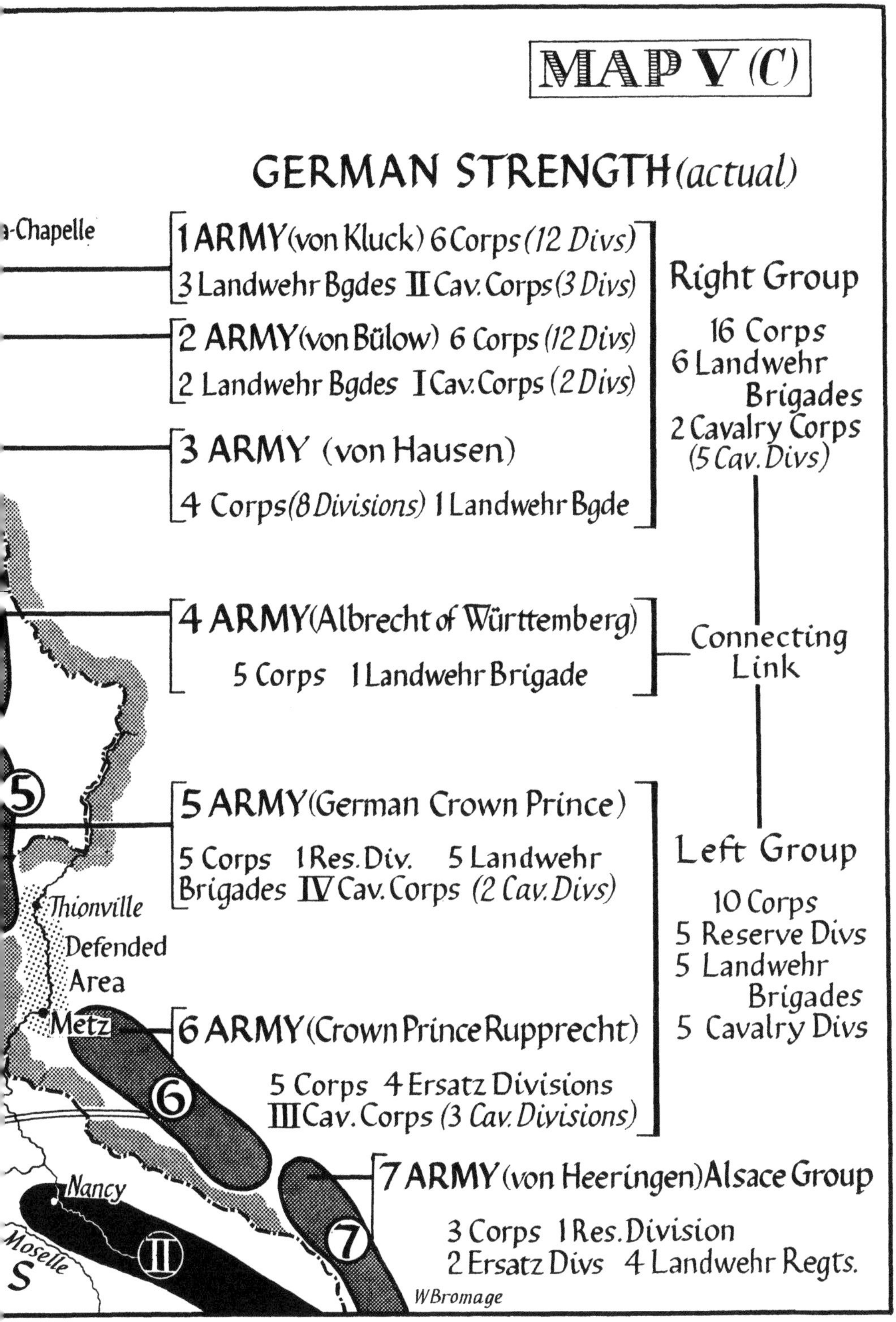

MAP V (C)

GERMAN STRENGTH (actual)

a-Chapelle

1 ARMY (von Kluck) 6 Corps (12 Divs)
3 Landwehr Bgdes II Cav. Corps (3 Divs)

Right Group
16 Corps
6 Landwehr
Brigades
2 Cavalry Corps
(5 Cav. Divs)

2 ARMY (von Bülow) 6 Corps (12 Divs)
2 Landwehr Bgdes I Cav. Corps (2 Divs)

3 ARMY (von Hausen)
4 Corps (8 Divisions) 1 Landwehr Bgde

4 ARMY (Albrecht of Württemberg)
5 Corps 1 Landwehr Brigade

Connecting Link

5 ARMY (German Crown Prince)
5 Corps 1 Res. Div. 5 Landwehr
Brigades IV Cav. Corps (2 Cav. Divs)

Left Group
10 Corps
5 Reserve Divs
5 Landwehr
Brigades
5 Cavalry Divs

Thionville
Defended
Area

Metz

6 ARMY (Crown Prince Rupprecht)
5 Corps 4 Ersatz Divisions
III Cav. Corps (3 Cav. Divisions)

⑤

⑥

Nancy

⑦

Ⅱ

Moselle
S

7 ARMY (von Heeringen) Alsace Group
3 Corps 1 Res. Division
2 Ersatz Divs 4 Landwehr Regts.

WBromage

least glimmering of the amplitude of the German sweep through Belgium.

Late in the evening an officer (Captain Fayolle) came in from the French Mission at British G.H.Q. with a letter from Colonel Huguet, which stated that the Field Marshal was preparing his forward movement, and asked whether, if the Fifth Army crossed the Sambre, the British right column could dispose of the Bavai-Nivelles road.* This message, from a French source, showed how ridiculous the British-hunting of the last few days had been.

Although we at Fifth Army H.Q. did not know it, that night the news from the Belgians was bad. The Belgian Government had withdrawn to Antwerp on the 17th. The Belgian Army was falling back and Belgian G.H.Q. had retired to Malines.†

On the morning of August 19th, Commandant Duruy returned from Namur. His news was pessimistic. He thought the morale of the Belgian Command very unsatisfactory and that a really determined and powerful attack would not be long resisted. He had been requested by General Michel to urge the Franco-British forces to cross the Sambre and assume responsibility for the defence of the north-western and south-western zones of the fortress, so that the Belgians might concentrate on the defence of the north-eastern and south-eastern sections.

Duruy would not be shaken in his opinion that the fortress could not be relied upon for a prolonged resistance, and, when Liège was cited, said that both the men and the circumstances were different. He suggested that some French troops should be drafted into the town for

---

* The answer, sent by the same officer, was that the British could have the use of this road when the general offensive north of the Sambre took place. The probable route of the XVIII. Corps was given, and it was stated that unless something unforeseen happened the heads of columns of the Fifth Army would reach the line Dinant-Mettet-Nalinnes on the following day.

† Colonel Adalbert, French Military Attaché in Brussels, had telegraphed to the President of the Republic:

"In the afternoon of August 17th the (Belgian) Government withdrew to Antwerp. I could only express my astonishment that this decision should be taken just at the precise moment when the French Cavalry Corps had appeared north of the Sambre and Meuse.

"The news available at Belgian H.Q. today, August 18th, which has been collected in some haste, is to the effect that troops of all arms belonging to the X. German Corps have crossed to the left bank of the Meuse over the bridge at Huy which has been repaired: 8,000 men of the IX. Corps passed through Landen at 11.30 a.m.; detachments of all arms attacked the Gette at Dies, Haelen and Tirlemont: other detachments are marching on Beverloo; the result of an action in the direction of Gembloux, in which the French Cavalry Corps and a Belgian Brigade participated, is still unknown.

"At 3 p.m. the Belgian G.H.Q. communicated to me their decision to evacuate the Gette, to fall back to the Dyle and move itself to Malines."

the purpose of heightening the morale of the garrison, and although this suggestion was not well received General Lanrezac was soon compelled to consider it, owing to the enormous importance of Namur as a *"point d'appui"* on the right of the Franco-British line. He did not do so at once, however, and when on the 20th General Joffre gave him leave to send a Reserve Division to co-operate in the defence of the fortress, he answered that, being ready to debouch north of the Sambre, he considered that he was meeting General Michel's wishes, for the latter had not actually asked for the entry of French troops into the town.*

General Lanrezac was, in fact, much put out by General Joffre's suggestion. Having been a lecturer, and a brilliant one, at the French Staff College, he had contracted the habit of expounding his views before an audience, and rather liked wandering into one of the rooms where the staff were working to hold forth on his impressions and theories. The Commander-in-Chief's proposals in the case of Namur gave rise to several such harangues, which might almost be said to have developed into indignation meetings. General Lanrezac kept repeating that to immobilize large forces in the defence of a fortress was a supreme mistake. He protested that he had always understood that fortified places were to be used as *"points d'appui"* for armies in the field. Any other conception meant the surrender of mobility and the abandonment of the possibility of strategic manœuvre. The bare idea of being involved in the defence of a fortress was particularly obnoxious to General Lanrezac, who had served in '70 as a subaltern in Lamirault's Corps, and to whom the events of that disastrous campaign were a very living memory.

General Lanrezac's arguments were no doubt sound, but took little account of General Joffre's reasons for wishing him to reinforce Namur. The only action that he took on the day of which I am writing, the 19th, (at which date of course General Joffre's message giving him leave to send a Reserve Division to Namur had not been despatched), was to send Duruy back to Namur in the afternoon, in company with Helbronner, to assure General Michel that the French troops were coming up fast on the Sambre, and to urge upon him the vital importance of putting up the strongest possible defence. Duruy and Helbronner returned that same evening, bringing a further request from General Michel that he should be given 30,000 rounds of 75 ammunition, which request General Lanrezac forwarded to General Joffre.

On this day, I saw a considerable number of units of the I., III. and X.

* See Appendix XV.

French Corps. The morale of the infantry was everywhere excellent. The men were cheerful and gay in spite of the fatigue imposed upon them by constant marching in torrid weather. The reservists were obviously getting fit, and indeed, under the gruelling they were being submitted to, it was a question of getting fit or dying of exhaustion, for the marches had been very long. How the French soldier could go on marching indefinitely wearing the heavy "*capote*", and carrying a big load on top of that, will always be a mystery to an Englishman.

It was impossible to say that any one unit was better than another, although some had better reputations. But from what I heard there seemed to be no doubt that the I. Corps (General Franchet d'Espérey's) was by far the best commanded and therefore the most valuable unit in the Fifth Army.

In the French Army, the fighting reputation of a regiment and the way it is led are of greater importance and influence its performance far more than its historic traditions. Nevertheless there are regiments which, although they have not the feeling of pride in their past that animates so many units in the British Army, can claim an ancient tradition and lineage: for instance there are two line regiments which trace their descent to Irish regiments in the French service in the eighteenth century, the Regiments of Dillon and Burke. Many claim as their forbears the old Royal Regiments; of these the 1st Regiment for instance is the lineal descendant of the Regiment of Picardie, which in the eighteenth century claimed to be the oldest in Europe; and in the sixteenth century the 5th Regiment was the famous Regiment of Navarre. Even our old friends the gendarmes are the descendants, as their name (*gens d'armes* – men-at-arms) implies, of the old feudal cavalry.*

It was a dogma in the French Army before the war that men from the south did not make such good fighters as men from the north, but the experience of the war, as time went on, was to show that this prejudice was not justified. As individuals the southerners were as good as men hailing from other districts, but when grouped together in Corps they were undoubtedly less warlike and less steadfast than the northerners or the men from the Centre. The fighting reputation of a unit, however, was of supreme importance.

Recruiting in the French Army was regional. All the recruits from the same province, with few exceptions, were drafted into the same Army Corps. But as the war dragged on and the regional system broke down

* See Appendix XVI.

to some extent, southerners were drafted into the XX. Corps, the crack formation of the French Army, and gave an excellent account of themselves.

Any regiment energetically commanded by able officers invariably fought well. The origin of the men who composed it, were they Gascons or Provençaux from the south, Touranjeaux from the centre, or stolid Picards from the north, was of comparatively little moment.

The overwhelming mass of men in the French Army were workers on the soil, peasants, hardy and strong, with tremendous powers of physical endurance. What is more they were big men. It came as rather a shock to those Englishmen who saw a great deal of the French, to observe, as the industrial population of England became absorbed in the British Army, that the French Army of '16, '17 and '18 was composed of bigger, burlier, and stronger men than the British, probably a stone heavier on the average, and an inch or so taller.

After my visit to the III. and X. Corps , I had to go and see the French Cavalry Corps. It had lost contact with the Belgian Army, owing to the retreat of the latter towards Antwerp. General Sordet, the G.O.C. of the Cavalry Corps, was very vague as to the intentions of the Belgians. The liaison, which would in any case have been difficult to establish, was non-existent.

An example of the difficulties of combined action had just occurred. An attack had been planned, in which a Belgian Brigade from the Field Army was to co-operate with the French Cavalry Corps on the left, and the garrison of Namur on the right. The result can hardly have been deemed successful. The Belgians on the left mistook the French for Germans and fired at them. Hardly had this contretemps been adjusted when the Belgians vanished completely. They were not seen again until the autumn in Flanders. Their disappearance seemed incomprehensible at the time; it was due to the fact that during the engagement they had received the general order to retire which had been issued to the whole of their Army, and had obeyed it without informing the French. The garrison of Namur had confined itself to sending forward a few cavalry patrols.

When I arrived, General Sordet's divisions, now north of the Sambre, were engaged in house to house fighting with German Cavalry supported by infantry, which formed part of a column that had been reported by an airman to be advancing from Grand Rosière to Perwez and Orbais. This kind of fighting was extremely unsatisfactory to the French Cavalry which was neither trained nor armed for dismounted work, and the casualties seemed to be pretty heavy. Indeed the French Cavalry was not equipped for modern warfare at all. The firearm was the *"mousqueton"*, a ridiculous little popgun. The cuirassier regiments, magnificent to look at in their armour, seemed accoutred to take on the bowmen of Agincourt. The dragoons had the same steel helmet as the cuirassiers, with a horse hair plume hanging down their backs.* This paraphernalia made fighting on foot very difficult. The Germans were almost as badly equipped, and were hung round with so many weapons that they never knew which to use.

There was a delightful spirit in the French Cavalry, and a splendid *esprit de corps* amongst the officers, many of whom belonged to the best families in France. Certainly something about them appealed to British cavalrymen. The common love of horseflesh may have carried the seed of mutual sympathy. Whatever it was, the French Cavalry were nice people to deal with, and the relations between officers and men were particularly happy, a mixture of good fellowship and respect that was pleasing to see. The officers almost invariably used the familiar *"tu"* when speaking to their men. They were gallant fellows. Later, in October, '14, in the country north of Béthune, upon several occasions dragoons, armed only with their lances, charged on foot across muddy fields against German riflemen. The pity of it, that such bravery should be so futile against bullets.

A story of that time comes to my mind. A French officer and I were walking across a ploughed field behind a village, when a German battery, less than a thousand yards away, began to cover the village and its neighbourhood systematically with shrapnel, evidently searching for a couple of 75s which were brazenly doing their worst in the village square. We had just seen these, decorated with a couple of shellcases placed on the limber and filled with flowers, a real French touch.

The field we were in became distinctly unhealthy. We threw ourselves down, each in a furrow. The bursts seemed to be getting ominously nearer. My French friend called to me to roll farther away, so that we should not both be hit by the same shell. A few minutes, long as centuries, elapsed, when to my amazement I heard a lively conversation taking place a few yards away. Carefully I lifted my head. My companion, resting on his elbow, was telling off an enormous cuirassier standing behind him, helmetless, but complete as to the very rusty

---

* For a long time the only attempt made to equip the French Cavalry for modern warfare was to supply them with canvas covers for their helmets.

cuirass. "Lie down at once, you idiot, you'll get killed if you stand there!" A sulky and almost insubordinate voice answered – "How can you expect me to lie down, *mon Capitaine*, when I have a bottle of *pinard** that's got no cork in my pocket?"

The French Cavalry had from the first established an undoubted ascendancy over their opponents in all mounted work. They had ridden them down whenever they met them, for the Germans showed neither initiative nor dash, seldom left the road, and when attacked galloped back to their infantry supports. As regards fire power, French and German Cavalry were about equal, but whenever the German infantry supports came up, and they were never far off, the enemy had the best of it. The advantage given to the French by their 75s was more than offset by the German machine-guns. The French troopers were exasperated against their invisible and elusive opponents. They all said the same thing – "If only they would get on to their horses and fight. They are supposed to be cavalry, aren't they?"

In consequence of their superiority to their opponents on horseback, the morale of the French Cavalry was high, although the horses were worn out. At this date the wastage was already so heavy that it amounted to the value of a regiment per division. Even in our own army, where horse management is so superior to the methods of the French, the wear and tear of useless marches and countermarches such as Sordet's Corps had been engaged in, would have spelt disaster to efficiency. The French cavalryman of 1914 sat his horse beautifully, but was no horsemaster. It did not occur to him to get off his horse's back whenever he could, so there were thousands of animals with sore backs, and the smell of some units, owing to this cause, was painful. A sixth of General Sordet's command had already melted away.

It was at this moment, when above all things his horses needed rest, that General Sordet was called upon to carry out every kind of mission. General Joffre wanted him to get into touch with Namur and to put in an appearance at Louvain to hearten the Belgian Army; he was also to stop the progression of the German Cavalry to the west. Sir John French was looking to him to cover the concentration and advance of the B.E.F. Meanwhile General Lanrezac was clamouring for the Cavalry Corps to carry out reconnaissances on his front, and protested against the political mission assigned to it by Joffre. General Berthelot assured him on the 17th that he could ask the Cavalry Corps to obtain any information he needed, and that its tactical duties were to take precedence over its

* *"Pinard,"* slang for wine.

strategical ones. In spite of this the following message was sent by the
G.Q.G. to the Fifth Army that night for transmission to Sordet:

"It is urgent that the Cavalry Corps should carry out the mission
assigned to it yesterday. Brussels is losing its head. The Belgian
Government is retiring on Antwerp. It is at all costs necessary to
prevent the Belgian Army following this movement, and consequently
it is indispensable that liaison should be established with it."

This was all very well, but whatever the requirements of the Higher
Command might be, and however much General Lanrezac might need
information, nothing could alter the fact that it was impossible to raise
a trot out of most of the Cavalry regiments. Sordet remained calm,
however, and did as much as his exhausted horses would let him. There
were rumours at this period that the G.Q.G. was much incensed against
him and accused him of dilatoriness. This was hardly fair, for between
August 5th and 9th, acting under the instructions of the G.Q.G., he had
been scouring the country east of the Meuse as far as Liège, and in the
last three days of this period the Corps had covered approximately 180
kilometres. The only day's rest it had had was on the 10th, and between
the 11th and 18th it was in constant movement: yet the result of its
activities, through no fault of General Sordet or his troops, was
practically nil. The G.Q.G. must bear its share of the blame for this
waste, for seldom has a fine force of Cavalry been more uselessly
squandered. The French Higher Command had but little idea of what
could be expected of Cavalry, or what horses could or could not do. A
criticism that can legitimately be levelled at Sordet himself is that he
carried out the orders he was given with his whole force, instead of
whenever possible detailing a single squadron or even when necessary a
division, for the duty in question.

It is to be regretted that the French Cavalry did not arrive earlier in
the region in which it found itself between the 16th and 18th. Had it
appeared there the week before with comparatively fresh horses, an
effective junction with the Belgians might have greatly influenced the
decision of the Belgian G.H.Q. The Belgian troops, under the direct
influence of and able to combine their operations with the French,
could have prolonged the Allied line, and the Germans would have been
compelled to deploy long before they intended.

On returning to Signy after my visit to the Cavalry, I heard that yet another hunt for the British Army had been organized and had failed. This was hardly to be wondered at, as the search took place in an area in which they were not, and had never intended to be on that date. This quest appeared all the more ridiculous when that night a letter came from Colonel Huguet stating that the British Army would begin its forward movement on the 21st, and enclosing a map showing the billeting areas for the 21st and 22nd, and also the march tables. This was extremely satisfactory, and the most sceptical began to believe that the English were now really coming up.

The Fifth Army had now reached the Sambre, which it held from Floreffe to Tamines. General Lanrezac appeared to be in no hurry to do more than deploy south of the river until his allies came up on his left. (Map IV, p. 60.)

Meanwhile his neighbour on the right, General de Langle de Cary, commanding the French Fourth Army, reported that evening that the central mass of the enemy on his front appeared to be slipping to the north-north-west, parallel to, and two or three marches distant from, the front of his Army. He informed the Commander-in-Chief that he was ready to debouch with five corps from the front Montmédy–Sedan.*

General Joffre replied to this communication as follows:

"I authorize you to take all measures forthwith which will facilitate your debouching north of the Semoy and in the clearing of Florenville, by pushing forward detachments to carefully selected points.

"I would draw your attention to the necessity of not revealing our manœuvre until it has been actually embarked upon. With a view to insuring this, the detachments envisaged in the above should remain masked, preferably in the woods, or in localities where it is possible to take steps to prevent any communication with the exterior . . .†

"JOFFRE."

*   *   *

Strolling into the 2ème Bureau that evening, I found it in a ferment of excitement. A German wireless message had been intercepted which stated that a paper had been found on a captured French officer of the

---

* General de Langle stated that the advance guards of his Army could reach in one march the front Paliseul – St. Médard – Tintigny – St. Léger.

† Telephone message from the Commander-in-Chief to the Commander of the Army Stenay (Fourth Army) dated August 20th, 9.30 a.m.

33rd Regiment, on which was written "I. Corps. Fifth Army. Hély d'Oissel." Our opposite numbers across the Sambre were evidently wide awake. They were as busy as we were, identifying, compiling, deducing. They had hit upon some valuable information. They probably now knew that there were five French armies and that the Fifth was on the left of the line. We had not been allowed to masquerade long as the "*Armée de Paris*". This *nom de guerre* was now but the merest *nom de plume*. I thought dubiously of my kitbag, on which this appellation had been painted in colours that would defy obliteration.

CHAPTER VIII

THE FIFTH ARMY IN POSITION ON THE SAMBRE

August 20th–21st, 1914

The Germans in sight – Visit to the Sambre valley – The French and entrench-ments – French adaptability – Comparison between French and British – A joint attack during the Somme – The Germans bombard Namur – The situation – The industrial area of Charleroi – Why it should have been occupied – General Lanrezac and Namur – The morale of the Fifth Army – The Intelligence and the German advance – Anxiety of General de Langle – The offensive of the Fourth Army ordered to begin – The British get into position – Joffre's report to the Minister – The "chenilles" – Will all be well with the British? – Fifth Army H.Q. leaves Signy for Belgium – And establishes its H.Q. at Chimay – Contrast between Belgian and French populations in occupied areas – First sight of British troops – A British infantry trap – Liaison work – Importance of personal meetings between Commanders – The G.V.C.s again.

THERE was a moment in the experience of every man in the war, when he realized suddenly the magnitude of the forces he was pitted against. It might come soon or it might come late, it might be screamed out with the distraught voice of a frenzied imagination, or whispered with the ashen lips of fear, but inevitably the time came when a cold hand gripped each man's heart: when each lonely soul gazed down into the bottomless abyss on the edge of which he suddenly found himself, and, seeing clearly what he had to face, measured the extent of the sacrifice demanded of him.

That moment came I think to two of us on the evening of the 20th. A French officer was sitting beside me on a hill from which we could see the great industrial area of Charleroi with the Sambre flowing below. Northwards the vast plain of Belgium spread as far as the eye could see. Mining villages dovetailed endlessly into each other until in the grey distance they all seemed to merge together into a vast, low, squatting town of smoke and mist, miles away, miles in extent. Much further than the horizon, far beyond the murky skyline, was the North Sea. To the right was more open country, possible country from a soldier's point of view, and beyond the villas and villages, invisible behind woods and copses, lay Namur. Farther still lay Liège and Germany.

We were speculating as to how great armies could possibly fight amid those streets, those endless houses. We began to wonder by what sign we would really know when the Germans were there. Hostile cavalry we had seen, but that had been absurdly like manœuvres. We imagined the endless columns of grey-clad men with spiked helmets, rolling forward, flattening out poor little Belgium in their overwhelming advance. But what would it be like when the great masses of infantry whose movements we had been marking down inch by inch on maps as they crept forward, were actually upon us? What form would the pressure take, what sort of an impact would there be?

The evening was still and wonderfully peaceful. The ominous rumble of guns from the direction of Namur, which had been going on all the afternoon, had ceased. A dog was barking at some sheep. A girl was singing as she walked down the lane behind us. From a little farm away on the right came the voices and laughter of some soldiers cooking their evening meal. Darkness grew in the far distance as the light began to fail.

Then, without a moment's warning, with a suddenness that made us start and strain our eyes to see what our minds could not realize, we saw the whole horizon burst into flames. To the north, outlined against the sky, countless fires were burning. It was as if hordes of fiends had suddenly been released, and dropping on the distant plain, were burning every town and every village. A chill of horror came over us. War seemed suddenly to have assumed a merciless, ruthless aspect that we had not realized till then. Hitherto it had been war as we had conceived it, hard blows, straight dealing, but now for the first time we felt as if some horrible Thing, utterly merciless, were advancing to grip us. It might have been a plague or an invasion of rats whose burning eyes were fixing us from right away beyond the river, and we understood, as our hearts missed a beat, that our people would have to fight, not to win a war, not for laurels and honours, but for the right to exist. Those fires over there told us something indescribably evil. The enemy who lit them would show no mercy. It came over us that each man would have to fight for something far more precious than life, for what each of us called home; remote things, far away and precious beings, were suddenly very near, very unprotected, almost in contact with this horror that had suddenly arisen. A peaceful river flowing between tall trees in a distant land, a group picnicking on the bank, pretty faces, laughter, what a frail barrier we were between what that stood for and this. We gazed as long, long ago other men must have gazed from these very hills perhaps, when they beheld with consternation other barbarians, the ancestors of those over there, who had also come swarming out of the east.

It suddenly became clear that to survive it would be necessary to go on beyond exhaustion, to march when the body clamoured to be allowed to drop and die, to shoot when eyes were too tired to see, to remain awake when a man would have given his chance of salvation to sleep. And we realized also that so to drive the body beyond its physical powers, to force the mind to act long after it had surrendered its power of thought, only despair and the strength of despair could furnish the motive force.

It was quite dark now. The distant fires glowed red against a violet black sky.

*   *   *

During the course of the day, I had had occasion to visit the Sambre valley, and saw various points occupied by the III. and X. Corps. The advance guards had reached the river the previous day, and the divisions were deploying to the south of it.

In my wanderings, somewhat to my surprise, I saw no attempt being made anywhere to dig entrenchments. The fact that the Germans might attack us was after all not an impossibility. A hostile army has been known to disturb the too-leisurely preparations of an opponent. An attack by the enemy in some strength was possible, and in any case if we were to advance across the Sambre it was an elementary precaution to prepare a strong position south of the river. Such, however, was apparently not the opinion of the commanders on the spot, for practically no digging was taking place. The troops evidently thought that as they were going to advance entrenchments would be useless. The whole pre-war training, or rather lack of training, of the French Army in this respect was telling. No soldier ever likes digging entrenchments. The French were particularly averse from the practice. Officers in whom the doctrine of the offensive had been diligently instilled were not only apprehensive of being thought lacking in dash, but feared that entrenchments would make their troops "sticky", and that men once behind earthworks would be reluctant to leave their protection to advance across the open. The absence of entrenchments at manœuvres has already been commented upon. No doubt it was said – what soldier has not heard the remark – "in war it will be different, then we will do this and that," whereas I for one was soon to learn that you apply in time of war the lessons you have learnt in peace; you may do less than you did in peacetime, you will certainly not do more. In war it is too late to remember theories and axioms which are all very well for officers on Staff rides; the soldier is either too tired or has no time to think; he will only do what comes to him naturally and instinctively, through long usage. In the Great War the new methods which were slowly evolved had to be taught the troops out of the line, under peace conditions.

It was a very long time before the French Army learnt the vital importance of entrenchments. Some units were much slower to learn than others. The more casual, the younger they were, the less they liked digging. Troops from Africa, trained in that free open country, seemed to prefer any amount of risk to this back-breaking business, whereas the old Territorials took no end of pains to make a trench snug and safe. As for the "Joyeux" (battalions of men who had been convicted and sent to prison before their military service), they were the worst of all. An officer who served beside them told me their casualties were so heavy at a particular point in Flanders that they used, on coming back into the line, to begin by telling off a fatigue party to dig the average number of graves which experience had taught them would be needed, but detailed no trench-digging parties. Graves were shallower and therefore easier to dig than trenches; that was all there was to it.

But although the young French soldiers remained temperamentally hostile to trench digging, and the lower standards of sanitation of the nation as a whole led them to tolerate conditions unacceptable to the British, their adaptability, of which I shall have occasion to speak later, kept them well ahead of us in the invention and adoption of new methods.

As liaison officer I brought in time and again new weapons, new flares, and the thousand and one new gadgets that the French evolved and manufactured with amazing industry and resource, either in the Army zone or in the interior, only to have them turned down by our own people, who too often lacked the imagination to visualize their utility.

Take for instance the steel helmet. Almost as soon as trench warfare began the French produced a kind of steel skullcap to be worn inside the cap. These were soon followed by steel helmets. We adopted these much later, but the type we finally decided upon was far better than theirs.

In the same way the French produced a quick-firing rifle and trained men to fire it from the hip in an advance; our Lewis gun appeared later, but was an infinitely better weapon.

Again, in the matter of rifle grenades, they were far ahead of us, having adopted by the time of the Battle of the Somme the "*Vivien-Bessière*", a simple and effective device much better and more practical than our own.

But when all is said and done, the most important invention of the war was ours: tanks. I remember the sceptical smile of the French General commanding near Arras when an important British personage told him that the Admiralty were working at land cruisers which would revolutionize trench warfare.

The final conclusion perhaps may be that the French were quicker than we were at seeing the advantages that were to be gained from inventions and innovations, but when we did finally adopt anything the article produced was of a far finer quality.

It was perhaps in evolving new tactical methods adapted to modern warfare that the French really had the advantage of us.

I remember well an incident during the Somme which illustrates how much we had to learn from them in this respect.

A joint attack by French and British had been ordered. At the appointed time they both sprang forward. The French had already adopted the self-contained platoon as a unit. Tiny groups, taking every advantage of cover, swarmed forward, intangible as will o' the wisps, illusive as quicksilver. The German artillery was baffled and their defences overrun by these handfuls of men who were everywhere at once. In a few minutes they had disappeared over the skyline. The attack had been successful.

Meanwhile, on their left, long lines of British infantry, at a few yards interval and in perfect order, were slowly advancing.

Wave after wave sprang forward from the trenches, joining in the parade, for that is what it looked like.

And they provided magnificent targets. The whole of the German artillery concentrated on the lines they could so easily see and range on. The British were soon enveloped in clouds of bursting shells. It looked as if they were advancing through the flames of hell. At times whole portions of the advance disappeared, and when the thick clouds of smoke were dispelled and the greatly thinned lines were once more revealed, they were seen to be far fewer, but still plodding forward over the deeply scarred and difficult ground at the same even pace. As a display of bravery it was magnificent, but how enraging to think of the irreparable waste. I remember a French artillery observation officer saying to me – "I thought of the Crimea today," and of what another French officer said then of the English – "*C'est magnifique, mais ce n'est pas la guerre.*"

*   *   *

On August 20th, the Germans began their attacks on the eastern defences of Namur. This onslaught caused some anxiety at the Headquarters of the Fifth Army, but it never entered anyone's head that the town, surrounded by its nine forts, would not hold out for at least a few days, long enough to enable General Lanrezac to cross the Sambre, when, resting his right on the fortress, he could deal a decisive blow at the attackers.

The possibility of the German right flank, now on the north bank of the Meuse, wheeling inward to attack the Fourth Army, thus exposing a flank to the Fifth Army, had become very remote; in fact no one with whom I had occasion to discuss the situation took it into serious account.

General Lanrezac's previsions seemed to be justified. The situation as it appeared to most of us was simple. Either the German right wing would wheel down on the Fifth Army, when the British would catch them in flank and the Belgians would make things uncomfortable for them in rear, or if their movement was on an even greater scale than was anticipated, and if in their attempt to outflank General Lanrezac they bumped into the British, then it would be up to the Fifth Army to anticipate this movement by attacking before the German manœuvre had had time to develop.

The position was satisfactory. The Fifth Army had reached the Sambre in time to fulfil its offensive role. But somehow, now that the supreme moment was drawing near, the spring of the Army was not being tightened to deliver the mighty blow everyone expected. There was a faint feeling of doubt, which was, however, confined to the Staffs of the higher formations, for the troops were in high fettle. Up till now the sensation in General Lanrezac's entourage had been of sailing swiftly and strongly forward with a firm hand on the tiller; but now it seemed as if the sails of our ship were flapping in the wind. There was a curious atmosphere of hesitation. Time, hitherto counted so valuable, appeared to be of less account. The period of maximum effort was at hand, yet there was a general relaxation. A slowing down was perceptible everywhere.

This impression may have been due to a slight uneasiness at the changing attitude of the Army Commander himself. All looked to him to provide the vital driving power that was to hurl the Army forward. A few days earlier none had doubted that this would be forthcoming, but now, though no word was spoken, there was not quite the same confidence. It was as if faith were escaping by tiny unperceived channels.

It is difficult to give a tangible reason for this impression: observation of the man himself, perhaps; probably also astonishment that the Army Commander had so much time on his hands, spent in sitting in his room, wandering about the offices, or pacing up and down outside his Headquarters. He did not take the opportunities that offered of going to see the troops, of making contact with and getting to know the Commanders of the new formations which constituted so large a part of his Army, or of consulting with those he already knew.

Again, from August 18th onwards, although the full German manœuvre was not yet revealed, it was clear enough over what ground to within a depth of twenty miles the Fifth Army would be engaged, yet General Lanrezac did little to make himself familiar with the country his Army was about to fight over. I believe he had been over it in peace-time, he probably knew it, but should not this opportunity have been taken for studying it anew? His inactivity at this time is one of the many strange things about General Lanrezac that have never been explained.

With the exception of the country immediately to the west of Namur, the region in which the Fifth Army now found itself was certainly difficult country for large units to deploy in or for troops to advance across. The river Sambre wound its way in and out at the base of low hills on the gentle slopes of which were very numerous villages, houses and factories. It would be difficult to give advancing troops artillery support owing to the impossibility of locating them exactly in the enclosed country, and the losses that would be involved in driving infantry with machine guns out of all those houses and from behind all those walls would be very great. On the other hand these very obstacles to an attacking army made it an easy country to defend. The hills south of the Sambre furnished a very fair defensive line, in spite of the lack, on a great part of the front, of an adequate field of fire. The numerous villages and houses could be turned into so many small forts.

The Fifth Army was not unfavourably situated in view of the mission

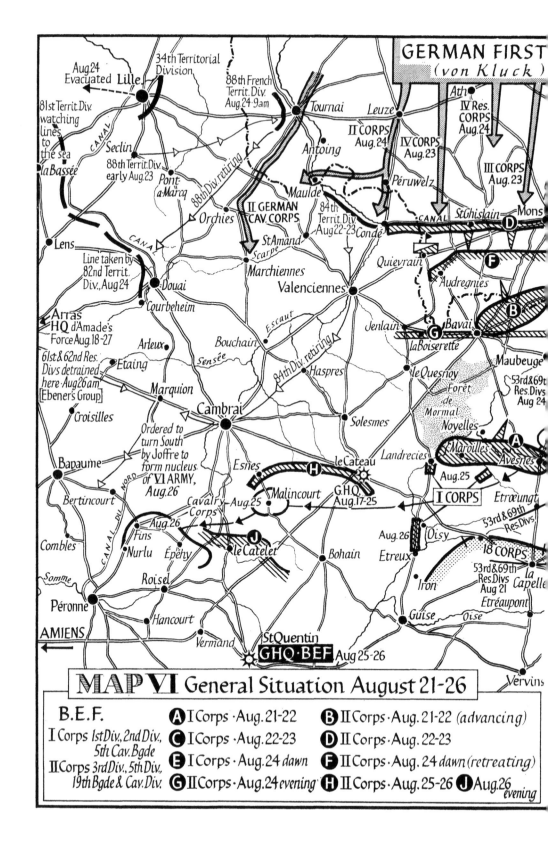

MAP VI General Situation August 21-26

B.E.F.

I Corps *1st Div., 2nd Div., 5th Cav. Bgde*

II Corps *3rd Div., 5th Div., 19th Bgde & Cav. Div.*

A I Corps · Aug. 21-22

B II Corps · Aug. 21-22 *(advancing)*

C I Corps · Aug. 22-23

D II Corps · Aug. 22-23

E I Corps · Aug. 24 *dawn*

F II Corps · Aug. 24 *dawn (retreating)*

G II Corps · Aug. 24 *evening*

H II Corps · Aug. 25-26

J Aug. 26 *evening*

GERMAN FIRST (*von Kluck*)

Aug.24 Evacuated Lille

81st Territ. Div. watching lines to the sea

la Bassée

Seclin

88th Territ. Div. early Aug.23

Pont a Marcq

34th Territorial Division

88th French Territ. Div. Aug.24·9am

Tournai

Leuze

Antoing

II CORPS Aug.24

IV CORPS Aug.23

Ath

IV Res. CORPS Aug.24

III CORPS Aug.23

Péruwelz

Maulde

II GERMAN CAV. CORPS

Orchies

84th Territ. Div. Aug.22-23

Condé

St Ghislain

Mons

D

F

Lens

Line taken by 82nd Territ. Div., Aug.24

Douai

Courbeheim

St Amand

Scarpe

Marchiennes

Valenciennes

Quiévrain

Audregnies

B

Arras HQ d'Amade's Force Aug.18-27

61st & 62nd Res. Divs detrained here·Aug.26 am [Ebener's Group]

Arleux

Etaing

Marquion

Bouchain

Sensée

Escaut

84th Div. retiring

Haspres

Jenlain

Bavai

la Boiserette

G

Maubeuge

le Quesñoy

Forêt de Mormal

53rd & 69th Res. Divs Aug 24

Croisilles

Cambrai

Solesmes

Noyelles

St Maroilles

A

Avesnes

Aug.25

Bapaume

Ordered to turn South by Joffre to form nucleus of VI ARMY, Aug.26

Esnes

le Cateau

H

Malincourt

G.H.Q. Aug.17-25

Landrecies

I CORPS

Etroeungt

53rd & 69th Res. Divs

Bertincourt

Cavalry Corps

Aug.25

Aug.26

J

Aug.26

Oisy

53rd & 69th Res. Divs Aug 21

la Capelle

Combles

Fins

Nurlu

Épéhy

le Catelet

Bohain

Etreux

Iron

18 CORPS

Roisel

Etréaupont

Péronne

Hancourt

Somme

Canal du Nord

Guise

Oise

AMIENS

Vermand

St Quentin

GHQ·BEF Aug 25-26

Vervins

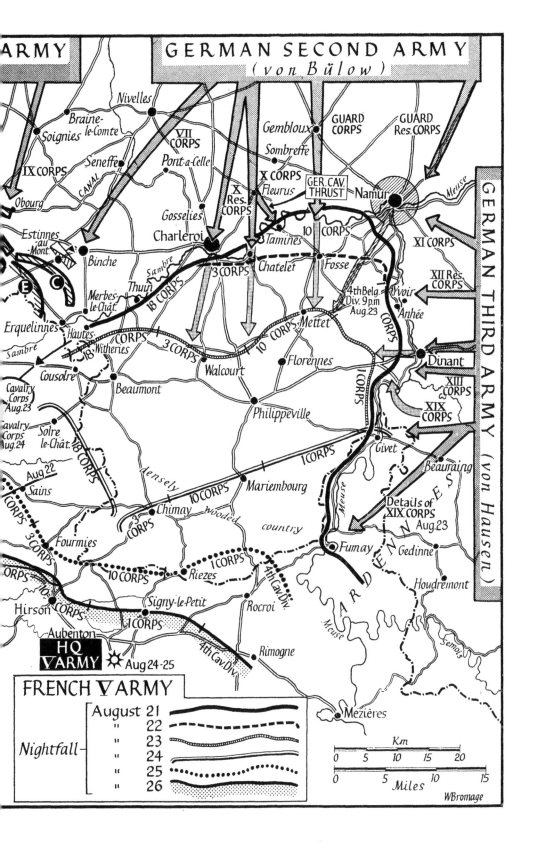

ARMY

GERMAN SECOND ARMY
(von Bülow)

Nivelles

Braine-
Soignies
IX CORPS
Obourg
Estinnes
au-Mont
E C
Seneffe

VII
CORPS
Pont-a-Celle
CANAL
Binche
Merbes-
le-Chât.
Thuin
Erquelinnes
Hautes-
Cousolre
Cavalry
Corps
Aug.23
Cavalry
Corps
Aug.24
Solre
le-Chât.
Aug 22
Sains
Fourmies
Chimay
Hirson
Aubenton
HQ
VARMY

Gemblouup
Sombreffe

GUARD
CORPS
Namur

GUARD.
Res.CORPS
Meuse

GERMAN THIRD ARMY (von Hausen)

X
Res.
CORPS
Gosselies
Charleroi
3 CORPS
Chatelet

X CORPS
Fleurus
Tamines

GER.CAV.
THRUST
10 CORPS
Fosse

XI CORPS
XII Res.
CORPS
Anhée
Yvoir
4thBelg.
Div. 9p.m
Aug.23

18 CORPS
18 CORPS
Witheries
3 CORPS
10 CORPS Mettet
Walcourt
Florennes
Dinant
XIII
CORPS
XIX
CORPS

Beaumont
Philippeville
Givet

1 CORPS
densely
10 CORPS Mariembourg
wooded
country

Beauraing
Details of
XIX CORPS
Aug.23

3 CORPS
Riezes
4thCav.Div.
Rocroi
Rimogne

1 CORPS
Signy-le-Petit

Meuse
Fumay
Gedinne
Houdremont

ARDENNES

Semois

★ Aug 24-25

FRENCH VARMY

August 21
"   22
Nightfall   "   23
"   24
"   25
"   26

Mezières

Km
0   5   10   15   20

0   5   10   15
Miles

WBromage

assigned to it by *Instruction Particulière No. 13*. Its right flank hinged on the fortress of Namur, and its right rear was protected by a great river, the Meuse, and was therefore easy to defend. Its left, beyond which the British were concentrating, was faced by a vast conglomeration of buildings covering many square miles, difficult for an enemy to hazard large forces in, easy to defend foot by foot, whereas immediately to the west of Namur, beyond the Sambre, extended ground open enough to allow of the deployment of large units.

Obviously if General Lanrezac were going to carry out the offensive mission assigned to him, he would attack here, his right flank protected by the Meuse, the right of his attack covered by Namur and supported by the guns of its forts, his left resting on the industrial area of Charleroi.* (Map VI, p. 112.)

I remember some comment at British G.H.Q. and some wonder on the Fifth Army Staff at the time as to why General Lanrezac made no attempt to hold the industrial area of Charleroi.

This is not to say it was thought that the whole of the Fifth Army need necessarily cross the Sambre until such time as the offensive was actually decided upon,† nor that carefully prepared positions should not have been dug on the hills south of the river: but it was felt that the outer fringe of the industrial area should have been held in sufficient force to prevent the enemy's seizing it with advanced detachments.‡ If the Germans once gained a footing there even with only a small force it would be difficult to drive them out, and the offensive of the Fifth Army might be fatally delayed. On the other hand, comparatively few troops could have compelled the Germans to deploy and it would have necessitated very large numbers to dislodge them. The enemy could not have neglected Charleroi and its suburbs so long as they were in French occupation, for to attempt the passage of a wider river defended by a powerful Army flanked by Namur on the right and a vast urban area in hostile hands on the left, would have been an impossible operation.

If it be argued, as it has been, that there was some danger in launching troops into all those uncharted streets, the answer is that the Germans

---

* Appendix XVII.

† It has been seen that on the 18th General Lanrezac had notified the Commander-in-Chief that he would, from the 20th onwards, be in a position to hurl any German formations that might attempt to cross the Sambre back into the river. But this merely referred to his possibilities on that particular date. It did not of course mean that he intended to assume a defensive attitude in the future, which would have been in flagrant contradiction to *Instruction Particulière No. 13*.

‡ There was not much time to be lost: early on the 20th hostile infantry had been reported within 20 km. of the Sambre.

themselves showed no hesitation in advancing through and occupying the district of Charleroi as soon as they got the opportunity, and that too under the orders of a most careful and even over-cautious commander, for such von Bülow proved himself to be.

What actually happened, of course, was that the Germans anticipated the allied offensive by attacking first themselves. They had intended to destroy the Fifth Army between the trip hammer of von Bülow's Second Army coming down from the north, and the thrust of Hausen's Third Army driving across the Meuse from the east. These attacks were not synchronized, and the Fifth Army escaped. Von Hausen's operation failed on his own showing against an inadequate defence, and had von Bülow found the industrial area of Charleroi occupied, there can be little doubt that this would have greatly embarrassed and delayed him. It might even possibly have broken up his attack and affected adversely the whole German plan. (Map VI, p. 112.)

We now know it would have been better had General Lanrezac awaited the German onslaught in a fortified position south of the Sambre; but it is not the purpose of this book to suggest in the light of present-day knowledge the ideal solution of the problems confronting him. In giving an account of events as they appeared at the time, as I am attempting to do, the only relevant point is that the Commander-in-Chief's plan demanded an offensive, and neither by word nor deed had General Lanrezac up to this time given the least hint either to General Joffre or to Sir John French that he did not fall in with this plan. It was therefore his duty to take all measures within his power to enable the Fifth Army to advance as soon as possible, and to do this it was necessary to hold the industrial area of Charleroi. Many competent officers who lived through those days and have studied the sequel, remain convinced that this is what he ought to have done.

When considering the situation of the Fifth Army and the part General Lanrezac was expected to play in General Joffre's scheme, it is interesting to note his attitude in the matter of Namur.

General Lanrezac had been urged by General Joffre to co-operate in the defence of the fortress, and his reply must have given the impression that he meant to do so. He stated his intention of supporting the Belgians within the fortress by advancing across the Sambre so as to be in a position to relieve the pressure on the north-western and south-western sectors.* If he remained inactive south of the river he would obviously be doing nothing to carry out the undertaking he had given.

* See Appendix XV.

It may be urged that he intended giving this support at a later date, and was entitled to believe that the fortress would hold out longer than it did. This may be so, but he was in constant touch with Namur and knew pretty well what its situation was. He was aware that General Joffre attached the greatest importance to holding the fortress, and that, should it fall, an offensive north of the Sambre in accordance with *Instruction Particulière No. 13* would be out of the question.

General Lanrezac's inaction as regards the occupation of Charleroi and the defence of Namur tend to show how little he entered into the Generalissimo's offensive plan. The distaste he was to reveal later for any offensive action was already manifesting itself.

*   *   *

The 20th was an exciting day for the troops. There was crisis in the air. Not a man but felt that a great battle was at hand. The morale of the Fifth Army was extremely high. Any doubts these same men might have had as civilians were forgotten. They felt certain of success. The march to the north and the welcome given by the Belgians gave the troops the impression of being already half victorious. They would give these Germans the lesson they so badly needed and then go back to work. The peasants talked of being back in time for the early winter sowings at the *métairie* or the farm.

Units were fast absorbing the reservists into their psychic being. The soul of regiments, what is called "*esprit de corps*" was being rapidly strengthened. Everyone, from the man in the last "*classe*" to the serious, worried staff officer, gave his fancy free rein and speculated hopefully about the Russians, who were visualized as immense masses of troops collecting to overrun Germany.

Tales of German inefficiency had spread, and all ranks were permeated with the idea that the vaunted discipline of that wooden soulless machine, the German Army, would avail little against the dash and enthusiasm of men who had come in their thousands to defend their country from unjust aggression.

But the defects so generously lent the Germans by the French did not appear to interfere with their advance, which the Intelligence was watching with ever-growing concern.

The British Intelligence reported that in the south the enemy's front was now only weakly held, whilst his main strength appeared to be concentrated in Belgium. It stated that at the moment five to six corps were probably north of the Meuse and that others were following.

Such information was reliable, but other reports were discarded as being nothing more than wild rumours: for instance General d'Amade sent in an unconfirmed report to the G.Q.G. that 600,000 Germans were expected in Brussels that day. This drew from General Joffre the retort that the information concerning the enemy's movements in Belgium was very much exaggerated, and that there was no occasion to get excited. As a matter of fact, the number of Germans in Belgium at this date was approximately 760,000, but by far the greater part of these did not pass through Brussels.

Further reports concerning the apparent flank march of the enemy across the front of the Fourth Army towards the north-west continued to come in, causing General de Langle, the Army Commander, the gravest concern. He asked General Joffre whether the moment had not come for his Army to gain by a night march the exits of the woods to his front.*

A little later he telephoned to the Commander-in-Chief that several important hostile columns had reached the front Neufchâteau–Bastogne and points farther north at 10 a.m. He said he could not tell if these columns would continue their march across his front or would wheel and face him. Was he to await the enemy on his present front Montmédy–Sedan or to seek battle in the clearings of Florenville and Neufchâteau? General Joffre answered, at 3 p.m., that it did not appear to him that the moment had yet come for the Fourth Army to advance,† but at 8.50 p.m. he sent a further telegram ordering the preliminary stages of the offensive to begin that night.

As for the British, it was confirmed that the B.E.F. would reach on the 22nd the line Mons–St. Ghislain–Estinnes-au-Mont–Villers-Sire-Nicole

* About Bertrix, Florenville, Tintigny.

† From the Commander-in-Chief to the Commander of the Army Stenay (Fourth Army), August 20th, 3 p.m.:

"The movements reported by air observers do not necessarily show that the enemy has begun his offensive. Information received from other sources does not reveal any important movements in the neighbourhood of Givet, Ciney, Huy. Nothing more than the convoys of the army corps which are marching against the Belgian Army appears to have crossed the Meuse below Namur.

"I understand your impatience, but in my opinion the time to attack is not yet. The more the district of Arlon, Audun-le-Roman, Luxembourg is bared of troops, the better will it be for us. I hold it to be essential that we should not begin our offensive until the right moment. It may, moreover, be to the interest of the enemy to provoke this offensive by drawing us on. We must not fall into such a trap.

"Accordingly the measures taken this morning are adequate for the present.

"J. JOFFRE."

–Gognies and Pont-sur-Sambre. At the end of that day's march the four divisions would be facing east. The Cavalry division was about Jurbise, and the 5th Cavalry Brigade would occupy the line Binche–Roeulx. (Map VI, p. 112.)

Things were going well according to the French Commander-in-Chief. In reporting the situation to the Minister of War, he said:

"The whole of our left is advancing between the Sambre and the Meuse; but I would ask you to keep this information strictly secret.

"To sum up, the situation appears to me to be favourable. There is reason to await with confidence the development of our projected operations. On account of the front upon which we are engaged, and the actual duration of the engagement, time is necessary for these operations to develop."

*   *   *

That evening at the 2ème Bureau we pored anxiously over the maps on which were being marked the German advance. The abominable red "*chenilles*" had ceased to crawl, they were beginning to move with alarming rapidity, making for the west across our front. They seemed to be heading for the British. Such was our impression. We who sat there, staring at the map, believed, or tried to believe that General Lanrezac would boldly throw his huge force against the flank of the columns marching across his front. We knew that the British, coming up in all haste on his left, absolutely relied upon his doing so. They had had every assurance that he would assume the offensive at the earliest possible moment. We told ourselves that the General knew what he was doing; he was only biding his time. It was inconceivable that, without striking a blow to hinder them, he would allow the Germans to carry out their plans unmolested and fall in their own time on the British.

So thought these men, as, grouped round the table, they gazed at the map and talked. It is a clear picture even now, after fifteen years have passed. The voices sound muffled and distant. Even straining the ear of memory it is impossible to hear what they say. The buzz of talk is remote and indistinguishable, the tone of this or that one is clearly recognizable, but the words themselves are blurred, whispers lost for ever, echoing faint and elusive down the road of time.

I who stood there with the others, thought as they did, and cast off the unpleasant doubts that had assailed me that afternoon.

*   *   *

It was on Friday, August 21st, at 8.30 a.m., that Fifth Army Head-quarters left Signy-le-Petit for Chimay in Belgium and installed itself in the *Athénée* (College) of that little town. It was a singularly unwhole-some, ill-ventilated building, with a large central hall covered in by a glass roof. In this hall were a number of beds where tired officers could snatch a little sleep. The different *bureaux* were in the adjoining class-rooms. The one in which I was allotted a corner was reminiscent of a rather unhealthy gaol.

The town itself was pretty, with one or two nice open spaces. The Château where General Lanrezac took up his quarters was charmingly situated, overlooking a little river. It belonged to the Prince de Chimay, who was still there when we arrived. The motor park was in one of the squares, and the cars, in order to screen them from air observation, were concealed under the trees which surrounded it.

A pleasant, peaceful, little place, with a population singularly un-aware of war, and much less mentally prepared for it than were French people of a similar class and in an analogous position. A machine-gun hoisted on to the roof of the *Athénée* galvanized them into a momentary sense of the realities of war. One man said to me, with his pronounced Belgian accent, as he pointed to the weapon and wisely shook his head: *"C'est la tactique, ça, c'est la tactique."*

It was very striking, the difference in the attitude of the Belgian and French people to the catastrophe threatening them. The French, realiz-ing what war meant, set their teeth and prepared for what they knew might befall. The Belgians had not the faintest idea of what would happen if the tide of invasion rolled their way. Hardly any news filtered through, and the Belgians behind the allied line imagined that nothing worse could possibly occur than having troops billeted on them, or more exciting than seeing a live general dash past in a motor.

That morning I had to go into the British zone and at last met with British troops. The first I saw were a small detachment of Irish Guards, enormous, stolid, in perfect step. What made them look even bigger and more dignified than usual was that they were being led to their unknown destination by a poor old, stumbling, shuffling, untidy little French

Territorial, who had to break into a trot every few minutes to keep ahead. The effect was extremely comic.

Leaving the Irishmen to follow their mascot, my companion and I went on our way and presently came on a column of artillery. I thought I should burst with inward gratification at the smartness of those gunners. They were really splendid, perfectly turned out, shining leather, flashing metal, beautiful horses, and the men absolutely unconcerned, disdaining to show the least surprise at or even interest in their strange surroundings.

Two or three years before, I had wandered over this same country and had conjured up a vision of British troops marching along these very roads. The dream had come true, the unbelievable was realized, for here they were in the flesh, supercilious and magnificent, riding along on the cobbled *pavé* between the tall poplar trees of the *chaussée*. I said nothing, but stole a glance at the French officer who accompanied me and was satisfied, for he was rendered almost speechless by the sight of these fighting men. He had not believed such troops existed. He asked me if they were the Guard Artillery!

Soon after this we received a shock, and my French companion was further impressed, but in a way he did not much like, for we drove head-long into a most effective British infantry trap. At a turn in the road we were suddenly faced by a barrier we had nearly run into, and found that without knowing it we had been covered for the last two hundred yards by cleverly concealed riflemen belonging to the picquet. Had we been Germans nothing in the world could have saved us. It was all extremely efficient and businesslike, less dangerous to the innocent but far more ominous than our old friends the G.V.C.s. My companion on his return gave a hair-raising account of how in the British zone rifle barrels were pointed at you from every bush, and people who looked uncommonly in earnest pounced out at you suddenly from nowhere. He shook his head and wondered what would have happened to him had not a British officer been with him, for these queer people insisted on strange formalities, hard to comply with as their language was incomprehensible, and, worst of all, positively resented anyone not speaking English.

This story of a new danger at the back of the front created quite a stir. The General himself was consulted. Many heads were scratched in perplexity. But it was not such a bad thing after all that it should be realized the British meant business and stood no nonsense in their area. *"Ces sacrés Anglais, tout de même!"* said the French staff good-humouredly, but funnily enough after this the polite scepticism of some concerning the British disappeared.

This incident has remained in my mind, for I was very much struck by the thought that, for the first time in the long history of the wars in France, a French soldier could answer "Friend" to the challenge of a British sentry. It was an interesting innovation, with the slight drawback that the sentry might not realize that a Frenchman would not have the faintest idea what he was expected to say when challenged in English.

*   *   *

Questions affecting operations and the movements of troops were now taking up more and more of my time. I had to report frequently to G.H.Q. and owing to the difficulty I found at times in obtaining information at Fifth Army Headquarters, I contracted the habit of visiting Corps and Divisional Commanders and seeing things for myself as much as possible.

I shall not dwell on the conditions under which we all worked. Were I to do so this narrative would be swallowed up in a boring and monotonous tale of never ending mechanical difficulties. But if the reader does not bear these constantly in mind he will gain a most misleading impression.

For instance, there was the problem of transmitting information; exasperating delays at the telephone, when every moment was of value; the connection obtained at last through a dozen exchanges, sometimes after several hours' delay, only to find it impossible to hear, or to be suddenly cut off. It was amusing, but a poor consolation, to get through to the Germans by mistake, as I did upon a number of occasions during the retreat, and it showed the danger of the telephone. My attempts to profit by the opportunity always failed, probably because my German was not good enough to deceive.

The difficulty of arriving in time with an urgent report, the frequent impossibility of locating the unit or the commander I was in search of, were exhausting mentally and physically. Like everyone else I was never off duty, and practically every night was on the road.

How can one convey what it was like to be constantly getting lost at night owing to inadequate maps, to be forced to stop when on urgent business, to strike lights to look at signposts, or to be blocked by endless transport columns and compelled to force one's way through a mad tangle of vehicles disposed as if they had been frozen into immobility in the midst of a wild dervish dance? And always the urgency, the frightful need for speed.

A constant source of exasperation were the cars supplied to the British. Bought straight out of shop windows, many of them had never been tuned up or run in, and broke down constantly. Several cars I had were equipped with lighting sets that worked for about ten minutes and then had to be refilled with carbide. The French, who had only requisitioned cars that were in use up to the time when they were taken from their owners, were handicapped by none of these contretemps.

The actual difficulties of transporting oneself from place to place were great and very exhausting, but they were nothing compared to the interminable vigils when it was necessary to be on the alert every minute, although there was nothing to do for hours but wait.

The sense of responsibility was overwhelming. A liaison officer, in those critical times when direct communication was impossible, often had to put forward an opinion as to what the future action of one Army or the other would be, and to give an estimate of its situation when hours had elapsed since there had been any news. Such an opinion as likely as not could only be based on previous experience, knowledge of a commander's character, or his own interpretation of events. He often had very slender facts to go upon, and the feeling that he might easily be wrong was terrifying.

One of my difficulties at this period was that General Lanrezac and the Operations Branch of his Staff were very reticent, and it was often impossible to obtain from them the information G.H.Q. asked for. My frequent questions as to whether there was any change of plan invariably met with the same answer: "General Lanrezac is carrying out with all celerity and dispatch the orders of the Generalissimo, which have been fully explained to and accepted by the British Commander-in-Chief." In this matter I had no personal ground for complaint, since much the same thing was being said to the G.Q.G. liaison officer. It was merely that the dragon of secrecy was at work breathing out a fog of war, doing his best to make it as difficult to know what our friends were doing as our foes.

The mania for secrecy, for which the system was more to blame than individuals, did not affect the 2ème Bureau of the Fifth Army, partly thanks to the broadmindedness of its chief, and partly because the very essence of the work consisted in comparing notes with as many authorities as possible. But the frankness with which Commandant Girard treated requests for information was almost unique. Complete confidence between men of different races cannot be built up in a moment, and in these early days the French and British staffs did not yet have that confidence in each other that developed later born of their common misfortunes and perils.

I remember reporting to my chiefs that at this stage of the operations something more than visits by liaison officers was needed. However often officers each aware of one aspect of the main problem travelled back and forth between the Fifth Army and G.H.Q., they could not insure unity of thought and action. They might arrange details, but they could not break down the watertight compartments in which each staff worked, nor had they the authority to determine whether any fundamental divergence of conception, any change of heart or mind, had occurred in the commanders. A short note made at the time reminds me that I ventured to urge General Lanrezac to see the Field Marshal, but I cannot remember the circumstances. It is evident that the suggestion was turned down.

In spite, perhaps because of the fact that the two commanders did not meet, there was much dashing about between H.Q.'s, generally by officers of the Fifth Army who reported to Colonel Huguet, or by those of Colonel Huguet's own Mission.

As I was included amongst these travellers by road, it came to me as a profound relief when it was at last decided on the 20th to disarm the G.V.C.'s in the neighbourhood of the British. Unfortunately this satisfactory though belated step was only taken after a tragedy had occurred. A post stationed at a railway crossing had opened fire on a column of British artillery peacefully marching down the *chaussée*.

I had several misadventures with G.V.C.s myself, and it was recognized by the French that it would be only a matter of time until the chauffeur and I got shot, so a fat, bearded reservist, who belonged to the cyclist escort of Fifth Army Headquarters, was attached to me. His uniform was to some extent a guarantee for mine, which no G.V.C. had ever seen. I had to transport his bicycle as well as his bulky person during the whole of the Retreat, but he was so cheery and resourceful, and such a tonic against the "falling back to the Mediterranean" spirit, that I soon felt I could not possibly do without him.

CHAPTER IX

THE EVE OF CHARLEROI

August 21st, 1914

The Western theatre of operations on August 21st – The French plan – What was known of the enemy – The British – General Lanrezac delivers another lecture – Its serious implication – Report to Le Cateau – Rumours of an attack by the enemy – Joffre's order to the Fifth Army and the British for an immediate offensive – The defeat of the First and Second Armies in Alsace – Lanrezac's reply to Joffre – Joffre leaves him free to decide when his offensive shall begin – Worse news from Namur – Duruy reports the fall of the fortress to be imminent – A regiment ordered to reinforce the garrison – Sordet asks for infantry support – Important information about the enemy from the Belgians – Joffre's message to Sir John French.

WE have now watched, as in a slow motion picture, the gradual development of the moves sanctioned by General Joffre for the Armies of the left. The players in the great game about to begin have so far been placing their pieces. They have gained no more than an inkling of what their opponents' actions will be. They have made all haste, yet their movements have seemed slow, and except for the crack of a few rifles and the booming of an occasional gun there has been silence on that part of the front that interests us.

All this is about to change. Speed and noise will soon confuse and blur the picture. Before the film moves on, reflecting something of the cataclysm, let us stop it and take stock of the position in the western theatre.

The Belgian Army is withdrawing on Antwerp. Part of the B.E.F. is now level with the Fifth Army, whilst the remainder is coming up fast. The Fifth Army is drawn up south of the Sambre, with the exception of the I. Corps, which is still keeping guard on the Meuse, and the Reserve Divisions which are far behind to the left. The Fourth and Third Armies, which had been impatiently awaiting the order to advance, have on the evening of the 20th received instructions to begin their offensive on the 21st. (Maps IV and V.)

We have seen how General Joffre, still in profound error as to the forces opposed to him, watching the Germans continuously slipping across the front of his armies, had concluded that the enemy was accumulating strength on his right at the expense of his centre. These movements on the part of the enemy appeared to him as auspicious as did those of the Russians on the eve of Austerlitz to Napoleon. At the G.Q.G. they rubbed their hands in glee. Mere civilians such as members of the Government who expressed concern at the evident massing of German troops in Belgium on the left of the French Armies, were patronizingly reassured: the enemy was doing exactly what suited the French best. The dangerous malady of underrating your opponent, of which I had seen some early signs at Vitry, had made rapid and alarming progress.

The French plan, be it remembered, consisted in outflanking the German right whilst a powerful thrust was launched at his centre. The difficulties of this operation would seem to have been somewhat lightly discounted at the G.Q.G., although they must have been well known. The formidable mountain barrier facing the French centre was hardly a favourable *terrain* to attack over. Great masses of troops would have to cross rugged and wooded country, with innumerable defiles easy for the enemy to defend, before reaching the open ground beyond the Ardennes.* In fact the French were aiming a blow at the enemy where he could most easily parry it.

Now what was known of the Germans?

It is important to realize that the Fourth and Fifth French Armies believed, as did Joffre, that the enemy was slipping across their front, dangerously thinning his centre in his endeavour to reach the Allied left. They believed that the Germans underestimated the strength of the Third, Fourth and Fifth Armies, relying upon being able to contain them with comparatively small numbers. The Intelligence thought it likely that the German blow would fall on the British. They estimated that there were five enemy corps north of the Meuse, whereas there were in reality thirteen.

The British, on the strength of General Joffre's instructions, expected the Fifth Army to assume the offensive at the earliest possible moment.

---

* Sir John French, wiring to Lord Kitchener some days later (the 26th) after seeing General Joffre at St. Quentin, said: "Joffre attributes failure of his first plan to precipitous and wooded nature of the country in the Ardennes and near the Meuse."

The enemy was in movement, getting ready but not ready yet. There seemed to be nothing but advantage in disturbing his plan by attacking as soon as possible.

With these facts in mind, the following occurrence which took place at Chimay on the afternoon of the 21st is significant.

I was in the 2ème Bureau going through the most recent Intelligence reports when General Lanrezac walked in. He halted opposite a large map which hung behind the place where the schoolmaster's desk had been, unhitched his pince-nez, which were hooked as usual uncomfortably and incongruously behind his ear, where they hung like a pair of cherries, put them on his nose, and began to call out the names of places on the Sambre as he located them on the map with his finger. Then he began to talk in his deep loud voice of what the Germans were doing. He was always interesting when he discoursed like this, for he was a brilliant speaker.

Presently he went on to talk of the situation of his own Army. We listened intently and respectfully, but he had not been speaking long before my interest changed to amazement and my amazement to incredulity. I could hardly believe my ears as it dawned on me that General Lanrezac was holding forth in eloquent language on the folly of attack. Pointing to the line held by the Fifth Army south of the Sambre and expatiating on its strength, he was saying that it would be madness for troops in such strong defensive positions to abandon these and attack.

To the reader who knows the sequel, General Lanrezac's point of view may seem inspired, but let it be remembered that he knew no more of the enemy's movements than had been stated above, that he had accepted General Joffre's plan without protest, that the role assigned to him was an offensive one and that the British were advancing in the belief that he was going to attack as soon as he could possibly do so.

The impression made by General Lanrezac on his hearers was very strange. When he had finished speaking, we who had been listening to him looked at each other with something like consternation. From that moment I felt that whatever orders he might receive General Lanrezac would be most unwilling to attack.

I was aghast as I thought of how this would affect the British. In the light of the situation as it was then known, a defensive attitude on the part of the Fifth Army could mean one thing and one thing only from Sir John French's point of view; that the enemy's corps believed to be slipping across its front would fall with full force on the British, who numbered some 80,000 men, whilst General Lanrezac, commanding a quarter of a million Frenchmen, stood by with folded arms.

I knew that Sir John would not accept General Lanrezac's attitude as being fair either to himself or to his Army, or as being compatible with the plan with which he was straining every nerve to comply.

I went to the 3ème Bureau to find out if there was a change of plan, but was told that nothing had been altered, and that orders preliminary to an advance were about to be issued.* I was nevertheless profoundly disturbed by what I had heard, and determined to go to Le Cateau forthwith. It seemed essential, in view of what General Lanrezac had said, that he and Sir John should come to a clear understanding as to each other's intentions. This point of view was shared by General Wilson, whom I eventually saw after an appalling drive with de Rose, for I had had the unfortunate idea of going first to the III. Corps to ascertain what their view of the situation was, and if they had further news of the enemy on their front.† I was especially anxious to know, as there were rumours that an attack by the Germans had taken place. Darkness fell as we got on to roads encumbered with transport. It was impossible to make any headway, so we gave up hope of reaching the III. Corps H.Q. and turned left, but soon got into the zone of the XVIII. Corps, where the road situation was even worse. Carts were drawn up all over the road, and the horses stood by, in many cases with their bits in their mouths, whilst the drivers slept sprawling on the waggons, or lay huddled under them, forming dark patches in the dust.

When de Rose and I returned to Chimay some time before dawn, we found confirmation of the rumours that the III. and X. Corps had been attacked during the afternoon. The reports were very vague, there was merely talk of contact having been established with the enemy on the Sambre. I don't think anyone from the General downwards knew more than this. Nothing precise had come in at a late hour that night, and the only definite information was that the engagement had started before General Lanrezac's orders, issued that afternoon, had been received.‡

Very puzzled, I determined to set out early next morning to find out what I could for myself. I had not the least idea that the Battle of Charleroi had begun.

* See Appendix XVIII.

† At Le Cateau we learnt that the Field Marshal had ordered the formation of an extra Brigade, the 19th, to consist of four battalions which till now had remained at Boulogne, le Havre, Rouen and Amiens; this brigade was expected to join the Army on Sunday, 23rd, about Mons. There was the further good news that the 4th Division was being sent out from England and was expected to join on the following Thursday or Friday.

‡ See Appendix XVIII.

On the principle of the more secrecy the better, I was not told at Chimay, although the order was addressed to the British as well as to the Fifth Army, that General Joffre had that morning sent out his order to launch the attack.

This was as follows:

"Ordre Particulier No. 15.

"The Commander-in-Chief to the Commander of the Fifth Army and the Commander-in-Chief of the British Army.

August 21st.

"1. The first eventuality envisaged in my *Instruction Particulière No. 13* [see Maps V and VI] appears to be coming to pass.

"2. The Third and Fourth Armies are beginning today, the 21st, their advance in the general direction of Neufchâteau (Fourth Army) and Arlon (Third Army), taking as their objective the enemy forces which have penetrated into Belgian Luxembourg and which appear to be moving westwards.

"3. The Fifth Army, resting on the Meuse and the fortress of Namur, will take as its objective the enemy northern group. The Commander-in-Chief of the British forces is asked to co-operate in this action, on the left of the Fifth Army, directing at first his main bodies in the general direction of Soignies.

"The line of demarcation between the zones of march of the Fifth Army and the British will be fixed by mutual agreement between the British Commander-in-Chief and the Commander of the Fifth Army. The information obtained by the Cavalry Corps and generally by the Fifth Army will be communicated to British G.H.Q. and vice versa.

"J. JOFFRE."

The immediate reason which had decided the French Commander-in-Chief to launch his offensive without further delay was the defeat of the First and Second Armies on the previous day. Up till then they had been gaining ground steadily in Alsace and Lorraine, but on the 20th they found themselves faced by very strong organized positions. They had reached the bottom of the traps carefully laid for them by the enemy, the spring had been released, the Germans had counter-attacked, and in a few hours the Second Army lost all the ground it had gained since its original advance on August 14th. It was now retiring on the Meurthe, and the First Army was obliged to conform to its movement. The battles of Morhange and Sarrebourg had been fought and lost.

General Joffre, true to the fundamental principle accepted as an axiom in the French Army that the initiative must be kept at all costs, was now attacking with his left and centre to counteract the defeat of his right.

Had I known of Joffre's order I should have realized that General Lanrezac's little lecture in the afternoon was his way of trying out his own ideas; he was expressing to his staff the views he would have liked to place before the Commander-in-Chief, instead of what he actually wrote, which was as follows (Map VI, p. 112):

"Chimay *August 21st*, 12.30 p.m.   *Note Secrète.*

"The Fifth Army has its advance guards on the Sambre from Namur to Thuin.

"It is ready to cross the Sambre, but it is obliged to leave one army corps on the Meuse between Givet and Namur, to guard its flank, so long as the Fourth Army has not crossed the Lesse, at least with its advance guards.

"The British Expeditionary Force has announced that it will have its heads of columns on the front Mons–Erquelinnes on the 23rd.

"If the Fifth Army debouches tomorrow, the 22nd, on the left bank of the Sambre (diminished by the I. Corps, left on the Meuse), it may be exposed to giving battle *alone*. If it is to act in liaison with the British Army, it must wait until the 23rd or perhaps the 24th.*

"The General Commanding the Fifth Army has the honour to ask whether he is to cross the Sambre tomorrow.

"LANREZAC."

This the Commander-in-Chief answered at 8 p.m. as follows (Map IV, p. 60):

"Commander-in-Chief to the Commander of the Army at Chimay, *August 21st, 1914*, 8 p.m.

* The relative position of the British to the Fifth Army can hardly be held to be an adequate reason for not attacking were there no others. On the 21st the B.E.F. already prolonged the line held by the Fifth Army, and General Lanrezac knew that on the 22nd the British left was to be well ahead of his Army on the front Mons – St. Ghislain. It was perfectly possible to synchronise as from the 21st the advance of the British with that of the Fifth Army.

"I leave you absolute judge of the moment when your offensive movement should begin. This evening the Fourth Army should reach the front Bièvre–Paliseul–Bertrix–Neufchâteau. I will keep you informed daily of the line reached by the Fourth Army.

"JOFFRE."

*   *   *

The news from Namur was disquieting. General Michel had sent a message that the Germans were attempting an "*attaque brusquée*" on the fortress and that the town was being bombarded. Duruy, who had gone again to Namur that morning, sent back several disturbing reports. It was becoming evident that unless something was done the town would not hold out long.

Late that night Duruy returned. In his opinion the fortress would not hold out another day unless help were immediately forthcoming. It seemed that the garrison and the population were extremely depressed by the bombardment, and the impression was gaining ground amongst them that they were being abandoned to their fate, that the French were not interested, having disregarded previous appeals, and that the forts and the city would be blown to pieces before the Allies bestirred themselves. "They must see French troops marching along with colours unfurled and a band playing, there must be a band," declared Duruy. At last he was heeded. The mandarins at Chimay became thoroughly alarmed, and the I. Corps was ordered to send an active, not a reserve regiment, into Namur immediately. Three battalions marched that night and reached Namur on the morning of the 22nd.

*   *   *

General Sordet's reports were optimistic. He stated that on the 22nd he would be ready to carry out any orders he might be given, as the morale of his troops was high and his regiments were now up to strength. He repeated his request for infantry support, a request which General Lanrezac had anticipated by ordering the 11th Brigade of the III. Corps to co-operate with the cavalry.*

General Sordet asked whether he might not be given leave to operate straight to the north of Nivelle so as to take in flank the German columns

* See Appendix XIX.

reported to be moving from east to west. He felt the danger these were to the British, and wished to do all he could to mitigate it.*

During the evening the Belgians had sent in very important information to the effect that the enemy corps operating in the neighbourhood of Brussels appeared to be carrying out a wheel to the south after passing the capital.†

General Joffre informed Sir John French that he believed the operations would develop as planned, and he added that he trusted they would be pressed with vigour.

The situation of the Fifth and British Armies at nightfall is shown on Map VI, pp. 112–13.

* In the afternoon the Cavalry Corps was attacked and lost the passages of the Charleroi Canal at Luttre and Pont-à-Celles, one division falling back on Gouy-le-Piéton; the other, driven out of Gosselies, still managed to hold Motte on the Canal.

† Belgian G.H.Q. 21/8, 8 p.m.:

"The German Army Corps operating in the neighbourhood of Brussels seem to be making a conversion towards the south after passing Brussels.

"Thus the IV. Corps, which occupied the capital yesterday evening, left by the Ninove road and has turned off towards Hal. Further north, the II. Corps after having marched from Vilvorde towards Alost, has not yet reached that town, and must therefore also have turned southwards.

"On the other hand, the 2nd Cavalry Division, which covers the advance of the marching wing, has left Malines during the day and arrived at Alost, throwing out reconnaissances north and west as far as Ghent.

"No news whatever of what is happening to the south of the IV. Corps."

CHAPTER X

THE BATTLE OF CHARLEROI BEGINS

August 22nd, 1914: – I

The refugees – The fighting on the front of the X. and III. Corps – The question of Army Reserves – The III. Corps area – The 19th Division at Auvelais – The X. Corps loses the heights south of the Sambre – The night attacks by the III. Corps – Meeting with Sir John French on the road to Le Cateau – Colonel Macdonogh's information about the enemy – A vitally important air reconnaissance – G.H.Q. at Le Cateau – The situation of the British.

AT dawn on the 22nd, I went over to the small hotel where we messed, in rather doubtful hope of getting something to eat, and possibly a cup of hot coffee.

To my intense surprise I found the place full of people, on the floor, under the tables, in chairs, sleeping or sitting up against the wall and staring vacantly before them. There were some men, but the majority were women of all classes and conditions, and many children; three tinies were asleep on the dining-room table. The white dust of the continental roads covered their faces and clothes. Those who were awake stared with the fixed, vacant, uncomprehending stare of utter fatigue, whilst the faces of the sleepers had the drawn, pinched look of corpses. One young woman, the only one who appeared to have any life in her, was attempting to put on her clothes behind the inadequate screen afforded by the open door.

These people did not know where they were going, and were quite incapable of explaining what had happened to them. They were from the neighbourhood of Charleroi, and had been flying all night and all the previous day from the Germans.

We were in contact for the first time with the Great Panic. These were the vanguard of a terrified uprooted population, running before some ghastly terror that killed and destroyed and burned all it met.

I went over to Headquarters, hoping to find out there what the latest news was. The fighting on the front of the X. and III. Corps had, it seemed, been far more severe than was thought at first. There appeared to be no doubt that the enemy had got across the Sambre and pushed well beyond it. Arsimont and the passages over the river at Ham-sur-Sambre, Mornimont and Franière had been lost by the X. Corps. There was also a report that on the front of the III. Corps Roselies had been evacuated after severe fighting. Neither the I. nor the XVIII. Corps appeared to have been attacked.* (Map VI, pp. 112–13.)

I was told that very late on the night of the 21st the Commander of the X. Corps had reported his intention of counter-attacking at dawn on the 22nd, his objective being to throw the enemy back into the Sambre. The Commander of the III. Corps, General Sauret, had sent in word that it was not his intention to put up a serious fight in the valley against forces that might attempt to cross the river, but to make his stand on the heights to the south of it.

The Staff did not appear unduly concerned at this news from the Sambre front. It was pointed out that General Lanrezac had not wished to fight in the valley. The general impression seemed to be that the enemy was doing little more than feel the front of the Army, and there was absolute confidence that he could be thrown back into the river with the greatest ease whenever this was desired.

I asked what reserves General Lanrezac had kept in his own hands, and was told that these were ample, although no units were named. In answer to a further question I was assured that the Army Commander's intentions were unaltered by the events of the preceding afternoon.

The question of Army reserves puzzled me. I knew the 37th and 38th Divisions had been allocated to the X. and III. Corps respectively,

---

* At 12.45 p.m. on the 21st the advanced guard of the X. Corps, drawn from the 19th Division, was sharply attacked in the bend of the river from Tamines to Auvelais. This attack was in the first instance repelled. A prisoner having stated that the attack was being carried out by five cavalry regiments, two of which belonged to the Guard, three infantry regiments, one battalion of Jägers and two regiments of artillery, General Desfforges, the G.O.C.X. Corps, ordered the G.O.C. 20th Division to establish his main body north of Biesme, and the 37th Division to hold itself in readiness to move forward. At 2 p.m. the attack was renewed, and the Germans crossed the river and gained ground towards Arsimont and Falisolle in spite of a French counter-attack.

Soon the Commander of the 19th Division, whose left was being hard pressed, asked for the support of the 20th Division.

At 9 p.m. Arsimont was abandoned in the face of what were reported to be superior forces. At 11 p.m. General Desforges ordered the 19th Division to hold the line Fosse, Vitrival, Aisemont, Cortil-Mozet, and the 20th Division the line Vitrival, le Roux. At daybreak the 37th Division was to be in immediate support of the 19th Division.

On the front of the III. Corps the outposts of the 5th Division were attacked at about 3 p.m. The enemy at his second attempt crossed the river at Roselies and gained a footing in Aiseau, but he was later driven out of the latter locality.

which, as far as I could make out, were giving them orders direct. I wondered if General Lanrezac intended to withdraw the I. Corps from the Meuse front and use it as a general reserve. Had I been told that the Army Commander had no reserves whatever in hand, and that no steps had been taken to use the heavy artillery for the obvious purpose of covering the river passages, I would not have believed it.

Faithful to my principle of seeing for myself whenever possible, I determined to go north before making for Le Cateau.

At Walcourt, the Headquarters of the III. Corps, a good deal of information concerning the engagements of the previous day was available. (Map VI, p. 112.)

The 19th Division of the X. Corps had been involved in some hard fighting. The village of Auvelais on the Sambre having been lost in the early afternoon, a regiment had been ordered to recapture it. As if at manœuvres, in dense formation, bugles blowing, drums beating and flags flying, it had dashed to the assault with the utmost gallantry. These brave men, in the face of machine-guns and artillery whose gunners can never have dreamed of such targets, actually reached the outskirts of the village, but the German Guards who were holding it had lost no time in organizing its defence, and the French who had dashed forward with but little artillery preparation were driven back in some confusion. This check led to the evacuation of Tamines.

From all accounts the hostile artillery fire had been severe and effective, and there was no doubt that the German Guards were tough customers (though perhaps not quite so formidable as they appeared to some of the staffs of the forces facing them).* The situation of the 19th Division might well have been difficult at nightfall owing to the loss of Roselies by the III. Corps, but this hardly seemed to explain the news that the X. Corps had abandoned Arsimont, thus leaving the enemy master of the heights south of the Sambre. Not more than seven or eight battalions out of a total of forty in the Corps appeared to have been engaged, although these had suffered severely. I sought an explanation of this retirement but got none, nor so far as I know has any explanation ever been given.

The morning's news was that the X. Corps had launched a counter-attack which was thought to be progressing. It was to be hoped that this

---

* "General Bonnier (19th Division) much perturbed, it seemed, at having to deal with the Prussian Guard, retired with some precipitation, evacuating Arsimont without much reason." – Lanrezac – "Le Plan de Campagne Français," p. 154.

attack would be successful, for unless the X. Corps regained the heights south of the Sambre on its own front it was unlikely that the III. Corps could retain its present positions.

The 5th Division of the III. Corps had been busy carrying out night attacks against the villages of Aiseau and Roselies, the former only having been recaptured.* An attack on the latter place was actually in progress whilst I was at the front. These night attacks had thrown the 5th Division into considerable confusion.† (Map VI, p. 112.)

I went forward, where exactly I do not know, but could see nothing. Fog lay thick in the Sambre valley. Heavy fighting was evidently going on, for the constant crackle of musketry could be heard a short distance ahead, with now and then the boom of a gun. No wonder the artillery was quiescent: they could not possibly see anything to shoot at, and can only have been loosing off an occasional shot "into the landscape", as the French say, to show the infantry they were there.

I met some units which had not been engaged. The men were excited at the prospect of fighting, and pressed round me with bits of information. They had heard that the engagements of the previous day had been fierce and the losses heavy, but this did not worry them in the least. They were like eager children, as gay as if this were the dawn of a holiday and they were presently going to march down the road to make a day of it at the local fair. What fine young fellows they were! Their lightheartedness and exuberance were contagious.

What I found seriously perturbing was that there was no sign of entrenchments: no one was digging. Surely, I thought, everyone ought to be working desperately now? What may come looming out of the fog presently?

Time was passing. I rejoined my car and made all speed for Le Cateau.

Presently, at a crossroads on the main Chimay–Avesnes–Landrecies road somewhere east of Avesnes, I passed the British Commander-in-Chief's car followed by another one. He signalled to me to stop, and he and his staff got out. I well remember the place: quite a number of French soldiers, a couple of companies perhaps, were halted on either side of the road, and stared suspiciously at these strange, khaki-clad, red-tabbed officers.

---

* See Appendix XX.

† The recapture of Roselies was of no military importance, but it transpired later that the Commander of the 5th Division believed that some of his men were still holding out in the village, and insisted upon being allowed to try to rescue them. This engagement led to three regiments (nine battalions) being engaged quite fruitlessly.

There was a small house by the roadside, a kind of combined cottage and estaminet, into which we all trooped. There was a table under a window to the left of the door, piled high with dirty plates and cups; these were cleared aside and a map spread out. Sir John bent over it and asked me for my news. I began to speak, but in spite of my best endeavours could not make myself heard. The lady of the house, who had watched our intrusion with a wide-open mouth from which no sound came, had noisily resumed washing up her dishes in a tub. Captain Guest persuaded her, not without difficulty, to postpone this important operation so that I might proceed with my report.

I began by giving the situation of the Fifth Army as it was known at Chimay when I left, adding the information I had gleaned at the front that morning. Sir John asked my opinion as to the condition of the X. Corps, and I said that I thought the units engaged had been knocked about a good deal, but that so far the fighting efficiency of the Corps as a whole had not been impaired.

The very important point of General Lanrezac's intentions then came up. As I expected, Sir John was relying on the Fifth Army's advancing at the earliest possible moment. This I feared was not General Lanrezac's intention, and I repeated what I had told General Wilson the day before.

I gave the Commander-in-Chief the view of the Intelligence Bureau of the Fifth Army that the far-flung German movement towards the west could mean one thing and one thing only, an enveloping movement on a huge scale. The danger this operation portended to the British Army, situated as it was on the left of the Allied line, was evident. Unless the French armies, by a vigorous offensive, interfered with the German manœuvre, its full force must fall on the British Army, which would not only be attacked in front but might possibly have its left flank threatened as well.

Sir John appeared to agree with this view.

He questioned me about the Cavalry Corps. He was very anxious to know when it was going to move to his left.* I told him that I understood it was somewhere about Merbes-le-Château, having retired there under the protection of the infantry brigade which supported it.

Sir John then said that he was on his way to see General Lanrezac, and wanted to know where he was to be found. On hearing he was to be at Mettet that day, Sir John looked at the map and decided he could not afford the time to go so far. This was most disappointing to me, for I

* See footnote, Chapter VII, p. 92.

had been thinking before I met him that when I got to G.H.Q. I must again do all in my power to persuade his staff to get him to see General Lanrezac. I felt certain that there was a most serious misunderstanding between the two men, and that this could only be cleared up by a personal interview at which representatives of the Staffs and properly qualified interpreters were present. Now this unfortunate chance meeting was going to spoil it all!

I tried very diffidently to persuade the Commander-in-Chief to change his mind. Perhaps I was not emphatic enough. I was only a subaltern, and much intimidated at having to deal with such important people. The glamour of the great still dazzled me, and I failed to gain my point. I was told to get into the Commander-in-Chief's car, which turned and made for Le Cateau at all speed. Sir John said it was fortunate he had met me, since had he found on arriving at Chimay that General Lanrezac was away he would certainly not have gone to look for him, his time was too valuable.

As we entered the town we passed some pipers belonging to the G.H.Q. Guard, the Camerons I believe they were. I thought them the smartest men imaginable, and the skirl of their pipes together with the perfect assurance of their demeanour gave one the warmest and most satisfying feeling of confidence. It was not fair to compare these Scotchmen with some of the tired and strained French units I had seen within the last few hours, but nevertheless the sight of them filled me with a sense of pride which I have not forgotten to this day.

Colonel Macdonogh, our Chief of Intelligence, whom I saw immediately on arrival, had most interesting news. Not only did his information confirm that collected by the 2ème Bureau of the Fifth Army, but it was still more precise. Several German Corps including the Guard had been identified by our people on the front of the Fifth Army, which was very helpful. A German Corps, believed to be the III., was reported to be marching down the Brussels–Mons road, and was expected to reach Braine-le-Comte, about thirteen miles north of Mons, that night. But this was nothing to the supremely important report brought in by a British aviator that day: a German Corps, thought to be the II. Corps belonging to the First Army, had been observed by the airman. He had seen it march westward along the Brussels–Ninove road and then turn southwards towards Grammont. This Corps was making straight for the British left. It was bound to outflank us. (Map III, p. 54.)

Now we knew. No possible doubt could subsist. The German manœuvre stood fully revealed.

Up to the moment when that report came in the impression had been that the German Corps were following each other in a long procession, turning inwards one after the other as they reached the Sambre. This was now shown to be an entirely erroneous conception. We were faced with something more grandiose and considerably more alarming. The German armies which had been projected into Belgium like rockets, were now falling back on us in an enveloping shower, each spark a corps. They had travelled far through the darkness of our ignorance before the beauty of the display was revealed. The great enemy formations, each advancing as if on the ribs of a fan, had been carrying out a gigantic wheel with the evident object of enveloping the Allied line. Would they succeed? That would appear soon enough. They had evidently prepared the manœuvre on a large enough scale to outflank the French. Did they reckon on finding us prolonging the line? Where had they found the troops for so ambitious a scheme? Might this not mean that their centre was so weak that General Joffre could drive it in with his Third and Fourth Armies?

The air reconnaissance that came back with this information was probably the most fruitful of the whole war. How nearly the invaluable revelation was entirely wasted I was to learn there and then. Quite accidentally it came to Colonel Macdonogh's ears that the Expeditionary Force was to advance to Soignies. He knew no more than I did that this was in accordance with General Joffre's request. (Map VI, pp. 112–13.) But what he did know was that we were not likely to get to Soignies before the Germans, and that the air report he had in his pocket made it clear that if by mischance we reached that place, our flank would certainly be turned and our communications threatened by the German corps coming down by Grammont. He therefore decided to see the Chief of Staff immediately, explaining to him the importance of the information he now possessed. As will be seen later, this information, strange as it may seem, did not affect in the least (for the time being at any rate) the decision of the British Commander-in-Chief and his advisers.*

I had a good many things to do at Le Cateau, various people to see

---

* The following is another curious example of how reluctant G.H.Q. was at this period to accept British Intelligence reports. In the information paragraph of Operation Order No. 6 of August 21st (drafted by Intelligence) it was stated that a column of all arms was reported moving on Mons from Brussels and that its head might have reached Braine-le-Comte. This was countered by the Operations section which issued an order on the same day (O(A)47) to the Cavalry Division which read as follows:

"The information which you have acquired and conveyed to the Commander-in-Chief appears to be somewhat exaggerated. It is probable that only mounted troops supported by Jägers are in your immediate neighbourhood."

and questions to ask, but this did not entail a long walk, for the greater part of the staff were housed in the school, but housed is hardly the right word, packed would be a more accurate expression. The whole of the General Staff were in two rooms on the first floor, Operations and Intelligence in one, and the clerks in the other. If my memory serves me rightly, these rooms were in the infant section, for I still visualize tall, very long-legged officers, attempting to work at desks made for small children of ten. On the other hand, Colonel Huguet's Mission, comparatively few in numbers and after all only a subsidiary liaison organ, had better accommodation than the Staff, having allotted to themselves (they had allocated the buildings) the larger of the two school-houses. I heard some very caustic comments on this arrangement.

The school looked on to a broad street which widened out into a square as you turned to the left. As I remember it, the little houses of the town clustered round it and spread along some streets, quickly merging into the country beyond. Down the street to the right, some little distance from the school, was the small château where the Commander-in-Chief had established his headquarters.

A sun-baked, drowsy little place it seemed, on the eve of being flung into history to the accompaniment of the roar of great guns. That afternoon, unconscious of its fate, the little town looked as if nothing could ever rouse it.

In the Operations Section, a glance at the map giving the positions to be reached by our troops showed that when the 1st Division, forming the right of our line, reached Grand Reng, which it would do sometime that night, there would be a gap of fully nine miles between it and the nearest units of the French XVIII. Corps, while of course the Reserve Divisions were still far behind.

While I was there a message came in from the Cavalry at Binche which caused a good deal of amusement. They asked if they were justified in loopholing the walls of a farmhouse they were stationed in. Evidently they thought they were still at manœuvres. The inveterate British respect for law, order and property could not be shaken by the mere fact of there being a war on. One wondered whether officers would not indent for coroners, complete with juries, to sit on the first casualties.

CHAPTER XI

THE BATTLE OF CHARLEROI

August 22nd, 1914: – II

On the road from Le Cateau to Mettet – Mettet – Communications during a battle – Information collected at Mettet – General Boé – Decision to report that the centre of the Fifth Army had fallen back some ten miles – The gap between the British and the XVIII. Corps – The Reserve Divisions – Report to Sir John – The British offensive cancelled – Lanrezac's extraordinary request to the British – And strange report to Joffre – Return to Chimay – Latest news of the battle.

As soon as I could get away from Le Cateau, I left for Mettet, the advance report centre of the Fifth Army. The first part of my journey was uneventful, being taken up merely with calculations as to how fast it was possible to go between the posts of G.V.C.s, but when I got into the areas first of the III. and then of the X. Corps, progress became at times extremely slow owing to convoys blocking the roads. Once or twice we took a chance and motored across the parched fields, trusting to luck to find an exit at the other end. Louder and louder grew the sound of guns, until it became obvious that a great battle was raging close at hand. It was strangely exciting, and an intense feeling of curiosity, a longing to know what was going on, a desire to be in it, seized us. The country we were now in was characteristic of the back area of a battlefield in a war of movement. Empty spaces with not a soul to be seen, under a sky of brass, shaking with the concussion of artillery, now a single heavy discharge, then a pulsation of the whole atmosphere, as if all the Gods in heaven were beating on drums the size of lakes. A little farther on one might come upon a man working in a field, apparently quite unperturbed; then two or three country folk dressed in their best, black suits and white shirts grey with dust, carrying odd packages, would hurry by. A farm lately occupied by troops, gates torn off or swinging wide open on one hinge, fences broken, signs of cooking, oddments lying about, the buildings looking strangely empty, forlorn and shrunken, after having evidently been filled to bursting point by men now perhaps in the centre of that hell over there. Then convoys hopelessly blocking the road, themselves stuck, not knowing where to go, awaiting orders. Farther on troops not yet engaged, the men eagerly watching anyone coming by, scanning the faces of passing officers to discover whether things were going well or ill, the officers serious, anxious, in little groups, talking in low tones.

Presently it became all too obvious that the French line must have fallen back since the morning, for we were now almost in the firing line, whereas, according to the morning's information, we should have been far behind it. We began to encounter long pathetic processions of wounded men hobbling along alone or helping each other, their cloth-ing torn, their faces black with grime or grey with dust, white bandages with an occasional bloody patch, masks of pain through which stared living and agonized eyes. Then came country carts on which lay on straw some seriously wounded men. We had got even closer to the fighting line than we had intended, for a few minutes later a couple of battalions in retreat crossed us. These were an even more poignant sight than the wounded. Hardly any officers, the men in disorder, terrible worn expressions on their faces, exhaustion dragging at their heels and weighing down their tired feet so that they caught on every stone in the roadway, but something driving them on. Was it fear? I do not think so – just the desire to find a place to rest, away from those infernal shells. These men were not beaten, they were worn out.

I remember thinking during that drive that officers in high authority, Army and even Corps Commanders, should avoid the proximity of the fighting line, and should not dwell in the atmosphere of the back area of a battlefield. It is unspeakably horrible, more depressing by far than the battlefield itself, for there is no excitement, only suspense. No com-mander can help being influenced by whatever misery or disorder comes within his limited field of vision. Nor can he, with the sight of the suffering of his own people before his eyes, console himself with the thought that the enemy is in the same plight.

Would the celebrated German, Lt. Colonel Hentsch, the liaison officer who came to von Kluck during the Battle of the Marne, armed with full powers from Headquarters, have given his emphatic order to retire, had he not met on his way convoys and wounded falling back in disorder?

Mettet square, where we arrived eventually, reminded one strongly of a picture of the war of 1870. A big oblong "*place*" in which some regimental carts and ambulance waggons were parked; along one side of it the main street, down which refugees were hurrying, meeting a counter-stream of troops moving in the opposite direction.

There was a church at the far end, with some steps leading up to the porch. On these steps stood several members of the X. Corps Staff, dominated by the tall figure of that splendid soldier, Colonel Paulinier, the Chief of Staff.*

A few yards in front of the steps General Lanrezac was standing by General Desforges, the Corps Commander. They were not talking. General Lanrezac, his hands behind his back, was looking towards the end of the "*place*", towards the enemy.

To the left of the church there was a convent, an arcaded building out of which a nun flitted now and then with downcast eyes and quick furtive footsteps. In this building, on the ground floor, the officers who had accompanied Lanrezac had found a room. The faces of all were furrowed with anxiety as they waited and waited and waited, with nothing to do and very little news. There were practically no reports, and those that came in were bad. Lack of information was exasperating, with the noise of battle growing ever nearer. Communications had apparently broken down.

It was the old story: the divisions, fully engaged, were evidently finding it hard to give a precise account of themselves. We were up against one of the great difficulties of modern warfare. There we were, in a friendly country, with all the equipment of a modern state at our disposal, yet the Army Commander was without news of a battle in which two of his corps were engaged less than ten miles away. There could be nothing wrong with the system of communications, it was perfect and undisturbed; on the contrary, the peacetime postal system had been reinforced by all the technical troops of the Army, and civil intercommunication had been suspended so that nothing should interfere with military messages. Any amount of motors were available besides.

The explanation? There could be only one, the difficulty subordinate commanders were finding in forming a clear idea of the situation of their own units. Time must pass before the Battalion Commander located his companies after they had been engaged; it would take more time to transmit the message to the Regimental Commander, who again would

* Mettet was also the Headquarters of the X. Corps.

have to wait for the reports from his other battalions before passing them on to the Brigadier, and so on to the top. How much time must elapse from the moment when a runner from the company or battalion, dodging shells, ran back with a pencilled message from the front line, until a report filtered through to Army Headquarters? No one man could actually see more than a small part of the battlefield, and the Army Commander would only have to guide him reports of events long past. With these as his sole information he must deal with future events.

I obtained a certain amount of information at Mettet. The liaison officers and others coming from the front confirmed my belief that, although some units engaged had had a fearful gruelling, the men believed they were opposed to greatly superior forces and did not accept for a moment the idea of defeat. They thought they had given as good as they got. Numbers had had the better of them, that was all. The Germans would meet their deserts presently. I was told of several satisfactory incidents when the French 75s caught the German infantry in fairly close formation and inflicted heavy punishment. Whenever this happened the sting was completely taken out of the German attack, if it was not stopped altogether. On the other hand, the liaison officers did not disguise the fact that the German heavy howitzers had taken the French infantry aback, and no wonder. The noise they made was appalling.

Imagine an express train, audible but invisible, coming down upon you from the sky, following an imperceptible corkscrew track at an immeasurable speed, and making straight for the top of your head (for if they were going to fall in your vicinity you always had the illusion that they were following an arc at one end of which you stood). Your quaking senses next perceived a terrific, an appalling noise as the shell burst, releasing hellish flames and great volumes of black smoke, whilst a geyser of earth and debris spouted into the air.

The French soldier was not slow to note the sooty characteristics of these shells, and called them "*marmites*" (cauldrons) whilst our men expressed the same idea in the appellation "Jack Johnsons". But at this early stage I don't think anyone had the stomach to be humorous about them: the beastly things appeared to be far more dangerous than they really were, though they could do enough damage, goodness knows. At a later date the exact punishing power of these missiles was accurately estimated by the troops, but at this time there was no doubt that they were having a most depressing effect, all the more so that owing to the nature of the country the French artillery could do little to silence the enemy guns, for they were completely concealed. It was very unfortunate that the men were gaining the impression that the German artillery was out of range of their own, and consequently unassailable.

Another factor already beginning to tell, whose effect on the morale of the troops increased as time went on, was the German aeroplanes. The men soon noticed with exasperation that the German machines, the *Taubes*, shaped like hawks, sailed the sky without interference, and that generally their passage was followed by salvos of shells landing on the troops they had flown over, proving all too clearly to the French soldiers that the hostile artillery had been accurately informed of their exact location.

Presently Captain Fort, the liaison officer to the III. Corps, came in. His news of the actual fighting was not too bad. A counter-attack by a brigade had relieved the pressure on the 5th Division, which had fallen back after being roughly handled in the morning. This onslaught seemed to have taken the enemy aback, for he had halted. Nevertheless in spite of this partial success it appeared that General Sauret, who commanded the Corps, was withdrawing his Headquarters five or six kilometres to the rear, and had ordered his command to fall back to the line Nalinnes–Tarcienne–Hanzinelle, which, he declared, it was his intention to defend with energy.

This retirement made an unfavourable impression, and indeed nothing seemed to justify it. There was of course no objection to the line Nalinnes–Tarcienne *per se* – after all it was the position General Lanrezac himself had selected for the III. Corps to fight on. But there was every ground for criticizing General Sauret for electing to fight farther north and then falling back, without adequate reason, to a line which had not been fortified. (Map VI, p. 112.)

As time passed the scene at Mettet became more and more depressing: groups of civilians, men carrying babies, women dragging tiny tots terrified by the din of approaching battle, hurried past with tired feet and frightened eyes. Horrible!

Inside, in the convent room where the staff was congregated, an occasional glimpse of the General, sombre and silent, could be caught; there appeared to be little or no definite news.

The tenseness of the moment may serve to explain the following incident. I was told of it at the time, and my memory has since been corroborated by officers who were present.

Several of the Staff were standing in the street, when a motor-car drove up coming from the north. It proceeded slowly round the *place* towards the Church steps on which General Lanrezac was standing. In it reclined a badly wounded man, with a face the colour of ashes. On seeing General Lanrezac he made a sign, and the car stopped. Many officers recognized General Boé, commanding the 20th Division belonging to the X. Corps. The wounded man made another sign. His hand lifted as if to salute, but dropped and hung over the door. General Lanrezac did not move. He turned to Hély d'Oissel, who was standing by him, and said – "You go and talk to him." The Chief of Staff stepped quickly forward, almost ran to the car, and clasped Boé's hand. He did not speak. Boé was silent for a moment, looking towards Lanrezac. Then he whispered – "Tell him," he gasped, then, speaking louder as he realized Hély d'Oissel could hardly hear him, he repeated, "Tell the General we held on as long as we could." His head fell back, his eyes were very sad. Hély d'Oissel grasped his hand again and said nothing. Still General Lanrezac had not moved. The car grated into gear, and drove slowly on.

It was not poor Boé's wounds that made such a tragic impression on the minds of all those who saw him at Mettet, though they were bad enough, a bullet through his arm and another through his stomach. It was the despair in his face that moved them. He was thinking of his men, and the sight of his emotion conjured up a vision of the division which had suffered so severely that even its commander had been stricken by rifle fire.

My chief preoccupation was of course how the position of the Fifth Army would affect the British. I asked the Operations people what the exact situation was, but could not get any definite news. I was told that no information could be given me without the General's permission, which was not forthcoming. I then sent in word to the General, asking him to give me a message or to explain his views either to me personally or through the Chief of Staff, so that I might convey them to Sir John, but I was told that he was too busy to do either. I should have felt lost indeed had not Commandant Girard, in his usual clear calm way, done all he could to help me weigh up the situation. Besides the opinion I obtained from him, conversations I had with various officers coming in from the front, and several short runs I took by car to various points in the area of the X. Corps, drove me to the conclusion that the centre of the Army had been driven back from five to ten miles south of the Sambre, which meant that the British forces were now about nine miles ahead of the main French line.*

The situation of the Fifth Army when I left Mettet is shown on Map VI, p. 112.

With no information beyond what I had been able to glean for myself, unarmed with any authority, I set out for Le Cateau at about 7 p.m., feeling anything but happy: the responsibility of having to report a situation so serious that it must necessarily profoundly influence British plans overwhelmed me with anxiety. But bad as the day had been, I

---

* On the right, the 51st Reserve Division was in process of relieving the I. Corps which was gradually moving up towards the Sambre on the right of the X. Corps. Several German attacks on the bridges of Dinant and Anseremme were easily repulsed without interfering with the relief. The presence of the XII. Saxon Corps in this area was notified.

The situation of the Fifth Army as reported to the G.Q.G. at 8.30 p.m. that night was as follows:

"Violent attacks on the front Namur–Charleroi. The X. Corps has been forced to fall back to the line Biesme–Saint-Gérard, which will compel the most northern forces of the I. Corps to fall back also and to abandon the defence of the Meuse below Yvoir.

"The X. Corps has suffered severely. General Boé (20th Division) has been very seriously wounded.

"Heavy casualties in officers.

"The 5th Division of the III. Corps heavily engaged before le Châtelet.

"The XVIII. Corps is intact.

"The Cavalry Corps, greatly exhausted, has had to fall back under cover of an infantry brigade which was acting in support of it and is in the neighbourhood of Thuin. The Cavalry Corps will only be able to maintain liaison with the Army W which is still in echelon in rear of the Fifth Army."

Telephoned by Commandant de Marmiès.
Received by Commandant de Partouneaux.

The only result of the German attacks on Dinant and Anseremme was that General Franchet d'Esperey asked leave to blow up the Meuse bridges with the exception of those at Givet, Hastière and Dinant. This permission was granted by General Lanrezac, who at the same time told General d'Esperey to take steps to reinforce the Sart–St. Laurent position as soon as possible. He was told that when this was done he should be in a position to support the X. Corps in this direction whilst at the same time opposing any attempt by the enemy to cross the Meuse between Givet and Namur, this remaining his principal duty.

During the day the X. Corps sent a pressing appeal for help to the I. Corps, but d'Esperey answered that the enemy was attacking on the Meuse, that he only had one brigade facing north, and that the situation did not appear to him to warrant taking a step which might dislocate the order of battle of the Army.

At 8 p.m. the I. Corps was ordered to withdraw the detachment from Sart–St. Laurent, and if necessary to withdraw its left as far back as St. Gérard so as to give strong support to the right of the X. Corps.

Following upon this order General d'Esperey increased his concentration to the north and ordered the 51st Reserve Division to assure the guard of the Meuse from Hastière to Anhée as from August 23rd at 3 a.m.

See Appendix XX.

was convinced that the Fifth Army was still unbeaten. The two wing Corps were quite intact, and the morale even of those units which had suffered most was good. There seemed every prospect that with any luck the two centre corps would be able to reorganize behind the 37th and 38th Divisions, and would in a short time be ready to give a good account of themselves.

The gap between the XVIII. Corps and the British, referred to in the previous chapter, was obviously a very serious matter. The only troops available to fill it were General Valabrègue's two Reserve Divisions whose headquarters were still at Vervins that morning, south of Avesnes, which is 10 miles south of Maubeuge. The divisions themselves were, on the early morning of the 22nd, in the region La Capelle–Hirson, 23 miles south of Maubeuge. At four in the afternoon an order was issued to them to advance level with and to the east of Maubeuge. I did not know the details of this order, and was only aware of the fact that they had been ordered forward, but I knew how far back they were and that they would probably be unable to reach the Sambre till late next day. (Map VI, p. 112.)

Why were the Reserve Divisions held back?

I did not know then nor has the matter ever been explained. Something will be said presently concerning the employment of these Reserve Divisions. All I would say here is that as General Lanrezac had decided to keep them on the left it is difficult to justify his letting them drop so far behind that they were useless when they were needed to span the gap between the British and the XVIII. Corps. Both flanks of the British were threatened, but their right flank more immediately so, as the formidable pressure on the Fifth Army, which I gathered had extended to Sordet's Cavalry Corps, opposite whom there were evidently large hostile forces, showed clearly enough. If the Germans succeeded in interposing themselves between the British and French Armies the British might be isolated and attacked on three sides. It was an awful prospect. I resolved to draw attention at Le Cateau to the fact that however badly the Cavalry Corps might be needed on the British left, its three divisions together with their infantry support and the Fifth British Cavalry Brigade constituted the only force available to fill the gap until the Reserve Divisions came up.* (Map VI, pp. 112–13).

* Sordet was covering the advance of the British as well as the left flank of the Fifth Army, but on the 21st he was not yet in contact with the former. General Joffre had sent a telegram (received at Chimay on the 22nd at 4 p.m.) which stated that it would be desirable for the Cavalry Corps to deal with the German Cavalry reported north of Mons, which was causing anxiety to the population of Lille. Meanwhile General Lanrezac had ordered General Sordet

When I reached Le Cateau I was in an almost exhausted condition. Luckily the first person I saw was Colonel Macdonogh, who said he knew of half a bottle of champagne, which he gave me. We then walked over to the Commander-in-Chief's château. Never have I felt more tired, but the feeling of being well-nigh spent was due far more to the news I bore, and to the responsibility of the report I had to make, than to actual lack of sleep. I felt more and more miserable: if I were mistaken in my deductions or in my observations the result might be terribly serious. Yet the situation, if I understood it rightly, was so perilous that I felt I must convince Sir John of two things; that General Lanrezac was not going to attack whatever happened, and that the position of the Fifth Army was dangerously exposing the British. It seemed to be my plain duty to inform the Commander-in-Chief that I was sure of this, whatever might be the consequences if I proved to be wrong, for if, as had appeared probable in the early afternoon, Sir John intended to attack in spite of Macdonogh's warning of the danger to his left, the British Army would be engaging in a Balaclava adventure on a huge scale.

At the Château the Commander-in-Chief was still at a very late dinner. We waited for him, standing in the drawing-room, but we were not kept waiting long, for a minute later he appeared, followed by Sir Archibald Murray. I reported the situation of the Fifth Army, but drew a by no means pessimistic picture of its condition. It was probably by this time half a day's march behind the main British line. There was a gap of approximately the same distance between the two armies, and in this space there was only at present Sordet's exhausted Cavalry, now sheltering behind its badly shaken infantry support. I pointed out that, quite apart from the danger on the right, the Intelligence reports of the Fifth Army tended to confirm that the threat to the left flank of the British was no less serious. This was confirmed by Colonel Macdonogh, who gave the Commander-in-Chief the information he possessed regarding

---

to operate on the left bank of the Sambre in liaison with the XVIII. Corps on the one hand and the British on the other. Before this order was received General Sordet had ordered the 5th and 3rd Cavalry Divisions to get into touch with the British Cavalry Brigade about Buvrinnes and Binche, and with the XVIII. Corps about Thuin. At 11 p.m. on the 22nd Sordet reported that his infantry brigade had suffered pretty severely whilst covering the retirement of the Cavalry Corps to the south of the Sambre. He stated that he would find it difficult, owing to the fatigue of men and horses, to carry out the orders given him for the following day. He could, however, form a detachment to operate on the left bank of the Sambre in liaison with the British and the XVIII. Corps.

the enemy, emphasizing once more the importance of the news brought in by the airman already referred to, which showed a whole German Corps marching down on the extreme left of the British line.

On being asked if I had anything further to say, I added, as I had resolved to do, that I felt convinced General Lanrezac had no intention of attacking, even were he in a position to do so, which he was not.

Sir John stood and listened in silence to our reports, glancing occasionally at a map spread out on a table by his side. General Murray looked grim. When we finished speaking they made no comment. Colonel Macdonogh and I were told to go to the dining-room and wait.

Then followed one of the most painful experiences of my life. We sat down on a sofa facing the door. Round the table, the empty coffee cups pushed out of the way to make room for maps, the Chiefs of Staff of the two Corps and of the Cavalry, with one or two officers of the Commander-in-Chief's personal staff, were in animated conversation. A sickly feeling came over me as I realized that they were discussing a plan, evidently already decided upon, for a general advance upon the following day. Representatives of neighbouring units were perfecting details, arranging communications, fixing time-tables, making notes in field service books. They paid no attention to the two individuals sitting on the sofa, whose mood was so strikingly different from theirs. Round the table keenness, suppressed excitement, joy and confidence, sparkled through the ordinary technical conversation of these men who already saw themselves marching to victory on the morrow, whilst we in our corner knew that their hopes must be dashed, that the advance we had all dreamed of would not take place, that, perhaps before it could even strike a blow at the enemy, the Army, *our* Army, might be forced to retire. My depression was increased by a gnawing doubt of my own judgement. I thought of the ill-fated Nolan who had brought the order to charge to the Light Brigade at Balaclava.

We waited for what seemed to be centuries but was really only about twenty minutes. Then the door opened suddenly and General Murray stood framed against the dark hall. Looking at the officers sitting round the table, he said – "You are to come in now and see the Chief. He is going to tell you that there will be no advance. But remember there are to be no questions. Don't ask why. There is no time and it would be useless. You are to take your orders, that's all. Come on in now."

They filed out without a word, and Macdonogh and I returned to the Headquarters building.

Later that night my sense of responsibility was relieved, for, a little before midnight I believe, a French staff officer came in. Not only did he confirm what I had said, but he requested Sir John to attack in flank the German formations that were pressing the Fifth Army back from the Sambre.

This was an extraordinary request to make in view of the situation of the British, on whom, as General Lanrezac well knew, large enemy forces were descending and who were threatened with being outflanked. Sir John very properly answered that it was quite impossible for him to do what General Lanrezac asked, but, anxious to help his Ally, he told the liaison officer that he would remain in his position on the Mons Canal for twenty-four hours.

Strange as was General Lanrezac's request, it appears stranger still in view of the following facts.

At 8.30 p.m. the Fifth Army sent a report to the G.Q.G. which contained the following paragraph:

"The Cavalry Corps, in a very exhausted condition, has had to fall back under the cover of a Brigade of Infantry which was acting in support of it, and which now occupies the region of Thuin. The Cavalry Corps will only be in a position to insure the liaison with the British Army, *which is still in echelon to the rear of the Fifth Army*."

This report is completely incompatible with General Lanrezac's request to Sir John to attack. Either the British were in echelon to the rear of the Fifth Army, in which case they obviously could not attack in flank the Germans who were pressing the Fifth Army back, or they were ahead of the Fifth Army, and the report to the G.Q.G. was an absolute misrepresentation of the facts. The exact position of the British was perfectly well known at Fifth Army H.Q. They were in possession of the march tables furnished by Colonel Huguet's Mission. The XVIII. Corps had that afternoon reported that the British II. Corps would that night be level with and east of Mons (miles ahead of the French line) and that the I. Corps on the right would be just north of Maubeuge (level with the French Cavalry Corps and ahead of the XVIII. Corps). Moreover Captain Fagalde and I had both been in to Le Cateau and had reported to the Fifth Army the more recent news that the 1st Division of the I. British Corps had been ordered to continue its advance to fill the gap between the British II. Corps and the XVIII. Corps.*

All this General Lanrezac knew. Why then did the Fifth Army state that the British were behind them? It is impossible to say, but if a surmise is permissible it may be suggested that General Lanrezac felt that the G.Q.G. was becoming critical of him, and that he succumbed to the natural tendency to forestall criticism by placing the blame on others. The British Army was a convenient whipping boy. Prejudice had assigned that role to it. After all, this message was but the echo of the words noted by Huguet on August 17th "If we are beaten it will be thanks to you."†

When I reached Chimay in the early hours of the morning of the 23rd, the officer on duty told me that the return of General Lanrezac and his officers from Mettet had been tragic. There was something terrible in the look of the men who had watched over the fate of the Army all day. Helpless witnesses of those catastrophic hours, near enough to be steeped in the horror of it all, too far to feel any of the exhilaration of the battle itself, their eyes were those of men who had stared at defeat. Indeed it was easy to understand that it was a harder test of nerves to have spent the afternoon at Mettet than to have fought in any one of those units that had been so badly hammered from early morning till late at night.

The Intelligence had ascertained that two German Corps were investing Namur. It seemed that the first line of defence between the fort of Marchovelette and Marche-les-Dames had been heavily attacked and the defenders driven out, but it was recaptured later.

* "Between five and seven the 1st Division continued its march, but did not reach its billets until far into the night, the 2nd and 3rd Infantry Brigades entering Villers-Sire-Nicole and Croix-les-Rouveroy . . . between 9 and 10 p.m., whilst the 1st (Guards) Brigade on the right did not arrive at Grand Reng until 2 to 3 a.m. on the 23rd. This was a long march which tried the troops severely." – *Official History of the War*, Vol. I, p. 55.

In support of the contention that General Lanrezac must have known the dangerous position of the British, it is only necessary to quote General Lanrezac's own book. On p. 158 he says, under date of the 21st: "The only black spot is that the British will probably have on top of them very superior German forces, so that they may be forced to beat a hasty retreat, which would compel me to follow suit as quickly as possible."

If this was true on the 21st, how much more true was it on the 22nd. Lanrezac's suggestion amounted to asking the British to commit suicide.

† It is strange to read the following statement in General Lanrezac's book under the date of the 22nd:

"I decided to abandon direct liaison with the British, by Binche, because the inadequate means available would not have allowed me to make it effective: I contented myself with an indirect liaison by Maubeuge."

Note by General Lanrezac: "There was also another reason: the difficulty of assuring agreement between the British and the French; allies who did not speak the same language and had different mentalities."

Heavy as were our hearts that night, black as was the cloud that overhung us, our anxiety would have been even greater had we known of the defeat of the First and Second French Armies away in the east. But we were in complete ignorance of this, and British Headquarters did not hear of what had happened until days afterwards. I do not know whether Colonel Huguet's Mission, which had constant liaison with Vitry-le-François, had any information on the subject, but if so they kept it to themselves.

CHAPTER XII

THE CENTRE OF THE FIFTH
ARMY DRIVEN BACK

August 23rd, 1914: – I

*Philippeville – Namur's first line of defence broken through – The Fifth Army
"to spend the day reorganizing" – Joffre sends news of the Fourth Army's progress
– The real position – Joffre's report to the Minister – An opportunity for a
counter-attack by the I. Corps – Lanrezac refuses to allow Franchet d'Esperey to
attack – Sir John French offers to attack on the 24th – General Henry Wilson's
calculations.*

I LEFT Chimay at about 6 a.m., with a section of the Staff who were
accompanying General Lanrezac to Philippeville. This was to be the
advance report centre of the Fifth Army on the 23rd.

Philippeville presented a strange sight that Sunday morning. There
was a cold mist, and I was none too warm in my khaki overcoat as I
stood about on the square, watching, fascinated, one of the saddest sights
I saw during the war.

The main street, a continuation of the great *chaussée* up which
Napoleon's IV. Corps had marched to Waterloo, led into Philippeville
from the north. It ran along one side of the *place*, and was packed with
people, all going in one direction, their backs to the north. A grey mob,
grey because the black clothes most of them wore were covered with
dust, was filing endlessly by; they occupied the whole width of the road,
pouring past like a crowd returning from a race meeting, but in absolute
silence, the only sound being that of very tired feet dragging on the
pavés. Each individual in that slowly-moving mass looked the embodiment of a personal tragedy; men and women with set staring faces,
carrying heavy bundles, moving on they knew not where, formed a
background of grim despair to this or that group or individual whose
more vivid suffering seemed to illuminate that drab flow of desolation.

I can still see a couple of young girls, sisters perhaps, helping each other, hardly able to drag themselves along, the blood from their torn feet oozing through their low silk shoes: a very sick woman, who looked as if she were dying, balanced somehow on a perambulator; a paralytic old man in a wheelbarrow, pushed by his sturdy daughter; a very old, very respectable couple, who for years had probably done no more than walk arm in arm round a small garden, now, still arm in arm, were helping each other in utter bewilderment of mind and exhaustion of body down the long meaningless road. I remember too a small boy playing the man and encouraging his mother, and an exhausted woman sinking under the weight of her two babies.

And none might stop: the gendarmes pounced on any who tarried and shoved them forward. The mass of refugees must be kept on the move. If they halted they would hopelessly block the communications they were already so seriously encumbering. Later perhaps it would become necessary to drive them off the roads into the fields, to clear the way for the troops, so on they had to stagger, men and tired cattle together, with here and there a huge cart drawn by oxen, packed with children. Some of these carts must have contained the entire infant population of a village thrown in pell mell. Were their parents trudging behind, or had they fallen by the way? The column of civilians must go endlessly on, whoever might drop out or get left behind, on and on and on, a wretched, racked, miserable mass of humanity, whose motive power was fear, and whose urge was a sound, the dull rumble of guns, ominously near, growling ceaselessly to the north.

Whenever there came a particular sharp burst of artillery fire rending the air like a sudden thunder clap, the whole miserable column trembled and staggered forward, all but the oxen moving faster for a moment, then relapsing into the former slow drag.

That morning typifies war as it really is. It destroyed once and for all such illusions as any of us may still have cherished concerning what is after all only a dreary massacre, a stupefying alternation of boredom, fatigue and fear.

When those who were at Philippeville that day meet and fall to talking of old times, they always end by saying – "Do you remember the square at Philippeville?" and there is a silence, for no words are needed and none are adequate to describe that dreadful scene.

General Lanrezac was one of those who stood on the *place* and watched; he was there nearly the whole morning. In his black tunic and red breeches, black gaitered legs apart, hands behind his back, he stared. The heavy folds of his face seemed to droop more than usual. He made no comment, but I have heard it said that what he saw that morning made a deep impression on him, as indeed it did upon us all. It was whispered that the sight of those people driven forward by the wind of defeat did much to shake his confidence.

Once he was startled out of his contemplation by some gendarmes who came up, bringing a couple of Zouaves they had in charge. Although I remember well the gendarmes saying they had found these men without arms behind the lines, and the Zouaves' explanation that they had been cut off and had dropped their rifles in escaping over walls they had climbed, I have entirely forgotten General Lanrezac's decision. I can see him shake his head, then speak looking away and over the heads of the prisoners and their escort, and I remember the Zouaves being led away, that is all.

If these men were guilty it is certain that they were not typical of their units, which behaved with much gallantry. That day I saw two battalions of them which would have done credit to any army.

During the morning I was able to ascertain the position of the Fifth Army at the end of the previous day's fighting. It had been driven back to the position shown on Map VI, p. 112.

The news from Namur was bad. A night attack on the north-eastern sector had broken through the first line of defence. It was hoped that the second line would hold out, although the Belgian field artillery on the front attacked had been completely destroyed. The entry of a French regiment into the town did not appear to have counteracted the demoralizing effect upon the garrison of the retirement of the Fifth Army. General Hély d'Oissel considered the situation of the fortress to be so precarious that he told Commandant Duruy there was no point in his attempting to return to the town.

I was informed, and reported to British G.H.Q., that the Fifth Army was to spend the day in reorganizing the units that had suffered in the previous day's fighting.

It was strange how often, at this early period of the war, Commanders who had been driven out of their positions by the enemy stated their intentions of spending some time in reorganizing. These declarations invariably came from the beaten side, which found it convenient to ignore the enemy for the time being. It was remarkable that generals in circumstances which should have led them to expect the enemy to drive home his advantage, allowed themselves such delusions. The explanation is, perhaps, that it is after all natural to give oneself a chance, to trust to luck, and on the basis of just one impossibility, in this instance the assumption that the enemy would leave one alone, to build a whole structure of plans and hopes. But upon this as upon other occasions the enemy did not behave as it was hoped he would.

Soon after our arrival at Philippeville, the following message was received from General Joffre. This message was also sent to the British.

"The Fourth Army has been engaged since yesterday morning under good conditions on the general line Paliseul–Bertrix–Straimont–Tintigny–Meix-devant-Virton."

This sounded cheerful. We should all have been less happy had we known the truth, that the slight successes gained at some points had been more than counter-balanced by the serious defeat of a great part of the Fourth Army, and that its commander, General de Langle, had himself reported it was unlikely that the positions held could be maintained.* (Map IV, p. 60.)

The result of the day's fighting in the Ardennes could hardly have been worse, and in the light of the information he had, General Joffre's message can only be explained by the fact that, still blind to the numbers of the Germans in the western theatre, he refused to believe in the collapse of his plan and the defeat of his armies. His first impulse was to attribute the Fourth Army's lack of success to certain derelictions of

---

* Bertrix, Jehonville and Assenois were in the hands of the enemy. One of the divisions of the Colonial Corps had suffered a serious check, the Commander of the XVII. Corps was entirely without news of one of his divisions, which appeared to have lost almost all its artillery except three guns, whilst his other division was retiring. During the night the retreat of the Colonial and XVII. Corps had compelled that of the neighbouring corps, and many units of the Fourth Army were already south of the Semoy.

General de Langle has sent the following report to the G.Q.G.:

"Stenay, *August 23rd*, 0.55 a.m.
"All corps engaged today (22nd). General result unsatisfactory. Serious checks in the direction of Tintigny and Ochamps. Success gained before Saint Médard and at Maissin cannot be maintained. Am giving orders to hold front Houdremont–Bièvre–Paliseul–Bertrix–Straimont – Jamoigne – Meix-devant-Virton. I am sending a fuller report by an officer in a car."

"GENERAL DE LANGLE."

A further report painted a hardly more cheerful picture. The Fourth Army had been heavily defeated. General de Langle stated that the clearings of Florenville and Jamoigne could not be held long and that the corps which had suffered most must be reformed outside the wooded region in a position enabling them to command the exits of the forests.

He proposed to take up a position on the line Montmédy–Thonne-le-Thil, Puilly–Messincourt–Villers Cernay–St. Menges.

The Semoy, fordable at many points, could not be held. He stated that he must consider the possibility of a retreat beyond the Chiers and the Meuse. General de Langle complained that his troops had not been able to make effective use of their artillery in the forests.

See Appendix XXI.

duty. He still believed the Army was attacking German columns marching west across its front. General de Langle was curtly informed that there were only about three corps in front of him and that he was to resume the offensive.*

General Joffre, telegraphing to the Minister at 7 a.m., said, after describing the situation on the remainder of the front:

"We have since the day before yesterday assumed the offensive with considerable forces between the regions of Longwy and Mézières.

"In the right sector (Longwy–Virton front) [see Map III, p. 54] the action is in progress, but we are only progressing slowly in spite of a marked superiority in numbers, and although our artillery has almost everywhere silenced that of the enemy.

"In the left sector (from Virton to the Meuse) [see Maps IV, p. 60 and V, p. 94] an action is developing over ground which is in parts difficult. Here also we have a marked superiority in numbers. Our progression is, however, meeting with considerable opposition. Nevertheless the enemy whose columns we are attacking whilst they are marching westward, must be in a difficult situation.

"To the north we are still holding the Meuse about Dinant. Violent attacks have enabled the enemy to debouch from the Sambre between Charleroi and Namur. We have kept in this area strong reserves which have not yet been engaged.

"Also the British Army is coming into action on our left.

Conclusion

"In the main the strategic manœuvre is now completed.

"Its object and its result have been to place the greater part of our forces at the point where the enemy would be most vulnerable, and to insure our having at this point numerical superiority. Everything is now in the hands of the troops and their commanders, upon whom it is incumbent to take advantage of this superiority.

"The result therefore depends upon the capacity of the leaders and the quality of the troops, and above all it depends upon perseverance in execution."†

* The Fourth French Army (for composition see Appendix II) was opposed by the Fourth German Army comprising five corps.

† On the 22nd the French Government had informed General Joffre that it considered it a national danger that the important centres of Lille, Roubaix and Tourcoing should remain at the mercy of German cavalry raids. General Joffre answered by requesting that a fourth Territorial Division should be sent to General d'Amade.

We at Philippeville knew nothing of all this; we were only too anxious to believe any good news concerning the army on our right, and the G.Q.G.'s report to General Lanrezac as to the situation of the Fourth Army was taken by us all to be the restrained expression of a considerable initial success.*

As the morning wore on, it became evident that a most interesting situation had arisen on the right of the Fifth Army. Excitement grew intense as it was realized that we were at last in a position to deal the enemy a heavy blow.

What happened was this.

The early morning reconnaissances disclosed no sign of enemy activity on the immediate front of the X. Corps. This quiescence on the part of the enemy had been of the utmost value, for it had given the comparatively fresh 37th Division time to deploy, and had enabled the disorganized units and transport of the rest of the Corps to collect behind it. It also meant that the front of the I. Corps, obstructed on the previous night and evening by the men and transport of the regiments belonging to the X. Corps which had suffered most during the day's fighting, was now clear.

The I. Corps was ideally placed to take in flank the enemy facing the X. Corps. General Franchet d'Esperey, who had come to the conclusion in the early morning that the enemy must have suffered very severely in his attacks on the X. Corps on the previous day, pointed out in reporting the situation to General Lanrezac at 7.30 a.m., that if the enemy advanced against the X. Corps an attack by his own I. Corps in conjunction with the 37th Division (the only unit of the X. Corps at that moment capable of offensive action) might yield important results. (Map VII, p. 159.)

---

* On the strength of this report the following letter was sent by General Lanrezac to General de Langle de Cary:

"Philippeville, *August 23rd*, 10.15 a.m.

"The Fifth Army has been violently attacked on the front of the X. and III. Corps by enemy forces which crossed the Sambre between Charleroi and Namur.

"The X. and III. Corps have had to fall back about 4 kilometres, and the Army is now on the line Thuin–Nalinnes–Biesme–Saint Gérard. It covers the bridges at Dinant and Hastière, and is in a position to give artillery support to an action by the Fourth Army on the lower Lesse.

"If the Fifth Army is compelled to fall back farther, it will be obliged to destroy the bridges at Dinant and Hastière.

"It is therefore of the greatest importance that the left of the Fourth Army should make its action felt as soon as possible in the neighbourhood of Dinant or at least on the Lesse, so as to free the Fifth Army from the anxiety of having to guard its right against attempts of the enemy to cross the Meuse between Givet and Namur.

"LANREZAC."

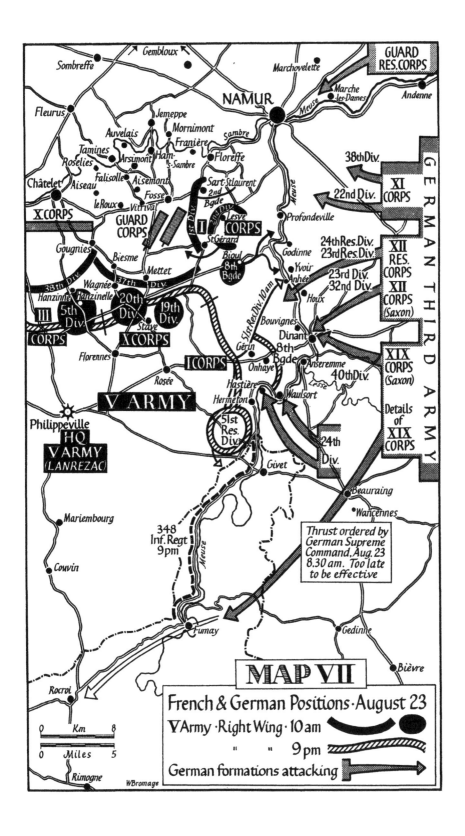

GUARD
RES. CORPS

Sombreffe · Gembloux · Marchovelette · Marche-les-Dames · Andenne

NAMUR

Meuse

38th Div.

XI CORPS

22nd Div.

Fleurus · Jemeppe · Mornimont · Auvelais · Franière · Sambre · Floreffe · Profondeville

Tamines · Ham-s-Sambre · Roselies · Arsimont · Aisemont · Aiseau · Falisolle · Châtelet · le Roux · Fosse · Vitrival · Sart-St-Laurent · 2nd · Bgde · Lesve · 24th Res. Div.

GUARD CORPS · 1st Div. · I CORPS · St Gérard · Godinne · 23rd Res. Div.

X CORPS · Gougnies · Biesme · Mettet · Bioul · 8th Bgde · Yvoir · Anhée · 23rd Div. · 32nd Div.

XII RES. CORPS

XII CORPS (Saxon)

38th Div. · Wagnée · 37th Div. · Houx

Hanzinne · Hanzinelle · 20th Div. · 19th Div. · Bouvignes

III CORPS · 5th Div. · X CORPS · Stave · Dinant

Florennes · Gérin · 8th Bgde · Anseremme · XIX CORPS (Saxon)

I CORPS · Onhaye · 40th Div.

Rosée · Hastière · Waulsort · Details of XIX CORPS

V ARMY · Hermeton

51st Res. Div.

Philippeville

HQ
V ARMY
(LANREZAC)

Givet · 24th Div. · Beauraing · Wancennes

Mariembourg

348
Inf. Regt
9pm

Couvin

Meuse

Thrust ordered by
German Supreme
Command, Aug. 23
8.30 am. Too late
to be effective

Fumay · Gedinne

Rocroi · Bièvre

MAP VII

French & German Positions · August 23
V Army · Right Wing · 10 am
"   "   9 pm
German formations attacking

Rimogne

WBromage

51st Res. Div. 10am

GERMAN THIRD ARMY

0 Km 8
0 Miles 5

To this proposal General Lanrezac gave no answer.

Very soon it became apparent that the situation was developing in the sense foreseen by General d'Esperey. At about 10 a.m., strong hostile columns were observed advancing from Fosse towards Mettet against the X. Corps. On hearing this d'Esperey immediately ordered the 2nd Division to prolong to the left the line held by the 1st Division.

Now was a unique opportunity. The Germans, in spite of heavy losses, were again pressing forward, to give the coup de grace, so they believed, to beaten troops. They were apparently quite unaware that they were advancing across the front of, and presenting their flank to, the crack corps of the Fifth Army, commanded by one of the best generals in France. The German Guard might have been smashed by the fist under whose shadow it was passing, but the blow never fell.

General d'Esperey sent Captain Malick, the Army liaison officer to the I. Corps, to Philippeville so that the position might be made clear to General Lanrezac. Malick used the strongest arguments to persuade the latter to unleash the I. Corps. He not only put forward the reasons that had been put into his mouth by General d'Esperey, but adduced others evolved in his own brilliant, eloquent, Gascon mind, all to no avail. General Lanrezac procrastinated, hummed and hawed, thought the moment not favourable. Malick left Philippeville bitterly disappointed, having failed in his mission.

It was now well on in the morning, getting on for 11 o'clock I think. The German columns were still advancing towards the X. Corps, and General d'Esperey, not receiving permission to attack, decided to manœuvre so as to minimize the risk to which the continued German advance was exposing him, whilst remaining well placed for attacking the enemy should leave be given him to do so. He could not afford to remain quiescent in his original position, for had the X. Corps retired farther, his own line of retreat might have been jeopardized. (Map VII, p. 159.)

Malick came in again before noon. He was determined, this time, to induce General Lanrezac to allow the I. Corps to attack. He jumped out of his car on the *place*, saw the General was not there, asked where he was to be found, and on being told ran across to a kind of barrack off the square, used in peacetime by the "*enfants de troupe*" of a Belgian regiment (the boys in training for the Army). There he found Lanrezac sitting in a bare room. The interview between them was stormy. Malick, young, full of fire, argued, pleaded with the Army Commander, who kept shrugging his shoulders and giving unconvincing reasons for withholding his consent, until Malick's distress changed to exasperation. Throwing all restraint and indeed even the forms of discipline to the wind, he told Lanrezac exactly what he thought. "If we retire now we shall not stop until we reach the Seine," he exclaimed, and finally burst out – "By not attacking now, *mon Général*, you are committing suicide."

Even in the light of the knowledge we now have that von Hausen's Third Army was at that very moment ready to strike across the Meuse at the right of the Fifth Army, many competent officers are of opinion, and it has always seemed to me they are right, that Franchet d'Esperey was justified in hoping for great things from the offensive he wished to see carried out that morning.

The I. Corps comprised its own two divisions, plus the 8th Brigade and the 51st Reserve Division. One division could have been spared for the attack, without, as it turned out, compromising in the least the safety of the Army. It might, with but little help from the rest of the Army, have rolled up the advancing German line, for the Germans had no reserves immediately available. As it was, von Bülow, commanding the Second German Army, although faced only by retiring troops on the Sambre, considered himself in so precarious a position that he appealed to von Hausen for help. Is it unfair to assume that the German Commander who paused and hesitated on the edge of an empty battle-field, might have called a halt to the whole advance had he been attacked with determination?*

Malick can barely have had time to rejoin his own H.Q. before we heard from him again. This time he sent a message to say that the 4th Belgian Division was evacuating Namur at midday.

At about this time a particularly violent cannonade was heard from the north. Little did we know that it was in all probability an echo of the battle taking place at that moment at Mons. General Lanrezac stopped in his walk up and down the *place*, to which he had returned, to look up and listen. Finally he ordered an officer to go up in an aeroplane and find out what was happening. The sky was now fairly clear and flying was possible. Captain Fournier, the officer entrusted with this mission, soon returned, saying he had observed nothing unusual, so with lighter hearts those who could get away trooped off in search of food.

Astonishing to say, an excellent meal was obtainable in the local hotel. It was packed as on a fair day, but the customers were all officers. The instinct to turn an honest penny was stronger than fear, so,

---

*At this period von Kluck's First Army was under the command of von Bülow, and would inevitably have been closely affected by an attack on the latter's army.

in spite of the battle, meals were cooked and served. It was surprising how often, as the war went on, women would be met with in the most unlikely places, even under shell fire, who, cheerful and unperturbed, were ready to cook a meal for hungry soldiers.

In the afternoon, at 3.10 p.m., I received over the telephone the following message from Colonel Macdonogh, with orders to transmit it to General Lanrezac. I was told that it had been dictated to Colonel Macdonogh by Sir John French himself, and was sent in answer to an inquiry by General Lanrezac as to British intentions.

"I am prepared to fulfil the role assigned to me when the Fifth Army advances to the attack. In the meantime I hold an advanced defensive position extending from Condé on the left, through Mons and Erquelinnes, where I connect with the two Reserve Divisions south of the Sambre.

"I am now much in advance of the line held by the Fifth Army, and feel my position to be as far forward as circumstances will allow, particularly in view of the fact that I am not properly prepared to take offensive action until tomorrow morning, as I have previously informed you.

"I do not understand from your wire* that the XVIII. Corps has been engaged, and they stand on my inner flank."† (Map VI, p. 112.)

The amazing thing about this message is that it proves that Sir John was unaware at the time it was sent, well on in the afternoon, that since 9 a.m. his forces had been engaged in the historic struggle to be known as the Battle of Mons. Just as Lanrezac had been ignorant for hours of the fact that the Battle of Charleroi was being waged a few miles away, so two days later French was envisaging an attack on the morrow when his Army had already been engaged for hours against very superior forces.

This message was astonishing from other points of view as well. It did not correspond with Sir John's decision of the night before to stand in his positions for twenty-four hours, nor with a very important letter concerning British intentions which Colonel Huguet had sent early

---

* No trace of this message can be found.

† In his book "1914" Sir John French inserts this message as having been despatched on the 22nd. This is a mistake, as there is no possible doubt as to its having been sent to me on the 23rd. The original text states that it was telephoned to me at Philippeville, and I was at Philippeville only on the 23rd. Further, the B.E.F. had not reached Condé by 3 p.m. on the 22nd. The 19th Brigade which prolonged the left towards Condé did not reach Valenciennes till 9 a.m. on the 23rd and then had to march on to Condé, nearly ten miles. For movements of Cavalry, see *Official History of the War*, Vol. I, p. 57.

that morning to General Lanrezac. I had not seen this letter, but was told something of its contents, which were to the effect that unless the early morning reconnaissances revealed very large forces on his front, and unless his left flank appeared to be seriously threatened, Sir John French intended to comply with General Lanrezac's request and to attack that day the flank of the German formations which were pressing back the Fifth Army.*

What could have happened to make the British Commander change his plans twice in so short a space of time? What had happened to re-assure him as to the threat to his left?

The explanation, which I only heard a long time afterwards, was really very simple: General Henry Wilson had become convinced that the right policy was to attack, and had brought the Commander-in-Chief round to his point of view. On what information General Wilson had based his conclusions, and whence this information came, will probably never be definitely known, but there seems to be little doubt that during the night he saw Colonel Huguet and that later they both conferred with Sir John. As a result of this conversation Colonel Huguet wrote the letter already referred to.†

What arguments were put forward to convince the British Com-mander-in-Chief at this interview I do not know. All that can be stated with certainty is that General Wilson was convinced that General Joffre was about to launch a series of offensives which he believed would dislocate completely the German centre, for he had adopted the French

---

* Colonel Huguet to the G.O.C. Fifth Army, Le Cateau, August 23rd, 1 a.m.:

"I have the honour to inform you that I have communicated to Marshal French the information brought me by Captain Loiseau (the officer who had brought General Lanrezac's request to attack on the previous evening).

"He asks me to say that it is difficult for him to engage his force fully without knowing what is in front of him.

"He will therefore send out aerial reconnaissances, at dawn today, north and north-west of Mons, to determine the enemy forces in the neighbourhood of Ath, Soignies, Nivelles, and he will make his decision accordingly.

"If these do not appear to be very considerable and do not threaten his left flank, he will carry out the movement you ask for: this movement might begin about midday.

"If he does not carry out this movement, he intends in any case to maintain for twenty-four hours his present position, and asks that the liaison between your army and his shall be assured by placing the reserve divisions under your command between his right, defined by the line Grand Reng, Buvrinnes, and the left of the XVIII. Corps.

                                                              "HUGUET.

"P.S. – I suggested to him that he should at least advance to the north of Mons and send his cavalry towards Ath, but he held to his decision without being willing to modify it, until he has fuller information."

† Sir John remained during the morning of the 23rd of the same mind as when Huguet left him, for at the Conference he held at Sir Douglas Haig's Headquarters at 10.30 a.m. he ordered the I. Corps to press forward.

point of view that the enemy had unduly weakened himself there in order to strengthen his right. Wilson also believed that General de Castelnau was preparing an attack on such a massive scale as was bound to insure its success. Moreover he was of opinion, which was not in agreement with the conclusions of the British Intelligence, that the enemy could not possibly oppose more than one, or at the outside two corps and one cavalry division, to the British. The miscalculation as to the German forces on the western front upon which General Wilson's arguments were based, was that of the G.Q.G. He seems to have been equally misinformed as to the French operations, for at that date, as has already been seen, the Fourth Army had been heavily defeated in its attempt to advance through the Ardennes, and Castelnau, far from preparing an offensive, had on the evening of the day before (22nd) received orders from Joffre to take up a defensive position on the Couronné of Nancy.

At the time, knowing nothing of these things, I was frankly bewildered: the night before, the decision had been taken that the British Army was to stand on the defensive; early next morning it was announced that it would attack that day if conditions were at all favourable; by the early afternoon we heard that the attack was postponed until the 24th!*

It seemed to me at the time, and I still believe, that Sir John had been led to think the Fifth Army would attack with its fresh corps on the 23rd, and only postponed his own offensive and dictated the message given above (p. 162) when he realized Lanrezac had no such intention. But he must still have believed the Fifth Army would attack on the 24th, or he would not have contemplated doing so himself.

---

* The explanation is given in General Wilson's Diary, Vol. I, p. 167. He writes under date August 23rd:

"During the afternoon I made a careful calculation that we only had one corps and one cavalry division (possibly two corps) opposite us. I persuaded Murray and Sir John that this was so, with result that I was allowed to draft orders for an attack tomorrow by Cavalry Division, 19th Brigade and II. Corps, to N.E. pivoted on Mons."

THE GERMAN THIRD ARMY ATTACKS THE I. CORPS ON THE MEUSE – LANREZAC ORDERS THE FIFTH ARMY TO RETIRE

August 23rd, 1914: – II

Von Hausen's Third Army delivers its attack across the Meuse – The German plan – The course of events on the Meuse – Hausen and Bülow – An urgent request for news from G.H.Q. – The French Cavalry Corps on its way to the British – An interview with Lanrezac – Lanrezac orders the retreat of the Fifth Army – Interview with Sir John French – The legend that the British decided to retire before the Fifth Army – Its possible source – Lanrezac's real reasons – Sir John French decides the B.E.F. must retire also.

DURING the afternoon I learned that a serious situation, how serious we did not realize at the time, appeared to be developing on the right of the Fifth Army on the Meuse. The thrust of von Hausen's Third Army, which might have proved the undoing of the Allied left wing, had been launched.

Happily the attack was so wanting in vigour, and the directing hand so nerveless, that the Fifth Army, unwarned and temporarily disorganized though it was, parried it easily. (Map VII, p. 159.)

On the 20th, the German Supreme Command had directed the Second and Third Armies to combine their operations west and south of Namur. These attacks were to have been synchronized, the two Army Commanders consulting together with a view to carrying out this operation. The combined attack was to have taken place on the morning of the 23rd, but on the 21st von Bülow, persuaded that he was only confronted by Sordet's Cavalry and small bodies of infantry, decided to take advantage of this situation by advancing without waiting for von Hausen. On the 22nd, still convinced that there were only cavalry divisions and their infantry supports on the Meuse, von Bülow determined "to seize the opportunity of the moment to throw his left wing over the Sambre that very day, occupying the extremely difficult river valley before the arrival of fresh enemy reinforcements."*† This advance led to the Battle of Charleroi.

On the 23rd, the date originally chosen by the Supreme Command for the combined advance of the Second and Third Armies, von Hausen delivered his attack on the Meuse.

All three of von Hausen's Corps which were now attacking had been identified by the French Fifth Army, and it had been supposed that they would be engaged against the Fourth Army. It was not realized that they formed part of an Army whose mission it was to drive in the Fifth Army's flank. To have thought so would have been to admit the G.Q.G.'s figures to be false.

When von Hausen's attack developed it was realized at Fifth Army Headquarters that the enemy had hit upon a vulnerable point, but that as the positions on the Meuse were naturally very strong an attack on this front could and should be held. It was also felt from the very first moment the Third German Army began its onslaught that the Saxons had no push. They fought well later, but on the Meuse they were singularly ineffective.

The situation of the Fifth Army was certainly perilous, even more so than we thought, but it might have been worse. Had the Germans let drive across the Meuse south of Givet, where the river passages were guarded only by three battalions spread over a front of about 15 miles (the enemy had known this as early as the 15th) they would certainly have got across the river. They would then have been in a position to march straight on to the communications of the Fifth Army and matters would have been serious indeed; serious, but not desperate, for the enemy could not have progressed fast through the rugged, wooded, abrupt and almost roadless country west of the Meuse. It would be a mistake to believe that had the enemy carried out this plan the Fifth Army would have been lost. It would have had to withdraw rapidly and would probably have lost a good many feathers, but it would have escaped. (Map VII, p. 159.)

---

* Bülow, *Mein Bericht zur Marneschlacht*, p. 22.

† The German Supreme Command had a very fair idea of the French forces west of the Meuse between Namur and Mézières. On the 20th the armies had been informed that these forces were estimated at four active corps, four reserve divisions, the Moroccan Division and three cavalry divisions.

Until the First German Army actually engaged the British, von Kluck knew only one thing about them, that there was a British squadron north of Mons. It was still thought that the British had disembarked at Boulogne and that they would be encountered coming from Lille.

The danger would have been far greater had the enemy thrown a large force of cavalry across the Meuse south of Givet; they would have quickly got across the wooded belt and found themselves athwart the Fifth Army's communications; fortunately this was impossible, for the I. German Cavalry Corps had been taken from the Third Army and sent north.

The actual course of events on the Meuse during the 23rd was as follows.

The Germans attacked during the night (of the 22nd) and in the early morning gained a footing on the left bank of the river. Before the measures ordered by General Franchet d'Esperey to drive them back had time to take effect, they gained further ground. Thereupon at 5 p.m., General d'Esperey decided to withdraw his Corps to the south, facing the Meuse. Whilst these orders were being carried out, General Mangin, commanding the 8th Brigade, who had been ordered to throw back the enemy over the river, reached the neighbourhood of the Meuse.* He found the Germans in occupation of the important village of Onhaye. His two battalions fixed bayonets and charged, driving the enemy helter skelter out of the place. This brilliant and timely intervention re-established the situation, which had got out of hand chiefly, it must be confessed, owing to the fact that the 51st Reserve Division had not opposed any very serious resistance to the enemy. (Map VII, p. 159.)

General d'Esperey informed General Lanrezac that he considered the danger had been exaggerated. Later, however, he reported that he was much concerned at the presence of small German detachments which had made their way into the dense and wooded country south of the Dinant–Philippeville road, but no great anxiety was felt on this score at Fifth Army Headquarters, as it was assumed that Franchet d'Esperey with his whole corps practically intact had the situation well in hand.

The immediate danger had been conjured, but what might not happen on the morrow? We at Philippeville, inevitably ignorant of the enemy's difficulties, were equally ignorant of the peril the Fifth Army had been in. If we could have spent some little time at von Hausen's elbow during the 23rd and the night of the 23rd–24th, it would have been particularly heartening.

---

* This Brigade now consisted of two battalions (three battalions had been drafted into Namur and one was on guard on the Meuse) and two cavalry regiments which were attached to it.

That Commander, far from happy at his own lack of success in cross-ing the Meuse, had been further perturbed by calls for help from von Bülow, who urged him to make every endeavour to advance across the river immediately. Things cannot be going well with the Second Army, thought von Hausen, and I have certainly failed in my objective. Then came a brighter interlude; he heard of the success of the Fourth German Army on his left and reports came in that the Fifth French Army was retiring. He thereupon resolved to advance to the south-west.* This was the dangerous direction for the Fifth Army, but the Germans were undertaking it too late. Hardly however, had von Hausen issued orders giving effect to this resolution, when a liaison officer from Bülow arrived. He reported that although the results of the day's operations had in the main been favourable, the X. German Reserve Corps had been success-fully attacked by the French. He requested, in view of the fact that the Second Army was continuing its offensive on the 24th, that the Third Army should attack immediately due west towards Mettet in support of von Bülow's left.

Von Hausen concluded that von Bülow's attack had been anything but successful, and that it was essential for the Third Army to lend him support. He reasoned that for his Army to advance south-west if the Second Army were held up would mean danger, possibly isolation. Accordingly he issued orders in compliance with von Bülow's request. This led to some confusion, but nevertheless the advance to the west was carried out in the morning and the Meuse crossed. Then it was realized that the French were in full retreat. The movement to the south-west was ordered once more, but any chance of its being effective had vanished.

*　　*　　*

To return to the immediate events of the 23rd.

At 4.55 in the afternoon I received an urgent request for news from British G.H.Q. They had had information that the X. Corps was streaming back, and expressed the gravest anxiety. It took a consider-able time to get through on the telephone from Philippeville Post

---

* The German Supreme Command did actually order von Hausen (in a wireless message received on the morning of the 23rd) to cross the Meuse south of Givet (at Fumay). Conse-quently what troops were available of the XIX. Corps were ordered to take this direction. Later when Hausen heard the Fifth Army was retiring, he ordered the whole of the XIX. Corps to advance in this direction, but the movement was abandoned when the Third Army was ordered to attack west at the call of von Bülow.

Office, which was naturally enough emptying itself rapidly of employés. I seized upon one of the few remaining clerks and absolutely refused to let him go until he had dealt with my business. His frenzied efforts led to my eventually getting through to G.H.Q. I suggested to the officer at Le Cateau to whom I spoke that aviators had in all probability mistaken the flying population for troops in retreat, as a similar mistake had been made by observers belonging to the Fifth Army earlier in the day. I was able to give a positive assurance that the X. Corps had only fallen back slightly, and that its losses appeared to be less than on the previous day.

When I came out of the Post Office, I had a strange impression. An hour or so before, the *place* had been alive with troops, bustling with Staff Officers. Now it was deserted, not a man in uniform to be seen. The civilian population seemed to have vanished also. Some belated and weary refugees were still trailing along the road, that was all. There was not a soul to say where the Fifth Army Staff had gone to. Eventually a despatch rider told me they had returned to Chimay. On arriving there I found that the Chiefs of Staff of the Corps had come in to see the Army Commander. Their reports were not pessimistic. Even the representatives of the III. and X. Corps, whilst admitting their losses to be severe, were convinced that the German losses were heavier still. With the exception of the III. Corps which needed time to reorganize, they were confident they could attack if called upon to do so.*

I had that morning sent through a message to British G.H.Q. to the effect that at last the French Cavalry Corps had been ordered to move to the left of the British, and that the order had been sent out by a car which left Philippeville at 9.45 a.m. By 4 p.m., relieved on the Sambre by the 69th Reserve Division, which took its place between the XVIII. Corps and Maubeuge, the Cavalry Corps had reached the neighbourhood of Beaufort, south of Maubeuge. The 53rd Reserve Division took up its position between the 69th Reserve Division and the British. Neither of the Reserve Divisions was attacked during the day.

Meanwhile at the 2ème Bureau reports from British sources had been received which convinced Girard that his worst fears were being confirmed, and that the Germans were closing in on the left of the Expeditionary Force. The danger Sir John was running was as clearly seen by the Intelligence of the Fifth Army as it was by Colonel Macdonogh and his Staff. It appeared evident to the 2ème Bureau as well as to some other members of the Fifth Army Staff, that not only was it out of the

* For details of fighting see Appendix XXI.

question for the British to attack to take pressure off the Fifth Army, but that the boot was, so to speak, on the other leg. The British seemed to these officers to be in such a perilous position that it was incumbent on the Fifth Army to assume the offensive, so as to delay, if it were not possible to dislocate, the German manœuvre.

Commandant Girard certainly had these considerations in mind when he asked to be received by General Lanrezac, but his purpose was to endeavour to give him a picture of the situation as he believed it must appear to the German higher command. The General consented to see him at once. Captain Fagalde accompanied him. As Intelligence officers their concern was with the enemy, and they based their arguments purely on the enemy's situation as they interpreted it. They tried to convince General Lanrezac of what they themselves were certain, that the enemy's losses in the previous day's fighting had been at least as heavy as those of the Fifth Army. They produced facts in support of their contentions, and endeavoured to impart some of their optimism to their Chief. Visualizing the condition of von Bülow's Army, they urged strongly that energetic action was certain to yield good results. The whole bias of their argument was in favour of an attack.

Lanrezac did not give a decision, and when the interview ended, neither Girard nor Fagalde nor anyone else had any idea of what he was going to do. One of these officers left his presence thinking that he was now at last inclined to attack; whereas the other gained the impression that he had been convinced by their arguments, but that his strong personal inclination was to do nothing.

Girard and Fagalde seem to have had a real intuition of the German position. Viewed from the French side, the enemy appeared successful and threatening, but, as we have seen, neither von Bülow nor von Hausen considered they had any reason for satisfaction. Whether General Lanrezac was right or wrong in the decisions he took, one cannot but admire these officers, who were representative of a large section of the Fifth Army Staff, for absolutely refusing to accept defeat or to be cowed and dispirited by reverses.

*   *   *

The evening dragged wearily on. One of the few incidents which broke the monotony was the arrival of a group of Belgian officers from Namur. They belonged to the garrison of the fortress, not to General Michel's Division. They arrived by car and were black with dust and much shaken. Their presence ahead of their men was unexplained, and their descriptions of terrific bombardments were received coldly by their French audience.

Little fresh information was received from the Corps, save that the liaison officer of the III. Corps reported it to be in considerable confusion, and General d'Esperey notified General Lanrezac that he had issued orders to his Corps to hold itself in readiness to assume the offensive next day.

The line reached by the Army that night is shown on Map VI, p. 112.

Presently, probably at about 9 p.m., the atmosphere of sickening inactivity and apprehension was disturbed by a current of suppressed excitement. There was a coming and going of liaison officers. Then, if I remember rightly, the whole of the Staff or at any rate many of its members, were called in to the General's room. It looked either as if some decision of importance had been taken, or an order from the G.Q.G. had come in.

The minute the conference was over I asked for information, and was told General Lanrezac was about to issue orders to the Fifth Army to retire.*

Whatever the reason for this decision, it seemed impossible that he really intended to fall back without reference to the British. They were much in advance of his Army and he knew they were preparing for offensive action on the following morning. To retire without consulting them was to abandon them to certain destruction. Yet that was apparently exactly what he was proposing to do.

It was obviously vital to warn the British Commander-in-Chief at the earliest possible moment, so without having been able to obtain an explanation or a direct message of any kind, verbal or otherwise, for Sir John, I drove to Le Cateau as quickly as a fast car could go.

At Le Cateau I saw Sir John French. In his book "1914" he gives the following account of the interview I had with him that night:

"At about 1 a.m. on the 24th Spears came in from the Headquarters of the Fifth French Army and told me they were seriously checked all along the line. The Third and Fourth French Armies were

---

* These orders were to the effect that the Fifth Army, which was holding the line Anthée–Florennes–Walcourt–Thuin, was to retire to the line Givet–Philippeville–Merbes-Le-Château, and that the movement was to begin at 3 a.m. (on the 24th). The Reserve Divisions were to hold the Sambre from Hautes Wiheries to Maubeuge. The H.Q. of the Fifth Army was to move to Aubenton.

retiring, and the Fifth French Army, after its check on Saturday, was conforming to the general movement."

I have no precise recollection of the details of this interview, but I think that Sir John is mistaken as to the time of my arrival at Le Cateau. My memory is that I was there much earlier than 1 a.m., probably about 11.

I cannot have been as emphatic as he says concerning the retreat of the French Third and Fourth Armies, because I did not know of it. What I think happened was that, not knowing why General Lanrezac had decided to retire, I hazarded the guess that he might have had bad news from the Armies on his right. That the news concerning the French centre was bad was only too true, but it was not the reason of General Lanrezac's decision, for he only heard it at 2 a.m. on the 24th.*

Much has been written and many theories have been advanced to explain this decision. It has even been said that General Lanrezac was compelled to fall back because the British Commander-in-Chief had previously decided to do so. This is simply absurd. Sir John French did not resolve to retire until after General Lanrezac had issued his orders.

What may have given birth to this legend is that General Sordet telegraphed at 8 p.m., to General Lanrezac as follows:

"British Army after engagement Mons has asked to cross Maubeuge to withdraw to front Bavai–Maubeuge. Shall I keep to my mission on its left?"

* General Lanrezac states in his book that he heard of the retreat of the Fourth Army at the same time that the news came in of the German attack on the Meuse. This must be a mistake, for there is not the least trace of such a communication. The conversation which took place between the Fourth and Fifth Armies at 2 a.m. on the 24th, which was as follows, bears every sign of being the first news the Fifth Army had of what was happening on the front of the Fourth Army:

Telephone conversation between Fourth Army (General Maistre, Chief of Staff) and Fifth Army.

"Our offensive towards the north has been defeated. A check in the centre has compelled the Fourth Army to give ground.

"To the question: Is it possible to give the line the Army is to retire to, more particularly as regards the left?

"(Answer): The Fourth Army is retiring to the Meuse, its left approximately on Mézières."

As will be seen (p. 173), General Lanrezac in giving the reasons for his decision to retire did not mention the retreat of the Fourth Army. If he had known the real situation he would probably have taken steps to withdraw his Army on the afternoon of the 23rd, and he would certainly have invoked the defeat of his neighbour as one of the major reasons for his own retirement.

This telegram was sent under a misapprehension, an inquiry by the British as to the possibility of crossing Maubeuge to take up a position farther south in case it was necessary to do so being mistaken for a statement that they were actually going to withdraw. It had not arrived when General Lanrezac issued his orders. (He answered it at 11.30 p.m. telling Sordet his mission was maintained.)

As a matter of fact, General Lanrezac gave the G.Q.G. his reasons for retiring, and they were perfectly clear. In the afternoon General Joffre had asked his opinion of the situation; he also inquired of him what Field Marshal French's opinion was, and what support the British could give the Fifth Army. At 9.30 p.m. Lanrezac answered the Commander-in-Chief's inquiry by the following telegram:

"The III. Corps, attacked at 4 p.m., did not hold its ground and has fallen back to Walcourt. Enemy threatens my right on the Meuse: an infantry detachment which crossed the river north of Hastière has succeeded in occupying Onhaye.* Givet threatened, Namur carried.† In view of this situation and the delay of the Fourth Army have decided to withdraw Army tomorrow to the front Beaumont–Givet."

It will be seen that in this message the withdrawal was attributed to its real and only cause, the situation of the Fifth Army itself. General Joffre's request for information as to Sir John French's views was left unanswered.

According to General Wilson‡ Sir John French only gave up the idea of an offensive on the 24th on hearing from the G.Q.G. at 8 p.m. on the 23rd that he was faced by overwhelming odds.§ Even then he did

---

* General d'Esperey's report to General Lanrezac that Mangin's Brigade had re-occupied Onhaye was only despatched at 11.30 p.m. that night.

† Namur did not surrender until the 25th, but the evacuation of the fortress by the field troops meant that the fall of the town would be only a question of hours.

‡ See *Sir Henry Wilson, His Life and Diaries*, Vol. I, p. 167.
"I was allowed to draft orders for an attack tomorrow (*i.e.* 24th) by Cavalry Division 19th Brigade, and II. Corps, to N.E. pivoted on Mons. Just as these were completed (8 p.m.) a wire came from Joffre to say we had two and a half corps opposite us. This stopped our attack, and at 11 p.m. news came that the Fifth Army was falling back still further."

§ The numbers the G.Q.G. thought might attack the British were three corps and two cavalry divisions. Actually, the First German Army, now engaged against the British, consisted of five corps plus a cavalry corps, and the VII. Corps of the Second German Army was also descending on the British forces.
Of these five corps, the II. was about Grammont, and the IV. Reserve did not take part in the battle. The actual forces opposed to the British were therefore the VII. Corps against the I. British Corps, and the IX., III. and IV. against the II. British Corps.

not decide to fall back, for at 8.40 p.m. he sent the following message to
the II. Corps:

> "I will stand the attack on the ground now occupied by the troops.
> You will therefore strengthen your position by every possible means
> during the night."

He only decided at midnight, after receiving my report, that as
General Lanrezac had issued orders to the Fifth Army to retire he must
withdraw his own force also.

These facts dispose once and for all of the legend that it was the
British decision to withdraw that compelled Lanrezac to follow suit.
General Lanrezac's decision was no doubt inevitable, in view of the
G.Q.G.'s dispositions and his own failure as a Commander. His Army
was beaten, and its position was even worse than he thought, for he did
not know of what had befallen the Fourth Army. But all this was no
excuse for his complete disregard of the British.

CHAPTER XIV

RETROSPECT

WITH the orders for retreat issued to their respective Armies by Sir John French and General Lanrezac, the battles of Mons and Charleroi ended. The British and French were now to retire, as they had fought, with but little reference to each other.

From that night the estrangement between the two Commanders, begun at Rethel, which had already had such serious results for both Armies, developed into a resentful antagonism.

The Englishman felt he had been badly let down, and ceased to trust the Commander of the Fifth Army. That he had some grounds for a belief that grew into a set conviction will probably be readily conceded, however much the result may be deplored. He had done his very best to play his part in General Joffre's plan, and, knowing something of the danger of his position, he had run grave risks to give what support he could to his neighbour. He had believed General Lanrezac would stand by the British as he himself had stood by the French. General Lanrezac, on the other hand, had known for days that the enemy was slipping across his front and making for the British. Under the date August 21st he writes in his book: "The one black spot is that the British are probably going to be attacked by superior forces; they might therefore be obliged to retire somewhat rapidly, which would compel me to do likewise as quickly as possible." Yet he never attempted to interfere in any way with the attack he tells us he saw coming, and did nothing to mitigate the blow. His retirement, leaving the British in the lurch, was a final and complete disillusionment for Sir John.

The narrow escape of the British Expeditionary Force is a matter of history. Now that the facts are known, it appears miraculous that the British should have slipped out of the gigantic embrace of the German right wing. There was an element of luck in this escape; the warning of the G.Q.G. came just in time, the reports of our own Intelligence having been disregarded; but what really saved the Army was the magnificent gallantry of the troops, who gave such a good account of themselves in this their first encounter with the enemy. Three and a half German divisions attacked the British 3rd Division, and two and a half divisions attacked the British 5th Division. Yet the only consequence of this overwhelming onslaught was that an unfavourable advanced position on the Mons Canal was evacuated, and the troops were able to withdraw to the main position a mile or two in the rear without undue difficulty, at a total cost of some 1,600 all ranks and two guns.

The British leaders would have been even better satisfied had they realized that the determined stand of their troops, and the severe punishment inflicted on the Germans, resulted in delaying the enemy's advance for one whole precious day.

The French Fifth Army, on the other hand, had on the evening of the 23rd completed its third day of hard fighting, and its losses had been incomparably higher than those of the British. The Army consisted of ten active and three reserve divisions, one extra brigade and the Cavalry Corps (three divisions). The greater part of this force had not been engaged until that afternoon (23rd) and the brunt of the fighting till then had been borne by only two corps (six divisions) the III. and X., which had been opposed by two German Corps, the X. and the Guard (four divisions). That is, 100,000 Frenchmen were attacked by 80,000 Germans.*

These figures show that during the first two days of the Battle of Charleroi a smaller number of Germans drove back a larger number of Frenchmen. Since nothing could have been more gallant than the behaviour of the French troops, the conclusion must be that at this stage of the operations the French were neither so well trained nor so well led as the Germans.†

By the afternoon of the 23rd, the balance of forces had changed in favour of the Germans. On the right, von Hausen's three Saxon Corps came into play, whilst the German VII. Corps began to advance towards the gap between the British and French Armies, (but distinctly heading towards the British right). This increase in the weight of the German attack occurred at the moment when the Fifth Army was weakened by the transfer of the Cavalry Corps to the British left, but on

---

* Compare with this the fine performance of the French Cavalry in a delaying action against the German X. Reserve Corps which was moving up to take its place in the German line on the right of the X. Corps. In this action 13,500 cavalrymen, of whom only two-thirds would be available in the firing line, plus some 7,000 infantry, opposed 40,000 Germans.

† See Appendix XXII.

the other hand the two Reserve Divisions had come up in the area vacated by the Cavalry. (Maps VI, p. 112 and VII, p. 159.)

The forces opposed to the Fifth Army on the 23rd were the X. Reserve X. Guard and von Hausen's three Corps, that is twelve German divisions were matched against eleven French divisions and one brigade.*†‡

Although the casualties of the French, due more to bad tactical employment of the troops than to anything else, were heavy, they undoubtedly inflicted severe losses on the enemy,§ and even on the 23rd there was not such a disproportion in the total opposing numbers as in itself to compel retreat. Yet the strategic position of the Allied left wing would have made retreat sooner or later inevitable.

In what follows I shall attempt to show that the retirement would have taken place under far better conditions for both French and British had General Lanrezac acted differently. I shall probably be held to be very much prejudiced, but I can only write of what I know. When I first arrived at Fifth Army H.Q. I had the most implicit faith in the Army Commander. At the end of the Battle of Charleroi I was living in agonized anticipation of what would happen next, watching every move in fear that the safety of the British would be further jeopardized.

*   *   *

It will be readily conceded that there were ample grounds for despondency.

The Fifth Army, comprising over a quarter of a million men, had marched to the Sambre under orders to strike a powerful blow at the enemy; it had been itself attacked by a force of approximately equal strength, and was now acknowledging its defeat by retreat.

---

* The 8th Brigade, attached to the I. Corps.

† As neither the VII. German Corps nor the VII. Reserve Corps, nor General Valabrègue's two Reserve Divisions were engaged, they are left out of this calculation, as are the German Guard Reserve and XI. Corps, which had been engaged against Namur and were transferred to Russia as soon as the fortress fell on the 25th.

‡ It should of course be borne in mind that the real fighting took place on the Sambre front between the German X. Reserve, X. and Guard Corps, and the French XVIII., X., and III. Corps. Only one division of the I. Corps was slightly engaged. On the Sambre therefore nine French Divisions fought six German ones. Hausen's Corps were opposed by the 51st Reserve Division and a part of Mangin's 8th Brigade.

§ The German Second Army acknowledged the loss of 11,000 men, but reckoned the French casualties far higher. It claimed to have taken 4,000 prisoners and thirty-five guns on the Sambre.

It is not disputed that the original errors of the French Higher Command were primarily responsible for the dangerous situation in which the Fifth Army found itself. But General Lanrezac's decision to retire was not due to the fact that, with profound military insight, he had realized these errors and understood the real position of the Allied left. There is absolutely nothing to show that on the eve of Charleroi he grasped the true situation any more than did the G.Q.G. There is no statement or order from him at the time that gives any sign of such knowledge. On the contrary, on his own showing he retired simply because his Army was beaten.

The battle itself was fought without any controlling authority. As it developed, General Lanrezac became obsessed as to what might happen to his right, which was *"en l'air"* it was true, but rested on a river the enemy was only able to cross in force when there was no longer any danger in his doing so. He was strangely indifferent concerning his left, where stood 80,000 Englishmen whom he abandoned to their fate without the least warning when he decided he must seek safety in retreat.

If General Lanrezac had had that confidence, courage and faith without which true leadership is impossible, he would, when the enemy attacked him, have imposed his will on his subordinates, co-ordinated their actions, and hurled his reserves against an enemy no stronger than he was, and upon whom had lain the onus of attacking powerful positions.

Even after the first enemy success on the 22nd, he could have selected a position farther back where he could have accepted battle, say on the 24th, in liaison with the British. A determined stand, even though a short one, would under the circumstances have been infinitely better than what actually happened.

The following are the main considerations affecting General Lanrezac's leadership up to the night of the 23rd, when the order to retreat was issued. For the sake of clarity they are arranged under separate heads.

I. In the early days of the campaign, General Lanrezac impressed all with whom he came in contact by his vigour and energy. The modifications he suggested in the Generalissimo's orders, which resulted in the Fifth Army's moving up to the Sambre, were wise and far-seeing, and were willingly agreed to by the latter. These modifications were based on an analysis of the situation which was certainly more acute than that of the G.Q.G.

But as the moment of crisis approached, the enemy loomed ever more formidable in General Lanrezac's eyes, while his mistrust of his own troops grew.

II. We have seen that when the Fifth Army neared the Sambre General Lanrezac was in no hurry to embark upon aggressive action. It can justifiably be held that he was right not to advance until the British were level with him and the Fourth Army had gained some ground on his right. This was the view he put forward to General Joffre on the 21st, and the latter left him free to judge when he could assume the offensive.

But here the question arises as to whether he had taken all possible steps to be in a position to attack as soon as possible in conformity with Joffre's plan. In this connection the importance of holding the industrial area of Charleroi has been dealt with; but there is another relevant consideration.

When orders to advance on the 21st were sent him, General Lanrezac pointed out that he had to leave a Corps (the I.) on the Meuse, to protect his right flank until the Fourth Army had crossed the Lesse. But would it not have been more in conformity with the plan of the French Higher Command had he grouped his forces for an offensive and endeavoured to secure the protection of his right flank without immobilizing his best Corps?

The line of advance laid down for the Fourth Army was far distant from the Fifth Army, and lay over country which General Lanrezac well knew to be extremely difficult. It was therefore at least possible that the advance of the Fourth Army would be slow and laborious. Under these circumstances it would have been normal for General Lanrezac, had he been determined to act offensively, to have provided for the safety of his right flank without depriving himself of the I. Corps. He had the means to do this. Had the three Reserve Divisions been sent to the Meuse as soon as they came under the orders of the Fifth Army on the 15th August, they could have reached the river on the 19th or 20th. Had they been made responsible for the defence of the river this would have been quite within their capacity. At this date they were hardly in a fit state to be effective in field operations, but they were perfectly capable of giving a good account of themselves on the defensive. They could have prepared a defensive position on the Meuse which might have been made well nigh impregnable.*

It may be argued that the 51st Reserve Division did not do so particularly well on the Meuse, and that there is no reason to suppose that the others would have done better, but in fairness to the 51st Division it must be remembered that it had only relieved the I. Corps on the 22nd and had not had time to organize itself. Moreover it suffered a great disability from being employed independently of its group, which had an excellent staff without whose controlling hand the 51st Division was rather lost. Had the whole Group been sent to the Meuse it could have been further strengthened by being given some of the heavy artillery of the Army, which was not used either there or on the Sambre. Von Hausen, who did so badly against a single Reserve Division spread out over eleven miles or so, would have achieved little or nothing against the three of them in positions they had had time to organize, under effective control and supported by a powerful artillery commanding the river passages†

III. General Lanrezac's lack of activity whilst the Fifth Army was marching north has been commented upon. He did not study the ground over which he might have to attack, or where the enemy might assault him. He did not make himself known to his Army, nor take advantage of the time available to gauge the value of commanders and

* If it be advanced that the Reserve Divisions could not be employed on the right because their support had been offered to the British, the answer surely is that in fact one division was actually sent to the right, and that on the 20th General Joffre suggested that another should be drafted into Namur. No one therefore considered there was any obligation to leave the Reserve Divisions on the left flank for the sake of the British.

† It is interesting to see what General Lanrezac himself has to say on the subject. In his book (p. 117) he publishes an order which he says he wrote on the 20th (incidentally no trace of this order can be found, and it is probably published in error: nevertheless it may be taken to show what his memory of the time was).

In this order it is stated that "the two Reserve Divisions of General Valabrègue will remain in rear and to the left of the XVIII. Corps to maintain liaison with the British."

(The order which General Lanrezac actually issued on the 20th ordered the two Reserve Divisions to advance in three stages to a position south and slightly east of Maubeuge.)

General Lanrezac states that the order he gives in his book was only sent out on the 21st. Now on the morning of that day the British had far outdistanced General Valabrègue's command, the nearest British units being some 15 kilometres to the north of it. There was no question therefore of liaison. The Reserve Divisions were well to the rear, and perfectly useless for that purpose.

This is probably the only case in history where at a decisive moment a commander thought of employing 36,000 men for the specific duty of keeping in touch to the rear with an army that was at the front. According to General Lanrezac himself, he was groping about behind him with the limp hand of his Reserve Divisions for the British who were jostling at his elbow.

of units. If he lacked faith in his troops, and it is only necessary to read his book to see how true this is, it was all the more necessary that he should endeavour by the greatest personal activity to remedy those defects which loomed so large in his eyes.

IV. When the Fifth Army was drawn up on the Sambre, it was in an exceptionally favourable position either for attack or defence, but General Lanrezac neither attacked nor organized himself for defence. Some orders were given to "organize positions" but these were vague and no steps were taken to see that they were carried out.

V. None knew better than General Lanrezac the great and invariable principles of war, yet he allowed the enemy to dominate him and impose battle upon him. He knew where he would meet the enemy; his zone of action lay within a clearly delimited area, his right and centre were covered by great rivers, his left by an Allied Army. Two extra divisions had been given him, the 37th and 38th, magnificent fighting units, which could have constituted an ideal Army Reserve, yet as we have seen he fought the battle without any reserves at all. His heavy artillery could have been so distributed as to cover the passages of the Meuse and the Sambre. If he had placed the Reserve Divisions on the Meuse, thus recovering at least one if not both divisions of the I. Corps, he could have attacked the enemy in flank after he had crossed the Sambre. But he did none of these things.

VI. His personal activity during the Battle of Charleroi was reduced to a minimum. The only Commander he saw whilst it was in progress was General Desforges, commanding the X. Corps.

VII. Little can be said in defence of his relations with the British. He viewed them with a mixture of distrust and suspicion. His profound indifference to what befell them save as it concerned his own command, and his disregard of that honourable understanding which makes soldiers stand by each other, could have but one result, a complete breakdown in co-operation, which profoundly affected the early stages of the campaign.

END OF PART I

PART TWO

*THE RETREAT
AND
THE BATTLE OF THE MARNE*

CHAPTER I

THE FIRST DAY OF THE RETREAT

August 24th, 1914 – I

General Lanrezac informed that the British will retire on their lines of communication if their left is threatened – The retreat of the Fifth Army to continue – Sir John French and Maubeuge – The Cavalry Corps to proceed immediately to the left of the British – A typical day's fighting during the retreat – The French Higher Command and the fighting capacity of the French soldier – Joffre's darkest hour – His report to the Minister for War – Measures to stem the enemy advance – The Belgian bank notes – The Chief of Staff of the Belgian 4th Division – Reports from the Fifth Army liaison officers.

AFTER reporting the retirement of the Fifth Army to Sir John on the night of the 23rd, I was told by General Murray to remain until a decision was taken. I hung about until the Chiefs of Staff, who had been summoned to Le Cateau, had been given their orders and had driven off again. (They came in at about 1 a.m. and were told that the Commander-in-Chief had decided upon a general retreat of about eight miles southwards.* No orders for this retreat were issued, the two Corps being told to make all arrangements between themselves.†) (Map VI, p. 112.)

Sir John's decision, and the line to which the Army was to retire, were communicated to me verbally. I was also told, to my great concern, "that I was to make it quite clear to General Lanrezac that should the left flank of the British Army be seriously threatened, the Commander-in-Chief intended to retire on his lines of communication, in

---

* To an east and west line from La Longueville through Bavai to La Boisserette.

† Extract from Sir Horace Smith-Dorrien's *Memories of Forty-eight Years' Service*, p. 387.
"At about 11 p.m. a message from G.H.Q. summoned my chief staff officer to Army Headquarters at Le Cateau, about thirty miles away, and it was past 3 a.m. when Forestier-Walker returned to my headquarters to say that the Commander-in-Chief had, in view of fresh information, decided that instead of standing to fight, the whole B.E.F. was to retire. I naturally asked him for the plan of retirement, and was told that G.H.Q. were issuing none, though he had gathered that the idea was for the I. Corps to cover the retirement of the II., but that I was to see Haig and arrange a plan with him."

which case General Lanrezac must look after his own left flank, as the British would no longer hold themselves responsible for covering it." Realizing its importance I wrote this message down.

It was some time after dawn when I arrived at Chimay. Duruy, the officer on duty, was asleep on a bed, his cloak thrown over him, a blue forage cap drawn down over his ears. He sat up as I entered, and I told him my news. He looked very grave. "The General should be told at once," he said.

We went over to the Château and walked straight upstairs to General Lanrezac's bedroom, which was in pitch darkness, both light and air being excluded. Duruy walked across the room, gingerly feeling his way along the shaft of light from the open door, and drew back the heavy curtains. The General jumped out of bed fully clad save for boots and tunic, and listened in silence to my message, which I delivered standing at attention. It did not take long. We waited a moment to see if he would make any comment, but he did not utter a word, so we saluted and walked out of the dark silent house into the daylight, in our minds the picture of a big heavy man, sitting on his bed, gazing absorbedly at the carpet at his feet.

I was relieved that the General had taken this severe blow so quietly, and grateful to him for not making me the victim of the message I bore. He might so easily have been explosive. Upon many occasions he had been caustic at the expense of the British, affecting to lump them in with Territorials, Reservists, and other by-products of the French military system, for which he had no use whatever, but now, faced with a situation that might easily lead to the parting of the ways between the two Armies, he had nothing to say. It may even have occurred to him, as he weighed the situation, that in disregarding his British neighbours he had made a mistake that might cost him dear.

The prospect opened up by the possibility of the British retiring along their lines of communication was a serious one. General Lanrezac now knew of the defeat of the Fourth Army. There was a big gap between it and his own forces, which would require careful watching. He could not possibly keep in touch with the British if they withdrew on Amiens at an angle of 45° to his own line of retreat in touch with the Fourth Army.

Although the British Commander-in-Chief had every reason to consider himself aggrieved, a withdrawal towards Amiens was not likely to help matters. Happily the British did not adopt a plan which would have been as dangerous to themselves as to the Fifth Army. What could be better, from the enemy's point of view, than to find the small British

Army isolated, so that it would either fall an easy prey to superior forces, or be masked whilst the First and Second German Armies fell on the French left?

There is some similarity between this contemplated action and the desperately anxious moment when in '18 the Germans tried to drive a wedge between the French and British Armies. They staked their all then on separating the French from the English, realizing that victory, final and absolute, would be theirs if they succeeded. Had we in 1914 done voluntarily what the enemy tried to force us to do four years later, the result might not have been fatal to Great Britain, since only the advanced guard of her forces were engaged, but the isolation and possible destruction of the B.E.F., and the consequences this would have entailed on the French Armies, would certainly have been disastrous to the Allied cause.

General Lanrezac's anxiety for his left would have been further increased had he known that but a few hours before von Bülow had ordered von Kluck to direct the IX. and III. German Corps to the west of Maubeuge, whence they were to carry out an enveloping attack against the left of the Fifth Army. This order was, however, never executed, for these corps had been engaged for some eighteen hours in fighting the British, who had thus saved the French left.

*   *   *

I went back to the *Athénée* and lay down on a bed in the Hall. After an hour or two of sleep the bustle of staff officers and orderlies coming and going awakened me. Outwardly nothing was changed. Everyone appeared to be calm and businesslike as usual, but there was a difference. So far, the prevailing feeling of optimism had been unshaken, but now, faced with the grim reality of retreat, each man felt that there was little left upon which to hang his optimism. Resolute they all were, but confident no longer.

I remember how, in those very bad days, hope, finding little comfort on the western front, turned despairing eyes towards Russia.

On this or the following day the liaison officer from the G.Q.G. must have dropped a hint that things were going well in the east, that great news might be expected. I do not know if he imparted the information received at the G.Q.G. that ten Russian armies were mobilized, seven of which were already engaged, and that two of these were to march on Berlin, but I do know that the worse things seemed on our front, the more hope centred in Russia. We should not forget the gratitude we owe to the distant and shadowy Muscovite for the great dollops of morale he poured out in generous doses to despairing souls on the western front.

All the steadfastness that could be mustered at Fifth Army Head-quarters was needed that morning, when it transpired that owing to the retreat of the Fourth Army to the Meuse, General Lanrezac had decided to continue his own retreat to the line Rocroi–Avesnes, and so informed General Joffre.*

General Joffre answered at 9.35 a.m.:

"The Fifth Army will manœuvre in retreat, resting its left on the fortress of Maubeuge, and its right against the wooded hills of the Ardennes.

"Keep in touch with the Fourth Army, which is withdrawing its left behind the Meuse, and is trying to keep in touch with you by its Cavalry towards Rocroi and Rimogne. Continue to maintain liaison with British Army." (Map VI, p. 112.)

But before receipt of this message General Lanrezac had given up all idea of resting his left on Maubeuge, and had notified the Governor by a wireless message in cipher that he must take all necessary measures for the defence of the fortress, which the Fifth Army would no longer cover.

Whilst General Lanrezac, who never forgot 1870, feared fortresses as a fox who has once been caught fears traps, the British Commander-in-Chief was sorely tempted to withdraw his Army into Maubeuge.

It is astonishing that this should have been so, for during the con-centration of his Army he had visited the place. The forts were old-fashioned and quite close to the town, which was a shell-trap. Trees and

* Cipher telegram from Fifth Army to G.Q.G., Chimay, August 24th, 6 a.m.:
"Violent fighting resumed yesterday evening, particularly on the fronts of the XVIII., III., and I. Corps. British Army informs me that it is retiring on line La Longueville–Valenci-ennes, and that in the event of its left flank being threatened it will retire on Amiens.
"On account of retreat of Fourth Army on Meuse will continue withdrawal towards line Rocroi–Avesnes.
"Please let me know the direction I am to retire to in case I have to fall back further."

To this the G.Q.G. replied in the evening as follows:
"Vitry, August 24th, 10.15 p.m.
"In the event of your being compelled to continue your withdrawal, the movement should be carried out in the zone indicated below:
"Between the line Maubeuge–Landrecies–Le Cateau– Bohain inclusive to the west, and the line Rocroi–Signy-l'Abbaye–Chaumont-Porcien inclusive to the east.
"This is merely for your information so that you can draw up your orders accordingly should the necessity arise.
"H. BERTHELOT."

woods everywhere obstructed the field of fire. Sir John may have thought
the Governor, who was active and efficient, had had time to remedy
some of these defects and had prepared gun emplacements and dug
trenches, but General Fournier had been unable in the time available to
do much in the way of making good the long years of systematic neglect
of the fortress.

Sir John often spoke to me in after years of the lure of the fortress, so
inviting, so protective with its belt of forts. It had loomed out of the fog
of war like a safe and welcoming haven in the eyes of the leader of the
small British force, who saw his command assailed in front by greatly
superior numbers, his left flank threatened, his Ally melting away to his
right. Why not take refuge in Maubeuge? As he reflected, so he told me,
faintly, insistently, a sentence, not clear at first but demanding attention,
began to echo in his memory. What was it he wanted to remember?
How did the sentence go? Suddenly he had it. It was a phrase out of old
Hamley's "Operations of War," read many years before; he did not
remember the exact words, but the sense of it was clear: "The Commander of a retiring Army who throws himself into a fortress acts like
one who, when the ship is foundering, lays hold of the anchor." Whether
Sir John took this as a warning, or whether the image evoked gave him a
truer picture of the situation, I do not know, but the fact remains, and
he often said so, that suddenly the fortress appeared to him as nothing
but a snare; the mirage of safety faded, the illusion of a place of refuge
vanished, and Maubeuge seemed to cry out: "I am Metz, would you be
another Bazaine?"

Psychologically the story is interesting, and two points arise out of it
which appear worthy of notice. The first is that had Hamley chosen an
image less vivid to express his meaning, it would probably not have
remained engraved in Sir John's memory. The second is that Lieutenant-
General Sir Edward Bruce Hamley is to be envied by all his countrymen:
it has been the privilege of many to serve their country in their lifetime,
but it has been the fortune of few to render a great service after death, to
stand invisible yet potent across a road leading to disaster and defeat.

*   *   *

To return to Chimay on the fateful morning of the 24th; General
Lanrezac, considering it necessary to fall back still farther, issued orders
at 10 a.m. to retire to the line La Capelle–Hirson–Mézières. In this
order, Sordet's Cavalry Corps was instructed to fall back *on the following*

day (25th) to Landrecies, keeping in touch with the right of the British. An absolute undertaking had been given Sir John that the Cavalry was on its way to cover his left, and we have seen that on the afternoon of the 24th it was already south of Maubeuge. This order would therefore have been a breach of faith with Sir John had it not been justified by his message to General Lanrezac that he might consider it necessary to fall back on his lines of communication, in which case the Cavalry would be badly needed on the left of the Fifth Army. Happily an hour or two later General Lanrezac changed his mind and sent off a further telegram requesting the Reserve Divisions to pass on to the Cavalry Corps an order to proceed as soon as possible to the left of the British. Later in the day General Lanrezac was notified that the Cavalry was to come under General Joffre's direct orders as from the 25th. (Map VI, p. 112 and XIII, p. 360.)

But it was one thing for General Joffre to issue an order to the Cavalry and quite another for it to be carried out: he had only a vague idea where it was, and at times lost it completely. On the 25th he sent a message to the Governor of Maubeuge – "Are you in touch with the Cavalry Corps? If so transmit urgently to it the Commander-in-Chief's order to go to the left of the British as soon as possible."

It was strange how often cavalry corps got mislaid during the war of movement. The Germans were even more careless than ourselves in this respect.

But General Sordet was not lost for long. That splendid little soldier never got rattled in the welter of contradictory orders he received. Somehow he brought his exhausted horses round the back of the British Army, and made a most welcome appearance on the left of their line on the evening of the 24th.

The explanation of the decision to fall back to the line La Capelle–Hirson–Mézières was the necessity of gaining elbow room for the Army, and above all to give the 75s a good field of fire. From now on this was to be the guiding principle, amounting almost to an obsession. I was told a dozen times by General Lanrezac that "our men are not sufficiently trained at present to stand up on equal terms against the Germans. On the other hand our field artillery is far superior to theirs, so our guns must do the work, they must do the fighting." So we fell back, for ever seeking ideal artillery positions.

Unfortunately, as the Germans began to realize the cost of attacks in close formation they offered fewer and fewer targets to the really formidable 75s, and made more and more use of their heavy artillery, which was as superior to that of the French as were the 75s to the German field guns. During the retreat, a typical day's fighting often consisted in being smothered all day by heavy shells from invisible German batteries, presumably out of range of our guns, and against which they could do nothing. There was always a generous interval for lunch, then the shelling would start again. It was maddening, all the more so that whenever any of our batteries did open fire they seemed to be located immediately by one of the ubiquitous *Taubes*. So the long day wore on, the constant shelling slowly exhausting the men's nerves. And all the time no sign of a single German. It was only when the long shades of evening lengthened on the plain that there seemed to be a movement as of hardly discernible shadows: far away along hedges and beneath trees, the field greys, almost invisible in the fading light, were creeping forward.

General Lanrezac's order of the 24th was the first of a series foreshadowing the reversal of the French pre-war conception of the employment of infantry.*

It may be that he himself, never a partisan of the forward school, saw such high-sounding phrases as "the irresistible infantry attack," "*offensive à outrance*", "the bayonet is queen of the battlefield" relegated to limbo without regret. There is, however, a great difference between disbelief in the potency of such shock tactics and acceptance as an established fact of the inferiority of French to German infantry.

The violent change in the fundamental theories upon which the infantry had been trained might well have proved the undoing of soldiers less brave, less adaptable than the French. To be taught shock tactics, and when these failed in a welter of blood to be shown plainly by his generals that they thought him no match for the enemy, might have been fatal had the French soldier lost faith in himself, which happily he never did.

It would be unfair to suggest that at this stage of the war the Commander of the Fifth Army was alone in thinking that the comparatively short service of the French soldier made him unable to stand on equal terms against his German opponent. General Joffre himself thought so for a time at least. Still convinced of the soundness of his plan, believing that he had succeeded in massing more troops than the enemy at the decisive points, he considered the failure of the offensive to be due to

* See Appendix XXII for instructions to Armies *re* tactics.

sheer ineptitude on the part of the executants. When he realized that this was not so, his confidence in the fighting ability of his troops was soon restored.

This was perhaps his darkest hour. On the previous day his confidence had remained unassailable, but as during the night (23rd–24th) report after report came in informing him of lost battles and of retirements, the real state of affairs in all its relentless grimness was revealed to him. There is a note of hopelessness in his report to the Minister:

"G.Q.G. August 24th, 9.35 a.m.

"The fears inspired in me during the last few days concerning the aptitude of our troops for offensive operations in the field have been confirmed by yesterday's events, which have definitely checked our offensive in Belgium. . . . We have made progress at certain points, but our retirement at others has compelled a general retreat.

"In the north, our Army operating between the Sambre, the Meuse and the British Army, appears to have suffered checks of which I do not yet know the full extent, but which have forced it to retire to the line Givet–Maubeuge–Valenciennes. . . .

"Conclusion

"One must face the facts. Our army corps, in spite of the numerical superiority which was assured to them, have not shown on the battle-field those offensive qualities which we had hoped for from the partial successes obtained at the beginning, successes obtained chiefly in operations in mountain country.

"We are therefore compelled to resort to the defensive, using our fortresses and great topographical obstacles to enable us to yield as little ground as possible.

"Our object must be to last out as long as possible, trying to wear the enemy out, and to resume the offensive when the time comes.

"J. JOFFRE."

His despondency did not last long. Having once realized the situation, he faced it boldly. Without losing a moment he began to take steps to strengthen his left at the expense of his right. To gain time, all the armies were ordered, whilst manœuvring in retreat, to use every endeavour to delay the enemy's advance. Each Army received precise orders and the zone allocated to each was defined.

Indefatigably, with marvellous energy and courage, General Joffre set about rearranging his pieces on the great chessboard of war. He perceived dimly what his counter-thrust would be. His brain had not yet evolved the great manœuvre that was to vindicate him, but his stern old heart, refusing to accept defeat, bade him fight grimly on until his opportunity came, as come it must.

Having issued his orders, General Joffre could do little more for the moment than co-ordinate the efforts of his Armies and withdraw all forces not essential in the fighting line to build up a mass of manœuvre. He also set about creating a barrage in northern France against German raids. The area about Dunkirk was to be flooded, and General d'Amade in charge of the thin barrier of Territorial troops extending from the British left to the sea was reinforced by two Territorial divisions. Steps were taken to destroy the railways in the north as the enemy advanced. Lille was declared an open town, from which all stores were to be evacuated or destroyed.

That morning there was a curious episode at Fifth Army Headquarters.

A couple of civilians were to be seen carrying from a motor-car standing outside the Headquarters building bundles of what looked like Bank notes, which they piled up in the yard. Backwards and forwards they went, gesticulating excitedly when their arms were empty, reduced to spluttering when their arms were full. They were representatives of the National Bank of Belgium who had come from Antwerp, and after making an immense detour along the coast, had followed behind the armies until they got opposite Namur. They had brought with them nine million francs in cash for the Governor. At first they would not believe that Namur had surrendered or was on the point of doing so. When they realized that there was no possibility of getting into the town they were in despair to know what to do with the money. It was suggested that they should hand it over to the paymaster of Fifth Army, but this they refused to do. They preferred to burn the notes, and presently the soldiers watching open-mouthed saw more money than they were ever likely to see again smouldering in the flames, fragments of crisp paper flying all over the place. For a moment they forgot the war in their astonishment at seeing such immense wealth being, as it seemed, destroyed.

Even when nothing was left but a heap of ashes the troubles of the Belgian cashier were not over, for he had also a million francs in gold, and these he could not burn. After a lot of argument he was at last persuaded to hand them over to the pay department of the Fifth Army on the understanding that they were to be used to pay the Belgian soldiers evacuated from Namur.

Later in the morning the Chief of Staff of the 4th Belgian Division from Namur came in to see General Lanrezac. I stood at the back of the room, which was packed with officers, so I could not hear very well what was going on. General Lanrezac was seated. The Belgian stood. It seemed to me that the reception accorded to our Ally was anything but cordial. None of us had yet experienced a bombardment by heavy artillery, so, not realizing the ordeal the Belgians had been through, no one was generous.

No news yet from the British, impossible to tell whether they were retiring in safety or not.

I was not the only person to feel anxious on their account, for it was impossible to look at a map showing the known movements of the enemy without being gripped by a sickening feeling of fear as one saw the long lines representing the German columns descending on the British flank. Would the impact come before the troops engaged frontally had had time to shake the enemy off?

Little news from the corps of the Fifth Army.

There were some signs of the enemy bringing pressure on the front of the X. Corps. The XVIII. Corps reported at noon that it was anxious at not being in touch with the III. Corps and that its right was threatened by a hostile column making straight for the gap between it and the III. Corps. Captain Bénazet, the liaison officer to the XVIII. Corps, who had come in earlier, said that the situation of the Corps was not bad, but that the men who had been fighting for twenty-four hours were very tired. He also told us that on the previous evening the enemy had advanced waving French and Belgian flags and shouting: "We are the English, your friends!" The Corps had been driven back, but only to the line assigned to it, where a position had been prepared.

At 3 p.m. Captain Leget, the liaison officer to the III. Corps, reported. He had been at Corps Headquarters at Barbançon when a civilian cyclist came tearing by yelling that the Uhlans were on them. Patrols of the Corps H.Q. escort dashed off to investigate, and came back with the news that these Uhlans were a pure invention. Leget concluded his report by remarking laconically that he had left Barbançon without again seeing the Corps Commander, who had taken his departure in a motor-car with one of his staff at the time the alarm was given.*

* Bénazet's report was forwarded to the G.Q.G. Leget's was not.

Leget's news was satisfactory in that he stated the *moral* of the men was excellent. He had been amongst the troops who had suffered most heavily on the 23rd, and although he considered them incapable of furnishing a heavy effort that day (24th) he found them all anxious to fight again and eager to advance. The various units were being sorted out, staff officers having spent all night collecting detachments that had got lost during the fighting. Most of these detachments had now rejoined their regiments, which were reforming behind powerful rearguards supported by the whole of the Corps artillery. The 6th Division, which it was now clear had retired somewhat precipitately on the previous day, had been withdrawn into Corps reserve.

CHAPTER II

THE FIRST DAY OF THE RETREAT
CONTINUED

August 24th, 1914: – II

Interview with General Lanrezac – Possibility that he may counter-attack – Orders issued to the XVIII. Corps and Reserve Divisions to halt – Joffre's suggestion to the British – And Sir John French's answer – Events on the British front on the 24th – The retreat of the British to continue – Aubenton – News of events on the front of the Fifth Army – The Fifth Army's retreat to continue – How General Lanrezac's orders to the Reserve Division miscarried – The situation that night.

THE news coming in from the Corps of the Fifth Army, scanty though it was, showed that the enemy had failed to hold them to their ground, and that they were all marching southwards according to plan, practically unmolested.

But the retreat of the Fifth Army was emphasizing the forward position of the B.E.F., and with every hour that passed the already alarming distance between the British right and the French left increased.* (Maps VI, p. 112 and XIII, p. 360.)

The British we knew had been heavily engaged by vastly superior forces. Hostile columns with nothing whatever to stop them were sweeping down on their left. Could Sir John shake off the enemy and retire in time, or would he be held until the German corps in the west had advanced far enough to turn inwards and overwhelm by a flank attack those troops already engaged against desperate odds? (Map VIII, p. 197.)

In the early afternoon I had an anxious conversation on these lines with Girard and Duruy. They agreed that although a great opportunity

---

* The map in the *French Official History* which gives the relative positions of the French and British at 6 a.m. on the 24th is somewhat misleading, for it shows the British as being farther back than they actually were. See *Official History of the War*, Chapter IV, p. 87.

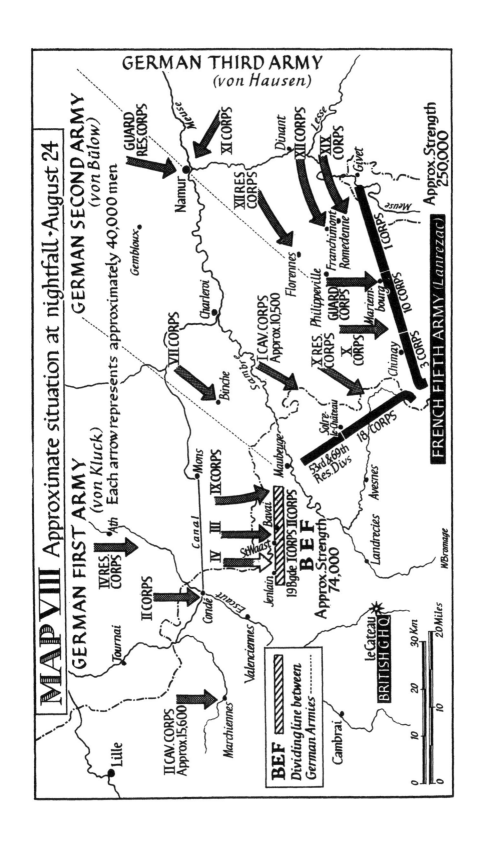

MAP VII · Approximate situation at nightfall · August 24

GERMAN THIRD ARMY
(von Hausen)

Approx. Strength 250,000

GERMAN SECOND ARMY
(von Bülow)

Each arrow represents approximately 40,000 men

GUARD RES. CORPS

XI CORPS

XII CORPS

XII RES. CORPS

XIX CORPS

GUARD CORPS

X RES. CORPS

X CORPS

I CAV. CORPS Approx. 10,500

VII CORPS

Namur

Meuse

Lesse

Dinant

Gembloux

Charleroi

Binche

Sambre

Florennes

Givet

Meuse

Franchimont

Romedenne

Philippeville

Mariembourg

Chimay

Solre-le-Château

I CORPS

10 CORPS

3 CORPS

18 CORPS

53rd & 69th Res. Divs

FRENCH FIFTH ARMY (Lanrezac)

GERMAN FIRST ARMY
(von Kluck)

IV RES. CORPS

II CORPS

II CAV. CORPS Approx. 15,600

IX CORPS

IV · II · II CORPS

19 Bgde I CORPS II CORPS

Jenlain

St. Waast

Bavai

Maubeuge

Mons

Condé

Canal

Escaut

BEF
Approx. Strength 74,000

Tournai

Valenciennes

Lille

Marchiennes

Ath

Avesnes

Landrecies

Cambrai

Le Cateau

★ BRITISH GHQ

W. B. romage

BEF
Dividing line between German Armies --------

0   10   20   30 Km
0   10   20 Miles

had been missed on the previous day, the Fifth Army still could and should strike a blow for the sake of disengaging the British, and they felt strongly that if General Lanrezac did nothing there was every chance that the British would meet with disaster. Duruy was very outspoken in his view that having regard to the position to which the British had been asked to advance, the French retreat was unjustifiable. "We had no business to clear out like that," he said gravely, "and it will be no thanks to us if the English escape."

It seemed to us not yet too late, that a counter-attack was still possible and should have every chance of success. The French officers believed that such an attack would not only take pressure off the British, but would be of the greatest benefit to the Fifth Army itself, heightening the morale of the troops and giving them confidence. There could of course be no question of an offensive by the whole Army. The threat to its right on the Meuse, the retreat of the Fourth Army, and the outflanking movement against the British left, precluded any such possibility. All we hoped for was a short sharp counter-attack by a part of the Army.

We went on arguing, but it all came to the same thing, our conviction that the General would do nothing. At last I suggested they should place all these considerations before him. They shook their heads. It was impossible. Girard explained that while perfectly entitled to lay before the General the situation of the Germans, and to expound the effect an attack would have upon them (as indeed he had done on the previous day), he had no right whatever to take any step implying criticism of General Lanrezac's orders. They both said that as members of his staff they could not do anything tantamount to finding fault with him. While evidently very unhappy about their Chief, they neither then nor at any time permitted themselves a word in disparagement of him.

Suddenly Duruy turned to me. "You ought to go and tell the General yourself," he said. I was horrified at such an idea and told him I thought he must be crazy. How could I, a British cavalry subaltern, form up before this French General, in whose hands lay not only the fate of a quarter of a million men, but possibly the very destinies of his country, and tell him what to do with his Army?

Duruy said: "It's worth trying anyway. It may be a question of saving your Army."

I felt it was *not* worth trying, that General Lanrezac would rightly consider my intervention as impertinence. He would pay no attention whatever to anything I said, and my action might make him still less inclined to help the British. I remember telling Duruy that I thought the General would be so angry that he would feel like having me shot. Duruy smiled and said he thought that was a risk worth taking, and that, as I was not a member of Lanrezac's staff, there would be nothing improper in putting my point of view before him. He agreed that it was a heavy responsibility to assume, but urged me to undertake it, adding that he would accompany me before General Lanrezac, as although he could say nothing his presence would show that he supported me. Girard said he would do the same.

We asked to be received by General Lanrezac, and almost immediately were shown in to him. He was sitting at a table in a small classroom lighted by a glass partition giving on to a passage. I advanced and saluted, while Duruy and Girard remained standing at attention on either side of the door.

Without mincing matters, I outlined the sequence of events which had led up to the present dangerous situation of the British Army. For the first time I felt perfectly at ease in speaking to General Lanrezac. I forgot everything except the danger of the British and that he could save them if he would.

Quite clearly I remember my last words, and I have never got over my astonishment at my sudden and quite unusual eloquence. "*Mon Général*," I concluded, "if by your action the British Army is annihilated, England will never pardon France, and France will not be able to afford to pardon you."

General Lanrezac exploded. He shouted and banged the table. What he said I do not know. I have never known. I was too strung up to take it in.

We got outside somehow. "You did well," said Duruy, and we waited.

This incident marked the beginning of my close friendship with Duruy. In the end he gave me his whole confidence, and nothing has ever honoured me more than the proofs he gave me of it. During the Battle of the Aisne, when he had become Head of the Operations Section of the Fifth Army, he called his officers together and said: "We shall have to cease attacking, and I want to tell you the real reason. We have run short of 75 shells. I have not put this down on paper as the English must not be told," and, looking at me, he added: "Of course our friend Spears will say nothing of this." I had to point out to him that he was placing me in an impossible position and that he must give me leave to tell the British Commander-in-Chief, which he ended by doing.

*   *   *

A very few minutes after we had left General Lanrezac's room, an officer came out and said to me: "Attack orders are about to be issued. They are to be taken by aeroplane to Le Cateau." I felt like turning somersaults.

The whole Staff began to buzz with excitement. The 3ème Bureau did not take long to draw up the orders, but when I saw them I was bitterly disappointed, for they were not attack orders at all, but a preliminary order to the XVIII. Corps not to retire beyond Solre-le-Château in view of a possible attack next day (25th) in co-operation with the British, in which the Reserve Divisions were to participate.* This was not at all what had been asked for, but there was this much to the good, that the XVIII. Corps, by not retiring farther for the moment, would diminish the vertical distance between the British right and the French left. And if the troops were in a position to attack, there was the possibility of their being ordered to do so.

When I arrived at Le Cateau with a copy of this order, the first person I met was General Wilson. I told him my news. He shook his head. "Too late," he said. "If only those orders had been issued for an attack yesterday or even today, but tomorrow is too late. We have just heard that a German Corps has entered Valenciennes on a level with our left."†

* The text of this order was as follows:

"Q.G., Chimay, August 24th, 15.15. (3.15 p.m.).
"Ordre Général.

"The XVIII. Corps will not fall back beyond Solre-le-Château. It is possible that it will be ordered to attack tomorrow in the direction of Thuin at the same time as the British Army, in the event of the latter's attacking towards Mons. It would in that case be linked up with the British Army by the Group of Reserve Divisions debouching from Maubeuge.

"The Group of Reserve Divisions will hold itself ready to debouch offensively, if it receives orders to do so, from the fortified camp of Maubeuge on the left bank of the Sambre so as to link up the attack of the XVIII. Corps with the offensive of the British Army towards Mons.

"LANREZAC."

This order was supplemented by the following, issued at 4 p.m.:

"Ordre Particulier.

"The III., X. and I. Corps will not continue tomorrow their movement in retreat unless ordered to do so by the Army Commander or compelled to do so by the enemy.

"The I. Corps will in any case send out very early tomorrow morning a detachment towards Rocroi to guard the Fumay road.

"GENERAL LANREZAC."

The 38th Division passed under the orders of the XVIII. Corps.

† This information proved inaccurate. It is not known whence it came.

Whilst at Le Cateau I learned that General Joffre had suggested to Sir John that the British should delay the enemy's advance between Valenciennes and Maubeuge, and should retire towards Cambrai if compelled to do so by superior forces, their left on the Denain–Bouchain–Arleux Canal, their right towards Le Cateau.*

To this Sir John answered:

"3 p.m. I am falling back slowly to position Maubeuge, Valenciennes which I hope to hold with assistance of your Corps of Cavalry on my left. If driven from these positions I will act in accordance with your wishes."

It will be observed that this message contains no reference to the British retiring on their lines of communication, and the subject was not mentioned to me again that day.

A communication from Major Clive, liaison officer attached to the G.Q.G. that "General Berthelot agreed with the British retirement, but suggested that it should take place as slowly as possible" and adding that "all the troops of the Fifth Army were engaged and would fight to the end," evoked the comment that the French Commander-in-Chief's information was singularly incomplete in some important respects.

For the sake of clarity, it is necessary at this point to summarize the day's happenings on the British front.

Von Kluck had ordered his Army to throw the British forces into Maubeuge on the 24th. By nightfall it was clear that it had failed. The British had not been enveloped "according to plan," and the German First Army had only been able to advance three and a half miles from the Mons Canal and had had to halt altogether in the middle of the afternoon.

The end of the day found the British withdrawn to the west of Maubeuge, with ample elbow room.† There had been severe fighting, and the story of that day is a fine page in British military annals.

The 5th Division, engaged on a front of six miles, had, together with

---

* Sir John was told that two Reserve Divisions would be brought up to Arras during the night. They were to be employed as reserves behind the barrage established between Arras and Valenciennes.

† The retreat had been so arranged that the 5th Division found its place taken in the line by the 3rd; this arrangement gave the former relief from the intensive pressure to which it had been submitted and also shortened its march. This movement was so well calculated by the Staff that there was not the slightest hitch, the divisions not even seeing each other.

the Cavalry Division and the 19th Brigade, completely held up von Kluck's attack, which had assumed ever more threatening proportions as the day wore on. Two battalions and a battery in flank guard had, with the help of the Cavalry, held up a whole German Corps. In some parts of the battlefield the infantry had held on till annihilated by sheer weight of numbers, but the results achieved had been worth the sacrifices involved, for the casualties, although severe, were small in proportion to the results obtained and the hurt inflicted on the enemy. (Map VI, p. 112.)

By its proficiency and valour the British Army had, unaided, arrested von Kluck's advance and thwarted his hope of enveloping our left. The troops were worn out. Many of them had had no food or sleep for twenty-four hours, but their morale was good, for these exhausted men knew well that they had proved themselves more than a match for the enemy.

The Army's achievement was the more remarkable in that the troops were already very tired when the day began. The 1st Division had been under arms almost continuously for eighteen hours on the previous day, most of the II. Corps had not got into billets until just before daylight on the 24th, and the 19th Brigade had only detrained at 2 a.m. The Army contained sixty per cent of Reservists, and anyone who has attempted to walk on the cobbled roads of Northern France and Belgium can imagine what a strain was put on these unfit men.

*   *   *

About 9 o'clock in the evening, whilst I was getting the news of the day from the Intelligence, I was sent for by Sir Archibald Murray.

Referring to the message I had brought from General Lanrezac, expressing his willingness to counter-attack in co-operation with the British, he told me that the British Army was to continue its retreat, since the development of the threat to its left made any other action out of the question. He pointed out that as the XVIII. Corps was ten miles in the rear of the British right, Lanrezac's condition that he would only attack if the British did so also, was absurd. An attack by Lanrezac with his left might be a great advantage and help us out, but to make it a condition that we should advance if he did was tantamount to offering to have a whack at the lion if we first put our head into its mouth. General Murray went on to say that the Commander-in-Chief was convinced the enemy wanted to drive us into Maubeuge, and that the only way of avoiding the trap was to fall back. In view of the difficulties presented by the Forest of Mormal, which formed a solid block some nine miles in length and three or four miles in depth, it had been decided to withdraw the I. Corps to the east and the II. to the west of it, to a position in the neighbourhood of Le Cateau.

It was important that General Lanrezac should be informed as soon as possible that the British were compelled to continue their retirement, so a cipher message was sent to the Fifth Army H.Q. giving them the information and saying that I was coming on with full details as rapidly as possible by car. I set off at once for Aubenton, whither Fifth Army Headquarters had by this time moved. An hour and a half later I was in the village, searching with the aid of a man carrying a lantern for the Chief of Staff's billet. We found it at last, and I made my report, upon which he offered no comment, save that the Fifth Army was to continue its retirement. I then went to the H.Q. building, where under fitful gas jets I repeated my news to the officers on duty, and found out what had been, or was supposed to have been happening, to the Fifth Army since I left.

The III., X. and XVIII. Corps had all reached in safety the line assigned to them, though the men were very tired. (Map VI, p. 112.)

There had been some disorder in the I. Corps, partly owing to the intermingling of units, but mainly because the 4th Belgian Division, almost officerless and in utter confusion, was pouring through the I. Corps area. Officers from the Fifth Army Staff were doing their best to deal with the situation. Duruy and Malick were amongst the unfortunate ones on whom this duty fell, and it nearly drove them out of their minds. There were no leaders to whom to give directions, so the unfortunate Belgians streamed on, taking up valuable room, obstructing vital roads, clamouring for food which it was impossible to provide. At the moment they were occupying the area allocated to the 51st Reserve Division, which had marched in after an exhausting trek to find every house occupied. To add to the general confusion, the Belgians had with them an immense number of motor-cars, taxis, touring cars and limousines filled with 75 ammunition. The problem of sorting them out was finally solved by the erection of large numbers of signposts directing them where to go.*

---

* These troops were, I believe, eventually shipped to Antwerp, with the exception of their artillery, which remained for some time with the Fifth Army, and did very well fighting side by side with the French.

In spite of these obstructions the I. Corps had carried out the movements assigned to it. There was no interference from the enemy.*

The danger to which the Fifth Army had been exposed by reason of its extended flank on the Meuse was now passed. The flank was much shorter, and the enemy had been held off all day. The greater part of what was left of the flank position was covered by practically impassable woods, the only possible point of danger being the passage at Fumay leading to Rocroi, which was easy to defend and strongly held. The only cause of anxiety General Lanrezac could now have for his right was the possible further retreat of the Fourth Army.

The message from Le Cateau that the British must continue their retirement was received at Aubenton at 10 p.m. on the 24th. At 7 a.m. next morning (25th) General Lanrezac issued orders for the retreat of his whole Army to the line La Capelle–Hirson–Mézières. The hopes raised by the order to halt were dashed, and thousands of disappointed men again turned their backs on the enemy with whom they were longing to come to grips. (Map VI, p. 112.)

*   *   *

We have seen that General Lanrezac issued orders to the XVIII. Corps and the Reserve Divisions to halt in view of a possible attack on the 25th, and then cancelled these orders. Until the morning of the 25th the Reserve Divisions, having received the order but not knowing that it was cancelled, remained level with Maubeuge and a day's march nearer the enemy than the rest of the Fifth Army. (Map IX, p. 207.) What happened shows the real conditions and difficulties of war and how uncertainly the machinery works, especially in a retreat. The imponderable human element plays a part even in such a simple business as the transmission of an order.

Battles are fought by hordes of men, generally footsore and hungry,

---

* By the evening of the 24th, it was known that the enemy held Tournai and Condé. Telephonic and telegraphic communications between Lille and Valenciennes were cut. The II. Corps had debouched from Ath on the British right. The British had been attacked by the IV. Corps, and troops belonging to another large formation had crossed the Meuse at Hastière, whilst pontoon bridges had been built at Anseremme and at Dinant.

It was at last admitted officially that German Reserve Corps might be following the corps, in the case of the Second Army at least. This was the view of Colonel Macdonogh. He had been insisting that this was the case for some time, and at last the G.Q.G. began to think there was something in it. It will be remembered that as early as August 17th we had had this information from the German airman we had captured.

It was thought that the 4th and 9th Cavalry Divisions had been opposed to the British.

each of whom had his own material preoccupations. As soon as the excitement or the danger is over, these preoccupations come to the surface. Have you ever seen rabbits scuttle away in terror before a weasel, the picture of panic, and then a few moments later return to the same spot to nibble contentedly? Men in war are just like that. Death is never far off, it may be hovering quite near to this man or to that. Some may just have had very narrow escapes, but they are not thinking of what has happened, or of what the future may hold. They know what their chances are, but they do not think about them. See them in billets. They are all taken up with the matter of the moment, material things loom large, much larger than in peace-time, for there are no other distractions, and the discomfort of their lives being very great, every little alleviation becomes important. Food is of course a matter of absorbing interest, while mishaps such as losing his kit are more annoying to the man at the front than the same misadventure at Victoria Station. All this the civilian seldom realizes, any more than he realizes how the machinery of an army functions. The armchair strategist no doubt imagines a general giving an order which is delivered by a bustling staff officer as a postman delivers a letter at the door, and sees divisions and regiments being moved on receipt of it like pieces on a chessboard. If the orders are good and the pieces well placed, then the game is won, provided the pieces do not take the moves into their own hands and run away.

Unfortunately war is not like this, as the following account of what happened to the Reserve Divisions on the 24th and 25th will show.

The order from the Fifth Army to the Reserve Divisions was received in the middle of the afternoon (24th) by the G.O.C., General Valabrègue, who at once took the preliminary steps necessary in view of a possible offensive.

As the offensive operation was to be carried out by the Reserve Divisions and the XVIII. Corps in co-operation it was necessary to establish a co-ordinated plan, so an officer named Wemaëre belonging to the Staff of the Reserve Divisions was ordered to go to Beaumont, where the XVIII. Corps H.Q. was thought to be, to make the necessary arrangements. He was greatly surprised to meet with neither troops nor convoys on the road; the country was deserted.

When within ten kilometres of Beaumont he met first an artillery officer and then an Army doctor. The first told him that the Germans had been in occupation of Beaumont since 11 a.m., the second that the XVIII. Corps had retired to the south, and that he thought the Corps

Commander was at Avesnes. Wemaëre therefore went to Avesnes, but when near the town found it impossible to advance faster than at a walking pace, and was constantly held up altogether, the roads being congested with troops and convoys. When at last he reached Avesnes it was only to be told that the XVIII. Corps Staff was at Senneries, some little distance to the east, where he arrived at about 7 p.m.

General de Mas Latrie, commanding the Corps, was at dinner. He was horror-struck at being told he was expected to attack next day. No instructions had reached him, yet his name appeared on the copy of the order received by the Reserve Divisions as one of those to whom it had been sent. It was obvious that the copy meant for him had gone astray.

In pursuance of the general order of retreat, he had withdrawn his troops by a forced march, and they were exhausted. How could he connect up again with the Reserve Divisions, which had halted and were now some 17 kilometres away to the north? And how could an attack for the next morning be arranged under the circumstances? Luckily Bénazet, the liaison officer from Army H.Q., was present. With much difficulty and after long delay he got through to Army H.Q. on the telephone and begged for instructions. The answer came that an officer would leave at once bearing orders, that he would arrive at La Capelle at about midnight and should be met there. Wemaëre decided to accompany Bénazet to La Capelle to find out what those orders were. The two officers waited at La Capelle until 2 a.m. (on the 25th) when the officer from Army H.Q. appeared. The envelope he carried was eagerly torn open. It contained a duplicate of the order to halt received by the Reserve Divisions in the afternoon! There was no explanation, and the bearer knew nothing.

As it was quite obvious by this time that no attack could possibly take place, Wemaëre rejoined the Reserve Divisions at 4 a.m. His report brought Colonel des Vallières, the Chief of Staff, his first news of the retreat of the XVIII. Corps. He was appalled, and at once pulled General Valabrègue out of bed. Together they drew up orders for an immediate retreat, which were carried to the two divisions by liaison officers.

The fact that his command was level with the British, they to the west and he to the east of Maubeuge, gave little comfort to General Valabrègue, who naturally enough took the gravest view of the situation in which he found himself, much nearer the enemy than the remainder of the Fifth Army, and out of touch with the neighbouring divisions.

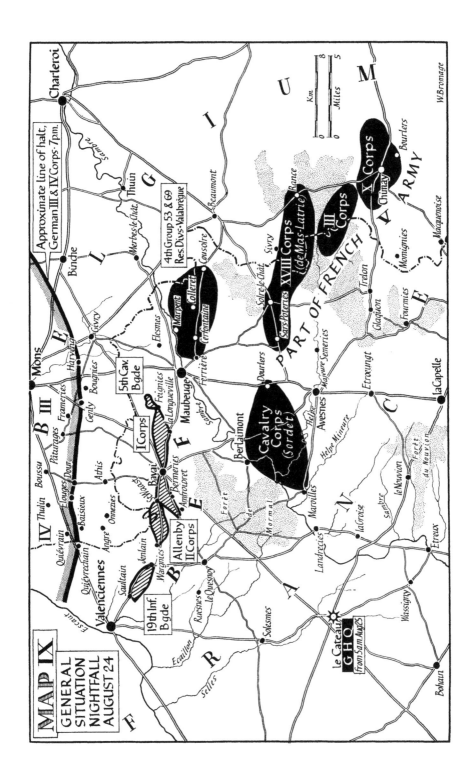

MAP IX

GENERAL
SITUATION
NIGHTFALL
AUGUST 24

Approximate line of halt,
German III & IV Corps·7pm.

4th Group 53 & 69
Res.Divs·Valabrègue

5th Cav.
Bgde

I Corps

Allenby
II Corps

19th Inf.
Bgde

PART OF FRENCH 5th ARMY

Cavalry
Corps
(Sordet)

Le Cateau
G H Q
from Sam.Aug.25

W.Bromage

I can find no trace of any message having been sent to the British at this juncture, although the orders which had caused all the confusion had as their object an attack in conjunction with them. What would have happened had the British been in a position to assume the offensive and had done so in the belief that the left of the Fifth Army would co-operate is a matter for interesting speculation.

General Lanrezac's order countermanding the offensive was never received by the Reserve Divisions.

That is how things happen in war. General Lanrezac contemplates a possible counter-attack and issues orders accordingly. Half the forces concerned never get the order. He changes his mind, and everyone remains as unaware of his new decision as if he were humming a tune on Mars.

On the evening of the 24th, when the first day of the retreat was over, the British were still a day's march nearer the enemy than the Fifth Army. They had for the time being escaped the German tentacles but the men were very tired.* Indeed the exhaustion of both British and French was a cause of great anxiety. The Germans must have been weary also, but what a difference between the fatigue of the advancing soldier whose feet alone are tired, and that of the retreating man, who with aching limbs and eyes gritty with sleeplessness, bears on his shoulders the added weight of a heavy nagging imp sitting on his knapsack and whispering "retreat, retreat, retreat". The endless humiliating drone of that terrible word makes the tired soldier feel the weight of each article of equipment and each round of ammunition as a living hostile thing conspiring to drag him down into the dust of the road, while pounds of lead seem to be where his heart was, and his heavy head droops wearily forward.

Through the night the column advances. An immense shuffling, rattling sound comes from it as if a gigantic tarpaulin was being dragged along the road. Shuffle, shuffle, the men stream past endlessly, hardly visible in the dust and darkness, looking like lost souls on an eternal hopeless march as Doré might have drawn them. They sway as they move. The column is irregular and keeps halting, and men stumble into the backs of those ahead. Here and there a man on a horse, an officer, sways in the saddle, clutching at the pommel, fighting sleep. Never a word, hardly

---

* Von Kluck's orders for the 25th, issued at 8 p.m. on the 12th, were as follows:
"The enemy's main position is believed to be Bavai–Valenciennes. The First Army will attack it with envelopment of the left flank. The II. Cavalry Corps against the enemy's rear."

even a curse from those parched lips, just the occasional click of equipment or of the harness of a regimental cart.

In the English column the men keep step. When the column starts off again after each one of the countless halts, there is an uneven irregular beat of feet until the rhythm is caught again. French troops on the march do not keep step, and the regiments pass by to a sound like the rain of pebbles on a drum. That is the only difference between French and British soldiers retiring through the night.

That first night of the retreat, men in khaki, in blue, in field grey, marched down the roads, whilst others, thousands upon thousands, slept in the fields, by the roadside, under any available roof. From Condé to the Meuse, the narrow strip of country containing the contending armies was packed with over a million armed men, whilst the waiting nations listened with straining ears for any sound that would give some indication of what was befalling their armies on that immense battlefield.

In the dark street of Aubenton, the nerve centre of the Fifth Army, two French officers of proved courage and poise were talking of service matters, arranging as they walked to the house in which they were to sleep some important details for the next day. They could not see each other's faces in the pitch blackness, the things they said were quite ordinary, but each could tell from the sound of the other's voice that he was crying.

CHAPTER III

THE SECOND DAY OF THE RETREAT

August 25th, 1914

Colbert and his band – Landing behind the German lines – Navarre – The Carrier Pigeons – Events on August 25th – Aubenton – Fifth Army H.Q. moves to Vervins – Lanrezac reports to Joffre – A conversation with Lanrezac – A memorandum "explaining" the retreat – Colonel des Vallières – News of the British.

THE Fifth Army was now about to leave behind for good and all the great forests of the Ardennes which we had crossed on our way north only a few days before.

As we fell back, we were to abandon many men lost or forgotten in their immense depths: stragglers, patrols that had missed their way, posts that had not been relieved, or detachments that had been cut off.

The story of what befell some of these men is a dramatic one. The ancient tales of robber bands which come naturally to the mind in that wild country, were to find an echo in the adventures of these modern outlaws. The German invasion had put the smugglers and hunters of pre-war days out of business, but their place was taken by roving bands of men cut off from civilization and hunted like wild beasts. They were outlaws in that if caught they would be treated as spies, for the Germans had announced that they would shoot any allied soldiers caught behind their lines.

Amongst the men cut off in this way during the retreat was a French officer with a great name and a greater heart, Captain de Colbert. He collected some three hundred soldiers of all arms, but mostly belonging to the 205th Infantry Regiment, and conducted with his little band a fierce and effective guerilla warfare against the German lines of communication. Never sleeping twice in the same place, moving from one fastness to another, he harried the enemy in this quarter or in that, and then vanished into the impenetrable thickets of the gloomy woods. His men came to know every path and glade in the forest, and learned to find their way about its rugged slopes as surely as the herds of wild pig lurking in its depths. Two whole divisions of Landwehr were sent against them to no purpose. The Germans tramped the woods in their heavy boots, fired at shadows, shouted "*Wehr da?*" as startled doe sprang from the undergrowth, but of de Colbert they could find no trace, and in the end they gave up the hunt.

The French knew nothing of the existence of Colbert and his men until the beginning of November, 1914. On the 13th of that month the G.Q.G. sent a note to the Armies reporting the presence of French troops behind the German lines in the neighbourhood of Signy-le-Petit, and asking that means of getting into touch with them should be studied. On the following day the G.Q.G. amplified the information concerning the "*enfants perdus*" the lost children, as they say in French, of Signy-le-Petit. They were believed to be 250 in number, and the name of their commander, de Colbert, was given. The 2ème Bureau of the Fifth Army immediately informed the G.Q.G. that they could get into touch with these men, and asked what instructions were to be transmitted to them.

The Intelligence of the Fifth Army was in a position to carry out the G.Q.G.'s wishes so promptly because during the previous month, on October 29th to be exact, Captain Démery, Head of the Intelligence of the I. Corps, then in line on the Pontavert, Berry-au-Bac front, called on the head of the Army Intelligence to express his great anxiety at knowing little or nothing of the enemy on this front, and proposed the experiment of sending an aeroplane over the enemy's lines to land a man who, after finding out what he could, would enter the Aisne about Guignicourt and swim with the current, until he could rejoin the French troops on the south bank of the river.

This proposal was treated with some scepticism at Army Headquarters, but Démery insisted. He was told that he must produce volunteers, since it was impossible to carry out such an experiment unless those participating in it were fully prepared to risk their lives.

Démery had thought of that. He had both the aviator and the passenger. The aviator was, I think, called Billard: the man to be dropped behind the enemy lines was *Maréchal des Logis* (Sergeant) Berthelot of the 27th Artillery Regiment.

When, therefore, the G.Q.G.'s request was received in November, it was possible, thanks to Démery's foresight, to comply with it without delay, and from that time Billard and Berthelot took practice flights together, the latter never having been in the air in his life before.

On November 17th the expedition started. Berthelot was to find de Colbert, ascertain what his men were capable of, and, if there was any use in so doing, give him the G.Q.G.'s instructions. If I am not mistaken, these instructions were that the German Supreme Command was at Mézières Charleville on the edge of the Ardennes and that if de Colbert with his men were to burst in upon the Hun strategists and settle accounts with them, it would be a highly gratifying and also a very useful feat.

On the 18th, the I. Corps reported that Berthelot, in uniform, had been safely landed in a forest clearing. The aviator was back, and was at once awarded the coveted Military Medal and congratulated by the G.Q.G.

I am not sure if de Colbert attempted to raid Mézières or not. I believe that either before or after hearing from the G.Q.G. he reconnoitred the place but found it too strongly defended.

By December 27th the G.Q.G. heard that de Colbert could no longer keep his men together. Hardship, and the fact that the Germans destroyed all villages suspected of providing them with supplies, made it imperative that they should break up. Individually, marching by night and hiding by day, they made for the Dutch frontier. Colbert himself fell into the enemy's hands.

Berthelot got to Amsterdam, whence he sailed to England and thence to Havre, where he was locked up as a suspect. It was some time before the Fifth Army heard of him and ordered him to H.Q. He was awarded the Legion of Honour.

After this first success, other attempts were made and by May, 1915, at least four more men had been landed behind the German lines.

The departure of one of these expeditions was always a striking event. First of all it was very secret: those who knew about it inwardly computed the risks and kept very quiet. Time was carefully calculated so that the German lines should be crossed before dawn and a landing effected as soon as it became possible to see. When things went well, the aviator was back reporting at H.Q. within four hours of his departure, and it was strange to think that he had stood behind the German lines on ground our millions could not reach.

One of the pilots selected for this work by de Rose, then Head of the Fifth Army Aviation, was a dare-devil called Navarre.

It was impossible for Navarre to land or indeed fly in an ordinary way. He simply had to go in for aerobatics of a nature to discourage any passenger, but volunteers prepared to face a German firing party were not to be turned from their purpose by a few somersaults in the air.

Dropping men behind the German lines was not the only scheme devised by the Intelligence for obtaining information.*

During the period of trench warfare, when miles of French territory were for years on end in German occupation, aeroplanes were sent over to drop parachutes behind the enemy lines. To these parachutes were attached baskets containing carrier pigeons. The baskets also contained directions as to the nature of the information that would be useful, and to prevent the despatch of false information by the enemy, the finder was requested to give a personal reference in unoccupied territory. To be found with the pigeons meant death, to disclose one's identity meant prompt execution if detected, yet there were few if any instances of civilians who, finding the pigeons, did not use them as directed regardless of the risk involved.

*   *   *

August 25th, the day on which the Germans sacked Louvain, was uneventful for the Fifth Army as a whole. It continued to retire without serious interference from the enemy, the only contact with him being that one division of the I. Corps was engaged by a German cavalry division and cyclists.† The line reached at nightfall by the Fifth Army and the British is shown on Maps VI, p. 112 and XIII, p. 360. Most of the troops were in good condition although tired: General d'Esperey reported his men full of ardour but in need of a day's rest.

The morning at Army Headquarters at Aubenton had been gloomy in the extreme. It started badly when we learnt that orders had been issued at 7 a.m. for the Army to retire to the line Maroilles–Avesnes–Fourmies–Regniowez, and that Headquarters would withdraw to Vervins.

The move took place at 2 p.m. in an atmosphere of deep depression. Girard and I travelled to Vervins in the same car.

Headquarters was established in a school. I learnt that Lanrezac had

---

* See Appendix XXIII for account of the adventures of British soldiers behind the German lines.

† The 4th Cavalry Division, now attached to the Fifth Army and placed by General Lanrezac under the orders of the I. Corps, also suffered some loss from artillery fire. This division had been assigned a special mission by the G.Q.G. It was to be the link between the Fourth and Fifth Armies.

sent a report to the Commander-in-Chief before leaving Aubenton, which was as follows:

"August 25th, 11.50 a.m.

"It is my intention to take steps to resume the offensive as soon as I am free of the wooded and very difficult country about Avesnes, where my infantry, tired and shaken by the recent fighting, could not receive effective support from my artillery which is intact. Further it is essential that, having up to now been compelled to manœuvre on a far too extended front in order to keep in touch with the British and to hold the Meuse, I should contract the front of the Army so as to make it possible to attack. Finally, according to your instructions, I have to join up with the British Army, which is retiring tomorrow to the line Le Cateau–Cambrai, and perhaps ultimately even farther back. Consequently I shall withdraw to the line De Cateau-Vervins and further if the British Army continues its retirement. This movement will obviously have as a result the creation of a gap between my Army and the Fourth Army, which cannot but widen, and I must insist on the fact that I cannot attack unless I have a front of attack."

It was true that the ground on which the Fifth Army now found itself was not suitable for a counter-attack on a big scale, but my impression at the time was that General Lanrezac was not anxious to attack under any circumstances. The whole history of his command was to prove this impression to be true.

I had a conversation at Vervins with the Army Commander in which he stressed once more the folly and futility of matching the less well trained French infantry against the Germans, and the necessity of making up for this disparity by the maximum use of the 75s. The Chief of Staff spoke in much the same sense. General Lanrezac also alluded to the great superiority of the enemy in machine-guns. Even in the matter of artillery he seemed to be less confident than he had been, and spoke of the terrible effect of the German howitzers, with which the French guns seemed unable to deal.

In the opinion of the responsible commanders and the liaison officers, General Lanrezac's statement that the infantry was much shaken applied only to a few units and to Valabrègue's Reserve Divisions, which were reported during the afternoon by their Chief of Staff, Colonel des Vallières, to be in a bad state, very tired and unfit to carry out serious fighting. He asked that they should be withdrawn from the line and placed in rear of the Army as a reserve. On hearing this General Lanrezac exclaimed for the *n*th time: *"Les divisions de réserve, c'est zéro!"**

The question of the numbers of machine-guns the enemy disposed of often came up during these days. I maintained that we in England knew pretty well the proportion of these weapons in the German infantry, and that in view of the technical training required to handle them, it was quite impossible for the enemy to spring any great surprise on us in this respect. My French friends were convinced that the Germans had far more machine-guns than seemed to me possible. This impression was perhaps due to the faulty way in which the French infantry was engaged, giving the Germans marvellous targets, and resulting in such casualties that the men, bewildered and shaken, put down their losses to machine-guns in astronomical numbers. I never heard anyone complain of the antiquity of the French infantry rifle, a weapon inferior to that of the Germans and especially to our own from the point of view of rapid fire.

The depressing effect of my conversation with General Lanrezac and his Chief of Staff was modified by what the latter told me later. He seemed confident that the German columns would be shattered by the 75s as they emerged from the woods. He conveyed the impression that careful plans were being made for a series of powerful artillery actions against the enemy as the latter emerged from the hilly wooded belt extending from Mézières to Hirson.

A memorandum given to the Army liaison officers to take out to the troops reinforced this impression. It ran as follows:

"You are to repeat that the retreat of the Fifth Army is due to the delay of the Fourth and British Armies in coming up, and that the necessity of finding ground where the attacks of the infantry can be supported by artillery, has compelled the Army to withdraw from the wooded region of Philippeville, Givet, Rocroi, and Avesnes.

"That this movement was imposed upon us, and was necessary in

---

* General Lanrezac was not the only French General who showed a prejudice against the reserve formations, which was to prove entirely unjustified. In the fearful ordeal of battle they proved their staunchness; in attack and in defence they displayed a heroism unsurpassed by the active formations. General Maunoury's Sixth Army, on whom the heaviest fighting fell during the Battle of the Marne, had an Army composed of Reserve Divisions (all except the 14th, 45th and 7th Divisions and the Moroccan Brigade (the 8th Division cannot be said to have taken any active part in the battle)), and during the Battle of the Frontiers the only success achieved by the French on August 24th and 25th was that of the Army of Lorraine composed almost exclusively of Reservists.

spite of the moral and physical fatigue a retreat necessarily implies for the troops.

"That an offensive spirit for the forthcoming fights should be maintained.

"The French artillery has shown itself to be clearly superior to the German.

"In the British Army it is said that if a British Battery Commander shot as the German Battery Commanders have been shooting in the last few days, he would be relieved of his command immediately.

"The Chief of the 3ème Bureau

"SCHNEIDER."

The reason given to explain the retreat of the Fifth Army was somewhat annoying to an Englishman, but excusable on the ground that it was better from the point of view of morale to lay the blame on others.

I had a long talk with Colonel des Vallières when he came to Vervins, and was greatly charmed and impressed by his personality, an impression that increased during years of intercourse. One of the most brilliant officers in the French Army, he was afterwards Chief of Staff to the Tenth Army, then Head of the French Mission at G.H.Q., and was killed later when commanding a division. He was partly Irish, though he spoke little or no English, very straight and tall, with a high forehead and a bald head, generally covered in those days by the tall steel helmet and hanging horsehair plume of the dragoons. A black tunic with white facings and red breeches completed his equipment. He had an earnest serious face, but an occasional twinkle in his eye bore witness to a substratum of humour which would come bubbling up in laughter, when his whole face lighted up and his grey eyes danced. He had a long moustache, which he stroked when in thought or about to produce a witty saying or observation. He was very sensitive and affectionate. One discovered in him all sorts of unexpected talents, for instance he drew very well. A most lovable man, and a great gentleman.

Late in the evening Helbronner returned to Fifth Army H.Q. from British G.H.Q., where he had been sent to give the line to which the Fifth Army was falling back. He was rather perturbed at the way in which he had been received. The fact of coming from General Lanrezac had ceased to be a recommendation in Sir John French's eyes, and Helbronner had been struck by the Field-Marshal's ominous silence.

He said that General Wilson appeared hardly more cordial than his Chief.

With the British the only cheerful news was the arrival of the 4th Division, which had detrained the night before at le Cateau. I had seen it myself, and anyone who did so will remember the joy of beholding those fresh troops. (Maps VI, pp. 112–13 and XIII, p. 360.)

The day had been an anxious one, for the B.E.F. had had to withdraw under conditions of extreme difficulty, the two Corps being separated by the great Forest of Mormal. The fatigue of the men had been increased owing to the congestion caused by the passage of Sordet's Cavalry Corps in rear of the columns, and the transport had been continually held up by masses of refugees.

On the western flank of the II. Corps there had been a running fight all day with every prospect of increased pressure to come, whilst several lively rearguard actions were fought. It was lucky indeed that the Germans were as weary as the British, for towards evening there were hopeless blocks at Solesmes and Viesly, and any considerable pressure would have been most serious.

It was on this day that General Robertson, the British Q.M.G., faced with the problem of keeping the retiring army supplied with food, and not knowing which roads would be followed by the troops, hit upon the ingenious solution of dumping supplies at crossroads on the most likely lines of retreat. Intelligence officers took charge of this work, two of whom were lost whilst carrying it out. It was an unavoidably wasteful method, but it answered very well, and had one entirely unforeseen and very important consequence which certainly influenced subsequent operations. The Germans, seeing enormous dumps of supplies by the side of the road, concluded that the British were thoroughly broken and disorganized, and very unwisely began to discount their fighting value.

On the right of the British I. Corps (Map IX, p. 207), the position of the unfortunate Reserve Divisions that night, was a very difficult one. By this time, they were nearer the enemy than either their British or French neighbours, and were to all intents and purposes squeezed out of the line. All day their Staff had heard the cannonade, violent and increasing in strength on the British front. Late in the evening news came that the British I. Corps had been attacked at Landrecies. What had really happened will be recounted in the next chapter. The information caused great anxiety: it was reported that the enemy had come up in motor lorries, from which it was deduced that he intended to press his attack with vigour and rapidity. Although Landrecies lay on the left of the British I. Corps, it was feared that this attack might lead to the retreat of the whole Corps, thus exposing the flank of the Reserve Divisions. General Valabrègue got into touch with the right of the I. Corps, and steps were taken to counter-attack any hostile force which might debouch in pursuit of the British should they fall back. Happily the necessity never arose, for as will be seen the British had no difficulty in repelling the attack, which was only a minor one. The Commander of the Reserve Divisions realized late at night that all immediate danger on his left had passed away. Nevertheless, before the situation was cleared up, General Valabrègue at Sir Douglas Haig's request relieved the British troops on the front Noyelles–Maroilles. This operation necessitated his calling on the XVIII. Corps for help.

Before leaving the Reserve Divisions, an incident showing the conditions of uncertainty affecting even the higher formations at that time, may be mentioned.

On the morning of the 25th, the H.Q. of the Reserve Divisions had moved from Obrechies and at 8 a.m. was installed at Prisches. About an hour after their arrival, down the main street of the village galloped a convoy, led by an officer of the gendarmerie shouting: "The enemy is upon us! He is pursuing us!" There was a moment of panic. A headquarters cannot be moved in five minutes, so Colonel des Vallières decided to defend Prisches. The place was quickly divided into sectors, each under a staff officer, with a few batmen and clerks as garrison. Barricades were erected. At the eastern one the officer in charge was giving the range, when the man next to him, a clerk, said timidly: "But, *mon Capitaine*, I don't know how to use a rifle!" That even a clerk should have been through his military service without learning the elements of musketry is a sad illustration of how uneven was the military training of the pre-war French Army.

Happily the alarm turned out to be false, and the enemy never appeared.

During the day the problem of the fleeing population had continued to cause much anxiety at Fifth Army Headquarters. One of its aspects was the question of espionage, for the enemy's intelligence service probably had drafted a number of spies into the immense unidentified anonymous mass of refugees, and the constant reports to this effect led to the following notice being circulated:

"It appears to be certain that amongst the great mass of people fleeing from the Belgian villages there are numerous spies who, on bicycles or in caravans, follow our troops and our convoys in complete security. It has been reported that in the evening, in certain of these caravans, too large for the needs of the persons occupying them, there are powerful lighting sets which send out coloured signals at night. People on bicycles who stated that they were Belgians driven from their homes, have been seen to watch artillery getting into position and infantry digging trenches; they follow with impunity every detail of the military operations and then move about freely in every direction. It is indispensable that most severe measures should be taken to put a stop to this. The foreign population must be stopped at the frontier, and must not be allowed under any circumstances to cross into French territory. The movement of civilians on roads followed by the columns must be absolutely forbidden. Troops must not under any pretext allow their movement or their operations to be watched by civilians.

"HÉLY D'OISSEL."

No doubt there were spies about, but certainly never as many as were reported. Perfectly absurd stories were solemnly believed and investigated, and quite unnecessary energy was expended in following up ridiculous rumours. The result was to engender a certain amount of unnecessary nervousness amongst the troops, so that every untoward or unexplained event, a sudden burst of artillery fire, for instance, or the shelling of billets, was put down to the work of spies. It is bad for morale that mysterious causes should be thought to be at the root of quite normal occurrences. The men get nerves, and nerves are the forerunner of unsteadiness and panic. It goes without saying that no caravan with signalling apparatus was ever found. That civilians should have watched with interest a battery coming into action was perfectly natural, it merely showed their ignorance of the danger involved. That such a battery should be spotted by the enemy was also quite natural, and had nothing to do with the gaping people who wondered what it was all about, although their presence may have attracted enemy attention to the guns.

*　　*　　*

In the morning, General Joffre had telegraphed to the Minister for

War. He said that the situation on the right was not modified. There had been some counter-attacks by the French. "The check suffered by our main offensive in Belgian Luxembourg has resulted in the enemy's being able to dispose of part of his forces operating in this region and to send these across the Meuse below Givet, thus enabling him to develop his movement on our left."

He went on to say that the failure of the main offensive was due to two divisions of the Third Army having allowed themselves to be surprised. The Army Commander, General Ruffey, had, however, re-established the situation. This Army if it had not progressed had at least not fallen back.

The failure of the Fourth Army was also attributed to the action of one division, the Corps to which it belonged falling back and dislocating the whole line. The Colonial Corps had then been violently attacked and had given way. This Army was being reconstituted behind the Meuse and the Chiers.

General Joffre concluded: "I am studying the means of stopping this movement by abandoning as much ground as is necessary and preparing a new manœuvre the object of which will be to oppose the march of the enemy on Paris."*

This message shows that the Generalissimo still laboured under his early illusions concerning the German numbers. He believed the blows delivered at the Fifth Army and at the British had been dealt by troops recovered by the enemy from his centre.

Meanwhile the Minister, Monsieur Messimy, had written to the French Commander-in-Chief before receiving his report. He said:

"It seems clear to me that the theatre of operations in the north is going to assume a real importance, strategic importance in the main, psychological importance also, owing to its proximity to Paris. An Army must be constituted to fight there. This is necessary in my opinion owing to the small power of resistance of the Territorials who do not hold their ground."

The Minister concluded:

"I enclose an order, the importance of which will not escape you –

---

* The movements of troops ordered this day were: two divisions from the Army of Alsace, and, as stated in a previous chapter, two Reserve Divisions to General d'Amade.
The Belgian Army had withdrawn into Antwerp since the 24th.

order to provide Paris with a garrison of three active corps in good condition in case the present operations should be unsuccessful.

"It goes without saying that the line of retreat of the Army must not be Paris but the centre or south of France.

"We are decided to fight on to the end, without mercy."*

* This letter also contained strictures on General Sordet:
"I am very surprised, I would say more, very displeased, at the rôle played by Sordet.
"The German Cavalry Corps is overrunning the north, ravaging everything, riding down the Territorials. Sordet, who has had little fighting, is asleep. This is inadmissible."

CHAPTER IV

THE CONFERENCE AT ST. QUENTIN

August 26th, 1914

Huguet's alarming report concerning the British I. Corps – General Lanrezac's response – The true story of Landrecies – The Battle of Le Cateau begins – La Capelle – Etroeungt – Lanrezac at le Nouvion – Lanrezac leaves for St. Quentin – A liaison officer's narrative – The Conference at St. Quentin – Instruction Générale No. 2 – Joffre and French – G.H.Q. departs southwards – Marle – The British "completely defeated" – The true situation – The feat of the British II. Corps at Le Cateau – Joffre's gratitude – Tension at Marle – The Fifth Army ordered to retire to Laon.

THE morning of August 26th was a nightmare.

A message sent by Colonel Huguet from St. Quentin at 5 a.m. to General Lanrezac, who received it at 6 a.m., started the ball rolling. This message, which was delivered by an officer named Armbruster, stated that the British I. Corps had been attacked in its billets between Landrecies and Le Cateau, and was endeavouring to fall back to the south in the direction of Guise. If this proved impossible it would retire south-east in the direction of La Capelle. Huguet concluded: "The British Commander-in-Chief asks General Lanrezac to come to his help by giving shelter to the I. Corps until it can rejoin the main body of the British Army."*

The first report of the fighting at Landrecies was received by Colonel Macdonogh at St. Quentin, to which G.H.Q. had removed, on the night of the 25th. He was called to the telephone and told that the operator at Le Cateau had been talking to the one at Landrecies, when suddenly the latter exclaimed that the Germans had entered Landrecies and that heavy fighting was going on. Colonel Macdonogh reported at once either to General Murray or to General Wilson, whose comment

* See Appendix XXIV.

was that it was an alarmist report. But presently the news was confirmed, and the Operations Section became thoroughly alarmed and despondent when I. Corps H.Q. reported the situation to be critical. News was actually circulated at St. Quentin that only a portion of the I. Corps had been able to cut its way through the enemy!

It is of course extremely difficult to determine the exact scope of an engagement fought in the night, but the completely erroneous impression gathered by the staff as to what was happening at Landrecies emphasized once more the importance of good liaison. Had there been a good G.H.Q. liaison officer at I. Corps H.Q. that night the nervousness at St. Quentin and the consequent confusion would have been avoided.

Colonel Huguet can hardly be blamed for the tenor of his alarming report to the Fifth Army. He only reflected the views of those around him.

The effect of his message, which was of course believed, was to upset completely the Fifth Army Staff. It evoked such a frightful picture of disaster, of irremediable defeat, that there is small wonder that a state of affairs bordering on panic reigned at H.Q. at Vervins. The British I. Corps was pictured streaming back towards the Fifth Army area as had the garrison of Namur, while the Germans poured through the gap left by the defeated British.

As a palliative to this grave menace, General Lanrezac issued the following order:

"Vervins, August 26th, 7 a.m.

"The British I. Corps is hard pressed by German forces debouching south and perhaps south-east from Landrecies.

"The Group of Reserve Divisions and the XVIII. Corps are ordered to face this attack with such forces as they can dispose of, and to counter-attack so as to disengage the British I. Corps which is retiring south from Landrecies.

"LANREZAC."

General Lanrezac should be given full credit for the neighbourly and generous help he tendered on this occasion.

As has been seen, General Valabrègue had not waited to receive orders to take action. The readiness with which subordinate formations almost always responded to appeals for support should be gratefully remembered.

After issuing his orders, General Lanrezac dashed into a car with his

Chief of Staff, and followed by Commander Schneider, disappeared down the road leading north in a cloud of dust. They had gone, it was said, to the report centre, but where was that? Some thought it was at La Capelle, others said at Etroeungt or Le Nouvion. Different destinations had been mentioned by distracted officers running to jump into the cars accompanying the General. The one thing that seemed certain was that General Lanrezac intended to see the Commander of the XVIII. Corps, General de Mas Latrie, but no one knew where he was.

Headquarters had been under orders to move to Marle at 10 a.m. but the disappearance of the Army Commander threw the machinery of the Army out of gear. Cars started in pursuit of him at frantic speeds, all liaison was disorganized, disorder reigned, and confusion became complete.

The real situation of the British was altogether different from that described in Colonel Huguet's message. The affair at Landrecies was merely a surprise encounter in which the British had the advantage. So little had the Germans expected to meet the British in Landrecies, where they had intended to billet, that the regimental transport trotted on ahead. The I. Corps had no difficulty in repulsing the enemy, and next morning and throughout the day (26th) carried out its retreat in perfect order, though the men were weary, having stood-to the whole of the previous night. The chief difficulty encountered by the Corps was the terrible confusion due to the fact that the same billeting areas had been allotted to it on the night of the 25th–26th as to the Reserve Divisions, and it had had to march on many of the same roads, for the G.Q.G. had not at this date laid down any line of demarcation between the Fifth Army and the B.E.F.

The danger to the British lay not on the right, as we thought, but farther to the left, where the II. Corps and the 4th Division were standing to fight the desperate battle of Le Cateau. (Map VI, p. 112.)

Sir Horace Smith-Dorrien had been informed late on the night of the 25th–26th by General Allenby, commanding the Cavalry, that the Cavalry Division could be of little help in covering the retreat next morning (26th), and also that as the enemy was pressing on in strength and was near by, the retreat should be begun before daylight if the troops were to be extricated. Simultaneously came news that the 3rd Division would be unable to march before 9 a.m. In face of these reports Sir Horace felt he had no choice but to stand and fight.*

He stood with 55,000 men against von Kluck who could bring against

* See Sir Horace Smith-Dorrien's *Memories of Forty-eight Years' Service*, p. 401.

him some 150,000, and who had a gun superiority of at least three to one.* Three British infantry divisions and one cavalry division were attacked in front and on both flanks by six German infantry divisions and three cavalry divisions, whilst the German II. Corps was descending on their left.† But of Sir Horace's fateful decision, and of the fight he was even then engaged in, we at Fifth Army H.Q. knew nothing.

I was one of those who started from Vervins in pursuit of General Lanrezac.

There were the usual heart-rending scenes on the roads, encumbered, like every highway leading north, with refugees who resembled all other refugees in their monotonous misery. Some were on the move, others camping by the road or sleeping under their waggons. When convoys met the slowly moving mass of the fleeing population there was a complete block, and wherever possible motor-cars cut across country.

At La Capelle I found other officers also looking for the Army Commander. No sign of him, and no one to tell us where he had gone, until we met a cyclist who thought he was at Etroeungt.

The roads were now more encumbered than ever. Retiring troops were pushing their way through the traffic under a torrid sun. Dust hung over the road, at times hiding even the high peasant waggons. Through the white choking cloud strained faces appeared and then were hidden again.

At Etroeungt, which I reached after seemingly endless delays, there were plenty of people about, but to my utter astonishment no one could direct me either to the *Mairie* or to the Post Office, where I hoped to find out where the General was. Exasperated, I walked into several houses and asked the people in them to direct me, with no better result. It seemed insane that none of the inhabitants should know the way to the most important buildings in the place. At last I grasped the truth. These were not the natives, who had abandoned the village some time ago. It was now occupied by refugees from villages and towns farther north, who had moved into the houses until such time as they should be forced to take the road again, which would be soon enough, for the enemy was perilously near. I now understood why everyone was in his Sunday best, for the peasantry when driven from their homes almost always put on their best clothes, either as the easiest way of carrying

---

* The British inferiority in numbers was reduced but slightly by the presence of some 4,000 French in Cambrai, and of Sordet's Cavalry on the left.

† The German account of the battle is given in the *Official History of the War*, Vol. I, p. 182.

them, or because it was a habit always to put on the Sunday suit when leaving the village.

Continuing my search for General Lanrezac, I at last found an officer who told me that he was probably at Le Nouvion, so thither I sped, and found him awaiting the Commander of the XVIII. Corps. The staff were installed in the dining-room of the Curé's house. The General, who appeared to be in a desperately bad temper, was wiling away the time by criticising with asperity an order his Chief of Staff had been drawing up. He also said that strong measures must be taken to deal with the fleeing population: they must be immobilized, or the whole Army would be paralysed. It certainly looked as if he were right.

My own impression of General Lanrezac at Le Nouvion has been confirmed from another source. An officer from the staff of a subordinate formation who had come in for orders, noted: "I found General Lanrezac on the *Place* of Le Nouvion surrounded by a number of officers. He seemed to be extremely displeased and expressed himself in violent language. He did not mince words in his criticism of the G.Q.G. and of the allies. He was much irritated against the former and the British. The gist of what he was saying was that all he required was to be left alone, that he would retire as far as was necessary, that he would choose his own time and then he would boot the enemy back whence he came." This officer goes on to say that he did not dare to approach the group, but watched the strange scene, which reminded him grotesquely of an umpire's criticism at manœuvres, for several minutes. The Chief of Staff, who had been standing by, beckoned to him and gave him his instructions. So struck was he by what he had seen that on returning to his formation he commented on it to his Chief.

No better description of Lanrezac at this time could be given. Such was his attitude and such were his methods. The officer who noted this scene was a mere captain. He was horrified. Discipline, faith in the leadership of the Supreme Command, alike seemed to be going by the board.

Whilst General Lanrezac was at Le Nouvion, he received information which enabled him to form a truer picture of the situation both of the British I. Corps and the Reserve Divisions. The former, far from being in a bad way, had, he learnt, inflicted a severe check on a German advance guard. This made it evident that Colonel Huguet's message had grossly exaggerated the peril of the situation, so General Lanrezac at once cancelled the order to the XVIII. Corps and the Reserve Divisions to go to the rescue of the British.

This satisfactory news from the left of the Army made it a matter of far less importance to see General de Mas Latrie, and General Hély d'Oissel reminded the General that the Commander-in-Chief had sent him an urgent summons to meet him at St. Quentin to confer there with Sir John French. General Lanrezac, after declaring that he would not go – it was absurd, he could not spare the time, it was unnecessary – was finally persuaded to change his mind. Once more he disappeared in a whirlwind of dust, accompanied by his Chief of Staff and Captain Besson.

The report centre at Le Nouvion was left in charge of Commandant Schneider, assisted by Girard. A few moments after General Lanrezac had left, General de Mas Latrie arrived. He seemed to be weary and unnerved. I gathered that Schneider received him rather badly.

An hour later, a very important cipher wireless message from the Eiffel Tower was handed in. It gave some precise details concerning von Kluck's advance. Schneider with but two or three officers and no clerks at his disposal, decided to send the original message in the first place to Le Cateau, and then to have it carried to the Commanders in conference at St. Quentin. Helbronner was entrusted with this mission. I am privileged to make use of the notes he made concerning what befell him that afternoon, and give them as an interesting example of the extreme difficulty of communicating at that time.

"To gain Le Cateau I crossed the Forest of Le Nouvion, which was full of our troops. There was an intense bombardment, and as I advanced the rattle of musketry and the rat-tat of machine-guns, together with the increasing noise of bursting shells, could be heard ever more distinctly.

"I now met British troops retiring, wounded men being carried by their comrades. I crossed Bergues and Catillon. I intended to reach the town of Le Cateau via Bazuel. Shells were dropping on the plain on British infantry, which appeared to be falling back rapidly. A British officer stopped me to ask who I was, and where I was going. When I told him I was going to Bazuel and then on to Le Cateau, he smiled and handed me his glasses, pointing out to me German patrols coming out of the village. He told me that Le Cateau was in the enemy's hands. He thought that British G.H.Q. was probably at La Fère and that the whole Army was retiring south of St. Quentin. I decided to go to the latter town. My intention was to make for Mazinghien and thence get on to the main Le Cateau–St. Quentin road if the enemy had not forestalled me. In the neighbourhood of Mazinghien shells were bursting on all sides. Some British troops were falling back in disorder. Wounded and dead were lying on the road and in the neighbouring fields. Four shells fell close to my car. From a neighbouring hill, along which I think the road from Le Cateau to Landrecies runs, I could clearly see the flash of the German guns firing directly at us. The road was congested with troops, on whom the German gunners were obviously concentrating. To gain time as well as to avoid extermination, my chauffeur left the road and drove across the fields. Shrapnel was bursting on all sides, and one of the wings of the car was blown off. The noise was deafening. At last we got clear of the British division, and I found myself on a narrow road in the neighbourhood of Bohain. A German monoplane spotted my car, dived towards it, and threw a small bomb which burst in a field without making much noise. We stopped the car and began a lively fusillade at the plane, which, however, flew off unharmed. The main road was completely deserted. I raced through abandoned villages. A little farther, in front of a solitary house, a woman and an old man were piling furniture on to a cart. They signalled to me to stop, begging me to help them, saying Uhlans had crossed the road ten minutes previously.

"At last I fell in with some outposts of French Territorials. I had not been aware that there were any in the neighbourhood. I asked whether I should find British G.H.Q. at St. Quentin, but no one knew. When I arrived there, I saw on the *Place* an officer wearing a red and white armlet. He was General Joffre's A.D.C."

*   *   *

The celebrated meeting at St. Quentin, the second and last between French and Lanrezac, took place in a house withdrawn from the main thoroughfare and decorated in a neo-pompeian style. The windows and shutters were closed in the dimly lit chamber where the conference was held, and everyone spoke in an undertone as if there were a corpse in the next room.

There were present at first Sir John, General Wilson, (General Murray was ill) Generals Joffre, Berthelot and d'Amade.

The French Commander-in-Chief asked to be told the present situation of the British, and General Wilson had just finished giving an account of it, when Fagalde arrived. The same question was put to him as regards the Fifth Army. He was in the midst of his report when General Lanrezac, accompanied by General Hély d'Oissel, arrived and took up the account. Lanrezac concluded his remarks by referring to the Instruction of the 25th (*Instruction Générale No. 2*)* which he had re-

* See Appendix XXV.

ceived while at Le Nouvion, saying with a touch of asperity that he could not be expected to carry out the order to rest his left on St. Quentin since the British barred his way, to which General Joffre answered that his left, instead of falling back on St. Quentin, was to retire to La Fère.

General Joffre then again turned to Sir John, who, irritated perhaps by the presence of Lanrezac, to whom he attributed so many of his difficulties, pointed out with acerbity the dangerous situation of the British Army. He had been ceaselessly attacked by overwhelming numbers, whereas the Fifth Army, attacked by an enemy inferior in strength, had continuously held back behind his own, and had finally retired headlong without warning or explanation.*

Sir John did not speak long. Realizing as his annoyance spent itself that he was not understood, since most of the Frenchmen present spoke no English, he turned to General Wilson and asked him to translate. Wilson did so, modifying and softening somewhat what his Chief had said. This bowdlerized translation did not efface the impression Sir John's tone had made on General Lanrezac, who appeared to sense the deep resentment of the British Commander against himself. He gave little sign, however, but shrugged his shoulders slightly, and made a few remarks which were neither an answer to the British Field Marshal nor an explanation of his own actions. He did not even mention the danger his right had run on the Meuse, but talked vaguely of the retreat as if it were an academic question.

The pointed way in which his remarks were ignored, the affectation of brushing aside what he had said, were, so he told me after the war, profoundly galling to Sir John. General Joffre looked hard at his subordinate but said nothing. After a pause during which everyone looked at him expectantly, he began in his blank even voice to summarize and explain his order (*Instruction Générale No. 2*)† in the following

---

* The following message from Colonel Huguet to the G.Q.G., sent off at 6.25 a.m., accurately reflects the point of view of the British G.O.C. at this time:

"Marshal French considers his position to be difficult because he has always been ahead of the Fifth Army, which has only been faced by numbers inferior to its own, whereas he himself is confronted by forces equal to his own, in addition to being threatened on his left by a large enemy force. He has consequently decided to retire tomorrow to the line Câtelet-Busigny, and will continue to fall back so long as the situation remains the same, but as soon as the Fifth Army stops and moves forward he is determined to push forward with all his force."

Incidentally, this message would tend to show that the overwhelming nature of the enemy's turning movement, and the grave import of General Smith-Dorrien's decision to stand and fight at Le Cateau, which had been known since 5 a.m., not to mention the actual strength of the enemy, were still not fully appreciated at British G.H.Q.

† See Appendix XXV.

sense: We have failed to carry out the offensive manœuvre we had in mind. The enemy's manœuvre is now clear, and there is but one way of defeating it: I must have a mass of manœuvre on my left capable of resuming the offensive. That mass will be constituted by the Fourth, Fifth and British Armies, to which I shall add troops withdrawn from the eastern front. The remaining armies will meanwhile contain the enemy, who is now extended to his maximum capacity. The armies of the left should keep in the closest touch with each other, conforming to each other's movements. They should do all they can to delay the enemy's advance. The best way to do this is to constitute powerful rearguards which will take advantage of every topographical feature and deliver short and violent counter-attacks the principal element of which will be artillery fire. The British Army will take up its position behind the Somme between Ham and Bray. The Fifth Army, astride the Oise, will hold the front between La Fère and Laon, whilst General d'Amade's Territorials will form a barrage to the sea.

By September 2nd the new Army (the Sixth), comprising one or perhaps two active corps and four reserve divisions, will be collected before Amiens. When we are ready to attack, the Sixth Army will advance either on St. Pol, Arras, or Arras, Bapaume, that is either north or north-east.

When General Joffre had finished speaking, he looked at Sir John, to whom General Wilson had been translating. The English Commander appeared puzzled. "I know nothing of this Order," he exclaimed. Everyone turned to General Wilson, who explained that the order had been received during the night, but had not yet been studied. General Joffre appeared disconcerted. He went over his instruction again, but his voice seemed lower even than before, and was very unemphatic. Somehow those who heard him formed the impression that he had lost faith in the success of his plan, whilst the French officers present were very critical of the fact that Sir John did not even know of the existence of *Instruction Générale No. 2*.

It seemed as if the projected operation would be stillborn, and that Joffre would do nothing to save it. He must have felt that his orders were being ignored, yet he made no effort to secure common action.

The sense of doom was as evident in that room as when a jury is about to return a verdict of guilty on a capital charge.

General Joffre must have felt himself helpless, unable to adjust differences he could only guess at, fettered by not being able to issue orders to the British soldier.

The atmosphere was heavy, embarrassed and almost hostile. There were long pauses. At last, when the strain had become almost intolerable, the juniors not daring to speak, some leaders mute because they could not think of anything to say, others because they had too much on their minds and could not trust their tempers, a particularly long and painful silence was broken by General d'Amade, who proposed to attack the German right flank with his Territorials and so delay the enemy's advance. His suggestion, which was listened to in brooding silence, was received with scepticism, for during the early part of the Conference he had declared that these same Territorials gave way as soon as they saw the German cavalry, and would be of no use until taken in hand and properly equipped with guns and machine-guns. He trailed on for a few minutes, then, sensing the critical atmosphere, faltered. General Joffre with a sign of impatience brushed the suggestion aside.

Extraordinary as it may seem, the Conference ended there. Although the *directive* prescribed close co-operation between the armies, not a word concerning co-operation was uttered. The Order which the British Commander-in-Chief had not heard of, nor his staff studied, was not gone into beyond the short exposition given by General Joffre. No attempt was made to study it, to take in its implications, or to see in what manner the then situation of the Armies permitted of its being carried out. Neither Sir John nor General Lanrezac addressed each other direct. The only practical result of the Conference was the decision that the left of the Fifth Army was to retire on La Fère and not on St. Quentin.

Yet the Order was perfectly clear. The Commander-in-Chief's idea was expressed with great lucidity, and the manner of its execution plainly indicated. The plan was sound in theory, indeed it has been rightly considered to foreshadow the battle of the Marne, but was it practical or even possible at the time it was issued?

The positions to be held, the high ground of Laon–St. Gobain, and the valley of the Somme, are of great strength: they are features which military writers have for years pointed to as providing the natural obstacles which should be used by an Army thrown on the defensive, to delay the enemy and furnish the screen behind which a counter-manœuvre could be organized. But time was necessary for this, and time was lacking. The development of events, and the rapidity of the retreat of both French and British during the next few days, were to render such an operation impossible. Again, Joffre's order prescribed a counter-offensive. But to debouch beyond an obstacle such as the Somme it would be necessary to maintain bridgeheads, and the order contained no mention of any such thing.

Instruction Générale No. 2 came too late. Alone the idea of strengthening the Allied left and basing a great manœuvre on this change of balance in the Franco-British order of battle was to survive in practice.

The truth was that events had moved faster than the minds at the G.Q.G. Many more departments were to be devastated, and thousands upon thousands of lives lost, before the initial errors of disposition and calculation could be remedied, before the G.Q.G. really grasped the German plan and realized the ponderous weight behind it.

When the Conference was over, Sir John invited everyone to lunch with him. Lanrezac declined, but Joffre accepted.[*]

Before he left St. Quentin, Joffre must have realized something of the desperate fight in which the British II. Corps was engaged, for through Huguet he ordered Sordet not only to cover the British left, but to intervene in the battle with all available forces and with the greatest energy, a call to which Sordet responded nobly.[†]

In one sense the Conference at St. Quentin was useful. It brought General Joffre and Sir John French closer together, and led each to a better comprehension of the other's point of view. Sir John told me much later that after Lanrezac had gone Joffre made it clear that he was anything but satisfied with the way the Fifth Army was being led. I think he also won Sir John by frankly admitting that his plans had miscarried. He put down his failure to the impossible nature of the Ardennes country, covered with forests and broken up by narrow and precipitous ravines where artillery was wellnigh useless. General Joffre emphasized the high morale of the regular troops, and dwelt also on the great results he felt sure would be obtained as soon as ground was reached on which the 75s could be employed to full advantage.

Another result of the Conference was that Joffre realized for the first time the exasperation of the British Commander-in-Chief and his staff at the way in which the Expeditionary Force had been treated. He saw

---

[*] For Colonel Huguet's account of the Conference, see Appendix XXVI.

[†] The transmission of this order resulted in poor Huguet's receiving a sharp rap over the knuckles from Sordet, who objected to receiving orders from him.

"Villers-Faucon, 27 août, 1914.

"MON CHER COLONEL,

". . . Je vous ferai observer que je ne vous reconnais pas le droit de me donner des ordres pour une action précise.

"Ma Mission générale est fixée par le Général Joffre, et je suis seul juge de la manière dont je dois et je peux la remplir. . . .

"Recevez, mon cher Colonel, l'expression de mes sentiments amicaux."

that something must be done to relieve the intolerable pressure that had been brought unremittingly to bear on the British, not only because the strain was greater than any human beings could bear, but also because they felt very badly let down, misled as they had been as to the enemy's plans and numbers, shepherded into what turned out to be the most dangerous part of the line, and abandoned there by the Fifth Army.

Relations had been strained to such a degree that the easing of tension resulting from the meeting of the two Commanders did not for the moment percolate to the Staffs. That afternoon at St. Quentin I was told that there was no point in my returning to the Fifth Army H.Q. and that the minimum of unavoidable correspondence would in the future be left to the Huguet Mission and to Colonel Bowes, who was a perfect French scholar, and occasionally came to the Fifth Army from the Operations Section of G.H.Q. As, however, I was not given a positive order to leave the Fifth Army, I decided, much troubled, to rejoin it. So perturbed was I, and so impressed by the talk of an independent retirement, that I well remember thinking that if the worst came to the worst I could eventually rejoin my own Army by sea!

St. Quentin was a gloomy place that afternoon. Sir John with his personal staff, General Wilson and Sir Archibald Murray, left in motors going south. To see the heads leaving, preceding the retreat, when no one knew anything but that things were going badly, had an immensely depressing influence on the remainder of the staff and on all the troops in the town.*

It was perhaps the worst day of all at G.H.Q. Nerves were bad, morale was low, and there was much confusion. The Staff wanted heartening, and Sir John's departure had the contrary effect. On the previous night the strain had been so frightful that the Chief of Staff, Sir Archibald Murray, exhausted by anxiety and overwork, had had a temporary collapse from shock when the false news was received that the enemy had attacked and defeated the I. Corps at Landrecies. Colonel Cummins, the M.O. at G.H.Q., was very anxious about him. He did not actually faint, but his pulse was very weak. He said to Colonel Cummins in a whisper: "They have got in between the I. and II. Corps. I have just heard, and it has been too much for me."

I have not attempted to describe in this narrative the racking anxieties and the terrible responsibilities of the Staffs, both French and

---

* Under similar circumstances I have known a French General drive out of the town he was leaving, in the direction of the enemy, then take a side road and drive south again. Such a dodge may or may not be worth indulging in for the sake of morale.

British, or the maddeningly difficult conditions under which their work had to be carried on, but something of their burdens may be gathered from a moment's consideration of the situations they had to deal with. Many officers collapsed completely. As I was not a Staff officer myself I feel it right to pay a tribute to a class of soldier whose services are not generally appreciated or understood, but whose task at a time such as the Retreat entailed a far severer strain and a more continuous effort than did that of the regimental officers, though of course the latter ran greater risks.

I learnt that day to what shifts G.H.Q. had been driven. The day before (25th) Colonel Macdonogh had had to send out his Intelligence officers in lorries to search for entrenching tools, of which there was a great shortage, with which to dig entrenchments somewhere about the Le Cateau–Cambrai road. The work was carried out by French civilians under French supervision. These trenches were long straight ditches without turns or traverses, and quite unusable, but the German artillery shelled them mercilessly, so they were perhaps of some service after all.

As the afternoon wore on the aspect of St. Quentin became very strange. It was a derelict town from which gradually the whole Staff had been withdrawn. Odd units, isolated men from different battalions, began to appear. I met several men belonging to my own regiment, one of whom, our adjutant's servant I think, told me a grisly story of some of our wounded having been found massacred by the enemy.

It proved to be none too easy to leave the town when the time came. Hostile patrols were reported, quite falsely as it turned out, on many of the roads leading out of it. It began to pour – I remember the drenching quality of that rain – and passing through very heavy showers I at last arrived at Marle, where the H.Q. of the Fifth Army had been established. It was one of the most dreadful places I have ever been in. I was greeted with the news that the British had been completely defeated. The hours I lived through then were perhaps the most painful of my life. Nothing can compare with the horror of feeling that your people have been beaten. No personal humiliation can equal this. It is impossible to overstate the bitterness of such news, especially when you are the sole representative of the supposedly beaten army, alone amongst men belonging to another Army and another nation, who, themselves under a great strain, feel temporarily estranged from you. This was a time of frayed nerves, when few resisted the temptation to place the blame for their misfortunes on their neighbours. I shall never forget the horror of Marle, nor the filthy room where we went to get something to eat. It was crawling with flies, a veritable plague of them. They covered everything, the ceiling was black, the air thick with them, droning and buzzing in endless gyrating swarms, making the very idea of food nauseating even had we not been too tired to eat.

The news that caused such despondency emanated from Colonel Huguet, who had sent the following telegram to the G.Q.G.

"Colonel Huguet from G.H.Q. Noyon, August 26th, 20.15

"Battle lost by British Army, which seems to have lost all cohesion. It will demand considerable protection to enable it to reconstitute. G.H.Q. tonight Noyon. Fuller details will follow."

I do not know how this message came to be sent. If only we had known the truth, which was that Sir Horace Smith-Dorrien had accomplished the stupendous feat of standing his ground, inflicting a check on an overwhelmingly superior enemy force, and then withdrawing in good order in broad daylight!

This wellnigh miraculous result was in great part due to the fact that the British had established themselves as such formidable fighters that the enemy simply did not dare to tackle them save with the utmost precaution, and only advanced against them with a prudence that sometimes amounted to timidity. Had von Kluck attacked boldly when he found the British, in apparently mad challenge, awaiting the onslaught of his immense force, the overwhelming torrent of his troops must have swept them away. He did not do so, nor did he pursue them when they withdrew.

After the battle the men of the II. Corps were scattered, and some of the units were broken up in that terrible and unequal duel, but only by the difficulty of the retreat, not by the direct action of the Germans. Only at one point, against the exhausted 5th Division, did the enemy succeed in interfering with the orderly withdrawal of the force. Elsewhere he was unable to make any impression: everywhere his infantry was met by the magnificently directed British artillery fire, the gunners stubbornly standing by the infantry, whilst all over the battlefield small units who had not received the order to retire hung on desperately to their ground, confusing and delaying the enemy's advance.

Von Kluck's failure to pursue was again due, as at Mons, to faulty Intelligence. He had been assured by his Intelligence service that as the British Army was based on Calais their lines of communication must run through Lille and Cambrai. He therefore concluded that as his troops were astride the Lille–Cambrai railway, the British Army, while fighting the battle of Le Cateau, was already cut off from its base. He manœuvred accordingly, that is he extended his right the more surely to prevent the British from connecting up with their supposed lines of communication farther north. Von Kluck, misled by his Intelligence, went on a wild goose chase, and meanwhile the British Army escaped. While his Army marched south-west ours retired south, and the German cavalry, which on this and the two following days might have operated with decisive results against the exhausted II. Corps, was occupied in cutting through our hypothetical lines of communication, and was directed on Péronne.

That night, Staff officers of the II. Corps sorted out the men who had lost their regiments as they streamed down the roads. Throughout the night, standing at the cross roads, they called out continuously: "Transport and mounted troops straight on, 3rd Infantry Division to the right, 5th Infantry Division to the left."* The men were then sorted into their proper units again, and before dawn the divisions were reconstituted, only to march on and on, officers and men weary beyond belief, beyond thought, almost beyond pain, but still disciplined and formidable. The II. Corps had fought, on that August 26th, as noteworthy a battle as did their ancestors at Crécy on the same date in 1346. The action cost the British 5,212 casualties and 2,600 prisoners, many of whom were captured because the order to retire did not reach them. But that the result amply repaid the sacrifice was acknowledged by ally and foe alike. Von Kluck in after years said to General Bingham, with special reference to the Battle of Le Cateau: "I always had the greatest admiration for the B.E.F. . . . The way the retreat was carried out was remarkable. I tried very hard to outflank them, but I could not do so. If I had succeeded the war would have been won."†

General Joffre expressed his gratitude next day. He telegraphed to Sir John, then at Noyon:

"The British Army, by engaging itself without hesitation against greatly superior forces, has powerfully contributed towards assuring the security of the left flank of the French Army.

---

* There was no need to do this in the case of the 4th Division. The 3rd and 5th coming off the battlefield struck diagonal roads and the units got mixed.

† Sir Horace Smith-Dorrien's *Memories of Forty-eight Years' Service*, p. 415.

"It has fought with a devotion, energy and perseverance to which I wish to pay homage, and which I am certain will be manifested in the future in assuring the final victory of our common cause. The French Army will not forget the service rendered. Animated by the same spirit of sacrifice and the same will to victory as the British Army, it will demonstrate its gratitude in the forthcoming combats."

This generous tribute did honour alike to the man who paid it and the men who received it. Above the heads of those who, in closer proximity to the battle, seemed deprived of any comprehension either of the magnitude of the achievement or of the heroism displayed, Joffre reached out his hand to the men who had fought so well.

Generous and chivalrous also was General Smith-Dorrien's recognition of the help he had received from the French. He was at pains at the time and afterwards to acknowledge the splendid service rendered by Sordet's Cavalry Corps on his left, which had arrived at its positions after a march of thirty miles on the previous day. General Sordet's artillery and cyclists had attacked the flank of the hostile forces attacking the British 4th Division.*

General Smith-Dorrien's voice was the only one raised in praise of the French Territorials, so much derided by their own countrymen. In his book he says: "General d'Amade's . . . advanced troops held up the German II. Corps for several hours . . . the delay and the brave front shown by these Territorials were of vital importance to us, as otherwise it is almost certain we should have had another Corps against us on the 26th." In an order of the day published on the 29th, Sir Horace, whilst telling the troops in simple but heartfelt words of his admiration for their prowess, did not forget to pay a public tribute to the support afforded by the French on his left at Le Cateau.

At a time when many people on both sides were inclined to blame their neighbours for all their misfortunes, General Smith-Dorrien's attitude was a notable and very welcome departure.

*   *   *

At Marle that evening, the visit of Colonel Alexandre, the liaison officer from the G.Q.G., to Fifth Army Headquarters, caused additional strain.

Short, rather stout, very square and powerful, fair-haired and hook-

---

* Sir John French's grateful thanks were conveyed to Sordet by Colonel Huguet on the 28th.

nosed, he impressed one as a man of strong personality. He went in to see the Army Commander, with whom he had a long conversation. After his departure the 3ème Bureau was nervous and irritable, as well it might be, for Alexandre had not concealed the fact that the G.Q.G. was, to put it mildly, critical of the way the Fifth Army had drifted back with never an attempt to deal a blow at the enemy.

Meanwhile, Maubeuge was completely invested by the enemy, and the Fifth Army, immune and unmolested, continued its retreat.

As the evening wore on, and neither the XVIII. Corps nor the Reserve Divisions reported anything abnormal, Duruy and others agreed with me that the news of the destruction of the British Army must be untrue.

* * *

That evening General Lanrezac ordered the Fifth Army to retire in three marches to the position of Laon.*

---

* That evening also the G.Q.G. modified the zones of action affected to the B.E.F. and the Fifth Army, and as a result the front of the British was to be more to the east than it had previously been.

General d'Amade, who had been told that in case retreat became unavoidable he was to occupy a line extending from Picquigny to the sea, was ordered in the afternoon, as the situation became clearer to the Commander-in-Chief, to withdraw immediately all his forces to the left bank of the Somme, the two Reserve Divisions about Bray, the Territorial Divisions between Amiens and the sea.

General Lanrezac, having received Joffre's instructions, issued his own orders, which were as follows:

"At Headquarters at Marle, August 26th, 9 p.m.

"Secret personal instructions for the generals commanding the 4th Group of Reserve Divisions, the I., III., X. and XVIII. Corps.

"By order of the Commander-in-Chief, the Fifth Army, endeavouring to break contact with the enemy, will retire in three marches to the position of Laon. It will occupy the front La Fère, Saint Erme, ready to resume the offensive with the British Army, from which it will be separated by the Oise, and with the Fourth Army established on the Aisne.

"Every obstacle will be taken advantage of to hold up the advance of the enemy, and should the pressure become too great he must be held up by violent counter-attacks principally conducted by the artillery.

"The Corps will take the greatest care to maintain contact with each other during the retirement, which will begin tomorrow at 3 a.m.

"LANREZAC."

He also sent for the Camp Commandant and the engineer officer in charge of Laon to give them orders for the defence of the position.

On this day the Belgians, who had been engaged in a sortie south of Antwerp since the 25th, withdrew on news being received that the Anglo–French forces were retiring.

On this day also, the two German Corps which had attacked Namur, the XI. and the Guard Reserve, began to move to East Prussia to parry the Russian invasion, an error for which the Germans were to pay dearly.

CHAPTER V

JOFFRE ORDERS A COUNTER-ATTACK

August 27th, 1914

The respective positions of the British and the French Fifth Army – Joffre orders the Fifth Army to counter-attack – General Hély d'Oissel's telephone conversation with the G.Q.G. – A difficulty concerning the allocation of roads – Another visit from Colonel Alexandre – Marle after the war – Joffre's message to the British – A telephone message from Huguet – Joffre's visit to French at Noyon – The British evacuate St. Quentin – Another pessimistic message from Huguet – The British Army may withdraw to Le Havre to reconstitute – Events on the British front during the day – Pessimism at G.H.Q. – Lanrezac's orders for the 28th – The G.Q.G. defines its orders for a counter-attack – Alexandre and Schneider fall out – The British retreat to continue.

ALTHOUGH on the 27th there was no fighting on the Fifth Army front and only rear-guard actions on that of the British, it was an important day from many points of view. Decisions of great moment were taken, but perhaps more important still, a distinct impression gained ground that the G.Q.G. was laying a firm hand on the direction of affairs, and that drift and vacillation were at an end. It was on this day that General Joffre's will and personality first began to impress themselves on the troops.

From this day too dates the complete reversal of the relative positions of the Fifth and British Armies. From now on many of the reproaches hitherto levelled at the Fifth Army could have been, and indeed were, made against the British.

It is not the purpose of this book to attempt to strike a balance in such matters, but the reader, when forming his judgement, will have to remember the plight and the circumstances of the British at this date.

They had been misinformed on every single matter of importance from the numbers of the enemy to the result of the French operations. Where they had looked for support they had found only shadows;

schemes, plans, operations, everything had melted away, leaving only one reality – the enemy, who in overwhelming strength and with relentless purpose had driven home blow after blow. Only one promise had matured in belated fruition. Plucky and indomitable Sordet had eventually appeared on the British left, but his force was exhausted and could only interfere by fire action.

In these circumstances it can hardly be wondered at that the British Command did not at once apprehend that a change had taken place and that the errors of the beginning were never to be repeated. How could they know? It was but natural that Sir John French, believing the B.E.F. had been exposed with complete wantonness, should have remembered the instructions of the Government: "That the greatest care must be exercised towards a minimum of losses and wastage," instructions placing an undue restriction on him perhaps, but justified in that the B.E.F. contained almost the entire nucleus from which the Armies of the Empire were to be trained.*

The first indication that the G.Q.G. really meant business was given in the following telephone message received by the Fifth Army at Marle in the early morning:

"Vitry, August 27th, 6.30 a.m.

"You have expressed to me your intention of throwing back by a counter-offensive, well supported by artillery, the troops which are following you, as soon as you have left the wooded region where the employment of your artillery is difficult.

"Not only do I authorize you to carry this out, but I consider such an attack to be indispensable. The state of your troops is good, their *moral* is excellent. It is necessary to take advantage of this. To act otherwise would diminish the *moral*, and might perhaps compromise the result of the campaign.

"The zone of Vervins into which you are moving lends itself well to such an operation.

"Do not take into account what the English are doing on your left.

"J. JOFFRE."

There was no possible doubt now that the Generalissimo, dissatisfied with General Lanrezac's conduct of operations, intended to impose a more aggressive policy. His message was a clever one, avoiding open criticism but pinning Lanrezac down to his own declarations, and

* See Appendix XXIX.

debarring him from using the British as a pretext for argument or negative action.

That General Lanrezac hardly jumped at General Joffre's suggestion is shown by what occurred on its receipt. (Map X, p. 266.)

At 6.40 a.m. General Hély d'Oissel got on the telephone to General Berthelot, when the following conversation took place.

1. *Question by General Hély d'Oissel.*
"We take it that it is on the *Southern bank of the Oise* that we are to counter-attack the Germans, because

(*a*) the ground on the north bank does not lend itself to the employment of artillery.

(*b*) in the Commander-in-Chief's telegraphic order of 6.30, August 27th, the following words occur "the zone of Vervins into which you are moving lends itself well to such an operation."

Answer by General Berthelot.
"Of course."

2. *Second question.*
"Therefore you do not ask us to recross the Oise, today the 27th, with a view to advancing towards the Germans on the north bank, over ground unfavourable to the employment of artillery?"

Answer.
"No."*

The effect of Joffre's message on Lanrezac was to make him very angry, as all those who like myself had to do with him that morning found to their cost.

The particular difficulty that brought me into contact with him was once more the question of the allocation of roads. The facts of the case are not clear in my mind, but had something to do with the French maintaining that the British I. Corps was retiring on the road allocated to the 53rd Reserve Division, whereas the British contended that an arrangement had been come to whereby this road, which ran through Guise, had been allotted to them. Apart from the suffering such disputes always inflicted on the troops, the Staffs were particularly nervous in this case, for a critical operation from the British point of view was

* *Les Armées Françaises dans la Grande Guerre*, Tome 1, 2nd Volume, Annex 887.

involved, firstly because of the gap between the two British Corps, which had widened since the previous day, and secondly because the enemy was reported to be in the immediate vicinity.* (He was even reported later in the day to be in great strength just north of St. Quentin, due west of the British I. Corps). Under these circumstances the difficulty of withdrawing a whole corps on one road, which our Allies were also using, will be readily understood. The negotiations involved led to some very acid criticism by General Lanrezac of the British and their Commander.

In the course of the morning Alexandre appeared, and the atmosphere, already charged with electricity, became dangerously tense.

General Lanrezac has described this interview in his book. Alexandre had come to see that the Commander-in-Chief's orders for an attack were carried out. He developed with great emphasis the spirit of those orders, and went on to say that the Fifth Army had all along been expected not merely to fall back but to fight and contain the enemy by vigorous counter-attacks. Hély d'Oissel replied with asperity that "by its rapid retreat the Fifth Army had disengaged itself and had gained the time necessary to enable it to establish itself in the prescribed positions."

These words have been recorded by General Lanrezac himself, and evidently met with his approval. There could be no better comment on his attitude. Ever since Charleroi, with his back to the enemy, the leader of the Fifth Army had been seeking for ideal positions, always further south.

Whilst Alexandre was in conference with the Army Commander, Girard was called in to give an appreciation of the situation from the enemy's point of view. He gave it as his opinion, an opinion confirmed by reports, that the enemy was slipping from east to west without pursuing the Fifth Army. This information could but strengthen Alexandre's contention that the Germans were being left free by the Fifth Army to carry out their manœuvre unmolested.

In view of the forthcoming attack, Fifth Army H.Q. remained at Marle instead of moving to Laon in the morning as had been intended.

A short time ago I revisited Marle, which had remained in my mind as a vision of horror. I thought I remembered it well. Could this sleepy

---

* The reports concerning the proximity of the Germans were inaccurate. The 1st Cavalry Brigade, forming part of the rearguard after the Battle of Le Cateau, which did not arrive at St. Quentin till midday on the 27th, had no difficulty in holding on to the town until the 28th.

little town be the place I remembered so vividly surging with troops, through which hurried gloomy staff officers with frayed nerves? I could not find my way about. I went to the school. It was quite different. "Are you sure this was where the staff was in 1914?" I asked the schoolmaster. He was quite sure. He thought he could remember the name of the General. "General – let me see – General von —" I then realized that we were not talking about the same thing. A German Commander had, it seemed, followed the Fifth Army in occupation of the town and made far more impression than we had. But still this was not the school I remembered. "Was there another one?" Yes, down a side street there was a girls' school, so thither I went. This was the place. The long balcony along which General Lanrezac had paced, his hands behind his back, and along which the Chief of Staff or Major Schneider had come almost at a run in search of their Chief, was unmistakable, but the remainder of the building was not as I remembered it, the entrance was quite different, so was the courtyard. So much for accurate memories.

General Joffre, having given his instructions to the Fifth Army, which was carrying out its movement in perfect quietude, turned his attention to the British, whose situation was giving him cause for ever-growing anxiety.

At 6.45 a.m. he sent the following message to Colonel Huguet:

"I am ordering the Fifth Army to carry out a vigorous attack from the line Guise–Vervins against the enemy who are following it.

"The left of the British Army will be protected from any outflanking movement by the Cavalry Corps. On the other hand, on your (the British) front the enemy seems to be exhausted and incapable of pursuit.

"Under these conditions it appears to me that the British Army runs no risks, and that its withdrawal can be methodical, and regulated by the movement of the Fifth Army in such a way as not to uncover the left flank of that Army."

Unfortunately this message struck the wrong note. The inference that the enemy had been dealt such a blow as to render him incapable of pursuit was flattering, but unfortunately the British knew this was not the case.

Colonel Huguet answered by a telephone message at 8.15 a.m. which reflected not only his usual pessimism but something of the resentment of the British Command as well. After stating that the situation was not clear and that it was hoped the II. Corps would be collected that night at St. Quentin and the I. at Origny-Ste. Benoîte, he went on to say:

"There is no news of the Cavalry Division which has suffered severely."* (It has lost fifteen men at Le Cateau.) "Effective support by Sordet's Cavalry Corps is relied upon. The 4th and 9th German Cavalry Divisions have been but little engaged. They may be very audacious and transform the retreat into a rout. It is therefore thought that Sordet's Corps should not only protect the retreat but attack if possible. If this co-operation is not very effective the appreciation of ourselves (by the British) risks being extremely severe."†

General Joffre realized when he visited Sir John French at Noyon at 11 a.m. that Huguet was right about the attitude of the British. No decision seems to have emerged from this meeting. On his return to his Headquarters he sent the congratulatory telegram referred to in the previous chapter. It may be that he hoped this would propitiate the British Commander, but it is certainly the fact that he sincerely believed such a tribute was due.

Before General Joffre had returned to the G.Q.G., news was received there that the British were evacuating St. Quentin. General Berthelot telephoned to Huguet to ask if this was the fact and to protest. "To uncover completely Lanrezac's left at the moment when his Army was about to attack would place him in a critical situation." He reiterated that the British left was amply covered.

Meanwhile Sordet was told to continue covering the B.E.F. principally to its rear and to the west until it had crossed the Somme. He was then

---

* G.H.Q. was absolutely without information about the Cavalry Division at this time. At about 8 a.m. the Colonel commanding one of the Regiments of the 1st Cavalry Brigade got on to G.H.Q. through a village telephone (north of St. Quentin). He asked if they could tell him the whereabouts of the 1st Cavalry Brigade, from which his Regiment had got detached during the night of the 26th. The officers to whom he spoke said: "We have heard nothing of any of the Cavalry for two days. Can you tell me where any of them are?" So the Colonel told him where they had been when he had last been in contact with them the night before, after the Battle of Le Cateau.

† The same alarmist note was sounded to General d'Amade:

"Colonel Huguet to General d'Amade at Bray-sur-Somme, August 27th, 1914, 9.15 a.m.

"Situation of British left Corps very precarious. It is hoped to reach St. Quentin this evening. Field Marshal asks when the Reserve Divisions will reach Péronne and be ready for action."

to remain about St. Quentin until he received fresh instructions from the G.Q.G.

As the day wore on, the horizon as seen from G.H.Q. grew ever darker, as was shown by yet another message from Huguet to the G.Q.G at 5.45 p.m. This time he announced that a German Cavalry Division had just entered Péronne, (which was not true) and cheerfully commented that the arrival of this mythical foe risked turning the British retreat into a rout. He also stated that Sordet had not left his billets at Villers-Faucon owing to the fatigue of his horses.* This extremely grave situation was leading, said Huguet, to very unfavourable comments on the part of the British. Again General Berthelot asserted that General Sordet had been ordered to protect the British retreat at all costs, and the British were informed that an Army Corps (the VII.) was detraining about Chaulnes.†

But the most staggering blow to General Joffre's hopes and plans was Huguet's final message. It was to the effect that the British Government might demand that the whole Army be withdrawn to its base at Le Havre to reorganize. (This was anything but the Government's intention; further, on the next day arrangements were discussed for changing the base from Havre to St. Nazaire at the mouth of the Loire.)

The gravity of this message was barely palliated by the further statement that should such a withdrawal take place it would only be temporary, the will to re-enter the conflict as soon as possible remaining unimpaired.

Colonel Huguet concluded by pointing out that under these circumstances the German policy of overwhelming the allied left would be carried out with ever-increasing success against a shorter line, and that General Lanrezac's left would soon be seriously threatened.

This communication, which reflected not only Colonel Huguet's own dejection but the discouragement and pessimism of a section of British G.H.Q., as well as the wildly inaccurate views current in some quarters concerning the state of the fighting troops, went on to say that while the I. Corps still presented a certain cohesion the II. could not offer the least resistance to the enemy. The British Army would therefore not be able to resume the campaign without a prolonged rest and a complete reconstitution, which would necessitate for at least three divisions out of five a delay of several days or even of some weeks. Undoubtedly this

---

* In a later message Huguet stated that Sordet's Cavalry Corps had moved to Estrées.

† This was the nucleus of the Sixth French Army under General Maunoury, which was to prolong the Allied left. The VII. Corps, which had belonged to the Army of Alsace, now consisted of the 14th and 63rd Divisions. The 13th Division had been left behind in Alsace.

dismal picture was largely coloured by the reports of stray staff Jere-miahs, both French and British, who in their wanderings saw stragglers and mistook them for units which had lost all cohesion.

The possibility envisaged in this report recalls vividly the extra-ordinary point of view held seriously in some quarters, a legacy of the South African War, that the British Army could withdraw and refit as and when it liked, as if it were possible to cross fingers and cease to play when the game became too hot. Even to entertain such an idea was to show a complete misunderstanding of the merciless and ruthless foe we were now opposed to.

To General Joffre, Huguet's report must have been a facer. It is remarkable, and typical of the man, that he adhered to his plan for an attack by the Fifth Army in the circumstances. He showed that day that he possessed the very greatest quality of all in a Commander, the courage to adhere to his plan when everything is going wrong and the only means of safety seems to consist in giving way and accepting a situation imposed by the enemy's action. What is involved, what tempering of soul is required, may be guessed at by those who have stood near the responsible Commander at such a time, but can only be known to the man who has had to make the decision.

*   *   *

The actual situation of the British, considering the ordeal the II. Corps had gone through on the previous day, was not unsatisfactory, and it is incredible that the description given in Huguet's message should have been applied to them. The I. Corps was weary but intact, having fought a brilliant rearguard action at Etreux, during which occurred yet another of those gallant stands culminating in a heroic sacrifice which were so characteristic of the British retreat. The II. Corps, after a sharp encounter in the morning, had carried out the noteworthy achievement of falling back in perfect order behind the Somme Canal. The men were worn and strained beyond belief, but their morale was extremely high.

The factor that was most in their favour was that von Kluck, just released from his subordination to von Bülow, was, as has been pre-viously explained (see Chapter IV, p. 235) inclining south-westwards, leaving the British free to reform unmolested. The British only found this out when news came through that von Kluck's troops were in conflict with Sordet's cavalry and d'Amade's Territorials away to the west about Péronne, but the information did not reach Sir John in time to influence his decision to continue his retirement.* (Map VI, p. 112.)

Whilst the B.E.F. was retiring, unmolested save for the sharp engagements already referred to, G.H.Q. was not far from thinking that all was lost. The following message shows the state of mind prevailing there:

"From Henry (General Wilson) to Snowball (General Snow), G.O.C. 4th Division: "Throw overboard all ammunition and impedimenta not absolutely required, and load up your lame ducks on all transport, horse and mechanical, and hustle along."†

This message was acted upon in some cases by formations which came to the conclusion that a danger they ignored was threatening them. In the case of the 4th Division great quantities of munitions and baggage were dumped and abandoned. Next day, realizing that the enemy was not within miles, lorries were sent back to recover it, but as German cavalry appeared after the baggage had been loaded up, the lorries had to drive away without the ammunition.

---

* It was learnt on the following day that Sordet's Cavalry had engaged the enemy on the Somme.

To the left of the Cavalry Corps d'Amade's two new Reserve Divisions were already marching on the Somme. One of them, the 61st, was engaged in a serious fight about Combles and was thrown back some distance, the other Division, the 62nd, reached Bapaume in the evening. From this day these two Divisions were attached to the Sixth Army which was being constituted under General Maunoury.

† This was later reinforced by the following order:

"Extract from Operation Order No. 9. G.H.Q., 27–8–14.

"All ammunition on wagons not absolutely required and other impedimenta will be unloaded and officers and men carried to the full capacity of all transport, both horse and mechanical.

"H. WILSON, Major-General, Sub-Chief of Staff."

See also Sir Horace Smith-Dorrien's *Memories of Forty-eight Years' Service*, pp. 416–17.

"Just before the Chief came up I had met an officer of the 4th Division whom I had known for years. I had a short talk with him, and, noticing that he was not quite in his usual spirits, asked him if anything was the matter. He replied it was *'the order'* he had just received from me. He then went on to explain that an order had come to his Division a short time before saying the ammunition on wagons not absolutely required and other impedimenta were to be unloaded and officers and men carried to the full capacity of transport. He went on to say that the order had had a very damping effect on his troops, for it was clear it would not have been issued unless we were in a very tight place. I told him I had never heard of the order, that the situation was excellent, the enemy only in small parties, and those keeping at a respectful distance, and that I was entirely at a loss to understand why such an order had been issued. Further, I would at once send to Divisional Headquarters to say that the order was to be disregarded. My counter order actually reached the 3rd and 5th Divisions in time, but the 4th Division had already acted on the order, burning officers kits, etc., to lighten their wagons. . . . It was unfortunate, for had I seen it (*i.e.* the order) I should have protested to G.H.Q. before circulating it, and I feel sure the Chief would have cancelled it on learning the true situation, and thus saved an increase of suffering to those who by acting on it sacrificed their spare clothes, boots, etc., at a time when they urgently needed them."

The truth was that G.H.Q. could not believe the II. Corps had recovered in the amazing way it had, a recovery probably due to the fact that the men realized the magnificent fight they had put up at Le Cateau and the punishment they had inflicted on the enemy. The danger had been great, but not so great as had been imagined by the directing staff, who concluded that a rapid retreat offered the only road to safety. This led to further efforts being demanded of the weary II. Corps, which thus lost the advantage of its short rest. The regiments rolled back, too weary to be allowed to halt, for any man who lay down dropped off to sleep in the road and could not be roused even to drag himself out of the way of the wheels of vehicles, or from under the hooves of horses.

*   *   *

Meanwhile the Fifth Army had withdrawn peacefully without interference from the enemy to the line assigned to it south of the Oise and Thon. (Map XII, p. 360.)

General Lanrezac, after awaiting the reports from the Corps, was taking steps for a very limited action on the following day. At 8 p.m. he issued orders to the Army to close in on the left, facing north-west, in readiness to attack any hostile columns crossing the Oise.

These orders had hardly been issued when a telegram despatched at 8.10 p.m. by the Commander-in-Chief was received at Marle. It ran as follows:

"Certain information received shows that elements of the VII. and IX. Corps forming part of the Second German Army which is opposed to you have been left in front of Maubeuge.

"It is therefore possible to come to the help of the British Army by taking action against the hostile forces which are advancing against it west of the Oise.

"You will therefore advance your left tomorrow morning between the Oise and St. Quentin, so as to attack all hostile forces marching against the British Army."

Having despatched this order, the Commander-in-Chief was informed of General Lanrezac's intentions of merely attacking those hostile columns which might follow his Army across the Oise, and he immediately telegraphed to insist that his order to the Fifth Army to attack in the direction of St. Quentin should be carried out. This message greatly incensed General Lanrezac, and indeed a most difficult and complicated manœuvre, necessitating a possibly dangerous change of front, had been imposed upon him. That he should have been pre-occupied and perturbed was comprehensible, but that he should have voiced his criticism as vehemently and openly as he did was less so. He had made it quite clear that even the restricted attack at first envisaged had not appealed to him, but the attack now ordered struck him as being almost insane, and he said so. What he feared was that whilst he attacked across the British front the German Corps which were follow-ing his Army might attack and overwhelm his right. He feared also that the enemy might advance into the gap between the right of his Army and the Fourth, and do to him on that flank what he was ordered to attempt against the enemy on his left.

Then came Alexandre, again evidently with the same purpose as earlier in the day, to see that General Joffre's orders were carried out, and that without delay or prevarication. His appearance was the signal for the storm, which had been brewing since the morning, to break violently. The immediate cause was Schneider. He thought that the G.Q.G. had no idea of the difficulty of the movement involved by the new order, and said so. Alexandre brushed aside all objections. Nothing extraordinary was being asked of the Fifth Army after all. They were facing north, well, they would face west, nothing very complicated in that, and, placing his hand flat on a map on the table, he slowly turned it round from the north to the west. Schneider, thoroughly imbued with the point of view of his Chief, became so exasperated at this that, forgetting the rank and position of the man he was addressing, he told Alexandre not to talk nonsense, to which the latter tartly replied: "You people can't be induced to do anything."

At this stage Lanrezac, who had been standing by biting his mous-tache, bounded into the dispute, and according to his own account told the representative of the G.Q.G. exactly what he thought of General Joffre's strategy and of the G.Q.G. generally. His terms were strong, his tone violent. General Hély d'Oissel intervened with tact and coolness. He drew Alexandre aside and explained the very real difficulties of the projected movement from the Staff point of view, but assured him that the attack would be carried out. Colonel Alexandre then left for the G.Q.G.

This scene revealed to the whole of the Fifth Army Staff not only that differences existed between the Army Commander and the G.Q.G., but that they were in strong opposition to each other, and the result was naturally deplorable, throwing a further burden of doubt and nervousness on the governing machine of the Army.

The prevailing feeling of tension and gloom was increased when that night the French Mission telephoned that on the following day the British Army was to continue its retreat and fall back behind the Oise between La Fère and Noyon. This meant that the left of the Fifth Army and the right of the new force now being formed about Chaulnes would be uncovered, for the British retirement must inevitably create a gap in the Allied line.

Naturally enough the news was very badly received. There is no point in recalling moments of almost unendurable strain, when men had to face ordeals that went beyond what they had imagined they could possibly stand. Suffice it to say that the French considered the British were running away at the critical moment, while the British were persuaded that they had been treated so badly that they could place no further reliance on their Allies.

CHAPTER VI

THE FIFTH ARMY PREPARES
TO COUNTER-ATTACK

August 28th, 1914

Joffre at Marle – Lanrezac and the Commander of the XVIII. Corps – General Hache – Colonel Lardemelle – Preparations for the counter-attack – A difficult manœuvre brilliantly executed – Lanrezac sends a liaison officer to investigate the position of the British I. and II. Corps – His report – Lanrezac's orders – Helbronner sent again to the British – Sir John French's refusal to allow Sir Douglas Haig to participate in the counter-attack – Colonel Macdonogh's visit to Laon – Events on the British front – The gap between the two British Corps – Von Kluck's view of the situation – Von Bülow – First fruits of the Battle of Mons – The situation at nightfall.

THE whole paraphernalia of Fifth Army Headquarters was despatched to Laon late in the morning, but the heads of sections only left Marle in the afternoon.

All morning the school there was a scene of the greatest activity. Busy officers dashed along the balcony which was the main thoroughfare, or dived off it into the classrooms where orders were being written, billeting areas allocated, wires decoded and Intelligence reports sifted. I was standing on this balcony when suddenly a large figure which took up its entire breadth appeared. It was General Joffre himself, and his appearance caused all the more of a flutter in that this was his first visit to the Fifth Army. As usual when travelling, he wore a great black overcoat which reached down nearly to his heels. He stopped to speak to Victor Duruy, and his manner was cordial and flattering in the extreme. He told him that he had heard of his splendid services at Namur and elsewhere. General Lanrezac, who was standing by, generously chimed in. Remembering this little scene, I was not entirely surprised when next day Duruy was appointed to take the place of Schneider, who was transferred to the Staff of his father-in-law, General Maunoury.

There was a long confabulation between the Generals, at the beginning of which Girard was called in. I don't think he had modified his opinion of the previous day that the Germans were using every endeavour to come to a decision by enveloping the Allies' left wing.

What happened at this interview between Joffre and Lanrezac I did not know until long afterwards.

The impression left by Lanrezac on the Commander-in-Chief was that he had lost his bearings, that he was fearful, did not seem able to control either himself or his Army, and was nervous for his right flank without being able to assign any very cogent reason for his fears.

He had been glum as usual before the arrival of his Chief. When he found himself alone with him he drew a dismal picture of the condition of his Army, emphasized the fatigue of the troops, told the Commander-in-Chief of the "nerves" of some units. General Joffre listened for a while, impassive, then without a moment's warning, exploded. His rage was terrific. He threatened to deprive Lanrezac of his command and told him that he must obey without discussion, that he must attack without this eternal procrastination and apprehensiveness.*

General Joffre's Olympian anger bore fruit: Lanrezac pulled himself together, and on that day at least a wave of energy vibrated down the nerves of the Army such as it had not known since it marched into Belgium.

The Commander-in-Chief left a written order confirming his verbal instructions. It was very short and ran as follows: "The Fifth Army will attack as soon as possible the German forces which advanced against the British yesterday. It will protect itself on its right with the minimum of forces, carrying out long distance reconnaissances on this flank."

As the Generals left the room where they had conferred, General Lanrezac was told that General de Mas Latrie, commanding the XVIII. Corps, had come in to see him. Mas Latrie began a long and dismal account of the state of his troops. He emphasized the fatigue of his men, and told the Army Commander of the nerves of some units.

---

* Monsieur Poincaré in his *Memoirs* (Vol. V, p. 206) writes of this day that –

"Unfortunately this Army (the Fifth) was so weary that General Lanrezac had expressed the desire to withdraw it south of Laon without fighting and there reconstitute it in view of further engagements. Joffre, who will not tolerate any delay at the moment, considered this proposal to be a sign of weakness. He has given Lanrezac definite orders to assume the offensive in the region of Guise; he has threatened to shoot him in case of disobedience or of hesitation. He has gone in person to the theatre of operations. He has, so Colonel Pénélon says, great hopes of this new battle."

The President was, I think, misinformed as far as Joffre's threat to shoot Lanrezac was concerned. It was the kind of exaggerated gossip likely to be current at that time. General Lanrezac never mentions it in his book. I can hardly believe that of the two men I remember seeing together after the interview at Marle, one had threatened to have the other shot.

General Joffre.

(*Bottom Left*) Lieut. E. L.
Spears (photograph taken
as Captain in 1915).

General Lanrezac.

Capt. The Marquis de Rose.

Capt. Helbronner.

Capt. Wemaëre.

Capt. Fagalde.

German Troops in Brussels.

German Infantry marching through Belgium.

Lieut.-General Sir A. T.
Murray, K.C.B., C.V.O.,
D.S.O., Chief of General
Staff, B.E.F., August 1914.

Colenel Macdonogh.
Head of British Military
Intelligence, G.H.Q.,
August 1914.

Plates issued to the French Troops to enable them to distinguish Allied from German uniforms.

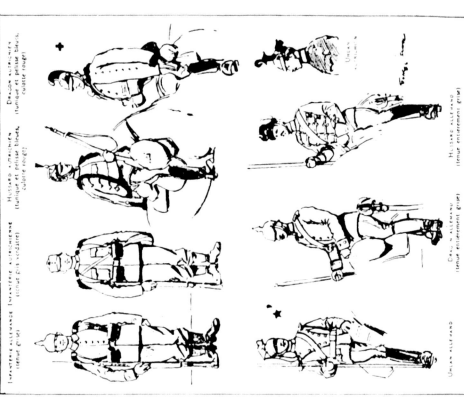

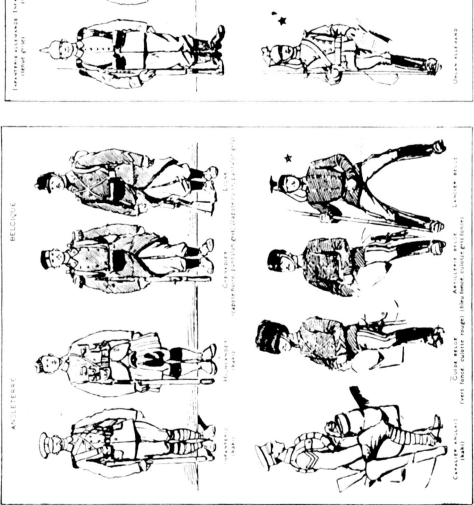

On board H.M.S. *Sentinel* in Boulogne harbour. Col. Huguet, Maj.-Gen. Sir W. Robertson, Lt.-Gen. Sir A. Murray, F.-M. Sir J. French, Maj.-Gen. H. Wilson (wearing cravat of Legion of Honour), Lt.-Col. Hon. G.W. Lambton, Lt.-Col B. Fitzgerald (in civilian dress), Major Sir H. Wake, Bt., The Duke of Westminster.

Field-Marshal Sir John French lands followed by Colonel Huguet.

Field-Marshal Sir John French,
G.C.B., G.C.V.O., K.C.M.G.
Commander-in-Chief, B.E.F.,
August 1914.

German Infantry.

British Cavalry. Lancers leading their horses.

British Infantry.

A patrol of Hussars.

Uhlans passing through a town.

A regiment leaving Paris on mobilization.

On the line of march.

French Cavalry.

A troop of French Dragoons halted whilst a cart which had been barricading the road is pulled out of the way.

Generaloberst von Bülow commanding the Second German Army.

(*Bottom Left*) Generaloberst von Kluck commanding the First German Army.

General Sordet.

Colonel des Vallières with
Generals Joffre and Castelnau.

Generals Joffre
and Hache.

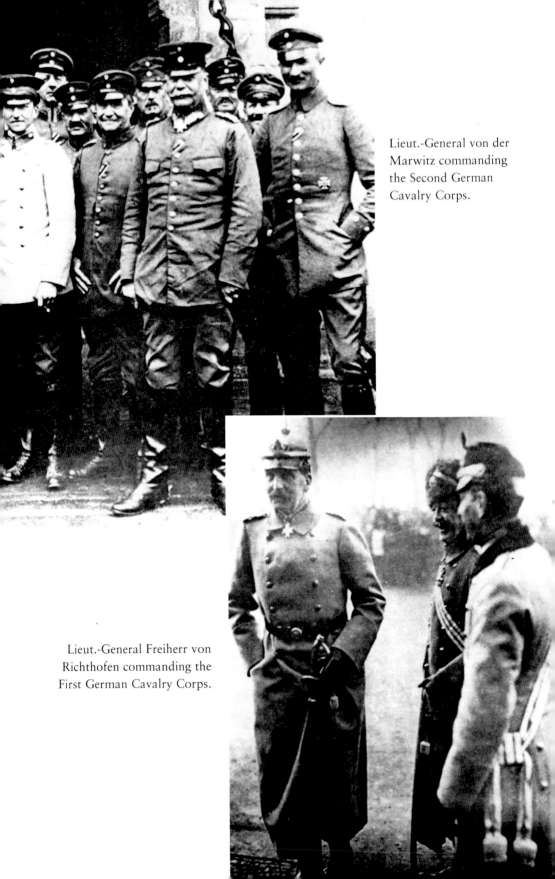

Lieut.-General von der Marwitz commanding the Second German Cavalry Corps.

Lieut.-General Freiherr von Richthofen commanding the First German Cavalry Corps.

Craonne – Before the War.

Craonne – After the War.

General Gallieni.

General Maunoury.

General Franchet
d'Esperey.

General Foch.

Pillage.

The battlefield of the Marne.

Général de Maud'huy.
Gouverneur de Metz, né à Metz rue Tête d'or nº 7.

General de Maud'huy.

General Lanrezac in 1925.

General de Maud'huy.

A column of German prisoners.

German prisoners being interrogated.

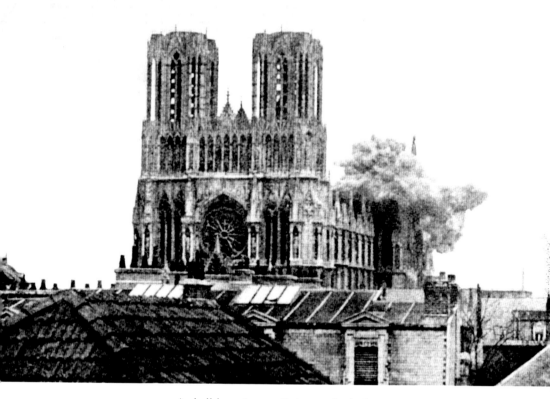

A shell bursting on Reims cathedral.

Reims after the bombardment.

Spies awaiting
execution.

Farm labourer
convicted of spying.

The *leitmotif* might have been plagiarized from General Lanrezac himself, who so short a time before had developed the same theme to General Joffre. The similarity of the two scenes did not end there. Lanrezac pulverized the wretched Corps Commander for his faint heart and pusillanimity. He growled and thundered, and no doubt knew exactly what to say. He had merely to pass on words and expressions fresh in his memory. General de Mas Latrie came off worse than his Chief, however, for General Joffre, approaching, chimed in with Lanrezac and completed the discomfiture of Mas Latrie, who withdrew like a man in a trance.

Thus was the truth of a French Cavalry proverb proved – *"C'est le bat-flanc qui trinque,"* which means that when the colonel is out of temper he upbraids the captain, who swears at the subaltern, who goes for the sergeant, who punishes the private, who beats the horse, whose only recourse is to kick the bail at the side of his stall. So it is always the bail that catches it in the end – *"C'est le bat-flanc qui trinque."*

A moment or two after General de Mas Latrie's departure, a very soldierly little figure, with white hair and a white moustache, stepped forward. This was General Hache, just appointed to take over the command of the III. Corps in succession to General Sauret. His appearance was very different from that of his predecessor. General Sauret had appeared on our balcony earlier in the morning, excited, dishevelled, gesticulating, and badly in need of a hair-cut. So heated was he that the icy reception accorded him, the coldest of cold shoulders presented by all with whom he came in contact, had apparently little effect.

General Hache was to prove an able and determined commander, firm, silent and reliable: I had to go to see him often and remember well his habit of walking up and down with his hands behind his back, his cap well forward, looking down on the ground. Today, he went up to Generals Joffre and Lanrezac and begged to be relieved of the terrible responsibility of taking over the command of a corps he did not know on the eve of a battle. Earnestly he begged the Commander-in-Chief to allow him to return to the division he had commanded so ably. But General Joffre would not have this, and told Hache that it was his duty to go to the III. Corps.

Then General Joffre left. I am not sure, but I think that one of his staff officers remained behind for some time, to see that preparations for next day's attack were pressed forward.

The next visitor was Colonel Lardemelle, Chief of Staff of the I.

Corps. He came to settle matters affecting the movement of his Corps. This officer was eventually, on the Aisne, to become Chief of Staff of the Fifth Army. Of medium height, dark, quiet, courtly and efficient, he was liked and admired by all who served under his orders.

During the course of the morning it was decided to employ part at least of the I. Corps on the left, but later this decision was reversed. Under the first hypothesis it was to have been moved by rail, and this led to an outburst of activity on the part of the Sub-Chief of Staff, Lieut.-Colonel Daydrein, which left all beholders quite dizzy. This small, efficient, grey-haired, grey-moustached artillery officer specialized in juggling with trains as a conjuror juggles with billiard balls, but how he had time to think whilst a ceaseless flow of words poured from him I don't know. His loquacity engendered fatigue, though not to himself. Upon this occasion his bubbling energy was wasted, for in the end it was decided to employ the I. Corps on the right and move it by road.

Preparations for the attack were being feverishly pressed forward.

The difficulties of the manœuvre now being carried out by the Fifth Army have not been sufficiently recognized. Had there been an extra day available, had twelve hours warning been given, it would have been possible to echelon the columns, which would have made the conversion comparatively easy. As it was no warning was given, and the manœuvre redounds greatly to the credit of both staff and troops, all the more so as it was not unhampered by the enemy.

The Army had been marching south on a front of some thirty kilometres in about thirteen infantry columns plus the cavalry. This great mass of troops was now being switched round, the whole of the left to face north-west, and concentrated on a much narrower front. The Reserve Divisions moved south and then faced west. The XVIII. Corps slipped into the position vacated by the Reserve Divisions and faced north-west towards St. Quentin. The III. Corps side-stepped to the left, following the XVIII. Corps and facing the same way, whilst the X. Corps closed in and faced north, protecting the right flank.* The I. Corps was placed, a welcome innovation, in reserve behind the right, one of its divisions in Army Reserve.† The 4th Cavalry Division,

---

* In the course of this movement the 38th and 37th Divisions from Africa, which had been attached the first to the III. and the second to the X. Corps, were transferred, the first to the XVIII. and the second to the III. Corps.

† The I. Corps was ordered to leave a Brigade in support of the 4th Cavalry Division. The 1st Division was to have its advance guard in the early morning on the Guise–Origny road ready to advance north-west.

together with the 51st Reserve Division, which was placed under the direct orders of the Army Commander, were to watch the right; the Cavalry was also to keep in touch with the Fourth Army, no easy task, as there was a gap of some twenty kilometres, which was increasing, between it and the Fifth Army. Happily there was no sign of any important enemy formations coming down from the hilly country opposite this gap. (Maps X, p. 266 and XIII, p. 360.)

Commandant Schneider was mainly responsible for this successful manœuvre, and it was hard on him to have to leave the Fifth Army at the moment of his best achievement. His departure (on the 29th) was an ominous reminder of the fact that it is unwise to quarrel with supreme authority or its representative.

Captain Helbronner had been sent out at 6 a.m. with the following instructions:

"To visit the area through which the two British Corps were retiring, and to get an impression of the state of the troops. If possible to see the Corps Commanders, to tell them of General Lanrezac's intentions and ascertain their frame of mind."

These instructions, ordering a French officer to deal direct with the British Corps Commanders without any reference to the British Commander-in-Chief, would appear extraordinary to an English soldier, but the French conception of liaison was different from our own, and in such an emergency, with so much at stake and communications so unreliable, there was much to be said for General Lanrezac's endeavour to find out for himself the real situation of his neighbours.

Captain Helbronner returned at 5 p.m. He has been good enough to give me the notes he made at the time concerning his mission.

He had found Sir Douglas Haig near Mont D'Origny. Sir Douglas seemed anxious about the II. Corps, and asked Helbronner to see him again after visiting Sir Horace Smith-Dorrien. Meanwhile the 1st Division was marching by, and Helbronner noted its excellent appearance. The men were tired and suffering from the extreme heat but marched in perfect order. "The regiments went by ceaselessly singing 'Tipperary', which was the song of the moment."

Helbronner then left for the II. Corps area. He presently encountered some regiments of the II. Corps, which presented, he wrote, a striking contrast to the I. Corps. The men looked harassed, there was some disorder, and some units were intermingled. Nobody was singing. He met a staff officer who told him the German Cavalry threatened to envelop the rearguards of the Corps and that his orders were to accelerate the retreat. "Guns were thundering to the north-west and at times the wind carried the distant sound of machine-guns."

He failed to find Sir Horace. On his way back he met General Monro, commanding the 2nd Division. The situation was not too serious for the French officer to note that General Monro was "jovial and in excellent temper, but was not shaved, an exceptional thing for a British officer."

Helbronner's narrative goes on:

"Eventually I found General Haig, north of Ribémont, near the little village of Lucy. He was standing on a mound, an orderly holding the horses beside the lance carrying the pennon, red with a white cross, which was planted in the ground. A British airman was reporting to Sir Douglas, who was very animated and conveyed to me the news he had just received from the aviator.

"This was that important German columns had been observed advancing south-west of St. Quentin. General Haig was good enough to mark these himself in pencil on my map. His words to me were: 'Go quickly to your General and give him this information. Let him take advantage of it without delay. The enemy is exposing his flank as he advances. Let him act. I am anxious to co-operate with him in his attack.'

"Sir Douglas thanked me for what I was able to tell him concerning the II. Corps, and gave me a rendezvous for that evening at La Fère. I left for Laon, expecting to find the Headquarters of the Fifth Army there, but was told that General Lanrezac was still at Marle, so I went on and found him there with General Hély d'Oissel. I made my report, laying stress on the very different appearance of the two British Corps. I gave General Lanrezac the information given me by General Haig concerning the German columns, and reported to him the suggestion made by the British General. He appeared to be delighted, and said some nice things concerning Sir Douglas Haig. He at once told his Chief of Staff to modify the orders for the following day so as to include the participation of the British I. Corps.

"An hour after my arrival General Haig's Sub-Chief of Staff, accompanied by Commandant Jammet, the French liaison officer, arrived at Marle. They both confirmed Sir Douglas Haig's intentions, but said that the I. Corps could not participate in the operation as early as 5 a.m. 5.30 a.m. was the time suggested. General Lanrezac accepted this modification and altered his plan accordingly."

The orders to which Helbronner refers were as follows:

"The First German Army is engaged frontally against the British Army. Its right flank is being attacked by the French Army of the north (Maunoury's Sixth Army). The Fifth Army will attack its left flank tomorrow morning and endeavour to outflank it by the north.

"General direction of the attack: St. Quentin and to the north.

"The attack will be carried out by the XVIII. and III. Corps, which will be supported on the left by the I. British Corps and covered on the right by the X. Corps and the 4th Cavalry Division. Leaving one division in Army Reserve, the I. Corps will be in second line, in rear and to the right of the III. Corps. The Group of Reserve Divisions will form a reserve to the left on the left bank of the Oise."

When he issued these orders, General Lanrezac knew little of what was going on at the front, although it was but a few miles away. There was heavy artillery fire in the direction of Guise. One of the Reserve Divisions had lost the Bridges over the Oise. This necessitated the intervention of a Division of the III. and of one of the XVIII. Corps: the latter suffered somewhat heavily in the action.

Shortly after the issue of this order, Helbronner was directed to return to the British I. Corps. His narrative continues:

"I went via Laon to give orders to our Sub-Chief of Staff, Lieut.-Colonel Daydrein.

"I arrived at 7 p.m. at La Fère. Sir Douglas was not there, nor was he at Danizy. I found him at St. Gobain. I conveyed to him General Lanrezac's thanks and told him of the latter's intentions for the following day. Sir Douglas expressed himself as satisfied, only making reservations concerning the hour at which his infantry was to attack. He decided to await the reports of his divisions before fixing me on this point. Meanwhile he asked me to dine. His Chief of Staff came in at the end of the meal saying that both General Lomax and General Monro asked that the men be allowed some rest before attacking. Sir Douglas then informed me that all his artillery and the cavalry he disposed of would intervene at 9 a.m. but that his infantry could only debouch at midday. He asked me to note that he had several heavy batteries at his disposal. He added that it would be necessary that, before participating in the attack, he should obtain Sir John French's sanction to the agreement he had come to with General Lanrezac. Sir Douglas Haig marked on my map in blue pencil the billeting areas occupied by his troops.

"I got back to Laon at 10 p.m. General Lanrezac was rather annoyed by all the modifications introduced by General Haig, but accepted them, saying – 'All I ask is that they should debouch whether it be at 9 or at noon.'"

After Helbronner had made his report, there was not a shadow of doubt in the minds of General Lanrezac and his Staff that the I. Corps would fight alongside the Fifth Army on the morrow. A telephone message sent out by Colonel Huguet in the morning (at 7.15 a.m.) stating that the British Army was to continue its retirement (a message which had been very badly received at Fifth Army Headquarters) was considered to have been superseded by the direct negotiations carried on since with the I. Corps. But knowing something of the point of view of British G.H.Q. I felt grave doubts as to whether the I. Corps would be allowed to co-operate, and ventured to emphasize the conditional character of Sir Douglas's agreement, which Helbronner had made perfectly clear. All my attempts to get into direct touch with G.H.Q. failed. I hoped and prayed that Sir Douglas's views would prevail with Sir John French but felt terribly uncertain. I should have felt less confidence still had I known that Colonel Huguet had written to General Joffre in the morning reiterating that the British Army was going to reorganize and would not be in a position to resume its place in the line for some time to come.*

Late in the evening my worst fears were confirmed. News came in from the G.Q.G. either over the telephone or through a liaison officer (I remember a very highly tried G.Q.G. liaison officer being present that evening, I think it was Brécart) that Sir John would not allow the I. Corps to participate in the offensive next day. For the first time I felt we were in the wrong. My impression was the stronger that I did not know what was going on at G.H.Q. and saw this particular situation from the French angle. General Lanrezac's anger was terrific. He said terrible, unpardonable things concerning Sir John French and the British Army, but these I was careful not to hear; nor did I ever report what occurred that evening. A violent outburst was to be expected, for even if General Lanrezac had not been engaged in an adventure for which he had no stomach, he would have had every excuse for exaspera-

* See Appendix XXVII.

tion. Indeed the message sent to the G.Q.G. from British G.H.Q. through Colonel Huguet was really amazing. It ran as follows:

"Compiègne. August 28th, 6.55 p.m.

"Marshal French regrets his inability to co-operate with you in tomorrow's general action in the measure desired by you.

"Troops very tired, must have at least one day's rest on the ground occupied tonight; after tomorrow they will be able to occupy the line of the Crozat Canal if necessary; if ultimately the French Army is victorious the Field-Marshal will place his troops at your disposal as a reserve."

This document showed clearly that the British Higher Command, thoroughly disillusioned, and mistrustful of understandings which as far as it was concerned had merely been misunderstandings resulting in the English receiving most of the blows, was determined not to risk a repetition of events which had well-nigh spelt disaster to its forces.

The news that the I. Corps would not be allowed to co-operate in the Fifth Army's attack was confirmed by a Staff officer from Sir Douglas Haig's Headquarters who arrived at Laon between midnight and 1 a.m. A further message addressed direct to the Fifth Army from G.H.Q. in English arrived at 1 a.m. This message, stating that the I. Corps was to enjoy a complete rest on the following day, added fresh flames to General Lanrezac's wrath, since he well knew the excellent condition of the Corps and the disposition of its Commander. Further, he had by this time received a message sent at 6 p.m. from the British to the G.Q.G. to the effect that the whole area, some fifteen kilometres deep, on the front of the British Army, was entirely free from any important bodies of the enemy.

To a dispassionate observer the situation would have appeared extraordinary.

The great complaint of the British against General Lanrezac had been that he could not be induced to attack. Now that he was about to do so nothing would persuade the British to co-operate. They were doing as they had been done by. If they were frank on the subject and gave him warning of their intentions, on the other hand they were not pressed by the enemy as he had been at Charleroi.

Sir John French's justification for allowing the Fifth Army to fight unsupported was the state he imagined the British II. Corps to be in. All his thoughts were with these badly mauled troops.

Moreover, regrettable though it may be that he should have refused to allow the I. Corps to co-operate in a plan largely intended to benefit the British, it must be remembered that at the outset General Joffre had not expected support from him, and that the offensive imposed on General Lanrezac was in Joffre's opinion necessary for the safety of the French Army itself.

The situation was strange, fogged by ill-will. The position of liaison officer had become almost impossible. Colonel Macdonogh, realizing something of my difficulties, took the time, overwhelmingly busy though he was, to come to Laon to give me moral support. The visit of this officer of high rank, completely self-possessed and superlatively competent, did much good and certainly eased things for me.

Nothing of great importance happened on the British front during the day.* Sir John heard that he was to receive the 6th Division from England about the middle of September, and a complete Corps from India later.

The only anxiety had been caused by the possibility of the enemy's Cavalry penetrating into the gap fifteen miles wide between the I. and II. Corps, but this did not happen. The British Cavalry again asserted its superiority over that of the enemy in a sharp fight. At Cerizy one of the few cavalry charges of the war took place. The Germans were ridden down and speared by the 12th Lancers. (Map XIII, p. 360.)

By nightfall the gap between the two Corps was still eleven miles across. It was covered by the Cavalry. According to a message received by the G.Q.G., the British Intelligence did not believe there were hostile forces of any importance on the front of the Army. In this they were right: the First German Army was moving south-west across the British front.

Von Kluck's view of the situation at midday was as follows:

"The left wing of the main body of the French is retiring south and south-west before the victorious Second and Third Armies. It is of decisive importance to attain the flank of these forces either during

---

* In the afternoon Joffre informed Huguet that the French outposts would cover the passages of the Somme between Péronne and Ham and those of the Oise at La Fère and above. He trusted the British would have their outposts at Ham, St. Simon and Jussy. General Wilson answered that they were further south but that he did not know their exact location. Later a message was sent that the 3rd Infantry and 3rd Cavalry Brigades were at Vendeuil and Choigny, the remainder of the Cavalry Division at Jussy on the Crozat Canal and at Cressy south of Nesle. The line of the Sambre between Ham and St. Simon was therefore abandoned.

their retreat or on any position they may take up, so as to cut them off from Paris and envelop them. This is of greater importance than cutting the British communications with the sea." (Kluck, p. 70.)

This meant that von Kluck assumed the British were by now separated from the French, and so far back on their lines of communication as to be out of reach of the sweep he projected.

He must have had different information in the afternoon, for he then sent a message to Bülow asking him to deal with the disorganized British forces which appeared to be falling back on La Fère.

There was nothing in this news to make him alter the plan he submitted to von Bülow, which consisted in the Second Army's advancing on Chauny, and the First on Compiègne and Noyon, that is south-east. But that evening orders came from the Supreme Command which gave the right wing armies objectives to the south-west.* Lack of a ruling conception and firm direction was making itself felt on the German side. Furthermore the Supreme Command had made a crowning mistake: believing that the decisive victory of the German text books had been won in the west, it ordered the transfer of troops from the western to the Russian theatre. (Six corps were detailed, but only two went.)

Bülow meanwhile was unhappy and considerably perplexed. He had resented Kluck's no longer being under his orders, and there was friction between the two Commanders. He was uncertain as to what the Fifth French Army on his front was doing, and fearful of gaps being created between him and his neighbours by von Kluck's action on his right and by that of the Third Army on his left, for the latter was marching south-east to the assistance of the Fourth Army.

Although we did not know it, and although everything appeared *couleur de rose* at Luxembourg, whence the Kaiser sent a wireless, which we intercepted, congratulating von Kluck on "approaching this day the heart of France," many factors were working in favour of the allies.

The severity of their long marches was telling on the Germans; unduly long lines of communication were absorbing more and more men; supplies and ammunition were already lagging behind the swift and mighty wave of invasion.

The Battle of Mons was also bearing fruit. Had not von Kluck's Army, pressing forward at its maximum speed, been delayed for twenty-four hours at Mons and given further severe punishment at Le Cateau,

* See Appendix XXVIII.

four of its corps instead of one division would have swung in against the left flank of the Fifth Army on the 29th, with disastrous results.

*   *   *

In spite of all this, the situation confronting General Joffre that night was anything but brilliant.

The British were apparently unresponsive to his appeals.

D'Amade's force was almost entirely nebulous.*

The situation of the Sixth Army was extremely precarious. General Maunoury informed the Commander-in-Chief that his offensive powers on the following day would be very limited.†

As if all this were not bad enough, Joffre heard that the enemy was massing forces opposite the gap between the Fourth and Fifth Armies.‡

Nothing daunted, instead of countermanding the attack orders to the Fifth Army, he decided to create the Ninth Army (at first known as the Foch Detachment forming part of the Fourth Army) to bridge this gap.§

Nowhere was there any relief, nowhere any good news, and his left appeared to be melting away. There lay his maximum danger at the

---

* On the evening of the 28th a part of d'Amade's Territorials had detrained at Abbeville. The remainder of his troops were moving by road and were to be in position in four days' time. That night he intended holding with those troops which were available the line of the Somme from Picquigny to the sea.

† Maunoury was absolutely without news of his 61st and 62nd Reserve Divisions. The Staff had attempted to locate them all day without result, their new Commander, General Ebener, sought for them in vain. The Germans were advancing in the zone where the troops transferred to the Sixth Army were to detrain.

Maunoury, who had by the evening been further reinforced by the 14th Division, the Ditte Brigade and the 55th Reserve Division, decided to detrain the 55th, 56th and 63rd Reserve Divisions farther south than had been originally intended.

During the day the French Cavalry Corps was submitted to a fairly violent attack about Péronne.

‡ The Fourth Army was itself engaged in a hard battle. On the previous day, columns marching south had been seen in the region of Chimay, as well as bodies of hostile troops in the region of Hirson, Chimay, Rocroi. It was therefore important that the Fourth Army, thus threatened on its left flank, should not delay further on the Meuse. Orders were sent to General de Langle that if he had not succeeded in throwing back the enemy into the Meuse before midday on the 28th he was to fall back to the Aisne, but these orders reached him when his Army was fully engaged. By evening it had been successful on the wings but not in the centre. Joffre ordered it to fall back progressively to the Aisne, keeping in touch with the Third Army and sending out Cavalry and light detachments to assure the liaison with the Fifth Army.

Joffre's orders to the First and Second Armies were "to last out."

§ It was not until the early morning of the 28th that General Foch was called to Vitry to receive the command of this force, which came into being on the 29th. It consisted of the IX. and XI. Corps from the Fourth Army plus the 42nd Division and the 9th Cavalry Division. During the retreat other divisions were temporarily attached.

moment, as well as his hope for the future. He concentrated upon sending every available man to that flank.*

The 28th was a terrible day for the Allies, a day during which the scales might have been definitely turned against them but for the iron will and faith of Joffre. Taking troops from here, throwing them in there, threatening this General, praising that one, he remoulded the Allied line now that at last he really understood the German manœuvre. But past mistakes had still to be paid for. The disastrous state of affairs whereby the Allied Armies withdrew by uneven jerks, exposing each other to the enemy's blows and uncovering each other's flanks, was not yet ended, and in spite of the Generalissimo's immense efforts risks were run which but for fabulous good luck would have resulted in irremediable rout.

Meanwhile the men of the Fifth Army, soldiers because of their uniforms, marched on weary but cheerful, for at last it seemed that the Mighty Ones in their omnipotence had decided to fight, and in spite of what had happened, to all those young hearts not yet aged by war, to fight meant "victory."

---

* The VI. Corps from the Third Army was ordered to join the Sixth Army, but this order had to be countermanded later, and other forces sent to the Sixth Army instead.

CHAPTER VII

THE BATTLE OF GUISE

August 29th, 1914

Laon – A further attempt to secure British co-operation – Lanrezac's new orders – Joffre at Laon – The Battle of Guise – The results – Lanrezac and the G.Q.G. – A strange telephone conversation – The dangerous situation of the Fifth Army – The order to retire does not reach it – British support requested – Joffre at Compiègne – General Wilson at the G.Q.G. – The situation that night.

COMING in to Laon, on the previous evening, I had been much struck by the place. The town proper rises on an immense ridge some 350 feet high, forming a wedge in the plain, which it commands like a great battleship anchored in a smooth sea. From the ramparts the view extends northwards far beyond St. Quentin, westward to the forest of St. Gobain and southwards over the country of Laonnais and Soissonais. There is a beautiful twelfth century cathedral with high towers, and from the upper platforms of one of these stone animals, amongst them a cow and a donkey, peer incongruously over the edge. The cathedral has lovely thirteenth century stained glass, and a rose window which must be one of the finest in France.

It was easy to realize how important the ridge on which the town stands must have been throughout the ages. Here the Gauls held off the Belgae, and the Romans, who fortified the place, stood on these heights to repel in turn the Franks, the Vandals and the Huns.

A story read to me as a boy came to my mind. It was about a small Duke of Normandy brought to this place by a Carlovingian King as a hostage, almost as a prisoner. He dreaded the grim towers and walls and wondered at the luxury of these French people, who transported their glass windows from place to place.

More recently, but still a very long time ago, in the Hundred Years War, the citadel had been held by the English.

The place gave a sense of security; the idea that it might once again prove to be the breakwater against which the tide of invasion would be shattered, gave some comfort. But historical reminiscence did not prevent my feeling sad at heart as, in the early hours of August 29th, I made my way to the fine modern school in the lower town where Fifth Army H.Q. was established.

Indeed I was very miserable. Since the firing of the first shot it had been my constant task to point out that the British Commander-in-Chief expected the Fifth Army to stand and fight. Frequently I had asserted that the British were only waiting for this to happen to take the offensive themselves. This had been true at the time, but now that the French were determined to come to grips with the enemy we hung back. Just as on previous occasions I had felt that the Fifth Army would slip back without fighting, so now I was convinced of the contrary. During the whole of the previous day officers of the G.Q.G. staff had been on the telephone asking for details, making sure there was no hitch, urging General Lanrezac and his staff to speed up the arrangements so that by no possible chance would the attack be postponed.

Yet present circumstances rendered this attack a pretty desperate adventure. The Fifth Army was unsupported on either hand; once engaged, could it extricate itself? . . . Such thoughts formed a background of depression to my immediate concern, the relations between the Fifth Army and our own and the situation of each at the moment.

It was evident from the atmosphere at Laon that morning that relations were being strained to breaking point at the very moment when the need for co-operation between the Armies was more vital than ever. Lack of it seemed likely to lead to the defeat of the Fifth Army, and the overwhelming of the British Expeditionary Force would inevitably follow.

I felt certain that the least demonstration of solidarity, the least gesture on our part, would hearten the French, make them feel safer on their dangerous left flank, and change the projected offensive from a desperate gamble into a rational if bold manœuvre. Accordingly I made one more attempt to obtain British support, and sent a telegram (I had sent several messages on the previous night) in which the following words occur:

"French thought they had unconditional promise of support. That support mentioned in yesterday's operation orders. Relying on our help, a division of the I. Corps, which was to have been moved to the left of the Army by rail, has remained with the I. Corps. All French

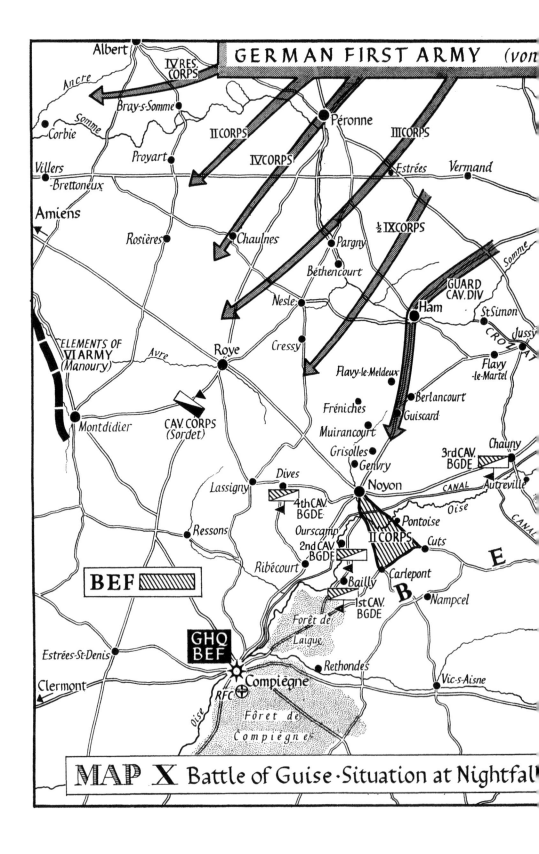

MAP **X** Battle of Guise · Situation at Nightfall

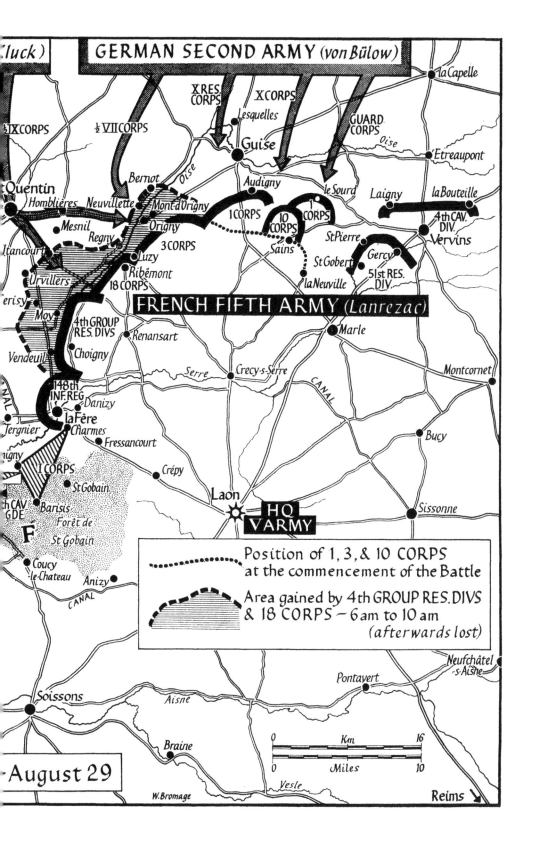

GERMAN SECOND ARMY *(von Bülow)*

(luck)

la Capelle

X RES. CORPS
X CORPS
GUARD. CORPS

IX CORPS
½ VII CORPS
Lesquelles
Guise
Oise
Etreaupont

Bernot
Audigny
le Sourd
Laigny
la Bouteille

Quentin
Homblières
Neuvillette
Mont d'Origny
1 CORPS
10 CORPS
1 CORPS
4th CAV. DIV.
Vervins

Mesnil
Origny
Regny
StPierre

Itancourt
Luzy
3 CORPS
Sains
St Gobert
Gercy

Urvillers
Ribémont
18 CORPS
la Neuville
51st RES. DIV.

erisy
Moy
4th GROUP RES. DIVS
Renansart
FRENCH FIFTH ARMY *(Lanrezac)*
Marle

Vendeuil
Choigny
Serre
Crecy-s-Serre
CANAL
Montcornet

148th INF. REG
Danizy
CANAL

Tergnier
laFère
Charmes
Fressancourt
Crépy
Laon
Bucy

igny
1 CORPS
St Gobain
HQ V ARMY
Sissonne

h CAV GDE
Barisis
Forêt de St Gobain
F'

Coucy le-Chateau
Anizy
CANAL

Neufchâtel -s-Aisne

Soissons
Aisne
Pontavert

Braine
Km   16
Miles   10

August 29
Vesle
Reims

W. Bromage

.... Position of 1, 3, & 10 CORPS
at the commencement of the Battle

╌╌╌ Area gained by 4th GROUP RES. DIVS
& 18 CORPS — 6 am to 10 am
(afterwards lost)

ask is a demonstration by guns and cavalry along the Ham–Jussy road and north of the river, direction: just west of St. Quentin, by 12 noon."

I cannot say I was hopeful that any result would follow, for I was aware of British G.H.Q.'s proposal to withdraw the Army to refit. Luckily the Fifth Army staff knew nothing of this, nor that so seriously had the possibility of withdrawing to a harbour been considered, that a Staff officer employed on railway duties, Lieut.-Colonel Marr Johnson, had been ordered by General Henry Wilson to reconnoitre and report on the bridges which might have to be blown up all along the immense distance to La Rochelle, on the Bay of Biscay, 250 miles south-west of Paris as the crow flies. What the effect of this information would have been on General Lanrezac and his Staff is beyond conjecture.

At 1.15 a.m. General Joffre had telegraphed to Lanrezac that the enemy, having thrown back the Reserve Divisions which were advancing on Péronne, had crossed the Somme moving westward, and was threatening the zone of detrainment of the Sixth Army. It was therefore essential that the action of the Fifth Army should be pressed with the utmost energy.

The receipt of this message, combined with the lack of British support, caused General Lanrezac to issue fresh orders at 7.30 a.m.

"The right of the First German Army attacked Péronne yesterday with its right. It is important that the attack we are launching against its left flank should be carried out with the greatest possible energy and with all the rapidity we are capable of.
"The initial movement will be directed on St. Quentin."*

At 9 a.m. General Joffre, flanked by Gamelin and de Galbert, appeared, clad in his long black overcoat. He spent all the morning at the school, a great deal of the time in Lanrezac's room, occasionally walking up and down the recreation ground accompanied by one or other of his orderly officers, the smooth Gamelin or the impulsive Galbert, but never a word did he utter; he watched.

* This order went on to prescribe that the XVIII. Corps should, once it had crossed the Oise, take the general direction of St. Quentin, its right a little to the east of Mesnil St. Laurent.
The III. Corps was to inflect its direction of attack towards the west, remaining in echelon behind the XVIII. Corps.
The Group of Reserve Divisions was to support the left of the XVIII. Corps and advance on Urvillers.

General Lanrezac was now grimly determined to attack, and was to prove himself an able commander. But no one who, having lived through those critical hours, has pondered over what occurred and read carefully the relevant documents and General Lanrezac's own book, can fail to conclude that he fought the battle with as wary an eye on the G.Q.G. as on the enemy. He was a man torn by conflicting emotions, ulcerated by the distrust of himself that he felt growing at the G.Q.G., exasperated by the British, by General Joffre's liaison officers, by the Commander-in-Chief himself, by every event that occurred. His clear view of the danger his Army was exposed to does his intelligence and comprehension credit, but does not justify his lack of faith in his own troops, demonstrated once more in his conversation with his Chief on the previous morning. Far-sighted he was, and clever, too clever perhaps, and certainly too critical. At Guise he manipulated his units with the consummate skill of an expert at the great game of war, but he played his hand without zest or faith, sardonically observant of the G.Q.G. which had forced the cards into his hand, and on whose entire responsibility, to his mind, the game was being played out.

I was told long afterwards that the Commander-in-Chief had come that morning determined to relieve General Lanrezac of his command. I imagine that when he saw him thoroughly master of the situation and carrying out the G.Q.G.'s instructions with energy and ability, he came to the conclusion that it would be madness to remove him from the head of his Army, now in full action.

This not being a military history, I shall not attempt to give a detailed account of what was to be known as the Battle of Guise. The following is a brief outline of the battle.

The French advanced in the direction of St. Quentin at 6 a.m.* The Oise was crossed by the Reserve Divisions and the XVIII. Corps without opposition. Some progress on the far bank had been made when a heavy German attack debouching from Guise and across the Oise east of the town, compelled the III. Corps to face north, and pressing back the right of the Army threatened to turn it. Before the morning was over all hope of progressing towards St. Quentin was at an end. Every available man was needed to parry the ever-increasing danger of the German advance from the north. (Map X, p. 266.)

* Two hours after the battle began the left-hand division of the XVIII. Corps was still looking for the British, whom they believed to be attacking on their left, a further illustration, if one were needed, of how incredibly slowly information travels in war.

General Lanrezac directed the battle from the schoolhouse at Laon with great decision and coolness, under the eye of Joffre who looked on never uttering a word.

Lanrezac maintained the attack on St. Quentin as he had been ordered to do, in spite of the threatening danger from the north. When it became evident that the original plan had miscarried, and that the Fifth Army must fight facing north to save its very existence, he rose to the occasion. Displaying the greatest quickness and comprehension of events, he decided to give up the attack in the direction of St. Quentin, and without any reference to the Commander-in-Chief, ordered the I. Corps to the rescue of the hard-pressed troops to the north.

At this stage of the battle General Lanrezac's worst previsions seemed about to be fulfilled. The attack on St. Quentin had yielded no result, whilst the German pressure on the right wing of the Army was proving extremely dangerous.

But worse was to come. The Germans attacked the French who had crossed the Oise. There was severe fighting in which the French were defeated, the Reserve Divisions on the left, where they had taken the place originally assigned to a division of the I. Corps, being severely handled. The Brigade at Urvillers lost its two colonels and fell back. The French counter-attacked gallantly, but failed to consolidate their position; the men, as always, were brave but ignorant, the officers uninstructed. It ended in something closely resembling a panic, when units, pouring back over the river, got jammed on the bridges and in the narrow passages beyond. Some regiments were not reformed east of the river till late at night by Staff officers riding on horseback amongst them.

The XVIII. Corps and the 6th Division of the III. Corps were driven back across the Oise, and the latter lost the high ground overlooking the river east of Mont d'Origny. There was panic here also, but the men were soon taken in hand and advanced again later under cover of the artillery.

Fighting was still very picturesque on our side at that time, full of colour, like a picture by Neuville. But the splendid pageant was a tragedy, for an endless number of actors who, uncounted to this day, flitted across the scene, achieved nothing beyond providing targets for an invisible foe.

Typical of the methods of those days, a vignette of this particular battle, the two divisional commanders of the XVIII. Corps were to be seen that morning, on the far side of the Oise, standing together under an apple tree in the middle of the deployed infantry, calmly discussing the situation under close infantry fire. An unlucky shell, a couple of bullets, might have laid them low and thereby paralysed the Corps.

On the right, General d'Esperey, quick of decision and impetuous in execution, was straining at the leash, circumstances as well as his own temperament impelling him to take action, only fear of running counter to the plan laid down by the Army Commander holding him in check.

He had watched all morning the X. Corps troops being driven back. When he saw their resistance about to collapse and the right of the Army threatened, he decided to attack with his 1st Division straight ahead towards Guise. His troops were about to carry out these instructions when about 1 p.m. he received a message from General Lanrezac telling him to advance on St. Quentin. He was only to intervene in support of the X. Corps if absolutely necessary.

This order was almost immediately superseded by two others in rapid succession, the first stating that "it was urgent that the I. Corps should be employed with the object of throwing back into the Oise the forces which have debouched and are attacking the X. Corps," and the second – "It has become imperative to throw back into the Oise the hostile forces which have crossed on to the left bank. The I. Corps will be engaged so as best to accomplish this, in conjunction with the III. and X. Corps."*

This was General d'Esperey's great opportunity, and he rose to it. He took immediate steps to carry out these new instructions, which he had anticipated. His divisional commanders were ordered to advance, rally the units of neighbouring Corps and lead them forward also. His indomitable personality made itself felt everywhere. No one

* The 2nd Division of the I. Corps had been at first in Army Reserve. When the attack began it was with its Corps on the right of the line. At 9 a.m. orders were sent to it to entrain for the extreme left to take the place of the absent British. This order did not reach the I. Corps till 11 a.m., when General d'Esperey constituted a provisional division with the 8th and 3rd Brigades and gave the command of it to General Deligny, G.O.C. of the 2nd Division. According to the *Historique of the I. Corps*, the reason why the 2nd Division was not moved in accordance with Lanrezac's order was that a sufficient number of trains could not be collected for the purpose. This is probably true and may have influenced General Lanrezac's decision to maintain this division with its own Corps. It turned out to be a happy factor in the events of the day and worked in with the decision to change the direction of the battle which General Lanrezac took in the afternoon, for this division found itself where it was needed at the critical moment, and at 3 p.m. was given back to the I. Corps. Only the 148th Regiment was in the end sent to the left of the line.

who served under him dared to have doubts or to question. Fiercely as
was his way he urged the men forward. His iron will carried his Corps,
the steel spring of his determination pressed it on. The men of the I.
Corps required no urging, but the little square man with the bullet
head, whose gestures were like cracking whips, as violent as dynamite,
was more feared than the Germans ahead. They were in front, he was
behind, and the enemy was the lesser evil. But he was respected, and
liked, too, for men love a real leader.

It was not till 5.30 in the afternoon that everything was ready, and
General d'Esperey, riding at the head of the 2nd Brigade, surrounded
by his staff on horseback, gave the order for the general attack.* It
was a magnificent sight. Strange, but very gallant, the bands were
playing and the colours were unfurled. The I. Corps troops, deployed
in long skirmishing lines, doubled forward with magnificent dash on
either side of the X. Corps. The X. Corps and the right of the III.
were carried forward in the splendid victorious wave, the men frantic
with joy at the new and longed for sensation. The Germans were
running away, there was no doubt about it. French artillery observers
reported the enemy's guns were limbering up, their infantry retiring
hurriedly. The gunners were almost the only ones who caught sight of
the German infantry all day. In spite of the severity of the fighting,
and the losses, it had been a fire action; the enemy's attacks had been
by fire, the French had been driven back by fire, and now the Germans
were retiring the fact was only patent to the French because the ground
in front of them was unoccupied and the hostile artillery fire had become
wild and desultory. It was said that the French guns had done such
execution that the bridge at Guise was heaped with dead, so numerous
that they lay up against each other in rows. Whether this was true
or not mattered little, the report heartened the French wonderfully,
and the men were tremendously proud, too, at the thought that they
had beaten the German Guard.

What had happened on the enemy's side was that the 2nd German

---

* I am unable to explain this delay. When more information is available, General Franchet
d'Esperey may be criticized for not having attacked earlier, on the grounds that had he done
so the action of the I. Corps would have been far more decisive than it was.

Of d'Esperey's activity and will to attack there can be no doubt, but it is possible that he
over-elaborated his arrangements and would not advance until every detail had been completed. The pomp and circumstance of the attack was also characteristic.

There is a story that seeing General Pétain, the future Commander-in-Chief, then in
command of a Brigade, who had been before the war a lecturer at the French Staff College,
d'Esperey called to him: "Well, *Monsieur le Professeur à l'Ecole de Guerre*, what do you think of
this movement?" I do not know whether this is true, but it might well be, it is so typical of the
man.

Guard Division had been busily engaged in attacking the right of the French X. Corps when d'Esperey launched his attack. A French battery got into position and enfiladed the Guard Division, whilst three companies attacked its uncovered flank and began rolling it up. This led to the hasty retreat of the Guards, and eventually to the withdrawal of the whole German line.* (Map X, p. 266.)

The I. Corps had carried the line forward five kilometres. On a front of 25 kilometres, from Mont d'Origny to Vervins, the Fifth Army had advanced. On the extreme right the 4th Cavalry Division had done good work in protecting the outer flank of the Army and in drawing large enemy forces to itself.

The Army had won its first victory, although not the victory that had been anticipated by Joffre. The Battle of St. Quentin was lost, but the Battle of Guise had been won. The lack of success on the left was more than compensated for by the tactical victory won by the I. Corps on the right. As a very brilliant French writer, Jules Isaac, has said: "There was a battle as willed by Joffre and not by Lanrezac, but as Lanrezac and not Joffre had foreseen, it turned out to be far more a battle of Guise than a battle of St. Quentin."

The results of the French success were immediate. The attacks against the Sixth Army ceased as if by magic, and British aviators observed German columns moving back. This respite enabled Maunoury to retire behind the Avre.†

More important still, the whole German advance was deflected. Von Bülow, who claimed that he was being attacked by superior forces, called for and obtained the help of the left of the First Army (i.e. of part of the IX. Corps), with the result that the line of von Kluck's

---

* Von Bülow stated that his losses were 240 officers and 5,800 men killed and wounded.

The 2ème Bureau of the Fifth Army believed that the German troops engaged on either side of the Oise were the X. Reserve Corps, perhaps the VII., and X. and Guard Corps. This estimate was correct, except that only half the VII. Corps was engaged, and that in addition to the above, half the IX. Corps from the First German Army also took part in the battle, but only with its artillery.

† When attacked in the morning General Maunoury decided to retire if necessary in the general direction of Moreuil, St. Just-en-Chaussée, and he asked the Commander-in-Chief for orders. He was told at 1 p.m. to withdraw behind the Avre, avoiding becoming involved in a decisive engagement. He was to reform his command behind the river between Montdidier and Moreuil, ultimately falling back towards St. Just-en-Chaussée. He was to watch the enemy with his Cavalry, and should the Germans withdraw he was to advance in the direction of Chaulnes.

General Sordet, whose Cavalry Corps was by now incapable of fighting as a whole, formed a provisional Cavalry Division under General Cornulier-Lucinière from those regiments which were still mobile, and placed it for two days at the disposal of General Maunoury.

advance was drawn down towards the south-east. Far-reaching in its effects also was the fact that von Bülow found it necessary to give his Army a rest of thirty-six hours after the battle.

During the day, as far as the British were concerned, only the Cavalry was engaged, and the Fourth Army, now some 50 km. south-east of the Fifth, was enabled to withdraw unmolested.

That night, the Fifth Army liaison officers were extraordinarily optimistic in their reports, both as to the results obtained and the morale of the troops, but much bitterness was felt towards the British, who, by continuing their retirement, were generally considered to be robbing the Fifth Army of the fruits of its success. Indeed their withdrawal was to have grave consequences, for it resulted in placing General Lanrezac's command in serious jeopardy.

For the moment, one thing was abundantly evident, the Fifth Army must retreat, and that rapidly. Although victorious it was in a more serious situation than ever, unsupported on either flank, on its left the British already a day's march behind, on its right an immense stretch of open country beyond which the Fourth Army was retiring.

But what chiefly preoccupied General Lanrezac at the moment were his relations with the G.Q.G. So piqued was he by the events of the last few days that he determined not to take any steps to extricate his Army without an express order from General Joffre. He was not going to have it said that he had withdrawn as soon as the Commander-in-Chief's back was turned, or that by lack of boldness he had deprived himself of the full fruits of his victory, although he knew that his Army could not possibly either stay where it was or continue to attack.

This unhappy state of mind led to his having a curious conversation over the telephone with General Belin, who answered in place of General Joffre, who was away when Lanrezac rang him up:

Lanrezac said:
 "Is the Fifth Army to delay in the region of Guise–St. Quentin at the risk of being captured?"

General Belin:
 "What do you mean, let your Army be captured, it is absurd!"

Lanrezac:

"You do not understand me. I am operating here by the express orders of the Commander-in-Chief to fulfil, so he told me, a mission of public safety. Are the events which have taken place in the last twenty-four hours of such a nature that I am to pursue the operation prescribed to me in spite of the growing risk I am running? I cannot take it upon myself to withdraw on Laon. It is for the Commander-in-Chief to give me the order to retire."

General Belin:

"I am not entitled to speak for the Commander-in-Chief under these circumstances. I will report to him as soon as he returns."

Lanrezac:

"Right. I will remain with a view to resuming if possible my attack on St. Quentin unless the Commander-in-Chief orders me to retire."*

A strange conversation, surely, and a stranger tone. Lanrezac was of course perfectly right to solicit instructions. He was not only entitled to keep in touch with the Commander-in-Chief and make certain that he was acting in conformity with his wishes, it was his duty to do so; but it is to be regretted that he, an Army Commander, should have thought fit to say in effect to the Commander-in-Chief – "Am I to go on with your plan? To do so means risking the capture of my force." He dissociated himself, at the end as he had at the beginning, from all responsibility for the battle of Guise, washing his hands of the only offensive the forces under his command ever undertook.

What would seem to prove that General Lanrezac was attempting to exacerbate the G.Q.G. by pointing out that his Army found itself in a very dangerous position owing to his having carried out General Joffre's orders, is that in spite of his declaration that he would be in readiness to resume the attack on St. Quentin, his orders to the Corps did not mention any such possibility.† He well knew such an attack to be impossible and that an order to withdraw must be sent him.

* This conversation is General Lanrezac's own version, taken from his book, *Le Plan de Campagne Français*, p. 241.

† The XVIII. Corps and the Reserve Divisions were alone facing St. Quentin, all the remaining Corps facing north. The orders were that all formations were to fortify the positions occupied and to throw back over the Oise any of the enemy who might attempt to cross. The III., I. and X. Corps were to press back into the Oise the Germans still on the left bank, but not to cross the river.

As General Lanrezac had anticipated, an order to retire was sent him, but the trouble was that he did not receive it, and consequently found himself in a fearful predicament. He had pledged himself out of sheer bravado to carry out an impossible operation, banking on the G.Q.G.'s being compelled to order him to withdraw, and now General Joffre was as silent as the tomb. Having stated his own view of the situation with such lucidity, there was nothing more for him to say. He could not and did not again solicit orders.

So the weary night dragged on, whilst the tired troops under the stimulus of the subordinate commanders got ready for further fighting in the morning, and the commanders of the corps facing north determined to carry on with the previous day's success to the uttermost limit allowed by General Lanrezac, namely to throw back into the Oise the Germans still south of the river.

Owing to an error which has not to this day been satisfactorily explained, the order to retire sent by the Commander-in-Chief to General Lanrezac at 10 p.m. was lost and has never been found. That it had been despatched was only discovered when a telephonic confirmation of it was sent on the following morning at 7 a.m.*

In his dire perplexity at hearing nothing from Joffre, Lanrezac turned once more to the British. At 2 a.m. Fagalde was ordered to go to British G.H.Q. at Compiègne. On arrival he woke Huguet who took him to see General Wilson. Fagalde explained the favourable result of the Battle of Guise, stressed the dangerous situation of the Fifth Army and pressed for British support, however limited, to safeguard the left of General Lanrezac's Army. This intervention had no result whatever, and Fagalde returned to Laon. It was unlikely that anyone would succeed where Joffre himself had failed: he had gone to Compiègne straight from Laon in the early afternoon, but found Sir John adamant in his resolve to continue his retreat.

Orders for the further British retirement to the line Soissons–Compiègne behind the Aisne were issued at 9 p.m. This step was taken

---

* The French Historical Section furnishes the following explanation of this incident:

"On account of delay in transmitting this order, dated August 29th, at 10 p.m., it did not reach its destination in its original form (that of a cipher telegram) . . . This delay in the despatch of an important order was due to an error committed by the postal service of the G.Q.G. Whereas the cipher telegram should have been sent off, this department thought that the telegram handed in was a written confirmation of a message which had already been telephoned by the 3ème Bureau. The error was only remedied next morning, the 30th. The telephonic communication figures in the documents of the Fifth Army as having been received at 7 a.m."

when Sir John heard of the lack of success of the French towards St. Quentin.*

The most satisfactory result of the day's operations from the British point of view, apart from a badly needed respite accorded to the troops, was that the gap between the two British Corps was reduced to seven miles.

Perhaps what had decided Joffre to go to see Sir John was a message from Duruy, who had gone in liaison to British G.H.Q. and reported that the British would not be able to resume the offensive till the 31st and would concentrate on the 30th south of the Oise. General Joffre begged Sir John to allow the B.E.F. to remain in line with the French Armies, but as has been seen he was unable to shake the Field Marshal's resolution. The satisfactory relationship established at St. Quentin was suffering a temporary eclipse.

On his way back to Vitry from Compiègne, General Joffre met General Henry Wilson, who, according to his own account, had been to the G.Q.G. with the object of persuading the Generalissimo to limit Lanrezac's attack to a mere demonstration.

General Wilson wrote in his Diary:

"I had two and a half hours with Belin and Berthelot. I spoke strongly about the madness of Lanrezac's attacking with four corps, because they would be met with seven corps. I spoke of the danger of eccentric movements like the VII. Corps detraining west of Péronne, of scattered Reserve Divisions, of the absolute necessity of bringing up corps from Alsace, and of gaining time. Of the urgent need of stopping Lanrezac from doing more than a demonstration. We had a long, at one time hot, discussion but I stuck to my points, and in the end I got my way. They agreed to the wisdom of my proposals, and said Lanrezac would be stopped from going beyond St. Quentin.

"Meanwhile Joffre had gone to Compiègne. On my way home after my long talk with Belin and Berthelot, I was met 10 km. outside

* On whose information British G.H.Q. was relying when this order was given I do not know, nor why the situation of General Lanrezac's Army was not considered as a whole. What I do know is that as early as 5 p.m. the situation of the Fifth Army at that time had been telegraphed to G.H.Q. and was stated to be satisfactory. Later a still more optimistic message was sent. It is a pity that an unauthorized and pessimistic report concerning a section only of the Fifth Army should have been given more weight than the official and responsible reports emanating from the H.Q. of that Army itself.

Reims by an officer who told me Joffre wished to see me in Reims on his way back to Vitry. I met him at the Lion d'Or at 7.30 p.m. under the electric light of the archway. I had a long talk with him, re-capitulating what I had said to Belin, and begging him not to commit Lanrezac irretrievably. He was tired but he insisted on the fact that Lanrezac must go '*au bout*'. I urged him to bring corps from Alsace. I don't know if my day's work has been any use, but I think Lanrezac will be withdrawn."*

Nothing I have said in this book better illustrates the confusion of the moment than this short note. It is extraordinary to find the Sub-Chief of Staff of the British Army, a force whose constant complaint had been that the Fifth Army could not be induced to attack, vehe-mently complaining when that Army was at last making a stand.

*   *   *

To General Joffre, the situation that night can hardly have seemed less gloomy than at the close of the previous day.

All hope of carrying out the manœuvre laid down in *Instruction Générale No. 2* had vanished.

The only encouraging news from any quarter was the partial tactical success of the Fifth Army, but this was offset by the fact that that Army was in greater danger than ever and was compelled to fall back, aban-doning the strong natural position of Laon and the hasty defences established there.

General d'Amade feared an attack from Amiens, and asked what he was to do if his Territorials could not hold the Somme.

General Maunoury reported that he was being violently attacked by two German Corps debouching from the front Bray–Péronne. (It

---

* Sir Henry Wilson's *Life and Diaries*, Vol. I, p. 172.

The idea of bringing up corps from Alsace can hardly have seemed a new one to the G.Q.G., as every available man was even then being transferred from the right to the left of the line.

There must have been some misunderstanding also between General Joffre and General Wilson in the talk he reports. General Joffre never intended Lanrezac to attempt more than a powerful counter-attack, a sudden blow. In the absence of British co-operation anything else was obviously impossible. Further General Joffre knew when he saw General Wilson some-thing of how the battle had progressed.

I imagine the misunderstanding may have been once more due to a language difficulty, for General Joffre can never have used the words "*au bout*". Had he meant to say anything like what General Wilson thought, he would have said "*jusqu' au bout*". What he probably said was that General Lanrezac must fulfil the role assigned him, "*aller au bout de sa tâche*", which is a very different thing.

was many hours before it was realized that the Fifth Army's offensive
had caused this attack to cease.)

General de Langle insisted that his troops needed rest.

Before Joffre left his Headquarters for Laon he had informed the
Minister that he had been compelled to order the Fourth Army to
retire on Reims. He told him that the offensive of the German right
wing might threaten Paris. He was attempting to hold it up by ordering
the Fifth Army to attack. So serious did he consider the situation that
he told the Minister he might have to reinforce the garrison of the capital
by part of Lanrezac's Army.* General de Langle was told that whether
his troops could rest or not depended on the enemy. General d'Amade
was ordered to blow up the Somme bridges at Amiens and below when
he judged it necessary to do so.

Whatever General Joffre's hopes and fears that night, there was little
to show him that his courageous stand was to yield important results,
and that over and above the check inflicted on the enemy, something
had happened to the German machine that would not be set right; he
could not know that in the incalculable lottery of events, in the infinite
repercussion of cause and effect, the blow he had dealt the enemy at
Guise had set the wheel of fate turning very slowly in his favour.

* He also told him that he was sending the 45th Division (formed in Africa) to Paris.

THE PERILOUS SITUATION OF THE FIFTH ARMY

August 30th, 1914

A visit to G.H.Q. – Sir John French at Compiègne – Joffre orders Fifth Army to retire behind the Serre – The Fifth Army escapes from a dangerous situation – The Reserve Divisions – The situation at nightfall – Lanrezac's orders for the 31st – Events at British G.H.Q. – Joffre informs French that the retreat is to continue – Sir John French decides to retire on his base – Joffre's protest – Sir John's letter to Lord Kitchener.

In the early morning Duruy came to request that I should accompany him immediately to British G.H.Q. His mission was of course to make yet another attempt to induce the Field-Marshal to await developments before retiring further. The position of the Fifth Army was growing more precarious every hour, and the G.Q.G. seemed to have forgotten its very existence.

I cannot remember why so important a man as the new Head of the Operations Section of the Fifth Army was sent on a journey that would take several hours. The reason may have been a cypher telegram sent by Huguet at 4.45 a.m. to the G.Q.G.,* the tenour of which may have been communicated direct from Compiègne to Laon or passed on from Vitry. In this Huguet said he had done his best to induce the Field-Marshal to change his orders for the 30th;† that the British I. Corps was retreating into the zone of the Fifth Army, and that the Field-Marshal had refused to modify his orders, as they were in course of execution.

---

* Colonel Huguet to the G.Q.G.: "As soon as I got in, I strongly pressed the Field-Marshal to change his orders for tomorrow (*i.e.* 30th), pointing out the importance of a forward movement by the I. Corps, and moreover (words missing in text) retreat into zone reserved to Fifth Army, and also great danger of blowing up bridges. Field-Marshal maintains his orders in spite of my insistence, saying that their execution has begun and that it is too late to modify them. The only point I obtained is that the bridges will not be blown up, and that the troops of the I. Corps may be stopped after the short march ordered, and then turn about. Will endeavour tomorrow (30th) to obtain at least this.

† See previous chapter, p. 276.

I have the clearest memory of that drive to Compiègne. Even today I can visualize Soissons, the Aisne, certain turns of the empty road as we flew along at terrific speed in a racing car. Once a puncture compelled us to stop, and I can still see the early sun flecking the woods with gold, and the dawn breaking on a landscape untouched by war, where the only sound was that of birds singing.

I think it was to that morning that another picture of this time belongs; of the Palace of Compiègne, where G.H.Q. was installed, through whose high windows the sun poured in on the British Staff, each section working in a different part of an immensely long gallery, whilst signallers were laying telegraph and telephone lines, stretching them from picture to picture. A scene of strange bustle and confusion, multiplied endlessly by the mirrors under the astonished gaze of the dignified portraits.

Many of the paintings had already been taken away. The removal had been in full swing when Joffre came to see Sir John on the 29th. Workmen on ladders were making such a deafening din with hammers, that they had to be stopped to enable the two Commanders-in-Chief to hear each other speak.

On arriving at Compiègne Duruy and I went to the hotel where the Commander-in-Chief was living. Duruy was kept waiting, rather unfortunately I thought, while I was ushered in to the Field-Marshal and his Chief of Staff. The former had been riding, and though his tunic was of the thinnest, the weather was so hot that I remember there was a great wet mark on his back. The interview took place in a corner room on the first floor. Sir John and Sir Archibald Murray both stood in front of a table on which maps were spread.

The impression Sir John made on me that morning was very reassuring. He was certainly one of the coolest and calmest people at G.H.Q. It was wonderful how he kept up his spirits in spite of the prevailing atmosphere of gloom.

I was questioned as to the events of the day before, and the position of the Fifth Army, but, uneasy that Duruy should be kept waiting in this obvious way, replied that he could answer better than I could and might be relied upon to be meticulously accurate. Nevertheless I was ordered to give my own impression. I placed the result of the previous day's fighting high, partly, no doubt, reflecting the enthusiasm of the liaison officers who had returned from the different parts of the battlefield, but also because I was persuaded that a very noteworthy event in the history of the campaign had occurred. I was able to pay tribute to the dash and bravery of the French in the small corner of the battle-field I had myself seen.

As I was speaking the door was flung open and a senior artillery officer ran in, seemingly on the verge of collapse. "All the guns in the division are lost," he almost sobbed. Sir Archibald Murray took a step towards him and getting hold of his shoulders shook him roughly. "To my own knowledge you have seven left," he said sternly.

The gunner was dismissed and I was told to go on, but to see anyone so far from the front suffering from nerves to this extent revealed the ordeal through which some of our units had passed.

I went on to say something of the obviously very dangerous situation in which the Fifth Army found itself, and showed my map, on which was marked the approximate line occupied on the previous night. Sir John asked my personal impression of General Lanrezac at the moment, and I repeated what I had reported the night before concerning the magnificent manœuvre that had preceded the battle and the masterly manner in which it had been conducted. On this head there could be no doubt whatever. As to what General Lanrezac's relations with the G.Q.G. now were, or what his subsequent action was likely to be, I preferred not to hazard a guess. The only thing I could confidently assert was that the events on the Sambre would not be repeated, for the Fifth Army was now far too closely controlled and watched for anything of the kind to be possible.

Duruy was then ushered in. He did not refer to the difficult position in which General Lanrezac had been placed on the previous day by the withdrawal of the British, but confined himself to describing the present precarious situation of the Fifth Army, and urged that a further British retirement would involve it in the most terrible danger. He submitted that even from the British point of view a halt would involve little risk, and would avert the possibility of a disaster not only to the Fifth Army but eventually to the B.E.F. as well, since it was obvious that if the former were overwhelmed in its advanced position the British would immediately be in great peril. For this reason he begged for some support from the I. Corps. He also said it was vitally necessary that the British convoys should keep to the west of the Chauny–Soissons road.*

* There was not a single main north–south road leading through the St. Gobain *Massif*. A road to the east of it connected La Fère with Laon and ran east-south-east. The road to the west of it was the Chauny–Soissons road. If at all pressed, therefore, it was difficult to see how the left of the Fifth Army could have extricated itself if deprived of the use of this road.

We were told that an answer would be given us presently, but we did not see either the Field-Marshal or his Chief of Staff again.

* * *

Duruy and I were soon on the road again under a broiling sun. In contrast to my vivid recollection of the outward journey, I remember nothing of our return, though it may have been then that we saw some terribly weary, bedraggled, unkempt men belonging to the II. Corps, hardly recognizable as soldiers, led by limping officers. In spite of their condition there was something martial in their bearing which Duruy recognized and paid tribute to. We also saw some magnificent rested troops, a little footsore perhaps, belonging to the I. Corps.

The impression we took away from British G.H.Q., though rather nebulous, was hopeful, but to Duruy's question as to whether I thought it would be all right I could answer nothing.

He told me of the following telegram sent by General Maunoury, G.O.C. Sixth Army, to Huguet. It had been communicated at 7 a.m. to the British Staff, and Duruy had seen it at the French Mission. (Map XIII, p. 360.)

"I have just learnt of the movement of the British Army on to the line Rethondes–Soissons. Under these circumstances my Army, still incompletely formed, remains isolated, faced by numerous forces. My intention is therefore not to allow myself to be engaged in another fight today, and to withdraw to the line Compiègne–Clermont, joining on to the British Army whose left I am covering."

When Duruy and I arrived at Laon at about 10 a.m. we found that the G.Q.G.'s orders to the Fifth Army to retire, which had gone astray as described in the previous chapter, had been received at 7 a.m.

These orders were as follows:

"The effect of the attack of the Fifth Army having made itself felt and having partially disengaged the Sixth Army, the Fifth Army will take steps to break off the fight and withdraw its forces behind the Serre.

"The breakaway will take place before dawn. Blow up as soon as possible the bridges of La Fère, Condren and Chauny (the latter if the British are no longer at Chauny)."

Since 5 a.m. the 3ème Bureau had been preparing an order to with-draw behind the Serre. It was almost ready for issue when Joffre's order was received. But it is one thing to issue an order and another to withdraw troops engaged in offensive operations. When the order to retire was received at Laon the right and centre of the Army were in process of driving the enemy back all along the line.* (Map X, p. 266.)

The III. Corps, which was to have participated in the offensive, had been unable to do so. As has been seen, these troops had been badly shaken on the previous day, and had not reached the assembly positions for the attack when the order to retire reached them. This Corps was therefore able to carry out the order without difficulty, and luckily for the troops of the Corps already engaged, the enemy had been so severely handled the day before, and the German Command so much taken aback, that they were able to withdraw pursued only by artillery fire.

The left of the Army was not escaping so easily as the right.

A German Corps was making a drive across the Oise and was pro-gressing. Until nightfall the situation remained critical, for the XVIII. Corps, which had been ordered to hold the heights of Renansart at all costs, appeared unable to maintain its position. The importance of these heights lay in the fact that if the enemy occupied them before the Army was across the Serre, he would command many of the river passages as well as the low ground between the river and Laon. (Map X, p. 266.)

During the afternoon the XVIII. Corps, which certainly did not fight well that day, lost more and more ground, many of its units retiring straight into III. Corps formations, and at 6 p.m. General Hache, commanding the III. Corps, who earlier in the day had been told to give what help he considered necessary to the XVIII. Corps, was ordered to advance immediately to its rescue.† Luckily by the

* The troops engaged were the 4th Cavalry Division, the 51st Reserve Division and the X. and I. Corps.

† General Lanrezac in his book judges the XVIII. Corps very severely. He says (p. 249): "My feeling is that the XVIII. Corps was perfectly capable of containing the Germans, who only engaged inferior forces against it and only progressed as it ceded ground before their cannonade. General de Mas Latrie imagined he had to deal with a very strong opponent; it will later be known who was right, he or I."

In fairness to the Commander of the XVIII. Corps it must be noted that at the time the H.Q. of the Army estimated the attack on the XVIII. Corps to be carried out by about a Corps, vide the following message sent out by a liaison officer to the III. Corps:

"Laon, August 30th, 3 p.m.

"The XVIII. Corps is engaged against a force of about a German Corps debouching from St. Quentin on Sery-les-Mézières-Ribémont . . .

The Chief of Staff, HÉLY D'OISSEL."

In point of fact the XVIII. Corps was opposed by the German X. Reserve Corps, which was advancing against it on Ribémont and Renansart on the left bank of the Oise, whilst half the VII. Corps was attacking it across the river from St. Quentin.

time the III. Corps was ready to intervene the enemy pressure had practically ceased.*

The Fifth Army had a lucky escape that afternoon, for the whole position of the left was precarious in the extreme. Not only was the XVIII. Corps giving way all too readily to the enemy, but farther to the left the Reserve Divisions were quite incapable of showing any fight, the only solid unit on that part of the front being the 148th Regiment (transferred to the left from the I. Corps on the previous day).

General Valabrègue's position was exceedingly difficult. His artillery alone had any fighting value. His infantry was disorganized, and he was so dissatisfied with some of his subordinate commanders, whom he held to blame for much that had occurred, that he was carrying out an investigation of their conduct. Whilst attempting to reorganize his command as it retired on St. Gobain, its right resting on the 148th Regiment, he was informed of the German attack on the XVIII. Corps. He was told that the river passage at La Fère was of vital importance to the security of the left flank of the Army and that he must cover it.† He at once took steps to do this by constituting a strong rearguard with all his artillery so as to be in a position to intervene should fighting develop in the neighbourhood of La Fère, but the necessity did not arise. (Map X, p. 266.)

In spite of all difficulties, by nightfall the Fifth Army found itself on the Serre between Marle and La Fère, its forces spread out like a hand laid flat on the map, the wrist at Laon, the fingers pointing north. Its position was most dangerous. On its right lay an immense gap, with not a man between it and an isolated division of Foch's group, some 26 kilometres due south of the right wing. To the east the Germans, to the south-east the Germans again, presumably by now in occupation of Rethel and bordering the Aisne.‡ In this direction the French troops nearest to the Fifth Army were a cavalry division at least 30 kilometres away. The Oise and its passages north of La Fère were in German

---

* On this day two officers who were to play an important part in the history of the war were appointed to the III. Corps. General Pétain took over command of the 6th and General Mangin of the 5th Division.

† Orders to blow up this bridge were issued in the evening. In the early afternoon the British Commander-in-Chief was authorized to blow up the Compiègne railway bridge if necessary, and the same permission was given to General Lanrezac concerning several bridges, etc., in the neighbourhood of Soissons. In the evening the Huguet Mission reported that the Oise bridges at Chauny, Condren, Beautor and Varesnes, the two bridges at Pontoise and the two bridges at Pont l'Eveque had been destroyed. Those of Ourscamp, Bailly and Compiègne were to be blown up that night or next day.

‡ These were presumed to be part of von Hausen's Army, which had not been in touch with the Fifth Army for some days.

hands, whilst those west of Chauny were undefended. West of the Oise and beyond it the First German Army was swerving south-eastwards at von Bülow's request to hurl itself against the left flank of the Fifth Army. Immediately behind the left of the Fifth Army, separated from it by the St. Gobain hills and woods, lay the British I. Corps some ten miles to the south-west. (Map XIII, p. 360.)

General Lanrezac issued orders at 8.15 p.m. that the whole Army was to be behind the Serre by the morning of the 31st, the delay in the transmission of Joffre's orders having thus held it back a whole day. Hardly were these orders issued when Joffre instructed Lanrezac to send a Corps of two divisions to Soissons, whence they were to be directed on Paris.*

Meanwhile events at British G.H.Q. had been working up to a crisis.

Duruy's intervention in the early morning would seem to have borne some fruit, since Joffre had received a message from Huguet that a halt had been called to the British retreat.† To improve the shining hour, he immediately sent Huguet the following telephone message:

"August 30th, 8.45 a.m.

"I request you to thank Marshal French warmly on my behalf for the order he has just issued.

* *Les Armées Française dans la Grande Guerre*, Tome Premier, Deuxième Volume, p. 518.

"This . . . measure was taken in response to a desire expressed by the Government. As early as August 25th, Monsieur Messimy, Minister of War, had, as has been seen, given General Joffre orders to direct an army of at least three corps on Paris in the event of our forces being compelled to retire 'to insure its defence.' On August 30th Colonel Pénelon, belonging to the military staff of the President of the Republic and attached to the G.Q.G., was ordered by Monsieur Millerand, who had replaced Monsieur Messimy at the Ministry of War, to obtain the views of the Commander-in-Chief as to whether the time had not come to provide the fortified camp of Paris with active troops which it lacked at the time, and also as to the possible transfer of the seat of the Government to Bordeaux.

"General Joffre answered that he fully intended to send to the Capital a sufficient number of active and reserve troops drawn from the armies of the left, and, as has been seen, he gave the necessary orders that same evening.

"On the other point, General Joffre saw only advantages in the Government's transferring to Bordeaux."

† Colonel Huguet to the G.Q.G. Compiègne, August 30th, 7.35 a.m.:

"Marshal French has just given orders to stop the retrograde movement of his Army.

"As regards the eastern column, the I. Corps (1st and 2nd Divisions) is by its rearguards to maintain contact with the left of the Fifth Army at La Fère. The main body is to halt as soon as the order reaches it, and in any event not to go beyond Coucy-le-Château.

"To the west, the 3rd, 4th and 5th Divisions are for the moment to remain within 10 km. of the Oise. It is not possible to hope that these three Divisions will be able to participate in the general action, but I think I can obtain that the 1st and 2nd Divisions will receive a little later orders to turn about and to attack.

"It is important in this connection that any turn for the better in the situation should be immediately made known here so that the Field-Marshal may be informed at once."

"Following upon yesterday's action (by the Fifth Army) when the two right-hand corps of that Army threw back towards the Oise at Guise and above that town the German Guard and X. Corps, I have ordered General Lanrezac, in view of the general situation of our forces, to withdraw behind the Serre.

"The Sixth Army is at present round Montdidier.

"I am considering the general withdrawal of the forces, avoiding all decisive action, so as to put up the most protracted resistance possible. But, whilst these movements are in progress, it is of the greatest importance that the British Army should keep in constant touch with the Fifth Army so as to be able to take advantage of all favourable circumstances to inflict on the enemy a severe lesson like that given yesterday.

"From reports received it appears that the Guard and X. Prussian Corps have suffered very severe losses.

"The zone of march will be communicated as soon as possible, but at the moment it is imperative that Soissons should be cleared of convoys, those of the British Army being deflected west of the St. Gobain–Landricourt–Loeuilly–Terny–Soissons–Longpont road.*

"Ask the Field-Marshal to blow up the Oise bridges between Chauny and Compiègne inclusively."

In the eyes of the British Commander-in-Chief the salient fact in the message was that the retreat of the French Armies was to continue. He saw his much shaken and weakened force framed by two allied armies the one whose physical strength and the other whose moral support he knew to be unreliable, and was determined that this time his Army should not be left behind. He at once sent for Huguet and desired him to forward to General Joffre a telegram he had himself written out.

Compiègne, August 30th, 1914, 12 noon.
"Colonel Huguet has just explained to me your new plan of retirement. I feel it very necessary to impress upon you that the British Army cannot under any circumstances take up a position in the front line for at least ten days. I require men and guns to make

---

* As has been seen, General Joffre intended to withdraw a Corps from the Fifth Army to send to Paris. The infantry was to be entrained at Soissons.

good casualties which have not been properly estimated owing to continual retirement behind fighting rearguards. You will thus understand that I cannot meet your wishes to fill the gap between the Fifth and Sixth Armies, *viz.* line Compiègne–Soissons.''*

It is comprehensible that this despatch not only perplexed but irritated the French. The idea of taking ten days to refit made them grind their teeth in exasperation at an attitude which seemed to take no account of realities. As for "estimating casualties" this seemed a bitter jest to the officers of an Army whose losses were such that to this day it is impossible to estimate with any accuracy how many men fell during any of those weeks in August, 1914.†

If Colonel Huguet's noon message had given Joffre grave anxiety, his subsequent ones caused real alarm. It appeared that the British intended to drop out of the line altogether.

At 3 p.m. Huguet telegraphed:

"Compiègne, August 30th, 1914, 3 p.m.
"Field-Marshal wishes to withdraw his troops behind the Seine, zone Mantes, Poissy, St. Germain, to refit. Wishes to know whether this proposal has the consent of the military authorities and of the Government; in event of affirmative British officers will be sent to prepare billets. Movement will be carried out by road in four or five stages save for the sick who will be sent by rail. The Field-Marshal proposes that Le Mans be chosen as advanced base in place of Amiens." (Map XIII, p. 360.)

Later in the day Huguet wrote a letter to the French Commander-in-Chief making it clear that it was the news of the French retirement that had caused Sir John to countermand his earlier orders and continue his withdrawal.

This letter concluded with the words:

* Our losses, as given by Sir John, were smaller than Kitchener had feared, and he had despatched to France more than enough drafts to make them good.
On August 25th the I.G.C. had telegraphed to G.H.Q. asking if he should forward from the advanced base the men forming the reinforcements and the guns into the line, but was told to keep them in hand for the moment.
See *Life of Kitchener*, by Sir George Arthur, Vol. III, p. 45.
† The only figures available are the total casualties for August and September. These amount to the enormous total of 329,000 killed, missing, prisoners and died in hospitals.
As the total casualties of the French during the war (exclusive of native troops) in killed, missing, prisoners and died in hospitals was 1,796,000, it will be seen that they lost in these first two months between a fifth and a sixth of their total casualties.

"The Field-Marshal proposes that the advanced base be transferred from Amiens to Le Mans; the British Government will itself propose to the French Government the harbour at which it desires to establish the base previously at Havre. The intention of the Field-Marshal is to remain there as short a time as possible, and as soon as he has been able to carry out his reorganization, to advance again."*

No other course was open to Joffre than to accept Sir John's decision to continue his retirement, but he pointed out to Huguet that the British intention of retiring towards Mantes and Poissy by following the Oise was impracticable, as this would mean cutting across the line of march of the Sixth Army. He suggested that in the first place the British should fall back east of Paris, that is behind the Marne between Meaux and Neuilly-sur-Marne, after which they could skirt the capital to the south and then march west.

Only one thing happened that day to show that the spirit of co-operation was still alive. On news, which turned out to be false, coming in to British G.H.Q. that a German force was advancing from Noyon to the south of Laon, the I. Corps was ordered to turn north-east so as to cover the left flank of the Fifth Army.

---

* This communication clearly indicated that the British were to retire on their base, but is in contradiction with the previous message stating that the B.E.F. was to refit about Paris.

It is not certain whether the above letter, written in Huguet's own hand, was ever delivered at the G.Q.G. There is no trace of it there. It is certain, however, that the gist of it was transmitted to Joffre, verbally if not in writing.

Proof that British G.H.Q. was making preparations for an immense retirement would seem to be found in the fact that either on that day or the next an order was sent to London for maps for the whole force as far as Angers, over 150 miles as the crow flies south-west of Paris.

On this day Huguet telephoned to the G.Q.G.:

"The British General Staff is anxious to know how far the British lines of communication on Havre are threatened, and requests that this information should be forthcoming as soon as possible in order that they may be able to take a decision as to changing these.

"There is occasion to make suggestions as to the choice of a new base; the Field-Marshal spoke to me a little while ago about establishing it at La Rochelle, but it may be possible to suggest a better harbour."

Received at 10.45, August 30th, 1914.

A. DEVILLE.

On the same day Sir John French informed Lord Kitchener that his base was now in the neighbourhood of La Rochelle.

What really occurred was that "the advisability of a change of base was foreseen by the Q.M.G., Major-General Sir William Robertson, as early as August 24th, and from that date all further movements of men and stores to Havre or Boulogne were stopped. By the 27th Boulogne had been cleared of stores and closed as a port of disembarkation; and on the 29th St. Nazaire on the Loire was selected as the new base."

Official History of the War, Vol. I, p. 263.

The following extracts from a letter which Sir John French sent to Lord Kitchener on this day, show his point of view concerning the French at this time.

"I cannot say that I am happy in the outlook as to the further progress of the campaign in France. My confidence in the ability of the leaders of the French Army to carry this campaign to a successful conclusion is fast waning, and this is my real reason for the decision I have taken to move the British Forces so far back. . . .

"Knowing what I do of the French soldiers' fighting capabilities and the immense amount of energy, skill, time and trouble which for many years has been brought to bear upon their training and efficiency, I can attribute these constant failures to no other cause than defective higher leading."

The truth was that that point in British psychology had been reached where complete and blissful confidence was replaced by almost irremediable suspicion and mistrust. Those who have had to negotiate with Englishmen, whether officials or otherwise, know how difficult it is ever to retrieve ground thus lost and to re-establish erstwhile confidence.

It may not be out of place here to underline how mistaken Sir John French was in attributing the French defeats to faulty leadership alone. The errors and mistakes in this respect have been frequently commented upon, but there is no doubt that the fearful losses of the French and their lack of success in so many encounters, in spite of great gallantry, was attributable largely to faulty training of the troops and to a complete misapprehension on the part of the officers of the conditions of modern warfare. A conscript Army will invariably be inferior in this respect to a professional one.

After writing these lines I had the opportunity of showing them to a French officer of great repute and mental integrity, and asked him for his honest opinion of them. I cannot do better than to quote his words, with which I thoroughly agree.

"There is much in what you say," he wrote, "but there is also something which only a Frenchman could understand. Since 1906 the Boche had so mortified us, so trodden on our toes, so spat in our faces, that every one of us, everyone, do you understand, even the poorest devil, even the humblest peasant from the depths of the mountains, had understood that it was necessary *once and for all to deal with the hereditary enemy.*

"It was then that the whole country under arms, that is the whole of the French infantry, hurled itself against the Germans, without taking into account, alas, that it is not possible to oppose solely men to material.

"This period of our history, my dear Spears, is finer in my eyes, owing to the enthusiasm we felt pulsating around us (and whatever our losses may have been) than the most moving moments of our Revolution."

* * *

Whilst the Fifth Army was at Laon I did some flying for the French. They had lost many machines and much material, and there was a shortage of observers, so that it was useful to have a volunteer. (I did not explain that I had only been up upon one occasion at Aldershot, and then only once round the Long Valley.)

I remember finding myself above St. Quentin, piloted by a remarkably fine flying officer, who at the moment was shaking with malaria. Visibility was perfect, and for endless miles we could see the enemy columns, black laces spread along the long white roads. Shell-bursts and clouds of dust made a long jagged line, showing where the struggle was going on at the moment. On our side of the shell-bursts the country was empty, and the effect was depressing in the extreme. It seemed as if nothing could stop an enemy so numerous. Here were the *chenilles* of the first days of the campaign translated from the map into horrible reality.

We released boxes of steel arrows on the enemy. These were a new invention and were about the size of a pen-holder, pointed at one end and with steel feathers at the other. They were packed tightly in a receptacle not unlike a petrol tin, and were released by pulling the bottom out. After release they spread wide, and, leaning over the side of the plane, one saw the sun glinting on the thousand steel shafts, transforming them into the likeness of a shoal of fish in a translucent sea.

Their use was soon discontinued, but not before the Germans had copied them and given us some of our own medicine. For a long time I kept some of these German arrows labelled "French invention, German manufacture."

When high up it was easy to realize that it would be practically impossible to hit a small target like that presented by a column on a road.

A further reason for discontinuing their use was that it was proved, unfortunately at our expense, by an aviator dropping some on a detachment of Zouaves, that they were poisonous, for the fall was not sufficiently rapid to clear them of the oil in which they were kept, and this infected the wounds they inflicted.

On one occasion we met a German *Taube* at very close quarters. My only weapon was a French cavalry carbine, hardly better than a pistol, with three shots in the magazine. My thoughts were that a megaphone would have been more useful to point out to the German that it was dangerous enough to be where we were without playing any tricks. But having no means of communication I fired at him and he at us: the usual thing in war, each tries to kill the other for fear of being killed himself.

CHAPTER IX

A GERMAN CAVALRY CORPS THREATENS TO CUT OFF THE RETREAT OF THE FIFTH ARMY

August 31st: – I

The Retreat enters on a new phase – A German Cavalry Corps crosses the Oise at Bailly – Why the Bridge at Bailly was not destroyed – Lanrezac sends a Brigade to Vauxaillon – And orders the 4th Cavalry Division to Vailly – Orders to the Reserve Divisions – Lanrezac appeals for help to the British – The British I. Corps Cavalry forms a screen north of the Aisne – The Fifth Army ordered to resume the retreat at 6 p.m. – A narrative of events on the left of the Fifth Army – How the Army escaped.

THE Retreat was about to begin in real earnest. So far it had been comparatively leisurely, an orderly withdrawal before an unhurrying and uninquisitive enemy. Now that phase was over, and in the days to come the safety of the Fifth Army was to depend on the powers of endurance and the marching capacity of the men, upon whom a terrific strain was imposed.

When the sun rose on the morning of the 31st it was evident that it was going to be another scorching day. The air was delightfully fresh and pleasant, but everyone realized that later the heat would be intense and would entail great additional fatigue for the troops, who were to carry out very long marches over shadeless plains, or through difficult hilly country where the valleys were dusty and airless and water anything but plentiful.

Nevertheless there was optimism in the air at Laon. The exhilaration generated by the success at Guise had not worn off, and was further enhanced by news sent by the G.Q.G. that according to an intercepted enemy wireless the German corps engaged had suffered a real defeat. This, coinciding with information confirming the transference of German troops to the Russian front, caused Joffre to take a more confident

view of the situation. General Maunoury was ordered not to retire farther unless he had reason to fear becoming entangled with superior
forces, and General Lanrezac was told only to give way under pressure,
and to rest his troops a little.

The optimism at Fifth Army Headquarters, which had been only
relative, did not endure long. We were suddenly faced with the news
that an enormous body of swiftly moving German Cavalry was making
straight for the gap between the British and the Fifth Army, advancing
towards the latter's open and undefended lines of communication.
(Map XI, p. 295.)

The seriousness of this will be realized when it is remembered that
the Fifth Army was isolated, nearer the enemy than either of its neighbours, its left flank in danger of an attack by von Kluck; and that from
this situation there was only one means of escape, an immediate and
rapid retreat, which the German Cavalry was now threatening to cut
off.

The first information of this new and terrifying development reached
us at Laon at 9.15 a.m., when the G.Q.G. telephoned that an enemy
wireless message had been intercepted ordering a German Cavalry
Corps* to cross the Oise at Bailly† and march on Vauxaillon, which lay
some fifteen miles south-west of Laon where we were sitting at that
moment. If the enemy cavalry moved at any speed they would reach
Vauxaillon hours before the retiring French infantry, completely outflanking our left. They would cut the Laon–Soissons Railway and be
only a very short distance from the Aisne, from which the main body
of the Fifth Army was separated by many miles of difficult hilly country.
If the Germans occupied the passages of the river before the Fifth Army,
they would cut off its retreat to the south. (Map XI, p. 295.)

It was extremely unfortunate that the bridge over the Oise at Bailly
had not been destroyed. Colonel Huguet had stated that it was to be
blown up either on the night of the 30th or the morning of the 31st.
The attempt ended in tragedy, and its failure placed the Fifth Army in
jeopardy for several hours. This is what happened:

News reached Compiègne on the afternoon of the 30th that the bridge
had not been destroyed, whereupon the British Sub-Chief of Staff,

---

* It was not known at the time which was the Corps in question. It proved to be the I.
(von Richthofen's).
† North-east of Compiègne and east of Ribecourt.

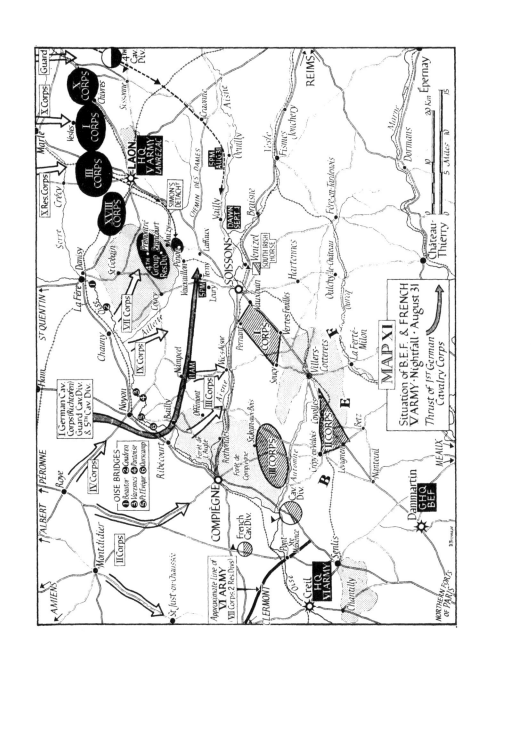

AMIENS   ↑ALBERT   ↑PÉRONNE

Guard

X Corps

I Corps

III Corps

X Res.Corps

Montdidier

Marle   Roye

St Just-en-Chaussée

III Corps

4TH Cav. Div.

Cluvres

Vervins

Crécy

LAON
HQ V ARMY
LANREZAC

Serre

Ham

St QUENTIN

La Fère

Danisy

St Gobain

IV Corps

OISE BRIDGES
1 Beautor   2 Condren
3 Varesnis   4 Dutaise
5 Pt l'Eveque   6 Manscamp

I German Cav.Corps(Richtofen)
Guard Cav.Div.
& 5TH Cav.Div.

Chauny

VII Corps

Noyon

Ribécourt

Forêt de l'Aigle

Forêt de Compiègne

COMPIÈGNE

French Cav.Div.

Cav.Automne
Div.

Pont Ste Maxence

Creil
HQ VI ARMY

CLERMONT

Chantilly

Oise

NORTHERN FORTS
OF PARIS

Approximate line of
VI ARMY
VII Corps 2 Res.Divs

MEAUX

Senlis

Dammartin
GHQ
BEF

Nanteuil

III CORPS

Crépy-en-Valois

Levignen

Betz

II CORPS

La Ferté-
Milon

Villers-
Cotterêts

I CORPS

Oulchy-le-Château

Fère-en-Tardenois

Château-
Thierry

Marne

Dormans

Épernay

REIMS

CHEMIN DES DAMES

Aillette

IX Corps

Bailly

Offémont

Rethondes

Scouaux-Bois

Soucy

Vertes Feuilles

Hartennes

Braisne

Fismes

Jonchery

Vesle

Vic-s-Aisne

Aisne

Pernant

Vauxaillon

SOISSONS

Venizel

SOUTH IRISH
HORSE

Vailly

DAWN
SEPT 1

Venilly

Aisne

Craonne

Soissonne

5 P.M.
AUG 31

III Corps

11 A.M.

Vregny

Leury

Laffaux

Vauxaillon

5 P.M.
AUG 31

Pinon

Anizy

Pontoise

Crécy

4TH
Premontre Forest
Group
Res.Div.

Crouy

SIMON'S
DETACHT

XVIII
CORPS

III
CORPS

I
CORPS

X
CORPS

X Corps

X Res.Corps

Guard

MAP XI
Situation of B.E.F. & FRENCH
V ARMY · Nightfall · August 31
Thrust of 1st German
Cavalry Corps

0   5   10   15 Miles
0   10   20 Km

B.Willoughby

meeting an engineer, Major Barstow, who was in Compiègne by chance, ordered him forthwith to collect sappers and explosives and proceed to Bailly to blow it up. Barstow drove off in a lorry with his detachment and arrived at his destination after dark, having no idea that the bridge might be held by the enemy. Unfortunately it was: the Germans allowed the lorry to get within fifteen yards of the bridge and then fired a volley, killing Barstow and nearly every man of his party.

*   *   *

As soon as news of the advance of the German Cavalry was received from the G.Q.G., General Lanrezac took what steps he could to parry the threat, but pointed out to the Commander-in-Chief that the position of his Army, now placed in a semi-circle round Laon, made it extremely difficult to deal with the situation. We all knew that the problem was complicated by the fact that in this grave emergency he could not rely on Valabrègue's Reserve Divisions on the left of the Army, which were far too shaken and exhausted (their rearguards had been fighting and marching incessantly for three days) to put up any serious resistance. The infantry of the main body of the Army, which was approaching the neighbourhood of Laon, had just carried out a day and night forced march. There was not a single unit capable of marching to the threatened point. The anxiety and nervous tension were extreme.

Colonel Daydrein, the short, bustling and voluble Sub-Chief of Staff of the Fifth Army, came to the rescue with a very useful suggestion. There were seven empty supply trains at Laon station and he stated that he could transport any brigade now in the neighbourhood to Vauxaillon by 5 p.m. (The railway line from Laon to Soissons runs through Vauxaillon.) Accordingly, the III. Corps was ordered to have an infantry brigade, a group of artillery,* and a troop of cavalry ready for entrainment, the head of the column to be at Laon station at 12.15 p.m. Colonel Simon's Brigade, belonging to one of the divisions from Africa, was designated for this duty. If all went well it was just possible for the Brigade to detrain at Vauxaillon in time to make its action felt before the enemy crossed the line running from Vauxaillon to Soissons. The strip of country between the Oise and the Aisne is hilly and narrow, and it was felt that the enemy would not advance very far if he saw that Vauxaillon at the head of the valley leading to Soissons was strongly held. If on the other hand he found no opposition there was nothing to

* Only one battery was entrained.

prevent his occupying all the river passages in rear of the Fifth Army. It was realized it would be a close thing which reached Vauxaillon first, Simon's Brigade or the German Cavalry.

Other measures taken were to order the 4th Cavalry Division, now on the right of the Army, to march forthwith via Craonne to Vailly on the Aisne, there to cover the left of the Army against German cavalry incursions,* and to tell General Valabrègue, commanding the 4th Group of Reserve Divisions, of the situation, giving him the special mission of covering the western flank of the Army. He was to withdraw immediately from his present position† and to send as soon as possible a brigade at least, reinforced by artillery, to the neighbourhood of Vauxaillon, there to co-operate with Simon's Brigade.‡ The Reservists, however shattered and unreliable, had to be made use of. (Map XI.)

Having done what he could with the forces under his own command, General Lanrezac naturally turned to the British for help in his most serious predicament.

G.H.Q. had been informed by the G.Q.G. of the advance of the German cavalry a quarter of an hour after the same information had been given to the Fifth Army, General Joffre pointing out that an action by the British rearguards might suffice to parry the danger. At 10.20 a.m. General Lanrezac sent a message to G.H.Q. asking that the British 1st Division (believed to be on the right of the British Army, and last heard of by the French in the neighbourhood of Anizy-le-Château) should oppose the advance of the German cavalry as it appeared to be well placed to do so.

At 11.15, hearing that the British withdrawal was continuing, and that the I. Corps was retiring across the Aisne at Soissons, he appealed to General Joffre to bring direct influence to bear on Sir Douglas Haig, with whom he, General Lanrezac, had already communicated. Joffre replied at 12 noon that the British had been requested to take steps to stop the German Cavalry, and instructed Lanrezac to come to a direct understanding with the British I. Corps. Huguet was informed of this, and told that it was urgent to inform Sir Douglas Haig that a further intercepted wireless revealed that the German Cavalry had crossed

* The 4th Cavalry Division only reached the Aisne, east of its destination, late at night, continuing its march on Vailly at dawn on September 1st.

† From the region of St. Gobain to that of Premontré (south of the St. Gobain hills and north of the Ailette river).

‡ General Valabrègue was to inform the G.O.C. XVIII. Corps of his orders, so that the latter might protect himself towards La Fère. The Reserve Divisions were also told that liaison with the British rearguards was to be sought about Terny and Leury, west of Vauxaillon (which the British had left in the morning).

the Oise at 11 a.m. and was moving east.* Huguet reported, however, that he had been unable to pass on any of Joffre's messages to Sir John. He was in the extremely trying position of not knowing where the British Commander-in-Chief was. G.H.Q. was in transit. It was to have opened at Dammartin, whence his message was sent, but not finding it there he started off for Crépy-en-Valois in the hope of finding Sir John.† Huguet does not appear to have realized the gravity of the immediate position, for he assured his Chief that he would do all in his power to induce Sir John to advance *on the following day*, September 1st.

The morning wore on, bringing report after report confirming the advance of the German cavalry towards the gaping undefended opening in rear of the left flank of the Fifth Army. Unfortunately news also kept coming in that the British right was steadily withdrawing, which caused bitter indignation at Fifth Army Headquarters. This was natural enough, for it was evident that the danger would have been greatly diminished if not dispelled altogether, had some of the comparatively fresh troops of the I. Corps merely halted north of Soissons.‡

The gravity of the position, which escaped no one, was agonizing to me, since the obvious counter-manœuvre, the only one that could be immediately effective, was British action. I was requested during the morning to bring the obvious peril of the Fifth Army to the notice of Sir John French, but I was no more successful than others had been, for G.H.Q. seemed to have disappeared into thin air, and no one knew where it was at the moment.

* This information was passed on to the Fifth Army at 11.55 a.m.

† Crépy-en-Valois had been decided upon as advanced G.H.Q. A section of both Operations and Intelligence arrived there during the morning, only to find that no arrangements had been made for communications of any kind. Eventually a British operator was installed in the telegraph office. Neither Sir John nor General Murray came to Crépy. General Wilson made a short appearance in the morning.

The British Mission at the G.Q.G. was naturally gravely concerned at the situation. In the late afternoon they wired that the French G.H.Q. were very anxious concerning the left of the Fifth Army, and asking for early information as to whether arrangements had been made for British forces to fill the gap at Soissons. The message went on to say that General Wilson had stated this would be done. There is, however, a note made on this message which states that "General Wilson explains he never made any such promise." This misunderstanding may have been due to the fact that General Wilson did not speak French as well during this stage of the war as he did later.

‡ It was not till 8.30 that Sir John answered Joffre's noon message requesting him to intercept the German Cavalry crossing the Oise at Bailly. His reply ran: "French Cavalry Corps with the Sixth Army now in neighbourhood of Compiègne. It is much nearer bridges at Bailly and the German cavalry moving west (*sic*) than any troops of mine."

Sir John was misinformed. The French Cavalry Corps was at that moment south of Beauvais, some forty miles west of Compiègne and some fifty miles from Bailly, whereas the 2nd Division was at the end of the day's march not more than fifteen miles from that place.

I was more fortunate in another direction. When the first news of the German cavalry advance came through I telephoned to the Post Offices in a number of villages in the area of the I. Corps, asking the Postmistresses if there were any British troops in the neighbourhood. The Postmistress at Vauxbuin said she thought there were British soldiers there, and that there was a gendarme in the building and she would ask him. He came to the telephone and proved exceptionally intelligent. He told me there were some British Cavalry in the place and offered to call their Commander.

A few minutes later the Colonel of the South Irish Horse, the Corps Cavalry of the I. Corps, was astonished to hear from a gendarme that he was wanted on the telephone, but I was still more astonished when I heard the voice of Burns-Lindow, an old 8th Hussar, a Regiment in which I had served. I told him I was at Laon and explained the situation, asking him to see Sir Douglas Haig and beg him to send or maintain some detachments north of the Aisne. This Burns-Lindow promised to do.

A mile down the road he found Sir Douglas, who, at once responding to the call, ordered Burns-Lindow to send detachments north of the river. The South Irish Horse accordingly established its H.Q. at Venizel on the Aisne and held the western portion of the Chemin des Dames north of the river till dusk. They were severely attacked during the afternoon, but eventually withdrew in safety to the forest of Villers Cotterets where they had some narrow escapes, being mistaken for Germans first by the Guards and then by the Sussex Regiment.

Their timely intervention played a considerable part in saving the Fifth Army, and was probably the main factor in blinding the enemy to the open gap behind the left flank of Lanrezac's command.

It was not till years afterwards that I learnt the result of my message. At the time, knowing nothing of what was happening, I remained troubled and anxious; perhaps too troubled and anxious. Steeped in the atmosphere of crisis at Laon, knowing little of what was occurring at British G.H.Q., I may have taken too one-sided a view of the situation. On occasions like the one I am describing, it is difficult if not impossible to give a balanced and impartial picture. My memories of those days are based upon the experiences I went through, and I am aware that the only account I can give may appear to be written from a rather French angle.

I remember gratefully that during the hours of this nightmare day spent at Fifth Army H.Q. I was not made to feel too keenly the difficulty

of my position, and my efforts to draw the attention of our own people
to the real situation were generously recognized.

Shortly after noon it became known that the German Cavalry had
already reached Nampcel,* some 12 kilometres east of Bailly. The whole
of the Fifth Army was steadily marching south, unhindered save that
the rearguard of the I. Corps had been attacked during the night. The
main bodies were near the region north of Laon which they were
to reach in the early afternoon. Many miles, much difficult country,
still separated the weary troops from the Aisne and safety. If the
German Cavalry maintained its rate of advance, and if it was
not stopped by Simon's Brigade or the British, it looked as if
the enemy would be across our communications before nightfall.
(Map XI, p. 295.)

It was in these circumstances that General Lanrezac issued orders
at 3 p.m. that the retreat was to be resumed at 6 p.m., the Army to
reach the region north of the Ailette river that night. It was there to
receive reinforcements and supplies.

Information that came in during the afternoon did nothing to allay
our anxiety. Intercepted enemy wireless showed that three German
Cavalry Divisions had grouped their first line transport about Compiègne. Von der Marwitz, commanding the II. German Cavalry
Corps, was sending messages to the Second Army from Offremont east
of the Forêt de l'Aigle, just east of Compiègne. One of these stated that
according to a German aviator the French had already reached Villers
Cotterets, and asked for confirmation and in which direction the cavalry
was to pursue. An immediate answer was requested as the divisions
were moving off at 5 p.m. (Map XI, p. 295.)

The Eiffel Tower heard the Second German Army passing on its
information to the Cavalry. "The aviation had seen that morning a
long cavalry column near Soissons marching south. This was presumed to be the left wing of the French. Also a Corps was marching

---

* At 12.35 General Lanrezac reported to the G.Q.G. that the air reconnaissances confirmed
that the German Cavalry Corps had crossed the Oise and reached Nampcel by 11 a.m. The
measures taken by him to parry the danger were given. He also informed the G.Q.G. of his
request to the British to send some troops to occupy the hills north of Soissons, but doubted
whether these would reach their positions in time to be effective. He went on to say that he
intended to change the axis of march of his Army so as to base it on the line Laon–Reims and
thus ensure its supplies in the event of the Laon–Soissons line being cut.

The G.Q.G. replied at 2.40 p.m. that the measures taken appeared adequate, and that it
was preferred that the Fifth Army should keep to its original zone. The message concluded
by stating that the question of the entrainment of the XVIII. Corps (for the defence of Paris)
was adjourned until the next day. (General Joffre was only informed personally of Lanrezac's
message at about 5.20 a.m. on the next day, but the G.Q.G.'s reply was sent in his name.)

from Vic-sur-Aisne, and Cavalry, presumably British, had passed Crépy-en-Valois."

Then the German Guard Cavalry Division reported that its horse-shoes were almost completely worn out, begging that three or four lorry loads be sent to Noyon, but above all that nails for shoeing be forwarded immediately.

The French aviation confirmed the rapid advance of the enemy's Cavalry. At 5 p.m. it had almost reached the Aisne in the neighbour-hood of Soissons, and was about a mile west of Vauxaillon, within striking distance of the main Laon–Soissons Railway. The aviators reported German cavalry swarming all over the country. Its columns on the roads were being passed by numerous motors. The airmen had landed to warn French parks and transport formations of the enemy's approach and of the need for immediate retreat. British aviators con-firmed and amplified these reports. They had seen several columns marching south-east, which turned out to be a German Cavalry Division marching on Vic-sur-Aisne, and long German infantry columns moving south.* (Map XI, p. 295.)

By the middle of this endless sweltering afternoon it was clear that the German Cavalry was south of the left wing of the Fifth Army. Of Simon's Brigade there was no news whatever.

The situation on the left of the Fifth Army was so critical that evening that I will give a detailed account of what happened there. Incidentally, the story affords an excellent example of the difficulties both of com-mand and of execution at that time.

As has already been noted, the Group of Reserve Divisions was covering the left flank of the Fifth Army (north of the St. Gobain Forest) on the morning of the 31st. It was protected on the Oise by the 148th Regiment, drawn out from La Fère to Chauny. It will be remembered that in the morning orders had been sent to General Valabrègue to move his command south of the St. Gobain woods and to send a brigade towards Vauxaillon to co-operate there with the infantry being sent by rail from Laon. General Valabrègue was also informed that the 4th Cavalry Division was on its way to take up a position on his left, to

* The II., III., IV. and IV. Reserve Corps.

West of the Oise the British reported a column on the Roye–Noyon road, its head on the Oise, and two big columns, the one on the Roye–Compiègne road, the other on the Mont-didier–Senlis road.

It is now known that only two German Cavalry Divisions, the 5th and the Guard, moved on Vauxaillon. The other three divisions followed the British and were unable to make any impression on them.

operate against the German Cavalry which had crossed the Oise at Bailly.

The H.Q. of the Reserve Divisions only received these orders, sent at 11.30 a.m. and 12.30 p.m., at about 4 in the afternoon, when steps were at once taken to carry them out in spite of the great fatigue of the men. Nevertheless no special anxiety was felt, especially as the orders in question gave the information that the British outposts were occupying Soissons, and that contact with them should be sought about Terny and Leury, several miles north of Soissons and just south of the Oise.*

The real seriousness of the situation was borne in on General Vala-brègue in the following way:

In the ordinary course of the retreat he had ordered his H.Q. to be withdrawn to Brancourt, north-west of Anizy-le-Château. Advanced elements were busy installing themselves there at about 2 p.m. under the orders of the subaltern in charge of the cavalry escort. A Captain on the Staff of the Group, who had been ordered to report, finding that no one in authority had arrived, was putting in time by having a bath, when the subaltern dashed in shouting: "*Les Boches!*" The captain was inclined to treat this as a joke. How could the Germans be about to enter the village where H.Q. was to be installed? If true, it would mean that the retreat to the south was cut off.

The subaltern was ordered to take a few men and reconnoitre to the west, where the enemy was reported to be. The Captain dressed in haste and went to the western exit of the village, but saw nothing. Presently the subaltern returned, saying he had seen about a thousand horsemen, but had been unable to make out in which direction they were moving. He had himself remained unseen.

Meanwhile more paraphernalia brought by men belonging to the Group Headquarters was being moved in. The alarm was given, the baggage hastily reloaded, and everyone ordered north again to Pré-montré, where the G.O.C. had been last seen. Happily he was still there, awaiting an early dinner which kindly but very flustered nuns were preparing for him in the convent.

It was then 6 p.m. The news from Brancourt was obviously very serious, and the General withdrew with his Chief of Staff to consider what should be done. Orders were drawn up but were not issued at once pending further information. At 8 p.m. Colonel Arnaud, the Sub-Chief of Staff of the Group, who had been to Fifth Army Headquarters, returned, evidently under the strain of great emotion. He at once

* The British were by this time well south of the Oise.

joined the General and the Chief of Staff and was closeted with them for an hour. It was only when they came out that the rest of the Staff became aware of the real position, and of the rapid advance of the German Cavalry during the morning and afternoon. The extreme gravity of the situation appeared horribly clear to every officer present. General Valabrègue, much moved, explained the danger of the whole Army. The earlier news from Brancourt was confirmed and amplified by what he had just learnt from Lieut.-Colonel Arnaud. German Cavalry might well be in rear of his divisions at that moment. (It was.) He told his officers that there was no news of the Reserve Brigade which, in conformity with the Army Commander's orders, he had directed on Vauxaillon,* there to co-operate with Simon's Brigade from Laon, nor did he know if the latter had arrived. Even were it in position, the country between Vauxaillon and the Aisne to the south was entirely open to the enemy pending the arrival of the 4th Cavalry Division, of which also there was as yet no sign.

All this General Valabrègue explained to his Staff, adding: "It is absolutely essential to get into touch with the Brigade (Simon's) which detrained at Vauxaillon this afternoon, and to explain the situation to its commander. He must be ordered to be in position at dawn at Laffaux and to establish there a strong flank guard under the protection of which the Reserve Divisions will withdraw." The General concluded: "The march to the south is to continue, the honour of our arms is at stake. The colours must be saved."

Colonel des Vallières then turned to the Staff and said – "Which of you will volunteer to carry out the mission the General has outlined?" It was certainly not an easy one. In all probability there was German cavalry between the Reserve Divisions and Vauxaillon. To find Simon's Brigade under such circumstances and convey to it an absolutely vital order required confidence and pluck. Yet all were ready to assume the task. The Chief of Staff's choice fell on Captain Wemaëre, a cavalry-man, lately instructor at Saumur; brave and dashing, this was emin-ently his task. A Reserve Officer, Captain Vivier, and two gendarmes were told off to accompany him.

I got to know Wemaëre very well later when he was forward liaison officer in the Notre Dame de Lorette Sector in Artois. I greatly admired him and will always value the friendship he extended to me. Not tall

* Whatever the reason, whether it was the lateness of the hour at which the order had been received, or the fatigue of the men, it had not arrived at its destination, and had in fact disappeared. Only some small detachments of infantry had reached the Oise Canal west of Anizy which they were lining facing *south*.

but very good-looking, he was a French Fleming from near Bailleul, a fine horseman, gay, earnest, and even-tempered. He had the clearest, most candid eyes I have ever seen, which looked out at you from a fresh face adorned by a big black moustache. He had the simple religious faith of a child, and, like nearly all French officers, an immense sense of duty.

I have obtained the following account of what happened that night from Wemaëre's own pen.

"The General and the Colonel both embraced me and told me to remain (with Simon's Brigade) and see the movement ordered by General Valabrègue carried out. We left the Abbey of Premontré on horseback at 9.30 p.m. and started off at a fast trot in the direction of Anizy-le Château in spite of the pitch darkness. This locality was held by one of our battalions. The southern exits were strongly barricaded and I was not allowed to pass. The battalion commander appeared and in a few words I explained my mission to him. As soon as I told him I was going to Vauxaillon he said: "That is madness. The Boches have been in Vauxaillon since 4 o'clock. You are walking into the lion's den." I insisted, obtaining leave at last to pass. I crossed the railway line and saw on my left a locomotive in the station. I asked the driver where he had come from. "From Vauxaillon," he said, "where I was shelled this afternoon. The tunnel has collapsed." Evidently the enemy must be at Vauxaillon. What was I to do? My mission was to go there, so go I must: if the enemy is there we will find out soon enough, I thought. Vivier was of the same opinion. We passed the junction of the roads Brancourt–Pinon and Anizy-le-Château–Vauxaillon. The map, read by the light of an electric torch, showed me that 2 kilometres to the west the Vauxaillon road crossed the railway line Anizy–Vauxaillon. "If the enemy is at Vauxaillon," I said to my companions, "he must be holding the level crossing, look out." We moved on. Two hundred metres from the level crossing I saw a light. It was the house of the level-crossing keeper, and the ground and first floors were both lit up. We approached the house, no sound, no movement: we got to within ten yards, still nothing. The barriers were open, the door of the house was open. I walked in, hoping to find a railwayman who might give me valuable information. There was no one. The house had not been abandoned long, however, for soup was still cooking on the stove.

"I mounted again. How could any troops be at Vauxaillon without holding this bridge, I wondered? At Premontré I had been told the

French were at Vauxaillon, at Anizy I was assured the Germans were there. Only one thing was evident. Both French and Germans kept pretty poor look-outs.

"We continued to advance on Vauxaillon at the trot when suddenly out of a wood which I guessed rather than saw lay on my right, horsemen debouched at the gallop. We drew swords and faced them. They were a stray patrol of *Chasseurs d'Afrique*. I was as pleased to be thus reinforced as I had been startled, and was particularly glad to fall in with these men, for I had served in their regiment for many years.

"We reached the northern exit of Vauxaillon and halted. No sound. No light. Nothing. Hardly a few distant barks. What could it mean? I was about to enter the village when I heard something on my left, a movement in the ditch. Before I had time to speak, a human shadow grew out of it, and I heard the unmistakable accent of a native of North Africa saying in broken French: "I have a message for Pinon." It was a *tirailleur* belonging to the African Brigade (*i.e.* Simon's) carrying an order. I opened the paper and found it was an order from the Colonel commanding the African Brigade whom I was in search of, to the artillery at Pinon. This was the battery which was to have joined him, but in this order he directed it to remain where it was. This would never do. It would make it impossible for the African Brigade to carry out the mission I had to convey to it. I put the order in my pocket and sent Vivier to Pinon to tell the artillery to join the brigade at Vauxaillon. I then told the *tirailleur* to lead me to the Brigade Commander. We began a most difficult climb in pitch darkness up the wooded heights to the east of the railway. I was completely lost and was beginning to suspect that the *tirailleur* could not possibly know his way either, when suddenly we found ourselves on a little plateau: a little farther on, in a kind of hole, was Colonel Simon, commanding the African Brigade; with him was the Colonel commanding the Regiment of Zouaves which formed part of the Brigade. I at once explained the situation and told Colonel Simon what General Valabrègue expected of him. It was then midnight. Colonel Simon said that his Brigade had been shelled by the German Cavalry as it detrained, and it was now dispersed on the plateau and could not be regrouped at the moment. He added that he had ordered the artillery placed at his disposal not to join him. He believed that the southern road (from Vauxaillon to the *Bascule de Laffaux*) was certainly held by the enemy, and that therefore any movement in this direction was impossible and would be stopped at once. His conclusion was that General Valabrègue's order could not be carried out. Again I explained to him the tragic situation in which the 4th Group of Reserve Divisions would find itself if it was not flank-guarded at dawn. I told him the artillery would be at Vauxaillon in two hours time. As my arguments made no impression I reminded the Colonel that I was speaking in the name of the General commanding the 4th Group of Reserve Divisions and that I was to remain on the spot to see his orders carried out.

"The Colonel commanding the Zouaves told me that I could rely on him, that he would be at the *Bascule de Laffaux* at 4 a.m. but asked leave to follow another itinerary than the one prescribed. He said he would go across country, and left us.

"It was 1 a.m. before I could get Colonel Simon to take action. He at last decided to move his regiment to the south of Vauxaillon along the itinerary given in the order. Having seen the men start I left him to meet the artillery, whose arrival I wished to hasten, and which should now have been somewhere north of Vauxaillon. I went north as far as the Brancourt–Pinon cross-roads. It was now 3 a.m. and the sight I was confronted with was painful. Dense columns of Reservists were pouring down the road from Anizy to the south. At the crossroads they met the artillery from Pinon marching north to Vauxaillon. A General, unaware of the situation, had ordered the guns to turn about. They had just done so, under conditions of extreme difficulty, causing a complete block, when I arrived. I knew the importance Colonel Simon attached to the presence of this artillery. I got it off the road, turned it about again, and led it on to the Vauxaillon road. Dawn was now breaking and there was a slight mist. The infantry of the Reserve Divisions was still surging through Anizy in ever denser, faster and more disorderly array. I had hardly rejoined the artillery group, when, a mile and a half from the crossroads, we found ourselves face to face with Colonel Simon's regiment of *tirailleurs*, who said they had found the southern exit of Vauxaillon barricaded and guarded and so had turned about, making for the *Bascule de Laffaux* via Pinon. It was now 4 a.m. I wondered whether the Reserve Divisions would soon clear Anizy. My fear was that they might be attacked from the right about Laffaux. In any case the regiment of *tirailleurs* could do nothing in that direction now, so I asked the Colonel to rearguard the column whilst I galloped down it. The spectacle was a sad one. The men were absolutely worn out, some fell and would not or could not get up, packs were thrown away. About 4.30 some shots, fired no doubt by German Cavalry patrols, hastened the laggards of the column; the enemy thus rendered us a real service, but I greatly feared a more serious intervention on his part further south, and so hastened to Laffaux, where I found that the Regiment of Zouaves had fortified the distillery and were ready for the enemy, who, however, did not appear. I wondered what had happened to the German Cavalry which had failed to turn us. It had missed a unique opportunity."

The Fifth Army owed its extraordinary escape partly to a lucky accident and the lack of initiative of the German Cavalry, and partly to the action of the British I. Corps Cavalry.

Owing to the heat of the day and the fatigue of the troops, the British had not retired so far as had been intended. The I. Corps had halted for the night on the northern instead of on the western side of the forest of Villers Cotterets, midway between it and the river Aisne. The Germans wasted time reconnoitring its outposts on the river instead of advancing into the undefended country about Vauxaillon and south of that place, and when night came withdrew westward to rest their tired horses. If the German Cavalry had had real dash and been well led, it is difficult to see how the Fifth Army could have escaped without very serious loss. (Map XIII, p. 360.)

*   *   *

Whilst the Fifth Army Staff was watching the western flank with bated breath, horribly aware of its own impotence, General Joffre, in optimistic mood, telegraphed General Lanrezac that he presumed he had taken all necessary steps to surprise and overthrow the German Cavalry Corps at daybreak!*

This is another example of how difficult it is in war for a commander to appreciate a situation correctly. All the Commander-in-Chief and the G.Q.G. knew were the orders issued by General Lanrezac. On paper they seemed adequate and were certainly the only ones possible. Had it been a game of chess the enemy's move would have been countered. But what the brain centre of the Army could not know were the thousand imponderable delays and difficulties involved, the weary men who could go no farther, orders that did not arrive, the constantly changing situation to be faced by subordinates unable to obtain fresh instructions. An Army resembles a giant with a quick and

---

* General Joffre telegraphed to the Government during the afternoon that the situation had not been modified since the morning, and that the transfer of the Government to Bordeaux could be adjourned at least until September 2nd.

brilliant brain, but whose nervous system is slow, lethargic, and inadequate. Something goes wrong with one of his distant limbs. Hours pass before he registers it. Once he has done so a counter-move is rapidly devised, but transmission is again slow, and before his arm or leg can receive and obey it, it may have been gnawed to the bone.

In the present instance, the G.Q.G. asked for von Richthofen's head on a charger, unaware that quite beyond reach of its orders a junior officer, guided only by his own common sense and initiative, was taking measures but for which the left flank of the Fifth Army would have been left without any protection save that afforded by the blindness of the enemy.

CHAPTER X

LORD KITCHENER
DECIDES TO GO TO PARIS

August 31st, 1914: – II

The right of the Fifth Army on the 31st – The Fifth Army ordered to retire behind the Aisne – Von Kluck advances south-east – Sir John French informs Lord Kitchener of his intention to withdraw the B.E.F. from the line – His telegram of the 31st – The Cabinet decides to send Lord Kitchener to Paris – Craonne.

ALTHOUGH all eyes were turned towards the left of the Fifth Army, were it was felt a crisis might occur at any moment, the position on the right was nearly as precarious, and only the absence of German Cavalry in this sector rendered the danger less pressing. Now that the 4th Cavalry Division had been ordered to the other flank of the Army there was nothing to fill the gap between General Lanrezac's right and Foch's left twenty miles to the south.* (Map XIII.)

The news of the enemy east and south-east of the Fifth Army was disquieting enough. As early as 10 a.m. a German infantry division had been located opposite Foch's left, half-way between it and Lanrezac's right; at the same time German advance guards were seen south of the Aisne about Rethel, level with Craonne which was to be the Fifth Army H.Q. that night. What would happen if they marched towards the latter place did not bear thinking of.

The situation of the Army led General Lanrezac to send out a personal and secret instruction to the Corps Commanders at 5 p.m. as follows:

---

* General Joffre had contemplated an offensive by the Fourth and Third Armies, supported by the Foch Detachment, but as Foch was probably opposed by three corps and unable to guarantee holding his position the Commander-in-Chief gave up this idea, all the more readily that the ground over which the contemplated action was to have taken place was unfavourable. The Fourth Army was ordered to retire during the night under cover of the Foch Detachment.

"By order of the Commander-in-Chief and in spite of the state of fatigue of the troops, to whose energy the Commander of the Fifth Army appeals, the Army will retire tomorrow behind the Aisne and will continue by forced marches the day after tomorrow its movement towards the south.

"This movement is necessary for the execution of the Commander-in-Chief's plan of operations and must be carried out at any cost and whatever may be the consequences."

A General Order issued at 6 p.m. amplified these instructions. By the morning of September 1st the whole Army was to be on the south bank of the Aisne. The forced march was to be kept up throughout the night and during the morning until the rearguards were in position on the heights immediately south of the river, and was to continue on the following days in the direction of the river Marne.* (Map XIII, p. 360.)

At 6 p.m. the Corps got under way, not to halt until their destinations south of the Aisne were reached.

Be it remembered that this effort was demanded of troops who had been fighting all day on the 29th, preparing for further action on the night of the 29th–30th, fighting and withdrawing on the 30th and marching during a great part of the night 30th–31st, as well as during the whole of the 31st. Exhausted men loaded like mules, and wearing the great flapping "*capotes*" were called upon to endure a strain which would have prostrated youthful athletes. At no time, during no battle, whether at Charleroi, Guise, or later on the Marne, did the soldiers of the Fifth Army prove themselves more heroic than on the endless forced marches during this period of the retreat. Yet they never lost faith nor abandoned hope of ultimate victory, but remained grimly determined

* The first paragraphs of this Order ran as follows:

I.

"Important enemy forces have crossed the Oise south of Noyon marching east. On the other hand German troops are marching on Chaumont-Porcien, Wasigny, Novion-Porcien. By the imperative order of the Commander-in-Chief the Fifth Army will withdraw during the night by a forced march south of the Aisne.

II.

"The march will continue on the following days in the direction of the Marne. Officers of all ranks are to exact the greatest possible display of energy by the troops."

The French Historical Section has noted in connection with this order that no trace whatever can be found either in the archives of the G.Q.G. or in those of the Fifth Army of the imperative order of the Commander-in-Chief to which General Lanrezac refers. On the other hand General Joffre does not appear to have protested either against the withdrawal of the Fifth Army or concerning the terms employed by General Lanrezac when ordering it.

(*Les Armées Françaises dans la Grande Guerre*, Tome Ier, Deuxième Volume, Annexes, p. 196.)

In a message sent by the G.Q.G. to General Lanrezac that evening he was ordered to requisition every possible conveyance to carry the men's packs.

to fight on as long as a single man remained to defend the soil of France.

* * *

The German movement on this day culminated in a change of orientation which set the stage for the victory of the Marne. British air reconnaissances established the important fact that von Kluck had attained the furthest limit of his western advance, and was now marching south-east while the British fell back south.* On the 27th, von Kluck by marching south-west had allowed the British, whom he thought were finally destroyed, to escape south after the battle of Le Cateau. Maunoury's force he believed to be dispersed. Now by marching south-east at the call of von Bülow (a splendid justification of the stand at Guise) he was abandoning all possibility of outflanking the allied line and enabling Joffre to do the one thing essential to his plan, to consolidate and strengthen his left.† (Map XII, p. 323.)

Throughout the day the British Army, under the same trying conditions that affected all the armies, friends and foes alike, was pursuing its retreat, its Cavalry in touch with the French Cavalry covering the right of the French Sixth Army.‡

G.H.Q., as was explained in the previous chapter, was on the move, with the result that Sir John received none of Joffre's messages until a late hour. In the first of these Joffre asked Sir John not to withdraw the British Army unless the French were themselves compelled to give ground, and requested that rearguards should at least be maintained, so as not to give the enemy the impression that a pronounced retreat was taking place nor that a void existed between the Fifth and Sixth Armies. He also said that there was a great deal of information which showed that the enemy was sending many troops to the Russian front.

We have seen that Colonel Huguet, being unable to deliver this or General Joffre's subsequent messages, left Dammartin for Crépy-en-Valois in search of Sir John.§ He found part of the G.H.Q. Staff

---

* The British Intelligence reports based on these reconnaissances were the first information that Joffre received of the German change of direction.

† Von Bülow's Second Army was meanwhile wasting time in preparing an attack on the "fortifications" of La Fère, only discovering the place to be unfortified on September 1st. It was also called upon by German G.H.Q. to come to the help of the Third Army, said to be engaged against superior forces, only to be told in the later afternoon, having diverted two Corps, that the French on the front of the Third Army were retiring.

‡ On the previous day the III. British Corps, under General Pulteney, was constituted. It consisted for the moment of the 4th Division and the 19th Infantry Brigade.

§ G.H.Q. spent the night at Dammartin, which it reached in the afternoon.

marooned at Crépy. It is unlikely that he remained there long, for the officers he saw, who for lack of better occupation were lying under the apple trees in a garden, were as ignorant as he was of the Commander-in-Chief's whereabouts.*

If G.H.Q., in the inaccessible region into which it had temporarily withdrawn, showed little interest in events not directly affecting the British Army, London in ever-increasing anxiety was far from sharing its detachment.

Lord Kitchener received from Sir John on the 31st a letter (parts of which have been already quoted) and a telegram in which the latter informed him of his intention to withdraw the B.E.F. from the line, and to retire independently of the French for at least eight days.†

* However trying to the Staff these frequent absences of the Commander-in-Chief may have been, their importance from the point of view of *morale* is illustrated by the following extract from an interesting little book, *Contemptible*, by "Casualty."

"A few miles south of La Fère, the Brigade was halted for its midday rest. . . . Three large Daimler limousines drew up opposite the lines. . . . An officer hurriedly got out, and held open the door with great deference, while a second alighted.

"The men were called round without any formality, and Sir John French began immediately to address them. . . .

"The Field-Marshal said that the greatest battle that had ever been fought was just over. It had rolled with the fury of a cyclone from Belfort to Mons. Nearly two million men had been engaged, and the British Army had emerged from the contest covered with glory, having for three days maintained an unbroken front in the face of an overwhelming superiority in numbers. Never had he been more proud to be a British soldier than he was that day. The Regiment had added yet another branch to its laurel wreath. It had more than sustained its ancient traditions for endurance and courage. He was proud of it. The enemy had been nearly five to one, and yet had been unable to inflict defeat upon them. If they had been 'broken' the whole of the French left would have assuredly perished. Thanks to their endurance and obedience in the face of great provocation and privation, the Allied armies were now free from the dangers that had threatened them. No one knew better than he did that they would continue to be as brave, as reliable and as soldierly in the future, as they had been in the past, until final victory had been fully accomplished!

"How they cheered him as he made his way to his car!

"At first the Tommies had not realized what was happening. There had been disturbing cries of 'What's this abart?' ''Oo's the ole bloke?' But they had soon ceased, and in a few seconds the men were crowding round with eager faces, hanging on the words of their leader. He commiserated with them upon their losses; he understood what they had been through. In a word he appreciated them, and in the Army appreciation is a 'rare and refreshing fruit.' Although they would have died rather than own it, there was a feeling of tears behind the eyes of a good many of those tough old warriors. The personality of the Field-Marshal, and his heartening words, had brightened many a grim face, and lightened many a heavy load."

† The following are extracts from this letter and telegram:
"MY DEAR LORD K.,

"Tonight a report has come in that the Fourth French Army has been driven back towards Rethel. This was the line which, as I explained to you in my wire this morning, was assigned to it in the new dispositions of General Joffre; and so the rumour that he was driven back may not be true, but still it is very disquieting.

"I feel most strongly the necessity for retaining in my hands complete independence of action, and power to retire on my base when circumstances render it necessary.

"I have been pressed very hard to remain, even in my shattered condition, in the fighting

These communications naturally aroused Lord Kitchener's gravest apprehensions. He telegraphed to Sir John asking if his proposals would not leave a gap in the Allied line, cause the French discouragement, and enable the Germans to carry out their plan of first crushing the French and then turning on the Russians.

The Cabinet shared Lord Kitchener's view that the proposed retirement might mean the loss of the war. Lord Kitchener was asked to telegraph requesting Sir John to co-operate closely with General Joffre and conform as far as possible to his plans.

Sir John answered by a long telegram in which the following passages occurred:

"If the French go on with their present tactics, which are practically to fall back right and left of me, usually without notice, and to abandon all idea of offensive operations, of course then the gap in the French line will remain, and the consequences must be borne by them. I can only state that it will be difficult for the force under my command to withstand successfully in its present condition a strong attack by even one German Army Corps, and in the event of a pause in my retirement I must expect two Army Corps at least, if not three.* If owing to Russian pressure the withdrawal of the Germans turns out to be true, it will be easy for me to refit north of Paris; but this I

* According to the *Official History of the War*, it would seem that Sir John French was influenced by information contained in a captured German order dated that day, that the French troops (Maunoury's) on the Avre having been defeated on the 29th had withdrawn; that the British were retreating south-eastwards (*sic*); that von Bülow had defeated at Guise the French Fifth Army, large bodies of which were retiring through La Fère; and that the task of the German First Army was to cut off its retreat. "Again, therefore, we call upon the troops for forced marches."

(*See Official History of the War*, Vol. I, p. 233.)

Concerning this the *History* notes: "At the moment the one thing clear to Sir John French was that the German First Army, which had practically left the British Army alone since the 26th, was again closing in upon it in great force, and that he must avoid serious collision with it until the time for General Joffre's counter-stroke should be ripe."

line, but I have absolutely refused to do so, and I hope you will approve the course I have taken. Not only is it in accordance with the spirit and letter of your instructions but it is dictated by common sense."

Telegram No. F54, dated August 31st, 1914.

"This morning I received an official communication that General Joffre has made a change in his plan of operations and now intends to take up a more backward position. . . . General Joffre appeared to me to be anxious that I should keep the position which I am now occupying north of the line Compiègne-Soissons. I have let him know plainly that in the present condition of my troops I shall be absolutely unable to remain in the front line, as he has now begun his retirement. I have decided to begin my retirement tomorrow in the morning, behind the Seine, in a south-westerly direction west of Paris. This means marching for some eight days without fatiguing the troops at a considerable distance from the enemy. . . ."

cannot do while my rearguard is still engaged, as it was up to last night. An effective offensive movement now appears to be open to the French, which will probably close the gap by uniting their inner flanks. But as they will not take such an opportunity I do not see why I should be called upon again to run the risk of absolute disaster in order a second time to save them. I do not think you understand the shattered condition of the Second Army Corps and how it paralyses my powers of offence. . . . Your second telegram today. If the French Armies are driven south of their present position, I could engage not to go back further than a line drawn east and west through Nanteuil. I shall reach this position tomorrow and will endeavour to refit there."

This despatch clearly justified Lord Kitchener's anxiety, for it revealed the abyss of misapprehension existing between Joffre and French. The Government realized that the situation did not permit of "exercising the greatest care towards a minimum of losses and wastage."* The statesmen did not perhaps make due allowance for the fact that their instructions had to some extent fettered Sir John, but they did see that whatever the cost the British Army must maintain its place in the line. It was therefore decided that night that Lord Kitchener should go to France to see the Commander-in-Chief.

It is common knowledge that Lord Kitchener's telegrams and his visit to Paris were resented at G.H.Q., as being in the nature of an invasion of the Commander-in-Chief's sphere. Nevertheless history will hold that the Government was justified, and that Lord Kitchener's intervention was necessary.

These were Sir John French's worst days. Those officers on his Staff who had based the most inordinate hopes on the French offensive were now a prey to correspondingly profound pessimism. Sir John himself was greatly influenced by the exaggerated reports he received concerning the state of the II. Corps. Further he did not understand what General Joffre's idea was, nor make allowance for his difficulties. Had he done so he would not have talked of the French "closing the gap by uniting their inner flank." Had the British withdrawn, and the Fifth and Sixth Armies closed in to take their place, General Joffre, who was endeavouring to strengthen and extend his left by every means in his power, would have had to abandon his plan and would have been outflanked.

* For "Instructions to Sir John French," see Appendix XXIX.

The blame for lack of comprehension of French plans and necessities cannot be laid entirely at Sir John's door. He was not taken into Joffre's confidence, nor was it made possible for him to see the situation as a whole. In the circumstances misunderstandings were inevitable. The British, an autonomous and not a subordinate force, a foreign Army set as a unit in the great French array, all their communications in French hands, befogged as to the situation, uncertain of what was expected of them, and still smarting under the thought that they had been sacrificed during the opening days of the campaign, became inevitably suspicious of the French. To make matters worse they had had as immediate neighbours on the right the Reserve Divisions, disorganized and counted of little use by the French themselves, and on the left for some time Sordet's Cavalry. I have already said something of the French Cavalry. Their first appearance had been very welcome. They were fine men and very well officered, but to the British at this stage of the war they were incomprehensible. Trained to headlong movements, they were here, there and everywhere. Knowing little or nothing of dismounted action, they seemed fluid in the extreme, and incapable of holding on to positions. The British gained the impression that on very little provocation they would bolt, and certainly the result of their movements was constantly to uncover their neighbours. The feeling of insecurity thus engendered accounts for much in the British attitude, which was further influenced by the conclusion that all plans emanating from the French always ended by resolving themselves into retreat.

Whatever the reason, Sir John's messages were, however, in some respects misleading. It was hardly accurate at this juncture to talk of "the present French tactics of practically falling back right and left of the British usually without notice," nor was it a true picture of the situation to declare that there was "an effective offensive movement now open to the French." The implication was that the Fifth and Sixth French Armies could close in on the Germans which were following the British, whereas such an operation was obviously impossible.

The decision of the British Commander-in-Chief, announced in his second telegram of the 31st to Lord Kitchener, not to retire farther on the following day than the Nanteuil line, was a compromise. It had little to do with the strategic situation, and was a concession to pressure from home and to General Joffre, whose protests were now backed by the French President. It was cold comfort, however, to the French, for Sir John stated that he would only remain on the Nanteuil line so long as the Fifth and Sixth Armies remained in their present positions, and

the Fifth Army was already in full retreat when his decision was communicated to it.*

*   *   *

I shall never forget arriving at dusk, at Craonne† where Fifth Army
H.Q. had not long been established. It was quite impossible to get into
the town except on foot, and that was not easy. An endless column of
motionless cavalry completely blocked the road. The great towering
cuirassiers, clumsy and massive in helmets and breastplates, sat impassive on their horses. Not a man dismounted. In the still evening air the
booming of the guns seemed very near. A gust of wind animated the
horsetail plumes that hung down each man's back, then the long steel-
clad column was still again. There was something stoical about these
men that was very striking, terribly reminiscent too of one of the well-
known pictures of the Franco-Prussian War of forty-four years ago.
When they had started, how long they had been standing there, I do
not know. They were part of the 4th Cavalry Division (Abonneau's)
on its way to the left of the Army, and were still 25 miles from their
destination.

Headquarters was installed in the small Château where Napoleon
stayed, so it was said, a hundred years ago when attempting to stem the
tide of another invasion.

I went on to the terrace where dinner was being served. It was an
ideal situation and a perfect night. The view extended over the Aisne
and across the plain to where the lights of Reims could be seen gleaming
20 miles away. The H.Q. telegraphists had fixed wires and lamps so
that the terrace was well lighted. There were two tables. At one sat the
General, who had nearly finished dinner. Coffee had been served, and
the orderlies had withdrawn. What talking there was went on in under-
tones. The mellow night, soft, impalpable, velvety, penetrated us all,
and in spite of everything we relaxed. Suddenly the voice of Lanrezac
was heard. It had a note new to me, soft and cadenced. He was speaking

* Decision of Field-Marshal French: "In deference to the desire expressed by General
Joffre the British Army will not withdraw tomorrow beyond the line Fontaine-les-Corps-Nuds
–Nanteuil-le-Haudoin–Betz. It will remain there as long as the Fifth and Sixth Armies continue to occupy their present positions. If they retire, the British Army will conform to their
movement. It cannot advance until it has been reconstituted and reorganized."

(Message telephoned to Fifth Army at 7 p.m. on August 31st from British G.H.Q.)

† The H.Q. of the Fifth Army was to have gone to Vailly on the Aisne, but the threat of
the German Cavalry had rendered this impossible.

Latin – reciting verses – Horace! And the burden of the lines he quoted was: "Oh how happy is he who remains at home, caressing the breast of his mistress, instead of waging war!"

There was a faint clatter outside, a metallic jingle, the beat of iron shod hoofs on the steep street of the little town; the cuirassiers were moving off at last.

A long way to the north a muffled gun boomed, firing its last round of the day.

On every road leading south the endless columns marched on and on without halt and without rest.

Over Paris a German aeroplane dropped a message announcing the arrival of the enemy in three days' time.

CHAPTER XI

HOW THE FIFTH ARMY LEARNT THAT VON KLUCK WAS ADVANCING SOUTH-EAST

September 1st, 1914: – I

The Retreat continues – The Fifth Army crosses the Aisne – The Fifth Army Intelligence learns from a captured German map that the German First Army is advancing south-east – A Cavalry Corps formed on the left of the Fifth Army – General Conneau – Fighting on the British front – Néry – The B.E.F. re-united – Results of the fighting on the British front.

FIFTH ARMY HEADQUARTERS left Craonne early under a cloudless sky. Evidently we were in for another torrid day.

Years later, when the war was over, I found myself in the same neighbourhood, but there was no trace of Craonne to be seen. Not a wall, not a stone where the pretty little town had stood. I came on a post to which a board was affixed which bore the word "Craonne". That board, and those green mounds and hummocks, were all that was left of the place through which the great retreat had once swept.

During the whole of September 1st, the men of the Fifth Army stumbled back, ever more slowly, under increasingly difficult conditions. They looked like ghosts in Hades expiating by their fearful endless march the sins of the world. Heads down, red trousers and blue coats indistinguishable for dust, bumping into transport, into abandoned carts, into each other, they shuffled down the endless roads, their eyes filled with dust that dimmed the scalding landscape, so that they saw clearly only the foreground of discarded packs, prostrate men, and an occasional abandoned gun.

Dead and dying horses that had dropped in their tracks from fatigue, lay in great numbers by the side of the roads. Worse still, horses dying but not yet dead, sometimes still struggling a little, a strange appeal in their eyes, looked at the passing columns whose dust covered them, caking their thirsty lips and nostrils.

As the heat increased and the air vibrated white under a sky of brass, many men, utterly worn out, overcome by fatigue or sunstroke, dropped and lay where they had fallen, yet the spark of duty, the spirit of self-sacrifice, survived and bore the Army on.

If Napoleon's *Grande Armeé* had withdrawn from some African Moscow, in torrid heat instead of through snow, the conditions would not have been dissimilar.

As was perhaps inevitable in a retreat of such magnitude, when every road had to be used, columns crossed each other, corps trespassed on to the roads of other corps. Inevitably also the fighting units in their cease-less march caught up with the transport columns, which, always a weak point, under-officered and lacking discipline, were often com-pletely lost, without maps and without orders. These columns sprawling over the roads, often blocking them completely, were a source of addi-tional and unendurable fatigue to the infantry. Enormous blocks were caused by the heavy artillery now also caught up and enmeshed with the infantry. Ammunition columns composed of every kind of vehicle drawn by any kind of horse, ill-harnessed, badly driven, and lacking direction, inordinately delayed the troops. Many vehicles and heavy guns were abandoned during the next few days, to be found where they had been left when the Army advanced over the same ground.

The confusion of the transport made the supplying of units a terribly difficult task, defying the skill of the ablest staff.

Everything seemed to conspire to increase fatigue and cause depres-sion.

General Maistre, who at the time was Chief of Staff to one of the Armies in retreat, and later achieved great distinction as a commander, has told me that upon several occasions during those terrible days, thinking all was lost, he contemplated suicide.

Had there been the same exodus of civilians as during the early part of the retreat, the Fifth Army would have been paralysed altogether. Happily the halt at Guise had given the majority of the population time to retire beyond the zone of the Army, but many could not bring themselves to leave their homesteads. Typical of these, I remember a middle-aged peasant woman at her gate; ugly she was with a hideous goitre, yet such a tragic figure as she wrung her hands and sobbed, as to be beautiful. Fear drove her to take the road – "But who will feed the pigs if I go?" she wailed.

Not all the troops resisted the strain and behaved like heroes, although the overwhelming majority did. The following incident, told me by Duruy, was exceptional, and I quote it only to illustrate what may happen when endurance has reached its limit and a panic occurs.

Near the Oise, Duruy fell in with a stream of men running away. He stood in the road, huge and stern, shouting to them to stop. It was of no avail. The stream of unarmed men pressed on unheeding, open-mouthed and with glazed eyes. Duruy, seeing that fear rode on those men's shoulders and panic reigned in their hearts, drew his revolver and fired; but the men merely stumbled over the prostrate ones and went on, hardly attempting even to dodge the levelled weapon.

Panic is certainly a paralysis of the mind. Extreme fear freezes the reasoning powers, while the subconscious mind alone functions to move the legs of the individual away from the danger until complete exhaustion throws him to the ground.

Later in the war I mentioned Duruy's story to a French officer whose comment was to tell me the following anecdote. "A curious and amusing thing happened to me one day," he said, "which would tend to show that all men who run away are not panic-stricken. I was attempting to stop a mob of men whose only preoccupation at the moment was to show a clean pair of heels to the enemy. I seized upon one man and shook him violently. 'Where is your regiment, your company?' I asked. The man was from the south, his quick brain reacted at once: he struck a dramatic attitude: 'Ah, *mon Capitaine*, they are all dead – or wounded –' then, cunningly, realizing by the look in my eyes it would not be wise to overstep the bounds of probability by too gigantic a stride, he hesitated, then concluded in a confidential whisper, 'or run away!'"

At this period of the retreat another manifestation of panic made itself felt. Bands of unarmed soldiers fled ahead of the Army, terrifying the population and pillaging. The G.Q.G. ordered the severest measures to be taken, and the gendarmes did what they could. There were executions, but the evil was too extensive, the forces of order too few, to stamp it out altogether until the Army halted. I saw villages completely gutted by these men.

*   *   *

All day the booming of guns on the whole front and away to the west gave the impression of a general engagement over a vast area, but at Headquarters there was little news. Anything might have been happening.

At 2 p.m. General Lanrezac informed the G.Q.G. that his Army had crossed the Aisne without serious difficulty, under the protection of the 4th Cavalry Division, now west of it, and that Simon's Brigade had enabled the Reserve Divisions to withdraw south of St. Gobain. His report was, however, premature, for after its despatch General Hache reported that his III. Corps, marching in two columns, was meeting with the greatest difficulties: the columns had crossed each other, and the fatigue of the men was so great that it was impossible to rely upon the Corps being collected south of the Aisne before 9 p.m. The I. Corps also had bitter complaints to make concerning the fatigue imposed on the troops by the overflowing of other Corps into its area. (Map XIII, p. 360.)

General Lanrezac, having received *Instruction Générale No. 4*, issued in the evening his orders for the 2nd. In these he stated that the Fifth Army, on the left of the French line, had, thanks to the energy and endurance displayed by all, reached the south bank of the Aisne. The movement of retreat was to continue in the direction of Dormans at 2 a.m. on the 2nd. The mission of the Fifth Army was to parry the attempted envelopment by the enemy on the left, so as to permit of a new grouping of the Armies with a view to resuming the offensive. The Fifth Army during the course of this manœuvre was to keep west of the line Reims, Romilly. It was to be supported on the right by General Foch's Detachment.†

A Brigade in Army Reserve was to be in readiness to support the XVIII. Corps.

At Jonchery, where Army H.Q. was installed that night, the impression was relatively good. There was a feeling of intense relief, all the greater that at one time during the day news had come in that the Fifth Army was threatened on its right, as it was on its left, by German Cavalry. This proved a false alarm, the "enemy" turning out to be the 9th French Cavalry Division. After this incident the feeling grew that the situation was improving and that the Army would escape after all.

As the evening wore on, the Intelligence officers of the Fifth Army, poring over maps, computing, comparing and weighing belated air reports, reports from the British, from the Cavalry, views expressed by the Intelligence of subordinate formations, and scraps gathered from refugees and agents of different kinds, came to the conclusion that the

* See next chapter, p. 333.
† See footnote, p. 309.

enemy was persisting in his endeavour to outflank the Fifth Army by the west. (Map XII, p. 323.)

This information was later confirmed, thanks to a dramatic windfall for the Intelligence. At about 11 p.m. Bourgine, the Head of the Intelligence of the III. Corps, arrived at Jonchery bringing the bag of a German officer supposed to belong to the Guard Cavalry Division. This officer, driving in a car, ran into a patrol of the 310th Regiment and was shot. His haversack contained food, clothing, and papers, all caked with blood. Girard and Fagalde shook out the bag and pounced upon a map. It was smeared with blood, but as they examined it they became immensely interested. It bore numbers and pencil lines. It was at once evident that the numbers referred to the Corps of the First German Army whose order of battle thus stood clearly revealed. This was interesting enough, but what made the document a find of inestimable value was that the pencil marks showed the lines of advance followed by each Corps and the point each column was to reach that night (1st–2nd September). The fact that the direction of advance of the whole Army was to the south-east was clearly exposed by the tell-tale lines.* (Map XII, p. 323.)

The German officer had evidently come straight from von Kluck's Headquarters, where he had been given the line of advance of the Army and had marked it on his map.

The change of direction of von Kluck's Army was now confirmed beyond all possibility of doubt. How important this was will be seen later.

That evening the Fifth Army halted between the Aisne and the Vesle, the rearguards holding the heights south of the Aisne.†

The decision of the G.Q.G. (see *Instr. Générale No. 4*, next Chapter) to form a Cavalry Corps on the left of the Fifth Army, greatly contributed to the wave of mild optimism at Fifth Army H.Q. The step was considered all the more opportune in that it was now known there were two German Cavalry Corps on this front, one commanded by

---

* The following movements were shown on the map. From west to east: IV. Reserve Corps (one column) was to reach St. Just-en-Chaussée; II. Corps (two columns) was to reach Verberie and the road junction south-west of the Croix St. Ouen; IV. Corps (two columns) was to reach Gilocourt and Rétheuil; the III. Corps (two columns) was to reach Taillefontaine, Vivières; the 18th Division should reach the region west of Longpont.

† The safety of the Fifth Army this day was largely due to the devotion of the 148th Regiment, which had already done such good work on the left flank. It lost half its numbers, not having received the order to retire.

On this day direct liaison was established with General Foch's detachment by Colonel Daydrein, who saw the former at Béthenville.

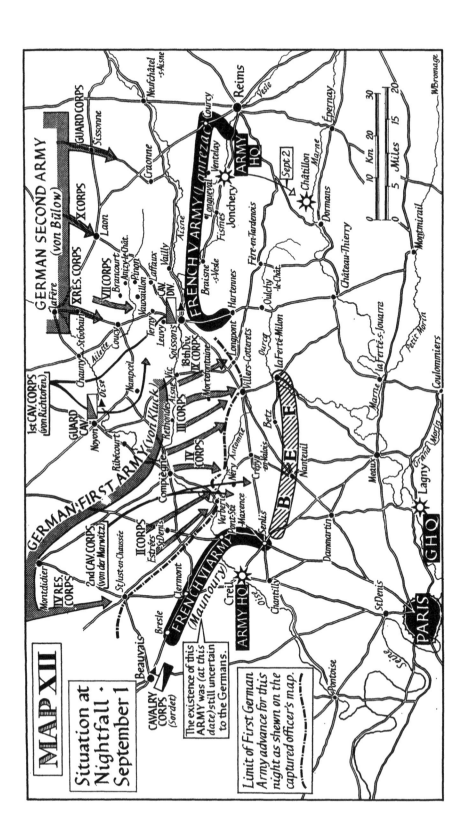

MAP XII

Situation at Nightfall · September 1

The existence of this ARMY was (at this date) still uncertain to the Germans.

Limit of First German Army advance for this night as shewn on the captured officer's map.

CAVALRY CORPS (Sordet)

GERMAN FIRST ARMY (von Kluck)

2nd CAV. CORPS (von der Marwitz)

IV RES. CORPS

II CORPS

IV CORPS

III CORPS

1st CAV. CORPS (von Richthofen)

GUARD CAV.

GERMAN SECOND ARMY (von Bülow)

X CORPS

X RES. CORPS

VII CORPS

GUARD CORPS

FRENCH V ARMY (Lanrezac)

ARMY H.Q.

18th Div.

IV CORPS

FRENCH VI ARMY (Maunoury)

ARMY H.Q.

B.E.F.

G.H.Q.

PARIS

W.Bromage

General von der Marwitz, the other by General von Richthofen.*
(Map XII, p. 323.)

We ended by forming a most peculiar picture of Richthofen and his
command. He seemed a will o' the wisp always just escaping the grasp
of Kluck or Bülow. The ether was constantly vibrating with the plaint
of the German wireless: "Where is Richthofen?" trailing off, when no
answer was received, into a querulous note: "But where on earth does
Richthofen now lie?" which literal translation from the German would
make us laugh. Richthofen appeared to us in the light of comic relief;
we saw him as a butterfly of war, flitting away gaily when Kluck or
Bülow seemed about to bring down their nets on him. I remember how
taken aback we were in the middle of some battle or other when
Richthofen suddenly trespassed on the air. What was he at now? The
experts pored over the puzzling cipher of the intercepted message. But
Richthofen remained true to his role. He was only sending fulsome birth-
day greetings to some Royal Highness, I think the Crown Princess.†

The new French Cavalry Corps, commanded by General Conneau,
was to be under the Commander-in-Chief's direct orders. It was formed
for the express purpose of covering the left flank of the Fifth Army, now
exposed by the retirement of the British.‡

Louis Napoléon Conneau, the Commander of the Corps, frequently
came into contact with the British in the course of the campaign. His
geniality and frankness made him very popular with them. Further, he

* Extract from Fifth Army Intelligence Report, dated September 1st, 3 p.m.:
"*On the left of the Fifth Army*, it appears there were this morning two cavalry corps, one of
three divisions, the other of two, the first in the neighbourhood of Crépy-en-Valois, Verberie,
the second in the district north of Soissons.
"The first of these is commanded by General von der Marwitz and comprises the 2nd, 4th
and 9th Divisions, commanded respectively by Generals von Garnier, von Schmettow and
von Krane. The II. comprises the 5th Division and the Guard, and is commanded by General
von Richthofen. The Guard Division has halted at Noyon to wait for horseshoes, those it has
being absolutely worn out."
(This information proved to be correct.)
† From about the time we reached Jonchery the Fifth Army Staff began to read themselves
many German wireless messages which were intercepted and brought to them by their
wireless officer Franck. The specialists in Paris who were handed intercepted messages by
the Eiffel Tower generally found the key to a new German code in forty-eight hours, and communicated it to the Fifth Army. The task was not difficult as many German messages were
partly in code and partly in clear. The German Cavalry movements before and after the
Marne were constantly followed by this means. Once, during the First Battles of Ypres, the
wireless announced the presence of the Kaiser at Tielt and aeroplanes were sent to bomb his
train. Thanks to the wireless, over a period of time the Fifth Army determined the arrival of
no less than seven German Corps. Captain Franck was a distinguished officer who rendered
most valuable services. It was notably he who perfected the wireless on board the Fifth Army
aeroplanes.
‡ The Corps, comprising two Cavalry Divisions (8th and 10th) and one infantry regiment
(three battalions) was to be fully constituted on September 3rd.

loved Englishmen. He had been brought up with the Prince Imperial from babyhood, and had followed him to Woolwich where he was enrolled as a cadet. He loved to talk of those times, which were, he said, amongst the happiest in his life. The tragic death in South Africa of his daily companion had affected him profoundly.

He was a splendid cavalryman, gaunt, huge, dark-skinned, with hair *en brosse*. He looked like a centaur on the big thoroughbred he liked to ride.

When he commanded the 8th Dragoons, a regiment of which he was very proud, he used to lead it each year to the frontier, when he and his men would spend the night by the post that marked the point beyond which lay Alsace.

In the autumn of 1914 there were hopes of a break through, and Conneau had two Cavalry Corps under him. "Murat himself never had such a command," he said. But alas, all hopes of mounted action were swallowed up, like so much else, in the mud of Flanders and Artois.

The end of the war did not fulfil General Conneau's high hopes. In 1917 he was given command of a Territorial region, and died some years later a disappointed man.

The cavalry of which he was given command in September '14 had already done heavy work and the horses were very tired. Still, the Germans were tired too, and the relief of knowing that soon a large mobile force would be opposing the enemy cavalry was great. What was less satisfactory was that the Corps could not be formed before the 3rd September, and would hardly be effective before the 4th.

*   *   *

From the point of view of the role played by the British this day was an important one.

For days von Kluck had been mercilessly driving his Army on, tacking now east now west in search of the allied flank. The distances covered had been enormous. The men were weary beyond belief, an exhausted, drunken, swaying mass, shackled together by an iron discipline, kept on their feet by the belief that Paris, if they kept on, would soon be at their mercy.

Some idea of the effort involved was given me in the autumn of 1914 by a German officer, an observer in an aeroplane which had been forced to land in the area held by the Indian Corps north of the La

Bassée Canal. I was ordered to take him to headquarters, and spent several hours with him. He was quite young and had been wounded in the very early days of the war. I put him a question which had puzzled many of us and was still unsolved. How did the German armies, full of reservists, manage to carry out such incredibly long marches over the cobbled roads of Belgium and northern France in the torrid heat of August, 1914? His answer took me aback. He said many men did fall out, and were shot by their officers. He had been under the painful necessity of shooting several himself, and described wretched men, their eyes starting out of their heads, foaming at the mouth, dropping in their tracks out of sheer exhaustion. When, seeking to find a formula that disguised disgust yet satisfied curiosity, I expressed doubt as to the wisdom of officers leading their men after having been guilty of such butchery, he said simply: "Oh, our men understood the necessity of the example." I cannot vouch for the facts, and am certain only of the statement as it was made to me.

The stupendous effort of the Germans seemed about to bear fruit, for the infantry of the First German Army was so placed on September 1st that it was in a position to drive straight at the flank of the Fifth Army. The Corps had only to march on, but instead of finding the road open they blundered into the British, and von Kluck's Army that day progressed only ten miles or less. Infantry and Cavalry were both kept busy, and this delay was a contributory factor of some importance in the escape of the Fifth Army.

There were many encounters and sharp conflicts during the day. Without method, and obviously without information concerning the movements of the British, von Kluck's troops, to the surprise both of themselves and of their leaders, kept bumping into our rearguards and our Cavalry. Each time this happened they were sternly repelled by troops disinclined to be in any way hurried, and evidently glad of an opportunity to punish their pursuers. The Germans were much taken aback. They had lost track of us, and as when last in contact with us they had thought they were dealing with an exhausted force, they had jumped to the conclusion that the British were an almost negligible quantity. The proof that they were wrong gave them a rude and disconcerting shock.

The first engagement of the day between the British and the enemy was the encounter of Néry, which had results out of all proportion to the numbers involved.

In the early morning fog, the British 1st Cavalry Brigade and the

German 4th Cavalry Division suddenly came into violent conflict. This chance engagement, in which the 4th German Cavalry Division was to all intents and purposes destroyed (four days later it could only turn out two squadrons for scouting purposes) proved of inestimable value to the Allies. The 4th Cavalry Division with the 4th Corps was von Kluck's flank guard: deprived of his "feelers" on the vital flank, he did not perceive Maunoury's force massing there. Had the 4th Cavalry Division remained intact, or had there been an adequate air force on this flank, there is little doubt that he would have located the French Sixth Army before September 5th, in which case he would have escaped Joffre's net.

The British Cavalry gave a splendid account of itself during the engagement, and L Battery R.H.A., which earned three V.C.'s, fought heroically till the last round was expended and the gun teams practically exterminated. Further east also the guns gave a fine account of themselves in the fighting which involved the British 5th Division; they were brought into action a hundred yards from the firing line and arrested the German advance.

The British I. Corps was also engaged. In this quarter the fighting, which in the morning had fallen to the 3rd Cavalry Brigade, soon involved the Guards and the 6th Infantry Brigade in a serious engagement in the thick woods, the Irish Guards receiving their baptism of fire. It was in the course of this fighting that two platoons of the Grenadiers were surrounded and killed at the Rond Point de la Reine, fighting to the last man. During the Marne I had to pass the scene of this fine display of British stubbornness, in which the Guards showed themselves worthy of their loftiest traditions. The terrible condition of the ground and the grim remains in the thickets told all too clearly how severe the fighting had been.

These sporadic engagements in no way interfered with the British withdrawal, which was carried out according to plan and achieved the important result that the Army, which had been divided since Le Cateau, was that night united once more. As at Le Cateau and again at Mons, von Kluck's Army lay opposite, this time six miles to the north.*

* It had been intended that the British should spend the night on the line La Ferté Milon–Betz–Nanteuil, but at 7 p.m. orders were issued that it should withdraw from its positions by a night march. This decision was not due to enemy pressure but to air reports, which all tended to confirm the previous ones as to the general wheel of von Kluck to the south-east. Heads of large columns reached Villers-Cotterets and appeared to be wheeling south, so it was deemed wise, especially as it was known that there were German Cavalry actually behind the British front, to withdraw beyond the reach of a night attack.

Neither French nor British realized at the time how extremely important the results of the fighting this day on the British front had been. Once more von Kluck had been prevented from achieving his objective. Had he been opposed less stoutly, it is doubtful if the Fifth Army could have escaped.

It has unfortunately become the fashion in certain quarters in France to accept as an axiom that in those early days the British were a negligible quantity. Such a point of view is ungenerous and untrue, and the verdict of history will be that but for the small British force, final and irremediable defeat would have overtaken France.

The shortcomings of the British have not been glossed over in these pages, but the mistakes which brought the British force to within an ace of destruction, the actions which led to such profound misunderstanding, originated with the French. The value of the British participation in these early days is too patent to be ignored even by the most prejudiced critics. The German marching wing, although attacking in overwhelming numbers, could not overcome their resistance, and as a result was fatally delayed. British valour and a training incomparably superior to that of either ally or opponent, achieved this result. By the sheer weight of the blows they delivered, the British held up a vastly superior force on their front, and the German line, stretched beyond its capacity, was never able to swing in in time to deliver the deadly thrust against the French left on which the success of the German plan depended. To keep the Germans extended, to hit them hard and delay them, was the role of the B.E.F. during the retreat. It can safely be said that no other force of anything like equal strength could have achieved this result without disintegrating, but as it was, the end of the retreat found the

---

At the same time, as the *Official History of the War* has it, "G.H.Q., to which the German Cavalry escaping from Néry had passed quite close, commenced to move back from Dammartin to Lagny." In the opinion of the German writer, von Baumgarten Crusius, this retirement was timely.

See also Appendix XXX.

French G.Q.G. was given by the French Mission in the evening, as was unfortunately too often the case, a depressing and completely inaccurate picture, unwarranted by the facts, of what had occurred on the British front. The version transmitted to the G.Q.G. of the events of the day was that the Brigade forming the rearguard of the 2nd Division had been violently attacked and thrown back with heavy loss beyond Villers-Cotterets behind the other Brigades of the Division which were still engaged at a late hour. Later a further message was sent stating that the I. Corps had been engaged against two German Corps.

Compare *Official History of the War*, Vol. I, p. 245.

"The British Commander-in-Chief, on returning to his Headquarters at Dammartin, found that the day's work had not been unsatisfactory; the enemy had been shaken off after several sharp actions, and the march, though long and exhausting to the men, had finally reunited the British Army for the first time since the I. and II. Corps had been separated on August 25th."

British still full of fight. At the Marne it was the British who were to be the only force available to advance into the gap in the enemy's lines. It was the wedge the British drove into the heart of the enemy's array that made the German retreat inevitable. Maunoury had all but failed. He was hanging on desperately, fighting a losing battle, waiting and hoping for the British advance that alone could save him and turn defeat into victory.

That the victory of the Marne would have been impossible without the B.E.F. will be the inevitable conclusion of posterity.

CHAPTER XII

JOFFRE BEGINS TO MAKE HIS PLANS FOR AN OFFENSIVE

September 1st, 1914: – II

The position of the Sixth Army – Liaison – Joffre's opportunity – Instruction Générale No. 4 – The part to be played by the Sixth Army – Joffre's telegram to the Minister – Paris to be under his direct orders – Reinforcements for the garrison – The Sixth Army placed under Gallieni – The Joffre-Gallieni controversy – Lord Kitchener's Meeting with Sir John French in Paris.

THAT evening General Maunoury summed up his position in a letter to Sir John French. He had, he said, remained all day on the positions he had held in the morning. The Germans had attacked him at Verberie at the time the British engagement at Néry was taking place. He had in consequence sent a native Brigade and a Reserve Infantry Division to that neighbourhood, and hoped that with the help of the British left, which had, he heard, brilliantly counter-attacked, the enemy columns would be prevented from debouching south of the forest of Compiègne.*

It will be perceived from the tone of this message how very different were the relations between the British and the Sixth Army as compared with the Fifth Army. General Maunoury was one of those rare leaders who at all times realized that his Army was not the only one engaged in the war, and that others as well as himself had their troubles and diffi-

---

* General Maunoury also informed the British Commander-in-Chief that in conformity with the orders he had received he was going to fall back slowly next morning on Paris, but that to carry out the movement it was necessary that he should maintain a strong position about Senlis.

With this end in view the Provisional Cavalry Division, reinforced by four Alpine Battalions, the Native Brigade and the 56th Reserve Division, were ordered to establish a very strong position north-east of Senlis. Maunoury concluded by saying he greatly hoped Sir John French would co-operate in this action, which would have the double effect of protecting his own movement whilst supporting the British left.

(The left of the Sixth Army, the VII. Corps and the 55th Reserve Division, was to fall back on the general line Creil, the heights south-west of Thérain and Noailles.)

culties. His courtesy, fairness and desire to co-operate were greatly appreciated by Sir John French, who always did his best to meet Maunoury's views. Sir John had an innate sense of chivalry, a generosity to which it was easy to appeal. Of late his hostility and mistrust had been aroused, but these soon disappeared when the cause of them was removed.

The human element, the personal relationship between leaders, plays a part in war that cannot be exaggerated. If commanders belonging to the same Army understand and have confidence in each other, so much the better the results they will jointly obtain. It is much more difficult to achieve understanding and mutual confidence between men of allied armies who speak different languages and have a totally different background, training and point of view.

To bring about such understanding and confidence is the problem of liaison, which, nominally concerned with the co-ordination of operations, is far more important as a method of interpreting commanders to each other. This is a difficult task, in which one generally gets more kicks than halfpence. The liaison officer has to stand up to both sides and defend the thesis of the one to the other and vice versa. He deals with all complaints. To one side he is always a foreigner. To his own people he seems to be for ever taking the side of the foreigner. His life is spent between the hammer and the anvil.

Whenever French and British commanders were "interpreted" to each other efficiently, and difficulties were not emphasized but studied and explained, misunderstandings disappeared. On the other hand, lack of understanding resulted in lack of candour and set up a vicious circle of mistrust. Absolute frankness on all points was essential to good relations, but this was difficult to obtain until confidence had been established.

The greatest difficulty of all was to demolish the theories of the French as to how to treat the British, and of the British as to how to treat the French. To the more nervous French temperament the British were often exasperating, appearing stolid, devoid of imagination, and unwilling on many occasions to assume what the French considered their proper share of the common burden.

Sometimes the French would sense an assumption of superiority on the part of their Allies which they found intolerable. On the other hand, they had to concede that the British were always where they said they would be, and that if they undertook to do anything they honestly endeavoured to carry it out. To the British the French often seemed unreliable. To be there one minute and gone the next suited their mentality but bewildered the British.

My experience was that when French Commanders had to deal with a British General whose mind was subtle enough to match their own, or who had the chivalry of manner that appealed to them, difficulties would disappear as if by magic, and all the cards would be laid on the table.

*   *   *

We have seen that on the evening of August 31st, General Joffre was made aware by British Intelligence reports of the German change of direction to the south-east, which was confirmed by the fortunate discovery of the map on the dead German officer.*

This information showed that as von Kluck advanced, he would present his flank to the Sixth Army and to Paris.

Here was the opportunity for which Joffre had been waiting. How exactly he would carry out the idea taking shape in his mind he did not yet know, but he began at once to make his preparations.

Since August 25th, when he had issued *Instruction Générale No. 2*, Joffre had realized that, to snatch the initiative from the enemy, he must accumulate a mass of manœuvre on his left. Further, the situation of Paris had to be taken into account. The Capital was, if not the first, at least the second objective of the enemy.

Paris loomed ever larger on the horizon as the theatre of operations receded. Not only was Paris the nerve-centre of a highly centralized state and the pivot of the entire railway system of the country, but it was the symbol of the nation.

The capital of France occupies a position which has no parallel amongst other nations. When an Englishman evokes a picture of England he sees his own countryside, his village or his town. London to him is merely the greatest town of all. A Frenchman thinking of France sees a beautiful land with a jewel set in its centre – Paris, his pride and his dream.

Now Paris was in danger. The people believed it to be mightily prepared, lying secure behind its multiple belts of forts; what would they do when they discovered it to be almost helpless?

No wonder the Government was anxious and constantly reminded

---

* The fact that von Kluck turned south again during the day (September 1st) confused the issue, which made this confirmation of vital importance to General Joffre.

the Commander-in-Chief of the vital importance of defending the city. And General Joffre understood. He sensed the danger. The enemy was not his only preoccupation, he had to consider the nation. The free democratic institutions of a critical people were being put to the test of defeat and invasion. The Government were not autocrats. Beyond them Joffre discerned the French people, now bewildered and dazed, but soon perhaps to become exasperated and ungovernable under the goad of disillusionment and despair.

These considerations were clouds in the background which would disappear with success; and now for the first time success seemed possible.

But if Joffre was to take advantage of the mistake he knew his opponents were making, it was necessary first to secure the safety of his own line by withdrawing the Fifth Army from the enemy's grasp, and to carry out a certain redistribution of forces.

With all this in mind, he issued on the afternoon of the 1st an order (*Instruction Générale No. 4*) which may be summarized as follows:

"In spite of the tactical successes achieved by the Second, Fourth and Fifth Armies on the Meuse and at Guise, the outflanking movement carried out by the enemy against the left wing of the Fifth Army, which the British and Sixth Armies failed to stop, has compelled the whole line to pivot on its right.

"As soon as the Fifth Army has escaped the threat of envelopment pronounced against its left, the Third, Fourth and Fifth Armies will resume the offensive.

"The retirement may lead to the armies having to withdraw in a southernly direction for a certain time.

"The Fifth Army, which forms the marching wing, must under no circumstances allow the enemy to fasten on to its left. The other armies which are less pressed can halt, face the enemy, and seize every favourable opportunity to inflict a check on him.

"No Army must, however, uncover its neighbour, and Army Commanders must constantly pass on information concerning their intentions, their movements and their intelligence reports to each other.

"The limit of retirement, without laying down that this limit will necessarily be reached, will place the Armies in the following position:

"A newly formed Cavalry Corps behind the Seine south of Bray.

"The Fifth Army behind the Seine, south of Nogent-sur-Seine.

"Fourth Army (Foch Detachment) behind the Aube south of Arcis-sur-Aube.

"The main body of the Fourth Army behind the Ornain east of Vitry.

"Third Army north of Bar-le-Duc. This Army will be reinforced by the Reserve Divisions from the Hauts de Meuse which will take part in the offensive.

"Circumstances permitting, portions of the First and Second Armies will be withdrawn so as to take part in the offensive.

"Lastly, the mobile troops belonging to the Paris garrison may also be called upon to take part in the offensive.*

General Joffre's intention, set forth in the above order, of using the garrison of Paris in the forthcoming offensive, was first hinted in a telegram to Gallieni (who had been appointed Governor of Paris on August 25th) despatched at 9 a.m. on September 1st. This informed him that Joffre had requested the Minister for War to place Paris under his (Joffre's) orders, with the object of enabling him to use the mobile garrison in conjunction with the field armies in the forthcoming operations.

General Joffre also telegraphed on the 1st to the Minister for War, Monsieur Millerand, explaining the situation to him. This communication conveys a further indication of his plan.† It stated that the pronounced retreat of the British on the previous day had uncovered the left flank of the Fifth Army, rendering the transport of the XVIII. Corps to Paris impossible, and added that another Corps was to be sent to replace it. Further the Minister was informed that the garrison of Paris would also comprise General Maunoury's Army (the VII. Corps and five reserve divisions); the latter, being very good behind entrenchments, could furnish the garrison of the field works.‡

---

* This order was issued to the Third, Fourth and Fifth Armies.

It is significant, as an indication of the relationship between the two G.H.Q.s, that all mention of an immediate offensive was omitted from the copy of this order sent to the British, as was the limit of retirement, nor was there anything to show them that the copy they received was not the complete version. See Appendix XXXI.

† "The Commander-in-Chief requests that the fortress of Paris be placed under his orders . . . so as to enable him, if the opportunity arises, to combine the operations of the mobile garrison of the fortress with those of the field armies; the garrison will not be sent so far from the fortress as to endanger its security."

(Extract from cipher telegram sent September 1st at 9.5 a.m. to the Minister for War.)

‡ Joffre had already ordered the 45th Algerian Division to Paris to reinforce the defence. He now directed the Third Army to send a Corps to the Capital instead of the XVIII. Corps, which was left with the Fifth Army. This Corps, the IV., was entrained on the 2nd.

The active Corps were to form the mobile defence with the possibility of being called upon to take part in the operations.

The Commander-in-Chief went on to say that if in the course of its retreat the British Army accepted to co-operate in a battle on the north front of Paris, this would be a great advantage – "But I cannot ask them to do this, having so far obtained nothing from them. In any case I do not know whether they would consent to this," he wrote.

In conclusion, General Joffre said that the direction of advance of the hostile columns was taking them somewhat further away from Paris, which would give some respite, but that nevertheless the Government should leave the capital that night or the following day. The G.Q.G. was moving that night to Bar-sur-Aube.

He placed General Maunoury's Sixth Army under General Gallieni, thereby obtaining the double result of reassuring the latter, who was very naturally desperately anxious concerning the weakness of the capital, and satisfying the demands of the Minister, who at Gallieni's instigation had been insisting ever since August 25th on the necessity of sending more troops to Paris.

Whilst Joffre was strengthening the garrison of the fortress for his own purposes, Gallieni, unaware that von Kluck's Army was no longer marching on the capital, was, very rightly and properly, entirely absorbed in the problem of organizing its defence.

His point of view at the moment is clearly shown in a conversation he had over the telephone with General Pellé on the 1st. He drew a gloomy picture. Two Reserve Divisions (General Ebener's) belonging to the Sixth Army, which he had seen, were, he said, completely disorganized. The fortress of Paris was absolutely incapable of providing for its own defence. Five or six days would be required before the defensive works could even be manned. That is, it would take this time before the guns would be in a position to fire, but even then they could only do so under very defective conditions, as the telephone lines would not be functioning. "General Joffre must know that if General Maunoury cannot hold the enemy we are incapable of resistance."

For years a steady and at times a violent campaign has raged, with the object of robbing General Joffre of the credit for the victory of the Marne and giving it instead to Gallieni. The documents referred to above, and others to be given in subsequent chapters, prove irrefutably that the claims put forward for General Gallieni by his supporters cannot be sustained. Gallieni's part in fighting the battle was an important one, but the conception and the responsibility were Joffre's alone.

The operation in its final form, which had to be prepared for by many preliminary movements, was based on one factor only, the change in the direction of the advance of von Kluck's Army to the south-east, which was not dreamed of by Gallieni till the evening of the 3rd, and only confirmed to him by Sordet's Cavalry and the Sixth Army aviation on the 4th, whereas General Joffre had been aware of it since the 31st.

From September 1st onwards, keeping his own counsel,* Joffre took all the necessary steps to place in Gallieni's hands, with an object all unknown to the latter, the means to take advantage of the German mistake. As, however, the possibility of an offensive depended upon many and complex factors, Joffre could not foretell the exact time or the exact place at which it would be launched.

*   *   *

Whilst the engagements described in the previous chapter were taking place, Lord Kitchener met Sir John French in Paris. This celebrated interview was a sequel to their exchange of telegrams, which has already been described.

After the meeting, Lord Kitchener drafted the following letter:

September 1st, 7.30 p.m.

"MY DEAR FRENCH,

"After thinking over our conversation today I think I am giving the sense of it in the following telegram to the Government I have just sent.

"French's troops are now engaged in the fighting line, where he will remain conforming to the movements of the French Army,

---

* General Joffre did not reveal his plan to anyone. Already on the 20th he had impressed on the Minister of War the importance of secrecy. His point of view in this respect is clearly revealed in the following extract from a letter he wrote to General Gallieni on September 7th:

"I shall be obliged if you will avoid sending to the Government information about operations. In the reports which I send them, I never tell them the objective of the current operations, or my intentions; or at least, in what I do tell them I indicate those passages which are secret. Otherwise, information about certain operations might come to the knowledge of the enemy in time for him to take advantage of it. It is for this reason that I consider it essential that I should be the only one to go into these matters with the Government, because I am best able to judge what may be said without disadvantage."

So little importance did General Joffre attach to Gallieni's being aware of what was in his mind, that Instruction Générale No. 4, issued on the 1st September, was not forwarded to Gallieni until the 4th, although he received on the 3rd the Note to the Army Commanders given in the following chapter on p. 353-4.

though at the same time acting with caution to avoid being in any way unsupported on his flanks.

"I feel sure you will agree that the above represents the conclusions we came to; but in any case, until I can communicate with you further in answer to anything you may wish to tell me, please consider it as an instruction.

"By being in the fighting line, you of course understand I mean disposition of your troops in contact with, though possibly behind, the French as they were today; of course you will judge as regards their position in this respect.

"I was very pleased to meet you today and hope all will go well, and that Joffre and you will make the best plans possible for the future, which you will, I hope, communicate to me. I leave the first thing tomorrow morning.

"Yours very truly,

"K.

"I hope you will do your utmost to refit as soon as possible from the Lines of Communication, and put in men and horses necessary to refill units to their proper strength."

This document in its terseness shows that Lord Kitchener had prevailed. Sir George Arthur states in his book that Lord Kitchener looked upon this episode as one of the most pregnant of the War, a view entirely justified by the result obtained, which was to break down the wall of mistrust which had surrounded General Headquarters, nullifying all attempts at co-operation between the Allied Armies.

CHAPTER XIII

CHÂTEAU-THIERRY

September 2nd, 1914

Fifth Army H.Q. leaves Jonchery for Châtillon-sur-Marne – Lanrezac at Châtillon – Information from the Corps of the Fifth Army – Fifth Army H.Q. leaves for Orbais – The situation on the left – What happened at Château-Thierry – How the Reserve Divisions crossed the Marne at Mézy – Sir John French's suggestions for a combined counter-attack – Joffre's answer – The gap between the British and the Fifth Army – Von Kluck's movements – His endeavours to destroy the British – The German Supreme Command's Orders – Joffre's Note to Army Commanders – Gallieni's difficulties.

THE Headquarters of the Fifth Army left Jonchery for Châtillon-sur-Marne at 7 a.m. on what was evidently going to be another mercilessly hot day. The transport of the III. Corps had bumped, eddied and swirled through Jonchery for a great part of the night, but happily was clear by the time we had to leave.

I left Jonchery a little later than the Army Commander, accompanied by a charming young French cavalry officer named Banéat, who was acting at the time as an air observer. He was one of the most attractive men I have ever met. Two days later, he, together with his pilot de Vienne, another fine soldier, were killed in the air. I felt his loss as if we had been friends from childhood.

We arrived in the beautiful Marne valley, which lay smiling in the sun, its soft lines still further softened by waves of heat radiating from the hot earth. Presently we turned up a steep hill into the little town of Châtillon-sur-Marne, perched starkly on the north bank of the river.

Watched over by a huge stern statue representing some ecclesiastic preaching a crusade (I think it was either Pierre l'Ermite or Pope Urban II) the place seemed to be completely deserted. No one in the houses, no one in the streets. The Staff was packed into some cottages separated from the street by diminutive gardens. I remember that a piano nearly filled the room in which the 2ème Bureau was installed.

Anxious to get in touch with G.H.Q., I went to the Post Office. To my amazement the Postmistress was at her post, dealing with the business of the soldiers thronging in to take advantage of the surprising fact that there was a Post Office open. Several men, some shyly, others in a benevolent bullying tone, urged her to go. She was the only civilian left in the place, they said. Soon it would be too late. But the quiet unruffled woman shook her head. No one had ordered her to go. She was responsible for Government property, for money, it was her duty to stay. So she went quietly on with her work. I felt for her an admiration and respect that is undimmed to this day. I never found anyone able to tell me what befell the little grey-clad woman in the ebb and flow of the great battle that rushed over, then receded, from Châtillon.

Mention of a post office recalls the unfortunate adventure which befell a smart young German cavalry officer a few days previously at La Fère. It was always difficult to know whether a given place was in one's own occupation or in that of the enemy, but this young man in his silver spiked helmet was badly misled when told La Fère was in German hands. That he got there at all does not say much for the way in which pickets, outposts or rearguards were doing their work, but the fact remains that he drove into the town in a motor car, when it was still in French occupation, got out at the post office and posted some letters and illustrated postcards. There were a good many French Territorials and reservists standing about, naturally unarmed, and he must have thought vaguely that they were prisoners. They gazed at his splendour in utter amazement and he was just about to re-enter his car when it occurred to a bright spirit amongst the Territorials to pounce upon him. The war was over then so far as he was concerned, which was heartbreaking for him, but not such a tragedy for his chauffeur, a big, garrulous, Berlin taxi-driver. I saw them both a few days later, when they were handed over to the Intelligence of the Fifth Army and put through an examination which scared them both, but to which their reactions were different. The officer kept a stiff upper lip and said nothing, but the chauffeur lost himself in a torrent of words and would gladly have told us all about the Kaiser and his plans had he known them. Owing to the strange way in which they had been captured, they both thought they would be shot as spies. I felt rather sorry for the officer as he was driven away in a cart, looking like a strange captive bird chained to its perch. Angry civilians surged round his incongruous conveyance and had to be kept off by the escort. But my feelings of sympathy diminished when a French officer maliciously showed me one of the postcards he had posted at La Fère, which said the British were running "like sheep" before the glorious and victorious German armies.

La Fère was the scene of another curious incident. One day Duruy wanted to locate one of the forts, probably with a view to making use of it as a strong point subsequent to the Battle of Guise. He asked his way of the inhabitants, who informed him that the garrison (two gunners), having no orders and no ammunition, had decided to withdraw whilst there was yet time. The yokels eagerly told the officer that if he wanted to go to the fort he should ask *Monsieur le Curé* for the key, which had been entrusted to his keeping by the garrison before their departure!

* * *

At Châtillon, as the morning wore on, the atmosphere became very depressing. The lack of news was oppressive, the increasing cannonade on the left, the danger point, was nerve-racking. Means of communication were practically non-existence. The drudgery of routine work went on unsparingly but with great difficulty, for the Staff was shorthanded, many officers being on special missions. The 2éme Bureau copied out their Intelligence Reports by hand, no typewriters having been unpacked.

The blinding sun poured down molten rays. The guns boomed exasperatingly, great rumbles first from one direction, then from another, but no news. It would have been difficult to be cheerful. The tired staff of the exhausted Army felt hunted, knowing that H.Q. was to move once more in the afternoon. It is impossible to convey how humiliating it was, how much it brought home the sense of defeat, to see the Commander and Staff of a huge Army so harried, so pressed by the enemy that they had to scuttle away twice in one day. But there was nothing else for it. General Joffre was urging General Lanrezac to withdraw beyond the Marne without loss of time so as to escape the threat to his left flank. He was told not to halt on the Marne but to continue his retirement towards the Seine.

After luncheon a section of the Commissariat butchers moved in and busily plied their trade, turning the market place into a shambles.

Presently, as several of us were standing in the little street outside the Staff offices, the Army Commander's voice was heard. It sounded at first as if once more he was roughly taking his Chief of Staff to task, but the words trailed off into a wail – *"Nous sommes foutus, nous sommes foutus!"* we heard him say, which freely translated and politely put means – "We are done for, we are done for!" Anyone might have heard. It was lamentable. Nothing could have been more utterly discouraging than to have thus brought home to one the attitude of the general to whom a quarter of a million men looked to lead them to safety and ultimately to victory.

In the early afternoon Colonel Alexandre arrived from the G.Q.G. and saw the General. I do not know what transpired but they probably discussed a matter to which General Lanrezac attached the greatest importance, the allocation to his Army of Épernay Bridge on the road from Épernay via Étoges to Sézanne. On his representing that his retreat would be seriously compromised were his request not granted, he obtained satisfaction.*

Meanwhile the withdrawal was being carried out with less interference from the enemy than might have been expected. In spite of the great strain the Corps were bearing up extraordinarily well. The morale was, as I saw for myself, good. The XVIII. Corps was not up to the level of the other Corps, but was not bad. The only units of the Army giving cause for real anxiety belonged to the Reserve Divisions. General Valabrègue himself thought that if attacked at all seriously they would disintegrate.

The usual difficulties incidental to the retreat arose. The III. Corps complained that its march had been retarded by the presence in its area of troops belonging to other corps. General Hache warned the Army Commander that the bridges were not being systematically destroyed, principally because each Corps had not been made individually responsible for the destruction of particular bridges.

The Army was ordered to continue its withdrawal during the night

* There was a good deal of feeling over this matter, which General Lanrezac refers to in his book as follows:

"My zone of march was already so poor in carriage roads that I ventured to ask the G.Q.G. to allot to me the road which follows the foot of the Falaise de Champagne by Épernay–Avize–Vertus–Sézanne–Anglure, which is less hilly and more direct than the western route, and would allow me to press on the march of my right corps, the X., so as to enable it to be in advance of the others and to be in a position to act as a reserve. The G.Q.G. answered me, with evident ill-humour, 'that it is accepted provisionally that I should use the route Épernay –Sézanne, but that if I find my zone of march too narrow, I have only to expand towards the west.'"

"This answer, which ignored the position of the enemy, caused me an annoyance which I did not attempt to conceal."

"LANREZAC."

Le Plan de Campagne Français, pp. 263–4.

September 2nd–3rd, the Reserve Divisions moving off at midnight, the remainder of the Army at 2 a.m.*

At about 5 p.m., H.Q. left for Orbais. I well remember the poignant sadness of abandoning the beautiful rich valley of the Marne, so typical of France, to the enemy, and the shame of seeing some girls by the bridge over the river shaking their fists at us. There, too, I saw an elderly woman trembling with rage as our car went by. She must have been a woman of education, for, parodying a celebrated line, she screamed *"La Garde ne se bat pas!"*†

We reached our new quarters at the same time as the first line transport of the 8th Cavalry Division on its way to Montmirail.

The situation on the left again gave rise to anxiety during the evening. A glance at Map No XIII, p. 360 will show how precarious it was likely to become if the enemy attacked at Château-Thierry. It was at Château-Thierry and at Mézy to the east of it that the Reserve Divisions were to cross the Marne. If the enemy seized the river passages before them, they would be cut off. Everything seemed to depend upon General Conneau's reaching the river in time. It was hoped that he would, for he informed the G.Q.G. and the British that he had agreed with General Lanrezac to assemble the Cavalry Corps in the neighbourhood of Château-Thierry that night.

But whilst the higher authorities hoped that Conneau's force was dealing with the situation, the most extraordinary series of events was taking place.

According to General Gendron, the Commander of the 8th Cavalry Division, the advanced guard of one of his Brigades arrived at Château-Thierry at about 5 p.m. Its instructions were to get in touch there with the Brigade of light cavalry which had crossed the river earlier, marching north to gain contact with the 4th Cavalry Division and the left flank of the Army. The patrols of the dragoons, so General Gendron stated in his report, were fired at a short distance outside the town and withdrew south of the river. General Gendron thereupon concluded that

---

* The X. Corps was responsible for keeping in touch with the Foch detachment.

The I. Corps, north of the forest of Enghien, was to be ready to move north of the forest and attack south-west if the enemy attacked from the west.

The III. Corps was to be prepared to support the XVIII. Corps, which was to be in readiness to debouch north of the Group of Reserve Division should these be attacked in strength. The Army Reserve was to consist of one division of the XVIII. Corps and one Brigade of the III. Corps.

The 4th Cavalry Division was to continue to cover the west flank of the Army and employ every means to delay the enemy should he attack. Conneau's Cavalry was to hold the entries into Château-Thierry by the evening of the 2nd.

† *"La Garde meurt, mais ne se rend pas."*

the Germans were attacking from the west, and withdrew without making any attempt to hold the river passage or to get into touch with the light cavalry. The engineers who were to have prepared the bridge for destruction withdrew also.

This is what actually occurred at Château-Thierry during those important hours.

Two Cavalry officers from the Staff of the Reserve Divisions, Captains Varroquier and Wemaëre, were ordered to inform the G.O.C. of the 53rd Reserve Division that a number of motor 'buses would be placed at his disposal during the afternoon. These were to transport a battalion to Château-Thierry, which was to arrive there not later than 7 p.m. to relieve the Cavalry which was supposed to be holding the bridge The two officers were further ordered to go to Château-Thierry to make all arrangements for the passage of the retiring columns, and to get into touch with Conneau's Cavalry Corps. They arrived at Château-Thierry from the north at 6 p.m., after fulfilling the first part of their mission. The inhabitants said there was no French Cavalry in the neighbourhood. They had seen some during the afternoon, but it had withdrawn to the south. There was no sign of any of General Conneau's troops or of the enemy.

The two cavalrymen strolled through the town to the Hotel de l'Eléphant where they hoped to get a meal. Wemaëre and Varroquier would have been astonished had they known that the G.O.C. the 8th Cavalry Division had reported that he considered his force inadequate to "attack and hold the locality from which he had been driven," half an hour before their arrival.

It is a well-nigh incredible story. The explanation can only be that one or two patrols of the Cavalry Division happened to meet some German Cavalry near the town. It is evident that the General commanding not only did not realize the situation, or the importance of the bridge at Château-Thierry, but had the strangest ideas concerning the conduct of warfare in general and the employment of cavalry in particular. He seems also to have had a lively imagination, for he reported that a troop of dragoons had been cut off in Château-Thierry at about the time our friends from the Reserve Divisions were driving in from the north. It is clear that this fighting occurred only in the imagination of the Staff of the 8th Cavalry Division, for the inhabitants of the town, the Territorial posts which surrounded it, and General Valabrègue's officers, were unaware of it.

At about 7 p.m. Wemaëre and Varroquier were crossing the bridge when a few Territorials came running after them shouting – "*Les Boches.*" The officers at first thought the men must have mistaken French troops for Germans. When questioned, they asserted they had distinctly seen German Cavalry from the position they had held on the heights north of the town. As these Territorials were still speaking others belonging to another picket appeared with the same tale to tell. It was evident that all these posts could not have made the same mistake at the same time. The officers were at first filled with consternation. For the second time German Cavalry was threatening the retreat of the ill-fated Reserve Divisions. A moment's reflection, however, brought calm. Things could not be so bad. The battalion to be transported in motor 'buses could not be far off and would soon turn up and deal with the German Cavalry. The only question was how to hold the bridges meanwhile.

Wemaëre, on being told that a hundred Territorials were detraining at Château-Thierry station, went there and explained the situation to the officer in charge, who had himself to leave at once on another mission. The men were handed over to Wemaëre together with a young civilian, an officer of the Woods and Forests Service, who proved extremely useful.

Wemaëre and his men reached the bridge over the Marne at 8 p.m. Still no sign of the Reserve Battalion or of the enemy. The bridge was barricaded and the Territorials spread out to either side of it. Only a few men were left to guard the barricade itself. Hardly had these preparations been made when shells began to fall near the bridge and in the town. Fires broke out in different places, and the boat used by the women of the town to wash linen in, the "*bateau lavoir*" close to the bridge, burst into flames. A shell tore a gaping hole in a house by the bridge a couple of feet from where a round cannon-ball was embedded. Under the cannon-ball was painted "1814." Modern progress was clearly demonstrated: the missile fired a hundred years ago had not been powerful enough to pierce the wall through which the shell of 1914 had crashed.

The shelling was too much for the old Territorials, some of whom were wounded. Men began to slink from their posts. It looked as if they might all run away. Wemaëre decided to make an example, and after that no man moved, but fear remained, and rifles held upright went off by themselves. Presently the shelling ceased and calm was restored amongst the men.

At 8.30 the sound of numerous horses could be heard on the far side of the river making for the bridge at the trot. There was a sudden silence as the cavalrymen dismounted, then distinctly the German command "*Achtung*" rasped out. Wemaëre answered at the top of his voice "*Garde à vous!*" (Attention!) and ordered a volley to be fired. A German machine gun opened fire, innocuously. The Territorials, now quite steady, fired volley after volley. This went on for ten minutes, then there was silence on the German side, followed by the sound of horses' hoofs withdrawing to the westward.

Wemaëre and Varroquier sat down and cogitated. The long-expected battalion was evidently not going to arrive. Either the 'buses had not materialized, or the convoy had been surprised by enemy cavalry. On the other hand the head of the 53rd Reserve Division ought by now to have arrived at Château-Thierry. The advance guard had no doubt heard the guns and must have seen the fires. Wemaëre thought the General might conclude that the town was occupied by the enemy, and take a road leading to another bridge farther east.

The two officers were very much puzzled. If they abandoned the bridge there was nothing to prevent the German Cavalry getting across and attacking at dawn the French columns which would then be cross-ing the Marne at Mézy. They therefore resolved to hold the bridge as long as possible. At 9 p.m. the German artillery again opened fire, followed a few minutes later by another attack. The Territorials, by this time old soldiers, were quite calm and fired steadily. The enemy again withdrew. After that there was dead silence. Some men crossed the barricade to reconnoitre a motor abandoned by the enemy at the nor-thern end of the bridge.

Soon after this it was realized that ammunition was running low, only three or four rounds per man remaining. Also it occurred to the officers that the enemy might cross the river by the railway bridge a little to the west of the town, thus turning the little garrison, so they decided to withdraw the defence to the canal some four hundred yards further south. A barricade was built on the canal bridge and the territorials withdrew to it.

Wemaëre sent off his chauffeur to the bridge at Mézy, and told him he was sure to find either a general or a staff officer there. He was to say – (1) that the battalion that was to have occupied the bridge at Château-Thierry had never appeared; (2) that the 53rd Reserve Division had not arrived either; (3) that the bridge was still in French hands; (4) that no French Cavalry had been seen since 7 p.m.

At 11 p.m. the chauffeur returned. He had seen a general who had said – "All right, the two Reserve Divisions would pass at Mézy." Nothing else.

At 11.15 there was another but less violent bombardment. The French, unable to see, answered by a very slow fire aimed in the direction of the first barricade. At 11.30 all was calm again. The two officers, who had not slept for three nights, were exhausted. What on earth were they to do with their Territorials in the morning, they wondered? At midnight they decided to send them to Montmirail, and started them off down the right road. Then they remembered that they had to get into touch with Conneau's Cavalry Corps and that the inhabitants had reported seeing some French cavalry which had withdrawn to the south during the afternoon. It was obviously of the greatest importance that General Conneau should be informed of the situation, so that he might take steps to stop the German Cavalry, which otherwise was certain to cross the river at dawn and attack the columns crossing at Mézy.

They therefore decided to go south in the hope of finding the Cavalry. Some distance was covered without meeting anything, then realizing the risk of missing the Cavalry altogether, they turned east. At 1.30 a.m., seeing a light in a house, they stopped and were lucky enough to find inside one of Conneau's Staff Officers. He did not, however, know where the General was. At 4.30 the alarm was given – the Germans again. Wemaëre and Varroquier jumped into their car and made for Mézy. On the road they met General Conneau himself, reported to him, and were told where their own General was.*

Whilst, thanks to a pure accident, the passage at Château-Thierry was being defended, General Lanrezac and his Staff continued to be much preoccupied concerning the position there. The report received from the Cavalry before 8 p.m. that Château-Thierry was being

---

* There was a sequel to this incident.

When Wemaëre reported to General Valabrègue on the morning of the 3rd and told him of what had occurred at Château-Thierry on the previous night, he exclaimed: "Then why on earth did the 53rd Reserve Division not cross there? It was reported to me just now that the right-hand column ran into the enemy in the evening before reaching the town."

As it happened the battalion commander who had led the advance guard of the right-hand column was at hand. He was sent for and confronted with Wemaëre. He asserted and reasserted with ever-increasing vehemence that Château-Thierry was in the enemy's hands at 8 p.m. on the previous night. The matter was only cleared up in Wemaëre's favour upon his producing witnesses.

What probably occurred – so some members of the Reserve Division Staff thought at least – was that the commander of the advance guard when nearing the town at about 8.30 saw the fires and heard the cannonade. He may even have had a brush with the German Cavalry, and concluding from this that Château-Thierry was occupied by the enemy, led the column to Mézy.

General Conneau had not received either the infantry support or the transport promised him by the Fifth Army.

The account in the *French Official History*, based on Gendron's report, is incorrect.

attacked, led General Lanrezac to conclude that the German Cavalry might precede a column of all arms. To avoid the danger of his retiring columns finding a strong enemy force in occupation of the bridge by which they were to cross, he ordered General Valabrègue to march at 8 p.m. and cross the river at Mézy with his whole force. He was then, that very night, to form up south of the Marne facing west in support of the cavalry.

General Lanrezac was rightly concerned lest the Reserve Divisions should be called upon for any serious effort, or indeed to fight at all. The idea of ordering them to advance along the north bank of the Marne to attack Château-Thierry had been mooted, but was abandoned on receipt of information (which turned out to be false) that a German infantry division was in the immediate vicinity of the town. General Lanrezac had opposed the proposal because he realized the Reserve Divisions could not carry out such a task. He was anxious to make the XVIII. Corps change places with them, but this was impossible at the moment owing to the rapidity of the retreat.

The Fifth Army Staff had reckoned that the Reserve Divisions would be in position south of the Marne by 4 a.m. on the 3rd, but at 6 a.m. they were still crossing the Marne at Mézy. To say they were crossing is an exaggeration. They were stuck. The spectacle was painful; such scenes can only be understood if they have been experienced. The infantry in a solid, struggling mass was literally wedged on the bridge, mixed up with artillery, all pushing wildly to get across. There were so many men in the narrow passage that they could hardly move. To make matters worse, elements of the 4th Cavalry Division, which was supposed to be keeping in touch with the enemy north of the river and protecting the retreat, appeared and joined the rush, to be at once swallowed up by the struggling mob, which was dominated here and there by small groups of horsemen squeezed in with the infantry. No one who has been caught in such a trap can ever forget the growing panic that inevitably seizes one, the feeling that the enemy is at one's heels, the wild desire to get on. General Valabrègue himself and his Chief of Staff stood in the street by the bridge trying to establish some sort of order, to disengage the exits, to get the column to advance. They were to some extent successful, for presently a slight movement was discernible, and then suddenly the whole human torrent swept forward, carrying with it in seemingly inextricable confusion, men, limbers and horsemen.

Thus the Reserve Divisions crossed the Marne at Mézy. But by the irony of circumstance, their Commander only received General Lanrezac's orders hours after he had unwittingly carried them out.

* * *

Following upon the meeting between Lord Kitchener and Sir John French in Paris on the 2nd, the latter prepared the following note in the presence of the French Minister for War and handed it to him:*

"It appears to me that the present situation demands that we should determine upon a plan which is well understood by all, so that we may all co-operate in carrying it out.

"I should like a line of defence on the river Marne to be chosen, extending for some kilometres to the west or to the north-west of Paris. The length of this line should be determined by the effectives available. The troops should be sufficiently numerous and so disposed in depth as to allow of both local and general counter-attacks.

"I should prefer that the force intended for the general counterattack, which ought to be as powerful as possible, should be concentrated in rear of the left flank.

"If a position of this kind is prepared I am willing to stand on my present line, that is east and west of Nanteuil, as long as the situation demands, provided however that I do not run the risk of my flanks being exposed to attack. I am prepared to do all in my power to co-operate in this plan, but I cannot in any circumstances place the British Army, owing to the condition of inferiority in which it now finds itself, in a situation in which it might be attacked by superior forces without being certain of its being supported and helped.

"If this plan is accepted, not a moment should be lost, and immediate steps should be taken to commence the defence of the position by all the means available."

This note was sent to General Joffre with a covering letter from Monsieur Millerand telling the Commander-in-Chief that the Government was unanimous in hoping he would accept the British proposals, but that, as he was solely responsible, he was entirely free to decide. Monsieur Millerand added that these proposals seemed the most favourable to the defence of the capital. They would, so it seemed to

---

* The text that follows has been translated from the French version.

him, have the further advantage of bringing the two headquarters into closer contact and ensuring better co-operation between the leaders. Sir John's memorandum and the Minister's letter reached Joffre on the 2nd. He was not able to accept Sir John's suggestion. The situation of the Fifth Army alone absolutely precluded the Franco-British forces from halting at the moment. The plan put forward by the British Commander-in-Chief was much the same as General Joffre's, but since it did not take into account the necessity of extricating the Fifth Army, it was premature. In his answer to the Minister General Joffre wrote:

"G.Q.G., September 2nd, 1914.

"I have received Marshal French's proposals which you were good enough to communicate to me; these are to organize on the Marne a line of defence to be held by forces of sufficient strength and in sufficient depth, particularly reinforced on the left flank.

"The actual position of the Fifth Army makes it impossible to carry out the programme suggested by Marshal French, and to assure to the British Army, in good time, effective support on the right.

"On the other hand, the British Army is certain of the support on its left of General Maunoury's Army, which is to defend the north-eastern front of Paris. The British Army could therefore remain on the Marne for a certain period, then withdraw to the left bank of the Seine, which it could hold from Melun to Juvisy; the British forces would thus participate in the defence of the capital, where their presence would be of the greatest value to the troops of the fortified camp.

"I should add that instructions have just been issued to the armies with the object of co-ordinating their movements, and it might be a disadvantage to modify these instructions; their object is to place our troops in a position to resume the offensive fairly soon. The date of their advance will be communicated to Marshal French, in order to enable the British Army to participate in the general offensive.

"JOFFRE."

General Joffre, anxious above all things not to reveal his plan sooner than was necessary, did not comment on the close resemblance of the British Commander-in-Chief's conception to his own. In sending Sir John a copy of his letter to the Minister, he thanked him for his suggestions and said:

"The present position of the Fifth Army does not allow of its lending the British Army sufficient support on the right.

"In view of the course of events of the last two days, I do not think it possible to envisage at the moment a general manœuvre on the Marne with the totality of our forces. But I believe that the co-operation of the British Army in the defence of Paris is the only plan which can yield satisfactory results."*

Next day (*i.e.* the 3rd) the British Commander-in-Chief responded with the utmost cordiality to General Joffre's letter, accepting without demur the laying aside of his suggestions. The alacrity with which he did so is sufficient proof that the G.Q.G.'s previous attitude towards him had been a mistaken one. So soon as he was no longer kept entirely in the dark, Sir John responded and turned his back on past disagreements.†

The pleasant picture of improving relations was completed by a cordial exchange of letters between Sir John and General Gallieni.

The fact remains, however, that this better understanding was due to the insistence of both Governments. Necessity had compelled them to assert themselves, and the results were excellent.

Sir John was now taking a far more cheerful view of the situation, and wired hopefully to Lord Kitchener. The withdrawal of the British during the day was entirely unmolested by the enemy, the only excitement being reports of German Cavalry ahead of the columns. These were in fact true, but abandoned saddles and equipment, and even four guns‡ showed that what Germans there were had but one idea, to escape through the thick woods.

The men were tired, the march of the I. Corps in particular having proved exhausting: it had followed the valley of the Ourcq, a defile whose heights it had to picket as in mountain warfare.

In the early afternoon Sir John French, who for some unexplained reason only received late in the evening *Instruction Générale No. 4*§ despatched at 2 p.m. on the previous day, and who was therefore still very much in the dark as to General Joffre's intentions, asked him

---

* A copy of this letter was sent to Gallieni.

† Monsieur Poincaré writes in his *Memoirs* under the date September 5th: "General Joffre himself freely recognized the necessity, indicated by the Minister of War, of keeping the British Commander-in-Chief better informed."

‡ These were the guns of the 4th Cavalry Division, which had been engaged at Néry.

§ See Chapter XII, p. 333–4.

through Huguet if the retreat of the French Armies behind the Marne was according to plan, and in particular why the Fifth Army was carrying out this movement, the reason for which he failed to understand. General Joffre answered that the Fifth Army was withdrawing because of the threat of envelopment aimed at its left wing by the First German Army.*

There was now a distance of some 25 miles between the infantry of the two armies. To diminish the danger of so wide a gap, Sir John ordered two Cavalry Brigades to march in the direction of Meaux that evening with orders to seek liaison with Conneau's Cavalry on the Meaux–Château-Thierry road, and he asked that the French Cavalry should get into touch with his own on this itinerary. With the object of further diminishing the gap on his right, the Field-Marshal notified the G.Q.G. that on the following night his Army would incline south-east.

He also took this opportunity of informing the French G.O.C. that the route followed by his columns was congested with refugees, and requested that steps be taken to clear them off the roads.

The distance between the Fifth and British Armies called forth another wail from the Huguet Mission. The German Cavalry, they reported, had on the preceding evening reached a point south-west of Nanteuil-le-Haudoin. It was therefore in a position to cross by the bridges at Meaux and above, thus turning the right of the British Army. This was true enough, but what is one to think of the conclusion of the message, which stated that the exhausted British Cavalry was incapable of offering serious resistance?†

The question of the formidable gap existing at this time between the Fifth Army and the British has excited some controversy. While Lanrezac in his book attributes it to the "precipitate retreat of the British," Sir John complained that Lanrezac by throwing back the left of his Army was responsible for it. The truth is that the gap was inevitable. The British Army had to endeavour to keep in touch both with the Fifth and Sixth Armies, but it was far more important for it to keep in

* Sir John's message is incomprehensible to me. Ever since the dangerous situation of the Fifth Army had arisen it had been constantly reported upon, by myself amongst others. Who can have led Sir John French to imagine the flank of the Fifth Army was no longer in danger I cannot imagine. It was certainly neither the G.Q.G. nor the Fifth Army. See Map XI, p. 245.

† The action of Néry the day before, when a British Cavalry Brigade played the leading role in crippling a German Cavalry Division, the subsequent work of the cavalry, their action from September 6th to 9th during the Battle of the Marne, and the use made of them during the Battle of the Aisne, where they took the place of French troops who could not hold their ground, is the best answer to such nonsense.

touch with the Sixth than with the Fifth, since to lose touch with the Sixth meant jeopardizing the British lines of communication. For this reason the B.E.F. had been marching south-west since the morning of the 1st. On the other hand it would be unjust to blame General Lanrezac for throwing back his left. He had no choice in the matter. Continuously threatened in that quarter, his sole protection, until Conneau's Corps came into being, one cavalry division and the entirely unreliable Reserve Divisions, he had perforce to refuse this flank as far as possible.*

As it turned out, the movement of the British could not have been more fortunate. Von Kluck had set apart this day for their destruction. He made this resolve when on the previous day (the 1st) he had unexpectedly bumped into them once again. The British two and a half corps were to be set upon frontally and on both flanks by five German corps plus von Marwitz's Cavalry Corps. The British happily withdrew in the nick of time and escaped this terrible danger. Moreover valuable hours were gained for the Allies, for von Kluck imposed a further enormous march on his Army and lost half a day before coming to the conclusion that "there was no longer any hope of dealing the British a decisive blow." It was only then, realizing the British had escaped him, that he wheeled his two easterly corps south-east against the flank of the Fifth Army, whilst the remainder resumed their advance in the original direction of Paris.

Von Kluck's changes of direction were sadly disturbing to the Allied Intelligence Services, which found it difficult to determine what his objective and plan really were. On the other hand the delay involved was most valuable to the Fifth Army, since von Kluck was, in spite of his erratic course, a full day's march ahead of von Bülow on the morning of the 2nd. Had he marched early that day, preceded by a Cavalry Corps, directly against the open flank of the Fifth Army, the result might indeed have been serious.

During the day, von Kluck's II. Corps engaged some troops of Maunoury's Sixth Army near Senlis. The German Intelligence failed to recognize that they were dealing with the same force that had disappeared on the 30th behind the Avre. Had they done so the danger threatening them in this quarter might have been realized. Once again

---

* As explained above, Sir John took steps on his own initiative on the 3rd to sidestep towards the Fifth Army, now that the Sixth Army was resting on Paris and the danger of the British being separated from it had disappeared. That this decision was mainly influenced by the alarming extent of country between his Army and the Fifth is certain, but a contributory factor was that had Sir John continued to retire south-west he would have brought his Army within the perimeter of the Camp of Paris, which he desired to avoid for a number of reasons.

their Intelligence Service was showing itself inadequate, badly organized and incapable of deducing conclusions from ascertained facts. Their psychology was as bad as their technique. It was their crowning error in this respect, in assuming that the Allied Armies were a beaten force, that underlay the order issued that night by German G.H.Q.:

"The intention of the Supreme Command is to drive the French south-east away from Paris.

"The First Army will follow the Second in echelon and will continue to cover the right flank of the Armies."

This order is self-contradictory. The First German Army was the only one able, owing to its forward position, to press the Allied left hard at the moment. To form an echelon behind the Second Army meant delay, for time would be necessary for the Second Army to draw level and then get ahead of the First. This delay would of course give the Anglo-French forces a respite and time to recover full liberty of action, thus rendering the rapid success desired by the Supreme Command impossible. But von Kluck, assuming that to drive the enemy away from Paris was the more important task, decided to press on south-east. He attempted a compromise by detailing the IV. Reserve Corps and the 4th Cavalry Division (the division which had suffered so much at Néry) to form a flank protection against Paris. In addition, the II. Corps was ordered to form echelon behind his right as a further cover against an attack from the capital. Von Kluck naturally thought the Supreme Command would not have contemplated ordering an advance south-east without conclusive information that the Allies were not in a position to concentrate troops in Paris. He had not enough troops both to pursue with vigour and to resist a serious onslaught from that quarter. He also believed that the German left Armies were at grips with the French and pinning them to their ground. When later he heard that this was not the case he began to realize the danger, but by then it was too late.

* * *

At 9.30 in the evening, General Joffre, thinking it expedient further to explain *Instruction Générale No. 4* (see previous chapter) issued on September 1st, sent the following personal and secret note to the Army Commanders:

"The general plan of operations which was the subject of Instruction No. 4 has the following objects:

"(a) To extricate the Armies from the enemy's pressure and to enable them to reorganize and fortify themselves in the zones in which they will be established at the end of the withdrawal.

"(b) To establish the main bodies of our forces on the general line Pont-sur-Yonne, Nogent-sur-Seine, Arcis-sur-Aube, Brienne-le-Château, Joinville,* on which line they will receive supplies and reinforcements from the depots.

"(c) To reinforce the right-hand army† by two corps drawn from the armies of Nancy and Épinal.

"(d) At that moment to assume the offensive on the whole front.

"(e) Cover our left wing with all available cavalry between Montereau and Melun.

"(f) Ask the British Army to participate in the manœuvre.

"1 – by holding the Seine from Melun to Juvisy.

"2 – by debouching from that front when the Fifth Army assumes the offensive.

"(g) Simultaneously the garrison of Paris will act in the direction of Meaux.

"JOFFRE."

This note goes further than *Instruction Générale No. 4* in specifically stating that the garrison of Paris would act in the direction of Meaux. This was in fact the direction in which General Maunoury did eventually attack.

The note did not extend the limit of retreat prescribed in *Instruction Générale No. 4*. It merely enumerated a number of railheads from which the armies were to draw reinforcements and supplies, and which obviously would have to be in rear of the furthest points the Corps would be likely to retire to.

* * *

Meanwhile, General Gallieni's fears, far from abating, were increasing. He warned all troops that the Germans might attempt to seize one of the gates of the capital by a surprise attack with armoured cars. Barricades and wire entanglements were erected to defend the roads leading

---

* By modification of the line given in paragraph 4 of *Instruction Générale No. 4*.

† *i.e.*, the right-hand attacking Army.

to the city. At noon he informed General Joffre that General Maunoury was withdrawing as far as possible towards the northern zone of Paris but that the German Cavalry was already on his flank and rear. In regard to the British he was equally pessimistic. He based his conclusions on the usual depressing report from Colonel Huguet* which he passed on to General Joffre in the following words: "The British Army has withdrawn to the Marne having been attacked by superior forces. Marshal French asks for the support of the Paris garrison." General Gallieni's conclusion was that the British Commander-in-Chief intended to withdraw without paying any attention to Paris. As far as the enemy was concerned, Gallieni thought he was trying to cut the Sixth Army off from Paris. He concluded by reminding the Commander-in-Chief that in conversation with the President, with the Minister of War and in a report to the Cabinet, as well as in three conversations over the telephone with Joffre himself, he had stated that "unless Paris received at least three active Corps as reinforcements it would be incapable of resistance."

In the evening Gallieni had contrary, though not much more accurate, information concerning the British. "Their retreat depended solely upon the retreat of the left of the Fifth Army," he telegraphed to Joffre. He said also that it was unlikely they would cross the Marne.

The withdrawal of the Sixth Army, practically unmolested, save for the right division which had been attacked, had greatly reassured him.

Gallieni's earlier and gloomy prognostications concerning the British had not unduly alarmed the G.Q.G. They had never believed the British would cross the Marne on the 2nd, having been informed early in the day that the passage of the river would only take place on the 3rd.

* * *

The seat of the French Government was this day transferred to Bordeaux.

---

* Huguet telegraphed to Gallieni at 7 a.m. that "the British, attacked by superior numbers on the previous day, had had to retire and the whole Army was going to cross the Marne." Huguet asked that if the British were pursued General Gallieni should diminish the pressure by intervening with that part of the garrison of Paris nearest to the west flank of the British.

All this so depressed Gallieni that he launched into the realm of morbid speculation concerning the British. He had the impression, so he telegraphed to Joffre, that Sir John did not intend even fulfilling the mission assigned him, adding truthfully and comically that he, Gallieni, did not know what that mission was.

In point of fact, the question of the possible intervention of the garrison of Paris had merely been raised by Sir John as a precautionary measure, the possibility of which should be considered, but the way in which it was put by Huguet aroused Gallieni's gravest concern.

CHAPTER XIV

THE DISMISSAL OF LANREZAC

September 3rd, 1914: – I

The situation on the left of the Fifth Army – Von Kluck resumes his advance south-east – Joffre sums up the situation in a personal letter to the Minister – A note to all the Armies on the coming offensive – Orbais – The German truce party – Reims abandoned – Fifth Army H.Q. falls back to Sézanne – Bad news of the XVIII Corps – Joffre at Sézanne – Lanrezac dismissed – General Franchet d'Esperey appointed to the command of the Fifth Army.

THE morning of September 3rd was particularly trying. We felt that in all probability little time separated us from the longed for moment when the Allies would turn on the Germans and the interminable retreat come to an end. But von Bülow's Second Army was bringing ever increasing pressure on the rearguards of the Fifth Army, and, to the north-west, behind a veil of mystery and uncertainty, von Kluck's First Army was straining every nerve to catch General Lanrezac's force in flank. Would the Germans reach their destination in time or would the French slip by before the blow fell? None could tell. Little or nothing could be done to weight the scales in our favour.

We knew what the troops were feeling. This flight had been incomprehensible to them. They believed they could beat the Germans if they were given half a chance; but meanwhile the Staff could do nothing but wait and wait, while the Army marched on to the cadence of weary feet that nothing could hasten.

General Lanrezac, who had thought a German attack in the direction of Condé-en-Brie was possible as early as 5 a.m., expressed to the G.Q.G. the fear that if nothing were done to delay the enemy they might arrive on the Seine at the same time as the Fifth Army, and before it had time to occupy and prepare positions on the south bank of the river.

But General Joffre could not help much: he could not lay his hands on any active troops to send Lanrezac. All he could do was to offer advice and some motor transport.* He told Lanrezac that with his own transport and what he proposed to give him, six thousand men could be transferred from that part of his front which was not threatened to his left, where, together with the Cavalry Corps which was placed under his orders, they should be able to delay the enemy. Joffre further suggested that the transport might also be utilized to move to the Seine those units which were to prepare a line of defence there. General Lanrezac was warned above all things to maintain the direction of his march within the zone indicated.

As has been seen, the Reserve Divisions had begun their movement at 8 p.m. on the night of the 2nd, and were to have been in position south of the Marne by 4 a.m. The conditions under which they crossed the river have been described. They only reached their destination at noon on the 3rd, worn out and incapable of fighting. It was impossible for the exposed flank to remain any longer under the illusory protection of General Valabrègue's command, so Mas Latrie's XVIII. Corps was ordered to throw out two strong flank-guards,† and to get into direct touch with Conneau's Cavalry Corps, to which the 4th Cavalry Division was now attached.

The prospect of the retreat being continued was depressing to all of us, and especially exasperating to Commandant Lamotte, the efficient little officer in charge of the distribution of maps for the Army. With the Army moving at such a rate, to supply all units with the vast quantity of maps required was no light task. Lamotte kept dashing off to Paris to exhort the map printing department, already working day and night, to even greater efforts. Maps of France, always more maps of France, were called for, whilst vast quantities of maps of Germany, carefully prepared for a successful offensive, filled the vaults, never to be disturbed.

At Orbais the special grievance of our little cartographer was that people would insist on fighting battles at the junction of two maps, thereby thoughtlessly and wastefully using two sheets where one should have sufficed.

The only positive information we had that morning, the only real

---

* The Staff of the Fifth Army hunted high and low, but were unable to find this motor transport. They finally concluded it must have fallen into the enemy's hands. It turned out that it had been detained by another Army and eventually it joined the Fifth.

† West and south-west of Corboin. The XVIII. Corps was further ordered to send out reconnaissances towards Essises and Château-Thierry. The Reserve Divisions were to take their place between the III. and XVIII. Corps.

contact with war, came from a civilian, the *"Conseiller Général"* from Condé-en-Brie, who arrived with a vivid description of how trains loaded with civilians going towards Château-Thierry had been fired at by the Germans. People evidently could not yet take the war in. They could not realize what it meant, nor that the enemy, advancing with giant strides, was so close to Paris. It seemed incredible that having bought a ticket as you had always done, and got into an ordinary train scheduled to arrive at a given time, you should actually be shot at on the way. Indignant passengers were asking what the police, what the Army, were doing anyway.

Presently information began to come in. The Cavalry Corps reported the enemy's infantry to be across the Marne at Château-Thierry and further west at Azy and Nogent-l'Artaud. The aviation reported numerous columns north of the river, all heading towards the left of the Fifth Army. (Map XIII, p. 360.)

All the news that came in tended to confirm General Lanrezac's gravest anxieties. The British aviation soon chimed in with information that became ever more precise, until it was evident that the whole of the First German Army was no longer moving south but had changed direction and was pressing on in a south-easterly direction.

At 5 p.m. the British Intelligence was able to confirm both to the G.Q.G. and to the Fifth Army that there were no more troops on the British front and that the whole of the First German Army* save the IV. Reserve Corps was advancing south-east to cross the Marne between Château-Thierry and La Ferté-sous-Jouarre and attack the left of the Fifth Army. Colonel Macdonogh thought it likely that the heads of at least three Corps would reach the Marne that evening. (Map XIII, p. 360.)

This information was of capital importance, since it proved that von Kluck, who on the previous day had distracted the Intelligence services by marching south, had resumed his advance south-east. Perturbed and misled by the elusive British, he had given them up and was once more aiming a thrust at the Fifth Army, but he had wasted too much precious time for his action to become effective now, though this of course we at Orbais did not know.

These movements on the part of von Kluck make September 3rd a crucial day in the history of the campaign. The Germans were now irretrievably committed to the manœuvre that was to be their undoing.

This was satisfactory on the broad strategic ground of General

* That is the II., and III. and IV. Corps and the 18th Division.

Joffre's conception, but the danger to the Fifth Army, acutely felt by its commander and staff, remained.

The X., I. and III. Corps got under way at 2 a.m., crossed the Marne in the early hours and reached the positions assigned to them, but the news in the afternoon was disquieting. The most westerly division of the Army (the 36th Division of the XVIII. Corps) came in for very severe shelling by heavy howitzers, and was so shaken that the mere threat of an infantry attack caused it to fall back eastwards. Nothing worse than this could have happened, since it involved the possibility that the whole Fifth Army might be squeezed out of the zone assigned to it by the G.Q.G., thereby jeopardizing its own retreat as well as that of the Foch Detachment, besides increasing the gap between the Fifth Army and the British. The only satisfactory report from this flank was that Conneau's three cavalry divisions were now grouped and appeared to be carrying out effectively their work of delaying the enemy. Night found them behind the Petit Morin in touch with the British Cavalry.

General Joffre summed up the situation at this date in a personal letter to the Minister, which is of great importance.

The Commander-in-Chief revealed just as much of his plan as was necessary to obtain a free hand. He described the situation in such a way as to ensure that the Government would accept without cavil a continuance of the retreat. While the possibility of an early offensive was foreshadowed, emphasis was laid on the necessity of gaining time to give the Russian offensive opportunity to develop.

Joffre said in effect:

"The German right wing is carrying out a wide enveloping movement against our left. We had hoped to meet this manœuvre by a powerful concentration of forces about Amiens with the help of the British and General Maunoury's Army, but the rapid withdrawal of the British which took place before General Maunoury's Army was able to participate in the operations under favourable conditions, has had deplorable consequences for the left flank of Lanrezac's Army. The German Cavalry, crossing the Oise by a bridge which was not destroyed in time by the British, was able to advance on to our lines of communication and carry off a convoy. To accept battle at present with any one of our armies would inevitably entail the totality of our forces being engaged, and General Lanrezac's Army would find itself pinned to a position which the line of advance of the First German Army renders most dangerous. There is the gravest

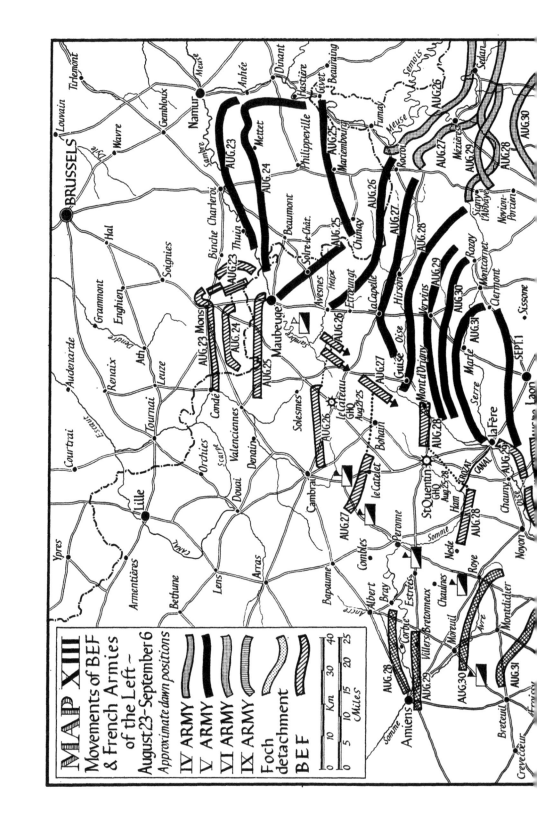

MAP XIII
Movements of BEF
& French Armies
of the Left –
August 23–September 6
Approximate dawn positions

IV ARMY
V ARMY
VI ARMY
IX ARMY
Foch
detachment
BEF

0   10   20   30   40
Km

0   5   10   15   20   25
Miles

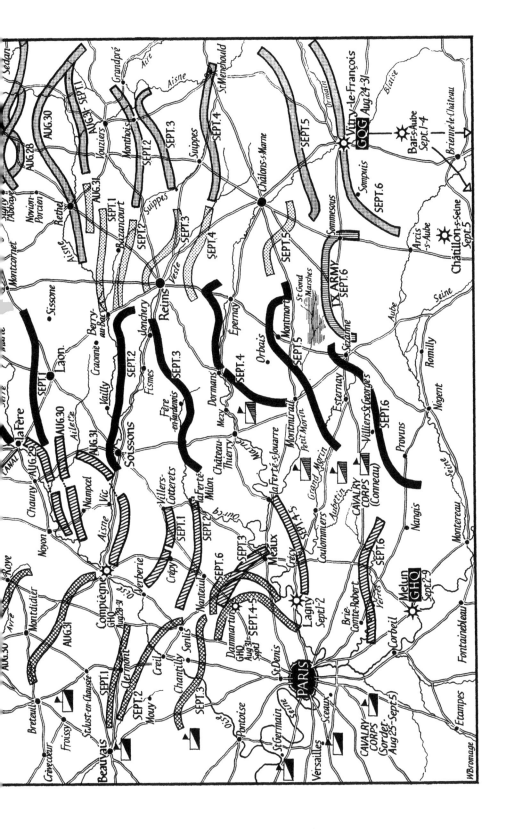

risk that at this stage the least check might degenerate into irremediable defeat, in the course of which what was left of our armies would become completely separated from the British. The great fatigue of the troops would further militate against success. Reinforcements are required, and Army Commanders are not in favour of an immediate engagement. Our position in the coalition imposes on us the duty of lasting out, to gain time and to compel the enemy to maintain the maximum of forces on our front. We can only do this by avoiding becoming involved in a decisive engagement unless the chances are greatly in our favour, and by wearing the enemy down by attacking him upon every favourable opportunity. This our Armies have constantly done. Even the necessity as a temporary measure of abandoning more territory is not a sufficient reason to compel us to accept a general battle under unfavourable conditions.

"These considerations have dictated my decision. I intend waiting a few days before engaging battle, retiring as far as is necessary to avoid our Armies becoming involved. The Armies of the right will be given strictly defensive missions, and I will take from them at least two corps. The troops will be rested as far as possible and reinforcements brought up.

"An offensive in the near future will be prepared in liaison with the British and the mobile troops of the Paris garrison. The zone of this offensive will be so selected that, by making use on certain portions of the front of defensive positions which are to be prepared, we may insure having numerical superiority in the theatre chosen for our principal effort. Facing an enemy who will weaken as he advances in a country where the means of communication have been partially destroyed we shall greatly increase our chances of victory."

General Joffre sent a note to the Armies urging them to do everything possible to spare the troops fatigue. He prescribed that itineraries should be carefully prepared. No column was to include more than one division. There should be wide intervals between the principal elements of each column. The infantry was to be lightened by requisitioning transport to carry knapsacks, etc. The troops might with advantage bivouac along the roads they were on. Parks and convoys were to be sent well ahead and food depots established along the roads the troops were to follow, and, finally, exhausted men were to be transported. At the same time the following order was sent out to all the Armies.

"G.Q.G., September 2nd.

"Part of our armies are falling back with a view to narrowing the front, obtaining reinforcements, and generally making themselves ready so that the offensive which I shall order to be resumed in the next few days may have the maximum chance of success.

"The salvation of the country depends upon the success of this offensive, which should, in conjunction with the effort of our Russian allies, break the German armies which we have already considerably weakened at various points.

"Everyone must be made aware of the situation and must concentrate all his energy on obtaining final victory.

"The most minute precautions, as well as the sternest measures, must be taken to insure that the retreat, while it continues, is carried out in perfect order, avoiding all useless fatigue to the troops.

"Men who abandon their units, if there be any such, are to be hunted down and immediately shot.

"Army Commanders will issue urgent orders to the depots for reinforcements which must be estimated for on a generous scale, to compensate for losses already incurred and those likely to be suffered in the near future.

"Effectives must be as nearly up to strength as possible. The cadres should be reconstituted by promotions, and the morale must be made equal to the demands which will be made upon it on the resumption of the forward movement which is to give us victory.

"J. JOFFRE."

Fifth Army H.Q. were installed in the pleasant Château at Orbais. I was pacing up and down the garden with Banéat after lunch when exciting news was brought in. Some Germans under a flag of truce were coming to see General Lanrezac. This struck most of us as an extraordinary event.

Shortly afterwards two cars drove up loaded with Germans, blindfolded according to the laws of war. They must have been nearly suffocated in the torrid heat, for the bandages over their eyes were of no ordinary size or thickness. I think they were hand towels. There were three officers, one of them with the carmine stripes and insignia of the German Great General Staff. There was also the chauffeur who had driven them to the French lines, and a large soft-looking N.C.O. of the Guard Cavalry, clutching a lance on which was a white pennon, a trumpet at his side. These were the emblems of the truce party.

It is difficult to look dignified when you cannot see where you are going, and it was a sorry little band of men who stumbled out of the cars, feeling their way and catching their feet. The N.C.O. looked scared, and the little chauffeur was so paralysed with fear that he could hardly walk at all. His knees were bent and he looked as if he would collapse. No one seemed to bother about him, so I led him along behind the others, who were each escorted by a soldier.

We went across to the Château, and the Germans stumbled up the stairs to the room where General Lanrezac was awaiting them. He sat at a large table, his Chief of Staff and some other officers standing behind him. The Germans stood in a row. Behind them were a number of curious members of the Fifth Army Staff, and my miserable little charge. The bandages were removed, the Germans saluted, and the Staff Officer said in good French that he had come to request the surrender of the town of Reims. The General who sent him made this demand so that the town should be spared a bombardment. I cannot remember whether it was then or later that he added that he wished to thank the Cavalry N.C.O. and the escort who at great personal risk had saved them from the fury of the population of Reims.

There was a dead silence. Then to my astonishment General Lanrezac said only: "Take them back to the lines."

That was all. The scene was one of much dignity. Everything was perfectly correct. I felt sure that the Germans must have been impressed by what they saw.

Their eyes were again bandaged and they were led down to their cars, now surrounded by gaping soldiers. In a few moments they were speeding north.

After they had gone I learned that, their orders being to deliver their message to the Military Governor of Reims, they had first been taken to the Commander of the X. Corps, but not wishing to assume the responsibility of giving an answer, he had sent them on to Army H.Q.

As a matter of fact there had never been any intention of defending Reims, which, together with its forts, had by then been evacuated. This was the only possible decision to take. The Army could not spare the troops to garrison the forts, which were old-fashioned and badly equipped. There had been no time to prepare field defences, and in any case the forts lay so close to the town that they would have afforded it no protection. Still it was horrible to have to abandon to the enemy a great historic city, perhaps second only to Paris from a sentimental point of view.

About the middle of the afternoon, the order was given for H.Q. to fall back to Sézanne. We piled into cars and were off in a very short time; by now, moving H.Q. had become a habit.

On our way we were all much interested in passing a Regiment of *Spahis Marocains* (Moroccan native cavalry). They looked very exotic, brown, hard-faced men with sparse moustaches and beards, great white turbans on their heads and flowing red cloaks trailing behind them. Their small mettlesome Arab horses jigged and cantered beneath them, whilst they, with knees right up, sat their mounts as if screwed on. One of their peculiarities was that their swords were passed under the left flap of their saddles. They were fine fighting material, but seemed singularly unsuited to European warfare.

In the late autumn of 1914 or early in '15, General de Maud'huy decided to use some *Spahis* to rush a house, the Château it was called, a few yards from the French trenches in some dismal little place, it may have been Vermelles, in the dreary valley between the Lorette ridge and Vimy. A small number of volunteers for this dismounted work were brought up, when it occurred to somebody that they did not know how to use rifles and bayonets. This entailed only a trifling delay. Standing behind what was left of a wall within a hundred yards of their objective, they were put through twenty minutes of intensive though silent drill. When let loose they rushed the building and killed the garrison in an amazingly short space of time.

The regiment of *Spahis* we passed on our way to Sézanne represented all the reinforcements the G.Q.G. had been able to raise for General Lanrezac, and was supposed to provide escorts for the convoys.

We arrived at Sézanne, an uninteresting little town of some 4,000 inhabitants, before 5 p.m.

Orders for the following day had been issued at Orbais. The line to be reached on the night of the 4th was level with Montmirail, some 20 kilometres south of that held on the 3rd. The cavalry of the corps was to cover the withdrawal, whilst Conneau's cavalry was to protect the left flank and use every endeavour to delay the enemy's progress.*
(Map XIII, p. 360.)

Soon after our arrival at Sézanne the anxiety as to what might be

* The X. Corps was to establish liaison with Foch's Detachment. The XVIII. Corps, now the left flank corps, was to be ready to act to the north-west, one of its divisions remaining in reserve.
  The 74th Brigade which was still attached to the Reserve Divisions was to rejoin the X. Corps. The Army was to continue its retreat on the 4th at 1 a.m., the XVIII. Corps alone marching at midnight.

happening on the left was intensified. The XVIII. Corps did not appear to be doing well, and General de Mas Latrie was severely criticized. His troops were reported to be retiring before a weak force of the enemy. More serious still, they had not only abandoned the high ground commanding the region over which the whole left of the Army was retiring,* but were falling back at right angles to the line of retreat.

Happily General Conneau seemed fully alive to the dangers of the situation. He had ordered his cavalry to attack the enemy at every opportunity, and was forming numerous small detachments, equipped with guns, which were to harass the enemy on every side and endeavour to enfilade his infantry and artillery. On receipt of the disquieting information concerning the XVIII. Corps, Conneau was ordered to be in position at daybreak to cover its left.†

* * *

At Sézanne, H.Q. was installed in a school in front of which was a playground.

In the late afternoon General Joffre suddenly appeared and sent for General Lanrezac. When the latter came out, the two Generals began to walk up and down the courtyard, whilst I and others watched with fascinated interest.

General Lanrezac was obviously dispirited and depressed. He talked a good deal and interrupted his walk now and then to make a point, but did not look at the Commander-in-Chief, and it was evident that the vigour he generally displayed in conversation was absent. His arms hung limp, he made no gestures except for an occasional movement of his hands.

General Joffre appeared to be talking a little more than was his habit, but even this unusual effort on his part did not amount to saying more than a few sentences. At first he seemed to be speaking emphatically, then, after long silences, to be remonstrating gently. One gathered he might be saying: "No, it is not as bad as that."

How the news got about I do not know, but the whisper passed round: "The Commander-in-Chief is dismissing the General."

For some time such a possibility had been in the air, and now the moment had come the atmosphere was electric.

* The high ground about Corboin. The XVIII. Corps now held the Condé-en-Brie-Montmirail railway.

† About Viffort.

The two big stout men, one fresh-coloured and calm, the other grey and haggard, continued to walk up and down, up and down. If the Commander-in-Chief were really dismissing Lanrezac his manner appeared to be very soothing and fatherly now.

I have no idea how long the scene lasted. It may have been short, but it appeared to be endless, every moment weighed down by the fate of the coming battle.

Suddenly the two Generals disappeared. Probably they walked out of the playground, but the picture left in my memory is that one moment they stood there and the next they were gone. I never saw General Lanrezac again; few of the Fifth Army Staff can have done so. He left for Paris almost immediately, accompanied by his personal escort, a black-uniformed non-commissioned officer belonging to the famous *"cadre-noir"* of the Cavalry School at Saumur, the great exponents of equitation in the French Army. I think Commandant Lamotte also went with him as far as Paris.

For a considerable time, but it may only have been a rumour amongst junior officers, one heard whispers that General Lanrezac's destination was one of the grimmest of the Paris forts, that he was under arrest and would be court-martialled. Nothing so dramatic happened; he was merely unstuck, ungummed, to use words coined later to meet the case of the long list of commanders who shared the same fate. The French called it *"Limogé"* from the fact that Limoges was generally assigned as the enforced residence of unsuccessful French generals, who were popularly supposed to while away the time by playing melancholy games of bridge together.

I know more now than I did then concerning this famous and painful incident.

General Joffre told Lanrezac as soon as he saw him at Sézanne that he had decided to replace him, saying that because of their friendship, because of the faith he had had in him, this was a particularly painful decision for him to take. Indeed it was no easy matter for the Commander-in-Chief, who had believed in Lanrezac, advanced his career, and trusted him with a high command, to dismiss him now, for to do so meant admitting his own failure in judgement.

Joffre went on to say that he had watched Lanrezac and had come to the conclusion that when he received an order he hesitated and did not know how to carry it out. He had all too obviously lost his grip, and events had proved to be too much for him, had in fact submerged him. He had no longer the decision, the energy, the determination or the morale to lead an Army.*

I know that Joffre received the impression (and was much astonished, for it seemed extraordinary to him) that Lanrezac's attitude when told he was no longer in command was that of a man immensely relieved, and that his whole face lighted up. General Joffre has been known to say that amazing as it might seem, Lanrezac told him in the courtyard at Sézanne that the decision he had taken to relieve him was the right one. General Lanrezac in his book gives a very different account, and I must say it was not my impression at the time that he appeared to be relieved or pleased. No one will ever know exactly what passed between the two men, for as so often happens, the picture left in the memory of the one was quite different from that remembered by the other.

General Lanrezac may have had a momentary reaction of relief when the burden of responsibility which had weighed him down was lifted from his shoulders. It may be that he had wondered how he could play his part in a great offensive battle when relations between himself and the G.Q.G. were so strained. It is not unlikely that, doubting and sceptical as always, he had little faith in ultimate success. Indeed, it is impossible to believe that, holding the views he did concerning the leadership of the French Armies, he was sanguine as to the future. The Commander-in-Chief may therefore have been right when he concluded that General Lanrezac's first reaction was to welcome relief from responsibility, relief that meant he would not be involved in the disaster his imagination pictured. But this is mere speculation, an effort to interpret the impressions of different people concerning one event.

General Lanrezac, as was his duty, went to Bordeaux to report to the Minister for War and receive instructions. On arrival he sent in his name to General Buat, then a member of Monsieur Millerand's staff (a most distinguished soldier who became eventually Chief of Staff in Paris). Buat was talking to General Gouraud, who had just returned from Africa. He asked Gouraud if he minded Lanrezac being received there and then, since he was very senior to both of them. Gouraud at once agreed, and General Lanrezac, in plain clothes, his face ravaged and drawn, was ushered in. He said: "An abominable thing has hap-

* Writing under the date of October 5th, 1914, when he saw General Joffre, Monsieur Poincaré notes in his memoirs: "The General spoke to me of Lanrezac, who is, he says, a perfect theoretician but who according to him lost his head in the field. He blamed him for the grave faults he had committed when in command. Monsieur Bénazet, Deputy, Captain on the Staff of General Franchet d'Esperey, told me recently that at times when his forces were in action Lanrezac had seemed unable to cope with the situation."

pened to me, but in the interests of the country no discussion or dispute is possible. Nothing must be said." The two younger men thought his attitude very fine.

Much later, in 1917, after the mutinies, General Gouraud was at Châlons where the H.Q. of the Army he was commanding was established. Hearing that General Lanrezac was visiting a relative in the neighbourhood, Gouraud, out of deference to his seniority, called on him. He found Lanrezac in a very different frame of mind from that he had been in at Bordeaux. He was extremely bitter, furious with Joffre and full of invective. He declared he was going to let the world know what was in his mind, that he was going to write a book. All this was extremely awkward for Gouraud. After listening for a while he respectfully reminded General Lanrezac of what he had said at Bordeaux, told him how much he had admired his attitude then, and plainly intimated how much finer and more dignified it had appeared to him than his present mood. "At Bordeaux you placed the interests of your country first, *Mon Général*; those interests have not changed." These were General Gouraud's concluding words as he took his leave.

From one point of view it is impossible not to feel sympathy for General Lanrezac. His fate was cruel indeed. The very night of his dismissal his army withdrew to safety. It had run great dangers and passed through a terrible ordeal, but the dangers were almost over, the ordeal nearly at an end. Was he not entitled to reap his reward for having piloted the Fifth Army into calmer waters? Many people think that he was. There is a school which considers his achievement to have been a very considerable one, and a legend of frustrated greatness has grown up about his name.

My own observation prevents my sharing this view, but in attempting to sum up the dramatic story of General Lanrezac's period of command, and to discern the main factors which influenced events when the Fifth Army was reeling back and the very life blood of France seemed to be pouring out unquenchably, it is impossible to maintain that the entire responsibility for the defeat of his Army should be placed on his shoulders alone.

Two main causes of failure stand out, both of which can be examined in the light of documentary evidence. One is the early action taken by the G.Q.G., the other is the actual handling of his forces by General Lanrezac.

Broadly speaking, on the first of these two counts the G.Q.G. was wrong and Lanrezac was right. On the second General Lanrezac merited the strictures passed upon him by the G.Q.G.

The early and almost fatal miscalculations of the G.Q.G. placed the Fifth Army in a position of great danger, which General Lanrezac sensed and did his best to meet. His foresight, which was greater than that of the Commander-in-Chief, at once led to divergence of views between himself and the G.Q.G. He felt that General Joffre's mind and his own worked on different lines, and that his Chief would not react as he did to a given situation. The more he felt this, the more morose did he become.

As soon as he began to differ from General Joffre, the inordinately high opinion the G.Q.G. Staff had had of him began to evaporate. They had thought him bold, but his objections made them first wonder if he was vacillating and then conclude that he was timorous. The French temperament is quick, apt in time of stress to fly from one extreme to the other. Soon General Lanrezac was but a fallen idol to the G.Q.G. He quickly realized their change of attitude and from that moment became hostile.

It would however be going too far to see in the attitude of the G.Q.G. a justification for General Lanrezac's conduct or an explanation of his failure.

If on the Sambre his tactical dispositions were poor, at Guise his conduct of the operations was excellent. Throughout the retreat, the staff work carried out under his direction was very efficient. But the constant factor, the trait that emerges constantly in the story of the retreat of the Fifth Army, is the reluctance of its Commander to fight. There were naturally always reasons for not doing so, just as there were reasons why a bold front should have been shown. Joffre could produce at least as good reasons for fighting as Lanrezac for withdrawing, but Lanrezac's mind invariably tended to prefer retreat to battle.

It may seem strange to think of General Lanrezac as a pedant rather than a man of action. His physique and his manner gave the contrary impression, yet the clue to his mentality may be that he was too much of a theoretician, too far removed from realities by long years of speculative and critical study, to assume suddenly the heavy responsibilities of actual command, when grip and character count for more than finely balanced arguments.

General Lanrezac knew his ability as a professor. He realized his power in argument. He had confidence in his own intelligence and in his effectiveness as a military critic. But these qualities only strengthened his tendency to cavil at the orders he received. The attitude of open criticism he allowed himself to adopt towards the Commander-in-Chief and the G.Q.G. made it impossible for him to retain his command.

There is nothing to add to what has been said concerning his relations with the British. There he reaped what he had sown, and was perhaps in command long enough to regret some of his earlier actions in regard to them, though I have no reason to believe that he did so. But seriously mistaken as his attitude to his Allies proved to be, it was an almost trivial error compared to his lack of faith in his own Army, which a few days after he left it gave such a splendid account of itself on the Marne.

Absorbed by the contemplation of great strategic moves and possibilities, he seemed little interested in the tactics of fighting, in the actual delivery of blows, yet hard knocks may upset the enemy's best laid plans.

The only thing he really believed in was the artillery. He loved the 75s. He never fully made use of the magnificent fighting qualities of his troops.

To those who say he saved his Army from a perilous position, it may be answered that if he did so, it was by the least glorious method a leader can adopt, continuous retreat. Not once of his own volition did he turn on the enemy between the Sambre and the Seine. The original mistake of the G.Q.G. would have imposed retreat in any event, but General Lanrezac adopted a continuous non-aggressive withdrawal as the answer to all moves of the enemy, the solution of all problems.

To quote Jules Isaac's final judgment of him: "Lanrezac found himself at the decisive moment with no faith in either his Chief, his Allies, or his troops."

*   *   *

General Joffre had ordered General Franchet d'Esperey, commanding the I. Corps, to meet him that afternoon at a crossroads a few kilometres from Sézanne. Said Joffre: I have decided to relieve General Lanrezac of the command of the Fifth Army. Tell me if you consider you have the strength to take up the burden of command? Are your shoulders broad enough and strong enough to carry it? – Franchet d'Esperey answered simply that he was ready to try, that he would do his best. Good, said Joffre, you are the commander of the Fifth Army from tonight.

CHAPTER XV

JOFFRE'S FIRST OFFENSIVE MOVE

September 3rd, 1914: – II

The Fifth Army reaches safety south of the Marne – The British retirement continues – Gallieni's anxiety – He is reassured by Joffre – Who sends him the Note to Army Commanders and copies of his correspondence with Sir John French – Joffre's personal letter to Gallieni ordering the Sixth Army to threaten the German right – Gallieni learns of von Kluck's change of direction and orders Maunoury to halt – On the morning of the 4th he takes steps in view of an offensive in co-operation with the British – The situation on the German side – The German truce party again.

WHILST the Fifth Army was carrying out its withdrawal successfully and was reaching comparative safety south of the Marne,* the British Army had also crossed the river, blowing up the bridges behind it, and by evening was between Nogent and Jouarre, having marched parallel to von Kluck. Its march had been trying, for the roads were still encumbered with refugees, and some units had been on the road for as long as eighteen hours.† Its right was now in touch with Conneau's Cavalry, but a gap of some twenty miles still separated the infantry of the two armies. The Sixth Army north of the Marne slightly overlapped the British front on the left.‡§

Sir John French, realizing that there was no immediate prospect of his being attacked, at first proposed resting on the following day and distributing amongst the units a reinforcement of 11,000 men which had just arrived, but later, finding the Fifth Army was still withdrawing and that the time for General Joffre's counter-stroke had not yet come,

---

* Only the 19th Division of the X. Corps was still north of the river.

† See *Official History of the War*, Vol. I, p. 254.

‡ On the right of the Fifth Army, the Fourth Army had withdrawn normally during the day, the only incidents being an attack against one corps of the Foch Detachment. The line reached is shown on Map XIII, p. 360.

§ See Appendix XXXII.

he ordered the Army to be in readiness to continue to retire south-wards on the 4th. Every precaution was taken to conceal the troops from aircraft, and in this the II. and III. Corps were completely successful.

General Gallieni, unaware of General Joffre's plans, continued to be extremely anxious as to a possible attack on the capital. The Com-mander-in-Chief reassured him in the morning. He told him that accord-ing to an intercepted wireless message, the German Cavalry Corps which had been engaged against Maunoury's Army on the 1st was now resting and could not therefore attack Maunoury's right flank or rear as he apprehended. General Joffre also informed Gallieni that the columns of the First German Army which had threatened Maunoury were now (September 3rd) south of the forest of Compiègne, and could not therefore be before Paris for several days. He added that it was quite out of the question to send an active corps to Paris.*†‡

That night, General Joffre wrote again to Gallieni.

It was not, he said, his intention to employ the Territorial troops in active operations in the neighbourhood of the Capital, owing to their poor manœuvring capacity. He intended, however, as foreshadowed in *Instruction Générale No. 4*, to call for the participation of the active and reserve troops of the garrison in operations in the direction of Meaux, when the offensive began.

He sent Gallieni a copy of a letter he was sending Sir John French, which was despatched at 8 a.m. on the following day.

* To this communication General Joffre attached his secret note of the 2nd to Army Commanders, and copies of his letters of that date to the Minister for War and the British Commander-in-Chief.

It will be remembered that the note foreshadowed an action by the mobile garrison of Paris in the direction of Meaux in conjunction with the offensive to be undertaken by the other armies.

† The garrison of Paris comprised at this moment the garrison proper, *i.e.* five Territorial Divisions occupying the defensive works, and General Maunoury's Army comprising the VII. Corps and three Reserve Divisions and the 45th Division from North Africa; also General Ebener's 61st and 62nd Reserve Divisions, much shaken at the moment. (In the 62nd Reserve Division four out of six colonels and lieutenant-colonels had been killed or wounded, and the same applied to two-thirds of the battalion commanders. There were only a few second-lieutenants of Reserve to take their places. Five thousand men were killed, wounded or prisoners.) The IV. Corps, which on the 7th joined Maunoury's Army, was in process of de-training in Paris.

‡ Sordet's Cavalry, which from September 1st to 4th was attached to General Gallieni's command, reverted on September 5th to the Sixth Army, to which it had been attached from August 30th to September 1st. It crossed the Seine between Mantes and Melun on the 3rd, and Sordet was ordered to have all his troops collected by September 7th in the region of Longjumeau–Brunoy, whilst General de Cornullier's Provisional Cavalry Division was to move east of Paris.

This letter ran as follows:

"MY DEAR FIELD-MARSHAL,

"I have just received your letter of September 3rd,* and I wish to thank you for the expression of cordiality which it contains, which touched me greatly.

"My intention, in the present situation, is to continue to carry out the plan which I had the honour to communicate to you, and only to engage battle on ground of my own choosing and with united forces.

"If the German forces pursue their advance south-south-east, thus swerving away from the Seine and Paris, perhaps you will share my opinion that your most effective action would be on the right bank of that river, between Marne and Seine.

"Your left, resting on the Marne, supported by the fortified camp of Paris, would be covered by the mobile garrison of the capital which would attack in an easterly direction on the left bank of the Marne.

"I have the honour to confirm to you the news of which I informed you yesterday, that General Franchet d'Esperey has been nominated to the command of the Fifth Army. I am certain that your collaboration in the battle will have the happiest results.

"Believe me, my dear Field-Marshal,

"Yours very sincerely,

"J. JOFFRE."

Joffre at the same time sent a personal letter to Gallieni in which he said: "Part of General Maunoury's active forces should be pushed out

* Sir John's letter was as follows:

"Montcerf, 3–9–1914. 12 a.m.

"MY DEAR GENERAL,

"I have the honour to acknowledge receipt of your very kind and cordial letter of September 2nd.

"I hesitated greatly about expressing my personal opinion on the subject of the general conduct of the future operations, and I am greatly obliged to you for the reception you have given to my point of view.

"I received your 'Instruction No. 4' and your 'Note for Army Commanders of September 2nd.' I understand clearly and absolutely your plans and the part which you wish me to take in their execution.

"You can count on my most cordial co-operation on all points.

"My troops appreciated very highly your most kind recognition of their services in sending them so many decorations.

"Believe me, my dear General,

"Very sincerely yours,

"J. FRENCH, Field-Marshal."

now towards the east to threaten the German right, so that the British left may feel it is supported on this side. It would be well to inform Marshal French of this, and to keep in close touch with him."

Joffre's mind was now made up. The moment at which the great turn-about was to take place was not yet determined, but the first offensive move had been ordered.

It was then that Gallieni proved himself a fine and capable Commander. Having himself drawn the conclusion on the evening of the 3rd, from information furnished him by Sixth Army patrols, that the whole of the First German Army (save perhaps the IV. Reserve Corps which it was surmised was to cover the movement) was moving south-east, he entered into the Commander-in-Chief's plans with the utmost vigour and determination. Before receiving Joffre's instructions, he told Maunoury of the German movement and ordered the Sixth Army to halt on the morrow (4th); but by 9 a.m. on the 4th, having meanwhile received General Joffre's letter and also confirmation concerning the enemy's change of direction, he informed General Maunoury that, as the German armies appeared to be slipping round the defences of Paris towards the south-east, he intended to drive into their flank, that is to the east, with the Sixth Army, in liaison with the British. He ordered General Maunoury to be ready to march that very afternoon and to prepare for a general movement to the east on the 5th. The direction of the march would be given as soon as that of the British had been ascertained. Cavalry reconnaissances were to be sent out immediately in the whole sector between Chantilly and the Marne. The 45th Division was handed over to General Maunoury, who was asked to come and see General Gallieni as soon as possible. Further, all available Cavalry in and about Paris was sent to the Sixth Army.

General Gallieni in his book (which unfortunately from every point of view he was unable to revise) gives himself, in his anxiety to prove that he was the instigator of the manœuvre of the Marne, a far less fine role than he actually performed. No great claim can be made on his behalf for having on the afternoon of the 3rd seen the obvious manœuvre indicated by the German mistake. But it can be truly said that the moment he realized the dangerous position in which the First German Army had placed itself, his every action showed intelligent anticipation, so that when on the night of the 3rd–4th, he received *Instruction Générale No. 4* and the Note to the Army Commanders, he was ready to act exactly in accordance with Joffre's intentions.

It is regrettable that in his book (see p. 100 French edition) Gallieni implies that it was the preliminary measures he took which forced the Commander-in-Chief to change his plans and to attack. The inadmissibility of this claim has been and will be further dealt with. It is extraordinary that Gallieni should contend that the Allied Armies had orders to withdraw behind the Seine as rapidly as possible, considering that *Instruction Générale No. 4* does not give this line as an objective but as the *limit* of a possible withdrawal, without any implication that this limit would necessarily be reached.

The fact is that within a few hours of receiving *Instruction Générale No. 4*, Gallieni was ordered to attack. Nothing he had done meanwhile had influenced the Commander-in-Chief.

It is beyond contention that General Joffre's orders of the 1st and 2nd, which set the pieces for the great offensive he had in mind, had necessarily to take into account the time that would be required for the Fifth Army to extricate itself from the threatened envelopment, for some re-organization in all formations to take place, and for the necessary movements to be carried out. Careful calculations resulted in the limit given in *Instruction Générale No. 4* being laid down. These calculations proved to be amazingly correct when the many imponderable factors that came into play are taken into account.

*   *   *

On the German side, the Second Army reported that the enemy on its front was falling back in complete disorder.

The German First Army Cavalry Corps reported that a battalion of Zouaves had fled, throwing away their arms as soon as they were shelled. Equipment in ever increasing quantities was found in the wake of the Fifth Army, and the German leaders concluded that the Allied retreat had degenerated into a rout. Reports such as these must have afforded them some consolation for having failed, in spite of the great efforts of the First and Second Armies, to pin the enemy to his positions and force him to fight north of the Marne.

The German Supreme Command was quite satisfied with the situation. It notified by wireless its approval of the measures taken by the Second Army and ordered it to advance south of the Marne.

As the German IX. Corps, the eastern corps of the First Army, was already south of the Marne and in contact with the enemy (the left of the Fifth Army), at Condé-en-Brie, von Bülow was justified in stating that he considered that instead of forming an echelon to the rear, as the

Supreme Command had ordered, with a view to covering the right flank of the German line, the First Army had in fact formed an echelon to the front.*

The whole situation emphasizes how much the Germans suffered because the Supreme Command was so far removed from the scene of the principal action, and lacked a Group Commander to co-ordinate the action of the Army Commanders. This deficiency was overcome to a certain extent on the Allied side by the great personal activity of the Generalissimo.

*   *   *

Late that evening news came to Sézanne that the Corps Commander responsible for conducting the German truce party back to their own lines, had refused to let them through. He reported that their papers were not in order and further that their behaviour before they were allowed into the French lines had been highly suspicious, for they had been observed inspecting them from various points before presenting themselves under the white flag. He asserted also that they had gravely abused the privileges of the white flag after leaving the French outposts. He therefore held them to be spies and was sending them back to Army Headquarters.

Here was a nice business. I had no doubt in my own mind that, however irregular their behaviour might have been, they were perfectly genuine emissaries under a flag of truce, and were therefore sacred under the laws of war. What were the Germans likely to do when they failed to return? What they did, though we did not know it then, was to shell the open and undefended town of Reims as a reprisal. General von Plettenberg commanding the Guard Corps, which in the evening was south of Reims, not seeing the emissaries, one of whom was his own

* It is not without interest to note the friction and lack of co-ordination existing between the First and Second Armies at this stage. (See page 352.)

Von Bülow writes: "The left hand Corps of the First Army had received an order to march not south but at a sharp south-east angle so that this Corps moved directly to the front of the right-hand Corps (the VII.) of the Second Army. This movement seriously interfered with the Second Army, for it compelled it to incline also in a direction which was believed not to be the right one. This was the fault of the First Army, and led eventually to increasing the gap which was to be created between the two armies."

The German writer, Baumgarten-Crusius, has observed that in these remarks Bülow forgets to point out that it was the Supreme Command that had ordered the direction of the march to be not south, but south-east. He also observes that personal contact between the two Army Commanders, or even a telephone conversation, would have dispelled misunderstandings which did so much harm to both armies. But no telephonic communication had been established between the two Headquarters.

A.D.C., turned some batteries on to the town and began a pretty heavy bombardment. But, unknown to von Plettenberg (the German liaison was decidedly bad) von Hausen's Saxons had swarmed into Reims. They, and not the inhabitants, who were in their cellars, sustained serious casualties which did not tend to improve their relations with the Prussians. Not knowing whence the firing came, the Saxons seized Monsieur Langlet, the Mayor of Reims, and declared they would shoot him because they were being shelled. He made the happy suggestion that they should find out who was firing at them. Struck by the idea, the Germans examined a fragment of shell. To their surprise and exasperation it had been manufactured by Krupps.

The Germans were not content to allow the matter to rest there. On the morning of the 4th an officer of von Bülow's Staff appeared at Reims and demanded of the Mayor the immediate appearance of the party. The Mayor had never even heard of them. "Very well," declared von Bülow's emissary, "if they are not found within one hour the town will be bombarded afresh, and you together with ten hostages will be shot. The town will also have to pay a heavy fine."

This was the Mayor's second though not his last experience of heading a list for imminent execution.

Happily two German princes, the Duke of Mecklenburg and Augustus William of Prussia, were also seeking the envoys. This entailed a gain of time. Together with the Mayor of La Neuvillette, M. de Tassigny, M. Kiéner of Reims and M. Pascal of Epernay, they made inquiries in every direction, and finally gained sufficient information to prove at least that the town of Reims had no responsibility for the detention of the truce party. The Princes' guides were, however, sent to Germany as hostages, where they remained until the middle of November.

Meanwhile news of the disappearance of the envoys had reached the Emperor, who gave orders that 300 French officers were to be shot should anything befall them.

All this, of course, we did not know at the time, but I felt extremely anxious as to the fate of these Germans. If the French decided that they had been spying, their fate was clear and would soon be settled. But to what fresh atrocities might not such a decision lead?

I was standing outside H.Q. at 11 p.m., when they were brought back, and a sorry, depressed band they looked, piled into one car together with their armed escort. This time their eyes were not bandaged. They got out of the car awkwardly. I wondered at their clumsiness until I saw that they were handcuffed and chained to each other. They looked utterly dejected and miserable, for they knew death to be close to them. They were taken off under guard. I at once went to see the Chief of Staff and notified him in the name of the British Commander-in-Chief that the fate of these Germans, whatever the case against them, was of as much moment to the British as to the French. To deal with them as spies would inevitably lead to reprisals which would affect the British as much as the French, for the Germans would certainly not differentiate between the Allies in a matter of this kind.

A preliminary interrogation of the Germans took place that evening, during which the Staff Officer in arrogant terms demanded his release. The answer he received was that if he could not prove himself to be a member of a properly constituted truce party he would be shot next morning.

The case against the Germans, which was investigated on the following day, was happily placed in the hands of Helbronner, a trained lawyer and a man of very unusual poise and clarity of mind. As far as I can remember he concluded that they were a genuine truce party, but that they had acted in a highly irregular manner, and had failed to observe the laws and customs of war. Their authority from the German commander was a scrap of paper written in pencil, with nothing to show it was an official document. It seemed clear they had observed the French lines for a long time before venturing forward under the white flag. I have always thought this was a perfectly natural thing to have done. Under modern conditions to have ventured down a road trusting someone would spot your white flag and decide you were a truce party before shooting you at long range, would have been highly dangerous. That these Germans should have carefully picked out by observation through their glasses the least dangerous point to appear at, seemed to me only common sense. What was far more serious was the accusation of attempting to collect information after they had left the French outposts. This charge appears to have been substantiated. They were watched by patrols of the French X. Corps and were seen observing the French lines and apparently noting the movements of French troops instead of returning immediately whence they came. The patrols decided to round them up and bring them back as prisoners.*

---

* I have reason to believe that in the memory of some officers the offence committed by the Germans took place before they ever came to Orbais the first time. The story is that they were stopped at the outposts just outside Reims (at La Neuvillette) whilst their message demanding the rendition of the town was conveyed to the Commander of the X. Corps, who

The whole case was submitted to General Joffre, who telegraphed his decision that they were to be treated as envoys, but as they had become possessed of valuable information they were to be detained for a period, then embarked for Germany in a neutral ship at Bordeaux. The officers' swords were to be returned to them. A highly equitable and, under the circumstances, honourable and generous solution.

I visited the Germans, I forget for what reason, soon after they had been told of this decision. Exiguity of space and the difficulty of providing guards, led to their being packed, higgledy-piggledy, in a very small room, officers, N.C.O.'s and privates together – anything but comfortable in the torrid heat. Yet they have left on my mind the impression of being amongst the happiest men I have ever seen, so greatly were they relieved at their lives being spared. I ascertained that the name of one officer was Captain von Arnim, and of the other, Captain von Kümmer. The former was small and had kept his dignity throughout. It was he who belonged to the Great General Staff. Von Kümmer on the other hand was fat and emotional. He was A.D.C. to the Commander of the Guard Corps. He had wept when he thought he was going to die, and he was now apt to weep from joy and relief. He wept again when given back his sword, which, he tactfully told the French, had belonged to his grandfather, the Governor of Metz. The third officer was a mere reservist and commoner, Schoelvinck by name, the head of the Benz motor works, and in charge of the motor service of the Guard Corps.

I remember seeing empty bottles of champagne – I have no idea how they managed to get them – with which the whole party had celebrated their change of fortune. They told me over and over again of their gratitude to their cavalry escort, and that the N.C.O. who had drawn his revolver in their defence at Reims was a real hero.

As for the ridiculous Guard Cavalry N.C.O. Carl Slewing, he turned out to be a music-hall singer in private life, and had been specially selected for the job because he had received that harmless French distinction the "*Palmes académiques*," for singing French comic songs in Berlin. He was actually wearing the violet ribbon of this decoration and

refused to answer it and ordered their return to their own Army. It was then, according to this account, that they attempted to carry out the spying which led to their arrest. This does not alter the material facts as given above. What I am certain of is that when they were brought to Orbais no complaint had been lodged against them, though this might be due to delay or to an error in transmission. I do not think that even a complaint concerning the way in which they had approached the French lines had been lodged.

was very proud of it. He could not understand why it did not cause the French to welcome him as one of themselves.

I heard an echo of this incident whilst lying in a London hospital early in 1915. I was given to read an account written by the pro-German Sven Hedin, of the bombardment of Ostend by the British Fleet. Sven Hedin was in the hotel on the front which the Germans used as a casino or officers' mess, and was in process of obtaining a colourful account of the above incident from the vocal N.C.O., who had long since been repatriated, when the British Fleet hove into sight and some well-directed shells landed in the great dining-room.

On May 15th, 1915, the *Journal de Genève* published a letter found on the body of a German officer killed near Lovitch, which had appeared in a Russian paper. The dead officer was a nephew of von Kümmer, and the letter, which was from his uncle, gave an account of his reception by the Emperor after he and his companions had been released. It was dated Mézières, October 1st. The Emperor had been delighted to see them, playfully calling fat Kümmer: "Kümmerchen," and keeping the whole party to lunch. He had been loud in his condemnation of the French, who were, it seemed, quite outside the pale. In his view international law was no longer applicable to such people.

The Kaiser appeared to look upon the release of the envoys as entirely his own doing. "We moved heaven and earth to obtain your release. We made Reims pay fifty millions. We arrested the Magistrates. Augustus William and Adolphus Frederick of Mecklenburg reconnoitred for you on horseback and pursued you to Sézanne. But it turned out the town had not been implicated in your arrest." (Nevertheless the fifty millions were not refunded.)

It took an experience such as that in the little room at Sézanne to break down the barriers of rank in the German Army. In pre-war days I have, in a limited experience, seen instances of brutality from superior to inferior, but never any real camaraderie. The relation between officers and men is best exemplified by an incident on the Somme in '16. A large batch of German prisoners had been marched a long way in very hot weather to the wire cages where they were sorted out. The men were halted by a watercart and began to fight amongst themselves as to who should be served first. There was pandemonium, and the very young French officer in charge did not know how to deal with the situation. A junior German officer, watching with some impatience his embarrassed and rather fluttering efforts to re-establish order, said, "Shall I manage them for you?" and on receiving an affirmative answer, seized the Frenchman's walking stick, and began to belabour his countrymen on the head, rasping out curses and commands at the same time, a method which quickly obtained the desired result.

The incident of the Reims' envoys was not the only occasion when I had to intervene for similar reasons.

When the Fifth Army advanced to the Aisne after the Battle of the Marne, it was found that there were many armed parties of Germans still behind our lines. Some indeed gave considerable trouble. For instance, the men who ranged about British G.H.Q. at Fère-en-Tardenois until the officer in command (who belonged to the *Garde du Corps* or the *Guard Kurassier Reg.*) was shot from an ambush laid by some of the troops forming the H.Q. Guard. As soon as their leader was killed, the men surrendered, heaving sighs of relief and saying what, literally translated, means: "We are colossally delighted that the Herr Lieutenant shot has been."

On reports coming in that these Germans were pillaging the back areas and had killed isolated men, the French took drastic action. They posted up notices in villages and at crossroads, etc. printed in French and German, stating that all enemy soldiers not surrendering at once would be treated as spies and shot if caught with weapons in their hands. I protested, on the grounds that the Germans would carry out reprisals on our own troops as well as on the French. After the posting of these notices I saw German soldiers who had been found in hiding brought in. I have a particularly horrible memory of seeing two Germans on their knees, dragging themselves along, and begging for their lives, saying they had wives and small children at home. They tried desperately to make themselves understood, though the only French word they spoke was "*Mossiou*". To the best of my knowledge the French never carried out their threat, and did not shoot any of these Germans. The Germans, on the other hand, did shoot unarmed British soldiers, who, however, never begged for their lives.*

* See Appendix XXIII.

CHAPTER XVI

GENERAL FRANCHET D'ESPEREY IN COMMAND OF THE FIFTH ARMY

September 4th, 1914

*General Franchet d'Esperey receives his Staff – His message to Sir John French –
His orders for the 5th and 6th – His Conference at Bray-sur-Seine with Sir Henry
Wilson and Colonel Macdonogh – The plans for the Battle of the Marne drawn
up – General Joffre decides to attack – Reactions of his Staff – Gallieni and
Maunoury at Melun draw up another plan with Sir Archibald Murray – Joffre
accepts d'Esperey's plan – Telephone conversation between Gallieni and Joffre –
Joffre's General Order No. 6 – Joffre receives Murray – Gallieni agreement –
Joffre sends General Order No. 6 and message to avoid confusion to Sir John
French – The French Sixth Army deploys facing east – Sir John French agrees to
co-operate – The German Side – Von Kluck's misgivings – He advances none
the less.*

THE period of apprehensive and bewildered waiting was over: General
Franchet d'Esperey, the new Commander of the Fifth Army, was
receiving his Staff.

I was to have the honour of a special interview, so was not present,
but I was soon given an idea of what was happening. I wager the war
was not long enough to allow any of those who met the General that
morning to forget the galvanic shock he gave them.

D'Esperey's words were short and to the point. He was going to
tolerate no weakness amongst the troops. Any dereliction of duty would
be visited with the extreme penalty. If this was to be the rule for the
troops who were exposed to every danger and of whom so much was
asked, was he to adopt a different standard for staff officers, especially
for his own? Far from it. Slackness, mistakes, lack of zeal or of intelligence were crimes in staff officers. Anyone who failed in his duty
would be shot. It was easy to see from the faces of the officers as they
streamed out of the Army Commander's room that they knew he meant

every word he said. A certain rather stout lieutenant-colonel who had come in for d'Esperey's unfavourable notice looked as if he had fallen down several flights of stairs.

The officer of gendarmerie attached to H.Q. also got into trouble. The H.Q. premises were not kept tidy enough. He was threatened with condign punishment. From then on passages and courtyards were kept as neat as an old maid's front parlour.

There was an amusing little scene when General d'Esperey went round the sections and met the junior officers. In the *"Section du Courrier"*, the postal department of the Staff which sent out, received and registered all messages, he came to a halt with a jerk in front of a Cavalry Captain and giving him a deadly look observed that the safe and sedentary job of a glorified postman was not one he considered suitable for a young, strong and healthy officer. Someone plucked him hurriedly by the sleeve, whispering: "It is Prince Louis of Monaco, *mon Général*, heir to the Principality. He is a volunteer." For the first and only time in my recollection the General looked nonplussed, and passed on rapidly.

I was received later. General d'Esperey, who could be very pleasant, was extremely courteous. He asked me to transmit a telegram notifying Sir John French that he had assumed his new functions (Sir John had of course already been informed of this by Joffre) and assuring him in cordial terms of his desire to co-operate with the British on the most friendly basis. D'Esperey pointed out that he had signed his telegram "Franchet d'Esperey, K.C.V.O.". He knew, he said, of the English custom of putting the letters of an Order after the name, and wished to convey in this way how much he appreciated the high honour conferred on him in April 1914 when he was carrying out a mission in England.

General Franchet d'Esperey was short and square. His hair was cut *"en brosse"*. Seen from the back, his head reminded one of a howitzer shell. His broad face, with high cheek-bones and straight jaw, was a series of parallel lines, straight top to his head, straight eyebrows, straight tooth-brush moustache, straight chin. He moved quickly, almost fiercely, bent arms keeping time like those of a runner with the movement of his legs. His dark eyes were piercing, his voice sharp, his diction precise. Olympian, the whole weight of responsibility rested on his shoulders alone. He kept all in their place by his manner. Never did he solicit or permit advice or suggestions, which indeed no one would have dared to offer. He was a genuine commander, the very man to lead the battered, discouraged but not demoralized Fifth Army.

As the stress of battle increased d'Esperey grew fiercer, more intolerant and more difficult of approach. He seemed almost to have instituted a reign of terror.

It was said that his method of dealing with the usual blocks, due to the bad and careless driving of the transport, which he was constantly confronted with as he dashed about in his great car, was to fire his revolver out of the windows at or towards the culprits.

Malick was appointed his A.D.C., but soon broke down under the strain.

Later in the war I found myself attached once more to General d'Esperey, and found him as the Commander of a Group of Armies an affable and even jovial gentleman. I often spoke of his attitude in 1914 compared with that of later years to officers who served with him, and their conclusion was that in the early days of his command he adopted a fierce and uncompromising manner of set policy. To deal with a terrible emergency, when the fate of his country depended upon his success or failure, to give the Army, depressed by retreat, the sensation of a strong hand on the helm, he deliberately banished everything that was kindly in his nature and became a fearsome demi-god of war. His success justified his method.

In the course of the morning Franchet d'Esperey informed me that he wished to meet Sir John French to discuss the situation that very afternoon. A rendezvous was first arranged at Provins, but was later changed to Bray-sur-Seine, at d'Esperey's request. It was to take place at 3 p.m. The General drove there accompanied by Malick, whilst I followed in my car. The procession was completed by the spare car that always followed the Army Commander in case of a breakdown, and by a powerful machine in which sat another officer, Commandant Maurin.* He was neither liaison officer nor did he belong to the Fifth Army Staff. His inclusion in this particular expedition was fortuitous. He belonged to the G.Q.G. and had been told to study the possibility of delaying the German advance by flooding certain areas. He had come to Fifth Army H.Q. to report, and, as he was to return to the G.Q.G., General d'Esperey told him to follow him to Bray as he might have an important message to send to General Joffre.

* In post-war years he became Minister for War.

We all arrived punctually and pulled up in the deserted *Place* in front of the Mairie.

Before he left for Bray, Franchet d'Esperey issued orders in the following sense:

"The Fifth Army in close touch with Foch's Army, is to continue on the 5th and 6th its withdrawal to the Seine in conformity with the Commander-in-Chief's orders, with a view to carrying out the manœuvre which is to culminate in the resumption of the offensive by the Allies. The objective is to reach the south bank of the Seine as soon as possible and with the minimum of loss. Consequently strong successive echelons of artillery will be placed with the rear-guards, and the fighting will be mainly carried out by the guns. The infantry must not be allowed to be drawn into serious engagements."*†
(Map XIII, p. 360.)

The first thing I remember seeing at Bray was Malick rushing wildly down the long narrow street of the town. A gendarme, sent by the Postmistress, had reported that Sézanne wanted d'Esperey urgently on the phone. The Chief of Staff had told the local people to be on the look out for the Army Commander, who must be found and brought to the telephone as soon as he arrived: meanwhile (the communication had been transmitted in a very roundabout way owing to the proximity of the enemy) the line must be kept clear at all costs.

Malick was told by General Hély d'Oissel that he must speak to the General personally, so off he raced once more.

General d'Esperey appeared round the corner looking as if he was on the last lap of a closely contested walking race, his legs twinkling, his clenched fists moving up and down at his sides.

Bouncing into the Post Office, he ordered the flabbergasted Postmistress, who was holding the receiver, and her assistant, out of the room – "*Sortez!*" he shouted as he pounced on the receiver.

I communicated with these ladies in after years and they confided to me that the door having remained open they heard General d'Esperey's side of the conversation.

What Hély d'Oissel said was that after the Army Commander had left, a cypher telegram of the highest importance had arrived at Sézanne

* While its Commander was at Bray and during the evening, the further retreat of the Fifth Army was carried out with some difficulty and at the cost of great fatigue and anxiety. The line attained by the Army that night is shown in Map XIII, p. 360.
† The operations of the Army during the day are given in Appendix XXXIII.

from the G.Q.G.; he had decoded it and was sending it on to Bray by an officer in the fastest car available. "I beg you not to settle anything with the British until you have seen it," he concluded.

One of the Post Office employees remembered General d'Esperey saying, "Tomorrow we will be ready," from which it may be inferred, if her memory is to be trusted, that, in spite of the frightful risk involved, the gist of the Commander-in-Chief's cypher telegram was given him over the telephone, but General d'Esperey, when I asked him seven years later, told me that he was positive the telegram was not read to him.

General d'Esperey returned to the *Placi*; no sign of Sir John. He was fuming with impatience and annoyance. Certainly this was no occasion to waste time. Every moment counted for the man who had only just taken over command of an Army about to play a leading part in one of the most momentous battles in history. He had, however, had time to think of a courteous gesture. He had put on the ribbon of a Knight Commander of the Victorian Order and thus adorned strode furiously up and down outside the Mairie, only stopping to ask me what had become of my Commander-in-Chief, a question to which I could not even hazard an answer. He also sent Malick to apologize to the Post-mistress for the brusque way he had literally bellowed her out of her own office. Malick must have been most successful in soothing ruffled feelings, for many years afterwards she could still look back on the incident with gratification. "*L'heure est si grave*," said Malick, "*vous comprenez*," and the excellent woman had understood.

Presently an officer, white with dust, jumped out of a car coming from the direction of Sézanne before it had quite time to pull up.

He handed the General the despatch forwarded by his Chief of Staff. The message was indeed important. It ran as follows:

Cypher telegram. Commander-in-Chief to Army Commander Sézanne, September 4th, 12.45 p.m.

"Circumstances are such that it might be advantageous to deliver battle tomorrow or the day after with all the forces of the Fifth Army in concert with the British Army and the mobile forces of Paris, against the First and Second German Armies.

"Please let me know if you consider your Army is in a fit state to do this with prospect of success.

"Immediate answer.

"J. JOFFRE."

After its receipt General d'Esperey, whose exasperation at being kept waiting had previously caused Malick and myself considerable alarm, now became positively dangerous.

At last when, nearly an hour late, a Rolls-Royce did drive up it contained only General Wilson and Colonel Macdonogh. I forget what explanation was given for Sir John's non-appearance, but I do remember that the delay was attributed partly to tyre trouble and partly to blocks on the road caused by refugees.

Happily General d'Esperey never knew that beauty in distress had been partly responsible for his long wait. General Wilson, seeing a halted car in which sat a French lady in obvious trouble, stopped to see what was the matter. She was flying before the Germans and had run short of petrol. This was easily though rather slowly put right by transferring petrol from the British car. It was then ascertained that the lady was on her way to some place near Provins. She was told that she might run into the enemy if she did so. Maps were produced and a new itinerary drawn up for her.

Perhaps General Wilson did not realize he was so late. He certainly cannot have had in mind a picture of the furious little man who was waiting for him, nor, it would seem, did he grasp the importance of the occasion.

We all made our way from the sunny *Place* into the deserted Mairie and found a large empty room, the *Salle des Mariages*, on the first floor. I remember posting as sentry on the door the Highlander who acted as escort on the British car. Colonel Macdonogh then proceeded to open the doors of adjoining rooms and looked round them carefully to make sure there were no eavesdroppers, then lifted the green baize cloth covering the large table in the room where we stood in case somebody was hiding there. This quiet and methodical search so astonished the French General that it did much to calm him. It remained so firmly impressed on his mind that he could never evoke what was perhaps the most momentous event of his career without conjuring up a picture of Macdonogh peering under the table.

Malick and I were rather awed by the importance of this meeting.

General d'Esperey asked without preliminaries for the latest news concerning the enemy. Colonel Macdonogh answered, and with his usual unrivalled mastery traced the march of the First German Army during the last few days, taking his auditors with him over to the German side until they felt that they had completely penetrated into the German mentality. When he had finished, the German movements appeared as clear as daylight. D'Esperey then, looking at General Wilson, asked what the situation of the British was, what were Sir John's intentions, and what arrangements, if any, had been come to between him and General Gallieni. To the astonishment of the Frenchman, General Wilson seemed very uncertain as to his facts and kept consulting Colonel Macdonogh, who finally answered General d'Esperey's questions himself.

With great clarity General d'Esperey then outlined the situation. His conclusions as regards the enemy were in complete agreement with those of Colonel Macdonogh. He read out General Joffre's telegram and said he considered a very great opportunity for a successful counterstroke had arisen. The First German Army had pushed south-eastwards across the Marne leaving only a comparatively small force north of the river. Since there was some interval between it and the Second German Army it was "in the air" with its communications exposed. In these circumstances a concentric attack eastwards from Paris and northwards from Sézanne might have decisive results. He proposed that next day, September 5th, the Fifth Army should take up the line Sézanne–Provins in readiness to attack on the front Sézanne–Courtacon. Meanwhile the Sixth Army and the garrison of Paris would advance to the Ourcq and endeavour to fall on the flank and rear of the First German Army. It was, however, vital to the success of this plan – and here d'Esperey rapped out his words with more emphasis than ever – that the British Army should co-operate and fill the gap between the Fifth and Sixth Armies. He suggested that it should move with its axis on Montmirail. The gap between the British right and the left of the Fifth Army would be filled by Conneau's Cavalry. If the scheme he suggested was approved, would the British Army play the part he had outlined for them, he asked. "I am going to tell the Commander-in-Chief that my Army is able to attack, and I am sure yours won't leave us in the lurch."

General Wilson replied that he was in entire agreement with the plan put forward by d'Esperey and would recommend it most strongly to Sir John French, but that he was unable to pledge the British Commander-in-Chief.

There was then considerable discussion as to how the British front was to be shortened as it advanced up the diagonal and the distance between the French Fifth and Sixth Armies diminished. The British officers insisted that the operation could only be undertaken if the British Army's left flank was supported by the Sixth Army. (Map XIV, p. 392.)

With this d'Esperey concurred, adding that the success of the operation depended above all upon the rapidity and vigour with which the Sixth Army attacked. He undertook to press this view on the French Commander-in-Chief. The moment the last points had been dealt with, without wasting a second, General d'Esperey burst open the door, causing the young Highland sentry to jump for his life, and rushed downstairs, his black-legginged legs twinkling as he ran.

On the *Place* stood Maurin, bearded and placid, looking at the trees, giving the impression of a disillusioned philosopher. I had met him several times and, like everyone else, felt drawn to this open-faced, bright-eyed officer. He had a well-established reputation throughout the French Army as a raconteur of rather *risqué* stories, but of late his fund of tales seemed to have run out. In present circumstances had he had the heart to tell them few would have been in the mood to listen.

Before he had time to move the General was at his side. "Is your car fast?" he exclaimed. "It can do 100 kilometres an hour, *mon Général!*" "Good. You can tell the Commander-in-Chief that the British are prepared to resume the offensive. Now write," said d'Esperey. Maurin, galvanized, plunged both hands in his pockets and produced his field service pocket-book.

The General then dictated the following message:

I

"The battle can only take place the day after tomorrow, September 6th.

II

"Tomorrow, September 5th, the Fifth Army will continue its retrograde movement on to the line Provins–Sezanne.

"The British Army will carry out a change of direction, facing east on the line Changis–Coulommiers and to the south, on condition its left flank is supported by the Sixth Army, which should advance to the line of the Ourcq north of Lizy-sur-Ourcq tomorrow, September 5th.

III

"On the 6th the general direction of the British offensive would be Montmirail, that of the Sixth Army Château–Thierry, that of the Fifth Army Montmirail." (Map XIVa, p. 392.)

He signed it "D'Esperey".

Maurin added at the end of the message, "Bray-sur-Seine, 4 p.m." But for some reason he made a mistake in this for it was nearer 5 than 4. He handed the paper to the General who read it and signed it. But after a moment's consideration d'Esperey concluded the message was not explicit enough and required amplification especially as regards the conditions of British preparation. "Write," he again said to Maurin, and dictated.

"For the operation to be successful it is necessary –

1. That the Sixth Army should co-operate as completely as possible, debouching on the left bank of the Ourcq north-east of Meaux on the morning of the 6th. The Sixth Army must be on the Ourcq tomorrow September 5th. Otherwise the British will not march.

2. My Army can fight on the 6th, but is not in brilliant condition. No reliance can be placed on the three Reserve Divisions. Further, it would be desirable that the Foch Detachment should take an energetic part in the operation, advancing on Montmort.

"Bray, September 4th, 4.45 p.m." (Map XIVa, p. 392.)

This message was written on the next sheet of Maurin's pocket-book. The General read it but did not sign it, evidently considering it a post-script to the first, but added in his own handwriting, "Bray" and this time the correct time: "4.45 p.m.".

When d'Esperey returned to Sézanne he sent a second telegram to the G.Q.G. confirming these messages and laying great emphasis upon the necessity of "absolute and energetic" action by the Sixth Army debouching north of the Marne, as a *sine qua non* of British participation.

It is truly remarkable that General d'Esperey, suddenly made aware of the Generalissimo's intention, should have had the grasp, the quickness of decision and the courage to elaborate there and then a plan which was adopted as the basis of the Marne manœuvre. It is all the more extraordinary in that he had only taken over command of his army the night before, and his staff was not with him to answer questions concerning his own forces. The mind that could so thoroughly weigh up the situation in a few hours was surely of exceptional quality. His army was being attacked, its situation was still precarious, he had been envisaging the continuance of the retreat for at least another forty-eight hours, yet he never hesitated. To have had the judgement, knowledge

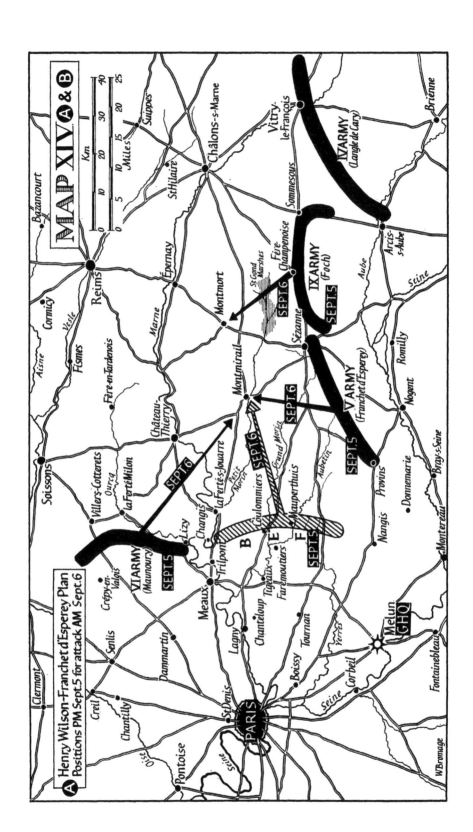

MAP XIV Ⓐ & Ⓑ

Ⓐ Henry Wilson–Franchet d'Esperey Plan
Positions PM Sept.5 for attack AM Sept.6

Km
0 10 20 30 40
0   5 10 15 20 25
Miles

Bazancourt

Clermont
Creil
Chantilly
Pontoise
Oise
Senlis
Dammartin
Crépy-en-Valois
Soissons
Villers-Cotterets
Ourcq
la Ferté-Milon
Aisne
Vesle
Cormicy
Reims
Fismes
Fère-en-Tardenois
Château-Thierry
Marne
Épernay
St Hilaire
Châlons-s-Marne
Suippes

VI ARMY (Maunoury)
SEPT.5
Lizy
Changis
Trilport
Meaux
Lagny
Chanteloup
Tigeaux
Farmoutiers
Coulommiers
la Ferté-s-Jouarre
Petit Morin
Grand Morin
Aubetin
SEPT.6
SEPT.6
SEPT.6
Montmirail
Montmort
St Gond Marshes
Fère-Champenoise
Sommesous
Vitry-le-François
Brienne

IX ARMY (Foch)
SEPT.6
SEPT.5
Sézanne

I ARMY (Langle de Cary)
Arcis-s-Aube
Aube
Seine
Romilly
Nogent

V ARMY (Franchet d'Esperey)
SEPT.5
SEPT.5
Provins
Nangis
Donnemarie
Bray-s-Seine

B E F
SEPT.5
Maupertuis
Boissy
Tournan
Yerres
Verneuil
Corbeil
Seine
Montereau

Melun
GHQ

St Denis
PARIS
Fontainebleau

W.Bromage

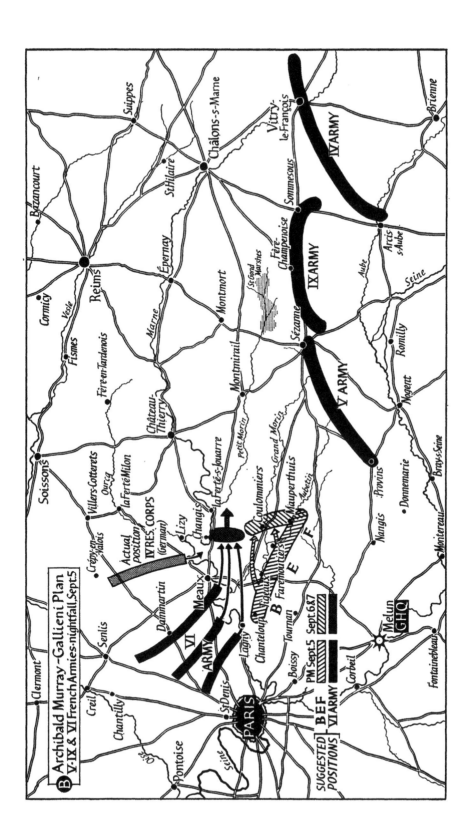

B Archibald Murray-Gallieni Plan
V·IX & VI French Armies-nightfall, Sept.5

SUGGESTED POSITIONS { B E F — VI ARMY
PM Sept 5 · Sept 6·7

and decision he showed that afternoon places General d'Esperey amongst the very great military commanders.

A curious commentary on my own impressions of the part played by General Wilson during the interview is furnished by the following entries in his diary. These were written in his own hand and were given me by Colonel Macdonogh.

"September 4th. With Macdonogh to Bray-sur-Seine at 4 p.m. Scheme – Franchet to fall back again tomorrow to the line Provins–Sézanne. He was to change front tomorrow from Jouarre–Lagny facing north, to Coulommiers–Nangis facing east. The Sixth Army was to move east and by tomorrow evening (5th) reach the line of the Ourcq. On the 6th we were all to advance."

Now Jouarre–Lagny happened to be the British front on the night of September 3rd and not that of the Fifth Army. Then he mentions "Nangis", due south of the British line and east of Melun, whereas Changis on the Marne was the place d'Esperey wished the British to make for.

The impression left is that the Sub-Chief of Staff of our Army had neither the situation nor the position of our own forces clearly in mind.

Meanwhile at the G.Q.G. at Bar-sur-Aube General Joffre spent the whole broiling afternoon sitting in the shade of a big weeping ash in the bare courtyard of the school in which the staff were working.

Voices could be heard faintly and occasionally through the open windows of the classrooms; now and then the clanging of a telephone bell was perceptible. From time to time a much louder tone broke into the droning silence as some exasperated officer tried to make himself heard down a bad line.

But in the courtyard no movement, nothing but waves of heat rising from the wide gravelled space where a big man was thinking. Those who watched him that day say that occasionally he would get up to walk to his office in the main building with his characteristic short uneven steps, which sometimes gave the impression when he hurried that his weight, which bore him forward, was too great for his legs. He would sit astride a kitchen chair in the little bare room which was his sanctum, peering from under the peak of his cap at the large maps on the walls. Then he would go out to the courtyard again.

He does not appear to have spoken to or consulted with anyone during those long hours, though it is probable that some messages were handed to him. It is likely that General Foch was consulted as had been General d'Esperey concerning the possibility of his Army's participating in the attack. Colonel Weygand, then his Chief of Staff, remembers that he was and that he agreed to do so that afternoon. Gamelin, many years later, thought Foch had been consulted through a liaison officer. I have not been able to find any written evidence that he was not but believe he must have been. Towards six o'clock General Joffre abandoned the shade of his tree in the courtyard for the last time. It must have been then that he finally decided in principle to attack, for although he had heard from neither the British nor d'Esperey he walked into the 3ème Bureau and directed draft orders for the offensive to be prepared. As yet neither the date nor the final line of the advance could be settled. For these to be determined the answer to the question he had put to the principal participants must first be received.

According to the evidence I have, General Joffre's decision came as a great relief to the officers of his Staff, who, at the usual routine conference held that morning, had urged that the time to turn on the Germans had come. Those who had held the opposite thesis, notably General Berthelot, maintaining that the Armies were too scattered, the gaps between them too wide, the troops too exhausted and the attitude of the British too uncertain to allow of a stand being made without the most serious risk, may have felt the gravest doubts but they said nothing. After all, the views of d'Esperey and of the British had yet to be received and General Berthelot's opposition to a general offensive had, amongst other things, been based on the lack of precise knowledge concerning the position and condition of many of the Fifth Army larger units. Obviously nothing could be finally settled until its Commander had answered the telegram despatched at 12.45 p.m.

No doubt General Berthelot still felt it would have been wiser to allow the Germans to advance farther into the pocket forming in front of their advance, the deeper the pocket the deadlier the trap, he had argued in the morning, but he was too loyal, too disciplined to formulate objections once his Chief had made up his mind.

It is interesting to note that it was the group of officers, whose opinion was voiced by General Berthelot, who had been the most intransigent advocates of fighting it out to a finish on the frontier, and who had refused to believe in the German manœuvre until after its purpose had been fully revealed, who now proved to be the least anxious to come to grips with the enemy. Commanders should watch in themselves and in others the most dangerous tendency of allowing undue optimism to be followed by exaggerated pessimism. There can be no greater disqualification in an officer. None ever knew what Napoleon felt when he opened, by the side of a road in Central Europe, the despatches informing him of the shattering of his plans at Trafalgar, for not a word, not a sign ever betrayed his feelings or his thoughts. A few weeks later he fought his greatest battle and won his greatest victory at Austerlitz.

At the moment when Joffre was taking his decision and Franchet d'Esperey was making all speed back to Sézanne, Generals Gallieni and Maunoury were hurrying back to Paris from Melun, where they had been propounding another scheme for joint Anglo-French action.

To explain how this occurred it is necessary to follow Gallieni.

Having received Joffre's instructions (see Chapter XV, September 3rd, p. 374-5), he decided to drive the Sixth Army into the flank of the Germans, and at 9 a.m. on the morning of the 4th advised General Maunoury of his intention, telling him to be in readiness to undertake a general movement to the east of Paris that very afternoon.

As a preliminary to the projected attack, Gallieni divided his forces into two distinct groups, a field army and the garrison of the fortress. He informed the G.Q.G. of the steps taken and asked if General Joffre would prefer that the Sixth Army should advance north or south of the Marne.

At 9.45 a.m. his Chief of Staff, General Clergerie, had the following telephone conversation with General Pellé at the G.Q.G.:

"General Clergerie intimates that according to his information the whole German Army is sliding south-east towards Lanrezac's Army, neglecting the fortified camp (i.e. Paris).

"In these conditions General Gallieni suggests that Maunoury's Army should move to the east, that he should reinforce it with all the available forces of the fortified camp, and that it could thus take part in the battle.

"If this were done, it would be necessary for the British Army to move on Montereau."

This suggestion was in conformity with Joffre's orders of the night before.

The offensive would have been launched within a few hours in any case, but it was after Clergerie had telephoned that Joffre sent the telegram to d'Esperey which the latter had received at Bray-sur-Seine, and it may have been the fact that General Gallieni not only shared the Commander-in-Chief's point of view, but was ready and eager to take advantage of the opportunity which had presented itself, that decided Joffre to ask d'Esperey when was the earliest moment at which the Fifth Army could participate in the attack.

British co-operation was as essential to the Sixth Army if it assumed the offensive as d'Esperey had realized it was to his own. Gallieni therefore summoned General Maunoury to accompany him to British G.H.Q. to discuss with Sir John the line of advance of the British upon which that of the Sixth Army depended.

Before leaving his Headquarters General Maunoury, anxious about his own left, gave instructions that every possible means should be employed to ascertain whether the enemy was strengthening his right by new forces brought up from the rear. He also left orders that no important steps were to be taken in his absence.

So it came about that while d'Esperey at Bray was drawing up one scheme in concert with the British Sub-Chief of Staff, Gallieni and Maunoury were drawing up another with Sir Archibald Murray at Melun. This naturally led to a good deal of confusion and loss of time.

On arrival at Melun, General Gallieni was handed the following telegram:

"September 4th, Bar-sur-Aube, 1 p.m.

"Of the two proposals you have made for the employment of General Maunoury's forces, I consider the most favourable will be to advance the Sixth Army to the left bank of the Marne south of Lagny. Will you come to an understanding with the Marshal Commanding-in-Chief the British Army with a view to carrying out this movement."*

* The following conversation on the telephone explains General Joffre's reasons for this decision:

"General Clergerie asks where the left of Lanrezac's Army is situated.

"He is informed that the left of the Army is and will remain today in the neighbourhood of La Ferté-Gaucher.

"Colonel Pont indicates, in guarded words, that of the two propositions made by General Gallieni that adopted by General Joffre is the attack by the south (i.e., south bank of the Marne).

"General Clergerie points out that this involves a delay of a day.

"Colonel Pont answers that the matter has been considered from this point of view, but that the delay of a day will mean that more forces will be available."

(Summary of a telephone conversation between General Clergerie, Sixth Army, and Colonel Pont, G.Q.G.)

The accession of strength alluded to by Colonel Pont refers to the completion of the movement of the IV., XV., and XXI. Corps. It was also thought at the G.Q.G. that the delay would mean a greater possibility of obtaining British co-operation.

It was decided at Melun, subject to Sir John French's approval, that the Sixth Army and the British should jointly attack the German forces that had crossed the Marne. The Sixth Army was to advance on the 5th, so that the heads of its columns reached the Marne between Lagny and Meaux the same evening. The British Army was to change front on the same day. It was to fall back to make room for the Sixth Army. On the 6th, the Sixth Army was to cross to the south bank of the Marne moving east. On that day also the British Army was to continue its movement and then pivot on its right wing, either on the 6th or 7th, so as to face east, its left joining the Sixth Army. Thereafter the two armies were to be in readiness to act together.

The following note was drawn up at the end of the Melun Conference. One copy was carried to the G.Q.G. by Lieut-.Colonel Brécard, who arrived there just before 10 p.m. Generals Gallieni and Maunoury each took away a copy:

"Plan of operations by the British Army and French Sixth Army, subject to Marshal French's approval:

"In compliance with the instructions of the French Commander-in-Chief, the French Sixth Army and the British Army have decided to unite their efforts against the German Army which has crossed the Marne.

"To this end, during September 5th the Sixth Army will march eastwards so that by the evening the heads of its columns will be on the Marne between Lagny and Meaux.

"The same day the British Army will change front to occupy the general line Mauperthuis–Farmoutiers–Tigeaux–Chanteloup, so as to give the Sixth Army the necessary room.

"On September 6th the Sixth Army will cross the Marne moving towards the east. The same day the British Army will continue its movement, pivoting on its right on either the 6th or 7th, to face east, its left joining the right of the Sixth Army. The two armies will be then ready to act conjointly."

Melun, September 4th, 4.40 p.m.

The difference between what may, for convenience, be called the Gallieni and the Franchet d'Esperey plans will be readily understood by a glance at Map XV, p. 416.

Gallieni's proposal entailed greater delay. The Sixth Army was to advance more slowly, and, far more important, with a view to gaining space for the Sixth Army, the British were to carry out a considerable retreat, whereas in Franchet d'Esperey's plan all that was required was that the British should pivot on their right (the I. Corps) while the II. and III. Corps advanced into line almost due south of it.

But the capital difference between the two plans lay in that Gallieni's suggestion amounted to little more than a local effort by the troops under his command in conjunction with the neighbouring British. It was a drive forward to take advantage of a local opportunity, whereas d'Esperey's conception embraced four armies and had as its object to surround and overwhelm the German right.

On one point d'Esperey and Gallieni had come to the same conclusion: that the Sixth Army should attack north of the Marne; but Gallieni as a result of General Joffre's decision had abandoned this proposal in favour of an attack south of the river. The "Melun" plan was therefore elaborated on the latter basis.

Sir John French returned to Melun at 7 p.m. and was informed of the plan decided upon by Gallieni, Maunoury and Murray subject to his approval. General Wilson and Colonel Macdonogh had not yet returned from Bray. Sir John found awaiting him a letter from General Joffre, despatched the night before, which seemed to fit in with General Gallieni's more recent proposals as General Murray explained them to him. Murray told his Chief that he had felt it was not possible to delay further issuing orders in the sense of the understanding he had come to with General Gallieni and had done so at 6.35. These orders Sir John sanctioned. They were for the British Army to move south-west on the 5th, pivoting on its left, its rearguards east and west of Tournon, to make room for the Sixth Army, in accordance with General Gallieni's request.

Then arrived General Wilson with the agreement he had come to with General d'Esperey. No doubt he advocated the acceptance of this plan, but he arrived too late for it to be adopted in its entirety even had Sir John wished to do so, for, as has been seen, the orders for the withdrawal had already been issued. Possibly, had he not been so late for his appointment with d'Esperey, he would have returned to Melun in time for the plan discussed at Bray to be considered before Murray issued his orders. It is likely and even probable that General Wilson gave the Commander-in-Chief a very misleading idea of what was in d'Esperey's mind owing to his having mistaken, as has been noted, the town of Nangis for the village of Changis, thus increasing the sense of confusion at British G.H.Q. Nangis is some twenty-five miles south of Changis. If

General Wilson told Sir John that the Commander of the Fifth Army wished him to occupy the line Coulommiers–Nangis, then the British Commander must have concluded that the proposals of each of the two French Generals had at least this in common: they both required the British to withdraw some distance.

Sir John must certainly have wondered what on earth was going to emerge from this welter of conflicting proposals. One course seemed not only safe but imperative, to retire to make room for the Sixth Army as General Gallieni desired. Apart from this, Sir John asked Huguet to inform the Generalissimo that in view of the constant changes in the situation he wished to study it further before deciding upon ulterior operations. Huguet's cypher telegram which was repeated to Gallieni and to the H.Q. of the Sixth Army, was as follows:

"The Marshal has decided to accept proposals for a retreat south of the Marne on the 5th and 6th. Prefers, in view of constant changes in the situation, to study it further before deciding on ulterior operations."

The different plans and suggestions that came in from the right, from the left, and from General Joffre in the rear, were enough to confuse anyone, or at least to make it natural for Sir John to wish to pause until it had been ascertained which counsel would prevail in the end. The orders he had issued had been based throughout on his interpretation of General Joffre's wishes. The only hesitation he felt was due to some considerable uncertainty as to what the French themselves were going to do.

Sir John was to remain in doubt for several hours after his return to Melun as to what exactly General Joffre's wishes and intentions were. Meanwhile, at Bar-sur-Aube, General Joffre was eating his dinner earlier than usual, for it was not yet eight o'clock. It was served in exactly the sort of dining-room you would have expected to find in the pleasant two-storeyed eighteenth-century Château where the Commander-in-Chief had taken up his residence. It went by the name of "Le Jard" and stood at the gates of the little town.

Seated round the table were the Commander-in-Chief's personal Staff and his more intimate collaborators. General Belin, the Chief of Staff, his clever face showing signs of almost unbearable strain, the Sub-Chief, General Berthelot, immense, bearded and unruffled, Muller, the stout, fair, round-faced, heavily-moustached A.D.C., de Galbert his colleague, whose dark face was quick and expressive, Commandant Gamme; and Commandant Gamelin, who had worked in close contact with the Commander-in-Chief since 1906 and possessed his complete confidence, self-possessed, enigmatic and supremely intelligent, who sat quietly saying nothing as was his wont. But somehow it was impossible not to notice and attempt to weigh up this unobtrusive little officer in his dark *Chasseurs-à-Pied* uniform. Perhaps it was the fact that he gave the impression of being completely sure of himself, that his steady blue eyes always looking straight ahead conveyed the impression of clear vision, of presenting an accurate picture of men and of things, that fascinated attention. One always felt curiosity to know what was the problem that absorbed him, all the more so that one also felt he would not readily tell.

The situation had not been such of late as to encourage conversation, and there had been little talk at meals, but tonight the silences were exceptionally long and oppressive. General Joffre himself, never loquacious, said nothing, indeed had he wished to do so he would have been faced with insuperable difficulties, for to either side of him sat two Japanese officers, guests that evening, and they did not utter a word. Since their arrival they had bowed and smiled, smiled and bowed again whenever anyone addressed them, but not a single intelligible syllable had passed their lips. Major Clive, our liaison officer to the G.Q.G., had also been invited. Monocled and urbane, this very able dark-moustached and dark-haired Guardsman, whose social qualities were as distinguished as were his professional attainments, who, under most circumstances, could be relied upon to make the most "sticky" party go, gave this one up as hopeless, and kept his long nose in his plate.

The heavy, brooding, strained atmosphere, as enervating as is the sultry silence before the first lightning tears across a storm-laden sky, seemed to affect General Joffre not at all. He sat relaxed and heavy, as if his black tunic concealed nothing more than a bag of flour plumped into his chair. His napkin was tucked in between two golden buttons. His pale blue eyes looking straight ahead of him shone as they caught the light of the lamp hanging overhead. Occasionally he wiped his big whitening moustache.

In front of him stood his favourite dish, a *gigot bretonne*, on his plate there was an ample helping which he was eating with quiet and slowly masticating concentration. His legendary appetite was being put to the test and not betraying its reputation.

Suddenly the door opened. Framed against the dark passage stood Maurin. His black uniform was grey with dust, so was his face and beard. It filled his eyes which were sore with it, and made him blink in the light.

He took a step forward, saluted and said, "Mon Général, General Franchet d'Esperey has asked me to tell you that the English are prepared to assume the offensive."

The Commander-in-Chief lifted both arms to Heaven "Then we can march!" he exclaimed. Maurin gave him General d'Esperey's two messages which General Joffre read, then handed to General Belin without comment. He in turn perused them carefully, then passed them on to General Berthelot. Belin and Berthelot looked at each other, then at their Chief. Joffre nodded. Words were unnecessary, nor were any uttered. Berthelot got up, making a sign to Gamelin who followed him out of the room.

The Commander-in-Chief resumed his dinner. Maurin, still standing by him, at first felt an immense sense of relief. Everything was going well evidently, then, as the Staff Officers left the room, he suddenly felt overwhelmingly weary and hungry. The smell of food filled his nostrils. He also had a penchant, never so marked as that evening, for *gigot bretonne*, but General Joffre, flanked by his grinning Japs, went on munching, staring in front of him, with the detached fixity of a bull chewing the cud as it stares at a passing train. There was nothing for it, Maurin, who would have given a fortune to sit down and eat, saluted and, swaying a little with fatigue, walked out. The remaining guests, with the exception of the Japanese officers who watched uncomprehendingly but incredibly alert, ready for anything demanded of them from Hari-Kari to endless bows, were a little "gêné" as they stared at their plates.

It was not long after 8.00 that the Commander-in-Chief took leave of his guests and followed by General Belin made his way to the 3ème Bureau where General Berthelot and Gamelin were already at work, redrafting the orders drawn up before dinner so as to bring them within the frame of d'Esperey's proposals. The first draft had been in conformity with the Gallieni plan and required radical amendments. The staff officers had known, without a word from their Chief, that these were his wishes.

General Joffre was studying the proposals put forward by his collaborators when General Gallieni asked to speak to him on the telephone. The time was not earlier than 8.30 and not later than 9 p.m.

It was common knowledge that the Commander-in-Chief hated to use that instrument and even pretended he did not know how to do so. This affectation concealed a sound underlying principle. He rightly feared misapprehension of instructions given in this way. Written instructions that could be referred to at a later date suited him better. Conversations that left no trace were, in his view, full of pitfalls and left the door wide open to misunderstanding, real or pretended, if things went wrong. Above all he feared leakages. When members of the Government called him to the telephone he could not refuse to answer, but, so says his A.D.C., he would on these occasions say as little as possible and refer his interlocutor to his official communications. On the rare occasions when an Army Commander insisted on speaking to him he would listen but not give an opinion. This is not to say of course that the Commander-in-Chief disdained the telephone as a most valuable instrument for Staff work, especially for the transmission of information; but when it had to be used to send reports or orders he insisted that they should be read from a written and signed paper.

He had occasion to regret the single occasion when he broke his rule and spoke to Gallieni without any of his usual safeguards, for what he said was certainly misrepresented. It was even said that there had been two telephone conversations between the Military Governor of Paris and the Commander-in-Chief, but this is not the case.

No one will ever be able to establish exactly what took place between the two Generals, for no record of the conversation was made, but it can be stated with certainty that the version put forward by General Gallieni at a later date from memory is inaccurate. The sequence of events had become telescoped in his mind, which is natural enough. This is his version of what occurred:

"As soon as I returned to Paris (i.e. after his visit to Melun) particularly in view of the tergiversations of British G.H.Q., I telephoned myself to General Joffre, to tell him of the dispositions made, of the march to the east of the Army of Paris, with the Meaux–Senlis road as the axis of march, of the attack to be made on first contact with the troops of the 4th German Reserve Corps, which was expected to take place next day in the afternoon, of the necessity for the co-operation of the British Army in the movement, and lastly of the hesitation I had encountered at British G.H.Q."

This in no way tallies with the facts. He cannot have told the Commander-in-Chief the Army of Paris was marching east, for it did not move that day (4th), nor can he have told him he intended it to take the Meaux–Senlis road as its axis of march.

This is obvious, as it was not the line of advance he had settled upon with General Murray but the one laid down by d'Esperey at Bray. It seems improbable that Gallieni should have told General Joffre of a plan he was not aware of or advocated proposals at variance with the arrangement he had himself so recently come to at Melun.

The simplest interpretation of what took place is also the most likely. It is probable that Gallieni began by giving General Joffre an account of what had occurred at Melun, but it may be surmised that the Commander-in-Chief cut him short to tell him of his decision, in general terms, for General Joffre only realized later, as will be seen, that there was some danger of confusion owing to the simultaneous interviews of Melun and Bray.

That Joffre told Gallieni he had adopted the Franchet d'Esperey proposals is proved by a telephone message sent by Gallieni to the Sixth Army at 10 p.m.

This is, incidentally, the only official record there is of this famous telephone conversation.

Gallieni's message was as follows:

"The Commander-in-Chief has just telephoned as follows:

"The Fifth Army, the British and the Sixth Army will attack on the morning of the 6th September in the following directions:

"Fifth Army on the front Courtacon (10 km. south of La Ferté Gaucher) Sézanne.

"British Army, on the front Coulommiers–Changis (11 km. east of Meaux).

"Sixth Army, north of the Marne, in the direction of Château-Thierry.

"Consequently, the orders given verbally are modified only in the sense that the Sixth Army will orient its columns tomorrow so as to reach the level of Meaux, remaining on the right bank of the Marne."

Nothing could be clearer than this. This message is the Franchet d'Esperey plan put in other words, and the strategic outline of the Battle of the Marne.

Gallieni's orders for the advance of the Sixth Army were only issued on the morning of the 5th. They were probably despatched before he received Instruction General No. 6 which was signed by Joffre at 10 p.m. It is obvious that Gallieni felt he was justified, as indeed he was, in issuing orders, as he had been in sending the message of the night before, on the verbal instructions of the Commander-in-Chief, without awaiting their confirmation in writing. Gallieni and Joffre were in complete agreement. Would that his subsequent urge to increase the importance of the part he had played (it was so great that it needed no amplification and there was ample glory for all) had not led him, all unwittingly it is certain, for he was a great man, to confuse a perfectly simple and clear sequence of events.

Ordre Générale No. 6, the order for the battle of the Marne, was as follows:

"Cypher Telegram
"G.Q.G., September 4th, 10 p.m.

I

"The precarious situation in which the First German Army finds itself is to be taken advantage of to concentrate against it the efforts of the allied armies on the extreme left.

"All dispositions will be taken on the 5th to attack on the 6th.

II

"The movements to be carried out on the 5th will be:

"(*a*) All the available forces of the Sixth Army to be north-east of Meaux ready to cross the Ourcq between Lizy-sur-Ourcq and May-en-Multien in the general direction of Château-Thierry.

"The available elements of the Cavalry Corps which are at hand will be under the orders of General Maunoury for this operation.

"(*b*) The British Army established on the front Changis–Coulommiers facing east will be ready to attack in the general direction of Montmirail.

"(*c*) The Fifth Army, closing in slightly on its left, will establish itself on the general line Courtacon–Esternay–Sézanne, ready to attack south–north.

"Conneau's Cavalry Corps will assure the liaison between the British and Fifth Armies.

"(*d*) The Ninth Army (General Foch)* will cover the right of the

---

* General Foch's Detachment was to form an autonomous army on September 5th.

Fifth Army by holding the southern exits of the St. Gond Marshes and by moving part of its forces on to the plateau north of Sézanne.

III

"The offensive will be assumed by these armies on the morning of September 6th.

"J. JOFFRE.

"Confirmation sent by officers in cars."

At 10 p.m., or shortly before, Colonel Brécard, a French Liaison Officer, arrived from Melun at Bar-sur-Aube with the Murray–Gallieni agreement. This was at once examined by General Joffre who then realized for the first time the dangerous confusion created by the simultaneous interviews of Melun and Bray. There could now be no question of altering the decision taken. The thought does not appear to have even crossed the Commander-in-Chief's mind, but he at once took steps to mitigate the effect of the muddle on the British. It is strange that the possibility of a misunderstanding did not emerge from General Gallieni's talk on the telephone. My impression is, as I have already suggested, that General Joffre, intent only upon explaining to him the essentials of the plan he had settled, did not give Gallieni time to launch into an explanation of the Melun interview. General Gallieni on his side, knowing nothing of the Bray interview, had no reason to suspect that any special difficulty would arise at British G.H.Q. His own plans had been superseded by one evolved by the Commander-in-Chief himself. It was the business of the G.Q.G. Staff to inform all concerned. He had enough on his hands without trespassing within this sphere.

General Joffre, anxious above all else to avoid a misunderstanding with the British, ordered Brécard to send a telephone message at once to Colonel Huguet. The draft was shown to the Commander-in-Chief. It ran as follows:

"I have arrived at the G.Q.G. I find rather a different solution has been adopted resulting from the conference at Bray between General Wilson and General Franchet d'Esperey, a solution which General Joffre has taken as the basis of his orders.

"A copy of these orders is being sent you by cypher telegram, which I beg you to transmit to Marshal French and ask his approval.

"Send acknowledgement of this and let us know as soon as you can that we are in agreement.

"Confirmation will be brought to you tonight by an officer."

Having read it Joffre added in his own handwriting:

"We will be in agreement to advance together in any case."

The words "Code telegram and officer follows" were appended and the message sent to the French Mission at Melun.

So anxious was Joffre to avoid all possibility of further confusion that the officer he sent to Melun to explain any points that might not be clear was his A.D.C., Commandant de Galbert.

This officer arrived at 5 a.m., two hours after the receipt at 3 a.m. of *Instruction Générale No. 6* by the French Mission.

De Galbert wasted his night's sleep. He only succeeded in reporting to Colonel Huguet, although his orders were to see Sir John French or at least his Chief of Staff. The Head of the Mission flatly refused to awaken them. It is possible he had learnt the lesson from previous experience that it was a precarious and dubious enterprise to disturb the slumbers of highly placed British officers; it is more probable he felt that if he himself were informed nothing further need be done till morning. As it turned out no harm was done, but had things gone wrong his responsibility would have been a grave one. To stand between a Liaison Officer who has a personal message to deliver and him for whom it is meant is a risk not to be lightly taken.

A similar incident had already occurred that night. As has already been noted, General Joffre's attack orders (*Instruction Générale No. 6*) were received by the French Mission at 3 a.m. and had been taken at once to General Wilson who, however, only showed them to Sir John French at 7 a.m.

Meanwhile, all night, while all but the officers on duty slept peacefully at Melun, the garrison of Paris poured out of the city and the Sixth Army marched, deploying facing east. These were vital hours, pregnant with the fate of nations. It was imperative that not a moment's delay should occur when it was a question of considering the implications of every new decision, every fresh move in this supreme game when the heritage of a thousand years was at stake, yet the Sub-Chief of Staff put this all important document by his bedside and only so far broke routine as to show it to his Chief before instead of after breakfast.

It was not, however, until 9.15 that Sir John French telegraphed his acceptance and agreed to retrace his steps and co-operate in the offensive, hours during which the French Army was being irretrievably committed to the great attack.

*   *   *

At Fifth Army Headquarters at Sézanne that evening there was strong, if suppressed, excitement. The new Commander had already infused something of his dynamic personality into all the Staff. Renewed confidence reigned, and there was a tendency to discount the danger still hanging over the Fifth Army. The continued retreat had assumed a new aspect. It was now the recoil before the spring.

*   *   *

We know from captured documents, prisoners' diaries, etc., that on the German side the officers and men of the German First Army were still very optimistic. This frame of mind was not shared by the Army Commander, as is shown by the following wireless message which he sent to the Supreme Command on this day:

"As a consequence of difficult and incessant fighting, the First Army has reached the limit of its strength. It is at this price only that it has been able to open the passages of the Marne to the other armies and to force the enemy to retreat.

"On this occasion the IX. Corps deserves the highest praise for the boldness of its operations. Now we may hope to exploit the success obtained.

"In the present situation it is not possible to conform to the order of the Supreme Command which prescribed that the First Army should follow the Second in echelon. The enemy can only be thrown back from Paris towards the south-east if the First Army moves forward. The necessity of covering the flank of the armies diminishes its offensive strength. Prompt reinforcements are urgently desired.

"Given the incessant changes in the situation, the First Army will only be able to take new and grave decisions if it is kept constantly informed of the situation of the other armies which appear to be further in the rear."

This was a grave message from the man who had deliberately elected to pursue the enemy, interpreting in that sense the contradictory order sent out by the Supreme Command on the night of the 2nd–3rd. (See Chapter XIII, September 2nd, p. 353).

In spite of this cry of alarm, von Kluck pressed forward with his usual energy during the whole of the 4th, and, on hearing that the Second Army was to advance on the 5th, decided to do likewise. No news of impending danger came to him. Once again the German Intelligence Service had failed.

CHAPTER XVII

THE EVE OF THE MARNE

September 5th, 1914

General d'Esperey's orders for the 6th – The British agree to play the part assigned to them by Joffre – Joffre at Melun – The British and the Sixth Army co-ordinate their plans – D'Esperey misinformed as to British intentions – D'Esperey's further orders for the 6th – His telegrams to Joffre – The situation of the Sixth Army – Lieut. de la Cornillière – Maunoury's orders to Lamaze – The Armies of the Right and Centre – Joffre's Order to the Armies – The German Supreme Command – Von Kluck receives his first warning of danger.

On the morning of the 5th the staff of the Fifth Army were in their offices before dawn. A start was made almost immediately for Romilly-sur-Seine, where we arrived before 6 a.m. On the way we passed columns of troops, amongst others the 110th Infantry Regiment, whose appearance, all things considered, was extremely good.

By 6 a.m. General d'Esperey had issued his orders. They were very simple:

"In view of the hazardous situation in which the First German Army has been placed, the General Commanding-in-Chief has pre-scribed, by an order received at 4 a.m. today, that the offensive against this army is to be launched tomorrow, September 6th, in conjunction with the British Army, the Sixth Army, and with the support of the Ninth Army (Foch's Army)."

The line to be occupied by the Army in view of the forthcoming offensive was then given, and is shown on Map XV, p. 416.

All the Corps, the XVIII. and the Group of Reserve Divisions in particular, were ordered to entrench themselves immediately on reaching their positions. The heavy artillery was to be moved up and placed in the zones of the corps to which it was attached (the III. and XVIII.), but the siege pieces (120 mm. long on platforms) were to remain south of the Seine, together with all transport not absolutely essential to the offensive.* All roads were to be kept clear so that there should be no delay in forwarding munitions and supplies.

By 11 a.m. General Joffre, whose H.Q. was now at Châtillon-sur-Seine, informed d'Esperey that the British had agreed to carry out his General Order No. 6 (*i.e.*, the order for the general offensive issued at 10 p.m. on the previous night, received by the British at 3 a.m. and by the Fifth Army at 4 a.m.) and would play the part assigned to them with but slight modifications of detail. The same telegram ordered General d'Esperey to carry out General Order No. 6 and to get in touch with the British Commander-in-Chief if he had not already done so. (A similar telegram was sent to the Sixth Army.) The vital and very welcome news of Sir John French's decision was conveyed in the following telephone message from the French Mission at British G.H.Q., timed 9.15 a.m.:

"The Marshal is going to conform to the intentions expressed in Order No. 6 of the G.Q.G., but by reason of the withdrawal carried out last night with the object of leaving more room for the Sixth Army to debouch south of the Marne, it will probably not be possible to occupy exactly the position Changis–Coulommiers but a position a little to the rear of it.

"The details of the marches are being studied. As soon as they are fixed they will be telegraphed to the G.Q.G.

"To sum up, tomorrow morning the British Army will be in position facing east but a little to the rear of the line at first assigned to it."

Nothing could be more definite. This message is evidence for all time that once the French Commander-in-Chief had made up his own mind and clearly conveyed his intention to Sir John French he obtained prompt and effective support from the British.

This message also disposes of all the legends concerning the further British withdrawal of the 4th. Sir John had carried out that movement fully and justifiably persuaded that he was acting in conformity with the Generalissimo's intentions and executing a necessary manœuvre to enable the Sixth Army to debouch. When General Joffre's Order No. 6

---

* The heavy artillery of the Army consisted of four batteries of 120 mm. long, six batteries 120 mm. short, and seven batteries 155 mm. short.

was received at 3 a.m. it was too late to countermand the orders issued the previous evening as a result of the Gallieni–Murray interview, for the II. Corps had begun its march at 10 p.m. on the 4th and the II. Corps at 3 a.m. on the 5th.

General Joffre's relief and gratitude on receiving Sir John's message were great, and a few minutes later he sent the following message to the French Mission at Melun:

"General Joffre is leaving for Melun, where he will arrive about 2 p.m. He wishes to make a point of going personally to thank Marshal French for the decision he has taken."

Just before receiving the promise of British co-operation General Joffre sent a long telegram to the Minister of War, which is worth reproducing *in extenso*:

"The situation which made me decide on a former occasion to refuse to engage a general battle, and to withdraw our armies towards the South has been modified in the following way:

"The First German Army has abandoned the direction of Paris and has deflected its march towards the south-east with a view to finding our left flank.

"Thanks to the steps taken it failed to find this flank, and the Fifth Army is now north of the Seine, ready to attack frontally the German columns.

"To its left the British forces are collected between Marne and Seine ready to attack. They will themselves be supported and flanked on their left by the mobile forces of the Paris garrison, acting in the direction of Meaux in such a way as to protect them (the British) from the threat of envelopment.

"The strategic situation is thus excellent, and we could not have better conditions for our offensive.

"That is why I have decided to attack.

"Marshal French has assured me that I can rely upon an energetic co-operation.

"A point of interrogation is nevertheless raised concerning the action of the British Army. Its Chief of Staff had an interview at Melun with the Governor of Paris whilst the Sub-Chief of Staff saw the Commander of the Fifth Army at Bray.

"The conclusions of these interviews appear to me to be somewhat divergent, but I have adopted dispositions capable of fitting in with either the one or the other of the solutions adopted.

"Be this as it may, the struggle which is about to take place may have decisive results, but may also have, in the case of a reverse, the gravest consequences for the country.

"To obtain victory I shall drive the blow home with all our forces, holding absolutely nothing back. It is essential that the British Army should act likewise, and I trust that you will be good enough to draw the Marshal's attention through diplomatic channels to the decisive importance of an offensive without *arrière pensée*.

"If I could give orders to the British Army as I would give them to a French Army holding the position it now occupies, I would attack immediately.*

"J. JOFFRE."

At about noon I had just located the mess where some food was available, when an orderly came up at the double saying General d'Esperey wanted to see Girard and myself. Girard, who had been ten minutes ahead of me and had had that much time to eat, came rushing out and we both proceeded at top speed to see the Army Commander.

We were told to go at once to Melun, get into touch with British G.H.Q., explain the orders issued by d'Esperey and find out the exact progress the British were making in the execution of Order No. 6. Further, General d'Esperey said that General Joffre was going to Melun and by hook or by crook we were to get there in time to see him. Girard was given a letter in which General d'Esperey placed before the Commander-in-Chief the suggestion that the Germans might anticipate the French offensive by themselves attacking. The Commander of the Fifth Army wished to know what his army was to do in such an eventuality.

A few minutes later we were on our way in a fast car, taking every sort of risk as we went. Some water in the petrol caused an exasperating delay, and at Nogent-sur-Seine we were involved in a terrible transport jam. Nevertheless we made quite good time, and on reaching Melun were directed to the Château of Vaux-le-Pénil, where the Field-Marshal was living. We arrived just in time to see the French Commander-in-Chief, accompanied by Gamelin, get out of his car. He walked straight

---

* All Joffre meant by this was that British co-operation was imperative. As has been seen it was materially impossible they should have attacked before they did. They were at the moment engaged in carrying out the manœuvre requested by General Gallieni. Further, as has been seen, Franchet d'Esperey had stated that he could not attack before the 6th.

into the Château, through the hall and into a small room where Sir
John stood awaiting him. There were not many officers present. I
remember besides the two Commanders, General Murray, General
Wilson, Major Clive, who was one of the liaison officers with the G.Q.G.,
keen-faced and intelligent, and Gamelin, smooth of face and of expression, but there were one or two more besides Girard and myself.

Everyone remained standing during the interview.

Sir John, with General Murray looking aloof and rather worried
almost behind him, stood by the corner of a table in the middle of the
room, facing the high French windows that gave on to the beautiful
park and the river beyond. General Wilson, tall, gaunt, his strange
enigmatical face expressionless at the moment, was on Sir John's right,
watching him.

General Joffre, his back half-turned to one of the windows, faced the
British Commander-in-Chief. He had placed his cap on the table.

At once he began to speak in that low, toneless, albino voice of his,
saying he had felt it his duty to come to thank Sir John personally for
having taken a decision on which the fate of Europe might well depend.
Sir John bowed. Then, without hurry or emphasis, Joffre explained the
situation, developing the story of the German advance, and the change
of direction of the First German Army. Here he interrupted his
narrative to say that the British Flying Corps had played a prominent,
in fact a vital part, in watching and following this all-important movement on which so much depended. Thanks to our aviators he had been
kept accurately and constantly informed of von Kluck's movements.
To them he owed the certainty which had enabled him to make his
plans in good time.

We looked at Sir John's face. Several officers were ready to translate,
and made as if to do so, but he signed that he had understood.

General Joffre, who had stopped speaking for a moment, began
again. He was now developing his plan. With one or two slight gestures
of his hands he explained what the Sixth Army was to do, and the action
of the Fifth Army.

We hung on his every word. We saw as he evoked it the immense
battlefield over which the corps, drawn by the magnet of his will, were
moving like pieces of intricate machinery until they clicked into their
appointed places. We saw trains in long processions labouring under the
weight of their human freight, great piles of shells mounting up by the
side of the ready and silent guns. And all this was taking place behind a
veil so thin and tenuous that none could perceive it, but through which

no German appeared able to see. Yet Joffre seemed to be pointing the Germans out to us – blundering blindly on, hastening to their fate, their huge, massive, dusty columns rushing towards the precipice over which they would soon be rolling.

Joffre was now foretelling what would happen on the morrow and on the day after and on the day after that, and as a prophet he was heard with absolute faith. We were listening to the story of the victory of the Marne, and we absolutely believed.

The atmosphere in the room grew tenser and tenser. General Joffre was talking now of the vital necessity of acting rapidly; the next twenty-four hours would be decisive. If not taken full advantage of at once, the opportunity, this great opportunity, would never occur again.

He spoke of the order he was issuing to his troops. The time for retreating was over. Those who could not advance were to die where they stood. No man was to give way even as much as a foot.

Again we saw the battlefield, the onward rush, the guns galloping up in the dust, the blinding flash; we heard the screech of bursting shells, and under the torn blue sky we saw the men who had been ordered to stand their ground falling on the thirsty earth and staining it with dusty dark red patches.

Joffre was now talking of the British. Again he thanked Sir John for his decision. His plan depended entirely upon British co-operation, its success on their action.

The still, even voice was eloquent now, with an intensity of feeling that drew our very souls out. British co-operation was demanded in words of exalted eloquence inspired by the feeling and the truth within the man. Everything the British could give, all they had, was asked for.

Then, turning full on Sir John, with an appeal so intense as to be irresistible, clasping both his own hands so as to hurt them, General Joffre said:

"Monsieur le Maréchal, c'est la France qui vous supplie."

His hands fell to his sides wearily. The effort he had made had exhausted him.

We all looked at Sir John. He had understood and was under the stress of strong emotion. Tears stood in his eyes, welled over and rolled down his cheeks.

He tried to say something in French. For a moment he struggled with his feelings and with the language, then turning to an English officer, I

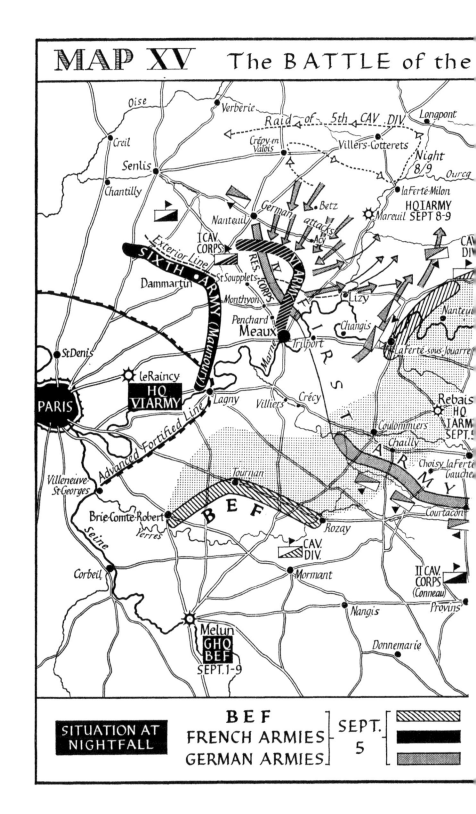

MAP XV   The BATTLE of the

Oise

Verberie

Raid of 5th CAV. DIV.

Longpont

Creil

Crépy-en-Valois

Villers-Cotterets

Night 8/9

Senlis

Ourcq

Chantilly

la Ferté-Milon

HQ ARMY Mareuil SEPT 8-9

Nanteuil

German attacks

Betz

Acy

CAV. DIV

I CAV. CORPS

Exterior Line

SIXTH ARMY (Maunoury)

RES. CORPS

St Soupplets

IV ARMY

Dammartin

Monthyon

Lizy

Nanteu

Penchard

Changis

Meaux

F

St Denis

Trilport

Marne

I

le Raincy

R

HQ VI ARMY

Lagny

Villiers

Crécy

S

Rebais

PARIS

Advanced Fortified Line

T

HQ I ARMY SEPT.

Coulommiers

Chailly

A

Choisy la Ferté Gauche

Villeneuve-St-Georges

Tournan

R

Brie-Comte-Robert

B E F

M

Yerres

Rozay

Courtacon

Y

Seine

CAV. DIV.

Corbeil

Mormant

II CAV. CORPS (Conneau)

Provins

Nangis

Melun GHQ BEF SEPT. 1-9

Donnemarie

B E F
FRENCH ARMIES
GERMAN ARMIES

SEPT. 5

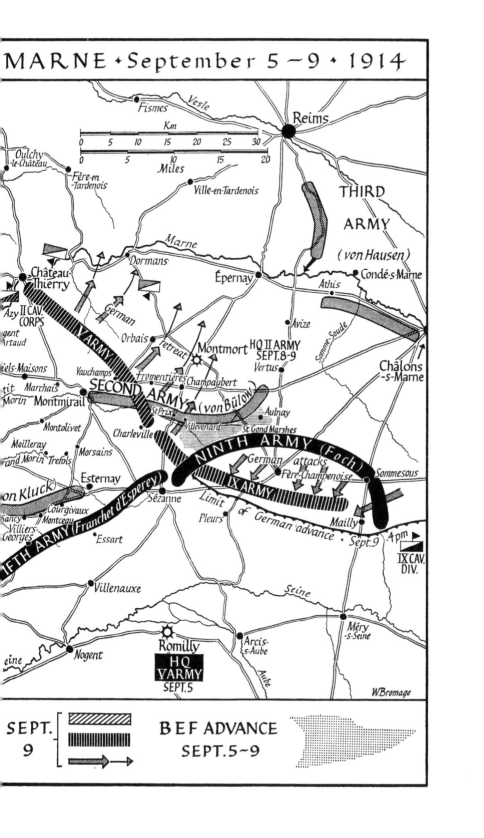

MARNE · September 5–9 · 1914

Fismes
Vesle
Reims

THIRD

ARMY

(von Hausen)

Km
0 5 10 15 20 25 30

Miles
0 5 10 15 20

Oulchy
-le-Château

Fère-en
-Tardenois

Ville-en-Tardenois

Marne

Dormans

Château-
Thierry

Azy II CAV
CORPS

gent
Artaud

German

V ARMY

Orbais

retreat

Vauchamps

Fromentières
Champaubert

SECOND ARMY

(von Bülow)

St Prix

els-Maisons

tit Marchais
Morin Montmirail

Montolivet

Morsains

Meilleray
and Morin Trefols

Charleville

Villevenard
St Gond Marshes

on Kluck

Courgivaux
Montceau

ancy
Villiers-
Georges

Esternay

FTH ARMY (Franchet d'Esperey)

Sézanne

Essart

Villenauxe

Epernay

Athis
Condé-s-Marne

Avize

Montmort HQ II ARMY
SEPT. 8-9
Vertus

Somme-Soude

Châlons
-s-Marne

Aulnay

NINTH ARMY (Foch)

German attacks

Fère-Champenoise

IX ARMY

Limit

Pleurs

of German advance · Sept. 9

Mailly

Sommesous

4pm

IX CAV.
DIV.

Seine

Romilly
HQ
V ARMY
SEPT. 5

Nogent

Arcis-
s-Aube

Aube

Méry
-s-Seine

W. Bromage

eine

Villenauxe

SEPT.
9

BEF ADVANCE
SEPT. 5~9

think it was Major Clive, who stood beside him, he exclaimed: "Damn it, I can't explain. Tell him that all that men can do our fellows will do."

There was an immediate anti-climax.

Sir Archibald Murray, evidently preoccupied by the practical difficulties involved and determined to avoid any possible misunderstanding, stepped forward to the side of Sir John and said coldly that it was quite impossible for the British to advance at 6 a.m. as General Joffre had asked. They could not be ready before 9 a.m. This was translated to Joffre. "It cannot be helped," he said with a tired shrug and movement of the hands. "Let them start as soon as they can. I have the Marshal's word, that is enough for me," and slowly, as one who is very tired, his head rather sunk and looking down, he made his way out of the room.

Girard went up to Gamelin and handed him d'Esperey's letter. Joffre was drawn aside to consider it. He beckoned Girard to him, and told him to tell d'Esperey that his mission on the following day was to form a barrage and to hang on at all costs to start with, then to engage his troops prudently and attack *à fond* as soon as he thought the action of the British Army had made itself felt. General Joffre added: "Tell General d'Esperey I rely upon him to do everything that it is possible to do, and I know I can count on him."

He added that an officer of the Fifth Army should be sent in liaison to the British Army next morning. (This duty was to fall upon Girard and myself.)

General Joffre then drove off.

Girard and I went back to Melun to find out the exact situation of the British forces. We ascertained that the British Army was to advance in three echelons preceded by its cavalry. (The note of what we were told is still in existence.)

The Army was to advance first on Rebais, then on Montmirail. The Cavalry which had moved from the left to the right of the Army was to get into touch with Conneau's Cavalry Corps.*

We found that General Maunoury had visited Sir John in the morning, and that the Sixth Army would be on the line of the Ourcq next morning by 9 a.m., from Lizy-sur-Ourcq to May-en-Multien. General Maunoury was in absolute agreement with the British Commander-in-Chief. It had been settled between them that the British Army should

---

* The only point of importance that arose subsequently was that at 7 p.m. Huguet reported the following modifications in the hours previously settled:

"The I. Corps was to be in position at 9 a.m. instead of at 8 a.m., and the II. and III. Corps at 10 a.m. instead of at 9 a.m. on the 6th."

advance on Rebais as soon as the Sixth Army gained a footing on the eastern bank of the Ourcq.*

The liaison between the Sixth Army and the British could hardly have been improved upon, for General Gallieni, reporting at 6.50 p.m. declared it to be perfect. This message concluded: "*Demain, en avant.*"

Having got into touch with most of the sections of the British Staff, we returned to the Fifth Army by roads encumbered with troops and transport.

We were both thinking of the interview at which we had assisted, and of the battle of the morrow, but little was said. I vaguely remember the remark that one day that meeting would probably furnish the theme of a great historical picture.

Not far from Romilly-sur-Seine we met a British officer, Baird, who signed to us to stop and jumped out of his car. "Your General" (Franchet d'Esperey), he said to me, "is in a terrible rage and fearfully upset. I have just seen him. Y (a British officer), who knows nothing about the plans, strolled into his H.Q. this afternoon, apparently under the impression, having seen some of our transport moving back, that the retreat was continuing. Anyway, when asked how far forward our troops had got, he calmly asserted that our Army was continuing to retire, and on d'Esperey protesting that this could not be so, said he had himself seen the troops falling back."

I exclaimed that everything was settled and that of course we were going to advance. "Well," said Baird, "you had better see d'Esperey as soon as you can. He is terribly angry and puzzled. He said he was going to hold up his orders for the advance of his own army."

We sped on faster than ever, and as soon as we arrived at Romilly I went at once to see the Army Commander.

He certainly was in a rage. Vainly did I point out that orders for the British advance next day had already been issued, and that there was no shadow of a doubt concerning British intentions, that it was impossible there should have been a change, that we came straight from British G.H.Q., and finally that Y, in spite of his rank and staff uniform, was totally unaware of what was on foot. D'Esperey would not listen. He said some very bitter, some unacceptable things concerning the British Commander-in-Chief in particular and the British in general.

I withdrew and telephoned to either the Chief or the Sub-Chief of

* Colonel Huguet in reporting the interview to General Gallieni at 11 a.m. added that it was the intention of Sir John to remain a little behind the Sixth Army. There was no question of any such thing when we were at Melun. General Maunoury in reporting to General Joffre never mentioned it, nor does it appear in any document other than this despatch.

Staff at Melun, who assured me that nothing was changed. Girard had probably been heard meanwhile, the atmosphere was calmer, my assurances were accepted, and orders issued for next day.

When sufficient time had elapsed to permit of the matter being considered calmly, I went to the Chief of Staff and requested an apology for what had been said concerning my Chief, stating that if this were not forthcoming I would leave Fifth Army H.Q. and would not be replaced. This I did in fear and trembling lest my action should be disowned by G.H.Q., but I was convinced it was essential for British prestige not to allow the incident to pass. The apology was given and my action subsequently upheld by Sir John French. The incident was never mentioned again, and relations between the two Staffs remained correct as long as the two armies were neighbours. A few days later I ventured to suggest to Sir John French that he should visit General d'Esperey, as the first gesture had been made by the French General when he proposed the meeting at Bray. This Sir John did.

As for the author of the mischief, Girard and I were told to inform British G.H.Q. that if Y was ever reported to be in the area of the Fifth Army he would immediately be shot. We gave this message to General Murray.

Later in the war I was greatly surprised when, meeting General d'Esperey, he exclaimed: "Well, and how is our excellent friend Y?" It seemed that by then Y, who had long since given up roving commissions and had exercised a command with distinction, had become quite a friend of his.

The orders issued by General d'Esperey were timed 6.30 p.m., and ran as follows:

"Tomorrow, September 6th, the Fifth Army will attack the First German Army frontally, whilst the British and Sixth Army will attack it in flank and threaten its retreat.

"On the success of this operation may depend the end of the first part of the campaign.

"The Fifth Army will attack in echelon, the right forward in the general direction of Montmirail. It will be supported on the right by the Ninth Army (General Foch).

"The operation will probably last several days. Corps Commanders will take the greatest care not to engage all their infantry at the outset." (Map XV, p. 426.)

The order went on:

"The advance is to begin for all Corps and the Cavalry Corps at 6 a.m. For the Reserve Divisions 7 a.m.

"If the enemy attacks in strength before we ourselves attack, the troops will stand their ground, and will resist with the utmost energy on the entrenched positions now occupied by the heads of the main bodies. The attack will be launched at the time given above.

"The attack will be supported –

"(1) On the left by the Cavalry Corps which will act in constant and *intimate* liaison with the XVIII. Corps. *It will take an effective part in the battle.*

"(2) On the right by the Ninth Army . . .

"The two corps on the wings (Cavalry Corps and X. Corps) will keep in constant touch, the one (Cavalry Corps) with the British Army whose cavalry will be at 8 a.m. on the 6th about Jouy-le-Châtel, the other (X. Corps) with the Ninth Army."

Then followed the allocation of the bridges over the Seine to the Corps.*

The order concluded:

"All impedimenta will be sent back. Only munitions, supplies for the day, and the sanitary formations will be allowed to follow the troops . . .

"All civilian conveyances must be pitilessly thrown off the roads

---

* The objectives of the Corps of the Fifth Army were given as follows in this order:
"XVIII. Corps will advance its right along the road Villiers-St. Georges–Baleine–le Vézier; general direction – Sancy–Meilleray–Montolivet. Corps reserves echelonned to the left rear.

"Group of Reserve Divisions will follow in second line between the XVIII. and III. Corps, resting its left on the road Villiers-St. Georges–Baleine, in readiness to support the neighbouring corps.

"III. Corps. General direction: Courgivaux–Tréfols–Marchais-en-Brie; one division to follow in second line as Army Reserve, behind the right of the III. Corps.

"I. Corps. General direction: les Essarts-le-Vicomte–Esternay–Champguyon–Montmirail.

"X. Corps. General direction: Moeurs–Soigny–Vauchamps, establishing contact on the Lachy-Charleville road with the 42nd Division (Ninth Army), the advance to be carried out by two linked divisions, the right division forming echelon to the front, the 51st Reserve Division following, at the beginning of the operation, to the right rear."

The Ninth Army was ordered to have a strong advance guard, from its left hand division, the 42nd, at Villeneuve-les-Charleville, on the 5th, ready to operate on the 6th in the direction of Vauchamps. The IX. Corps was to be ready to operate in the direction of Baye.

and no military conveyances are to be allowed to remain stationary on the roads save those belonging to the heavy artillery."

It was expressly stated that Corps Commanders as they advanced their H.Q.'s were to inform Army H.Q. of their new positions, and that communications by telegram or telephone must remain uninterrupted.

The different H.Q.'s were then fixed, and the order ended with these words:

"It is important that every soldier should know before the battle that the honour of France and the salvation of the homeland depend upon the energy he displays in tomorrow's fighting.

"The country relies upon every man to do his duty. *Any weakness will be punished immediately with all the rigour of martial law*: acts of courage and energy will be reported without delay so that they may be rewarded on the spot."

Later each Corps was told to send small detachments to guard the bridges allocated to them.

As far as the preparation of a position south of the Seine was concerned, little was done beyond digging a few trenches at four or five strong points (*centres de résistance*).

At 9.45 p.m. General Franchet d'Esperey was able to send the following cipher telegram to the G.Q.G.:

"All measures taken to attack tomorrow, direction Montmirail. Very energetic and very rapid action by Sixth Army is essential to success plan envisaged. Request you insistently give it positive order in this sense. Fifth Army starting from front Sézanne–Courchamp."

The line occupied that night by the Fifth Army is shown on Map XV, p. 426.

All the movements during the day were carried out undisturbed by the enemy and without incident, save that other corps frequently borrowed the roads allotted to the Group of Reserve Divisions, with the result that their commander reported that an intolerable strain was being imposed upon troops who had reached several days before the furthest limit of endurance.

Tactical instructions for the following day were issued in the evening.*

These clearly show that the faults committed in the earlier stages of

* For these instructions see Appendix XXXIV.

the campaign had been detected, but it is lamentable to think that such very simple commonsense rules should have had to be laid down at all, especially as there was extremely little chance of their arriving in time to be applied on the morrow. Happily both subordinate commanders and troops had learnt some lessons for themselves and worked out methods which, without being in any way ideal, were far removed from the follies of the early days of August.

The circumstances under which the Sixth Army was being marshalled for its heavy task were none too favourable.*

As events developed, this Army, which was to have provided the left hand punch of the allied attack, became the fulcrum of the whole battle, against which the trapped German forces surged and raged in their effort to shake themselves free. (Map XV, p. 426.)

At the eleventh hour a new difficulty arose. The IV. Corps was to have joined up at latest on the previous day, but owing to the difficulties of entraining in the Argonne in face of an advancing enemy, difficulties complicated by the destruction of railway lines and general congestion, only one division of this Corps, the 8th, had detrained north-west of Paris, and that was in a bad state. Its commander reported his troops to be worn out. They had fought for two days, marched for two days, and had had a long railway journey. Reservists had been poured in until the companies were three hundred strong and quite beyond what the depleted cadres could deal with.† The Commander requested forty-eight hours rest for his men, saying the offensive power of the division was small, and that it might become disorganized if engaged too soon.

In spite of this General Gallieni ordered the division to march next day (the 6th) to the east of Paris, where the remainder of the Corps was being detrained.

In the course of the afternoon General Maunoury committed two mistakes. At 3 p.m. he reported to General Gallieni that his troops had reached a line‡ which in reality they were far short of and did not even occupy by evening.

---

* It consisted on this date of the VII. Corps, 5th Group of Reserve Divisions, 55th and 56th Reserve Divisions, 45th Division, Moroccan Brigade, the Provisional Cavalry Division and Sordet's Cavalry Corps.

† This question of over-reinforced units came up at different times during the war. On the whole it was proved that, in the case of units which had to be immediately engaged, it was worse policy, because more wasteful, to over-reinforce units than to leave them under strength. Experience proved it to be essential to give the new men time to be absorbed into their units. There is nothing to be said in favour of units so swollen as to be unwieldy.

‡ Penchard–Monthyon–St. Soupplets–Lessart–Eve and Ver.

Secondly, he issued his orders for the next day at 4 p.m., although he had little information concerning either his own troops or the enemy on his front. As a matter of fact, some of the troops were checked whilst others suffered a reverse.*

During the fighting in this quarter a battalion of the 276th Regiment was ordered to charge to disengage the Moroccans, who were retiring. The captain in command was instantly killed as he led his men at the double over absolutely open ground under a withering machine-gun fire. The command devolved on Lieut. de la Cornillière, who led his men forward a couple of hundred yards. The men then lay down, but he remained standing directing the fire. In the middle of giving the order: "At five hundred yards independent fire," he fell mortally wounded. A colour-sergeant who dashed to his rescue was instantly killed. There were cries amongst the men: "The lieutenant is killed, the lieutenant is killed," and some signs of panic. Then Lieut. de la Cornillière made a supreme effort, and raising himself to his knees, shouted: "Yes, he is killed, but advance all the same," then, as the men sprang forward, he fell dead.

*   *   *

General Maunoury, having by evening obtained some idea of what had happened during the afternoon, and fully realizing the vital importance of the mission assigned to the Sixth Army, sent a message to General de Lamaze commanding the 5th Group of Reserve Divisions. Maunoury, evidently fearful lest a local check might slow up the advance of the Army upon which so much depended, reminded Lamaze that the mission assigned to the Sixth Army was an offensive "*à fond*". Lamaze was told to renew his attacks before daylight next day at those points where this could be done with advantage.†

It has been seen that General Joffre had assigned to Foch's Ninth Army an important role in the attack of the allied line. The Ninth

---

* Towards evening the advance guards of the VII. Corps did reach the line assigned them, but the Reserve Divisions met with serious resistance and were unable to occupy St. Soupplets, Monthyon and Penchard. Worse still, the Moroccan Regiments were thrown into some confusion and driven back a considerable distance. The Provisional Cavalry Division had to be called in to support the right of the Reserve Divisions, whilst the Moroccan Regiments were reformed behind its protection. The Provisional Cavalry Division was to have rejoined Sordet but had not done so.

† The right of the VII. Corps was to make its action felt at daybreak, and a brigade of the 45th Division was sent to support the right of the Reserve Divisions. General de Lamaze was told to make use of all the means at his disposal, including the Provisional Cavalry Division, to carry out a vigorous attack that must lead to the Ourcq.

Army was at nightfall on the 5th in the neighbourhood of the Marshes of St. Gond. General Foch informed the G.Q.G. that on September 6th he intended, whilst holding the Marshes of St. Gond and defending the approaches from Châlons and Vertus, to attack north-west in conjunction with the Fifth Army.

Although the main attack was to be delivered by the armies of the left, the armies of the right and centre had important parts to play in Joffre's plan. (See Map XVI, p. 426.)

The Fourth Army was to hold the enemy whilst the Third Army on its right made a drive westward into the flank of the German forces marching to the west of the Argonne.

Castelnau's Second Army was to defend its positions at all costs. Considerable anxiety was being caused by the violent attacks to which it had been subjected since the evening of the 4th.

A glance at Map XVI, p. 426 will make clear how important Castelnau's role was. If he failed to hold the Couronné of Nancy the enemy would find the way open for an advance in rear of the main French line. On the other hand, the very violence and strength of the German attacks against the Second Army were reassuring from the point of view of Joffre's plan, for whilst they continued the enemy could not parry Joffre's manœuvre by withdrawing troops to meet it. The danger was that Castelnau might not be able to hang on long enough to enable Joffre to drive his blow home.

On the afternoon of the 5th Castelnau reported that he was still being hard pressed, especially on the Grand Couronné of Nancy, and that, owing to the fact that the enemy's artillery, which had been further reinforced by a siege train, was greatly superior to his own in numbers, power and range, he could not guarantee a prolonged resistance. He submitted two alternatives to the Commander-in-Chief.

1st. He could, if the enemy pressed his attack home, resist on his present lines, but then his units would lose all fighting value for the future.

2nd. He could break off the fight and fall back on two successive positions which he indicated, lasting out as long as possible whilst continuing to cover the right of the line.

General de Castelnau expressed his preference for the second alternative, and, whilst awaiting orders, prepared to carry it out.

On the evening of the 5th the enemy again attacked on the Couronné of Nancy, in spite of a counter-attack by the XX. Corps.

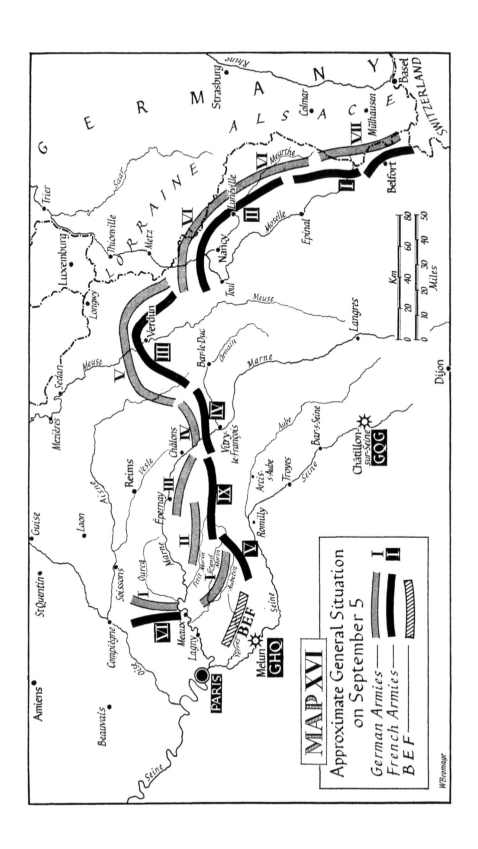

It was not till the following day, the 6th, that General Joffre answered General de Castelnau.

He told him that the principal mass of the allied forces were engaged in a general battle too far removed from the Second Army for the latter to participate in it. Under these circumstances General Joffre preferred the first alternative, but added that he approved of the steps General de Castelnau proposed to take in the event of being compelled to abandon the Grand Couronné of Nancy.

Meanwhile, behind the battle line, troops withdrawn from other fronts were being rushed forward to the vital points as fast as an over-taxed and disorganized railway system would allow.

The IV. Corps detraining near Paris has already been mentioned.

The XV. Corps from the Second Army, 24 hours late, was being sent on with the utmost speed to General Sarrail.*

Individual units, especially infantry, were rushed forward anyhow, as they came up.

The XXI. Corps (from the First Army) was also in the zone of the Third Army, but remained at the disposal of the Commander-in-Chief.

* * *

General Joffre, confident that his plan was well and truly laid and that he had chosen the right moment to throw down his challenge to the invader, issued a proclamation to the troops breathing the determination and the conviction that inspired him.

"At the moment when the battle upon which hangs the fate of the country is about to begin, all must remember that the time for looking back is past; every effort must be concentrated on attacking and throwing the enemy back.

"Troops which can no longer advance must at any cost keep the ground that has been won, and must die where they stand rather than give way.

"Under present conditions no weakness can be tolerated.†

"J. JOFFRE."

* * *

* The Commander of the Third Army.

† This order was not sent to the First and Second Armies as not being in conformity with their instructions.

The German Supreme Command had issued orders to all the Armies which were received on the evening of the 5th.

These were an amplification of a wireless message which ran as follows:

"The First and Second Armies will remain on the eastern front of Paris, the First between Oise and Marne, holding the passages of the Marne west of Château–Thierry; the Second Army between Marne and Seine, holding the passages of the Seine between Nogent and Méry inclusive. The Third Army will march to Troyes and to the east of it."

As will be seen below, the Supreme Command was aware of the possibility of a French attack from Paris. It is extraordinary that on mention of such a contingency is found in this wireless message which was by way of being a summary of the order. The explanation probably is that no immediate danger was anticipated.

Kluck and Bülow received this wireless on the morning of the 5th. Bülow (whose Army had only been ordered to carry out a short march on the 5th owing to the Third Army having fallen behind) took steps to obey it. He halted and began to wheel gradually so as to change front from south to west. He believed von Kluck would conform, but the latter concluded that the best means of parrying any danger there might be in the west was to attack straight before him, and he so informed the German Great Headquarters. In any case, had he acted as the Supreme Command desired and taken up a position between the Oise and the Marne, he would have had to withdraw for two days, as his main force was already south of the Marne. Von Kluck, reasoning that to halt would give the enemy time to reorganize, ignored his own pessimistic message of the 4th,* and pressed on. He still believed that it was possible to throw the enemy back over the Seine, the First and Second Armies waiting till then to wheel and face Paris.

In the evening, von Kluck received the full text of the Supreme Command Order, the opening paragraphs of which ran as follows:

"To all the Armies,
"The enemy has evaded the enveloping attack of the First and Second Armies, and a part of his forces has joined up with those about Paris. From reports and other information, it appears that the enemy is moving troops westwards from Toul–Belfort, and is also taking them from the front of the Third, Fourth and Fifth Armies. The

* See Chapter XVI, p. 408.

attempt to force the whole French Army back in a south-easterly direction towards the Swiss frontier is thus rendered impracticable. It is probable that the enemy will bring up new formations and concentrate numerous forces in the neighbourhood of Paris, to protect the capital and to threaten the right flank of the German Army.

"The First and Second Armies must therefore remain facing the eastern front of Paris. Their task is to oppose any operations of the enemy from the neighbourhood of Paris and to give each other mutual support to this end."

He then made an attempt to stop the IV. Reserve Corps which was acting as flank guard, but his orders did not reach it until it had completed its march for the day. The Second Cavalry Corps was also ordered to halt.

The news during the day had been reassuring for von Kluck. There was no sign of danger on the right flank, and reports came in that the Allies were continuing to withdraw along the whole front. At 10 p.m., although persuaded there was no immediate cause for alarm, he began in leisurely fashion to conform to the orders of the Supreme Command.*

---

* These orders met with the approval of the liaison officer of the Supreme Command, Lieut.-Colonel Hentsch, who arrived in the evening, and reported as follows:

"The general situation was dubious. The left wing was held up before Nancy-Épinal, and, in spite of heavy losses, could not get on. The Fourth and Fifth Armies were only making slow progress. Apparently transfers of troops were being made from the French right wing in the direction of Paris. It was reported that further British troops were about to land, perhaps at Ostend. Assistance to Antwerp by the British was possible."

"When Colonel Hentsch was informed of the preparations that had been made to stop the advance, he said 'that they corresponded to the wishes of O.H.L. and that the movement could be made at leisure; no special haste was necessary.'

"At 10 p.m. von Kluck gave the following orders preparatory to getting into position between the Marne and Oise to face Paris. They were to take effect at 5 a.m. next day. Whilst his left Corps, the IX., and the flank guard stood fast, the other three Corps were to face about, and begin wheeling to the right on the IX. Corps. Very full directions were given as regards transport, which was to be got clear at once; the withdrawal was to be covered by the 2nd and 9th Cavalry Divisions and weak rear-guards of the II. and IV. Corps on the Grand Morin. In detail, the III. Corps was to march on La Ferté-Gaucher, the IV. to Doué and the II. in two columns to Isles-les-Meldeuses and Germigny, in the loop south of the Marne, north-east of Meaux.

"On receipt during the night of the information that the IV. Reserve Corps had been in action with strong French forces, instructions were sent to General von Linsingen, commanding the II. Corps, to start as soon as possible to its assistance, and his two divisions crossed the Marne at Vereddes and the Ourcq at Lizy, respectively, and co-operated with the IV. Reserve Corps on the 6th. During the day the IV. Corps also, instead of halting at Doué, was moved back over the Marne north of La Férte-sous-Jouarre, and at 10.30 p.m. was ordered to make a night march to the assistance of the right wing. Thus by the morning of the 7th, the II., IV. and IV. Reserve Corps were engaged against Maunoury, but the III. and IX. Corps were still south of the Marne."

(*Official History of the War*, Vol. I, p. 297.)

On hearing that the IV. Reserve Corps had been in action against strong forces during the afternoon of the 5th (the fighting about St. Soupplets), he immediately issued orders to hasten the movements of the different Corps, but by then it was too late; the blow was about to fall with practically no warning.

CHAPTER XVIII

WHAT MADE THE VICTORY
OF THE MARNE POSSIBLE

The Miracle of the Marne – Italian neutrality – French casualties in officers –
The 75s – The part played by the British – The mistakes of the Germans –
Gallieni, Maunoury, Foch and d'Esperey – Joffre – His plan – The situation on
the Eve of the Battle – A brief outline of the action.

I t had been my intention to close my narrative on September 5th with
the end of the Retreat, when hundreds of thousands of weary men were
holding themselves in readiness for the great offensive. It may, however,
be useful to the reader who has followed me so far to give a summary of
the battle, together with some notes and orders which may not be
generally known. A few, a very few incidents which came under my
personal observation have also been added.

I have in no way attempted a critical military study of the battle,
still less to give an impression of the "atmosphere" of the Marne. Deeds
speak for themselves. The achievement of those men, whose courage
transformed defeat into victory, who learnt the secret of modern warfare
in retreat and forged the will to win as they withdrew, entitles them to
a place in history by the side of the hosts of the past who in their day
also saved a civilization: the men of Marathon, the soldiers of Aëtius
who finally defeated the Huns in 451, and those who at Poitiers drove
the Moors back into Spain.

What made the victory of the Marne possible? Factors of a psychological
as well as of a material order, brain and brawn, courage physical and
moral, at least one political factor, but above all the impulse of a great
and ably seconded leader carrying out a well-conceived plan. To these
elements might perhaps be added luck, if the enemy's mistakes and the
ability to take advantage of them may be so called.

The political factor, often forgotten but never underestimated by
Joffre himself, concerned Italy. Had not Joffre been certain that the

Italians would remain neutral he would have been compelled to leave on the Franco-Italian frontier troops without whom the Battle of Marne could not have been fought.*

The Marne has been called a miracle. The world wondered to see a great victory born of a great defeat, a defeat which indeed seemed to have developed into an irremediable rout.

The Germans themselves were certainly the actors who were the most taken aback by the *dénouement* of the tragedy they had so carefully staged.

It seems to me that the real miracle was the feat of the French private soldier. The battle proved the genius of the French race for instantaneous comprehension and adaptability. It is hardly too much to say that when they fought in the latter half of August the troops though well disciplined knew less than nothing. The little training they had had served but to bewilder and confuse them. Yet in a fortnight of almost unparalleled disasters they succeeded in so altering and improving their methods that their tactics became at least equal to those of their opponents. No people but the French – the most adaptable and intelligent race in the world – having started so badly could in so short a time have learnt so much.

Had the French attacked at the Marne as they did at Charleroi, they could not have advanced, and all Joffre's strategy could not have won the battle.

Moreover the French troops adapted themselves to a new conception of warfare, whilst suffering under one of the greatest disabilities from which an Army can suffer, a great dearth of officers. Their losses in the commissioned ranks were enormous. Near Reims one day General d'Esperey, watching a long infantry column march by, company after company led by a second lieutenant or an N.C.O., seemed for once to lose control, and lifting his arms, exclaimed – "*Mais où sont mes officiers, où sont mes officiers!*"

During the month of August alone, 1,041 officers were killed, 2,679 wounded, and 1,058 reported missing, in all 4,478, that is ten to eleven per cent of the total strength of 44,500 officers both regular and reserve.

These figures apply to the Army as a whole, so that the proportion of losses in the infantry was far higher. Some examples may be given. At the engagement of Flaxon on August 19th, the 26th Division lost two-thirds of its officers. On August 24th at Neufchâteau the 21st Regiment lost 37 officers out of a total of 65.

---

* The Army of the Alps consisted of five regular divisions and one Territorial Division. Its commander was General d'Amade. It was dissolved on August 17th.

The fact that there were so many educated men in the ranks stood the French in good stead in making good this deficiency. A crop of excellent subaltern officers was immediately forthcoming from amongst the men themselves.

A "moral" factor of great importance should not be overlooked – the 75s. The deadliness of their high explosives and the rapidity of their fire, immediately established their ascendancy as field pieces. But the German howitzers and heavy artillery were as superior to those of the French as the 75s were to the German 77 mm.; the two might have cancelled each other but that the French infantryman trusted his guns and believed they could do anything, shatter resistance and defeat attack, which indeed they often did.* The reliance that the private soldier placed on these weapons made them a factor of the highest psychological importance.

The most superficial study of the battle shows that the victory of the Marne could not have been won without the British Army. No soldier, French or German, would deny this, but politicians and journalists have taught the French nation to believe that the role of the British during the battle was negligible, and that the Marne was entirely a French victory. Nothing could be further from the truth. I have shown Joffre's extreme anxiety concerning British participation, which he considered of vital importance. His plan would have collapsed at its inception without their co-operation.

Fortunately the B.E.F. found itself where its superior training made it most effective. Although it had received incomparably rougher treatment during the retreat than any other part of the allied line, and had had to face an enemy far more numerous than had opposed any other Army, it was still, in the opinion of many competent enemy observers, the most formidable force for its size on the western front.

During its advance it had to overcome considerable obstacles and deal with serious and well organized resistance in country admirably adapted to defence. On the ground over which the B.E.F. advanced the 75s would have proved no substitute for the British soldier, admirably trained to manœuvre and whose fire capacity was so superior to that of

---

* The accounts of the First, Second, Third and Fourth German Armies all say that they were held back by the French artillery. The Second, Third and Fifth Armies all made dawn and night attacks in order to avoid its fire.

friend or foe that the enemy were constantly mistaking our rapid fire for machine-gun fire.

British Cavalry, rapid moving, armed with the same kind of rifle as the infantry and trained to fight dismounted, was able to play a role the French Cavalry would have been incapable of, in spite of its dash and gallantry.

The opposition encountered by the B.E.F. was less stubborn than that encountered by either the Sixth Army or the right of the Fifth Army, but it would have held up for longer troops less well-trained than the British.

The only criticism which may perhaps survive when present-day incomprehension and – it is not too strong a word – ingratitude, due to lack of knowledge, have been dissipated, is that the British suffered at this stage from an excessive prudence in leadership, a prudence engendered by bitter previous experience. Nevertheless the British Army crossed the Marne thirty hours before any French infantry.

The major strategic mistakes of the Germans are dealt with elsewhere, but no attempt to sum up the considerations affecting the Marne would be complete without reference to their consistent weakening of their right wing.

Two corps, some 80,000 men, were immobilized by Antwerp and by fantastic yarns of British and even Russian landings on the Belgian coast. Two more corps were withdrawn to face the Russian threat against East Prussia, but did not get there until after the Battle of Tannenburg. Had they remained in the west, their intervention might have been decisive, as it was they were entirely wasted. Yet another corps was besieging Maubeuge. All these troops belonged to the right wing, which was further weakened in a greater degree than any other German forces by having to guard longer lines of communication, which moreover were on the exposed flank.*

* The wastage caused by the fatigues of the advance, and the necessity of leaving troops on the lines of communication, as well as the difficulty the Germans found in replacing the casualties, is shown by the strength of some of the German Corps during the battle, which was as follows:

VII. Corps	14,522
X. Reserve Corps	12,774
X. Corps	10,839
Guard Corps	12,366
32nd Division	6,566
XII. Reserve Corps	17,165

The establishment of a Division was 17,500 and of a Corps about 36,000 men. No corps, therefore, except the XII. Reserve was up to half establishment.

The Germans were slow to repair their error in weakening their right. Von Moltke, who had hoped to trap the French Armies between the Sixth and Seventh Armies on the left, and the First and Second Armies on the right, while the Third, Fourth and Fifth Armies contained or drove in the French centre, persisted in his barren attacks in Lorraine against Castelnau, when every available man should have been sent to meet the deadly allied thrust. It was not until September 9th that at last two corps were withdrawn from this front to be sent to the west.

That von Kluck was compelled to face west under the pressure of Maunoury's attacks while von Bülow withdrew his right, thereby increasing the gap between the First and Second German Armies, also decisively contributed to the German defeat.

Whilst the Germans were piling mistake on mistake, and their Army Commanders, in surly aloofness, were enclosed in watertight compartments, the French Generals were working in the closest and most enthusiastic accord. General Joffre's task was greatly facilitated by the energy, organizing ability and intelligent anticipation displayed by General Gallieni, the courage of Maunoury and the dogged will to victory of Foch, and not least, by the emergence at the supreme moment of decision of that dynamic personality, General Franchet d'Esperey.

Not only did he galvanize his weary troops, saturated by the depression of retreat, into a fighting force in which every man suddenly became the equal, then the superior, of his erstwhile pursuer, not only did he drive his victorious and stubborn opponents before him, but, as has been seen, he elaborated a plan which fitted in exactly with the Generalissimo's own conception, a plan which he declared he could and would carry out, in which nothing was left vague, and which laid down precisely when and how he himself, the commander of the force which had been in greatest danger, could turn on the enemy.

But when all these elements have been assessed, one figure emerges, dominating the greatest battle of all time – Joffre: for the Battle of the Marne was essentially Joffre's achievement.

After the disastrous mistakes and miscalculations of the beginning of the campaign, General Joffre, although weighed down by the responsibility of having to abandon France's fairest provinces to the invader, set himself with admirable fortitude to build, laboriously and obstinately, an instrument with which he could strike back.

Massive and enigmatic, he watched hour by hour the respective positions of his own and his adversaries' forces, impervious to cries for help from Gallieni, unmoved by opportunities offered at one point or desperate situations developing at others, deaf to suggestions and regardless of the desires even of part of his own entourage.

His plan from the beginning was simple in the extreme, and he never allowed himself to be diverted from it. It was the same on the eve of the battle as it had been on August 25th: accumulate forces on the left till superiority in numbers was achieved, then attack. So successful was he in this that in spite of the original German superiority in numbers, the actual Battle of the Marne was fought by forty-nine allied divisions and eight cavalry divisions against forty-six German divisions and seven cavalry divisions.

Instruction Générale No. 2 of August 26th, it will be remembered, stated that – "It having been found impossible to carry out the projected offensive which had been planned, the next operations will have as their object to reform on our left a mass capable of resuming the offensive."

Instruction Générale No. 4 of September 1st and the note to the Minister of War, sound the same note. Whatever plan the Germans adopted, whatever their line of advance, Joffre's basic idea of an attack by his left would have been maintained. If von Kluck had marched on Paris, the capital, instead of being the left of the line, would have been included in it, and the Sixth Army would have attacked to the west of it. Chance, luck, the German mistake, all favoured Joffre's plan. Von Kluck contrived his own trap. Joffre was not compelled to seek the German flank, von Kluck presented it to him, so that all Maunoury had to do was to advance straight ahead.

*   *   *

At the dawn of the battle the Allied Armies stretched and sagged like an immense sheet firmly fixed on the left to Paris and on the right to Verdun, and into the pocket of this sheet the enemy advanced, like someone falling into a blanket held firmly by men intent on bouncing him out as soon as he landed. (Maps XV, p. 416 and XVI, p. 426).

Paris and Verdun were the massive piers on which the two extremities of the line rested, but the latter fortress by itself did not cover the extreme right. South of it was an opening through which, if he penetrated, the enemy could turn the whole Allied line. Barring this passage stood Castelnau hanging on desperately to the Couronné of Nancy, whilst farther south stood Dubail solidly entrenched in the Vosges.

From the pillars upon which the two wings of the allies rested, General Joffre intended to drive straight into the flanks of the enemy with Maunoury's, French's and Sarrail's Armies, whilst the remainder of his array attacked the enemy frontally. Thus the Allied Armies, in the guise of that old instrument of torture the Iron Maid of Nuremberg, were about to fold the enemy in a deadly embrace. But were the hinges of the machine strong enough to hold so powerful a prey? Would he bend back the arms that were gripping him? Could he escape?

Mighty were the blows rained by the Germans on Castelnau to turn the Allied line, on Foch and de Langle de Cary to break the centre, on Maunoury to bend back the arm of the trap. A fearful strain was put on some of the links in the chain, and had any one of them snapped the Germans and not the French would have been the victors.

Day after day the struggle raged. Many times it seemed as if the Germans would prove too strong, and in their struggle to escape from the wide embrace would carry everything before them. But whilst the Germans fought furiously to break through, driving the indomitable Foch to within an ace of defeat and that magnificent fighter Maunoury to his very last gasp, the advance of the left of the Fifth Army and of the B.E.F. into the fatal gap in their line was beginning to tell, until finally their whole array collapsed.

A glance at Map XV (p. 416) will show what befell. There was a vertical gap between von Kluck's left and von Bülow's right. This gap constantly increased as von Kluck was compelled to transfer troops from his left to his right to meet Maunoury's attack. The pressure of the Fifth Army on von Bülow's right, while the latter endeavoured to carry out the Supreme Command's orders and face Paris, led to the right of the Second Army being gradually thrown back, which in turn contributed to widen the already alarmingly wide space between the First and Second German Armies.

Maunoury's attack was a magnet which gradually attracted the whole of von Kluck's Army, until there was an immense area, guarded only by Cavalry and some infantry detachments, between von Kluck and von Bülow.

Into this gap the B.E.F. advanced, and it was the Contemptible Little Army which on the confession of the Germans themselves caused the retreat of the whole German line from Verdun to Paris.*

* For Diary of the Battle of the Marne, see Appendix XXXVI.

CHAPTER XIX

EPISODES OF THE BATTLE OF THE MARNE AND THE PURSUIT TO THE AISNE

September 6th–12th, 1914

Preamble – (I) *The first day – In liaison with the British* – (II) *The second day – Coulommiers* – (III) *The third day – Villiers St. Georges* – (IV) *The fourth day – Montmirail – Franchet d'Esperey's Proclamation – Joffre's movements* – (V) *The advance to the Aisne – The weather breaks – The XVIII. Corps – Vielmaison – French and British Cavalry co-operate – Gallieni's Staff Officers on the British – High hopes* – (VI) *General de Maud'huy.*

THE sketches that follow are mere fragments, drawn from memory; trivial perhaps, some of them, but it is thus memory works, often discarding the important to cherish incidents that probably failed to make an impression at the time.

It is impossible for me to give a complete picture of the battle.

In each of its hours there were many thousands of episodes, of which I only witnessed a few. Perhaps too many threads have been broken and too many voices stilled for the complete and detailed story ever to be related.

I have not even attempted to describe the conditions under which we worked, or the strain put upon the Staffs, the maddening perplexities and seemingly insoluble problems arising minute by minute. These things must be taken for granted, just as in a description of the fighting many blanks have to be filled in by the imagination.

I. THE FIRST DAY

September 6th was a day of wonderful exhilaration. Both French and English were advancing, and from all sides good news came in.

Girard and I were sent to the British area carrying General d'Esperey's orders, with instructions to get into personal touch with Sir John and the British Cavalry.

We went to Melun first, sent back by motor cyclist a copy of British orders, then went on to Tournon to find Sir John. He was not there, so we went forward in search of the Cavalry. On the way I experienced the joy and pride I always felt at meeting British troops when accompanied by a French officer. It was indeed good to see these fine unruffled battalions (I think they belonged to one of the Guards Brigades), calm in the advance as they had been steady in the retreat.

Near Rozoy we came upon some infantry entrenching an advanced position, the men working stolidly whilst the officers walked up and down, to all appearances as detached as if this, the first day of one of the decisive battles of the world, were a rather boring field day.

We saw the G.O.C. of the 1st Division, and Sir Douglas Haig, and witnessed a pretty little fight in which the 3rd Cavalry Brigade was engaged. It was splendid to see the squadrons dashing forward to drive the enemy from the village just ahead. The rapidity of their movements and the excellence of their dismounted work were good to behold. How well they knew their job! It was just like manœuvres at home. The only figure one missed was that of the Umpire with his white cap band. One almost expected him to ride out from somewhere and spoil this excellent little show by sending everyone home. The only creatures who seemed to feel that anything unpleasant was going on were ourselves and several coveys of partridges who shared our dislike for the shrapnel that kept bursting in the field where we stood. The birds shifted their ground with a rapidity we almost succeeded in emulating.

We returned to Tournon to await the Commander-in-Chief. As we stood in the street we watched our Signal Service setting up their lines. They were also being watched by a rather good-looking Frenchwoman, who kept up a running fire of comment of a kind I have never heard equalled in the lightest cavalry circles. The English soldiers, uncomprehending but appreciative, grinned.

At 2.30, Sir John and General Murray appeared. As was too often the case, Girard, because of the difficulty of language, was almost instantly dismissed, whilst I was told to remain and explain the progress of events with the Fifth Army.

Later in the afternoon we visited the British II. Corps, and saw the G.O.C. of the 3rd Division, General Hubert Hamilton (who was killed two months later at Béthune), at Crèvecœur. We watched the British Cavalry driving the enemy out of Tourquin.

II. THE SECOND DAY

Girard and I were again sent in liaison to the British. After reporting to G.H.Q. we were to see if the liaison between the fighting forces was satisfactory.

The change in the appearance of the British troops, now that they were advancing, was remarkable. The exhilaration of victory had already wiped out the horror of the retreat. The men of the II. Corps showed by their faces and their soiled and tattered clothing the ordeal they had been through. Hardly any of them had greatcoats, many had lost their caps and puttees and wore the most disreputable head-gear, some evidently borrowed from scarecrows. They looked incongruous but gay. As for the hats, an Army Order soon put an end to the variety and fantasy of those first few days of the advance.

Collecting information as we went, we were told the cavalry were beyond Coulommiers, and made straight for that place, arriving between 2 and 3 p.m. We had been misinformed: there was no cavalry ahead. We did not know that the 3rd Cavalry Brigade was held up a short distance east of where we were. On our right guns were firing. Of the infantry there was no sign. The only British in the place were an Intelligence and an Engineer officer, who had just reached the station in an engine.

The town presented an extraordinary spectacle. The streets were so littered with empty bottles that it was impossible to drive the car through them. The escort had to walk ahead kicking them out of the way. It was easy to believe the inhabitants when they said there was an enormous amount of drunkenness amongst the Germans, and that the last troops to leave swayed as they marched. The town had been thoroughly pillaged, all portable articles carried away, and the remainder smashed. We had a talk with some hostages just released by the Germans. They had walked back into the town a few moments before our arrival. I had never seen before, and hope I will never see again, men so shaken, men who had just stepped out of the shadow of an unmerited sentence of death. One of them, a town official who spoke German fluently, though the enemy did not know this, had heard a group of German officers debating for a long time and in the end arguing angrily as to whether they should be shot.

The inhabitants pointed out to us a house which they said had been German headquarters until that morning. They described the German General, whose appearance had evidently impressed them. He was probably either the Commander of the Second Cavalry Corps or one of its divisions. As one Frenchman said: "He is like one of Offenbach's Generals who slept on the '*Champ de bouteilles*'."

We went on in the hope of discovering something of interest from the Intelligence point of view. We were confronted with a strange and very nauseating spectacle. In parts of the house, in corners, were signs of unspeakable filth. On the floors of the outer rooms there was straw everywhere, large numbers of men evidently having slept there. The parts of the building which had been occupied by the officers were less dirty but in a state of disorder – drawers on floors, tables upset, etc., which gave us great pleasure as the outward and manifest signs of a very hasty departure. What I could not have believed had I not seen it, was that there were lumps of grease and butter lying about in bits of paper on tables and window sills which had been eaten "*nature*" as was evident from the imprints of teeth on them. We left the house feeling quite sick.

Happily before we went away some British officers appeared, for the inhabitants, who had given us a touching welcome, clung to us in fear they would be abandoned once more.

Only once again was I so moved by the greeting of the inhabitants during the war. It was at Noyon in 1917, when the Germans withdrew to the Hindenburg line. The weight of the German occupation had been so heavy and so prolonged that the voice of the people had been stilled and they could only stand silent, the old men bareheaded, all with tears in their eyes, as the first French troops marched in. Some did not know British uniforms and had to be told we were friends. Women held up their children to touch our coats, and one young girl turned in silence to pick some laurel leaves and gave me one, which I treasure to this day. But never a word was spoken in the grim dead little town, where the only gay note was struck by the spick-and-span German sentry boxes freshly painted in black and white stripes.

That evening (September 7th) I heard of an interesting suggestion made by the Intelligence of the G.Q.G., showing with what care information had been collected before the war. They warned the Sixth Army, and the message was repeated to the British, of a manœuvre carried out by von Kluck at the Imperial Manœuvres in 1910. Von Kluck had commanded the First Army, operating against the XVIII. Corps commanded by von Mackensen. Von Kluck's tactics, which were crowned with success, had consisted in leading his adversary on to an entrenched position occupied by a small force behind which the main body was drawn up, then by a night march he advanced in echelon against the enemy's flank. The implication was that having found this manœuvre successful once, von Kluck might be laying a somewhat similar trap at this moment.

On our way back to Fifth Army Headquarters, Girard and I met a man whom I had seen several times already, a British private soldier who, having lost his regiment early in the retreat, had attached himself to a French battalion. He was a tall, thin, red-headed young Irishman with a most winning grin, who, according to his French comrades, fought like a tiger. Officers and men of his adopted regiment were very fond of him, apparently looking upon him as a mascot. I sent his name to his unit so that he should not be reported missing, but it was not practical to repatriate him at the time. Indeed he was better where he was. Head and shoulders above his French friends, he was a queer figure in his khaki in the ranks of dark blue, but to such French soldiers as saw him British participation in the war was a reality. This was a matter of some importance. General de Maud'huy thoroughly understood this, and later in the war when commanding the Tenth Army, he asked British G.H.Q. to send some French Canadians to spend a few days in the different units of his Army, so that their presence might enable his men to visualize the fact that the British Empire was in the war as a whole. The reason he asked for French Canadians was so that they should be able to make themselves understood.

III. THE THIRD DAY

On the night of September 8th, Fifth Army Headquarters was at Villiers St. Georges, which had been thoroughly pillaged and turned upside down by the Germans. Even poor little faded photographs hanging on the walls had been pulled down and torn in tiny pieces. The contents of cupboards were strewn about, and women's underclothing lay on the floor in pieces.

I saw there, as I often saw in other villages which had been occupied by the Germans, the inscription chalked in pointed Gothic characters on the doors of some of the houses – "*Gute Leute*". Presumably its purpose was to protect the inhabitants from some of the worst vexations, but what of the others? To be the subject of such a recommendation was at best a doubtful boon, and apt to engender the suspicion of the other villagers.

I was given a room in a house whose only occupant was a young woman, its owner, who had trudged in after the troops, carrying her child. There was no door to the house, nor I think were there doors inside it. When I tip-toed in to lie down, fully dressed (since the beginning of the retreat I had scarcely had my clothes or even my field boots off), I had to cross the room where she lay sleeping, her child in a basket by her side. That child, quite defenceless, asleep in its wrecked home, so close to the battle line, made me think that however much men might endeavour to destroy their race, life would have its way and would survive, persistent and unconquerable, although it seemed at the moment as if the whole world were collapsing in the awful roar of the great guns.

*   *   *

That evening I saw General de Maud'huy, the Commander of the XVIII. Corps, for the first time. His artillery had co-operated in the capture of Montmirail, which had just fallen to General Hache's III. Corps. In spite of the usual horror of dead and wounded, that battlefield was inspiring, for all who had been fighting, wounded and sound alike, had the conviction that they were victorious. The guns, the fires on which men were cooking at the end of the day, regimental carts coming up with supplies, and the lightly wounded men hobbling back, made an extraordinarily fine picture, and, strange to say, the evening, perhaps because of the contrast with all the violence of the day, was wonderfully peaceful. It looked, as the dusk blotted out the gruesome details, like an idealized battlefield, for the soil was not pocked with shell-holes nor the ground strewn with debris as was the case in the battles in trench warfare.

Next day in Montmirail, I saw de Maud'huy again and had a long talk with him. He was very pleased with the way things were going, pleased too at having contributed to the capture of the town, for his guns had carried out a night bombardment, the first of its kind in the war, he said.

He asked me what I thought of the war, and I answered that there was one good thing about it; I had not received a single dunning letter from my tailor since it began. I do not know why this appealed to him, but years later he used to burst out laughing, describe the battlefield of Montmirail and then say that he had met an Englishman there who praised the war as an escape from tradesmen's bills.

Later, when he commanded an Army, I was attached to his Staff and had my meals with him. It was impossible not to like and admire him, and I feel it has been my privilege to meet at least one man utterly devoid of personal ambition, whose entire mind and soul were consecrated to the service of his country.

I shall have more to say concerning him later.

IV. THE FOURTH DAY

On the morning of September 9th, the report centre of the Fifth Army moved to Montmirail. Everywhere on the way were traces of the battle. I stopped several times to shoot wretched horses abandoned with broken legs. Unburied bodies lay thick in places; hundreds of little combats were explained by the position of the dead who had taken part in them: here a shallow trench or ditch full of Germans who had been caught by the 75s, there a group of Frenchmen lying in the open where a machine-gun had caught them; then five or six Germans lying by a haystack. And always, in the German trenches, an incredible quantity of empty bottles – how such numbers could have been carried I cannot imagine.* Some German trenches were far better than others. It was interesting to see how astonished the French were to observe that if the Germans had time to do more than just scratch the ground they built traverses in their trenches. The French thought this elementary precaution marvellous.

The German dead, strange to say, turned absolutely black a few hours after death, so much so that it was difficult to believe they were not negroes. Different theories were advanced to account for this. Some said it was the result of being killed by the French 75s, others that it was the effect of drinking so much wine.

A perfectly horrible sight were the maimed cattle. It was thought at the time that with wanton cruelty living animals had had feet and legs cut off, but it is far more likely that the animals had been wounded by shell fire.

It may seem strange, but it is quite true that it was not until this day that we fully grasped the fact that a great battle had been fought, was still in progress and was being won. Even at the H.Q. of an Army where the Commander-in-Chief's plan, or at least that part of it affecting our own and neighbouring armies, was known, the battlefield was so vast, the section of it one could see or even hear about was so reduced compared to the whole, that it was quite impossible to gain a general idea of what was happening. It had seemed to most of us that the fighting since

---

* A favourite German book which recounts the adventures of a Bavarian officer named Tanera in 1870–1 describes how his battalion marched out of Reims each man carrying two bottles of champagne.

September 6th, heavy though it had been, was merely a series of preliminary engagements, the opening phase of the great struggle, which we inevitably pictured as something far more dramatic. It was difficult to realize that these engagements, together with others we had not even heard of, made up the battle. We should have been very astonished had we been told that this day, the one we were then living, was the most important one in the whole battle.

The southern approaches of Montmirail were a wonderful sight. Troops in great numbers, the reserves of the III. Corps, stood in massive squares on the trampled wheatfields, waiting to advance.

In company with some French officers, I walked into the Château, which presented an extraordinary spectacle. A direct hit by a shell, probably on the night of the 7th, must have been the signal for the hasty departure of the German Corps Staff occupying it. The General and his Staff must have been at dinner when it happened. It was easy to visualize the whole scene. At the head of the table had sat the Commander. He must have come in punctually, for by his plate was an empty cup belonging to the fine china service of the Rochefoucaulds, the owners of the Château. In the saucer were cigar ashes. The place next to him, perhaps that of the Chief of Staff, showed that the occupant was only a trifle behind his Chief, for he had completed his meal, all but the coffee, which remained in his cup. Down the long table the rank of each diner could be divined, for the more junior officers had come in late. Near the Commander one had started to eat an apple which lay half peeled. A few places farther down was a plate of untouched meat, while at the end of the table the soup-plate of an unfortunate junior was quite full.

Upstairs, the names of the late occupants of the rooms were written in chalk on the doors. Piles of trampled and soiled linen on the floors of the linen cupboards showed where the orderlies had pulled piles of sheets down to get what they wanted for the officers' beds.

I forget what orders we were attempting to carry out, but I remember that Helbronner and I, leaving Montmirail, and relying on some information given us in the neighbourhood, started to motor out beyond the village of Vauchamps. There were fewer and fewer troops, but we had been told positively that the French were at least as far forward as Orbais, so we did not worry. Presently we noticed only a scattered line of skirmishers lying down to either side of the road in perfectly flat and open country. Some waved to us in greeting. The car was still tearing forward. I shouted to the driver to stop and investigate. No sooner had we done so than we heard the peculiar hum and bee-like noise of bullets, too numerous to be at all pleasant. Four shells dropped immediately afterwards in close proximity to us. It seemed very likely that the next salvo would be closer still. We began to turn the car in the very narrow road, having to reverse several times. Happily the English chauffeur, Johnson by name, kept perfectly calm and did not put us into the ditch. Whilst this was going on we realized we were between the French and German lines and some two or three hundred yards from the latter. Strange as it may seem, the Boches were such bad shots that not only was no one hurt but the car was little damaged, only the windscreen being smashed. This little adventure was typical of the difficulties of getting from one part of the line to another owing to the uncertainty as to where our own people really were at any given moment.

*   *   *

It was on this day that Franchet d'Esperey issued his fine proclamation to the Fifth Army, which sounds like a trumpet-call. It heartened all who read it and made them feel that victory lay within their grasp.

It was drafted by Girard and submitted to the General, who may have made alterations before signing it. It was as follows:

"SOLDIERS,

"On the historic fields of Montmirail, Vauchamps and Champaubert, which witnessed a hundred years ago the victory of our ancestors over the Prussians of Blücher, your vigorous offensive has broken the German resistance.

"Held on his wings, his centre broken, the enemy is flying to the east and to the north by forced marches.

"The most renowned corps of Old Prussia, the contingents of Westphalia, of Hanover and of Brandenburg have withdrawn hastily before you.

"This first success is but a preliminary. The enemy is shaken but not completely beaten. Great tests of your endurance lie ahead of you, you will have to carry out many long marches, to take part in many bitter fights. Let the evocation of the Motherland, defiled by the barbarians, remain ever present before your eyes. Never was the sacrifice of all for her sake more necessary.

"Whilst paying homage to the brave men who have already fallen in the struggle of the last few days, my thoughts turn to you, the instruments of the forthcoming victory.

> "Forward, soldiers, for France,
>
>> "The General Commanding the Fifth Army,
>>
>>> "FRANCHET D'ESPEREY.*

"Montmirail, September 9th, 1914."

General d'Esperey's faith in victory was justified by events. His own successful advance was a good augury: but at the moment the fate of the battle was trembling in the balance. Foch on his right, and Maunoury far to the west were barely holding their own. These were the danger points of the line. Which of the two adversaries, each almost victorious at one point and almost defeated at the other, could by sheer grit hold on and so achieve definite success? If no relief came, if there were no diversion, defeat stared the French in the face, for on Maunoury's and Foch's fronts the enemy seemed to be winning. Everything depended on the British advance.

This advance did, that very day, bring about the German retreat. When it was reported to von Bülow that the British were across the Marne, he realized he could not remain in his present position and ordered his Army to fall back. Whilst this was happening von Kluck, although he had reason to believe he had beaten Maunoury's left, was also compelled by the advance of the British in his rear to order a retirement. (Map XV, p. 416.)

In spite of grave anxieties and uncertainties and stupefying fatigue, an immense wave of optimism swept over us all. I can still recall the exhilaration we felt at this time. Susceptibilities were getting blunted, horror no longer gripped. Death was taken as a matter of course. However deeply a comrade might be missed, a self-protecting instinct prevented the mind dwelling on the pain caused by his loss. We were all in the same boat. Today you, tomorrow me.

At Fifth Army Headquarters we used to sing with immense gusto the German song:

> "Ach du liebe Augustin, Augustin, Augustin,
> Ach du liebe Augustin, alles ist hin.
> Geld ist weg, Mehl ist weg, alles weg, alles weg,
> Ach du liebe Augustin, alles ist hin!"

* See Appendix XXXV.

It seemed to depict adequately the plight the Germans were in. And de Rose banged the table with his fist, yelling, "That's the way the shells go!"

For the first time jokes and stories, some of them grim enough, were passed from one to the other. I remember one, of a man who in a bayonet charge had a leg blown off by a shell. Another wave of attacking men swept past and he begged a man running by to carry him to an ambulance, or he would bleed to death. "I can't," said the other, "I must go on, I am not allowed to stop and carry wounded. The stretcher-bearers will be coming." But the wounded man begged so hard that his companion, a giant, put down his rifle, hiked him painfully on to his back and started plodding laboriously back with him. Unfortunately on the way a stray shell splinter carried off the head of the wounded man all unknown to his benefactor. Presently he encountered an officer, who took him to task for having left the attacking line. "But, *mon Capitaine*, I am carrying a poor wounded man who said he would die if I did not take him to the dressing station." "A wounded man, you are carrying a headless corpse!" The soldier put down his burden slowly and gazed at it in amazement. "And he did tell me quite distinctly it was his leg that was blown off!" he said.

It may have been at this time, or perhaps a little later, that I witnessed a scene illustrative, not of hardness but of sheer incomprehension of war by some civilians. A cavalryman had been badly wounded in the stomach. He was put on a ladder lying nearby, and two of his comrades carried him towards a cottage a short distance away. A good many shrapnel shells were bursting in the vicinity, and just before we reached it the bullets of one rattled on its tiled roof. We knocked on the door, and as it was not immediately opened burst it open and all got in just as the next shell burst viciously overhead, breaking more tiles on the roof. As we stood in the tiny hall, the wounded man occupying its entire length, a door opened and an old man's head appeared, his wife behind him. He looked at the wounded man and at the ladder, then, pointing to a door opposite him on the other side of the improvised stretcher, he said in a querulous, trembling voice: "And how do you expect me to get to the kitchen now?"

*   *   *

All day and every day, General Joffre was here, there and everywhere.

It is right and necessary that every individual in an Army should be worked to his last ounce of strength, only allowed to rest, like the infantryman about to attack, so that he will have the more energy to expend at the critical moment. But it is also necessary that the responsible head of an Army and his advisers should live in quiet, under conditions best suited to brain work. This is not always possible. Joffre for instance covered incredible distances by car during this period, seeing Army Commanders personally along the whole front, and he was right to do so. The encouragement he gave, the better understanding of the situation he formed on the spot, his appreciation by personal contact of the mentality of his subordinates, made the fatigue involved worth while, and gave him a great advantage over his opponent von Moltke, who, in far-distant Luxembourg, was no doubt well placed to nurse his debilitated frame, but was thoroughly out of touch both with the situation and with his Army Commanders. His choice of H.Q. likened him to one who, having to observe a distant scene through a telescope, deliberately looks through the wrong end, thus still further increasing the distance between his eye and its objective.

The moral of this is that the Commander-in-Chief should be a strong man capable of withstanding great fatigue without his mental powers being impaired. The mileage covered by Joffre at this period is incredible. When it became historically important to ascertain his movements it seemed impossible to do so. These would have remained a mystery for ever, but for the fact that his chauffeur, a careful man who liked to note his menu and the price paid for his meals, kept a diary, and the long list of inns and restaurants gave the required clue to the Commander-in-Chief's itineraries.

V. THE PURSUIT

I have but little to say concerning the pursuit from the Marne to the Aisne. I was on never-ending liaison duties, often seeking commanders at places they had never been at, or endeavouring to locate troops that seemed to have disappeared into thin air, and almost invariably finding the situation I had been sent to deal with completely changed by the time I arrived on the scene. And this went on day and night. Countless cumbersome lines of transport blocked the roads as usual, and long columns of infantry plodded by in the mud, for the weather had broken.

When the rain came our first feeling was of delight at being rid of a sun that had proved so implacably cruel to armies whose safety had depended upon the rapidity of their marches. But soon, when it was realized that an early autumn had set in, we felt the elements were again playing us false.

The rain took some of the zest out of the pursuit, and was particularly cruel to those British troops who had lost their greatcoats. The men, both French and British, protected themselves as best they could. Many wore sacking, others I saw had to be content with old skirts picked up in abandoned houses. They were chilled to the bone, and their sodden clothes drew what heart there was out of their bodies. It was often impossible to build a fire to cook by.

One of my clearest recollections of this time, of which I remember very little, is of coming upon General de Maud'huy standing on the steps of the *Mairie* at Château-Thierry reviewing some troops under the gaze of a huddled group of German prisoners in charge of gendarmes. It was long since I had seen troops step smartly by to martial music, and it did me good, as it did the men who were taking part in the parade. You could see their pride being roused, their keenness and enthusiasm stimulated.

I remember Viels-Maisons, where the Fifth Army Staff arrived on the 10th. It had of course been sacked. In the church were a hundred and fifty terrified prisoners in charge of Moroccans. Thinking of them I compare them to some other wretched prisoners I saw in 1916, crowded together in a small wire compound or cage, surrounded by squatting Senegalese who were engaged in sharpening their enormous three-foot knives, the "*coupe-coupe*", on the soles of their feet, interrupting their work occasionally to make the significant gesture of cutting a throat, and saying with wide-mouthed grins "*Nach Paris*".

There was a disappointing incident on the morning of the 10th.

General de Maud'huy notified Sir Douglas Haig that fifty-four German heavy guns were moving from Lizy-sur-Ourcq to Oulchy, and wished to co-operate with the I. Corps in capturing them. Most unfortunately both British divisions were heavily engaged at the time, and later, when action was possible, the enemy had escaped. But in the afternoon the right-hand brigade of the British Cavalry Division co-operated successfully in the neighbourhood of Latilly with one of Conneau's Cavalry Divisions supported by infantry in motor lorries, against a strong German cavalry and infantry column.

On the 11th, to everyone's astonishment, a group of middle-aged Englishmen arrived at Château-Thierry. Whence had they come? No one knew. They wanted to fight the Germans and were disappointed when told that if that was their desire they must return to Paris and join the Foreign Legion.

More precise in my memory is an incident that occurred on the afternoon of the 12th.

Some officers of General Gallieni's Staff appeared at Fifth Army H.Q. They made in my hearing some most unseemly remarks concerning the advance of the British. The burden of their comment was that the British advance had been unconscionably slow, and that their Cavalry had been consistently held back. These statements showed so little knowledge of what had actually occurred as to render the speakers ridiculous in the eyes of the French officers who heard them and who knew the facts. They knew, for instance, that Conneau's Cavalry Corps, until it drew level with the British on the 10th, had never been less than 15 miles behind the British Cavalry.

It was easy to turn the tables on these gentlemen from Paris, but their hostile attitude made a marked impression, and explains the very biased accounts of the British part in the Battle of the Marne which have since emanated from that source.

The little fighting I saw was a replica of all other engagements during the past week. Cannonades, occasional shelling of points by guns whose positions could only be vaguely guessed at; here and there infantry advancing in long skirmishing lines: reserves grouped out of sight; that was all. And the rain came down in torrents, turning the roads into quagmires. The weather not only delayed the advance but made flying almost impossible, thus blinding the Allies at a time when bold and rapid movements were of especial importance.

Everywhere dead men and horses marked the path of the advance. A living tide had swept forward, leaving where each wave had broken a flotsam of human and animal remains. The ground in some places was strewn with helmets and weapons of all kinds. The ditches were still lined with German dead, but surrounded by a noticeably diminished number of bottles compared to those seen on previous days. In front of them small groups of Frenchmen lay huddled, shot down as they attacked: but they had died on ground reconquered from the enemy and would be laid reverently to rest by their own people.

We were beginning to realize that a great strategic victory had been won. Hope had deserted the grey-clad masses and was now leading the men in blue and the men in khaki, who, following her, forgot their weariness.

British and French were advancing, their heads held high, a new look in their eyes. They knew they could beat the Germans, and the Germans, who had thought themselves invincible, found themselves having to acknowledge defeat at the hands of a despised enemy.

The Germans were beaten not only because they were outmatched, but because they made the same mistakes as had the French during the Battle of the Frontiers. On the immense battlefield of the Marne, when the Germans attacked they did so without reconnaissances and without artillery support, with the result that they were almost invariably stopped by the French artillery.

Some idea of how high the enemy's hopes had been was shown by postcards and letters addressed to German soldiers "in or near Paris". These had been conveyed by an impartial postal service through Switzerland and dumped in Paris.

During these days, the dominant thought of the Staffs was – would the Germans halt and fight on the Aisne or withdraw still farther? The tone was extremely optimistic, not only at Fifth Army H.Q. but at G.H.Q. Those who had been most downhearted during the retreat were now busily proving that the enemy could not possibly halt till he reached the Rhine.

General Joffre had the highest expectations of what General Maunoury's Army might accomplish.* He hoped that it might still outflank the German line, or at least keep von Kluck so engaged as to prevent his junction with von Bülow, from whose Army he was separated by a gap of some 18 miles. In this it was successful, for when von Bülow ordered the First Army to close in on the right of the Second, von Kluck replied that being threatened by the French Sixth Army he could not comply. The gap between the German First and Second Armies remained, and the Allies would have driven a wedge between them on the Aisne had not reinforcements arrived just in time to save the Germans from complete defeat.†

VI. GENERAL DE MAUD'HUY

When I look back on the Battle of the Marne, I find, and this is only natural, that I remember more about the French than about the British,

---

* This Army had now been reinforced by the XIII. Corps from the First Army.
† See Appendix XXXVI.

for I saw far more of them than of my own people. But my most abiding impression is not of the fighting, nor yet of the country over which the Armies advanced, it is of a man, General de Maud'huy, who will always be to me the embodiment of all that is finest in the French soldier's character.

General Count de Maud'huy belonged to an ancient Lorraine family and was born in Metz. When he was nine years old his native town was taken from France and his parents went to live in that country. His whole childhood was overshadowed by the tragedy of his lost home, and the idea of winning it back became his dream. Brought up as he had been on tales of chivalry, the reconquest of Lorraine assumed for him the romantic guise of a knightly quest.

In due course he went to St. Cyr and obtained a commission in the infantry. As a young lieutenant it occurred to him that he was allowing the thought of his native town, now under the Germans, to fade from his memory. He was horrified to find that days sometimes passed without his giving a thought to the lost provinces of France. Thereupon he resolved never to enter a place of amusement until Metz was French again. Thus whenever anyone mentioned a play or he saw a notice of a concert or an *"affiche"* of any of the theatres, he remembered his oath, and the idea of the great *"revanche"* recurred to his mind.

It was my privilege to see General de Maud'huy enter a theatre once more. With a great sense of the fitness of things, the Government appointed him Governor of Metz as soon as the French occupied the town, and one of his first actions was to announce that he was going to the play, which he did. Preceded by twenty trumpeters of his beloved *"Chasseurs à pied"*, who made it seem as if they would blow the roof off as they marched in playing their regimental tune *"La Sidi Brahim"*, General de Maud'huy walked into a theatre for the first time in nearly forty years.

He had the outlook on life of a knight errant, and lived his life in a dream of military chivalry. His two heroes were Bayard and du Guesclin, the embodiment of all the virtues he admired. Anyone who was not a soldier, or anything that did not appertain to soldiering, he simply did not understand. They moved in another dimension that escaped him. He was a religious man, but his saints wore armour, and it is fact that Bayard and du Guesclin were so alive to him that he felt no anomaly in imagining them involved in the complications of twentieth-century existence.* And he was right when he maintained that their principles of truth and honour were as applicable now as they had been in their day.

He was fond of quoting Bayard, the knight *"sans peur et sans reproche"*, and du Guesclin, who, captured by the English and asked to name his own ransom, stated an enormous figure, and, seeing the astonishment on his captors' faces, said: "There is not a woman in France who will not spin for the ransom of du Guesclin."

On the whole, de Maud'huy preferred du Guesclin, who had been an ugly man, perhaps because he himself was no beauty, perhaps because they both greatly enjoyed giving and receiving hard knocks.

He brought up his two sons according to his own tenets. In their prayers they were taught to say: "Pray God that we may become like Bayard and du Guesclin, and preserve us above all things from lying, for lies are the characteristic of slaves."

The war found him commanding a brigade. I think it was at Maurange that he was ordered to carry out a night attack. Quite unable to remember that his duty was to remain in the rear when there was fighting going on, he went forward into the front lines. The Germans were on the alert, machine-guns opened fire on all sides, and the French had to lie down. Soon de Maud'huy gave the signal to advance again. To his disgust the men lying on either side of him did not respond, and lay quite still. He stooped and shook first one then the other; they were both dead.

On the eve of the Marne he was given command of the XVIII. Corps. The Generalissimo told him that it was a good Corps but the men did not much like being shot at. He added that if they were properly led they were all right, and so it proved, but de Maud'huy never got over his dislike of those of his countrymen who hailed from the south, as did most of the men in this Corps.

He was merciless whenever he had to deal with a dereliction of duty, and death was too good for anyone who committed a crime against France.

When his Corps reached Château-Thierry during the Battle of the Marne, the indignant inhabitants dragged before him two women accused of having consorted with the Germans during their occupation

---

* Incidentally, Bayard so disliked the new-fangled firearms that were becoming popular in his day, and that in his view were not only unsporting but threatened to turn war into a noisy brawl quite unfit for gentlemen to participate in, that he took the somewhat extreme line of torturing and putting to death all musketeers he captured.

of the town. I rather think that he had them drummed through the streets; he certainly had them inscribed officially as prostitutes, which in France means reports to the police stations, constant police supervision, the petty tyranny of minor officials and humiliating bi-weekly medical inspections.

Battles and shells suited him; he loved danger. I can see him now, during the battle of the Aisne, on the tower of the Château of Roucy, within full view of the enemy and within range of his guns. Obviously longing to lead his men himself, he stood there looking as if by sheer will he would drive them over the river on to the hills beyond. Whenever he got a chance of exposing himself he did. I remember a very uncomfortable afternoon spent with him at Arras. The Germans were shelling hard. Whenever a shell fell de Maud'huy walked to the spot and began a conversation with whoever he could lay hands on. Example, he called it, no doubt excellent, but this sort of thing cost the French dear. For instance, when General Maunoury was inspecting some trenches with another general, they were warned not to approach a particular loophole. They at once put their heads to it, and a German bullet went through Maunoury's eyes and killed his companion.

It was on the Aisne I witnessed a very strange incident.

General de Maud'huy had just been roused from sleep on the straw of a shed and was standing in the street, when a little group of unmistakable purport came round the corner. Twelve soldiers and an N.C.O., a firing party, a couple of gendarmes, and between them an unarmed soldier. My heart sank and a feeling of horror overcame me. An execution was about to take place. General de Maud'huy gave a look, then held up his hand so that the party halted, and with his characteristic quick step went up to the doomed man. He asked what he had been condemned for. It was for abandoning his post. The General then began to talk to the man. Quite simply he explained discipline to him. Abandoning your post was letting down your pals, more, it was letting down your country that looked to you to defend her. He spoke of the necessity of example, how some could do their duty without prompting but others, less strong, had to know and understand the supreme cost of failure. He told the condemned man that his crime was not venial, not low, and that he must die as an example, so that others should not fail. Surprisingly the wretch agreed, nodded his head. The burden of infamy was lifted from his shoulders. He saw a glimmer of something, redemption in his own eyes, a real hope, though he knew he was to die.

Maud'huy went on, carrying the man with him to comprehension that any sacrifice was worth while if it helped France ever so little. What did anything matter if he knew this?

Finally de Maud'huy held out his hand: "Yours also is a way of dying for France," he said. The procession started again, but now the victim was a willing one.

The sound of a volley in the distance announced that all was over. General de Maud'huy wiped the beads of perspiration from his brow, and for the first time perhaps his hand trembled as he lit his pipe.

He was so simple-minded, so completely unselfconscious, that, always being perfectly at ease himself and treating each individual with whom he came in contact as a comrade, he obtained the very best out of everyone.

When things were going badly he would walk up and down with short quick steps, his hands behind his back, his face rather red, his prominent blue eyes staring, and invariably puffing at his pipe. He was short, and never looked down or elsewhere than into the eyes of whoever he spoke to. That look was so friendly, so confiding as to draw you to him and make you his friend for ever. Only in case of something he considered dishonourable did his eyes blaze with fury.

After dinner he loved to relax and talk, both elbows on the table, puffing at his enormous pipe. (When on leave I used to search London for the largest models available.) He used to call me "*l'ami Spears*" and told me many interesting things, but nothing was more exhilarating than to feel his absolute confidence in ultimate victory. He could not conceive of defeat so long as a single Frenchman remained alive.

He had been a lecturer at the War College and knew his classics well. He had a soft corner in his heart for the Athenians because of their system of military service and because of the oath the young men took that they would defend their fatherland to the death and never allow its territory to be diminished.

I once ventured to ask him if he liked the Republican form of government. His answer was that from the thirteenth century till the revolution his family had served the King in alternate generations. The Maud'huy of the day would take service and end his life utterly ruined, having pledged field and mill so that he might follow the King. His son would lead a meagre and sparing existence repairing the family fortunes and accumulating wealth to be spent by his son in the King's service. "And all during that time," said de Maud'huy, "not one of my ancestors rose above the rank of captain. Since the Revolution we have had forty generals and marshals in the family. Which system do you think I prefer?"

And certainly he was a true democrat, seeing no distinctions in the great fraternity of fighting men. It would have been useless to explain the meaning of the word snobbery to him, he would not have understood it.

He was fond of developing his theory that when the French could beat the English at football they would be the first race in the world. Could he but teach his countrymen team-work, the sacrificing of the individual to the side – and he would sigh.

He told me of a colonel he had known who, when he carried out an inspection and found fault with a man, punished him then and there; after which he would look at the man fixedly for a few moments, and add "the same to you". The explanation of this strange procedure was that the Colonel knew well the mentality of the French soldier; he was certain that the man in the ranks he had just punished was saying in his own mind, although his lips did not move as he looked straight in front of him in a soldierly fashion: "Stuff it up" (or the much ruder French equivalent); so the Colonel had adopted this plan of answering the man's unuttered expletive.

De Maud'huy was naturally involved in the frightful controversies which rent the French Army at the time of the separation of Church and State. The system of the "*fiches*" already alluded to, the spying system inaugurated by General André, drove him mad with rage, and his hatred for that Minister was unbounded. He had concealed his views so little that his career had been compromised. When General André lay very ill, dying in fact, de Maud'huy went to his house and left a card on which he had written: "Major de Maud'huy alive and well has called on General André who is almost dead." At the same disturbed period he had a duel with a journalist, whom he considered unworthy to cross swords with him. De Maud'huy, single-stick champion of the French Army, hobbled on to the field saying he had sprained his leg but would fight nevertheless. He must, however, have a stick to support himself. As soon as his adversary was in position his lameness disappeared. In a trice the whirling stick had sent his opponent's sword flying and Maud'huy was belabouring him as hard as he could. The wretch was half dead before the witnesses recovered sufficiently from their astonishment to intervene.

When he commanded the Tenth Army I came to him one day in the winter of '14-'15 from the H.Q. of the British I. Corps next door to the Tenth Army. I had a grave matter to lay before him. Sir Douglas Haig had no cook. The officer who ran his mess was in despair. The whole Corps had been searched but no cook was forthcoming. Now all Frenchmen were cooks. Would General de Maud'huy be very kind and neighbourly and lend the I. Corps a soldier who was also a cook? General de Maud'huy was extremely embarrassed. The regulations were explicit, no single man could be detached from the army, yet he so wanted to help *"ce bon Haig"* (he pronounced it "Eg"). After some reflection his face brightened. "I have it," he said. "I can't lend *ce bon Eg* a soldier, but there is nothing to prevent my detaching a battalion from my Army and attaching it to his Corps. I will send him Territorials, all good cooks. He can use discernment and select the best." And so it was. A thousand elderly Frenchmen were marched off to the La Bassée Canal and attached to the I. Corps. They had hardly been installed when the enemy attacked the Indians in front of them, who gave way, and the gallant old Territorials, suddenly confronted with a crisis, put up an excellent fight and stopped a rather dangerous German rush at a delicate point in the line. So it all turned out for the best.

The latter part of the war was not a happy one for General de Maud'huy. He was relieved of the command of the Tenth Army at the moment when it was preparing for the great attacks of the spring of 1915, and given command of an army in a quiet sector in the eastern part of the line. Later still, and to his great indignation, he was told he was ill, tired, and sent to rest. He besieged the Ministry in Paris, begging for any command, a company would do. He was finally given a corps, one from the south to his disgust. He exchanged this for another one later.

His incomparable magnetism was fully used to re-establish order at the time of the mutinies of 1917, when he and his corps were sent to the disaffected area, and finally the Governorship of Metz worthily crowned his career. He probably had not the capacity to lead an army, but as the chief of a formation not too large for his personality to make itself felt he had no equal. He was a survival from another age, an age of simpler impulses and simpler needs, when men believed that the accomplishment of brave deeds and the pursuit of honour were an end in themselves.

CHAPTER XX

THE BOMBARDMENT OF REIMS AND THE END OF THE ADVANCE

September 13th–14th, 1914

General Franchet d'Esperey's entry into Reims – A German proclamation – An attempt to get to G.H.Q. – Return to Reims – The bombardment begins – Fifth Army H.Q. leaves the town – Romigny – Spies – Reims burning – Finis.

IT was a wet morning but cleared up later. The weather was chilly and damp when the Staff of the Fifth Army reached Pargny, some eight miles from Reims. From the side of the hill the city and its great cathedral were visible. Anxiously we scanned the hills beyond, watching the smoke from bursting shells, and debating the problem of whether the Germans would make a stand between Reims and the Aisne, or abandon the heights between the Vesle and Aisne rivers, north-west of where we stood. The cannonade was particularly heavy towards Berru to the east and the fort of Brimont to the north of Reims.

General d'Esperey had evidently made up his mind that the Germans would not or could not hold their present positions, for presently the word went round that we were to make a triumphal entry into the Ancient City as soon as the enemy had fallen back. This gave us all a great thrill, though we were careful to maintain an air implying that we were quite used to riding in state through rescued cities to the acclamations of the populace.

But time passed and nothing happened. The trouble was that the Germans appeared to be in no hurry. They hung on. The horses of the Staff had been taken to the entrance of the town in readiness for the pageant, but unfortunately there was no visible sign of the enemy's withdrawing.

Whilst we waited a long column of German prisoners came by,

miserable and derelict as prisoners always looked.* They halted near us, and an officer of the escort began, within General d'Esperey's hearing, to tell how some men had behaved with callousness to a wounded German. The General turned on him. "Your story is revolting," he said. "If you saw this happen and did nothing you are unworthy to wear the uniform of a French officer."

It must have been after one o'clock when the Staff were suddenly ordered forward in cars. Either a report had come in that the enemy was retiring, or the General had come to the conclusion that he would take a risk.

Just before reaching the first houses in Reims we got on our horses. I don't think anyone knew that at that moment fighting was still going on at the northern extremity of Reims in the Faubourg Cérès. General d'Esperey led the way. Half a horse's length behind him came his Chief of Staff, then Colonel Alexandre, representing the G.Q.G., and myself representing the British Army.

The streets were almost empty at first. Then people began to come out timidly, evidently still scared and bewildered. The enemy had only just left and they could hardly make out what was happening. The whole thing was pathetic and rather depressing. The triumphal entry was not coming off as a piece of ceremonial pageantry; the essential element in such affairs, an enthusiastic and care-free mob, was entirely missing.

At one point we encountered a small group of people who gathered up enough courage to cheer. One old man held out a small bunch of flowers to d'Esperey and called out: "*Vive le Général Pau.*" "*Vive le Général Pau,*" echoed the others. Now the one-armed General Pau had been a popular figure before the war, the only General whose name was widely known, and the people of Reims jumped to the conclusion that their deliverer must be he. The cheer excited Alexandre's horse, which very nearly threw its rider. General d'Esperey looked furious. Whether to be taken for another annoyed him, or whether he feared that more cheers would be Alexandre's undoing, was not apparent. With an imperious gesture of the hand he called out to the people: "*Taisez-vous!*"

---

* I remember one occasion when this was not true. Early in 1915 General Pétain's Corps belonging to the Tenth French Army took many hundreds, maybe thousands, of prisoners about Souchez and Ablain St. Nazaire. The Army Commander, General d'Urbal, ordered them to march past him under their own N.C.O.'s. It was an unforgettable sight to see these enemy soldiers doing the goosestep before a French General as if they had been at Potsdam. Personally I was rather awed by their discipline and fine bearing.

Presently we found ourselves in the great square of the Town Hall, which was entirely empty save for a burnt-out motor-car against a wall.

Our entry had not been a success, and I was told later that General Joffre was very much annoyed when he heard about it. Such a proceeding did not tally with his ideas, and he considered it an unjustifiable waste of time.

Army H.Q. was established in a school near the Town Hall Square, in a small street called, I think, the *"Rue des Boucheries"*.

Pasted on to the Town Hall wall was a very striking large green poster put up by the Germans. It was to the effect that if there was the least disturbance, the seventy hostages whose names were printed at the bottom would be shot.* The poster had been printed in the town, so I made a note of the printer's address to obtain a copy later.

Soon after our arrival I was given a number of questions to settle at G.H.Q., so I started off for Fère-en-Tardenois where Sir John now had his H.Q. As regards the situation of the Fifth Army, I knew only that it was engaged in driving the enemy from the heights north of Reims. I was also told by some French aviators that the aerodrome was being heavily shelled. I was anxious to acquire more detailed knowledge on my way to G.H.Q., and to this end attempted to leave the town by the north-east.

By a big champagne factory on the outskirts of the town was a battery of 75s, battered and abandoned. This looked ominous. I stopped the car and asked a soldier peering round a wall if he knew what was happening hereabouts. He answered laconically that the Germans were at the bend of the road, and that at the rate at which my car had been going I would have been amongst them in a minute or so; also that the battery by which we stood had been knocked out of action within the last half hour. There seemed to be nothing to stop the Germans had they taken it into their heads to march back into the town at this point.

* Notice to the Population:

"With a view to ensuring sufficiently the security of our troops and the calm of the population of Reims, the persons named have been seized as hostages by the Commander of the German Army.

"These hostages will be shot should the least disorder break out.

"On the other hand, if the town remains absolutely calm and quiet, these hostages and the inhabitants will be placed under the protection of the German Army.

"THE GENERAL COMMANDING-IN-CHIEF.

"Reims, September 12th, 1914."

Here followed the names of the hostages.

Beating a hasty retreat, I met a Staff Officer who informed me that the situation in the sector I had just come from was "obscure". To me it had seemed unpleasantly obvious. He assured me that the road to Bétheny was clear, and that I could go from thence to La Neuvillette.

I set off again. The outskirts of this part of the town were packed with troops who cheered as we went by. This I noted as a pleasing manifestation of the spirit of the Entente, but learnt later that the men had considered it a huge joke to see a single car apparently on its way to assail the forts which they knew to be still held by the enemy.

Some way beyond the town we came upon a gypsy van, whose occupants had been killed by a shell. Farther on, a high explosive had broken off some branches, which lay obstructing the road. We got out to clear them away, but at that moment attracted the enemy's unwelcome attention, at a range whose shortness was in inverse ratio to the rapidity with which we turned about and got back into Reims. Heavy shells were dropping into another part of the city.

Weary of experimenting, I went to British G.H.Q. by a more southerly route. Whilst I was there the following message from the Fifth Army came in:

"Situation of Fifth Army at 10 p.m.

"The III., I. and X. Corps were stopped tonight on the line Brimont-Berru–Nogent–l'Abbesse–la Pompelle. Tomorrow the attack will be resumed at dawn."

Unfortunately, the Germans did not evacuate the line referred to in this message for nearly four years.

I returned to Reims after midnight and found the whole Staff lying on mattresses in the different classrooms in the school. This was called the "*cantonnement d'alerte*", and was a measure fully justified by the proximity of the enemy. It is neither usual nor satisfactory for an Army Staff to be established within less than five miles of the enemy's positions.

I was lucky in securing a couple of mattresses, one of which, in the absence of blankets, served as covering. Before I went to sleep I was told by the Intelligence Officer on duty that it was as yet impossible to say if the Fifth Army was faced by strong rearguards or by the main bodies of the enemy's forces determined to fight on their present position.

Next morning we had bread and coffee at about 4.30 a.m., and for once de Rose's hitting the table and imitating the sound of bursting shells did not strike me as very amusing. The talk was that the gendarmes had had trouble, and even armed fights, with men who had found their way into the vast champagne cellars under the town.

There was a good deal of work to do both from the point of view of Intelligence and Operations, and having got through this I went to the printing office where the German proclamation had been printed. I was able to procure a copy, and two days later it was read in Parliament by the Prime Minister, Mr. Asquith.

Finding myself at last in a town with a semblance of normal life, some shops open, and people walking about ignoring or genuinely ignorant of the fact that they were still under the very muzzle of the German guns, I went to have my hair cut. Business was good, handicapped only by a shell having blown a large hole in the floor of the coiffeur's establishment and destroyed two of the seats. The barber had remained during the German occupation, and the shop had been, he said, much patronized by German officers. He told me that several of them when they entered had stamped the dust off their boots, saying: *"Poussière de France."* "Dust of France."

On returning to H.Q. I found that the order issued earlier to move Army Headquarters to Jonchery had been cancelled.

To the Chief of Staff I remarked that the shelling prophesied by some had not materialized, and asked if in his view the enemy was merely carrying out a rearguard action as General Wilson thought. He only answered me concerning the possible bombardment, and said, looking worried: "The day is not over yet."

It was then 9.30 a.m. I went upstairs to the schoolroom allotted to the Intelligence. Colonel Alexandre was there, but after examining a large assortment of German shoulder straps taken from prisoners, he went away. Finding a mattress I flung myself down for half an hour's sleep. The only other occupant of the room was Commandant Lamotte, the Maps Officer, who was writing at a table. At 9.45 a.m. I was almost asleep when there was a formidable explosion that made me jump up as our window was blown in. Lamotte, waving the paper he had been writing on so as to catch the dust that filled the room, quoted one of Napoleon's Generals, who, when the despatches he was writing were covered with sand by a cannon ball, thanked the enemy for drying his paper for him.

As I dived downstairs another explosion rocked the building. I made for the Town Hall Square, passing in the street two men carrying an officer in the striking uniform of a Spahi, red tunic and sky blue breeches.

They were running, holding him by the feet and arms. I looked at him in wonder, for such uniforms were rare and I did not recognize the wearer, whose face was distorted and grey. Yet I knew him well: he was Colonel de Laborie, in charge of one of the sections of the Staff. Wounded in the stomach and liver, he died that night.

A shell had landed at the corner of the square, killing and wounding some soldiers and some women who had been haggling over the merchandise on the little push-cart of a street vendor. Now the push-cart lay flat, its contents scattered wide, and torn human remains were plastered high up on the houses.

The bombardment increased in violence. Screeching like a dozen express trains playing ladies' chain high overhead, eight-inch shells crashed down on the houses with the noise of planets colliding; some exploded inside the houses whose fronts, changed into a hail of stones, were driven with terrific force into the houses on the other side of the street.

This was my first experience of a heavy bombardment in a town, and it was terrifying. Many small details remain in my mind: for instance, how very small the soldiers lying about on the ground appeared: they looked like boys dressed up as soldiers resting after too strenuous a game.

I must have stood about taking shelter for some time, for presently I noticed that the air had become thick and yellow like a London fog and stank of explosives. Through this fog I saw something which made me wonder if the enemy had rushed the town: a German officer loomed close to me through the foul smoke, and then appeared to kneel down suddenly. Another shell burst and I saw no more. I must have run, for when I looked again there was no sign of him. I heard afterwards that he was a prisoner being escorted across the square by a gendarme when the latter was badly wounded. The German remained by him and finally dragged him to shelter. I hope his fine action was recognized.

*   *   *

The bombardment seemed to increase in intensity. Dodging my way back to H.Q., I saw a little soldier whose arm had been blown off. He looked small and light. For minutes I struggled to lift him. At last, by lying almost flat and holding him by the belt, I got him on to my back. Then I was seized with panic. I longed to run and tried to do so, but could only stagger forward under the weight. More shells were falling every moment. I got to a door and kicked at it. It gave way. In the hall a family of people were on their knees praying. I put down my burden amongst them, asking them to do what they could for the man. There was no dressing station anywhere near.

The sentry at the door of H.Q. remains in my mind. He was laughing. There may have been a touch of hysteria in that laughter, but it sounded gay.

The strange thing about the bombardment was that the enemy seemed to be aiming at the block of houses in which H.Q. was situated. The Town Hall, in which were 1,500 German prisoners, was less than two hundred yards away, and in the direct line of fire, but had not been touched. Incidentally, the prisoners, not being in the secrets of their own command and fearful of the shells, became panicky and the guards had to be reinforced.

The enemy began to bombard the Cathedral. As a retaliation and to save the building, the General ordered that the German wounded should be collected there. I suppose the Red Cross flag was hoisted, but am not sure. The bombardment went on undiminished, and I believe I am right in saying that many Germans were burnt to death when the straw on which they lay was set on fire by shells from their own guns. Many were saved, thanks to the devotion of some French priests who at the risk of their lives carried them to safety when they realized that the bombardment was continuing. The Germans claimed that they were justified in shelling the Cathedral because the French used it as a signalling station. I know this was not true. The French never used the building for any military purpose. The only colour that can be given to the story is that a couple of French aviators who happened to have nothing to do climbed up to one of the towers to have a look round. It is possible the Germans saw them, but there was nothing whatever to justify the assumption that they were signalling.

Soon it became evident that it was quite impossible for H.Q. to remain in Reims, and the order to evacuate was issued. The Staff was given a rendezvous in one of the suburbs, the Faubourg de Vesle. Meanwhile I had been waiting in a doorway, and remember well becoming acquainted with a sensation I was often to feel again, that of lighting a pipe and finding it tasted horribly nasty, a common effect of nerves.

To walk, or rather run in spurts, to the motor park in an avenue of trees a short way from H.Q., was a little adventure in itself, and the rapid scaling of houses that had collapsed into the street provided good exercise. Some shells had fallen amongst the cars, and one or two were on fire. I found mine, the phlegmatic driver, Johnson, at the wheel. I told him to drive off, but he said we could not do that, as the French soldier, our escort, was not there. He had gone off to get our windscreen, smashed at Vauchamps, replaced, and had not been seen since. This was most annoying, for the place we were in did not make dallying desirable, and I told Johnson that our stout friend must have taken refuge in a cellar. I decided to give him five minutes grace, and long minutes they were, but before they were quite up a large bearded figure running for dear life appeared, carrying, *mirabile dictu*, a new windscreen. I shall never forget my pleasure at seeing the Frenchman alive, nor the absurdity of his emergence from that inferno of destruction clasping the only unbroken piece of glass in the neighbourhood.

At last we were off, but had not gone a hundred yards when we pulled up to let a column of infantry, which was being withdrawn into safety, go by. With characteristic French courtesy, and perhaps a touch of sardonic humour, they stopped to let us pass, waving us on, whilst I, standing in the car, begged them with many bows to proceed.

For some time the Staff stood about at a street corner in the Faubourg de Vesle, then, as it became evident that the French attack was having no effect and that the Germans remained exactly where they were, bombarding the town with renewed vigour, the report centre was removed to Pargny, H.Q. itself being sent to the horrible little village of Romigny, where it was to spend many weary months. Next day I noticed a hole as big as a hand through the bottom of my British warm. A large splinter of shell must have passed between my knees without my noticing it at the time. I pointed this out to de Rose, who maintained that rats and not Germans had spoilt my coat. After all, this was quite possible in the loft in which I had slept.

There were some painful scenes at Romigny that evening. A spy hunt was in full cry. That the enemy had known the position of Army H.Q. in Reims seemed evident. It was ascertained that the only part of the town besides the Cathedral that had been shelled was the quite unimportant corner where H.Q. was established; it was also reported that the telephone lines between the forts occupied by the enemy and the town had not been cut. It was suspected that someone had communicated, probably by telephone, the exact position of H.Q. to the enemy. There were rumours that German officers in plain clothes had remained in the town. If there were any they were not caught, but at least twenty people, men and women, accused of spying, were condemned to death and shot in batches next morning. I remember the Chief of Staff consulting de Rose about one couple accused of making light signals to the enemy. He appeared very doubtful concerning their guilt. De Rose, who had had something to do with their arrest, was positive.

I recalled lamentable stories of the siege of Paris, when an accidental light reflected in a mirror swinging in a draught, or some similar mischance, led to accusations such as these. The scene has remained unpleasantly vivid in my mind. General Hély d'Oissel and de Rose were standing in the village street, and the older man, perhaps unconvinced himself, laid on the younger one the burden of responsibility for the decision on which a couple of lives depended.

I had a conversation with one of the officers connected with the court martial that condemned these people, and shudderingly remarked that the evidence was slight, the accusation often improbable, and how could guilt be established in such cases without the possibility of error? His answer made a profound impression on me. "You English don't know what war is. The existence of France is at stake. A single spy may cause such harm as to imperil the fate of the nation. Justice has little to do with it. Our duty is to see that no spy escapes whatever the cost may be. If a proportion of those who are executed today are guilty, even one or two, we have every reason to be satisfied that our duty to the country has been done."

These executions and drastic methods were not ours, but on the other hand it would hardly behove us to criticize them, for often when doubtful cases arose in our own area, difficult to deal with by our more deliberate procedure, the suspected persons were handed over to the French, not merely because it was best to let them deal with people who might turn out to be their own nationals, but also on account of the expeditiousness and rapidity with which we knew they would handle such matters.

To my mind one of the most ghastly things in the war was having anything to do with people accused of spying. I saw the famous shepherd who had been accused of giving away the position of French guns by moving his flock about according to a prearranged plan, as well as an accused man (supposed to be a German officer) who hanged himself in his cell, and many others.

During the advance to the Aisne I witnessed a particularly horrible scene, the questioning of several German civilian prisoners who had fallen into the hands of the French in their advance. They were chained together, and I have an unpleasant memory of their cringing and terrified anxiety to please the French officers. One was a seminarist, who had kept a diary in which were such entries as: "Today we set foot on the soil of the hated nation," etc. "The executions I saw carried out today are just retributions which will humble our loathsome enemies." These extracts were read out to him, and it was ghastly to see him, with a nimbleness of wit born of agonized fear, explaining that the hated nation did not refer to the French at all, but to the Belgians, and that the executions were a mere figure of speech and referred to the burning of some obscene books whose discovery had shocked German susceptibilities. I never knew what happened to these people, for I fled long before a decision had been come to.

The French method of dealing with military offences early in the war was on the same hasty system as that practised in the case of suspected spies, and the sad list of rehabilitations of the memory of men proved in subsequent years to have been wrongly executed is proof enough of this.*

*　　*　　*

Late that night, standing on a hill, we watched Reims burning. The town seemed to be wrapped in flames. At times huge shafts of fire rose higher than the great Cathedral, which stood out etched against the night; then the flames, driven down by a gust of wind, would spread low, an immense blue, red and yellow fan laid flat on the city. At moments the Cathedral disappeared in the darkness, and then would be lit up again suddenly by another great torch of light.

And all the time, from the road which was hidden from us by a hedge, came the sound of a whispering shuffle. Hundreds of people were hurrying by: the inhabitants of Reims were flying from their homes.

*　　*　　*

* Later in the war French methods changed and executions became very rare, especially after General Pétain became Commander-in-Chief.

Disciplinary companies were formed, one per division, into which men who would otherwise have been condemned to death or to long terms of penal servitude were drafted. These Companies were commanded by specially selected officers who received accelerated promotion for their services. They were continuously employed in the hardest and most dangerous tasks and no man was released from them until the officer in command was satisfied that he would give no more trouble.

Invariably those who survived begged to be allowed to return to their units, promising to give no further cause for complaint.

My narrative must come to an end as the last wave of the advance died out on the banks of the Aisne.

On 14th September, 1914, we did not know that the pursuit was at an end. Far from being over, the battle seemed only to be beginning. We imagined that the Allies were about to press on in real earnest, and that the hour of the cavalry had come. We did not guess that the very contrary was the case and that the long siege of the Central Powers lay before us.

A wave of optimism was sweeping over the Allies, which grew in magnitude the farther it moved from the battlefield. The troops were confident; the erstwhile pessimists at Headquarters speculated as to whether the enemy would be able to hold out on the Rhine; the G.Q.G. was becoming lyrical in its communiqués; and in far-distant Bordeaux, where teeming and cheerful crowds thronged the streets, the Government's policy was hardening in a fixed determination to obtain a victory that would restore her lost provinces to France. Further afield still, in Washington, the German Ambassador, Count Bernsdorff, now that the great blow had been delivered and failed, was, under instructions from his Government, seeking American intervention on the basis of a return to the *status quo*. But to these overtures the French Ambassador, Monsieur Jusserand, answered that France would accept the *status quo* when Germany, to re-establish it, gave back their lives to the dead.

No one foresaw what the war was going to develop into, its horror, its duration, its dreariness. No one foresaw trench warfare, and it occurred to none that the day of the mighty manœuvres of armies in which cavalry, artillery and infantry combined in grandiose operations was over for ever.

Looking back, I am deeply thankful that none of those who gazed across the Aisne on September 14th had the faintest glimmering of what was awaiting them. They were untroubled by visions of mud and soaking trenches, nor were they borne down in despair by a vision of the years of misery ahead.

There was nothing to show them that the most dramatic period of the war was over, and that between them and the victory they believed awaited them across the river, stretched four weary years of stalemate on the western front.

APPENDICES

APPENDIX I

ORDER OF BATTLE OF THE BRITISH EXPEDITIONARY FORCE,
AUGUST, 1914

(Taken from British Official History)

Commander-in-Chief – Field-Marshal Sir J. D. P. French, G.C.B., G.C.V.O.,
K.C.M.G.
Chief of the General Staff – Lieut.-General Sir A. J. Murray, K.C.B., C.V.O.,
D.S.O.
Major-General, General Staff – Major-General H. H. Wilson, C.B., D.S.O.
G.S.O.1 (Operations) – Colonel G. M. Harper, D.S.O.
G.S.O.1 (Intelligence) – Colonel G. M. W. Macdonogh.

The Cavalry Division.
    G.O.C. – Major-General E. H. H. Allenby, C.B.
    1st Cavalry Brigade – Brigadier-General C. J. Briggs, C.B.
    2nd Cavalry Brigade – Brigadier-General H. de B. de Lisle, C.B., D.S.O.
    3rd Cavalry Brigade – Brigadier-General H. de la Poer Gough, C.B.
    4th Cavalry Brigade – Brigadier-General Hon. C. E. Bingham, C.V.O., C.B.
    5th Cavalry Brigade – Brigadier-General Sir P. W. Chetwode, Bart., D.S.O.

I. Corps – Lieut.-General Sir D. Haig, K.C.B., K.C.I.E., K.C.V.O., A.D.C. General.
    1st Division – Major-General S. H. Lomax.
    2nd Division – Major-General C. C. Monro, C.B.

II. Corps – (1) Lieut.-General Sir J. M. Grierson, K.C.B., C.V.O., C.M.G.,
A.D.C. General. (Died in train, between Rouen and Amiens, 17th
August, 1914.)
    (2) General Sir H. L. Smith-Dorrien, G.C.B., D.S.O. (Took over
command at Bavai, 4 p.m., 21st August, 1914.)
    3rd Division – Major-General Hubert I. W. Hamilton, C.V.O., C.B., D.S.O.
    5th Division – Major-General Sir C. Ferguson, Bart., C.B., M.V.O., D.S.O.

III. Corps (formed in France, 31st August, 1914) – Major-General W. P.
Pulteney, C.B., D.S.O.
    4th Division (landed in France, night 22nd–23rd August, 1914) –
Major-General T. d'O. Snow, C.B.
    6th Division (embarked for St. Nazaire 8th September, 1914) – Major-
General J. L. Keir, C.B.

The total ration strength of the B.E.F. in August, 1914, was approximately 110,000.

$$* \begin{cases} \text{Rifle strength} & 66,000 \\ \text{Sabre strength} & 7,600 \\ \text{Guns} & 400 \end{cases}$$

NOTES ON THE ORGANIZATION OF SOME OF THE PRINCIPAL FORMATIONS OF THE B.E.F. IN AUGUST, 1914

Cavalry – Regiment = 3 Squadrons = 12 Troops (two machine-guns were an integral part of each Regiment).

Artillery – Royal Horse Artillery – Brigade = 2 R.H.A. Batteries and Brigade Ammunition Column. Battery = six 13-pdr. Q.F. Guns and 12 Ammunition Wagons. Royal Field Artillery – Brigade = 3 R.F.A. Batteries and Brigade Ammunition Column. Battery = six 18-pdr. Q.F. Guns (or six 4·5-inch Howitzers) and 12 Ammunition Wagons. Royal Garrison Artillery – Heavy Battery = four 60-pdr. Guns, 8 Ammunition Wagons and Battery Ammunition Column.

Infantry – Battalion = 4 Companies = 16 Platoons (two machine-guns were an integral part of each Battalion).

Cavalry Division – 4 Cavalry Brigades = 12 Cavalry Regiments, and Divisional Troops.

        Strength 9,269 all ranks.
              9,815 horses.
              24 13-pdrs.
              24 machine-guns.
        Marching depth (about) 11½ miles.

Division – 3 Infantry Brigades = 12 Infantry Battalions and Divisional Troops.

        Strength 18,073 all ranks.
              5,592 horses.
              76 guns (fifty-four 18-pdrs., eighteen 4·5-inch howitzers and four 60-pdrs).
              24 machine-guns
        Marching depth (about) 15 miles.

Army Troops

3 Squadrons Irish Horse.

Engineers – 3 Signal Companies; A to E Air Line Sections; F to P Cable Sections; Q Wireless Section; two Bridging Trains.

4 Aeroplane Squadrons.

1 Battalion Infantry.

A.S.C. Army Troop Train.

2 Field Ambulances.

    * *i.e.* First five divisions.

Lines of Communication Defence Troops – These comprised 5 Battalions, but 4 of these were formed into the 19th Infantry Brigade at Valenciennes on the 22nd August, 1914.

There were in addition the Lines of Communication units, including railway companies, 2 fortress companies, ammunition parks, supply columns, horse and mechanical transport depots, reserve parks, field butcheries and bakeries, clearing, stationary and general hospitals, ambulance trains, etc.

COMPOSITION AND ORDER OF BATTLE OF THE FRENCH ARMY, 1914

The French Army when moblized comprised:

20 Army Corps each of 2 Divisions.

1 Army Corps of 3 Divisions (the Colonial Corps).

3 Independent Divisions (two of these were the 37th and 38th Divisions from North Africa, which were attached to the Fifth Army).

25 Reserve Divisions (4 of which were to reinforce the fortresses of the north-east).

12 Territorial Divisions (8 of these were to take the field, and 4 were to act as fortress troops).

1 Territorial Infantry Brigade.

10 Cavalry Divisions.

Army troops, including heavy artillery, railway troops, aviation, etc.

The garrisons of the fortresses, which comprised 1,643 battalions, 596 squadrons, 1,527 batteries, 528 Engineer units.

The numbers in round figures were:

29 Corps of 2 Divisions, 44,000 men each ⎤	
1 Corps of 3 Divisions, 60,000 men　　　 ⎦	940,000
3 Independent Divisions of 18,000 men each	54,000
25 Reserve Divisions* of 18,000 men each	450,000
12 Territorial Divisions (field and fortress)	184,600
10 Cavalry Divisions at 5,250 men each	52,500
Army troops	187,500
†Garrisons of the fortresses	821,400
Men mobilized to guard communications (G.V.C.'s)	210,000
In the depots	680,000
Making a total of	3,580,000

These figures do not include either the Staffs or the forces in North Africa, except the 37th and 38th Divisions, which were to serve in France, nor the numerous auxiliary services not included in the garrisons of the fortresses. 82,000 men left in Morocco are not included in these figures.

The approximate fighting strength of the French Armies, conservatively estimated in the *Official History of the War* (see figures of active and Reserve Divisions above) is given as:

First Army	256,000 men
Second Army	200,000 ,,
Third Army	168,000 ,,
Fourth Army	193,000 ,,
Fifth Army‡	254,000 ,,
Total	1,071,000 men

* The Reserve Divisions were numbered by adding fifty to Corps area number from which they were drawn, *i.e.*, the I. Corps area provided the 51st Reserve Division.

† The garrison troops were as follows:

Infantry	433,405
Cavalry	9,825
Artillery	148,155
Engineers	33,150
A.S.C.	7,940
Workmen and clerks	31,220
Medical Corps	9,710
Staff clerks	1,130
Gendarmes	1,750
G.V.C.'s	16,215
Customs officials and forest guards mobilized in Army	9,230
Fortress auxiliaries	99,395
Navy personnel	20,275
	821,400

‡ The ration strength of the Fifth Army, on mobilization, including lines of communication troops, was 300,000.

ORDER OF BATTLE OF THE FRENCH ARMIES, AUGUST, 1914

Commander-in-Chief – General Joffre.
Chief of General Staff (Major-Général) – General Belin.
Sub-Chiefs of Staff (Aides-Major-Généraux) – General Berthelot, Colonel Pellé.

First Army – General Dubail.
  VII. Corps (14th and 41st Divisions) – General Bonneau.
  VIII. Corps (15th and 16th Divisions) – General Castelli.
  XIII. Corps (25th and 26th Division) – General Alix.
  XIV. Corps (27th and 28th Divisions – General Pouradier-Duteil.
  XXI. Corps (13th and 43rd Divisions) – General Legrand-Girarde.
  44th Division.
  An Alpine Group.

1st Group of Reserve Divisions (58th, 63rd and 66th) – General Archinard.

6th and 8th Cavalry Divisions.*

Second Army – General de Castelnau.
> *IX. Corps* (17th and 18th Divisions, with Moroccan Divisions attached) – General Dubois.
> *XV. Corps* (29th and 30th Divisions) – General Espinasse.
> *XVI. Corps* (31st and 32nd Divisions) – General Taverna.
> *XVIII. Corps*† (35th and 36th Divisions) – General de Mas-Latrie.
> 2nd Group of Reserve Divisions (59th, 65th and 70th) – General Durand (Léon).
> A mixed Colonial Brigade.
> 2nd and 10th Cavalry Divisions.

Third Army – General Ruffey.
> *IV. Corps* (7th and 8th Divisions) – General Boëlle.
> *V. Corps* (9th and 10th Divisions) – General Brochin.
> *VI. Corps* (12th, 40th and 42nd Divisions) – General Sarrail.
> 3rd Group of Reserve Divisions (54th, 55th and 56th) – General Durand (Paul).

Fourth Army – General de Langle de Cary.
> *XII. Corps* (23rd and 24th Divisions) – General Roques.
> *XVII. Corps* (33rd and 34th Divisions) – General Poline.
> *Colonial Corps* (1st, 2nd and 3rd Colonial Divisions) – General Lefèvre (Jules).
> 9th Cavalry Division.

Fifth Army – General Lanrezac. A.D.C., Captain Besson.
> *Chief of Staff* – General Hély d'Oissel.
> *Sub-Chief of Staff* – Lieut.-Colonel Daydrein.
> *Head of Operations Section* (3ème Bureau) – Commandant Schneider.
> *Head of Intelligence Section* (2ème Bureau) – Commandant Girard.
> *II. Corps* – (transferred to Fourth Army before fighting began) General Gérard.
> *XI. Corps* – (transferred to Fourth Army before fighting began) General Eydoux.
> *I. Corps* – General Franchet d'Esperey.
> > 1st Division – General Gallet.
> > 2nd Division – General Deligny.
> *III. Corps* – General Sauret (replaced on 25th August, 1914, by General Hache).

---

* Early in September two of the Cavalry Divisions of the First and Second Armies, plus the 4th Cavalry Division, were formed into a Cavalry Corps under General Conneau.
† The XVIII. Corps was transferred to the Fifth Army in August, 1914.

5th Division – General Verrier (replaced on 31st August, 1914, by General Pétain).

6th Division – General Bloch (replaced on 31st August, 1914, by General Mangin).

X. Corps – General Desforges.

19th Division – General Bonnier (replaced on 5th September, 1914, by General Bailly).

20th Division – General Boé, wounded 22nd August, 1914. Division temporarily commanded by General Menissier. General Rogerie was appointed to the command on 5th September, 1914).

XVIII. Corps – General de Mas-Latrie (replaced on 4th September, 1914, by General de Maud'huy).

35th Division – General Exelmans (replaced on 4th September, 1914, by General Marjoulet).

36th Division – General Jouannic (replaced on 19th September by General Bertin).

4th Group of Reserve Divisions – General Valabrègue.

51st Reserve Division – General Boutegoud.

53rd Reserve Division – General Perruchon (replaced on 7th September, 1914, by General Journée).

69th Reserve Division – General Le Gros (replaced on 8th September by General Néraud).

37th Division – General Comby.

38th Division – General Muteau (replaced on 13th September by General Brulard).

Cavalry Corps – General Sordet (replaced on 8th September by General Bridoux). (The Corps was for a time attached to the Fifth Army.)

1st Cavalry Division – General Buisson.

3rd Cavalry Division – General de Lastours.

5th Cavalry Division – General Bridoux (succeeded by General Lallemand du Marais).

Conneau's Cavalry Corps (attached to the Fifth Army at the beginning of September, 1914) – General Conneau.

10th Cavalry Division – General Conneau (succeeded by General de Contades-Gizeux).

8th Cavalry Division – General Mazel.

4th Cavalry Division – General Abonneau. (Attached to Fifth Army except for a short time, when it was attached to Fourth Army, and on 3rd September became part of Conneau's Corps.)

On mobilization the Fifth Army comprised 172 battalions (40 regiments), 58 squadrons (14 regiments), 190 batteries, 17 heavy batteries, 22 engineer companies.

Total ration strength including line of communication troops, 300,000 men, 110,000 horses, 21,000 vehicles of all kinds.

In round figures – total fighting strength on mobilization, 160,000 rifles, 8,000 sabres,* 800 guns.

Sixth Army – General Maunoury.

Composition on 28th August, 1914

    VII. Corps – General Vautier.

        3rd bis Group of Reserve Divisions (55th and 56th Reserve Divisions) – General Beaudenom de Lamaze.

        6th Group of Reserve Divisions (61st and 62nd Divisions) – General Ebener (passed under orders of Governor of Paris on 1st September).

On the 5th September, 1914, the Army comprised –

    VII. Corps

    5th (ex 3rd bis) Group of Reserve Divisions.

    45th Division – General Drude.

    Sordet's Cavalry Corps.

On the 7th September, 1914,

    IV. Corps – General Boëlle – joined the Army.

On the 8th September, 1914 –

    62nd Division, which had been engaged on defensive works, rejoined the Army.

On the 9th September –

    37th Division joined the Army (from the Fifth Army).

On the 10th September the Army comprised –

    VII. Corps.

    IV. Corps.

    5th Group of Reserve Divisions.

    6th Group of Reserve Divisions.

    45th Division.

    37th Division.

On the 11th September

    XIII. Corps – General Alix – joined the Army.

Sordet's (later Bridoux's) Cavalry Corps was attached to the Sixth Army from the 30th August, as was also the Provisional Cavalry Division – General Cornulier-Lucinière – which was dissolved on the 8th September, 1914, and replaced by the 5th Cavalry Division.

---

* *i.e.* The 4th Cavalry Division and Divisional and Corps Cavalry.

To make the changes in the composition of the Fifth Army clear, they are enumerated together here:

The Fourth Army took over from the Fifth Army: II. Corps, XI. Corps, 52nd and 60th Reserve Divisions; a Cavalry Division.

The Fifth Army, to make up for this, received the 37th and 38th Divisions from Africa; the XVIII. Corps from the Second Army, and General Valabrègue's 4th Group of three Reserve Divisions. So that the Corps it comprised on August 20th were the I., III, X., XVIII., with the 37th Division attached to the III. Corps, and the 38th to the X. Corps, and the 4th Group of Reserve Divisions.

APPENDIX III

ORGANIZATION OF SOME OF THE PRINCIPAL FRENCH FORMATIONS
AND UNITS IN 1914

(From British Official History)

Cavalry

Cavalry Brigade = 2 Regiments and machine-gun section.
Cavalry Regiment = 32 officers, 651 all ranks, and 687 horses = 4 squadrons.
Cavalry Squadron = 5 officers, 145 other ranks, 143 horses.

Artillery

Field – Regiment (Divisional) = 3 *groupes*; Regiment (Corps) = 4 *groupes*;
    Groupe = 3 batteries; Battery = 4 guns, 12 wagons, etc.
*Heavy** – Regiment, strength variable; those in Second and Fifth Armies
    consisted of six 120-mm. batteries and seven 144-mm. batteries. The
    4th Regiment had 5 *groupes* each of four 120-mm. batteries.
    Groupe = 3 or 4 batteries.
    Battery = 4 guns, 8 wagons, observation wagon, etc.

Infantry

Brigade = 2 regiments.
Regiment = 3 battalions and H.Q. company.
Battalion = 4 companies and a machine-gun section (22 officers and 1,030
    other ranks), etc.
Company = 2 *pelotons* each of 2 *sections*.

Cavalry Division

3 Cavalry Brigades.
1 Horse Artillery Brigade (of two 4-gun batteries).
Groupe cycliste (4 officers and 320 other ranks).
Telegraph detachment, etc.
    4,500 all ranks and 8 guns.

Division

2 Infantry Brigades.
1 Squadron.
3 Field Artillery *groupes*.
Engineer Company, etc.
    15,000 all ranks, 36 guns and 24 machine-guns.

---

* Allotted to Armies and Corps.

Reserve Division

2 Brigades.
1 Squadron.
3 Field Artillery *groupes*, etc.
  Reserve Brigades = 3 regiments and a *chasseur* battalion.
  Reserve Regiment = 2 battalions.

Corps

Normally 2 Divisions.
1 Cavalry Regiment.
Field Artillery Regiment.
1 *Groupe* of 155-cm. Howitzers.
1 Engineer Company.
Reserve Infantry Brigade of 2 Regiments of 2 Battalions each.

APPENDIX IV

When war broke out the Belgian Army was in process of reorganization with the object of raising the Field Army to 150,000 men and the garrison troops to 130,000 men, but in 1914 only 117,000 men could be mobilized in the Field Army.

Belgian plans were based on the contingency of having to face either France or Germany or even England, and had the purpose, in M. de Broqueville's words, of inclining the scales in favour of those countries which had not been the first to violate Belgian territory.

Liège and Namur were barrier forts which were intended to prevent either the French or the German Armies from crossing the Meuse.

Field troops were intended to co-operate in their defence.

Antwerp was the greatest fortress in Belgium, to which as a last resort the Army could retire.

ORDER OF BATTLE OF THE BELGIAN ARMY, AUGUST, 1914

Commander-in-Chief – His Majesty King Albert.
Chief of the General Staff – Lieut.-General Chevalier de Selliers de Moranville.
  1st Division – Lieut.-General Baix.
  2nd Division – Lieut.-General Dassin.
  3rd Division – Lieut.-General Leman.
  4th Division – Lieut.-General Michel.
  5th Division – Lieut.-General Ruwet.
  6th Division – Lieut.-General Latonnois van Rode.
  Cavalry Division – Lieut.-General de Witte.

The Strength of a Division varied between 25,500 and 32,000 all ranks, with 60 guns and 18 machine-guns.

The Cavalry Division had 2 cavalry brigades (each of 2 cavalry regiments), 3 Horse Artillery batteries (12 guns), a cyclist battalion, a cyclist pioneer bridging company, telegraphists and transport.

The strength of the Cavalry Division was 4,500 all ranks, with 3,400 horses and 12 guns.

APPENDIX V

COMPOSITION AND ORDER OF BATTLE OF THE GERMAN ARMY, 1914

(*Information taken mainly from French Official History*)

From 1871 until 1893 the peacetime effectives of the French and German Armies were approximately equal, but after that date the German numbers were constantly increased.

In 1893 the strength of the German peacetime Army was raised from 467,000 to 549,000, and by 1912 the real figures for the peacetime Army were 715,000 all ranks; two more Corps were created.

In 1913 the numbers were further increased by 168,000, making a total of approximately 880,000 men with the colours in peacetime.

At the same time great efforts were made to improve the auxiliary services; the technical services and the foot artillery were reinforced. By the beginning of 1914 most of the programme laid down the previous year had been realized.

The French had deduced from a study of the German mobilization plan that these additions and improvements would enable an "*attaque brusquée*" to be made but would not enable the different armies to mobilize more rapidly.

The French knew the Germans were to create Reserve Corps on mobilization. They were also aware how these were to be employed, since the new German mobilization plan stated: "The Reserve troops will be employed as the active troops." They estimated that the Cavalry Divisions would be mobilized on the second day and certain special Brigades on the fourth day. The mobilization of the covering troops would be completed on the sixth day, as also that of the first line defences. Normal concentration, they knew, would begin on the 5th and 6th days and be complete on the 15th day.

They calculated that 20 active Corps, 10 Reserve Corps, 8 Reserve Divisions and 8 Cavalry Divisions would be concentrated against them, whereas in reality the Germans placed on the Western front 22 active Corps, 13 Reserve Corps, 7 Ersatz Divisions, 14 Landwehr Brigades and 10 Cavalry Divisions. The French thought they would have to deal with 60 Divisions, whereas they were opposed by 78 Divisions plus 14 Landwehr Brigades and 2 more Cavalry Divisions than they had reckoned with.

The Army was organized into 25 Active Corps (50 Divisions), *i.e.*, the Guard Corps and Corps numbered I. to XXI., plus 3 Bavarian Corps.

On mobilization 14 Reserve Corps were added, and 3 Reserve Brigades.

On the 16th August the formation of 6 new Reserve Corps and 1 new Reserve Division was ordered.

The Germans further mobilized from *Ersatz* and *Landwehr* Brigades and

Regiments the equivalent of 16 Divisions, making a total of 111 Divisions plus 3 Brigades, and 11 Cavalry Divisions.

The approximate mobilizable strength was in round figures –

Trained officers and men	4,300,000
Partially trained	100,000
Untrained	5,500,000
	9,900,000

The original Reserve Corps were formed mainly of Reservists supernumerary to the requirements of the active Army, with some *Landwehr*, but the Guard Reserve Corps contained an active Division and the V., VI. and VII. Reserve Corps, each contained an active Brigade, as the active Corps of these numbers each had in peacetime an extra Brigade and others had similarly an active Regiment.

The *Ersatz* Reserve consisted of men fit and liable for military service but who, for different reasons, had not been called up.

The *Landwehr* units were formed of men who had completed seven years with active Army and Reserve and were under 39 years of age.

The active Corps on mobilization did not include more than a third of reservists belonging almost all to the last liberated class.

The approximate numbers of the German Armies on the Western front, excluding the higher Cavalry formations, were:

First Army	320,000	men
Second Army	260,000	,,
Third Army	180,000	,,
Fourth Army	180,000	,,
Fifth Army	200,000	,,
Sixth Army	220,000	,,
Seventh Army	125,000	,,
	1,485,000	

The density of the different German Armies on the original front on the 17th August, 1914, is of interest.

First Army front,	18 miles,	about	18,000	men per mile			
Second Army front,	20 ,,	,,	13,000	,,	,,	,,	
Third Army front,	15 ,,	,,	12,000	,,	,,	,,	
Fourth Army front,	30 ,,	,,	6,000	,,	,,	,,	
Fifth Army front,	40 ,,	,,	5,000	,,	,,	,,	
Sixth Army front,	70 ,,	,,	3,100	,,	,,	,,	
Seventh Army front,	35 ,,	,,	3,500	,,	,,	,,	

ORDER OF BATTLE OF GERMAN ARMIES, AUGUST, 1914

Chief of Staff – Generaloberst von Moltke.
Deputy Chief – General von Stein.
Chief of Operations Bureau – Oberst Tappen.
Chief of Intelligence – Oberleutnant Hentsch.

(1) ARMIES OPPOSED TO THE B.E.F., THE FRENCH FIFTH ARMY
AND THE BELGIAN ARMY IN AUGUST, 1914

First Army – Generaloberst von Kluck.
  II. Corps – von Linsingen (3rd and 4th Divisions).
  III. Corps – von Lichow (5th and 6th Divisions).
  IV. Corps – Sixt von Arnim (7th and 8th Divisions).
  IX. Corps – von Quast (17th and 18th Divisions).
  III. Reserve Corps – von Beseler (5th and 6th Reserve Divisions).
  IV. Reserve Corps – von Gronau (7th Reserve and 22nd Reserve Divisions).
  *IX. Reserve Corps – von Boehn (17th Reserve and 18th Reserve Divisions).
    10th, 11th and 27th *Landwehr* Brigades.
    1 *Pionier* Regiment.

Second Army – Generaloberst von Bülow.
  Guard Corps – von Plettenberg (1st Guard and 2nd Guard Divisions).
  VII. Corps – von Einem (13th and 14th Divisions).
  X. Corps – von Emmich (19th and 20th Divisions).
  VII. Reserve Corps – von Zwehl (13th and 14th Reserve Divisions).
  †Guard Reserve Corps – von Gallivitz (3rd Guard and 14th Reserve Divisions).
  X. Reserve Corps – Graf von Kirchbach (2nd Guard Reserve and 19th Reserve Divisions).
    25th and 29th *Landwehr* Brigades.
    4 Mortar Battalions.
    1 10-cm. Gun Battalion.
    2 Heavy Coast Mortar Battalions.
    2 *Pionier* Regiments.

Third Army – Generaloberst Freiherr von Hausen.
  XI. Corps† – von Pluskow (22nd and 38th Divisions).
  XII. (1st Saxon) Corps – d'Elsa (23rd and 32nd Divisions).
  XIX. (2nd Saxon) Corps – von Laffert (24th and 40th Divisions).
  XII. (Saxon) Reserve Corps – von Kirchbach (23rd and 24th Reserve Divisions).
    47th *Landwehr* Brigade.
    2 Mortar Battalions.
    1 *Pionier* Regiment.
  I. Cavalry Corps – Lieutenant-General Freiherr von Richtofen.
    Guard Cavalry Division.
    5th Cavalry Division.

* This corps was originally left behind in Schleswig to oppose landings, and as it was hurried up behind the advance it sacked Louvain, August 25th, 1914.
  † These two corps (Guard Reserve and XI.) began to move to the Russian front on August 26th, after the fall of Namur.

II. Cavalry Corps – Lieutenant-General von der Marwitz.
    2nd Cavalry Division.
    4th Cavalry Division.
    9th Cavalry Division.

(2) NOT OPPOSED TO THE BRITISH IN AUGUST–SEPTEMBER, 1914

Fourth Army – Generaloberst Duke Albrecht of Württemberg.
    VI. Corps* – von Pritzelwitz.
    VIII. Corps – von Weidenbach.
    XVIII. Corps – von Schenk.
    VIII. Reserve Corps – von Egloffstein.
    XVIII. Reserve Corps – von Steuben.
        49th *Landwehr* Brigade, 2 Mortar Battalions and a *Pionier* Regiment.

Fifth Army – Crown Prince of Germany.
    V. Corps – von Strantz.
    XIII. Corps – von Fabeck.
    XVI. Corps – von Mudra.
    V. Reserve Corps – von Gündell.
    VI. Reserve Corps – von Gossler.
        33rd Reserve Division.
    IV. Cavalry Corps (3rd and 6th Cavalry Divisions) – von Hollen.
        13th, 43rd, 33rd and 9th Bavarian *Landwehr* Brigades.
        4 Mortar Battalions and 2 *Pionier* Battalions.

Sixth Army – Crown Prince Rupprecht of Bavaria.
    XXI. Corps – Fritz von Below.
    I. Bavarian Corps – von Xylander.
    II. Bavarian Corps – von Martini.
    III. Bavarian Corps – von Gebsattel.
    I. Bavarian Reserve Corps – von Fasbender.
    III. Cavalry Corps (7th, 8th and Bavarian Cavalry Divisions) – von Frommel.
    Guard *Ersatz* Division.
    4th, 7th and 8th *Ersatz* Divisions.

Seventh Army – Generaloberst von Herringen.
    XIV. Corps – von Heiningen.
    XV. Corps – von Deimling.
    XIV. Reserve Corps – von Schubert.
        Strasbourg Reserve Division.
        19th and Bavarian *Ersatz* Divisions.
        109th, 112th, 114th and 142nd *Landwehr* Regiments.

* To Fifth Army, August 28th.

Total on Western front –
    45 Divisions.
    27 Reserve Divisions.
    10 Cavalry Divisions.
    6 *Ersatz* Divisions (17 Brigades).
    14 *Landwehr* Brigades.
    15 Artillery Battalions.
    7 *Pionier* Regiments.

(3) RUSSIAN FRONTIER

Eighth Army – Generaloberst von Prittwitz.
    I. Corps – von François.
    XVII. Corps – von Mackensen.
    XX. Corps – von Scholtz.
    I. Reserve Corps – Otto von Below.
    3rd Reserve Division.
    1st Cavalry Division.
    5th *Ersatz* Division.
    6th and 70th *Landwehr* Brigades.
    von der Goltz's *Landwehr* Division.*

* Originally in Schleswig to oppose landings; arrived in East Prussia on August 28th, 1914.

APPENDIX VI

NOTES ON THE ORGANIZATION OF SOME OF THE PRINCIPAL GERMAN
FORMATIONS AND UNITS IN 1914

(*Taken from British Official History*)

Air Force –
Field Balloon Detachment = 2 balloons.
Gas Column.
Flying Detachment = 12 aeroplanes.
(One Balloon Detachment was allotted to each Army and one
Flying Detachment was allotted to each Army and Corps.)

Cavalry –
Cavalry Brigade = 2 Regiments.
Cavalry Regiment = 36 officers, 686 other ranks, and 765 horses.
4 Squadrons, Telegraph Detachment, and 1st and 2nd Line
Transport.
Squadron = 6 officers, 163 other ranks, and 178 horses.

Artillery, Field –
Brigade = 2 Regiments (72 guns).
Regiment = 2 *Abteilungen*.
Abteilung = 3 Batteries and Light Ammunition Column.
Battery = 6 guns, 6 ammunition wagons (4 of each in horse batteries),
1 Observation Wagon, and 1st and 2nd Line Transport.

Artillery, Foot (Heavy) of the Field Army –
Regiment = 2 Battalions.
Battalion = 4 Batteries of 5·9-inch (15 cm.) howitzers, or 2 Batteries
of 8·27-inch (21 cm.) mortars.
Battery = 4 guns.

Infantry –
Brigade = 2 Regiments.
Regiment = 3 Battalions and a Machine-gun Company of 6 guns and
1 spare gun.
Battalion = 4 Companies (26 officers and officials and 1,050 other
ranks) and 1st and 2nd Line Transport.

Battalion of *Jäger* = 4 Companies and a Machine-gun Company
(4 officers and 104 other ranks) and a Cyclist Company (3
officers and 113 other ranks).
Company = 3 Platoons (5 officers and 259 other ranks).

Cavalry Division –
3 Cavalry Brigades.
Divisional Troops –
Horse Artillery *Abteilung* (three 4-gun batteries).
1, 2 or 3 *Jäger* Battalions, each with Machine-gun Company of
6 guns.
Machine-gun battery (mounted).
Pionier Detachment.
Heavy and Light Wireless Stations.
Motor Transport Column.
5,200 all ranks, 5,600 horses, 12 guns, 6 machine-guns.

Infantry Division –
2 Infantry Brigades.
Divisional Troops –
1 Field Artillery Brigade (72 guns).
1 Cavalry Regiment.
1 or 2 *Pionier* Companies (3 per Corps).
1 Divisional Bridging Train.
1 Divisional Telephone Detachment.
1 or 2 Medical Companies (3 per Corps).
17,500 all ranks, 4,000 horses, 72 guns, 24 machine-guns.

Cavalry Corps –
2 or 3 Cavalry Divisions.

Corps –
2 Infantry Divisions.
Corps Troops:
1 Foot Artillery Regiment.
1 *Jäger* Battalion.
1 Corps Bridging Train.
1 Telephone Detachment.
1 Searchlight Section.
1 Flying Detachment.
4 Infantry Ammunition Columns.
9 Field Artillery Ammunition Columns.
8 Heavy Artillery Ammunition Columns.
12 Field Hospitals.
6 Supply Columns.
7 Transport Columns.
2 Horse Depots.
2 Field Bakeries.

Reserve Division –
> Same as Active Division, except that it had 6 Field Batteries instead of 12.

Reserve Corps –
> Same as Active Corps, except it has 12 Field Batteries instead of 24, no heavy guns, no aeroplanes and correspondingly fewer ammunition columns.

Landwehr Brigade –
> 2 Regiments of 3 Battalions.
> 1 Squadron.
> 1 Battery.

APPENDIX VII

THE LACK OF TRAINING OF FRENCH INFANTRY

The alarm felt by the Higher Command at the indifferent training of the French troops at the beginning of the war is shown by the following:

On August 16th General Joffre sent the following communication to the Army Commanders:

"The engagements which have taken place so far have served to display the admirable qualities of our infantry. Without in any way wishing to impair this dash, in which lies the principal factor of success, it is of the greatest importance, especially when it is a question of carrying fortified positions, to learn to await artillery support and to prevent the troops from hastily exposing themselves to the enemy's fire.

"It is further necessary that at no time should the direction of the fight escape the control of the generals. The infantry must feel its way when attacking strong points, then turn them if possible, and not be content merely to attack frontally.

"As many guns as possible should be engaged from the beginning of an engagement. The attacks will be all the more successful, all the less costly in proportion to the care with which they have been prepared.

"Every time that this has been done and that the commander has known how to operate with method and rapidity, combining the action of the two arms, the undoubted superiority of our artillery together with the irresistible force of our infantry have insured immediate success."

See Les Armées Françaises dans la Grande Guerre, Tome I., Vol. 1, Annex 352.

APPENDIX VIII

GENERAL LANREZAC'S MEMORANDUM TO THE GRAND QUARTIER GENERAL
WITH REFERENCE TO THE OFFENSIVE OF THE FIFTH ARMY AND THE
PROBABLE MOVEMENTS OF THE ENEMY

"Paris, July 31st, 1914.

"The mission entrusted to the Fifth Army, in the eventuality of the violation of Belgian neutrality by the Germans, is to develop a counter-offensive in the general direction of Neufchâteau.

"The conditions under which such a counter-attack may be envisaged are as follows:

"1. The Fifth Army ought, before becoming engaged in the wooded defiles of the Ardennes and of the Semoy, to be certain not only of being able to debouch from these defiles without encountering opposition, but further to be able to get sufficiently far to be able to deploy beyond them.

"In practice, this means that it should be able to reach with its four left corps the front Paliseul–Maissin–Bertrix–St. Médard before the enemy.

"This front is three days march from the German frontier.

"The Fifth Army, according to the dates laid down for the detrainment of its units, could not reach this front until the thirteenth day." (*i.e* of mobilization.)

"2. It is essential that the 2nd Corps should be relieved of its mission as a covering force early enough to participate, on the right of the Fifth Army, in any action in which the latter may be engaged as soon as it is clear of the defiles.

"3. It is not less essential that the offensive of the Fifth Army should be reinforced by the *simultaneous* offensive of the army to be stationed on its right.

"An offensive by the Fifth Army on Neufchâteau would meet the eventuality, which seems probable, that the German right would be directed on Sedan. But it is possible that it may be directed much farther to the north. This evidently depends upon the amplitude which the Germans would or could give to their enveloping movement through Belgium.

"In recent German military studies (notably the *Kriegspiel* of 1911 of the General Staff) the passage of three German armies through Belgium is envisaged, of which the northernmost would be directed towards Dinant, so as to be able to cross the Meuse between Givet and Namur.

"On the other hand, the obstacle of the Meuse is reinforced between Mézières and Givet by a formidable wooded belt, which it would take a day's march to cross, in which no army would become involved if it knew the exits were guarded.

"From this it follows that the army forming the right of the German right wing group can only be directed either above the barrier, that is on Sedan, *or below it, that is on Givet and further north.*

"It is obvious that once the Fifth Army is engaged in the direction of Neufchâteau it could not meet this latter eventuality, which is only envisaged here in order that it may be noted.

"LANREZAC."

APPENDIX IX

INSTRUCTION PARTICULIÈRE NO. 6

Grand Quartier Générale, August 13th.

Instruction Particulière No. 6 to the Commanders of the Third, Fourth and Fifth Armies.

1. The situation of the enemy as it is known to us makes it appear possible that we may not have time to seek battle beyond the Semoy and the Chiers under good conditions.

2. Consequently, the following dispositions will be made, beginning on the 14th August, in view of the battle which may be joined on the 15th or 16th.

3. The Third Army, holding with its reserve divisions the positions organized north and south of Verdun, will dispose its forces so as to be able to counter-attack all forces debouching from Metz with its two right corps (in which action the XVIII. Corps, under the direct orders of the Commander-in-Chief, will co-operate) or to participate in the attack of the Fourth Army with the IV. and V. Corps, in a northerly direction (keeping to the west of the wooded region Gremilly, Billy-sous-Mangiennes).

4. The Fourth Army will push the heads of its main bodies on the 14th August up to the front Sommauthe, Dun-sur-Meuse.

The II. Corps will conform to the dispositions prescribed for it in *Instruction Particulière No. 1*, but will confine its retreat to the line of the Hauts-de-Meuse, from Ecurey to Brandeville (if it is hard pressed by superior forces).

5. The Fifth Army will have the heads of its main bodies eight or ten kilometres behind the Meuse in front of and above Mézières. It will not attack until the enemy has engaged a considerable part of his forces on the left bank. The attack must be organized, and, once begun, sharply pressed.

Below Mézières as far as Givet, the passages of the Meuse must be energetically defended and destroyed if need be. It is left to the Commander of the Fifth Army to decide when and if they are to be blown up.

The I. Corps will cover the left of the Fifth Army and will give support to the Cavalry Corps. It will, by its position, cover the detrainment of the divisions from Africa.

6. The Cavalry Corps will remain on the left of the Fifth Army and will continue to carry out its original mission, but it will not cross to the left bank of the Meuse unless it is unable to remain on the right bank.

7. The 37th Division will detrain between the 13th and 16th August in the region Tournes–Auvillers-les-Forges, billeting area during concentration, about Rocroi.

The 38th Division will detrain between the 13th and 16th August in the region Anor–Hirson billeting area during concentration, about Chimay.

These two divisions will be at the disposal of the Fifth Army, which can attach them to its two left corps, and modify accordingly the billeting areas.

8. Should the necessity arise, the group of Reserve Divisions at Vervins will use its fortified position to protect the withdrawal of the left of our forces.

9. If the enemy is still some distance off, the Fourth and Fifth Armies must take all necessary steps, as from the 15th August, to be in a position to advance rapidly, as soon as they receive the order, to the front Beauraing–Gedinne–Paliseul–Fays-les-Veneurs–Cugnon (Fifth Army), Tétaigne–Margut–Quincy (Fourth Army).

The route Létanne, Mouzon (exclusive), Tétaigne, will be reserved to the Fourth Army.

J. JOFFRE.

APPENDIX X

INSTRUCTION PARTICULIÈRE NO. 10

August 15th, 1914.

To the Commanders of the Fourth and Fifth Armies and the Cavalry Corps.

1. The enemy seems to be making his main effort by his right wing north of Givet. Another group of hostile forces seems to be marching on the front Sedan–Montmédy–Damvillers.

2. The Fifth Army, leaving its right corps in the region south-west of Sedan and its reserve divisions to defend the line of the Meuse, and leaving the 4th Cavalry Division at the disposal of the Fourth Army, will move the remainder of its forces to the neighbourhood of Mariembourg and Phillippe-ville, to operate together with the British and Belgian forces against the enemy forces to the north.

The Cavalry Corps is placed under the orders of the Fifth Army. The Group of Reserve Divisions at Vervins is also at the disposal of the Commander of the Fifth Army.

3. The Fourth Army, to which the XI. Corps is attached until further orders, as are the 52nd and 60th Reserve Divisions, will establish itself facing north-east so as to be in a position to debouch on the front Sedan–Montmédy in the general direction of Neufchâteau.

The 4th Cavalry Division is placed under the orders of the Fourth Army.

JOFFRE.

On August 16th, the above order was modified by the extension of the Fourth Army to Jametz. The Fourth Army was also ordered to organize its present position defensively whilst awaiting the order to advance.

APPENDIX XI

GENERAL JOFFRE'S MEMORANDUM FOR SIR JOHN FRENCH

G.Q.G., August 16th, 1914, 2.25 p.m.

Secret and Personal

For the British Commander-in-Chief

The enemy appears to be making his main effort with his right wing and his centre, on the one hand north of Givet, on the other on the front Sedan–Montmédy–Damvillers. South of Metz, he seems to be on the defensive.

General Lanrezac, commanding the Fifth Army, has as his objective to operate against the enemy forces to the north, in co-operation with the British Army and the Belgians.

General Lanrezac disposes of the following forces to carry out this mission:

The Fifth Army, which has one corps on the Meuse facing Dinant, two corps plus two African Divisions which are marching on Philippeville, of which the last corps will detrain about Maubeuge and will be in position on the evening of August 20th about Beaumont.

The Cavalry Corps (three divisions) under General Sordet.

The Group of Reserve Divisions (three divisions about Vervins) under General Valabrègue.

The fortress of Maubeuge is under General Lanrezac's orders.

It is not possible as yet to determine precisely the form the manœuvre will take, in view of eventualities which may arise between now and the 21st, but on general lines the idea of this manœuvre for the British Army in particular will be as follows:

As soon as the fighting forces are assembled, that is to say by the morning of the 21st, the British Army will advance north of the Sambre, in the area of Rouveroy, Harmignies, so as to be in position to march in the general direction of Nivelles:

Either on the left of the Fifth Army as the main body of our forces moves up towards the north, or in echelon to the rear of the Fifth Army if the direction of the latter's march inclines farther to the east.

In any case the Cavalry Corps will cover to the north of the Sambre the movement of the British Army, whose Cavalry Division might co-operate with the former.

On coming into contact with the enemy, the Cavalry Corps will disengage itself so as to be able to place itself on the left of the British Army.

With reference to the co-operation of the Belgian Army, it might be asked, while covering Brussels and Antwerp, to operate under all circumstances on the far flank of the German forces, or against their rear if need be.

JOFFRE.

APPENDIX XII

August 17th, 1914.

Telephone message from General Hély d'Oissel to the Grand Quartier Général:

1. General Lanrezac has had an interview with Field Marshal French. He ascertained at this interview that the British Army will be ready at the earliest only by the 24th.

2. The British Cavalry will never be available to participate in the operations undertaken by General Sordet's Corps. It will be employed as mounted infantry in the line, and cannot be counted upon for any other purpose.

3. General Lanrezac calls attention to the fact that the Cavalry Corps which has been placed under his orders has received a special mission from the Commander-in-Chief. The Fifth Army is therefore left without Cavalry. General Lanrezac asks that the mission of the Cavalry shall be temporary.*

4. As the area of detrainment of the British Army is very close to the Sambre, the Fifth Army, which would not have at its disposal enough roads in the event of a retirement would be obliged to make incursions into the British area. To avoid the confusion which would result, would it not be possible to *study* the concentration of the British Army further back?

---

* On August 16th, General Lanrezac had been instructed by General Joffre to direct the Cavalry Corps to proceed on the 17th to the region Eghezée-Tirlemont to get into touch with the Belgian troops occupying Namur and the Belgian field forces at Namur and Tirlemont.

APPENDIX XIII

(*"This paper is to be considered by each soldier as confidential, and to be kept in his Active Service Pay Book.*)

"You are ordered abroad as a soldier of the King to help our French comrades against the invasion of a common enemy. You have to perform a task which will need your courage, your energy, your patience. Remember that the honour of the British Army depends on your individual conduct. It will be your duty not only to set an example of discipline and perfect steadiness under fire but also to maintain the most friendly relations with those whom you are helping in this struggle. The operations in which you are engaged will, for the most part, take place in a friendly country, and you can do your own country no better service than in showing yourself in France and Belgium in the true character of a British soldier.

"Be invariably courteous, considerate and kind. Never do anything likely to injure or destroy property, and always look upon looting as a disgraceful act. You are sure to meet with a welcome and be trusted; your conduct must justify that welcome and that trust. Your duty cannot be done unless your health is sound. So keep constantly on your guard against any excesses. In this new experience you may find temptations both in wine and women. You must entirely resist both temptations, and, while treating all women with perfect courtesy, you should avoid any intimacy.

"Do your duty bravely,

"Fear God,

"Honour the King,

"KITCHENER, *Field-Marshal.*"

APPENDIX XIV

INSTRUCTION PARTICULIÈRE NO. 13

8 a.m., August 18th, 1914.

To the Commanders of the Third, Fourth and Fifth Armies.
Communicated to the C.-in-C. British forces.
Communicated to the C.-in-C. Belgian forces.

1. The Third, Fourth and Fifth Armies, acting together with the British and Belgian Armies, are to take as their objective the German forces concentrated in the neighbourhood of Thionville, in Luxembourg and in Belgium.

These latter would appear to comprise a total of thirteen to fifteen corps. They seem to form two main groups.

In the north, the right wing group seems to comprise seven to eight army corps and four cavalry divisions. Farther south, the centre group, between Bastogne and Thionville, may comprise six to seven army corps and two or three cavalry divisions.

2. The Third and Fourth French Armies have already received their orders and been given the initial direction of their offensive.

3. As far as the Fifth French Army, the British Army and the Belgian Army are concerned, two main eventualities may be envisaged.

(1) The enemy northern group, marching along both sides of the Meuse, may try to cross between Givet and Brussels, and even possibly accentuate still further its movement towards the north.

In this event the Fifth French Army and the Cavalry Corps attached to it, operating in complete liaison with the British and Belgian Armies, will oppose itself directly to this movement, attempting to outflank the enemy by the north. The Belgian Army and the Cavalry Corps are already in position for such an outflanking movement.

Meanwhile the French Armies of the centre (Third and Fourth) would in the first place attack the enemy central group so as to put it out of action. Once this result has been obtained, the greater part of the Fourth Army would march immediately against the left flank of the enemy northern group.

(2) The enemy may engage only a fraction of his right wing group north of the Meuse. While his centre is engaged frontally by our Third and Fourth Armies, the other part of his northern group, south of the Meuse, may seek to attack the left flank of our Fourth Army.

Under this second hypothesis, the Fifth Army wheeling on Namur and Givet in the general direction of Marche and St. Hubert, would leave to the British and Belgian Armies the task of dealing with the German forces to the north of the Meuse and of the Sambre.

In view of this possibility, it would be well to organize a strong bridgehead east of Givet on a line which might be marked by Falmagne–Finnevaux–Beauraing–Sevry Wood.

The Group of Reserve Divisions of the Fifth Army might co-operate in whole or in part with the British Army north of the Meuse.

JOFFRE.

APPENDIX XV

Vitry, August 20th, 1914, 7.45 a.m.

Telephone message from the Commander-in-Chief to the G.O.C. Fifth
Army, Signy-le-Petit.

"You sent me on August 19th a report from Commandant Duruy regarding the defence of the fortress of Namur. This report was enclosed with
a letter written at the dictation of the Governor of Namur, and in it the latter
asked for the participation of the French Army in the defence of the fortress.
If you find it possible to do what General Michel asks by drafting one of the
Reserve Divisions attached to your Army into the town, I readily authorize
you to do so.

"Apart from the fact that the possession of Namur is of undeniable importance for the development of our operations, I hold that the co-operation
of French and Belgian troops might be, from another point of view, very
beneficial to both.

"JOFFRE."

To this message General Berthelot added: It might be possible to use for
the transport of a certain number of battalions the sections of motor transport
and some trains *via* Chimay and Charleroi.

General Lanrezac to the Commander-in-Chief, August 20th.

"In reply to your telephone message No. 44913 of August 20th, I have
the honour to report that the wish expressed by General Michel, commanding
the forces at Namur, relates to the co-operation of the French Armies in the
protection of the north-western and south-western sectors of the fortress in
order that the efforts of the Belgian defence may be concentrated on the
north-eastern and south-eastern sectors which are more seriously threatened.

"Since yesterday, the 19th, the Army under my command has infantry on
the Sambre from Floreffe to Tamines. Today, the 20th, a large force of all
arms is at Fosse, ready to debouch north of the Sambre.

"Under these circumstances I consider that the co-operation of the French
Army in the defence of Namur as envisaged by General Michel is assured.
The latter did not ask that French troops should actually be drafted into the
town of Namur itself.

"A second demand from General Michel requests the despatch of 30,000
rounds of 75 ammunition to Namur for the batteries of the mobile defence.

This request was written down by Commandant Duruy at the dictation of General Michel and was sent on to you yesterday, the 19th, together with a printed notice concerning the use of our 75 ammunition in the Belgian guns. This notice was distributed to the Belgian Army when operations started.

"It is not for me to give a decision in the matter of this request.

"LANREZAC."

APPENDIX XVI

The French infantry regiments, the first hundred at least, are descendants of the old pre-revolution army. The last were raised in 1776. A good many are much older. Before the Revolution every regiment had a name, either that of a province or that of the founder or great leader.

From 1791 on there were several general modifications.

1. In 1791 all the regiments lost their names and were given a number and designated as infantry regiments.

2. About 1794 the name regiment was done away with, and the famous *demi-brigade* took its place.

There were battle *demi-brigades* and light *demi-brigades*.

In principle each *demi-brigade* was composed of one battalion of the old Royal Army and two battalions of the Revolutionary levies (volunteers or conscripts – *requisitionnaires*). This was known as the *Amalgame*.

3. In 1803 the First Consul re-established the name of "Regiment".

There were Infantry of the Line Regiments and Light Infantry Regiments.

4. In 1815 the Restoration abolished the Regiments and replaced them by the Departmental Legions (*Légions départementales*).

5. In 1820 the Regiments were finally re-established.

The history of some of the Regiments included in the Fifth Army was as follows:

1st Regiment (1st Division, I. Corps).
> *Picardie* (1569) formed from the old French bands of Picardy commanded by Philippe Strozzi.
> Regiment of *Picardie* (1585).
> Regiment *Colonel Général* (1785). In principle the *Colonel Général* gave his name to the oldest regiment in the army.
> 1st Infantry Regiment (1791).
> 1st Battle *Demi-brigade* of Infantry of the Line (1796) (formed from the 136th Battle *Demi-brigade*).
> 1st Regiment of Infantry of the Line (1820).

2nd Regiment (20th Division, X. Corps).
> *Provence* (1776) formed with the 2nd and 4th Battalions of *Picardie*.
> Regiment of *Picardie* (1780).
> 2nd Regiment of Infantry (1791).
> 2nd Battle *Demi-brigade* (1795–96).

2nd *Demi-brigade* of the Line (1796).
2nd Regiment of Infantry of the Line (1803).
Legion of the *Aisne* (1816).
2nd Regiment of Infantry of the Line (1820).

5th Regiment (6th Division, III. Corps).
> *Navarre* (about 1569) formed from the remnants of the bands of *Guyenne*.
> Regiment of the Guards of Young Henry (1569) in the pay of the King of Navarre (Henry IV) till 1589.
> Regiment of *Valirault* (1589).
> Regiment of *Navarre* (1594).
> 5th Infantry Regiment (1791).
> 5th *Demi-brigade de Bataille* (1794–96).
> 5th Regiment of Infantry of the Line (1803).
> Legions of the *Aveyron* and of the *Drôme* (1815).
> 5th Regiment of Infantry of the Line (1820).

6th Regiment (35th Division, XVIII. Corps).
> *Armagnac* (1796) formed with two Battalions of the Regiment of *Navarre*.
> 6th Infantry Regiment (1791).
> 6th *Demi-brigade de Bataille*.
> 6th *Demi-brigade* of Infantry of the Line (1794–96).
> 6th Regiment of Infantry of the Line (1803).
> Legion of the *Bouches du Rhône* (1816).
> 6th Regiment of Infantry of the Line (1820).

8th Regiment (2nd Division, I. Corps).
> *Austrasie* (1776).
> 8th Infantry Regiment (1791).
> Legion of the *Cantal* and of the *Vendée* (1816).
> 8th Regiment of Infantry of the Line (1820).

12th Regiment (36th Division, XVIII. Corps).
> *Auxerrois* (1692).
> 12th Regiment of Infantry (1791).
> Legion of the *Côtes du Nord* (1815).

18th Regiment (36th Division, XVIII. Corps).
> *Royal Auvergne* (1776) formed from the 2nd and 4th Battalions of the Regiment of *Auvergne*.
> *Régiment du Gâtinais* (1776).
> *Royal Auvergne* (1781).
> 18th Half-brigade of the Line.
>> At Rivoli, Bonaparte, inspecting them said: "Brave 18th, I know you, the enemy will not hold you up."

25th Regiment (20th Division, X. Corps).
> *Poitou* (1616) formed from a corps raised by the Choiseul-Praslin
> family (1585).
> Regiment of *Poitou* (1682).
> 25th Regiment of Infantry (1791).

33rd Regiment (2nd Division, I. Corps).
> *Touraine* (1625).
> Regiment of *Touraine* (1636).

39th Regiment (5th Division, III. Corps).
> *Isle de France* (1629) raised in Belgium as the Guard of the Prince
> Bishop of Liège. Foreign Regiment in the French service. Became
> French in 1647.

43rd Regiment (1st Division, I. Corps).
> *Royal Vaisseaux* (Royal Ships) (1638) raised for service at sea by the
> Bishop of Bordeaux, Henri d'Escoubleau de Sourdis, Admiral of
> France. Received the name "*Royal des Vaisseaux*" for gallantry in
> 1638.

45th Regiment (Mangin's Brigade).
> *Régiment de la Couronne* (1643).

48th Regiment (19th Division, X. Corps).
> *Artois* (1610).
> Regiment *d'Artois* (1673).

GENERAL LANREZAC'S PLANS FOR THE OFFENSIVE

General Lanrezac thus describes in his book the offensive he says he intended
to carry out on August 23rd:

"(1) General Boutegourd's Division (51st Reserve Division) was to guard
the Meuse above Namur. It was to have at its disposal the batteries
of 120 mm. guns on platforms.

"(2) The right of the Army (I. Corps reinforced by Mangin's Brigade,
X. Corps reinforced by an African Division, the heavy artillery, an
African Division to be withdrawn from the III. Corps and kept under
my direct control) was to attack to the west of Namur, where the
country is comparatively open and where it is possible to take
advantage of the protection of the guns of the fortress.

"(3) The centre and left (III. and XVIII. Corps and General Valabrègue's
two Reserve Divisions) were to contain the enemy on the front
Ham-sur-Sambre–Fontaine-l'Evêque."

From *Le Plan de Campagne Français et le premier mois de la Guerre*, p. 118.
It may be noted that the fact that the XVIII. Corps was still somewhat
behindhand, its foremost division only reaching Thuin on the Sambre on the
night of the 21st, need have influenced General Lanrezac's plan but little had
he wished to assume the offensive earlier than the 23rd. It has been pointed
out that the III. Corps could easily have occupied the industrial area with
detachments. Had this been done its left would have been secure on the canal,
and further would have been protected by the leading division of the XVIII.
Corps, now close at hand.

General Lanrezac himself appears to have felt that his decision not to
advance across the river requires some explanation, for in his book, under the
date 20th August, he says that already on the 20th the Germans were holding
the exits of the "*Borinage*" – the district round Charleroi – but he must have
made a mistake in dates owing to a lapse of memory. His remarks are
applicable to the 21st, but not to the 20th.

"So the Fifth Army, continuing its movement to the north, would have
come up against the *Borinage* between Charleroi and Namur, the Germans
already holding the exits of this region, which is tactically so difficult."
Le Plan de Campagne Français, p. 120.

As a matter of fact, the French Cavalry Corps on the 19th was still fighting
as far north as Perwez, and was only opposed by cavalry with infantry supports. It was not until the evening of the 20th that German infantry was

reported to have advanced south of Gembloux as far as Balâtre–St. Martin–Mazy–Bothey, Corroy-le-Château, with cavalry towards Boignée. On the 20th, therefore, General Lanrezac, whose troops had reached the Sambre the day before, could, had he so desired, have seized the exits of the industrial area. It was not till the next day that German infantry was in the immediate neighbourhood. At any time on the 20th infantry could have established itself in a position anywhere between Charleroi and Gembloux.

APPENDIX XVIII

GENERAL LANREZAC'S ORDERS FOR THE OFFENSIVE

PERSONAL AND SECRET INSTRUCTIONS FOR THE GENERALS COMMANDING THE CAVALRY CORPS, 4TH GROUP OF RESERVE DIVISIONS, AND THE I., III., X. AND XVIII. CORPS

Fifth Army H.Q. at Chimay, August 21st, 1914, 4 p.m.

The Army will hold itself in readiness to assume the offensive as soon as it receives the order, by crossing the Sambre and advancing on the front Namur–Nivelles.

As this offensive is dependent on that of neighbouring armies, the moment when it will take place cannot at the moment be fixed.

Consequently the Corps will tomorrow close in their main bodies on their leading units, and will take up the following positions so as to be in readiness to oppose, if need be, any hostile forces which might debouch south of the Sambre.

The X. Corps will organize the general position Fosse–Vitrival–Sart–St. Eustache. It will dispose of the group of 120 mm. long and the group of 155 c.t.r. (quick firing short) . . .

On its right the I. Corps will occupy and organize the position Sart–St. Laurent by a brigade. It will continue to hold the passages of the Meuse on its present front.

On the left of the X. Corps the III. Corps will organize on its present front a position which will enable it to oppose an advance by the enemy either by Châtelet or on the Charleroi–Philippeville road. It will also take steps to support in flank the action of the X. Corps or eventually that of the XVIII. Corps. It will dispose until further orders of the groups of the 1st Regiment of Heavy Artillery . . . two groups of 120 mm. long and one group of 155 c.t.r.*

The XVIII. Corps will organize the position Thuin–Gozée–Ham-sur-Heure. The Corps will hold by posts the bridges of the Sambre on this front. The orders of these posts will be not to resist columns of all arms in the bottom of the valley, but simply to stop possible incursions of cavalry. They will be reinforced as soon as the order to cross the Meuse (*sic*) has been given.

---

* As has been seen in the text of my narrative, the heavy guns were not used to defend the river passages. The fault may be largely imputable to the Corps Commanders, but General Lanrezac took no steps to make his intentions clear, and had no personal contact with the Corps Commanders.

The General Commanding the 4th Group of Reserve Divisions will direct tomorrow his right-hand division towards Solre-le-Château so that it can on the 23rd move in the direction of Beaumont or in that of Cousolre. The other division advancing as has been prescribed towards the region south-west of Maubeuge.

LANREZAC.

APPENDIX XIX

GENERAL SORDET'S REQUEST FOR INFANTRY SUPPORT

Fontaine l'Evêque, August 21st, 1914.

The Cavalry Corps is ready to undertake on the 22nd any mission whatsoever with its effectives complete and morale excellent.

The covering troops of the Corps continue to be employed north of the Sambre.

In opposing the German Cavalry, which always remains close to its infantry supports, it is necessary, *if we want to destroy it*, that the Cavalry Corps should dispose of infantry sufficiently numerous to form a screen behind which it can take refuge; without this it is compelled, after attacking, to retire far enough to put between it and the enemy infantry distance enough to ensure being left in peace at night. For lack of infantry, the Cavalry Corps is obliged to start a long way from its objective, and to envisage a long retreat. It has not sufficient time or strength to undertake for instance, in the space of a day, an attack against the flanks of a position held by the enemy cavalry.

A considerable force of infantry would therefore allow it, even if this force did not co-operate in the attack, to obtain much better results at the expense of far less effort.

The necessities of feeding, protecting the transport, the need of halting at times to see to shoeing the horses, all lead to the same conclusion: necessity for the Cavalry Corps, when it is operating over considerable distances, to have an infantry support which should be increased as the distance of the Cavalry from the base increases.

GENERAL SORDET.

Co-operation with the British?

Would it not be a good plan to operate straight to the north, on Nivelles, so as to take in flank the columns which are reported to be advancing from east to west?

APPENDIX XX

The following account of an action by part of the III. Corps was given by General Schwartz, who commánded the 12th Brigade, to General Lanrezac. (*Plan de Campagne Français*, p. 165.)

"At ten o'clock General Sauret gave me over the telephone an order to push an attack home immediately in the direction of Châtelet, to retake this place and throw the Germans back over the Sambre. As soon as this order was received I attempted to locate, without success alas, those units of the III. Corps which I was to support. Having got into touch with the commander of the artillery who was to support me, I asked him what he could do, and he answered: 'I cannot attempt to silence the German artillery, for I have not the faintest idea where it is, nor is there any chance of my locating it. On the other hand in the very enclosed country in which your brigade is going to advance I cannot see a single infantry objective. Nevertheless, if you wish I will order my guns to fire so as to make a noise.' I answered that my troops were courageous enough to be able to dispense with this. My battalions, which by now were in attack formation, advanced resolutely towards Le Châtelet and soon found themselves under intense artillery fire. They advanced nevertheless and carried the first houses of the town, but in spite of every endeavour could not succeed in turning out the hostile infantry belonging to the X. German Corps which had entrenched itself there. On our way we had come upon a few very small detachments of the III. Corps, some of which joined in the attack. The battlefield appeared to me to be empty or very nearly so. At about two o'clock, threatened with being out-flanked on my right and my left, I ordered my brigade to retire, stopping whenever the lie of the country allowed me to do so. At nightfall, having got behind the outposts of the III. Corps, I collected my people near Gerpinnes and rejoined my division. I lost more than a third of my men in killed, wounded and missing.

APPENDIX XXI

In the afternoon the Germans attacked the X. Corps on the right and left, but not more than a couple of kilometres of ground were lost. The situation of the III. Corps was much less satisfactory. The 6th Division (one Brigade only) which had fought extremely well on the previous day, gave way under strong pressure in the afternoon. It may be that one of the main causes of this retirement was the reaction of the troops after their extremely trying experience of the previous day, when they had been ordered to retire a considerable distance after what they believed to have been a successful counter-attack. Threatened on its left, this division was driven back in some disorder, and its artillery which on the previous day had brilliantly supported the infantry, pushing forward guns into the firing line, had, owing to some misunderstanding, retired so far as to be useless. This was all the more disappointing since the Corps Commander, General Sauret, had declared in the morning that "he held and would hold *coûte que coûte* the position he then occupied." It is notorious that all was not well with this Corps, and that its weakness had nothing to do with the troops; there was shortly afterwards a change of command.

Late that night General Sauret reported the serious news that the III. Corps was no longer in touch with the X. Corps, and that the 6th Division was incapable of putting up the slightest resistance during the night: to remedy this situation he was withdrawing comparatively fresh units from his right to send them to his left. He said a day's rest was necessary to reconstitute his units.

The retirement of the 6th Division compelled that of the 38th, which had also been violently attacked. Further to the right, the 5th Division had not moved during the day.

The XVIII. Corps had been attacked during the afternoon. The 11th Brigade of Infantry, which had been acting as support to the Cavalry Corps and was now attached to the XVIII. Corps, lost the bridges over the Sambre at Lobbes and Fontaine Valmont. Gallantly the Brigade attempted a counter-attack which failed. In this action one of the regiments of the Brigade lost one battalion altogether, and of the other two battalions, one had lost three-quarters and the other half of its men. The machine-guns had no munitions, and there were only thirty rounds per man left. The second regiment of the Brigade was hardly in better case.

The retirement of the 11th Brigade exposed the left of the 36th Division, which had so far held up the enemy on its front by its artillery fire. The 35th Division, finding the enemy advancing, counter-attacked and threw back the enemy some distance towards the river, thus relieving the 36th Division of the danger on its left and enabling it to hold its ground all the afternoon. It was probably these attacks which gave General von Bülow so much concern.

During the night the 35th Division was compelled to fall back 5 kilometres as some badly shaken units had to be withdrawn under cover of darkness.

APPENDIX XXII

THE G.Q.G.'S INSTRUCTIONS ON TACTICS

A. TO THE ARMIES

Grand Quartier Général
des Armées de l'Est

At the G.Q.G., August 24th, 1914.

État Major

3è Bureau

2083

NOTE FOR ALL THE ARMIES

The lesson to be learnt from the fighting up to date is that the attacks are not carried out with an intimate combination of infantry and artillery.

Every combined operation comprises a series of minor operations which have as objective the gaining of *points d'appui*. Whenever it is desired to occupy a *point d'appui* the attack must be prepared by artillery, the infantry must be held back and the assault must only be launched from such distance as will permit the objective to be reached with certainty. Whenever the infantry attack has been launched at too great a distance, and without the artillery having had time to make itself felt, the infantry has fallen under machine-gun fire and has suffered losses which might have been avoided.

When a *point d'appui* is occupied it must be immediately organized, entrenchments must be dug, and artillery must be brought up to prevent a counter-offensive by the enemy. The infantry appears to ignore the necessity of organizing itself for long-drawn-out encounters.

The practice has been to throw forward immediately numerous units in dense formation, which become immediately exposed to hostile fire and are decimated, with the result that the offensive is stopped dead, and the infantry is often left at the mercy of a counter-attack.

The combat must be carried out by a line of skirmishers in sufficiently extended order, continually fed from the rear and supported by artillery. The fight can thus be carried on until the moment when the assault can be launched under the most favourable conditions.

The German Cavalry Division always operates preceded by some infantry battalions transported in motor-cars. Up to date the main bodies of these cavalry formations have never allowed themselves to be approached by ours. They advance behind their infantry and then throw forward detachments of cavalry (patrols and reconnaissances) which fall back upon their infantry as soon as they are attacked. Our cavalry pursues these detachments and comes up against barrages strongly held.

It is important that our cavalry divisions should always have infantry detachments to support them and to increase their offensive capacity. Time must be allowed for the horses to eat and sleep. If this is not done the cavalry is worn out prematurely before it has been employed.

JOFFRE.

B. NOTE BY THE G.Q.G. ON THE EMPLOYMENT OF ARTILLERY

Basing his information largely on the reports of his liaison officers, General Joffre said:

Army Commanders will once more and in the most emphatic way possible call the attention of the troops under their orders on the *absolute necessity* of ensuring complete co-operation between infantry and artillery. Up to the present this co-operation has not been achieved in all cases. The one has attacked in too much of a hurry, the other is often engaged after much delay, hesitatingly and sparingly. It is to this capital error that the greater part of the losses sustained by the infantry are imputable.

Further, the work of the batteries is inadequately co-ordinated. The impression is often given that the batteries are engaged singly, depending for their action on the initiative of the captains.

The use made by several corps of the 75s *firing at a maximum range*, with the trail dug in, should be more general.

Finally, we must copy our adversaries in using aeroplanes to prepare artillery attacks.

These aeroplanes fly over the ground, beyond the front, directing the artillery so that it can bring our assembled forces and our columns under its fire at its maximum range, without our being able to determine, even approximately, the position of the batteries.

Now that contact has been established along the whole front, the number of aeroplanes needed for strategic reconnaisances has very much decreased. Army Commanders will therefore henceforward put at the disposal of commanders of corps and groups of reserve divisions a certain number of aeroplanes, which will be specially employed –

1. To discover targets;
2. To give the batteries the necessary information for directing their fire.

The experiments carried out in this connection during recent years have been sufficiently frequent for it to be possible for the artillery commander of each corps or group of reserve divisions to be able to take the necessary measures to carry out this step, after having obtained the necessary information from the aviation service.

I had intended to include the following stories in the text of my narrative, but for reasons which will appear later decided to relegate them to an Appendix.

The Strange Story of Trooper Fowler and Corporal Hull, XIth Hussars.

Fowler and two other men got cut off after the battle of Le Cateau, and rode about aimlessly, completely lost. That they were behind the German lines became evident, for they caught glimpses of German guns in position. The roads were covered with German convoys, the villages full of German troops, and as their horses made concealment impossible, they left them at a farm. The farmer provided them with food, and the three men then separated, each to try his luck at rejoining the British lines.

Fowler made for the woods, and how he existed there until winter was well advanced will always be a mystery. Utterly lost, not knowing the language, with the vaguest ideas as to his whereabouts, in dread of every living soul, he remained hidden in the thickets until some time in January, 1915.

Then one day he had the good fortune to be discovered by a really splendid fellow, Louis Basquin, who hid him in a haystack and brought him food. Basquin lived in a tiny house, too small to conceal anyone, in the little village of Bertry on the battlefield of Le Cateau. He could not take anyone in, yet the Englishman would certainly have died of exposure if he had remained in the woods. Basquin consulted his wife's mother, Madame Belmont-Gobert, who lived in the same village. The Belmont-Gobert household consisted of Madame and her daughter Angèle. Another daughter, Euphémie, was in unoccupied territory, completely cut off from her family. Angèle and her mother were very poor, for all they had was what the girl could earn by her embroidery. When they heard Basquin's story they found themselves faced with a terrible problem. Outside an unknown soldier, a foreigner, lay in hiding; they were amongst the very poorest in the village, food was scarce, expensive and strictly rationed; to shelter an allied soldier meant the risk of death if discovered. Why should they undertake this task? Yet they did. The soldier had fought for France, although he did not understand the French tongue. He would die if they did not take him in, so resolutely they staked their lives for his. Truly a heroic decision. And in the long dreary years they were to shelter him, they never flinched, never regretted their action, rather they became more steadfast in their resolve. A long-drawn-out martyrdom of suspense, the daily risking of their lives for another, was their existence for four years.

The material difficulties would have seemed to most people insurmountable. There were four rooms in the cottage, and at that very moment twenty German soldiers were sleeping in the two upper rooms. Yet Basquin was sent to fetch Fowler as soon as night fell. He returned with a creature hardly human, who by no conceivable stretch of the imagination could have been connected with the smartest cavalry regiment in the British Army. The Hussar was bearded and unspeakably dirty, his uniform torn and soiled. His face and hands were scarred and plastered with the dried up blood of innumerable cuts and scratches. Dazed and bewildered, not comprehending the rapid flow of whispered words, he was put straight into what was to be his hiding place for nearly four years. The women had prepared a niche for him in the great wardrobe that stood in the kitchen living-room. This piece of furniture was about five and a half feet high, five and a half feet long, and some twenty inches in depth. It was divided into two sections, the one forming the right-hand compartment having shelves. It was in the left-hand compartment that Fowler was hidden.

The alarms and anxieties that the Englishman, in his prison two and a half feet long and one and a half feet wide, had to endure, were probably not as excruciating as those experienced by the two women who sheltered him, for they saw dangers that he had no inkling of in the darkness of his cupboard. He could not see when the hand of a German soldier was on the latch of his door, nor did he know how Angèle or her mother would distract the man's attention. He could not understand the ponderous joke of the *Feldwebel* who told Madame Belmont-Gobert that she must have a hidden store of food in the cupboard for which Fritz would search as soon as her back was turned. He did not see the neighbour's dog sniffing round his hiding place.

In great emergencies Madame Belmont-Gobert resorted to an inspired trick that never failed. When the house was being searched, as it often was, when every nook and cranny was being peered into and bayonets poked into the bedding and into the sacking and clothing hanging on pegs in the corner, when finally a German was making straight for the cupboard, the *"armoire"*, then Madame Belmont-Gobert would play her last card. She would draw the attention of the soldiers to a photograph of her second daughter, Euphémie. Euphémie was good-looking, furthermore Euphémie was safely away in Marseilles, and she was a sure draw. The Germans forgot the cupboard and crowded round the photograph with eager inquiries as to where the young lady was to be found. Madame Belmont-Gobert led them to believe that her daughter would soon be back, and the wardrobe door remained unopened, except just once, when a German patrol demanded admittance suddenly. Fowler was sitting in the room, and the women, acting under some amazing intuition, pushed him away from the cupboard towards the bed and concealed him in the heavy framework, underneath the mattress. The Germans made straight for the *"armoire"* and pulled both doors open. Then they poked bayonets into the bed, but mercifully Fowler was not touched.

In spite of this escape, the household did not lose faith in the wardrobe, in which Fowler continued to spend most of his time. A hole in the partition between the two compartments gave him air, and through this food was passed in to him, often when German soldiers were actually sitting in the room. What probably contributed more than anything else to the continued success of the scheme was that Madame Belmont-Gobert always kept the shelved half of the wardrobe partly open and frequently got things out of it in the presence of the Germans. Anyone watching her would naturally suppose that the shelves ran right across the wardrobe, in which case of course nothing bigger than a cat could have been concealed there.

The nights were particularly trying for Fowler. Sleep was out of the question, for the German soldiers upstairs were apt to creep down to steal the potatoes that were kept on top of the wardrobe.

One day the Belmont-Goberts were ordered to clear out of their house and move into a smaller one. Nothing daunted, the two women and Basquin moved the furniture to the new home, to which Fowler was brought at night, and the same life, if life it can be called, was resumed. Even in this small house Germans were billeted in the loft.

This miserable existence began to have its effect. Fowler, who could only sleep during the day in the cupboard, became frequently ill. The local chemist, Monsieur Baudet, a remarkable man, was confided in and provided medicine. Then Madame Belmont-Gobert began to show that she too felt the strain. She would never admit to fear, but she began to have alarming nervous collapses. One awful day she had an attack when the Germans were actually in the house upstairs, and Fowler frantically tended her. After that she was never left alone in the house.

A few neighbours were in the secret. These helped with an occasional potato or two, a little milk. There were some very hungry days. The Goberts had two hens and had to give the Germans an egg a day. If they failed to do so they were fined a mark. When this happened Angèle had to work half the night to earn the money.

It came to Fowler's knowledge that another man in his regiment was also hiding in Bertry. This was Corporal Hull, who was concealed in the house of a Monsieur and Madame Cardon. Fowler and Hull met one night and planned to escape to Holland, but this was never to be. Hull was betrayed to the Germans by a woman, and tragedy engulfed him and his protectors.

Fowler and the Belmont-Goberts escaped a like fate: discretion, ready wit, and above all luck served them well till the end of the war.

In 1918 the first allied troops that re-entered Bertry were met by a de-liriously-shouting, bent individual who they could not believe was what he claimed to be, a British soldier. They arrested him as a spy and sent him back under escort. Luckily the first officer he met was Major Drake, who had been his own troop officer in 1914. Fowler was released, and that night Colonel Anderson, commanding the XIth Hussars, came to fetch him, for the regiment was advancing over the same ground it had retired from after Mons.

The end of Corporal Hull's story was far more tragic.

The woman who betrayed him, Irma Ferlicot (and the less said about her the better) was known all over the district as "*la mauvaise française*". The finger of scorn which was pointed at her during the invasion became the finger of accusation as soon as the Germans retreated. Public opinion indicted her, she was condemned to penal servitude for life by a French court martial, and died in gaol not long ago. She deserved her fate, for her betrayal of Hull cost him his life, and resulted in untold misery to the Cardons who hid him.

One night in September, 1915, acting on information furnished by the traitress, a posse of Germans went to the Cardons' house and made straight for Hull's hiding place, Cardon, seeing all was up, knocked down the nearest German and made good his escape. His quickness saved his skin for the time being, but a long-drawn-out agony worse than death was in store for him. Till the end of the war he hid in the woods. He wandered about, getting occasional scraps of food from people who did not dare give him shelter. Once or twice he managed to get work, but always had to abandon it and fly to the woods for fear of being arrested. He never had any news of his family, his health was ruined, his reason became unhinged. Always he kept repeating the names of his wife and children and of Herbert Hull. The end of the war found him a wreck, quite unable to support his family: he died seven years ago.

Cardon has left a curious document giving an account of his adventures. In spite of his tribulations, in spite of the sufferings of his family, he never regretted having taken home the British soldier he had found collapsed on the battlefield of Le Cateau. He wrote how "obeying the voice of his conscience", fully aware of the risk he ran, he carried Hull to his cottage and arranged a clever cache in a small loft over a coal-hole, the trapdoor of which was concealed by a strip of canvas whitewashed to match the ceiling.

When Cardon disappeared into the night, the Germans who had come to arrest him and his protégé, thinking the Frenchman would be caught easily enough next day, proceeded to carry off Madame Cardon and Hull. They were conveyed to Caudry, and, according to Madame Cardon, to their mental torture was added physical brutality. Hull in particular was shamefully treated. He was half-starved, and kept in a damp nauseating hole. So miserable was their plight that the villagers attempted to pass them food, and ran considerable risk in so doing.

At the end of eight days, the French peasant woman and the English corporal were taken before a German court martial. They had no one to defend them. They were both condemned to death, but Madame Cardon's sentence was later reduced to twenty years hard labour in Germany.

After their trial, they were kept in adjacent cells, Hull in chains except when his hands were freed to allow him to eat.

Through a chink in the wall the prisoners were able to talk at times, and the noble woman did everything in her power to keep up Hull's spirits. He had no hope. Madame Cardon tried to convey to him in words he could understand that his sentence might be remitted after all, but he knew better. He had one great preoccupation. He feared that his parents would never know his fate. He made Madame Cardon promise that she would let them know – afterwards. He was not allowed to write, and it was terribly difficult to get the address of his family into Madame Cardon's head. It took a great effort on her part to memorize the barbarous English words, to learn the address which the agonized Hussar repeated over and over again in a whisper through the chink in the partition. Spelling was no good, English letters meant nothing to her, they had to rely on the sound of the words.

But she did remember. She remembered when on the night of October 21st she heard the Germans go into Hull's cell and take him away, whilst she lay choking on the floor of her prison, unable even to call farewell to him. She remembered next day when told that Herbert Hull had been shot and had met his death like a soldier. She remembered in the gaol of Aix-la-Chapelle, to which she was conveyed, and she did not forget in the prisons of Delitzch and Siegburg where she was sent later. Always the vision of the tragic British soldier haunted her: he was inextricably mixed in her mind with those others of whom she had no news, her husband Gustave, her little children, Marie Jeanne, Gustave and baby Gabrielle.

1927 found Madame Cardon a widow, living in a hovel at Le Cateau, in extreme poverty. She and little Gabrielle, now fourteen, had to work long hours in a factory to keep body and soul together. The other two children had been helped by friends and have been fitted to earn their livings. The parents of Corporal Hull wanted to adopt one of the Cardon children, but the indomitable mother determined that while she had strength she would bring up her family, and the offer was gratefully refused.

I had had something to do with the case of Madame Belmont-Gobert immediately after the war, as my regiment, greatly moved by her devotion, asked me to get into touch with her. Officers and men subscribed silver plate, for which I wrote a suitable inscription. Then, hearing that she was in dire poverty, I laid the case before the War Office. This appeal led to a great deal of cogitation and scratching of heads in London. There was much goodwill, fettered unfortunately by red tape. The answer when it finally came was to the following effect. There was no precedent for the case of Madame Belmont-Gobert, no regulation met her case, consequently no payment could be made to her. On the other hand, in somewhat irregular circumstances it was true, Fowler might be said to have been billeted on her for four years. In spite of the distressing anomaly that the only properly constituted authority in Bertry had been German, and that therefore the correct return had not been made at the right time, a point was stretched, and it was ruled that Madame Belmont-Gobert was entitled to Fowler's extra messing allowance at the rate of 2d. a day, and that the requisite forms might be dispensed with. Two thousand and forty-four francs and fifty centimes were therefore sent her. It should in fairness be added that the War Office drew the attention of the King to her heroism, and that she and her daughter each received the O.B.E.

It presently transpired that the sum paid by the War Office had been absorbed in repaying debts to neighbours incurred in keeping Fowler alive and in paying for his illness. Upon hearing this the officers of the XIth Hussars subscribed a further sum, which, however, did not last very long.

These women, Madame Belmont-Gobert and Madame Cardon, were poor, uneducated, hard-working peasant women. They were typical of their class. They seemed hard, parsimonious, and narrow, but they had hearts of gold.

They were just ordinary French peasant women, there are thousands like them who, when put to the same test reacted in the same way. Heroism such as theirs must have been frequent, for the attitude of the invaded provinces was magnificent throughout the war. Whenever there was an opportunity of showing devotion to the Allied cause it was eagerly seized upon.

But for the accident of this book these stories would probably have been long forgotten. The French peasant works too hard and is too near the soil to talk much about the past. After all, were not these episodes part of the war, when all did what they could, when all suffered, so why dwell on one incident more than on another?

Remembering the wonderful devotion of the Belmont-Gobert family, and wishing to give their heroism due prominence in my narrative, I had some inquiries made to verify the facts. These revealed that the women were living in dire poverty and want and with impaired health as a direct result of their sacrifices on behalf of British soldiers. It appeared only right to place the facts before the British public, whose response would, I was certain, be immediate and generous. I decided to approach Lord Burnham, who immediately had the stories investigated and published in the *Daily Telegraph*. Thanks to his efforts justice has been done, and a sufficient sum of money has been collected to keep the French women from want. They were brought to London, and a magnificent reception was accorded them by the King and Queen, the Lord Mayor, and the British public generally, proving to the whole French nation that England knows how to recognize and honour heroism and self-sacrifice.

Only one thing remains to be done. I hope that somewhere in England, if not a statue, at least a tablet commemorating these fine deeds will be erected one day. These women deserve the honour, and we owe it to them and to ourselves. To keep their memory green will be to perpetuate the finest trait known to human nature. "For greater love hath no man than this . . ."

APPENDIX XXIV

Colonel Huguet to General Lanrezac, at Vervins:

St. Quentin, August 26th, 5 a.m.

The I. Corps has been violently attacked during the night (night of 25th–26th) in its billets between Le Cateau and Landrecies, and is falling back, if it can, on Guise, to the south; if not, south-east in the direction of La Capelle.

The cavalry division, billeted at Catillon (8 km. south-east of Le Cateau) is going to retire on Bohain; the II. Corps and the 4th Division, billeted in the zone Caudry, Le Cateau, is going to withdraw to the line Le Catelet, Beaurevoir.

Tomorrow, 27th, the general retreat will be continued on Péronne.

Under these circumstances, Field-Marshal French asks you to come to his aid by sheltering the I. Corps until it can rejoin the main body of the British forces.

HUGUET.

Received at Vervins, August 26th, 6 a.m.

APPENDIX XXV

G.Q.G.
Des Armées de l'Est

G.Q.G., *August 25th, 1914.*

———
Etat Major

———
3ème Bureau

———
2349

It being impossible to carry out the offensive manœuvre which had been projected, future operations will have as their objective to reform on our left a mass capable of resuming the offensive. This will consist of the Fourth, Fifth and British Armies, together with new forces drawn from the eastern front, whilst the other armies contain the enemy for as long as is necessary.

In the course of its retirement, each of the Third, Fourth and Fifth Armies will conform to the movement of its neighbours, and each will remain in liaison with the others. The retirement will be covered by rearguards established on favourable topographical positions so as to take advantage of every obstacle to arrest or at least delay the advance of the enemy by short and violent counter-attacks, the principal element of which will be the artillery.

Limits of zones of action between the Armies:
The British Army will operate north-west of the line Le Cateau–Vermand–Nesle (inclusive).

Fifth Army between this line (exclusive) to the west, and the line Rocroi–Liart–Rozoy-sur-Serre–Craonne (inclusive) to the east.

To the exteme left, between Picquigny and the sea, a barrage will be formed on the Somme by the northern Territorial divisions, which will have the 61st or 62nd Reserve Divisions as a reserve.

The Cavalry Corps will be on the Anthie ready to participate in the forward movement on the extreme left.

A new group, comprising formations transported by rail (VII. Corps, four reserve divisions and perhaps in addition another active corps) will be formed between the 27th August and the 2nd September in front of Amiens, between Domart-en-Ponthieu and Corbie, or behind the Somme between Picquigny and Villers-Bretonneux. This group will be in readiness to assume the offensive in the general direction of St. Pol–Arras or Arras–Bapaume.

The British Army in rear of the Somme, from Bray-sur-Somme to Ham, will be prepared to advance either north on Bertincourt, or east on Le Catelet.

The Fifth Army will have its main forces grouped in the region Vermand–St. Quentin–Moy (offensive front) in readiness to debouch in the general direction of Bohain. Its right will hold La Fère–Laon–Craonne–St. Erme (defensive front).

APPENDIX XXVI

COLONEL HUGUET'S ACCOUNT OF THE ST. QUENTIN CONFERENCE, AUGUST 26TH, 1914

Colonel Huguet, in a posthumous book recently published, gives an account of this interview, but his recollections differ on several points from those of others who were present.

For instance, he states that Sir John was late at the rendezvous. This is a mistake. It was General Lanrezac who arrived after the other Generals.

Huguet is also in error on another point.

He quotes Lanrezac's book (p. 209) where the latter, describing the scene, states that General Joffre concluded his remarks to Sir John French by saying: "But have you not received my directive of the 25th?" The Field-Marshal then turned to his Chief of Staff, who acknowledged having received the document in question. "These words," says Huguet, "were not spoken, and could not have been, as General Joffre himself had brought the directive to the Field-Marshal, and handed it to me *two hours later* when he left St. Quentin with orders to have it translated and its content conveyed to the Field-Marshal as soon as possible."

But it is Huguet and not Lanrezac who is mistaken. Lanrezac is inaccurate on only one point. For Chief of Staff he should have said Sub-Chief of Staff, as General Murray was absent, but General Lanrezac of course would not have known one from the other as they had only met once.

Huguet's version is wholly fantastic. It would be incredible that General Joffre should produce an order of this importance out of his pocket to be dealt with *after* his departure. Nothing of the sort happened. The *Official History of the War* states that the French Commander-in-Chief confirmed the directive already sent to British G.H.Q.

Huguet's mistake in all probability is explainable by the likelihood that when the French Commander-in-Chief found that the British Staff had not dealt with this important order, he gave Huguet another copy as he left, telling him to see to it himself that Sir John was made acquainted with it as soon as possible.

On yet another point Huguet is inaccurate. He describes the British Commander as being so dissatisfied that "alleging the necessity of his presence with his troops he withdrew; the French Generals did likewise, and the conference then immediately terminated," whereas in fact Sir John issued a general invitation to lunch which Lanrezac declined and Joffre accepted.

APPENDIX XXVII

Noyon, August 28th, 1914, 8.45 a.m.

Following upon my letter of yesterday, I have the honour to report that the retreat of the British Army was carried out yesterday, the 27th, under better conditions and without being seriously interfered with, thanks to the help afforded by General Sordet's Cavalry Corps on the one hand and General d'Amade's two Reserve Divisions on the other.

An effective intervention by General Sordet's artillery on the afternoon of the 26th at Séranvillers and Florenville south of Cambrai had the happiest results in facilitating the retreat of the 3rd and 5th Divisions. General Smith-Dorrien commanding these Divisions expressed his warmest thanks.

Yesterday, the 27th, a new intervention north of Péronne against an attack launched by the Germans on Villers-Faucon and Saulcourt was equally successful.

General d'Amade's two Reserve Divisions also made their action felt with good results towards the end of the afternoon of yesterday, the 27th, in the region Combles–Bertincourt, and forced a German column of all arms, which had debouched from Cambrai, to turn about.

As a result, the retreat has been carried out in this region without difficulty, and in the evening the 3rd, 4th and 5th English Divisions are billeted south of the Sambre at Ham-sur-Sambre. They are going to be reconstituted in two divisions (3rd and 4th, (sic)).

Three trains were able to leave Tergnier during the night for Ham and neighbouring stations to bring back to Compiègne those men who were too weary to march.

The remainder of the three divisions will arrive today at Noyon.

The 1st and 2nd Divisions, in contact with the left of the Fifth Army at Origny-Ste.-Benoite, were able to carry out their retreat without difficulty.

This evening they will be at Chauny. Having to a great extent preserved their cohesion they seem to be in a fairly good state (*sic.*).

Under these conditions the British Army will be able to reconstitute itself and to reorganize, but it still remains unable to take the field for a fairly long period. I informed General Lanrezac of this situation this morning, so that he should know that his left flank is no longer covered and that he may soon have to meet a most serious attack on this side by the whole of the German forces operating in this part of the theatre of operations. . . .

HUGUET.

The following is a summary of the orders of the Supreme Command to the German Armies issued on August 27th, which reached the armies on the 28th:

The French, at least their northern and centre group, are in full retreat towards the west and south-west, that is on Paris. It is likely that they will put up during their retreat a renewed and vigorous resistance. All the information reaching us from France goes to show that the French Army is fighting to gain time, and their objective is to keep the majority of the German forces fixed on their front, so as to facilitate the offensive of the Russian Armies.

The objective of the German Army, therefore, must be to advance as rapidly as possible on Paris, not to give the French Army time to recover, to prevent it from forming fresh units, and to take from France as many of her means of defence as possible.

His Majesty orders that the German Army advance on Paris.

The First Army will advance on the lower Seine, marching west of the Oise. It will be prepared to intervene in the offensive of the Second Army. Its mission will be, further, to cover the right flank of the armies.

The Second Army, having the I. Cavalry Corps under its orders, will advance across the line La Fère–Laon and march on Paris.

The Third Army, advancing across the line Laon–Guignicourt, will continue its march on Château-Thierry.

The Fourth Army will advance by Reims on Epernay. The IV. Cavalry Corps, placed under the orders of the Fifth Army, will send its information to the Fourth Army as well. The VI. Cavalry Corps will pass to the Fifth Army.

The Fifth Army will advance across the line Châlons–Vitry-le-François. It will be echelonned to the rear and to the left, and cover the left flank of the army until this duty can be taken over by the Sixth Army on the left bank of the Meuse. Verdun will be invested.

The Sixth Army, having under its orders the Seventh Army and the III. Cavalry Corps, will have as its first mission to oppose an advance of the enemy into Lorraine and Alsace. It will rest on Metz. If the enemy retires, the Sixth Army, with the II. Cavalry Corps under its orders, will cross the Moselle between Toul and Epinal and advance in the general direction of Neufchâteau. The task of covering the left flank of the armies will then fall to the Sixth Army.

The Seventh Army will remain, to begin with, under the orders of the Sixth Army. If the Sixth Army crosses the Moselle, the Seventh Army will become independent of it. Its mission will then be to prevent the enemy's advancing between Epinal and the Swiss frontier.

If the enemy puts up a strong resistance on the Aisne and later on the Marne, it may be necessary to abandon the south-western direction of the advance and to wheel south.

It is urgently desirable that the army should advance as rapidly as possible, so as not to give the French time to reform and organize a serious resistance.

Any national resistance will be stamped out at its inception.

(*Signed*)   VON MOLTKE.

Thus the original plan to sweep round Paris was maintained, but was being varied by the new rôle assigned to the Sixth Army. This meant that the Germans were now attempting to envelop the Allies on both flanks, whereas in the original plan the outflanking attack against the French right was only to be attempted after the complete success of the sweep against their left, but already the movement was showing signs of being beyond the capacity of the German Armies.

Owing to the infringement of the neutrality of Belgium by Germany, and in furtherance of the Entente which exists between this country and France, his Majesty's Government has decided, at the request of the French Government, to send an Expeditionary Force to France, and to entrust the command of the troops to yourself.

The special motive of the force under your control is to support and co-operate with the French Army against our common enemies. The peculiar task laid upon you is to assist the French Government in preventing or repelling the invasion by Germany of French and Belgian territory and eventually to restore the neutrality of Belgium, on behalf of which, as guaranteed by treaty, Belgium has appealed to the French and to ourselves.

These are the reasons which have induced His Majesty's Government to declare war, and these reasons constitute the primary objective you have before you.

The place of your assembly, according to present arrangements, is Amiens, and during the assembly of your troops you will have every opportunity for discussing with the Commander-in-Chief of the French Army the military position in general and the special part which your force is able and adapted to play. It must be recognized from the outset that the numerical strength of the British Force and its contingent reinforcements is strictly limited, and with this consideration kept steadily in view it will be obvious that the greatest care must be exercised towards a minimum of losses and wastage.

Therefore, while every effort must be made to coincide most sympathetically with the plans and wishes of our Ally, the gravest consideration will devolve upon you as to participation in forward movements where large bodies of French troops are not engaged and where your force may be unduly exposed to attack. Should a contingency of this sort be contemplated, I look to you to inform me fully and give me time to communicate to you any decision to which His Majesty's Government may come in the matter. In this connection I wish you distinctly to understand that your command is an entirely independent one, and that you will in no case come under the orders of any Allied General.

In minor operations you should be careful that your subordinates understand that risk of serious losses should only be taken where such risk is authoritatively considered to be commensurate with the object in view.

The high courage and discipline of your troops should, and certainly will, have fair and full opportunity of display during the campaign, but officers may well be reminded that in this their first experience of European warfare, a greater measure of caution must be employed than under former conditions of hostilities against an untrained adversary.

You will kindly keep up constant communication with the War Office, and you will be good enough to inform me as to all movements of the enemy reported to you as well as those of the French Army.

I am sure you fully realize that you can rely with the utmost confidence on the wholehearted and unswerving support of the Government, of myself, and of your compatriots, in carrying out the high duty which the King has entrusted to you and in maintaining the great tradition of His Majesty's Army.

KITCHENER, *Secretary of State.*

The following amusing account of G.H.Q.'s departure from Dammartin was given me by Colonel Lyle Cummins, then M.O. at G.H.Q.:

"I fancy that G.H.Q. was rather hurried when it left Compiègne on August 31st; at least I got the impression of undue haste through the fact that I got no notice that we were leaving, and that no provision was made for my transport by car as usual. I was, in fact, left behind, and was lucky in catching a train which happened to have waited at the station for some of the G.H.Q. clerks and details. This impression of haste was confirmed a few days later when Colonel S. told me that, on driving into Compiègne in his car on the evening of the 31st, with messages for the Chief, he found the Germans taking over our offices in the *Hôtel de Ville* and had rather a narrow escape of being captured.

"On September 1st the day opened, for me, as a rather placid one after a very strenuous few weeks, and in the afternoon I obtained leave to ride out and see a little of the country. I had only ridden about a mile when I met an agitated French officer galloping in with half a dozen troopers. He told me that a large force of German cavalry was approaching the town, and then rode on in considerable haste. This report seemed to me so unlikely as not to merit any further attention, so I continued my ride in a northerly direction, keeping to fairly high ground so as to get a view in case there were really any troops about.

"After riding a few miles I did come in sight of what appeared to be a large force of mounted troops, rendered visible by the long cloud of dust in which they moved. I concluded that they were probably some of our own cavalry, but decided not to get too near them, so turned and rode back towards Dammartin intending to report what the French officer had said and what I had seen.

"When entering Dammartin, I met an A.S.C. officer driving in an open car with a Uhlan trooper by his side. (I don't think he was an officer, my recollection is that he was a trooper.) He slowed down and asked the way to the G.S. offices, adding that he had captured his Uhlan a mile or two out and brought him in 'as a specimen'. He had tied the German's thumbs together behind his back, which rather took away from the appearance of '*camaraderie*' so marked at a little distance!

"I rode with him to the 'G' offices, outside which we met Major X. of O.B. To him we told our stories, but without any effect upon the sangfroid of the perfect Staff Officer. He merely looked at or through us with an air of detached omniscience and said with conviction: 'There are *no* Germans within twenty miles of Dammartin.' This seemed to settle the matter, so I directed the A.S.C. officer to the Provost-Marshal's quarters and went back to my work.

"A few hours later, towards 7.30 p.m. as far as I can remember, I went up to Sir John French's quarters as there was one of his orderlies ill and I had intended to see how he was getting on. To my surprise, however, I found the building deserted and learnt from some orderlies that the General Staff had left Dammartin. This struck me as queer, as I had only just left Colonel O'Donnell on his way to dine with the Adjutant-General. I hurried down to Sir Nevil Macready's quarters and found him sitting down to dinner with his staff, and quite innocent of any idea that G.H.Q. was on the move! On hearing that the General Staff had departed he showed more annoyance than surprise, and decided, on verifying my report, to catch them up if possible. I left his quarters after ascertaining that there was no room for *me* on any of the A.G. cars, and went off to see about handing over the key of my billet. This proved impossible, as the *Mairie* was already deserted, so I left the key on a table, hoping that it might help some tired German to a comfortable room. As I stood in the street with my few articles of kit, wondering how I was to get away and where to go to, a big car with two French Under-Officers in it dashed into sight, and the driver kindly slowed down to my signal. The occupants proved to be Princes Michel Murat and Ney, both of whom were attached to the French Mission. Murat, to whom the car belonged, told me that he believed the Staff were on their way to Lagny, and very politely invited me into his already full car. So I fled from Dammartin with the descendant of 'the bravest of the brave', and found a comfortable billet at Lagny for the night."

APPENDIX XXXI

THE DIFFERENT VERSIONS OF INSTRUCTION GÉNÉRALE NO. 4
SENT TO THE BRITISH AND TO THE FRENCH ARMIES

G.Q.G., 1st September, 1914.

(1) In spite of tactical successes won by the Third, Fourth and Fifth Armies on the Meuse and at Guise, the outflanking movement against the left wing of the Fifth Army, insufficiently arrested by the British Army and the Sixth Army, constrains the forces as a whole to [pivot on our right.*]
[As soon as the Fifth Army has escaped the menace of envelopment against its left, the Third, Fourth and Fifth Armies will resume the offensive.]

(2) The withdrawal may lead the armies to retire from north to south for some time to come. The Fifth Army on the marching wing must not on any account allow its left to be held. [The other armies, less pressed in the execution of their movements, will be able to halt, face the enemy, and seize all favourable occasions to inflict a check on him.]

The movement of each army must in any case be such as not to uncover the neighbouring armies, and army commanders must constantly interchange information as to their intentions, their movements and their intelligence reports.

(3) The lines separating the zones of march of the different armies will be as follows:
Between the Fifth and Fourth Armies (Foch's Detachment) route Reims, Epernay (for the Fourth Army) route Montmort, Sézanne, Romilly (for the Fifth Army).
Between the Fourth Army and the Third Army, route Grande Pré, St. Ménéhould, Revigny (for the Fourth Army).

In the zone of the Fourth Army, the detachment under General Foch will maintain constant liaison with the Fifth Army: the interval between this detachment and the main body of the Fourth Army being watched by the 7th and 9th Cavalry Divisions attached to the Fourth Army and supported by infantry detachments furnished by that Army.

The Third Army will carry out its movement under cover of the Hauts-de-Meuse.

[4. It is possible to envisage as the limit of the movement of retreat, and without any implication that this limit will necessarily be attained, the moment when the armies will be in the following positions:

---

* In the copy sent to the British the words "to retire" were substituted.

A newly-formed cavalry corps behind the Seine south of Bray.

Fifth Army behind the Seine, south of Nogent-sur-Seine.

Fourth Army (Foch detachment) behind the Aube, south of Arcis-sur-Aube.

Fourth Army (main body) behind the Ornain, east of Vitry.

Third Army, north of Bar-le-Duc.

The Third Army will at that moment be reinforced by the Reserve Divisions which will abandon the Hauts-de-Meuse to take part in the offensive movement.

If circumstances permit, parts of the First and Second Armies will be recalled in due course to participate in the offensive; finally, the mobile troops of the fortified camp of Paris may also take part in the general action.

J. JOFFRE.

For the Fourth Army, it should be observed that it must not expose the entraining points of the IV. Corps.

The armies are urged to requisition vehicles to avoid fatigue to the men as far as possible.]

NOTE. – The words underlined between square brackets were omitted in the copy of this order sent to the British.

APPENDIX XXXII

September 3rd, 1914.

Monsieur le Maréchal,

In General Joffre's letter No. 3332 of September 2nd, on the subject of the co-operation of the British Army in the operations of the French Armies, the Commander-in-Chief anticipated that the British Army would be in position on the Seine on the general line Juvisy–Melun.

If the British Army bases its left on Juvisy it will impinge on the fortified camp, and inevitably confusion will ensue.

It seems to me therefore to be necessary that the front of the British Army on the Seine should be above the zone indicated by General Joffre, and that its left should be at Corbeil instead of at Juvisy. The British Army could thus extend from Corbeil as far as Moret.

I have further the honour to draw your attention to the passages in General Joffre's letter No. 3331 to the Minister of War, in which the Commander-in-Chief expects that the British Army will be able to remain for some time on the Marne. It seems to me indeed most desirable that the retreat of the British Army from the Marne towards the Seine should be as slow as possible, and should only begin when compelled either by the attack of superior forces or by the necessity of remaining in contact with the Fifth French Army.

In remaining on the Marne as long as possible, the British Army would contribute powerfully to the defence of the fortified camp of Paris, by menacing enemy troops which might attack it from the north-east.

In conclusion, I have the honour to assure you that all steps will be taken to avoid confusion while the British Army is moving in front of the fortified camp.

I should be greatly obliged if you would let me know as early as possible what your dispositions will be.

Please accept, *Monsieur le Maréchal*, the expression of my highest consideration and my cordial comradeship.

GALLIENI.

The sequence of events during the day was as follows:

Early in the morning General Joffre had telegraphed to know the situation of the Fifth Army and of the Cavalry Corps, to which General d'Esperey answered that the retreat was continuing according to orders, the Cavalry Corps attacking to cover the withdrawal of the left.

As reports from the XVIII. Corps came in later, General d'Esperey became somewhat anxious at the way in which the situation was developing in that quarter. The Germans were pressing on fast, and columns of all arms had reached the Marne from Château-Thierry to La Ferté-sous-Jouarre. The XVIII. Corps was in a dangerous situation and appeared to be doing little to retard the enemy's advance.

As it was essential that the enemy who was threatening the left of the XVIII. Corps should be delayed, General Conneau was told he must constantly engage the hostile columns by artillery and machine-gun fire and with his cyclists, without, however, becoming involved in a general action. He was told that the XVIII. Corps required both material and moral support, and that the Cavalry Corps, by its presence and action, was to give it that feeling of security of which it stood so badly in need.

The outposts of the X. Corps were attacked in the late afternoon, but held their ground.

At the I. Corps, rearguards of the 2nd Division did nothing more than exchange rifle shots with the enemy, and the 1st Division was unsuccessfully attacked.

The III. Corps did not escape so easily. Hearing the sound of a heavy cannonade to the left in the direction of the XVIII. Corps rearguards, the divisions manœuvred in echelon to the rear in readiness for an attack from that quarter. On the cannonade diminishing the retreat was resumed, but the enemy attacked one of the divisions with sufficient vigour to necessitate a counter-attack. The troops finally reached their destinations in a state of great fatigue. The Reserve Divisions luckily were not attacked. The enemy brought strong pressure to bear upon the division acting as rearguard to the XVIII. Corps, driving it considerably eastwards. Under the protection of a powerful artillery, however, it crossed the Petit Morin without mishap, but later was driven back beyond the line it was to have occupied by hostile artillery fire. The G.O.C. was wounded.

The Cavalry Corps had been allocated the duty of relieving pressure on the left of the XVIII. Corps. With this end in view two divisions attacked the enemy crossing the Marne, which had the effect of holding up his advance for an hour. The Cavalry Corps was later compelled to cross the Petit Morin, the passages of which it defended whilst also attacking in flank the hostile bodies which were making for Montmirail in the zone of the XVIII. Corps.

In the afternoon the hostile pressure against the cavalry increased, and the 3rd Cavalry division, which till then had been covering the withdrawal of the XVIII. Corps, had to be recalled into reserve of the remainder of the Cavalry Corps. At dusk the Cavalry Corps crossed the Grand Morin blowing up the bridges. The horses were quite worn out.

APPENDIX XXXIV

GENERAL D'ESPEREY'S TACTICAL INSTRUCTIONS FOR THE BATTLE OF
THE MARNE

Fifth Army Q.G., September 5th, 5 p.m.

PERSONAL AND SECRET INSTRUCTION

Tomorrow, September 6th, the Fifth Army, the British Army and General Maunoury's Sixth Army will attack the First German Army.

To ensure victory, the closest attention must be paid to the lessons learnt from the fighting since the campaign began.

1. The corps must march on the various objectives on a narrow front of attack. There is no disadvantage in leaving a space between two neighbouring corps, provided liaison is maintained between them.

2. Attacks on a number of objectives at the same time must at all costs be avoided. Success can only be obtained by concentrating upon successive objectives all the resources of both infantry and artillery, and by taking care to cover the attacking troops.

3. At the beginning of the engagement, the attack must be carried out by infantry in small numbers supported by the whole of the artillery. The main bodies of the infantry must not advance until the artillery has prepared the way for them as thoroughly as possible.

4. As soon as a strong point has been carried, the troops which have captured it must organize it strongly: the attack on the next objective must be carried out by fresh troops, which will provide a reserve strong enough to establish a rallying point in case of failure. In any case it is indispensable that the assembly of troops at easily recognizable points should be avoided.

To sum up, the attack must be carried out methodically, and the action of the command must make itself felt at all times with a view to securing the co-operation of subordinate formations.

D'ESPEREY.

GENERAL FRANCHET D'ESPEREY'S PROCLAMATION TO THE FIFTH ARMY
ON THE MARNE

Ve Armée

———

État Major

SOLDATS,

Sur les champs mémorables de Montmirail, de Vauchamps, de Champaubert, qui virent il y a cent ans, la victoire de nos aïeux sur les Prussiens de Blücher, votre vigoureuse offensive a triomphé de la résistance allemande. Contenu sur ses ailes, forcé à son centre, l'ennemi fuit vers l'est et vers le nord à marches forcées. Les corps d'armées les plus réputés de la Vieille Prusse, les contigents de Westphalie, du Hanovre, du Brandenbourg, se sont retirés en hâte devant vous.

Ce premier succés n'est qu'un prélude. L'ennemi ébranlé n'est pas encore complètement battu.

Vous aurez encore de dures épreuves à subir, de longues marches à faire, de rudes combats à livrer.

Que l'image de la Patrie, souillée par les barbares, soit toujours devant vos yeux. Jamais le sacrifice de tous pour Elle ne fut plus nécessaire.

En saluant les braves déjà tombés dans les luttes de ces derniers jours, ma pensée se tourne vers vous, artisans de la prochaine victoire.

En avant, Soldats, pour la France!

Montmirail, le 9 Septembre, 1914.

Le Général Commandant la Ve Armée,
FRANCHET D'ESPEREY.

APPENDIX XXXVI

DIARY OF THE BATTLE OF THE MARNE

I

September 6th.

Girard and I were ordered to go in liaison to the British. We handed in the following information to G.H.Q. when we arrived at Melun in the morning:

"The Fifth Army attacked at 6 a.m. The XVIII. Corps on Sancy–Meilleray–Montolivet. The III. Corps on Courgivaux–Tréfols–Morsains. The I. Corps on Essart-le-Vicomte-Esternay. Group of Reserve Divisions in second line. The attack was to be supported on the right by the Ninth Army and on the left by the Cavalry Corps."

We were told the situation of the British, which was as given in the following message to General Maunoury despatched by Huguet at 11.30 a.m.:

"The British Army established itself this morning facing east, the right towards Rozoy, the left south of Crépy, attacking eastwards at this moment. Left on Grand Morin. Enemy forces supposed to be the Corps reported last night bivouacking between Coulommiers and Crécy, supposed to have resumed march southwards first thing this morning.

"British left should be protected by Sixth Army pushing forward troops as soon as possible in region of Meaux and Grand Morin."

At 5.15 p.m. Sir John French informed General Joffre of the position of his forces and of his intentions:

"In accordance with what I understand to be your wishes, I have pushed the British forces today as far as the line Choisy–Coulommiers–Crécy-Villiers-sur-Morin. On the river Grand Morin we have encountered slight opposition, but the enemy columns have retired north. I am marching at daybreak, and should be glad if you would indicate the direction you desire me to take in combination with the Sixth and Fifth French Armies."

In addition to this, Girard and I heard before we returned to the Fifth Army that hostile columns had been observed going north, evidently to meet Maunoury's attack.

The British were engaged on this day against the rearguards of the II. and IV. Corps and the 2nd and 9th Cavalry Divisions.

That night General Joffre answered Sir John. After giving the line attained by the Fifth Army and reporting the presence of the III. German Corps and 18th Division, he wrote:

"These troops according to information found on the enemy are asking for reinforcements. The attack seems to be progressing favourably. This result is certainly due to the protection afforded by the British forces. Under these conditions the continuation of the offensive by your forces will greatly facilitate the attack of the Fifth Army tomorrow, but it seems that your action might be usefully directed a little more to the north, by orienting your offensive against the German right wing, remaining in liaison with the XVIII. Corps by your cavalry and that of General Conneau. It is possible that your direction of attack may have to be diverted still more towards the north if the enemy falls back on the Marne. In any case the Sixth Army will support your left, and you can ask it to co-operate closely in your attack."

On the left of the British, the Sixth Army had been engaged against the German IV. Reserve Corps during the afternoon of the 5th. At 10 p.m. von Kluck, unaware that anything serious had occurred, issued orders to his army to face Paris between the Marne and the Oise in accordance with the orders of the Supreme Command. When he heard during the night of the attack against the IV. Reserve Corps, he ordered the movement to be accelerated so that his corps should be supported as soon as possible.

(By the morning of the 7th, the II. and IV. German Corps had joined the IV. Reserve Corps against Maunoury, but the III. and IX. Corps were still south of the Marne.)

On the morning of the 6th Maunoury's troops were getting the best of it, and the IV. German Reserve Corps was falling back, but during the afternoon German reinforcements belonging to the II. Corps began to appear in support of the IV. Reserve Corps. Thanks to this support the Germans still clung to the west bank of the Ourcq, but nevertheless the Sixth Army gained some ground during the day.

General Joffre reminded Maunoury at 6 p.m. that it was essential he should constantly support the British left and remain in liaison with the British. Maunoury informed Sir John that he hoped to cross the Marne on the following day (7th) between the Grand Morin and Germigny l'Eveque.

The Fifth Army had achieved a very marked success during the day. At 5 p.m. it gave its situation to the British in the following telegram:*

"Fifth Army, Romilly-sur-Seine. Situation at 5 p.m. Serious opposition met with about Montceaux-les-Provins, Courgivaux and Esternay. Montceaux-les-Provins supposed to be evacuated by enemy. Courgivaux carried. Esternay still holds out. At end of day Fifth Army established on

* At 6 p.m. the Fifth Army telegraphed to the British that a German column of all arms was advancing from La Ferté Gaucher towards Courtacon and Champcenest. The message continued: "This column is therefore marching straight to the south between the left of the French Army and the right of the British. G.O.C. Fifth Army trusts attention of British will be directed to results that might be obtained by British action on the flank and rear of this column."
This was not a column of all arms, but was the Guard Cavalry Division which came into violent conflict with the French Cavalry at Courtacon and got the better of the engagement. There were no British troops within ten miles of Courtacon.

general line Coupderdrix–St. Bon–Courgivaux–Montceaux-les-Provins, heights south of Esternay, Château de Désirée and Charleville. It seems that at Esternay there was at least one division, the 17th of the IX. Corps. Troops belonging to the III. Corps reported at Courgivaux.''

The news on the remainder of the front may be summarized as follows: At the Ninth Army, in spite of all efforts, St. Prix, Villevenard and Joches were lost, thanks to a turning movement of the German X. Corps west of the St. Gond Marshes. The XI. Corps was violently attacked, and the IX. Corps retired south of the St. Gond Marshes. A hard day for Foch.

On the front of the Fourth Army, the enemy violently attacked the II. Corps, which held its ground. The Colonial Corps, also attacked, managed to gain a little ground. The XVII. Corps beat the XIX. Saxon Corps.

At the Third Army there was heavy fighting, which in the main did not go in favour of the French. The enemy captured Revigny.

II

September 7th.

Girard and I were again sent in liaison to the British, We had been standing to awaiting orders at dawn, but were not ordered to go till 7 a.m.

We saw Generals Murray and Wilson, and were informed of the following instructions issued by General Joffre to the British Army:

"G.Q.G., 2 a.m. Supplementary note on the subject of the general rôle requested of the British Army.

"The role of the British Army is to be constantly prepared to attack the right flank of the German forces should these accept battle on the front of the Fifth Army. The Sixth Army on the extreme left has a similar role. It is as yet impossible to know whether the Fifth Army is only confronted by rearguards, or whether it is going to come into conflict with the main bodies of the Corps which are opposing it.

"Under these circumstances it would seem that the British Army should march approximately north, its Corps in pronounced echelon left forward, so as to be in a position to face right at once as soon as the Germans accept battle.

"If it should turn out that the enemy is withdrawing to the north behind the Petit Morin or even beyond, the British Army will then have to form advanced echelon on the left of the Fifth Army, the axis of its movement being Coulommiers–La Ferté-sous-Jouarre, its left towards the Ourcq, but the main consideration to be dealt with remains the battle which the Germans may accept on the front of the Fifth Army."

This note shows plainly both what was in the Generalissimo's mind, and the information at his disposal. Evidently it was not clear if von Bülow was withdrawing behind strong rearguards to a selected position where he intended to accept battle, or being pressed back by d'Esperey's attacks and the threat of the British advance. Before the receipt of this communication, which did not arrive till 11 a.m., the British Commander-in-Chief had ordered his army to advance north-east on Rebaix.

As Girard and I had orders to see that the liaison between the fighting troops of the French and British Armies was satisfactory, we went forward to Coulommiers, which we reached before the cavalry.

On returning to British G.H.Q., we gathered that the reports from the whole front showed that the greater part of the fighting had fallen on the cavalry, and that the whole army had made good progress.

We also heard that after very heavy fighting ground had been gained by the Sixth Army, but lost again later. The IV. German Reserve Corps gave way in the morning before the French left. The 61st Reserve Division (French) arriving on the left, the French pressure increased, whilst the Cavalry Corps gained ground farther north. But German reinforcements arrived from the south, and after very heavy fighting the French were driven from Acy-en-Multien.

The fighting had been very severe. Near the cemetery of Acy-en-Multien 150 French and German dead were found in an area of 200 square metres, and Hill 139 at Vareddes, where there had been fierce bayonet fighting, was like a slaughterhouse.

It was on this day that Gallieni rushed forward in taxis and motor-buses from Paris, three battalions of the IV. Corps, which had been sent to him from the Third Army.

There were reports that the enemy was withdrawing his main bodies to the east bank of the Ourcq. The British artillery greatly helped Maunoury by taking in flank the German forces opposing him, causing him severe losses and drawing the fire of the whole of the heavy artillery of the German III. Corps.

The effect of General Manoury's attacks, resulting in the drawing of German troops to his front, was beginning to tell. The German line was being dangerously thinned on the front both of the British and Fifth Armies. Aviators had seen many German columns marching north and north-west. (These were the III. and IX. Corps, claimed back by von Kluck from von Bülow.) *

The news from the remainder of the front was that the Fifth Army had been pressing towards the Petit Morin, attempting to cut off von Bülow's line of retreat on Montmirail. Von Bülow's right, giving way with heavy loss

---

* At 10 a.m. the German First Army telegraphed to the Second:
"The II., IV. and IV. Reserve Corps are engaged in heavy fighting west of the Ourcq."
This was followed at 11.15 a.m. by:
"The intervention of the III. and IX. Corps on the Ourcq is urgently necessary. The enemy is being heavily reinforced. Please order the two corps to march on La Ferté Milon and Crouy.
A little later, owing to the increasing gravity of the situation, these Corps were ordered to the Ourcq battlefield by the shortest route.
In the hope of delaying the British advance von Kluck ordered the destruction of the Marne bridges. This order was only carried out at La Ferté-sous-Jouarre and below, owing to lack of explosives.
Von Kluck himself was nearly captured by a raid of General Cornulier Lucinière's Provisional Cavalry Division near La Ferté Milon.
When von Kluck's left hand corps, the IX., withdrew behind the Marne, von Bülow's X. Reserve Corps retired behind the Petit Morin.

before the attacks of d'Esperey's left, began to fall back covered by strong
rearguards. The Fifth Army was thus in a very favourable position at the
moment, able to threaten von Bülow's right with envelopment, this flank
having been weakened by the withdrawal of the III. and IX. Corps. Von
Bülow, however, met this danger by swinging back his right when these two
corps were withdrawn and crossed the Petit Morin at 8 a.m.

But on the eastern flank of the Fifth Army events had been profoundly
affected by the violent attacks the Germans were launching against Foch.
When d'Esperey heard that German forces were attacking Foch's left from
St. Prix, he ordered the X. Corps to gain ground to the right and attack
these forces, but the X. Corps was not able to progress until the I. Corps had
in its turn intervened.

General d'Esperey's task was thus not an easy one. He was compelled to
support Foch at this critical stage in the operations, but to do so precluded
him from taking advantage of the obvious gap now opening on von Bülow's
right.

Foch had intended attacking but was himself violently attacked. The Fifth
Army came to his help to the west, but to the east he had to withstand unaided the formidable assault of the German Guards, supported by the right
wing of the German Third Army, east of the Marshes of St. Gond. Thanks
to the timely aid furnished by d'Esperey, Foch not only withstood these
attacks but managed to counter-attack in the direction of Aulnay. This
counter-attack had the happiest results, for, unknown to us, it caused von
Bülow to transfer half his VII. Corps from his right to the neighbourhood of
the St. Gond Marshes. This further weakened the right of the second German
Army, with very grave consequences to the enemy.

General de Langle's Fourth Army also suffered from the violent efforts of
the enemy to smash the French centre. How difficult his task was is best
shown by the fact that even before the German attack began, the XII.
Corps, for instance, had only six battalions capable of taking their place in
the line. On his right, at the point of junction between his army and the
Third Army and on his left, the German attacks were particularly violent.

Facing the Fourth Army was half the German Third Army (the western
half was engaged against Foch) and the German Fourth Army.

General de Langle, realizing that his greatest danger lay on his left, reinforced it as much as possible, especially with artillery, with the result that
the situation in this quarter was saved, the Germans being unable to gain
sufficient superiority in artillery to launch their infantry attacks.

III

September 8th.

The battle was working up to its climax in a swelter of tropical heat.

The news that came in during the morning from the Fifth Army front was
good. Girard and I, who had been told to await the return of the air reconnaissances before setting out to go to the British, were able to inform
General Wilson that at 1 p.m. the Fifth Army had been progressing easily, and

that it was believed that the Ninth Army was again being violently attacked*, for the X. Corps had once more had to intervene in its favour.

On the previous night General Joffre had ordered the main bodies of the armies of the left to follow the enemy, but in such a way as to be in a position to envelop the German right wing. Consequently the Sixth Army was to gain ground towards the north on the right bank of the Ourcq, the British were to cross the Grand Morin, the Petit Morin and the Marne, whilst the Fifth Army was to increase the pressure on the enemy with its left wing, and with its right support the Ninth Army.

In conformity with these directions Sir John ordered the advance to be continued against the line of the Marne from Nogent l'Artaud to La Ferté-sous-Jouarre. The cavalry was to press on in pursuit, keeping in touch with both the Fifth and Sixth Armies. The British were already across the Grand Morin, but very difficult country and the Petit Morin and the Marne lay ahead.

The British Cavalry moved off before dawn and made some progress, but were soon held up by strong German rearguards of infantry and artillery, which made excellent use of difficult ground admirably suited to defence.

The G.Q.G. was watching the progress of the British with the greatest anxiety, realizing that the result of the whole battle depended upon whether they could advance with sufficient rapidity. Major Clive, liaison officer at the G.Q.G., telephoned at 8 a.m. to Major Wake at G.H.Q. as follows:

"All eyes are turned today on the British Army. They attach the very greatest importance to our action today in the corner between the Marne and the Ourcq. The position of the Sixth French Army is regarded as uncertain in view of the fact that the Germans have sent two more corps against them, making three, and because it is probable that by tomorrow one corps at least will appear on their flank from Maubeuge.‡ The armies on our right have not made much progress yesterday. They suggest that we have not much more than cavalry in front of us. Major Clive gave me to understand that the action of the British Army today in connection with the attack on the Sixth Army, that is against the left rear of the German forces along the Ourcq, would in the opinion of the French Staff relieve a situation that might easily become critical. They are trying to send another Corps by rail to help the Sixth Army, but it cannot arrive just yet."‡

Though it was not apparent at the time, even to themselves, much less to

* The Guard and Saxons had attacked it at dawn.

† Maubeuge surrendered on the evening of September 7th with effect from noon on the 8th. The VII. Reserve Corps which had been besieging the fortress was at first ordered to the Flanders coast because of a possible British landing there. These orders were, however, cancelled and the Corps ordered to La Fère, there to form the nucleus of the Seventh Army.

‡ General Joffre's points of view was further emphasized in the following telegram:

"3.30 p.m. From General Joffre to Marshal French.

"German forces which were on front of British are moving to the north against the Sixth Army. So that Sixth Army be not forced to fall back, I consider it indispensable that the British forces should attack on La Ferté-sous-Jouarre and debouch to the north of the Marne no later than six this evening."

the French, the British had inflicted a serious defeat on the enemy. Indeed, the Germans only confess to one important reverse that day, that of von Richthofen's I. Cavalry Corps, which was hurled back in two separate parts by the British. This, according to the enemy themselves, was the crux of the whole battle, since it determined the breach in their line that ultimately led to their retreat.

To the left of the British the battle had reached its crisis. Von Kluck was striking with all his might at the claw Maunoury had fastened into the flank of the German line. His blows were the more violent and fell with increasing speed in that he was fighting against the inexorable enemy, time.* Slowly and relentlessly, whilst the hours sped by in his fight with Maunoury, the British, forcing their way through forests, up and down precipitous and wooded glades and across rivers, were gradually gnawing their way into his very vitals.

Before noon the British were in sight of La Ferté, but large forces to the north of the river, and a strong bridgehead to the south, prohibited any advance till the artillery had cleared the way. There was hard fighting in difficult country before the British infantry reached the Petit Morin, but by nightfall they had forced their way over the river, and their left had occupied that part of La Ferté-sous-Jouarre which lies south of the Marne, with their right half-way between the Petit Morin and the Marne. Their guns had wrought much havoc on the retreating Germans, whom the aviation reported to be withdrawing in a continuous stream over the Marne. These were evidently troops on their way to reinforce the enemy corps facing Maunoury.

To von Kluck the situation must have appeared very serious. His line was rent. Divisions had to be thrown in as they became available owing to the increasing gravity of the situation, and thus became separated from their corps. Before the battle ended his whole army was facing west, and this combined with the fact that von Bülow had weakened and thrown back his right, resulted in a gap of some thirty miles between the First and Second German Armies. This was filled by four cavalry divisions and their infantry support.†

The Fifth Army had progressed after hard fighting. The XVIII. Corps had crossed the Petit Morin, occupied Marchais-en-Brie, and progressed to within four miles of Montmirail. The III. Corps captured this celebrated little town after very hard fighting, thus establishing the undoubted ascendency of the Fifth Army over their opponents. The I. Corps gained a footing on the famous plateau of Vauchamps, where it covered the left of the X. Corps which had been heavily engaged in protecting the left of the Ninth Army. A

---

* Maunoury failed to gain ground, his left suffering from heavy enfilade fire from the south, as did his right from German heavy artillery in the bend of the Marne. His centre could not progress against the entrenchments the enemy had thrown up. It was in fact driven back. The VII. Corps, which had fought gallantly from the beginning and was nearly exhausted, was attacked violently and lost Betz and Thery-en-Valois, the enemy advancing on Nanteuil. Maunoury sent the 8th Division from his right to his left.

† Von Kluck sent a composite Brigade (Kraewels), formed of units of the IX. Corps, and on the 9th and 5th Division, to fill the gap. It is noteworthy that the Germans appointed no commander over all the troops in the gap. Even the cavalry was not under a single leader. This grave omission was a contributory factor in their defeat.

good many prisoners were taken. The X. Corps had captured a whole battalion and a machine-gun company.*

The orders issued by Joffre at 8.7 p.m. that evening were as follows:

"(1) The retiring German forces seem to constitute two distinct groups; one apparently comprising the IV. Reserve Corps and II. and IV. Active Corps, is fighting on the Ourcq facing west against our Sixth Army, which it is endeavouring to outflank to the north. The other comprises the remainder of the First German Army, the III. and IX. Active Corps. The Second and Third German Armies remain facing south opposed to the Fifth and Ninth French Armies. Connection between these two groups appears to be carried out only by several cavalry divisions supported by detachments of all arms facing the British."

"(2) It seems essential to deal with the extreme right of the Germans before it can be reinforced by elements which the fall of Maubeuge may render available. The Sixth Army and the British will undertake this mission. The Sixth Army will pin the troops facing it on the right bank of the Ourcq to their positions, and the British forces crossing the Marne between Nogent l'Artaud and La Ferté-sous-Jouarre will advance on the left and rear of the enemy on the Ourcq."

"(3) The Fifth French Army will cover the right flank of the British by pushing forward a detachment on Azy and Château-Thierry. The Cavalry Corps, crossing the Marne if necessary behind this detachment or behind the British columns, must carry out effectively the liaison between the British and the Fifth Army.† On its right the Fifth Army will continue to support the action of the Ninth Army so as to enable this army to assume the offensive. The main body of the Fifth Army marching straight to the north will throw back beyond the Marne the enemy opposing it."

On the front of the Ninth Army, where the fighting of the previous day continued with great violence, the situation was critical. The German Guard and Saxons attacked at dawn. The position was unfavourable on the French right, and there were no more reserves. It required some optimism to envisage with equanimity the possibility of renewed assaults by the Germans.

Bülow, facing d'Esperey and Foch, was not cast in the same mould as his opponents. From the beginning of the battle he had thought only of the safety of his army and had done nothing to help von Kluck. As the French Fifth Army advanced he began to throw back his right with the double purpose of facing Paris in compliance with the orders of the Supreme Command, and of securing his own flank, regardless of the fact that by so doing he was placing his army at right angles to the French attacks. These forced him to accentuate the movement and pivot on his centre instead of on his right as he had intended, so that the gap between his army and the First was widened.

---

* This battalion, of the 74th Reserve Regiment, was overlooked and forgotten in a wood when Bülow ordered the X. Reserve Corps to swing back.

† This part of the order was not carried out, but part of Conneau's Cavalry Corps crossed the Marne at Château-Thierry on the afternoon of the 9th.

Bülow was already depressed on the 7th, when he reported to the Supreme Command that his army only represented the value of three corps. In the forward position in which his H.Q. was situated, what he saw at the back of the fighting line must have discouraged him, and at one time during the afternoon he ordered the H.Q. transport to be turned about ready to fall back to the north. The Commander of the Second German Army felt himself beaten, and he communicated this attitude of mind to Moltke's emissary, Lieut.-Colonel Hentsch, on the evening of the 8th.*

On the remainder of the front the situation, from the point of view of the Allies, was obscure.

The Fourth French Army was heavily attacked and had to call on the Third Army for help. General Sarrail responded, and the situation on the right was re-established. But on Langle de Cary's left the position remained serious. Luckily the XXI. Corps, sent by Joffre, was near enough to make certain that it could intervene next day (one of the divisions of this corps carried out a forced march of fifty kilometres to reach the battlefield).

On the front of the Third French Army the day revealed a new danger to the French. The enemy was attempting to cut off Verdun from the east.†

Castlenau's Second Army was holding out magnificently, all German

* The fourth official German monograph on the Battle of the Marne (1914) summarizes Bülow's orders for the 9th, issued by telephone between 10 and 11 p.m. on the 8th as follows:

"The attack was to be continued by the left wing of the Army, whilst the right wing was to be withdrawn. The 13th Division and the X. Reserve Corps (*on the right*) were to be in position by 6 a.m., right flank at Margny (*some nine miles in rear of where it was on the morning of the 8th*) left in touch with the right of the 19th Division (*X. Corps*) in the neighbourhood of Le Thoult. The X. Corps and 14th Division (*centre*) were to maintain the position won (*this is hardly an exact description*) on the 8th. The Guard Corps was to continue to the 9th September its attack movement on a broad front on both sides of the Fère–Champenoise–Sézanne road (*i.e., south-west*) right flank on Sézanne via St. Loup; left on Chichay via Pleurs. Kirchbach's group (*32nd, 23rd Reserve and 24th Reserve Divisions of the Third Army*) was to co-operate in the attack on the immediate right of the 2nd Guard Divisions.

(My italics throughout.)

The following remarks on these orders appeared in the *Army Review* of October, 1929:

"The compiler remarks that the order contained no information about the intentions of the Second Army nor any task for the 1st Cavalry Corps (Richthofen) under Bülow's command because there was no news of them. It might equally be remarked that Bülow made no statement as to his own intentions. We may, however, conclude, as his centre was to stand still, the right to go back and the left forward, that he meant to align his army facing Paris, as ordered by the Supreme Command on September 5th, regardless of the fact that by so doing he would place his Army at right angles to the general front of the French."

At 1.30 p.m. on the 8th von Bülow sent an urgent message to the Commander of the Third Army to push forward energetically in a south-western direction towards Fère-Champenoise, "as the enemy was threatening to envelop the right wing of the Second Army which had no more reserves."

† The Germans had threatened St. Mihiel on the previous day. A glance at Map XVI, p. 426, will show how dangerous a successful advance in this region would have been. If Verdun were isolated, the right of the French attack would be taken in flank, and the French Third Army separated from the Second. True, the upper reaches of the Meuse were defended by a line of forts, but the history of forts had not so far been a happy one.

General Sarrail blew up the Meuse bridges, and sent a Cavalry Division towards Troyon, whilst another Cavalry Division and the mixed brigade from Toul guarded the country south of St. Mihiel.

attacks failing against his defence. He was not only guarding the gap of Nancy, but was filling the invaluable role of retaining German troops on his front whose presence farther west might well have reversed the situation there.

IV

September 9th.

The progress realized by the Fifth Army on this day was very satisfactory.*

The XVIII. Corps occupied Château-Thierry that night.
Messages sent by the Fifth Army to British G.H.Q.:
"Whole of Cavalry and XVII. Corps on way to Château-Thierry have been ordered to cross Marne today in order to give best possible assistance to British forces."
"7.35 p.m. Cavalry of XVIII. Corps was at Château-Thierry at 7 p.m. Infantry XVIII. Corps will be there later on and cross the river today."

The Reserve Divisions which till then had been kept in second line, were sent forward; the III. Corps advanced,† as did the I., which reached the plateau of Vauchamps, when it became apparent that things were not going well with the Ninth Army. It was stated that the X. Corps, which had been lent to Foch, was encountering violent resistance, the repercussion of the struggle being waged farther to the east.

General d'Esperey, realizing the importance of the moment, directed his I. Corps to divert its line of advance so as to drive into the flank of the German X. Corps, which he feared might join the Guard in attacking Foch. This manœuvre was a powerful help to the Ninth Army, enabling it to hold its own on the left.

Whilst these movements were taking place, the Moroccan Division, forming the left of Foch's Army, fought so nobly that its reputation as a premier assault unit, to be called upon when it was necessary to hold or to win, was established for the whole war.

The support so readily lent by d'Esperey enabled Foch to recoup a division with which he planned to launch a counter-attack to relieve the sorely pressed XI. Corps. This, however, proved unnecessary, for the Germans

* That evening General Franchet d'Espercy was extremely anxious to know in which direction he was to launch his army in pursuit. At 6.30 p.m., he asked the G.Q.G. for orders. At nine he had still not received any. The delay was nerve-racking owing to the difficulty there would be in getting his own orders out in time. At last, at 10 p.m., he received them: the army was to march straight on to the Marne.

† According to the Germans, their 13th Division facing the III. Corps withdrew in obedience to von Bülow's orders during the night of the 8th–9th. They were completely unmolested whilst carrying out this movement, and next morning (9th) the French, who were completely unaware of what was happening, continued to fire at the positions the enemy had evacuated.

The divisions of the X. Reserve Corps also retired unobserved at 1 and 3 a.m., and were dug in by 10 a.m. on the 9th. This Corps did no fighting on the 9th.

On the front of the X. French Corps the German 19th Division reported that the French infantry did not attack.

retired before the French were in position, and all Foch's troops could do was to fire a few shells after them.

For hours the battle raged, and on Foch's right it seemed that his exhausted men must give way before the German assaults. In this part of the battlefield, the enemy apparently advanced between two and three miles. If the German claim is correct that they covered this distance between 8.45 a.m. and 2 p.m., the French must have been incapable of offering any great reistance in this quarter.*

On the morning of the 9th the Sixth Army was in the gravest danger.† Things looked bright for the enemy, and it may well have appeared to von Kluck that a tactical victory would retrieve his hazardous situation. Opportune reinforcements were coming down from the north to be hurled at the exposed French line, determining the withdrawal of the French in this quarter. Von Kluck and Maunoury were both attempting to outflank each other from the north. Maunoury threw in a reserve division on his left, but unfortunately a German brigade belonging to the IV. Reserve Corps which had been left behind in Brussels suddenly appeared almost behind his left flank. Air reports showed the Germans that the French reinforcements were exhausted, as indeed they were. The only support General Maunoury could afford his left, now consisting of the remnants of six infantry and four cavalry regiments, was the much exhausted 8th Division released from the right, where it was supposed to have been co-operating with the British; owing, however, to its state of fatigue, it had not done so.‡ Eight and a half French divisions were fighting it out against ten German divisions. The French Cavalry Corps was falling back, and ammunition was running short. (This was true of both sides.) The time seemed to have come when there was no hope left and the troops would have to die where they stood.

Then something very dramatic happened. The pressure first on Maunoury then on Foch relaxed. As if by magic von Kluck's grip on the Sixth Army

* It is interesting to note the German version of what has been described as the heroic struggle of Mondemont on Foch's left. The 164th Regiment of the 39th Brigade, the 20th Division of the X. Corps, advanced through the morning mist, and coming upon the Château of Mondemont occupied apparently only by a French advanced post, captured it and repulsed all French counter-attacks. The Germans state they evacuated the Château at 7.30 p.m. without being interfered with. If this account is correct, the oft-described storming of the place by the French is a fable.

The Germans also claim that their 14th Division (facing the IX. French Corps) crossed the causeways over the St. Gond Marshes in columns of fours with arms at the shoulder, preceded by scouts, and occupied some villages beyond.

† So hard had things been going with Maunoury that on the previous evening he had contemplated falling back to a position he was having prepared in rear. He was discouraged from doing so by Gallieni, who suggested to him that if he really had to fall back on the 9th he should do so in such a way as to compel the enemy to remain facing west, thereby facilitating the task of the British and rendering their advance more decisive.

‡ "The 8th Division arrived in Paris on September 5th, and billeted in the area Asnières, Gennevilliers, Colombes (north-western suburban area). General de Lartigue, its commander, considered that on account of the fatigues due to two days' battle in Lorraine, and long journeys in the train, the 8th Division packed (*bourrée*) with reservists recently arrived from the depots, and without sufficient officers and non-commissioned officers (many had been killed) had only a feeble offensive value, and to engage it too soon would be to risk disorganizing it." – *Les Armées Française dans la Grande Guerre.*

slackened. Under the compulsion of the British advance in his rear, his blows weakened, then ceased. News came that the British were across the Marne, advancing on Montreuil. One brigade was already four miles beyond the river, well behind von Kluck's left flank, at the moment engaged against Maunoury, twelve miles to the west. There was nothing for it, his flank was turned.*

The British advance saved the Sixth Army, and by so doing turned the scale of victory in the Allies' favour.†

The actual order of the First German Army to retire is said to have emanated from the representative of the Supreme Command, Lieut.-Colonel Hentsch.

The Supreme Command which had issued no orders whatever between ·the 5th and the 9th, suddenly awakened to the gravity of the situation developing 130 miles away, and sent Hentsch to investigate, investing him with full powers to co-ordinate a retirement if this proved necessary.‡

Hentsch met with nothing but encouraging reports until he reached the Second Army, where he heard the situation of the right wing was serious. Next morning he left for the First Army. He and the Chief of Staff of the Second Army had come to the conclusion that as von Kluck had withdrawn the III. and IX. Corps from the Marne and sent them to his right wing, the Second Army would have to fall back to that river. According to Hentsch the Second Army was prepared to halt on the Marne, but only if the First Army undertook to protect its right flank.

But while Hentsch was on his way to von Kluck's H.Q. Bülow heard the British were over the Marne. He concluded that it was no longer possible to hold the river, as he had hoped. The British advance had turned von Kluck's left. Evidently, therefore, he would be unable to lend the Second Army any support. Von Bülow had told von Kluck on the previous day that his right wing was falling back. Now that the passage of the Marne was forced, he realized that the strategic position was impossible and that he must withdraw

---

* When von Kluck heard that the British were across the Marne he ordered the formation of a defensive flank on the line Crouy-Coulombs. It would seem that the troops who received this order mistook it for an order to retire, but this was of little moment, for the real order to retire was issued soon afterwards.

† Corroboration of this is contained in the following passage from Gallieni's *Mémoires:*

"Meanwhile General Vauthier, who had been engaged in furious fighting on the eastern front, noticed about the middle of the afternoon a slowing down of the German offensive. At 3 p.m. powerful batteries installed about Torcy ceased firing, and reconnaissances reported that the German trenches about Prisieux had been evacuated. Evidently the enemy, under the threat of the British Army which had just crossed the Marne, was abandoning the eastern front of the Sixth Army."

‡ His instructions were to order a general retirement on the line Ste. Ménéhould–Reims–Fismes–Soissons if he found it necessary, and if any of the German forces had already begun to withdraw.

The Supreme Command was not only ill-informed and uncomprehending of the situation of the right wing of its armies, but appears to have pinned its faith until the evening of the 8th on the success of the Sixth and Seventh German Armies against Castelnau. The French right was to be turned and the Armies composing it captured. Such was the pleasing picture evoked at H.Q. at Luxembourg, a delusion which kept troops riveted in Lorraine when their intervention might have been decisive in Champagne against Foch, or nearer Paris.

his whole force and confess defeat. It may be true that von Bülow, a man of sixty-eight, was not equal to the situation, but his decision was probably right, at any rate it was not questioned by the Supreme Command at the time. Having made up his mind, not a minute was lost and the retreat was ordered. He so informed his neighbours. In the case of von Hausen's Third Army he went so far as to take the extraordinary step of issuing direct orders to the right-hand group of that army to retire also.*

But of all this Hentsch knew nothing. He followed the Reims, Fismes, Fère-en-Tardenois road, and the impression he gathered as he went was anything but reassuring. Everywhere in rear of the gap between the First and Second Armies there were signs of panic and retreat. Fleeing men and fleeing transport, frequent reports that the British Cavalry were upon them.

Hentsch only reached the H.Q. of the First Army at midday. After examining the situation with the Chief of Staff of the Army he came to the conclusion that retreat was inevitable if envelopment by the British was to be avoided. He therefore ordered the First Army to withdraw.

German writers may declare that the decision to retire was all wrong, and may derive some satisfaction from so doing, but it was not only von Bülow and Hentsch who considered retreat essential: all the German authorities who were aware of the real situation at the time concurred with them.

Even had von Kluck been successful in driving Maunoury from the field, he could not have exploited his success, for he would have been stopped almost immediately by the exterior line of the Paris defences.†

The far-reaching results of their advance were not immediately apparent to the British themselves. When they reached the Marne disappointment awaited them.

The III. Corps found bridges destroyed and the river too wide to be crossed with the material at its disposal and in face of the enemy defending the passages. The corps fought all day to get over the river, but by nightfall

* General von Kuhl, Chief of Staff of the First Army, in his *Marne* writes:
"After it was established that the Second Army had decided in the morning to retire, and as at midday the troops were already in retreat, the First Army Command had to conform as there was no means of reversing this decision. Even a victory over Maunoury could not prevent us from having our left flank enveloped by superior forces, and from being driven away from the main army. The First Army stood isolated." – (p. 219.)

† Hentsch wrote in his report: "The break through of the British and French would have succeeded at Craonne on September 13th if the VII. R. and XV. Corps, thrown into the battle battalion by battalion, had not closed this breach (between the German First and Second Armies). If carried out on September 10th, that is three days earlier and fifty kilometres farther south, and at a time when the VII. R. and XV. Corps could not have intervened, this break through would have enabled the enemy to obtain a complete success. This is a fact which history will in all probability some day establish."

In other words, Hentsch's contention is that had the Germans stood their ground and accepted battle on the Marne on the 10th, instead of on the Aisne on the 13th, they would have courted disaster, for the First Army would have been separated from the Second.

The VII Reserve Corps, released by the fall of Maubeuge, arrived just in time on the Aisne on September 13th to prevent the I. British Corps penetrating into the gap between the First and Second German Armies north of the Aisne. It was a matter of hours, the German Corps arriving a couple of hours before the British.

On the following day the XV. Corps from the Seventh Army stopped the French advance on the right of the British under similar circumstances.

only ten out of sixteen battalions were across. On the right the advance of the I. Corps was held up in the morning by the threat of strong German columns advancing against its right flank. The fact that there was no sign of the French coming up on their right also delayed their advance, and in consequence they only reached the Château-Thierry–Montreuil road in the afternoon. The II. Corps progressed in spite of heavy fighting. One of its brigades reached the Château-Thierry–Montreuil road early, but finding itself unsupported was unable to advance. It was infinitely disappointing that circumstances prevented a rapid forward movement on this day, for had the III. and I. Corps been able to progress as far and as rapidly as the II., the First German Army might well have been annihilated.*

On the front of the other French armies there was heavy fighting without any important modification.

On the front of the Third Army, apart from some progress on the left in conjunction with the right of the Fourth Army, the situation remained unchanged. Anxiety was still felt concerning the situation on the Meuse. Verdun reported that the fort of Gemicourt had been bombarded. At one moment came the report that the fort of Troyon (through which contact with Verdun was maintained) had ceased firing. What had actually occurred was that the fort had been assaulted unsuccessfully.

September 10th.

On the 10th I was ordered to find the points of junction of the French and British forces to insure good liaison.

The British had marched at 5 a.m. As early as 7.15 a.m. it was realized that the enemy had evacuated the valleys of the Ourcq and Marne. He had a long start. The III. Corps was greatly delayed by having only two passages over the Marne, a floating bridge and a railway bridge. It took the troops nearly all day to cross the river. Bad visibility in the morning, which rendered early air reconnaissances impossible, was a further handicap to the pursuit. Nevertheless, the British pressed on, meeting considerable resistance from strong rearguards well provided with artillery, which necessitated frequent deployments and consequently further delays. The army progressed some ten

---

* The German troops driven back by the British were hardly inferior in numbers to their pursuers. They consisted of four Cavalry Divisions, not less than eight Jäger Battalions, the 5th Division, a composite Brigade of the IX. Corps, and a detachment of the III. Corps. These troops were fighting on ground eminently suitable to defence, but they failed to prevent the British crossing such notable obstacles as the Ourcq and the Marne.

British G.H.Q. received the following from the G.Q.G.in the evening:

"Enemy seems to have fallen back partly on the heights north of Château-Thierry and on the Marne, partly on the line Etrepilly–Courchamps where he appears to be fortifying himself. Tomorrow the Fifth and Sixth French Armies will prepare to attack the enemy's positions. British forces will endeavour to reach the heights and the south bank of the Clignon between Bouresches and Hervilliers, and will be supported on the right by the XVIII. Corps, which will organize a *tête de pont* at or about Château-Thierry

"The Fifth Army will support the movement of the XVIII. Corps by throwing back the enemy towards the north, whilst maintaining liaison with the Ninth Army, and will endeavour to get up to the Marne and its bridges between Château-Thierry and Dormans.

"The Cavalry Corps operating with the XVIII. Corps will keep in constant touch with the enemy, and will endeavour to break through in the general direction of Oulchy-le-Château."

miles during the day, and the increasing signs of disorder amongst the enemy, abandoned supplies and numerous stragglers, greatly heartened the men.* It was, however, frankly disappointing that the First German Army should have been able to retreat practically across the front of the B.E.F. without the latter being able to intercept it. But the German withdrawal was too rapid: just as in August French and British had been able time and again to break off engagements and withdraw, so in their turn the Germans were able to do likewise.

Conneau, on the left of the Fifth Army, was pressing on. The French cavalry horses, although showing every sign of extreme fatigue, seemed to have imbibed something of the spirit of the chase.

The main bodies of the Fifth Army reached the Marne, and the I. Corps, no longer needed by the Ninth Army, turned north and marched in its turn on the river.

On this day General Maunoury, after balancing so long on the edge of defeat, at last felt victory within his grasp, and issued his famous order:

"COMRADES,

"The General Commanding-in-Chief asked, in the name of the Mother-land, that you should do more than your duty. Your response went even beyond what was thought to be possible. If it has been given to me to do some good, I have been rewarded by the greatest honour received during my long career, that of commanding men such as you."

The enemy had withdrawn on the front of the Sixth Army and succeeded in reaching the safe cover of the forest of Villers Cotterets after a couple of rearguard actions.

* Whilst the Fifth Army was also pressing on, its left well forward and now, together with the British, marching into the gap between the First and Second German Armies, von Bülow opposite drew the conclusion, a conclusion based on an air report which stated that two hostile corps were marching against the German Third Army, that the French intended to attack at the junction of the Second and Third Armies. This led him to accumulate forces on his left, a very strange action when it is remembered that the main reason advanced for the German retreat was the gap between their First and Second Armies. Every effort should surely have been made to fill this gap, still sixteen miles wide, whereas here was von Bülow strengthening his left, on the opposite side to the gap! The Supreme Command supported von Bülow's decision, ordering him to incline north-east, which had the consequence of further widening the gap, and compressing the Third and Fourth Armies.

It was only at 1.15 p.m. on the 10th that von Bülow heard that the Supreme Command approved of the retirement and of Hentsch's action.

On this day the Supreme Command again placed von Kluck under von Bülow's orders. [He was also given command of the newly formed Seventh Army which came into being on the following day.]

Von Bülow received the following orders at 5.45 p.m.:

"Second Army will go back behind the Vesle, left flank Thuizy (ten miles south-east of Reims). First Army will receive instructions from Second Army, and will hold the line Mourmelon-le-Petit–Franck.

"Fourth Army in touch with Third north of the Rhine–Marne Canal as far as Revigny area.

"Fifth Army will remain where it is. The positions reached by the Armies will be entrenched and held."

Great credit is due to the Germans for their successful withdrawal in this quarter, and it is the strongest proof of their discipline and organization. Von Kluck's soldiers had been engaged in a continuous forced march for three weeks, interpolated with frequent fighting; they had been drawn from one front to fight hard on another, and they were now retreating. The units were inextricably mixed. Their escape was a truly wonderful performance, which would probably have been impossible had not the Sixth Army been worn out.*

They were a happy band of warriors at Fifth Army H.Q. that night, for now it was quite clear that the enemy was in full retreat. The only question was where would he, or could he, attempt to hold us up? The whole army was filled with just pride as it realized its achievement and the importance of its victories of the last few days.

The G.Q.G. Intelligence supported the view of the Fifth Army and the British that the enemy was in general retreat. German wireless reports all pointed this way, for different wireless stations were all issuing orders to fall back.

At 5 p.m. General Joffre issued orders to press forward and exploit the success with the utmost energy.

The British were to pursue "their victorious career" between the road Fère-en-Tardenois–Bazoches on the right and La Ferté-Milon–Longpont–Soissons (exclusive of the latter town) on the left.

The Fifth Army was to press forward on the right of the British.

The British were to incline north-east, as the front indicated was very narrow and necessitated more than one division marching on each road.

Foch's Ninth Army was, it goes without saying, also ordered to press forward. That night Foch moved his H.Q. to Fère Champenoise where many of the enemy, including Guards officers, were captured, too drunk to move.

The French Fourth Army also progressed, reaching the Marne south of Châlons that night.

The Third Army also advanced, and the Fort of Troyon repelled two attacks.

The Battle of the Marne was over. The pursuit had begun.

VI   *September 11th and 12th.*

The great question now was, would the Germans halt on the Aisne or withdraw still farther?

The view of the Intelligence was that the enemy intended to make a stand on the Aisne, since for the last three days large bodies of enemy troops had been moved eastwards from Soissons to the north of Reims, with the manifest intention of strengthening the centre against the British and Fifth Armies. Alternatively, it was thought possible that he might halt not on the Aisne but farther back on the La Fère line.

Uncertainty concerning the enemy's intentions imposed great caution on

* Von Kluck sent a Cavalry Division back to the Aisne, towards which all the convoys of the Army were converging. Its duty was to keep the bridges clear and maintain discipline and order in the back areas. It would seem that this measure was amply justified by the results achieved.

the Commanders of the pursuing armies, for, while a headlong pursuit is justified when dealing with a thoroughly beaten enemy, such a course of action may lead to defeat at the hands of one who, in spite of appearances, has his troops in hand. The German mistake in this respect was too recent to be forgotten.

Both G.H.Q. and the G.Q.G. were very optimistic. Great emphasis was laid on the success of the Fifth Army at Montmirail.

Major Clive reported that the reason why Joffre had requested the British on the 10th to turn half right and march north-east, which involved a difficult and troublesome operation, was due to his uncertainty as to what was on the Aisne. The B.E.F. advanced some ten miles, in pouring rain, over sodden roads which were badly congested owing to the change of direction.

Sir John had given orders for the pursuit to be continued on the 12th, the passages of the Aisne seized and the high ground north of the river occupied, but this proved to be impossible. The ground was favourable to defence, and there was a good deal of sharp fighting during the day. By nightfall the British had crossed the Vesle, but were still a short distance from the Aisne.

The British were not the only ones suffering from fatigue and delay due to traffic blocks. According to an intercepted German wireless sent out on the night of the 10th–11th, the German cavalry divisions south of Soissons were blocked by transport and their horses exhausted.

On this day we received news that a small German cavalry detachment had entered Lille in the morning, but later withdrew.

On the 11th the Fifth Army, now marching north-east, pressed forward. At the beginning of the day its left-hand corps, the XVIII., had been level with the British whilst the remainder of the army was still in the neighbourhood of the Marne. It did not encounter any resistance worth mentioning.

General d'Esperey offered the British the support of the XVIII. Corps to facilitate their advance. Its commander, General de Maud'huy, full of heart as usual, informed his English neighbours that the German retreat on his front was almost a rout. Similar reports came in from Maunoury's Sixth Army.

The Fifth Army reached the Vesle, but Fismes on the left was only captured after very heavy fighting. There were many reports (later proved to be incorrect) that the enemy was throwing up great entrenchments on the Aisne.

Early on the 12th General d'Esperey issued orders for the pursuit to be continued next day in the same direction, but at 6 p.m. fresh instructions were issued by the G.Q.G. and, in accordance with these, orders were issued for the army to turn northwards again.

During the 11th, the Sixth Army was engaged in changing front to the north. On the 12th it lined up on the Aisne preparatory to crossing the river; all the bridges had been destroyed on its front. Its Cavalry Corps was still engaged in endeavouring to envelop the German right, and was driving towards the Oise between Chauny and Noyon.

On this day the Ninth Army had nothing more serious than rearguards to deal with. The Fourth Army reached the Marne. On the following day both Armies again progressed, and the Fourth Army crossed the Marne.

The Third Army also advanced. The bombardment of the fort of Troyon was continued. On the 13th the enemy was still falling back on the fronts of both the Fourth and Third Armies.

The only task now left for the Third Army was to drive the enemy from the vitally important Ste. Ménéhould–Verdun line, and this was accomplished by a fine effort.

The problem for the Germans resolved itself into whether to seek safety and reunion by continuing to fall back, or to make a stand on the strong position afforded by the Aisne. To impose further retreat on the already weary and disheartened troops might be to run the risk of complete disintegration.

The gap between the First and Second German Armies was now some eighteen miles wide. Von Bülow, being very anxious as to the safety of his right wing, endangered owing to the forcing of the Vesle by the British right and the left of the Fifth Army, withdrew north of the Aisne to the neighbourhood of Berry-au-Bac on the night of the 12th.

The fate of the campaign was once more in the balance, but this time luck was with the Germans. Their reinforcements came up a few hours before the Allies were able to penetrate into the gap between the First and Second German Armies.

INDEX